National Football League 1981 Media Information Book

Published by the National Football League.
Compiled by the NFL Public Relations Department
and the 28 NFL Public Relations Directors.
Produced by NFL Properties, Inc., Creative Services Division.
Edited by Fran Connors, NFL Public Relations.
Workman Publishing, New York

National Football League, 1981

410 Park Avenue, New York, N.Y. 10022   (212) 758-1500

Commissioner: Pete Rozelle
Executive Director: Don Weiss
Treasurer: Bill Ray
Counsel to Commissioner: Jay Moyer
Director of Operations: Jan Van Duser
Assistant to President: Al Ward
Director of Public Relations: Jim Heffernan
Director of Information: Joe Browne
Director of Broadcasting: Val Pinchbeck, Jr.
Director of Security: Warren Welsh
Assistant Director of Security: Charles R. Jackson
Director of Personnel: Joel Bussert
Administrative Coordinator: Peter Hadhazy
Supervisor of Officials: Art McNally
Assistant Supervisor of Officials: Jack Reader
Assistant Supervisor of Officials: Nick Skorich
Director of Special Events: Jim Steeg
Assistant Director of Special Events: Maxine Isenberg
Special Projects Manager: Bill Granholm
Director of Player Relations: Buddy Young
Auditor: Tom Sullivan
Director of Office Services: Wayne Rosen
Officiating Assistant: Stu Kirkpatrick

American Football Conference

President: Lamar Hunt, Kansas City Chiefs
Assistant to President: Al Ward
Director of Information: Fran Connors

National Football Conference

President: George Halas, Chicago Bears
Assistant to President: Joe Rhein
Director of Information: Dick Maxwell

Photography Credits
Cover: Rod Hanna.
Bill Amatucci 88, 126; Vernon Biever 118; David Boss 122; Thomas J. Croke 76; Dave Cross 72; Scott Cunningham 102, 138; Gin Ellis 114; Robert Harmeyer, Jr. 52, 56, 150; Andy Hayt 92, 134; Paul Jasienski 64; Kansas City Chiefs 68; Al Messerschmidt 130; New York Jets 80; Ron Ross 44; Russ Russell 110; Bill Smith 106; Robert L. Smith 48; Tony Tomsic 154; Corky Trewin 96; Herb Weitman 142; Michael Zagaris 60, 84, 146.

Workman Publishing Co.,
1 West 39th Street, New York, N.Y. 10018
Manufactured in the United States of America.
First printing, July 1981.

10 9 8 7 6 5 4 3 2 1

Contents

American Football Conference

Eastern Division

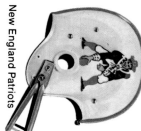

New York Jets

New England Patriots

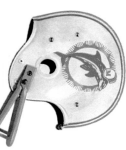

Miami Dolphins

Buffalo Bills

Baltimore Colts

Central Division

Pittsburgh Steelers

Houston Oilers

Cleveland Browns

Cincinnati Bengals

Western Division

Seattle Seahawks

San Diego Chargers

Oakland Raiders

Kansas City Chiefs

Denver Broncos

National Football Conference

Eastern Division

Dallas Cowboys

New York Giants

Philadelphia Eagles

St. Louis Cardinals

Washington Redskins

Central Division

Chicago Bears

Detroit Lions

Green Bay Packers

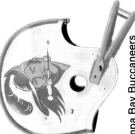
Minnesota Vikings

Tampa Bay Buccaneers

Western Division

Atlanta Falcons

Los Angeles Rams

New Orleans Saints

San Francisco 49ers

Waivers

The waiver system is a procedure by which player contracts or NFL rights to players are made available by a club to other clubs in the League. During the procedure the 27 other clubs either file claims to obtain the players or waive the opportunity to do so—thus the term "waiver." Claiming clubs are assigned players on a priority based on the inverse of won-and-lost standings. The claiming period normally is 10 days during the off-season and 24 hours from early July through December. In some circumstances another 24 hours is added on to allow the original club to rescind its action (known as a recall of a waiver request) and/or the claiming club to do the same (known as a withdrawal of a claim). If a player passes through waivers unclaimed and is not recalled by the original club, he becomes a free agent. All waivers from July through December are no-recall and no-withdrawal. Under the Collective Bargaining Agreement, from February 1 through October 13 any veteran who has acquired four years of pension credit may, if about to be assigned to another club through the waiver system, reject such assignment and become a free agent.

Active List

The Active List is the principal status for players participating for a club. It consists of all players under contract, including option, who are eligible for preseason, regular season, and postseason games. Clubs are allowed to open training camp with an unlimited number of players but thereafter must meet a series of mandatory roster reductions prior to the season opener. Teams will be permitted to dress up to 45 players for each regular season and postseason game during the 1981 season. The Active List maximums and dates for 1981 are:

August 18	60 players
August 25	50 players
August 31	45 players

Reserve List

The Reserve List is a status for players who, for reasons of injury, retirement, military service, or other circumstances, are not immediately available for participation with a club. Those players in the category of Reserve/Injured who were physically unable to play football for a minimum of four weeks from the date of going onto Reserve may be re-activated by their clubs upon clearing procedural recall waivers; in addition, each club will have three free re-activations for players meeting the four-week requirement who were placed on Reserve following the final cutdown. Clubs participating in postseason competition will be granted on additional free re-activation. Players not meeting the four-week requirement may not return in the same season to the Active List of the club which originally placed them on Reserve, but may be assigned through the waiver system to other clubs. Early in 1982 all clubs who had players on Reserve/Injured must declare a maximum of three players, from those meeting the four-week requirement, as tradeable in that year; others who were on the list cannot be traded until 1983. Players in the category of Reserve/Retired may not be reinstated during the period from 30 days before the end of the regular season on through the postseason.

Trades

Unrestricted trading between the AFC and NFC is allowed in 1981 through October 13, after which all trading will end until February 1, 1982.

Annual Player Limits

NFL

Year(s)	Limit
1978–80	45
1975–77	43
1974	47
1964–73	40
1963	37
1961–62	36
1960	38
1959	36
1957–58	35
1951–56	33
1949–50	32
1948	35
1947	35*–34
1945–46	33
1943–44	28
1940–42	33
1938–39	30
1936–37	25
1935	24
1930–34	20
1926–29	18
1925	16

*35 for first three games

AFL

Year(s)	Limit
1966–69	40
1965	38
1964	34
1962–63	33
1960–61	35

Tie-Breaking Procedures

The following procedures will be used to break standings ties for postseason playoffs and to determine regular season schedules.

To Break a Tie Within a Division

If, at the end of the regular season, two or more clubs in the same division finish with identical won-lost-tied percentages, the following steps will be taken until a champion is determined.

Two Clubs

1. Head-to-head (best won-lost-tied percentage in games between the clubs).
2. Best won-lost-tied percentage in games played within the division.
3. Best won-lost-tied percentage in games played within the conference.
4. Best won-lost-tied percentage in common games, if applicable.
5. Best net points in division games.
6. Best net points in all games.
7. Strength of schedule.
8. Best net touchdowns in all games.
9. Coin toss.

Three or More Clubs

(Note: If two clubs remain tied after a third club is eliminated during any step, tie-breaker reverts to step 1 of two-club format.)

1. Head-to-head (best won-lost-tied percentage in games among the clubs).
2. Best won-lost-tied percentage in games played within the division.
3. Best won-lost-tied percentage in games played within the conference.
4. Best won-lost-tied percentage in common games.
5. Best net points in division games.
6. Best net points in all games.
7. Strength of schedule.
8. Best net touchdowns in all games.
9. Coin toss.

To Break a Tie for the Wild Card Team

If it is necessary to break ties to determine the two Wild Card clubs from each conference, the following steps will be taken.

1. If the tied clubs are from the same division, apply division tie-breaker.
2. If the tied clubs are from different divisions, apply the following steps.

Two Clubs

1. Head-to-head, if applicable.
2. Best won-lost-tied percentage in games played within the conference.
3. Best won-lost-tied percentage in common games, minimum of four.
4. Best net points in conference games.
5. Best net points in all games.
6. Strength of schedule.
7. Best net touchdowns in all games.
8. Coin toss.

Three or More Clubs

(Note: If two clubs remain tied after other clubs are eliminated, tie-breaker reverts to step 1 of applicable two-club format.)

1. Head-to-head sweep. (Applicable only if one club has defeated each of the others, or if one club has lost to each of the others.)
2. Best won-lost-tied percentage in games played within the conference.
3. Best won-lost-tied percentage in common games, minimum of four.
4. Best net points in conference games.
5. Best net points in all games.
6. Strength of schedule.
7. Best net touchdowns in all games.
8. Coin toss.

Tie-Breaking Procedure for Selection Meeting

If two or more clubs are tied for selection order, the conventional strength of schedule tie-breaker will be applied, subject to the following exceptions for playoff teams.

1. The Super Bowl winner will be last and the Super Bowl loser will be next-to-last.
2. Any non-Super Bowl playoff team involved in a tie moves down in drafting priority as follows:
   A. Participation by a club in the playoffs without a victory adds one-half victory to the club's regular season won-lost-tied record.
   B. For each victory in the playoffs, one full victory will be added to the club's regular season won-lost-tied record.
3. Clubs with the best won-lost-tied records after these steps are applied will drop to their appropriate spots at the bottom of the tied segment. In no case will the above process move a club lower than the segment in which it was initially tied.

7

Figuring the 1982 NFL Schedule

As soon as the final game of the 1981 NFL regular season (Oakland at San Diego on December 21) has been completed, it will be possible to determine the 1982 opponents of the 28 NFL teams.

Each schedule is based on a formula initiated for the 1978 season that uses the team's won-lost-tied percentage from the current season as the primary guide.

For years the NFL has been seeking an easily understood, balanced schedule that would provide for both competitive equality and a variety of opponents. It is easy to segregate groups of teams into tight divisions, have them play the majority of their games within those divisions, and let the division winners emerge into a structured playoff system. But the result is that many attractive teams with star players never appear in other cities unless those clubs happen to be matched in the playoffs.

The new approach to scheduling gives the fans the best of both systems, a neat competitive format and variety at the same time. It also reduces inequities in the strength of schedules that popped up too often in the past under the system of rotating opponents over a period of years.

Under the new format, schedules of any NFL team are figured according to one of the following three formulas. (The reference point for the figuring is the final standings. Ties for position in any of the divisions are broken according to the tie-breaking procedures outlined on page 7. The chart on page 9 is included for use as you go through each step.)

A. First- through fourth-place teams in a five-team division (AFC East, AFC West, NFC East, NFC Central).

1. Home-and-home round-robin within the division (8 games).
2. One game each with the first- through fourth-place teams in a division of the other conference. In 1982, AFC East will play NFC Central, AFC Central will play NFC East, and AFC West will play NFC West, (4 games).
3. The first-place team plays the first- and fourth-place teams in the other divisions within the conference. The second-place team plays the second- and third-place teams in the other divisions within the conference. The third-place team plays the third- and second-place teams in the other divisions within the conference. The fourth-place team plays the fourth- and first-place teams in the other divisions within the conference (4 games).

This completes the 16-game schedule.

B. First- through fourth-place teams in a four-team division (AFC Central, NFC West).

1. Home-and-home round-robin within the division (6 games).
2. One game with each of the fifth-place teams in the conference (2 games).
3. The same procedure that is listed in step A2 (4 games).
4. The same procedure that is listed in step A3 (4 games).

This completes the 16-game schedule.

C. The fifth-place teams in a division (AFC East, AFC West, NFC East, NFC Central).

1. Home-and-home round-robin within the division (8 games).
2. One game with each team in the four-team division of the conference (4 games).
3. A home-and-home with the other fifth-place team in the conference (2 games).
4. One game each with the fifth-place teams in the other conference (2 games).

This completes the 16-game schedule.

The 1982 Opponent Breakdown chart on page 9 does not include the round-robin games within the division. Those are automatically on a home-and-away basis. The dates and sites of all games will be announced by the NFL.

1981 NFL Standings

AFC

EAST AE
1 _____
2 _____
3 _____
4 _____
5 _____

CENTRAL AC
1 _____
2 _____
3 _____
4 _____

WEST AW
1 _____
2 _____
3 _____
4 _____
5 _____

NFC

EAST NE
1 _____
2 _____
3 _____
4 _____
5 _____

WEST NW
1 _____
2 _____
3 _____
4 _____

CENTRAL NC
1 _____
2 _____
3 _____
4 _____
5 _____

A Team's 1982 Schedule

Team Name _____

_____
_____
_____
_____
_____
_____
_____
_____
_____
_____
_____
_____
_____
_____
_____
_____

1982 Opponent Breakdown

AE — AFC EAST

AE-1	AE-2	AE-3	AE-4	AE-5
NC-1 NC-2	NC-1 NC-2	NC-1 NC-2	NC-1 NC-2	AC-1 AC-2
NC-3 NC-4	NC-3 NC-4	NC-3 NC-4	NC-3 NC-4	AC-3 AC-4
AC-4 AC-1	AC-3 AC-2	AC-2 AC-3	AC-1 AC-4	AW-5 AW-5
AW-1 AW-4	AW-2 AW-3	AW-3 AW-2	AW-4 AW-1	NE-5 NC-5

AC — AFC CENTRAL

AC-1	AC-2	AC-3	AC-4
NE-1 NE-2	NE-1 NE-2	NE-1 NE-2	NE-1 NE-2
NE-3 NE-4	NE-3 NE-4	NE-3 NE-4	NE-3 NE-4
AE-1 AE-4	AE-2 AE-3	AE-3 AE-2	AE-4 AE-1
AW-1 AW-4	AW-3 AW-2	AW-2 AW-3	AW-4 AW-1
AW-5 AE-5	AE-5 AW-5	AW-5 AE-5	AE-5 AW-5

AW — AFC WEST

AW-1	AW-2	AW-3	AW-4	AW-5
NW-1 NW-2	NW-1 NW-2	NW-1 NW-2	NW-1 NW-2	AC-1 AC-2
NW-3 NW-4	NW-3 NW-4	NW-3 NW-4	NW-3 NW-4	AC-4 AC-3
AE-4 AE-1	AE-3 AE-2	AE-2 AE-3	AE-1 AE-4	AC-5 AC-5
AC-1 AC-4	AC-2 AC-3	AC-3 AC-2	AC-4 AC-1	NC-5 NE-5

NE — NFC EAST

NE-1	NE-2	NE-3	NE-4	NE-5
AC-1 AC-2	AC-1 AC-2	AC-1 AC-2	AC-1 AC-2	NW-1 NW-2
AC-3 AC-4	AC-3 AC-4	AC-3 AC-4	AC-3 AC-4	NW-3 NW-4
NW-4 NW-1	NW-3 NW-2	NW-2 NW-3	NW-1 NW-4	NC-5 NC-5
NC-1 NC-4	NC-2 NC-3	NC-3 NC-2	NC-4 NC-1	AE-5 AW-5

NC — NFC CENTRAL

NC-1	NC-2	NC-3	NC-4	NC-5
AE-1 AE-2	AE-1 AE-2	AE-1 AE-2	AE-1 AE-2	NW-2 NW-1
AE-3 AE-4	AE-3 AE-4	AE-3 AE-4	AE-3 AE-4	NW-4 NW-3
NE-4 NE-1	NE-3 NE-2	NE-2 NE-3	NE-1 NE-4	NE-5 NE-5
NW-1 NW-4	NW-2 NW-3	NW-3 NW-2	NW-4 NW-1	AE-5 AW-5

NW — NFC WEST

NW-1	NW-2	NW-3	NW-4
AW-1 AW-2	AW-1 AW-2	AW-1 AW-2	AW-1 AW-2
AW-3 AW-4	AW-3 AW-4	AW-3 AW-4	AW-3 AW-4
NE-1 NE-4	NE-2 NE-3	NE-3 NE-2	NE-4 NE-1
NC-4 NC-1	NC-3 NC-2	NC-2 NC-3	NC-1 NC-4
NC-5 NE-5	NE-5 NC-5	NC-5 NE-5	NE-5 NC-5

AFC Active Statistical Leaders

(Numbers in parentheses denote rankings on NFL top 10 lifetime list.)

LEADING ACTIVE PASSERS, AMERICAN FOOTBALL CONFERENCE
1,000 or more attempts

	Att.	Comp.	Pct. Comp.	Yards	TD	Had Int.	Pct. Int.	Avg. Gain	Rate Pts.
1. Bert Jones, Balt. (6)	2038	1138	55.8	14569	101	77	3.8	7.15	79.2
2. Ken Stabler, Hou. (7)	2938	1779	60.6	22280	163	171	5.8	7.58	78.3
3. Ken Anderson, Cin. (10)	3060	1736	56.7	21808	114	131	4.3	7.13	78.0
4. Brian Sipe, Clev.	1149	607	52.8	8136	45	59	5.1	7.08	76.9
5. Dan Fouts, S.D.	2191	1239	56.5	15207	93	107	4.9	6.94	76.0
6. Greg Landry, Balt.	2594	1489	57.4	19454	112	112	4.3	7.50	75.5
7. Craig Morton, Den.	2251	1251	55.6	15658	97	99	4.4	6.96	73.4
8. Joe Ferguson, Buff.	3384	1810	53.5	24520	125	125	3.7	7.25	72.1
9. Terry Bradshaw, Pitt.	2552	1320	51.7	17355	112	112	4.4	6.80	69.8
10. James Harris, S.D.	3283	1692	51.5	23257	171	185	5.6	7.08	68.5
Steve Grogan, N.E.	1972	1006	51.0	14626	59	96	4.9	7.42	67.3
Jim Zorn, Sea.	2126	1121	52.7	14548	107	124	5.8	6.84	67.3
Jim Plunkett, Oak.	2329	1155	49.6	15605	103	104	4.5	6.70	61.8
Dan Pastorini, Oak.	2898	1492	51.5	17796	147	147	5.1	6.14	61.0
Richard Todd, N.Y.J.	1347	693	51.4	9571	91	91	6.8	7.11	59.2

TOP 10 ACTIVE RUSHERS, AFC

	Yrs.	Att.	Yards	TD
1. Franco Harris, Pitt. (3)	9	2220	9352	76
2. Calvin Hill, Clev.	11	1448	6060	42
3. Mark van Eeghen, Oak.	7	1436	5756	33
4. Delvin Williams, Mia.	7	1312	5598	33
5. Greg Pruitt, Clev.	8	1127	5372	25
6. Earl Campbell, Hou.	3	1043	5081	45
7. Mike Thomas, S.D.	6	1087	4196	19
8. Chuck Muncie, S.D.	4	923	4052	32
9. Don Calhoun, N.E.	7	803	3354	21
10. Mike Pruitt, Clev.	5	747	3231	21

Other Leading Rushers

	Yrs.	Att.	Yards	TD
Boobie Clark, Hou.	8	802	3032	25
Sherman Smith, Sea.	5	664	2974	25
Pete Johnson, Cin.	4	762	2959	31
Ronnie Coleman, Hou.	7	679	2678	15
Jon Keyworth, Den.	7	699	2653	22
Greg Landry, Balt.	13	427	2643	20
John Cappelletti, S.D.	6	733	2610	20
Archie Griffin, Cin.	5	632	2606	3
Don McCauley, Balt.	10	760	2590	40
Clark Gaines, N.Y.J.	5	581	2552	8

TOP 10 ACTIVE PASS RECEIVERS, AFC

	Yrs.	No.	Yards	TD
1. Harold Jackson, N.E. (7)	13	532	9577	75
2. Haven Moses, Den.	11	433	7845	55
3. Charlie Joiner, S.D.	12	425	7288	40
4. Reggie Rucker, Clev.	11	420	6633	43
5. Ken Burrough, Hou.	11	381	6434	42
6. Cliff Branch, Oak.	8	364	6378	57
7. Ray Chester, Oak.	9	351	4920	47
8. Riley Odoms, Den.	8	346	5095	36
9. Bob Chandler, Buff.	9	344	4785	44
10. Richard Caster, Hou.	10	310	5330	45

Other Leading Pass Receivers

	Yrs.	No.	Yards	TD
Nat Moore, Mia.	8	305	4749	45
Isaac Curtis, Cin.	8	302	5466	48
Don McCauley, Balt.	10	297	2679	15
Steve Largent, Sea.	5	290	4817	37
Dave Casper, Hou.	6	285	3791	36
Lynn Swann, Pitt.	7	284	4692	46
Frank Lewis, Buff.	10	263	4551	31
Greg Pruitt, Clev.	8	258	2386	13
Calvin Hill, Clev.	11	254	2711	21
Ron Jessie, Buff.	10	250	4078	26
Jerome Barkum, N.Y.J.	9	236	3727	26
Roger Carr, Balt.	7	216	4186	32
John Stallworth, Pitt.	7	209	3765	32
Franco Harris, Pitt.	9	204	1507	6

TOP 10 ACTIVE SCORERS, AFC

	Yrs.	TD	FG	PAT	TP
1. Don Cockroft, Clev. (8)	13	0	216	432	1080
2. Toni Fritsch, Hou.	9	0	138	247	661
3. John Smith, N.E.	7	0	105	253	568
4. Efren Herrera, Sea.	6	0	96	222	510
5. Franco Harris, Pitt.	9	82	0	0	492
6. Nick Mike-Mayer, Buff.	8	0	108	161	485
7. Harold Jackson, N.E.	13	75	0	0	450
8. Pat Leahy, N.Y.J.	7	0	89	168	435
9. Chris Bahr, Oak.	4	0	81	171	414
10. Calvin Hill, Clev.	11	63	0	0	378

Other Leading Scorers

	Yrs.	TD	FG	PAT	TP
Steve Mike-Mayer, Balt.	6	0	67	161	362
Cliff Branch, Oak.	8	57	0	0	342
Don McCauley, Balt.	10	56	0	0	336
Haven Moses, Den.	11	56	0	0	336
Rolf Benirschke, S.D.	4	0	63	116	305
Isaac Curtis, Cin.	8	48	0	0	288
Lynn Swann, Pitt.	7	48	0	0	288
Ray Chester, Oak.	9	47	0	0	282
Earl Campbell, Hou.	3	46	0	0	276
Richard Caster, Hou.	10	45	0	0	270
Nat Moore, Mia.	8	45	0	0	270
Bob Chandler, Buff.	9	44	0	0	264
Ken Burrough, Hou.	11	43	0	0	258
Reggie Rucker, Clev.	11	43	0	0	258

TOP 10 ACTIVE INTERCEPTORS, AFC

	Yrs.	No.	Yards	TD
1. Ken Riley, Cin.	12	47	413	2
2. Mel Blount, Pitt.	11	46	596	1
3. Thom Darden, Clev.	8	42	752	2
4. Glen Edwards, S.D.	10	37	916	3
5. Dick Jauron, Cin.	8	25	432	2
6. Burgess Owens, Oak.	7	25	372	2
7. Gary Barbaro, K.C.	4	31	589	3
8. Clarence Scott, Clev.	10	30	332	2
9. Jack Ham, Pitt.	9	30	193	1
10. Bill Simpson, Buff.	6	26	427	0

Other Leading Interceptors

	Yrs.	No.	Yards	TD
Ted Hendricks, Oak.	11	26	332	1
Lester Hayes, Oak.	4	25	486	2
Steve Foley, Den.	5	25	330	2
Willie Buchanon, S.D.	9	23	334	2
Isiah Robertson, Buff.	10	23	247	3
Monte Jackson, Oak.	8	23	338	3
David Brown, Sea.	5	23	364	2
Mike Reinfeldt, Hou.	5	23	372	1
Mike Haynes, N.E.	4	21	296	2
Donnie Shell, Pitt.	7	20	213	3
Lyle Blackwood, Balt.	8	20	416	2
Mario Clark, Buff.	5	20	296	0

TOP 10 ACTIVE PUNTERS, AFC
35 or more punts

	Yrs.	No.	Yards	Avg.	LG
1. Ray Guy, Oak. (7)	7	558	24022	43.1	74
2. Luke Prestridge, Den.	2	159	6634	41.7	63
3. Bob Grupp, K.C.	2	173	7204	41.6	74
4. Pat McInally, Cin.	5	406	16768	41.3	67
5. George Roberts, Mia.	5	227	9307	41.0	71
6. Don Cockroft, Clev.	13	651	26258	40.3	71
7. Craig Colquitt, Pitt.	3	195	7859	40.3	61
8. Herman Weaver, Sea.	11	693	27922	40.3	69
9. Chuck Ramsey, N.Y.J.	4	282	11336	40.2	79
10. Rick Partridge, S.D.	2	117	4680	40.0	61

Other Leading Punters

	Yrs.	No.	Yards	Avg.	LG
Cliff Parsley, Hou.	4	328		39.9	59
Mike Bragg, Balt.	13	978		39.8	74
Dan Pastorini, Oak.	10	316		39.7	74
Johnny Evans, Clev.	3	214		39.5	65
Greg Cater, Buff.	1	73		39.5	65
Mike Wood, S.D.	1	63		38.7	69
Mike Hubach, N.E.	1	82		36.8	81

TOP 10 ACTIVE PUNT RETURNERS, AFC

	Yrs.	No.	Yards	Avg.	TD
1. Lynn Swann, Pitt.	7	61	739	12.1	1
2. Rick Upchurch, Den. (6)	6	220	2651	12.1	6
3. J.T. Smith, K.C. (7)	3	102	1226	12.0	4
4. Greg Pruitt, Clev.	8	56	659	11.8	0
5. Bill Thompson, Den. (10)	12	157	1814	11.6	0
6. Mike Fuller, S.D.	6	212	2388	11.3	1
7. Stanley Morgan, N.E.	4	71	844	11.9	2
8. Mike Haynes, N.E.	4	105	1147	10.9	2
9. Bruce Harper, N.Y.J.	4	125	1335	10.7	1
10. Keith Moody, Oak.	5	88	920	10.5	3

Other Leading Punt Returners

	Yrs.	No.	Yards	Avg.	TD
Dick Jauron, Cin.	8	44	447	10.2	0
Roland James, N.E.	1	33	331	10.0	1
Dino Hall, Clev.	2	35	336	9.6	0
Tony Nathan, Mia.	2	51	484	9.5	1
Glen Edwards, S.D.	10	103	958	9.3	0
Theo Bell, Pitt.	4	139	1259	9.1	0
David Brown, Sea.	5	33	291	8.8	0
Will Lewis, Sea.	1	41	349	8.5	1
Larry Brunson, Den.	6	75	630	8.4	1
Carl Roaches, Hou.	1	47	384	8.2	0
Nesby Glasgow, Balt.	3	67	539	8.1	1
Jim Smith, Pitt.	2	68	533	8.0	1
Ira Matthews, Oak.	2	80	586	7.3	0
Cleotha Montgomery, Cin.	1	31	223	7.2	0

TOP 10 ACTIVE KICKOFF RETURNERS, AFC

	Yrs.	No.	Yards	Avg.	TD
1. Raymond Clayborn, N.E.	4	57	1538	27.0	3
2. Horace Ivory, N.E.	4	44	1172	26.6	2
3. Ron Jessie, Buff.	10	47	1237	26.3	2
4. Greg Pruitt, Clev.	8	55	1441	26.2	1
5. Nat Moore, Mia.	8	33	858	26.0	1
6. Duriel Harris, Mia.	5	55	1396	25.4	2
7. Mel Blount, Pitt.	11	36	911	25.3	0
8. Keith Wright, Clev.	3	70	1767	25.2	0
9. Bill Thompson, Den.	12	46	1156	25.1	2
10. Bruce Laird, Balt.	9	137	3406	24.9	0

Other Leading Kickoff Returners

	Yrs.	No.	Yards	Avg.	TD
Rick Upchurch, Den.	6	95	2355	24.8	1
Larry Anderson, Pitt.	3	85	2041	24.0	0
Lou Piccone, Buff.	7	106	2478	23.4	0
Larry Brunson, Den.	7	87	2022	23.2	0
Tony Nathan, Mia.	2	50	1118	22.4	0

NFC Active Statistical Leaders

(Numbers in parentheses denote rankings on NFL top 10 lifetime list.)

LEADING ACTIVE PASSERS, NATIONAL FOOTBALL CONFERENCE

1,000 or more attempts

	Yrs.	Att.	Comp.	Pct. Comp.	Yards	Avg. Gain	TD	Pct. TD	Had Int.	Pct. Int.	Rate Pts.
Ron Jaworski, Phil.	7	1693	873	51.6	11587	6.84	80	4.7	69	4.1	72.2
Pat Haden, L.A.	5	1096	593	54.1	7481	6.83	43	3.9	47	4.3	70.7
Tommy Kramer, Minn.	4	1161	649	55.9	7454	6.42	47	4.0	52	4.5	70.0
Joe Theismann, Wash.	7	1617	864	53.4	10726	6.63	67	4.1	69	4.3	70.0
Archie Manning, N.O.	9	3096	1714	55.4	20284	6.55	110	3.6	143	4.6	68.4
Jim Hart, St.L.	15	4704	2387	50.7	32154	6.84	193	4.1	225	4.8	66.5
Steve Bartkowski, Atl.	6	1723	884	51.3	11673	6.78	78	4.5	91	5.3	66.0
Steve DeBerg, S.F.	3	1201	670	55.8	7220	6.01	37	3.1	60	5.0	63.1
Doug Williams, T.B.	3	1112	493	44.3	7014	6.31	45	4.0	48	4.3	60.7
Lynn Dickey, G.B.	8	1354	721	53.2	9080	6.71	40	3.0	85	6.3	58.1
Bob Avellini, Chi.	5	1005	507	50.4	6554	6.52	32	3.2	63	6.3	55.7
Mike Phipps, Chi.	11	1782	875	49.1	10335	5.80	53	3.0	108	6.1	51.8

TOP 10 ACTIVE RUSHERS, NFC

	Yrs.	Att.	Yards	TD
1. Walter Payton, Chi. (5)	6	1865	8386	65
2. John Riggins, Wash.	9	1666	6822	42
3. Robert Newhouse, Dall.	9	1123	4638	30
4. Tony Dorsett, Dall.	4	1026	4624	36
5. Dexter Bussey, Det.	7	961	4183	18
6. Wilbert Montgomery, Phil.	4	835	3693	28
7. Wilbur Jackson, Wash.	6	921	3663	13
8. Rickey Young, Minn.	6	909	3398	20
9. Don Woods, S.F.	7	763	3087	16
10. Ricky Bell, T.B.	4	790	2977	16

Other Leading Rushers

	Yrs.	Att.	Yards	TD
Ottis Anderson, St.L.	2	632	2957	17
Roland Harper, Chi.	5	720	2931	14
Tony Galbreath, N.O.	5	760	2865	27
Cullen Bryant, L.A.	8	692	2681	19
Joe Washington, Wash.	4	688	2559	5
Wayne Morris, St.L.	5	626	2427	26
William Andrews, Atl.	2	504	2331	7
Archie Manning, N.O.	9	355	2030	18

TOP 10 ACTIVE PASS RECEIVERS, NFC

	Yrs.	No.	Yards	TD
1. Harold Carmichael, Phil.	10	455	6895	66
2. Ahmad Rashad, Minn.	8	414	5714	37
3. Drew Pearson, Dall.	8	378	6281	37
4. Rickey Young, Minn.	6	340	2752	13
5. Mel Gray, St.L.	10	320	6300	43
6. Tony Galbreath, N.O.	5	284	2221	6
7. Charley Young, S.F.	8	262	3300	17
8. Sammy White, Minn.	5	240	4009	37
9. Billy Joe DuPree, Dall.	8	229	3168	36
10. Alfred Jenkins, Atl.	6	227	4066	25

Other Leading Pass Receivers

	Yrs.	No.	Yards	TD
Pat Tilley, St.L.	5	218	3275	16
John Riggins, Wash.	9	216	1891	12
Wallace Francis, Atl.	8	214	3254	23
Ike Harris, N.O.	6	209	3272	16
Joe Washington, Wash.	4	209	1865	5
Henry Childs, L.A.	7	207	3224	27
Walter Payton, Chi.	6	202	1791	5

TOP 10 ACTIVE SCORERS, NFC

	Yrs.	TD	FG	PAT	TP
1. Jan Stenerud, G.B. (6)	14	0	282	397	1243
2. Garo Yepremian, T.B. (9)	13	0	208	438	1062
3. Mark Moseley, Wash.	10	0	170	262	772
4. Ray Wersching, S.F.	8	0	92	159	435
5. Bob Thomas, Chi.	6	0	85	167	422
6. Walter Payton, Chi.	6	70	0	0	420
7. Harold Carmichael, Phil.	10	66	0	0	396
8. Joe Danelo, N.Y.G.	6	0	79	141	378
9. John Riggins, Wash.	9	54	0	0	324
10. Frank Corral, L.A.	3	0	58	118	292

Other Leading Scorers

	Yrs.	TD	FG	PAT	TP
Mel Gray, St.L.	10	44	0	0	264
Benny Ricardo, N.O.	4	0	51	109	262
Tony Dorsett, Dall.	4	41	0	0	246
Drew Pearson, Dall.	8	39	0	0	234
Ahmad, Rashad, Minn.	8	39	0	0	234
Tim Mazzetti, Atl.	3	0	45	95	230

TOP 10 ACTIVE INTERCEPTORS, NFC

	Yrs.	No.	Yards	TD
1. Bobby Bryant, Minn.	13	51	749	3
2. Lemar Parrish, Wash.	11	45	453	4
3. Rolland Lawrence, Atl.	8	39	658	1
4. Charlie Waters, Dall.	10	38	563	2
5. Roger Wehrli, St.L.	12	36	301	2
6. Tom Myers, N.O.	9	34	551	2
7. Joe Lavender, Wash.	8	29	382	3
8. Ken Stone, St.L.	8	27	445	0
9. Bill Bergey, Phil.	12	27	397	0
10. Stan White, Det.	9	27	370	2

Other Leading Interceptors

	Yrs.	No.	Yards	TD
James Hunter, Det.	5	24	246	1
Rod Perry, L.A.	6	22	311	4
Allan Ellis, Chi.	7	22	185	1
Jimmy Allen, Det.	7	22	184	0
Randy Logan, Phil.	8	20	294	0

TOP 10 ACTIVE PUNT RETURNERS, NFC

	Yrs.	No.	Yards	Avg.	TD
1. Neal Colzie, T.B.	6	168	1747	10.4	0
2. James Jones, Dall.	1	54	548	10.1	0
3. Mike Nelms, Wash.	1	48	487	10.1	0
4. Cullen Bryant, L.A.	8	71	707	10.0	0
5. Wally Henry, Phil.	4	74	732	9.9	1
6. Freddie Solomon, S.F.	6	130	1285	9.9	4
7. Eddie Payton, Minn.	3	96	905	9.4	1
8. Lemar Parrish, Wash.	11	131	1205	9.2	4
9. Butch Johnson, Dall.	5	146	1313	9.0	0
10. Pat Tilley, St.L.	5	30	265	8.8	0

Other Leading Punt Returners

	Yrs.	No.	Yards	Avg.	TD
John Sciarra, Phil.	3	89	763	8.6	0
Tony Davis, T.B.	5	67	566	8.5	0
Bobby Hammond, Wash.	5	67	566	8.4	1
Alvin Garrett, N.Y.G.	1	35	287	8.2	0
Rich Mauti, N.O.	4	75	610	8.1	0
Johnnie Gray, G.B.	6	76	599	7.9	0
John Arnold, Det.	2	47	368	7.8	0
Vaughn Lusby, Chi.	2	36	274	7.6	0
Len Walterscheid, Chi.	4	56	418	7.5	0
Roger Wehrli, St.L.	12	42	310	7.4	0
LeRoy Irvin, L.A.	1	42	296	7.0	0
Willard Harrell, St.L.	6	116	814	7.0	2

TOP 10 ACTIVE KICKOFF RETURNERS, NFC

	Yrs.	No.	Yards	Avg.	TD
1. Cullen Bryant, L.A.	8	66	1760	26.7	3
2. Wilbert Montgomery, Phil.	4	31	802	25.9	4
3. Wallace Francis, Atl.	8	84	2077	24.7	2
4. Lemar Parrish, Wash.	11	61	1504	24.7	1
5. Len Walterscheid, Chi.	4	34	833	24.5	0
6. Brian Baschnagel, Chi.	5	84	2026	24.1	1
7. James Owens, S.F.	2	72	1728	24.0	2
8. Roy Green, St.L.	2	73	1750	24.0	1
9. Eddie Payton, Minn.	3	105	2507	23.9	1
10. Rolland Lawrence, Atl.	8	29	685	23.6	0

Other Leading Kickoff Returners

	Yrs.	No.	Yards	Avg.	TD
Dave Williams, Chi.	4	65	1533	23.6	3
Rich Mauti, N.O.	4	111	2596	23.4	0
Mel Gray, St.L.	10	51	1191	23.4	0
Butch Johnson, Dall.	5	79	1832	23.1	0
Wally Henry, Phil.	4	38	876	23.1	0
Wes Chandler, N.O.	3	39	896	23.0	0

TOP 10 ACTIVE PUNTERS, NFC

35 or more punts

	Yrs.	No.	Avg.	LG
1. Tom Skladany, Det.	3	168	42.2	67
2. Dave Jennings, N.Y.G.	7	611	41.8	72
3. Tom Blanchard, T.B.	10	797	41.3	71
4. Jim Miller, S.F.	4	77	40.9	65
5. John James, Atl.	9	786	40.8	75
6. Larry Swider, Det.	2	187	40.8	72
7. Danny White, Dall.	5	373	40.2	73
8. Bob Lee, L.A.	12	156	39.7	58
9. Frank Corral, L.A.	3	76	39.5	65
10. Max Runager, Phil.	2	149	39.4	58

Other Leading Punters

	Yrs.	No.	Avg.	LG
Russell Erxleben, N.O.	2	93	39.2	57
Greg Coleman, Minn.	4	283	39.1	70
Bob Parsons, Chi.	9	633	38.5	62
Mike Connell, Wash.	2	181	38.2	59
David Beverly, G.B.	7	586	38.1	69

Active Coaches' Career Records
Start of 1981 Season

Coach	Team(s)	Regular Season					Postseason				Career			
		Yrs.	Won	Lost	Tied	Pct.	Won	Lost	Tied	Pct.	Won	Lost	Tied	Pct.
Don Shula	Baltimore Colts, Miami Dolphins	18	183	70	5	.718	10	8	0	.556	193	78	5	.708
Tom Flores	Oakland Raiders	2	20	12	0	.625	4	0	0	1.000	24	12	0	.666
Chuck Noll	Pittsburgh Steelers	12	109	64	1	.629	14	4	0	.778	123	68	1	.643
Bud Grant	Minnesota Vikings	14	131	66	5	.660	9	11	0	.450	140	77	5	.641
Chuck Knox	Los Angeles Rams, Buffalo Bills	8	77	40	1	.656	3	6	0	.333	80	46	1	.633
Don Coryell	St. Louis Cardinals, San Diego Chargers	8	73	40	1	.644	1	4	0	.200	74	44	1	.626
Tom Landry	Dallas Cowboys	21	184	108	6	.627	17	12	0	.586	201	120	6	.623
O. A. (Bum) Phillips	Houston Oilers, New Orleans Saints	6	55	35	0	.611	4	3	0	.571	59	38	0	.608
Ron Erhardt	New England Patriots	2	19	13	0	.593	0	0	0	.000	19	13	0	.593
Ray Malavasi	Denver Broncos, Los Angeles Rams	4	36	24	0	.600	3	3	0	.500	39	27	0	.590
Sam Rutigliano	Cleveland Browns	3	28	20	0	.583	0	1	0	.000	28	21	0	.571
Leeman Bennett	Atlanta Falcons	4	34	28	0	.548	1	2	0	.333	35	30	0	.538
Dick Vermeil	Philadelphia Eagles	5	41	35	0	.539	3	3	0	.500	44	38	0	.536
Neill Armstrong	Chicago Bears	3	24	24	0	.500	0	1	0	.000	24	25	0	.489
Forrest Gregg	Cleveland Browns, Cincinnati Bengals	4	24	33	0	.421	0	0	0	.000	24	33	0	.421
Monte Clark	San Francisco 49ers, Detroit Lions	4	26	36	0	.419	0	0	0	.000	26	36	0	.419
Mike McCormack	Philadelphia Eagles, Baltimore Colts	4	23	34	1	.405	0	0	0	.000	23	34	1	.405
Marv Levy	Kansas City Chiefs	3	19	29	0	.395	0	0	0	.000	19	29	0	.395
Jack Patera	Seattle Seahawks	5	29	47	0	.381	0	0	0	.000	29	47	0	.381
Walt Michaels	New York Jets	4	23	39	0	.370	0	0	0	.000	23	39	0	.370
Bart Starr	Green Bay Packers	6	31	57	2	.355	0	0	0	.000	31	57	2	.355
Bill Walsh	San Francisco 49ers	2	8	24	0	.333	0	0	0	.000	8	24	0	.333
Ray Perkins	New York Giants	2	10	22	0	.312	0	0	0	.000	10	22	0	.313
Jim Hanifan	St. Louis Cardinals	1	5	11	0	.312	0	0	0	.000	5	11	0	.313
John McKay	Tampa Bay Buccaneers	5	22	53	1	.296	1	1	0	.500	23	54	1	.301
Ed Biles	Houston Oilers	0	0	0	0	.000	0	0	0	.000	0	0	0	.000
Joe Gibbs	Washington Redskins	0	0	0	0	.000	0	0	0	.000	0	0	0	.000
Dan Reeves	Denver Broncos	0	0	0	0	.000	0	0	0	.000	0	0	0	.000

Coaches With 100 Career Victories
Start of 1981 Season

Coach	Team(s)	Regular Season					Postseason				Career			
		Yrs.	Won	Lost	Tied	Pct.	Won	Lost	Tied	Pct.	Won	Lost	Tied	Pct.
George Halas	Chicago Bears	40	320	147	30	.674	6	3	0	.667	326	150	30	.674
Earl (Curly) Lambeau	Green Bay Packers, Chicago Cardinals, Washington Redskins	33	231	133	23	.627	3	2	0	.600	234	135	23	.626
Tom Landry	Dallas Cowboys	21	184	108	6	.627	17	12	0	.586	201	120	6	.623
Don Shula	Baltimore Colts, Miami Dolphins	18	183	70	5	.718	10	8	0	.556	193	78	5	.708
Paul Brown	Cleveland Browns, Cincinnati Bengals	21	166	100	6	.621	4	8	0	.333	170	108	6	.608
Steve Owen	New York Giants	23	151	100	17	.595	3	8	0	.273	154	108	17	.582
Bud Grant	Minnesota Vikings	14	131	66	5	.660	9	11	0	.450	140	77	5	.641
Hank Stram	Kansas City Chiefs, New Orleans Saints	17	131	97	10	.571	5	3	0	.625	136	100	10	.573
Weeb Ewbank	Baltimore Colts, New York Jets	20	130	129	7	.502	4	1	0	.800	134	130	7	.507
Chuck Noll	Pittsburgh Steelers	12	109	64	1	.629	14	4	0	.778	123	68	1	.643
Sid Gillman	Los Angeles Rams, San Diego Chargers, Houston Oilers	18	122	99	7	.550	1	5	0	.167	123	104	7	.541
George Allen	Los Angeles Rams, Washington Redskins	12	116	47	5	.705	2	7	0	.222	118	54	5	.681
John Madden	Oakland Raiders	10	103	32	7	.750	9	7	0	.563	112	39	7	.731
Raymond (Buddy) Parker	Chicago Cardinals, Detroit Lions, Pittsburgh Steelers	15	104	75	9	.577	3	1	0	.750	107	76	9	.580
Vince Lombardi	Green Bay Packers, Washington Redskins	10	96	34	6	.728	9	1	0	.900	105	35	6	.740

1981 Trades

Interconference Trades

Los Angeles traded linebacker **Bob Brudzinski** and a 1981 second-round choice previously acquired from Oakland to Miami for the Dolphins' second- and third-round choices in 1981 and a 1982 second-round choice previously acquired from Tampa Bay. Miami subsequently selected running back **Andra Franklin** (Nebraska). Los Angeles subsequently selected linebacker **Jim Collins** (Syracuse) and then traded the 1981 third-round choice to Washington (4/28).

Baltimore traded running back **Joe Washington** to Washington for a 1981 second-round choice the Redskins previously acquired from Los Angeles. Baltimore subsequently traded the second-round choice to Minnesota (4/28).

Minnesota traded its 1981 first-round choice to Baltimore for the Colts' 1981 second- and fifth-round choices and a 1981 second-round choice Baltimore had previously acquired from Los Angeles through Washington. Baltimore subsequently selected defensive tackle **Donnell Thompson** (North Carolina). Minnesota subsequently selected wide receiver **Mardye McDole** (Mississippi State), running back **Jarvis Redwine** (Nebraska), and defensive end **Wendell Ray** (Missouri) (4/28).

New England traded guard **Sam Adams** to New Orleans for the Saints' 1981 eighth-round choice (4/23) and New England selected kicker-punter **Ken Naber** (Stanford) (4/29).

Cleveland traded a 1981 tenth-round choice it previously acquired from Washington and a 1981 tenth-round choice it previously acquired from New England to Washington for the Redskins' eighth choice in 1982. Washington subsequently selected quarterback **Phil Kessel** (Northern Michigan) and tackle **Allan Kennedy** (Washington State) (4/29).

Defensive tackle **Wilbur Young** from San Diego to Washington for tackle **Jeff Williams** (5-15).

AFC Trades

Buffalo traded its 1981 first-round choice to Oakland for the Raiders' 1981 first- and third-round draft choices. Oakland subsequently selected tackle **Curt Marsh** (Washington). Buffalo subsequently selected running back **Booker Moore** (Penn State) and defensive tackle **Robert Geathers** (South Carolina State) (4/28).

Kansas City traded running back **Tony Reed** to Denver for a 1981 third-round choice the Broncos previously acquired from Cleveland and the Broncos' 1982 fourth-round choice. Kansas City subsequently selected tackle **Roger Taylor** (Oklahoma State) (4/28).

Punter-quarterback **Johnny Evans** from Cleveland to Buffalo for a draft choice (5/5).

Running back **Terry Miller** from Buffalo to Cleveland for draft choices (5/5).

Defensive end **Mel Lunsford** from New England to Cincinnati for cash (6/19).

NFC Trades

Los Angeles traded its 1981 first, second- and fourth-round choices to Washington for the Redskins' 1981 first-round choice. Los Angeles subsequently selected linebacker **Mel Owens** (Michigan). Washington subsequently selected tackle **Mark May** (Pittsburgh) and traded the Los Angeles' second to Baltimore and the fourth to Green Bay (4/28).

San Francisco traded its 1981 second-round choice to Chicago for the Bears' 1981 second- and fifth-round choices. San Francisco subsequently selected defensive back **Eric Wright** (Missouri) and running back **Arrington Jones** (Winston-Salem). Chicago subsequently selected linebacker **Mike Singletary** (Baylor) (4/28).

Washington traded its 1982 first-round choice to Los Angeles for the Rams' 1981 fifth-round choice, a 1981 third-round choice the Rams previously had acquired from Miami, a 1981 fifth-round choice the Rams previously had acquired from Green Bay, and the Rams' 1982 second-round choice. Washington subsequently selected center **Russ Grimm** (Pittsburgh) and guard **Gary Sayre** (Cameron, Okla.). Washington returned the Green Bay choice to the Packers in a subsequent trade (4/28).

Washington traded the 1981 fourth-round choice it previously acquired from Los Angeles and a 1981 fifth-round choice it previously acquired from Green Bay through Los Angeles to Green Bay for the Packers' 1981 fourth-round choice. Washington subsequently selected quarterback **Tom Flick** (Washington). Green Bay subsequently selected defensive tackle **Richard Turner** (Oklahoma) (4/28).

San Francisco traded its 1981 seventh-round choice to Philadelphia for past consideration (3/24) and Philadelphia selected kicker **Alan Duncan** (Tennessee) (4/29).

Tight end **Henry Childs** from New Orleans to Washington for a 1982 draft choice (4/30).

Defensive tackle **Ted Vincent** from San Francisco to Tampa Bay for a 1982 draft choice (4/30).

Tight end **Henry Childs** from Washington to Los Angeles for 1982 draft choices. (5/6).

Running back **Terry Metcalf** from St. Louis to Washington for a 1982 draft choice (5/13).

Quarterback **Guy Benjamin** from New Orleans to San Francisco for a 1982 draft choice (7-13).

Look for in 1981

Things that could happen in 1981:

• Franco Harris, Pittsburgh, needs 185 rushing attempts to exceed the career record of 2,404 held by O. J. Simpson. Harris is 648 yards short of the 10,000-yard mark, previously achieved only by Jim Brown (12,312) and Simpson (11,236).

• Walter Payton, Chicago, is only 614 yards short of 9,000 yards rushing, and needs 135 carries to reach a career total of 2,000. Payton is looking to add to his streak of five consecutive NFC rushing titles.

• Jim Hart, St. Louis, needs seven touchdown passes to reach the 200 mark, a level achieved by only nine passers. Hart needs only 83 completions to move into third place on the all-time list ahead of John Brodie, who had 2,469.

• Harold Jackson, New England, who is in third place on the all-time list for yards gained on pass receptions, needs 423 yards to reach the 10,000-yard plateau. Don Maynard (11,834) and Lance Alworth (10,266) are the only players ahead of him.

• Mel Gray, St. Louis, has a current streak of 105 games catching passes and has matched the streak of Danny Abramowicz, the second-longest in NFL history. The record is 127 games by Harold Carmichael; that streak ended in the Eagles' final regular-season game of 1980. Carmichael needs 45 catches to reach 500 for his career. He would become only the tenth NFL player to reach that mark.

• Rick Upchurch, Denver, starts the season with 220 career punt returns; the all-time leader is Emlen Tunnell (258). Upchurch is already the leader in punt return yardage (2,651). Mike Fuller, San Diego, is second with 2,388.

• Jan Stenerud, Green Bay, starts the season in a third-place tie with Fred Cox and Jim Bakken in career field goals. Each player has 282. The only players to have kicked at least 300 field goals are George Blanda (335) and Jim Turner (304).

• Mike Bragg, Baltimore, who is in second place on the all-time list for most punts, needs 22 to reach the 1,000 mark. Jerrel Wilson is the all-time leader with 1,072.

Monday Night Football, 1970–1980

(Home Team in capitals, games listed in chronological order.)

1980
Dallas 17, WASHINGTON 3
Houston 16, CLEVELAND 7
PHILADELPHIA 35, N.Y. Giants 3
NEW ENGLAND 23, Denver 14
CHICAGO, 23, Tampa Bay 0
DENVER 20, Washington 17
Oakland 45, PITTSBURGH 34
N.Y. JETS 17, Miami 14
CLEVELAND 27, Chicago 21
HOUSTON 38, New England 34
Oakland 19, SEATTLE 17
Los Angeles 27, NEW ORLEANS 7
MIAMI 16, New England 13 (OT)
LOS ANGELES 38, Dallas 14
SAN DIEGO 26, Pittsburgh 17

1979
Pittsburgh 16, NEW ENGLAND 13 (OT)
Atlanta 14, PHILADELPHIA 10
WASHINGTON 27, New York Giants 0
CLEVELAND 26, Dallas 7
GREEN BAY 27, New England 14
OAKLAND 13, Miami 3
NEW YORK JETS 14, Minnesota 7
PITTSBURGH 42, Denver 7
Seattle 31, ATLANTA 28
Houston 9, MIAMI 6
Philadelphia 31, DALLAS 21
LOS ANGELES 20, Atlanta 14
SEATTLE 30, New York Jets 7
Oakland 34, CINCINNATI 21
HOUSTON 20, Pittsburgh 17
SAN DIEGO 17, Denver 7

1978
DALLAS 38, Baltimore 0
MINNESOTA 12, Denver 9 (OT)
Baltimore 34, NEW ENGLAND 27
Minnesota 24, CHICAGO 20
WASHINGTON 9, Dallas 5
MIAMI 21, Cincinnati 0
DENVER 16, Chicago 7
Houston 24, PITTSBURGH 17
ATLANTA 15, Los Angeles 7
BALTIMORE 21, Washington 17
HOUSTON 35, Miami 30
Pittsburgh 24, SAN FRANCISCO 7
SAN DIEGO 40, Chicago 7
Cincinnati 20, LOS ANGELES 19
MIAMI 23, New England 3

1977
PITTSBURGH 27, San Francisco 0
CLEVELAND 30, New England 27 (OT)
Oakland 37, KANSAS CITY 28
CHICAGO 24, Los Angeles 23
PITTSBURGH 20, Cincinnati 14
LOS ANGELES 35, Minnesota 3
ST. LOUIS 28, New York Giants 0
BALTIMORE 10, Washington 3
St. Louis 24, DALLAS 17
WASHINGTON 10, Green Bay 9
OAKLAND 34, Buffalo 13
MIAMI 16, Baltimore 6
Dallas 42, SAN FRANCISCO 35

1976
Miami 30, BUFFALO 21
Oakland 24, KANSAS CITY 21
Washington 20, PHILADELPHIA 17 (OT)
MINNESOTA 17, Pittsburgh 6
San Francisco 16, LOS ANGELES 0
NEW ENGLAND 41, New York Jets 7
WASHINGTON 20, St. Louis 10
BALTIMORE 38, Houston 14
CINCINNATI 20, Los Angeles 12
DALLAS 17, Buffalo 10
Baltimore 17, MIAMI 16
SAN FRANCISCO 20, Minnesota 16
OAKLAND 35, Cincinnati 20

1975
Oakland 31, MIAMI 21
DENVER 23, Green Bay 13
Dallas 36, DETROIT 10
WASHINGTON 27, St. Louis 17
New York Giants 17, BUFFALO 14
Minnesota 13, CHICAGO 9
Los Angeles 42, PHILADELPHIA 3
KANSAS CITY 34, DALLAS 31
CINCINNATI 33, Buffalo 24
Pittsburgh 32, HOUSTON 9
MIAMI 20, New England 7
OAKLAND 17, Denver 10
SAN DIEGO 24, New York Jets 16

1974
BUFFALO 21, Oakland 20
PHILADELPHIA 13, Dallas 10
WASHINGTON 30, Denver 3
MIAMI 21, New York Jets 17
DETROIT 17, San Francisco 13
CHICAGO 10, Green Bay 9
PITTSBURGH 24, Atlanta 17
Los Angeles 15, SAN FRANCISCO 13
Minnesota 28, ST. LOUIS 24
Kansas City 42, DENVER 34
Pittsburgh 28, NEW ORLEANS 7
MIAMI 24, Cincinnati 3
Washington 23, LOS ANGELES 17

1973
GREEN BAY 23, New York Jets 7
DALLAS 40, New Orleans 3
DETROIT 31, Atlanta 6
WASHINGTON 14, Dallas 7
Miami 17, CLEVELAND 9
DENVER 23, Oakland 23
BUFFALO 23, Kansas City 14
PITTSBURGH 21, Washington 16
KANSAS CITY 19, Chicago 7
ATLANTA 20, Minnesota 14
SAN FRANCISCO 20, Green Bay 6
MIAMI 30, Pittsburgh 26
LOS ANGELES 40, New York Giants 6

1972
Washington 24, MINNESOTA 21
Kansas City 20, NEW ORLEANS 17
New York Giants 27, PHILADELPHIA 12
Oakland 34, HOUSTON 0
Green Bay 24, DETROIT 23
CHICAGO 13, Minnesota 10
DALLAS 28, Detroit 24
Baltimore 24, NEW ENGLAND 17
MIAMI 31, St. Louis 10
WASHINGTON 24, Atlanta 13
Cleveland 21, SAN DIEGO 17
Los Angeles 26, SAN FRANCISCO 16
OAKLAND 24, New York Jets 16

1971
Minnesota 16, DETROIT 13
ST. LOUIS 17, New York Jets 10
Oakland 34, CLEVELAND 20
DALLAS 20, New York Giants 13
KANSAS CITY 38, Pittsburgh 16
MINNESOTA 10, Baltimore 3
GREEN BAY 14, Detroit 14
BALTIMORE 24, Los Angeles 17
SAN DIEGO 20, St. Louis 17
ATLANTA 28, Green Bay 21
MIAMI 34, Chicago 3
Kansas City 26, SAN FRANCISCO 17
Washington 38, LOS ANGELES 24

1970
CLEVELAND 31, New York Jets 21
Kansas City 44, BALTIMORE 24
DETROIT 28, Chicago 14
Green Bay 22, SAN DIEGO 20
OAKLAND 34, Washington 20
MINNESOTA 13, Los Angeles 3
PITTSBURGH 21, Cincinnati 10
Baltimore 13, GREEN BAY 10
PHILADELPHIA 23, New York Giants 20
St. Louis 38, DALLAS 0
Miami 20, ATLANTA 7
Cleveland 21, HOUSTON 10
Detroit 28, LOS ANGELES 23

Monday Night Won-Lost Records, 1970-1980

Team	Total	1980	1979	1978	1977	1976	1975	1974	1973	1972	1971	1970
Baltimore	8-4			2-1	1-1			1-0	1-0	1-0	1-1	1-1
Buffalo	2-5		1-0			0-2		0-1	1-0		0-1	0-1
Cincinnati	3-6	1-1	1-0		0-1	1-1				0-1	0-1	0-1
Cleveland	6-3	1-2	1-0		1-0			1-0	0-1			2-0
Denver	3-8-1		0-2	1-1	1-0	0-1	1-1	0-2	0-0-1		0-1	0-1
Houston	6-4		2-0	2-0		0-1	0-1	1-0	1-1			0-1
Kansas City	7-3	1-1				1-0	1-1	1-0	1-0	1-0	1-0	0-1
Miami	13-6	1-2		2-1	0-1	1-1	1-1	2-0	1-0	1-0	2-0	2-0
New England	2-9	1-0	0-2	0-2	0-1	1-0	0-1	0-1			0-1	0-1
New York Jets	2-8		1-1	0-2	0-1	0-1		0-1		0-1	1-0	0-1
Oakland	16-1-1	3-0	2-0	1-0	2-0	2-0	2-0	2-0	0-0-1	2-0	0-1	
Pittsburgh	10-7	0-2	2-1	1-1	2-0	2-0	1-0		0-1	2-0	0-1	0-1
San Diego	5-2	1-0	1-0	1-0		0-1		2-0				0-1
Seattle	2-1	0-1	2-0									
Atlanta	4-6		1-2	1-0	1-0			0-1	1-1	0-1		0-1
Chicago	4-8	1-1		0-3	1-0	0-1	0-1	0-1		1-0	1-0	0-1
Dallas	8-9	1-1	0-2	1-1	1-1	1-0	1-1	1-0		0-2	0-1	2-0
Detroit	4-4-1					1-0	0-1	0-1	0-0-1	0-1	1-1	2-0
Green Bay	4-6-1		1-0		0-1	1-0	0-1	0-1	0-1	1-0	0-1-1	1-0
Los Angeles	8-10	2-0	1-0	0-2	1-1	0-2	1-0	1-1		0-2	0-2	2-0
Minnesota	8-6		0-1	2-0	0-1	1-1	1-0	1-0	0-1	0-2	2-0	1-0
New Orleans	0-5		0-1		0-1		0-1	0-1				0-1
New York Giants	2-6	0-1	1-1		0-1	0-1	1-0	0-1		0-1		
Philadelphia	4-4	1-0	0-1			0-1	0-1	1-0	1-0		1-0	0-1
St. Louis	4-5				2-0	2-0	0-1		0-1	0-1	0-1	0-1
San Francisco	3-7			0-1	0-2			0-2	1-0	0-1	1-1	1-0
Tampa Bay	0-1		0-1									
Washington	12-6	0-2	1-0	1-1	1-1	2-0	1-0	2-0	1-1	1-0	1-0	1-1

Monday Night Syndrome

1980

Of the 15 winning teams:	8 won the next week	
	7 lost the next week	
	0 tied the next week	
Of the 15 losing teams:	7 won the next week	
	7 lost the next week	
	1 tied the next week	

Of the 30 NFL teams:	15 won the next week
	14 lost the next week
	1 tied the next week

1970-80

Of the 147 winning teams:	81 won the next week
	63 lost the next week
	3 tied the next week
Of the 147 losing teams:	77 won the next week
	69 lost the next week
	1 tied the next week
Of the 4 tying teams:	4 won the next week
	0 lost the next week
	0 tied the next week

Of the 298 NFL teams:	162 won the next week
	132 lost the next week
	4 tied the next week

Thursday-Sunday Night Football, 1978-1980

(Home Team in capitals, games listed in chronological order.)

1980
TAMPA BAY 10, Los Angeles 9 (Thur.)
DALLAS 42, San Diego 31 (Sun.)
San Diego 27, MIAMI 24 (OT) (Thur.)
HOUSTON 6, Pittsburgh 0 (Thur.)

1979
Los Angeles 13, DENVER 9 (Thur.)
DALLAS 30, Los Angeles 6 (Sun.)
OAKLAND 45, San Diego 22 (Thur.)
MIAMI 39, New England 24 (Thur.)

1978
New England 21, OAKLAND 14 (Sun.)
Minnesota 21, DALLAS 10 (Thur.)
LOS ANGELES 10, Pittsburgh 7 (Sun.)
Denver 21, OAKLAND 6 (Sun.)

Regular Season Interconference Records, 1970-1980

American Football Conference

Eastern Division	W	L	T	Pct.
Miami	29	5	0	.853
New England	18	16	0	.529
Baltimore	18	16	0	.529
Buffalo	14	17	1	.453
New York Jets	11	23	0	.324

Central Division	W	L	T	Pct.
Pittsburgh	24	10	0	.706
Cincinnati	21	14	0	.600
Cleveland	19	16	1	.543
Houston	15	18	1	.456

Western Division	W	L	T	Pct.
Oakland	27	7	1	.786
Seattle	8	5	0	.615
Denver	19	15	1	.557
Kansas City	12	14	2	.464
San Diego	15	19	0	.441

TOTALS 247

National Football Conference

Eastern Division	W	L	T	Pct.
Dallas	25	9	0	.735
Philadelphia	18	16	0	.529
Washington	16	18	0	.471
St. Louis	14	20	1	.406
N.Y. Giants	12	18	2	.400

Central Division	W	L	T	Pct.
Minnesota	19	15	0	.556
Detroit	18	15	1	.543
Green Bay	18	16	0	.530
Chicago	13	21	1	.386
Tampa Bay	5	13	0	.229

Western Division	W	L	T	Pct.
Los Angeles	22	13	0	.629
San Francisco	14	21	0	.400
Atlanta	13	22	0	.371
New Orleans	4	29	2	.143

TOTALS 199

AFC vs. NFC (Regular Season), 1970-1980

	1970	1971	1972	1973	1974	1975	1976	1977	1978	1979	1980	Totals
Miami	2-1	3-0	3-0	2-1	2-1	3-0	2-0	2-0	4-0	4-0	4-0	29-5
Oakland	2-1	3-0	3-0	3-0	2-1	3-0	3-0	1-2	3-1	3-1	2-2	27-7-1
Pittsburgh	3-0	1-1-1	1-2	2-1	2-1	2-1	2-1	3-1	3-1	2-2	2-2	24-10
Cincinnati	1-2	3-0	3-0	0-3-1	2-2	3-0	2-1	1-2	2-2	2-2	2-2	21-14
Cleveland	2-1	0-3	1-2	1-2	0-3	3-0	2-1	3-1	2-2	2-2	3-1	19-16-1
Denver	1-2	0-3	0-3	2-1	4-0	2-1	1-1	3-1	2-2	2-2	2-2	19-15-1
Baltimore	3-0	2-1	3-0	2-1	0-3	1-2	2-0	0-2	1-3	2-2	2-2	18-16
New England	2-1	1-2	1-2	2-1	2-2	1-2	2-0	2-0	2-2	1-3	2-2	18-16
Houston	2-1	1-2	0-3	1-2	1-2	3-0	1-1	1-1	2-2	1-3	2-2	15-18-1
San Diego	2-0-1	0-3	1-2	1-2	1-2	1-2	0-2	1-1	2-2	2-2	4-1	15-19
Buffalo	0-3	0-2-1	2-1	3-0	2-1	0-3	0-2	2-0	0-4	2-2	3-1	14-17-1
Kansas City	2-1	1-2	1-2	2-1	2-1	1-2	0-2	1-1	0-4	1-3	1-3	12-14-2
New York Jets	2-1	0-3	1-2	0-3	1-2	0-3	2-0	1-1	1-3	1-3	1-3	11-23
Seattle							0-1	1-0	3-1	1-3	3-1	8-5
TOTALS	12-27-1	15-23-2	20-19-1	19-19-2	23-17	23-17	16-12	19-9	31-21	36-16	33-19	247-199-6

NFC vs. AFC (Regular Season), 1970-1980

	1970	1971	1972	1973	1974	1975	1976	1977	1978	1979	1980	Totals
Dallas	3-0	3-0	3-0	2-1	2-1	3-0	2-0	1-1	3-1	3-1	3-1	25-9
Los Angeles	3-0	3-0	2-1	2-1	2-1	2-1	1-1	3-1	1-3	2-2	1-3	22-13
Minnesota	3-0	3-0	2-1	3-0	0-3	1-2	0-2	2-0	1-3	2-2	2-2	19-15
Washington	2-1	1-2	3-0	1-2	2-1	3-0	1-1	1-1	0-4	1-3	1-3	16-18
St. Louis	1-2	2-1	2-1	1-2	3-0	1-2	2-0	0-2	2-2	0-4	1-3	16-18
Philadelphia	1-2	1-2	1-2	2-1	2-1	2-1	1-1	2-0	2-2	2-2	2-2	18-16
San Francisco	2-1	1-2	2-1	2-1	0-3	0-3	2-0	0-2	0-4	2-2	2-2	14-21
Green Bay	3-0	1-2	0-3	2-1	2-1	0-3	0-2	1-1	1-3	2-2	1-3	13-21
Atlanta	2-1	1-2	2-1	1-1-1	0-3	1-2	0-2	1-1	2-2	1-3	2-2	13-22
Detroit	2-1	2-1	2-1	2-0-1	2-1	1-2	1-1	1-1	2-2	1-3	1-3	17-16-1
Chicago	1-2	1-2	1-2	0-3	2-1	1-2	0-2	1-1	0-4	2-2	1-3	13-21
N.Y. Giants	1-2	1-2	1-2	2-1	1-2	2-1	0-2	1-1	1-3	0-4	1-3	12-18-2
New Orleans	0-3	2-1	0-3	0-3	0-3	1-2	0-2	0-2	1-3	1-3	0-4	4-29-2
Tampa Bay							0-2	1-0	1-3	1-3	1-3	5-13
TOTALS	27-12-1	23-15-2	19-20-1	19-19-2	17-23	17-23	12-16	9-19	21-31	16-36	19-33	199-247-6

Interconference Victories, 1970-1980

Regular Season

	AFC	NFC	Tie
1970	12	27	1
1971	15	23	2
1972	20	19	1
1973	19	19	2
1974	23	17	0
1975	23	17	0
1976	16	12	0
1977	19	9	0
1978	31	21	0
1979	36	16	0
1980	33	19	0
Total	247	199	6

Preseason

	AFC	NFC	Tie
1970	21	28	1
1971	28	28	3
1972	27	25	4
1973	19	35	2
1974	23	25	0
1975	35	26	1
1976	30	31	0
1977	38	25	0
1978	20	19	2
1979	25	18	4
1980	22	20	3
Total	299	280	12

1980 Interconference Games

(Home Team in capital letters.)

AFC 33, NFC 19

AFC Victories

DENVER 41, Dallas 20
Miami 20, ATLANTA 17
Buffalo 35, NEW ORLEANS 26
OAKLAND 24, Washington 21
PITTSBURGH 38, Chicago 3
Cleveland 34, TAMPA BAY 27
PITTSBURGH 23, MINNESOTA 17
Seattle 14, WASHINGTON 0
New York Jets 14, ATLANTA 7
DENVER 20, Washington 17
CLEVELAND 26, Green Bay 21
CINCINNATI 14, Minnesota 0
SAN DIEGO 44, New York Giants 7
HOUSTON 20, Tampa Bay 14
Denver 14, NEW YORK GIANTS 9
KANSAS CITY 20, Detroit 17
CLEVELAND 27, Chicago 21
PITTSBURGH 22, Green Bay 20
MIAMI 35, LOS ANGELES 14
PITTSBURGH 24, TAMPA BAY 21
Baltimore 10, DETROIT 9
Houston 10, CHICAGO 6
MIAMI 17, San Francisco 13
Kansas City 21, ST. LOUIS 13
SAN DIEGO 22, Philadelphia 21
BUFFALO 10, Los Angeles 7 (OT)
Cincinnati 17, CHICAGO 14 (OT)
Houston 22, GREEN BAY 3
Buffalo 18, SAN FRANCISCO 13
New England 20, Minnesota 16
New England 38, NEW ORLEANS 27
Oakland 33, NEW YORK GIANTS 17

NFC Victories

PHILADELPHIA 27, Denver 6
Tampa Bay 17, CINCINNATI 12
Atlanta 37, NEW ENGLAND 21
GREEN BAY 14, Cincinnati 9
St. Louis 17, BALTIMORE 10
DALLAS 42, San Diego 31
Atlanta 30, BUFFALO 14
Los Angeles 17, NEW ENGLAND 14
PHILADELPHIA 10, Oakland 7
DALLAS 51, Seattle 7
SAN FRANCISCO 21, New England 17
LOS ANGELES 38, New York Jets 13
Dallas 19, OAKLAND 13
New York Giants 27, SEATTLE 21
WASHINGTON 40, San Diego 17
MINNESOTA 28, Cleveland 23
New Orleans 21, NEW YORK JETS 20

History of Overtime Games

Preseason

Aug. 24, 1962	Denver 27, Dallas Texans 24, at Fort Worth, Texas
Aug. 10, 1974	San Diego 20, New York Jets 14, at San Diego
Aug. 17, 1974	Pittsburgh 33, Philadelphia 30, at Philadelphia
Aug. 17, 1974	Dallas 19, Houston 13, at Dallas
Aug. 17, 1974	Cincinnati 13, Atlanta 7, at Atlanta
Sept. 6, 1974	Buffalo 23, New York Giants 17, at Buffalo
Aug. 9, 1975	Baltimore 23, Denver 20, at Denver
Aug. 30, 1975	New England 20, Green Bay 17, at Milwaukee
Sept. 13, 1975	Minnesota 14, San Diego 14, at San Diego
Aug. 1, 1976	New England 13, New York Giants 7, at New England
Aug. 2, 1976	Kansas City 9, Houston 3, at Kansas City
Aug. 20, 1976	New Orleans 26, Baltimore 20, at Baltimore
Sept. 4, 1976	Dallas 26, Houston 20, at Dallas
Aug. 13, 1977	Seattle 23, Dallas 17, at Seattle
Aug. 28, 1977	New England 13, Pittsburgh 10, at New England
Aug. 28, 1977	New York Giants 24, Buffalo 21, at East Rutherford, N.J.
Aug. 2, 1979	Seattle 12, Minnesota 9, at Minnesota
Aug. 4, 1979	Los Angeles 20, Oakland 14, at Los Angeles
Aug. 24, 1979	Denver 20, New England 17, at Denver
August 23, 1980	Tampa Bay 20, Cincinnati 14, at Tampa Bay

Regular Season

Sept. 27, 1976—Washington 20, Philadelphia 17, at Philadelphia; Eagles win toss. Jones punts and Eddie Brown loses one yard on return to Redskins' 40. Bragg punts 51 yards into end zone for touchback. Jones punts and Eddie Brown returns to Redskins' 42. Bragg punts and Marshall returns to Eagles' 41. Boryla's pass intercepted by Dusek at Redskins' 37, no return. Bragg punts and Bradley returns, Philadelphia holding penalty moves ball back to Eagles' 8. Boryla pass intercepted by Eddie Brown and returned to Eagles' 22. Moseley kicks 29-yard field goal at 12:49.

Oct. 17, 1976—Kansas City 20, Miami 17, at Miami; Chiefs win toss. Wilson punts into end zone for touchback. Bulaich fumbles into Kansas City end zone, Collier recovers for touchback. Stenerud kicks 34 yard field goal at 14:48.

Oct. 31, 1976—St. Louis 23, San Francisco 20, at St. Louis; Cardinals win toss. Joyce punts and Leonard fumbles on return, Jones recovers at 49ers' 43. Bakken kicks 21-yard field goal at 6:42.

Dec. 5, 1976—San Diego 13, San Francisco 7, at San Diego; Chargers win toss. Morris runs 13 yards for touchdown at 5:12.

Sept. 18, 1977—Dallas 16, Minnesota 10, at Minnesota; Vikings win toss. Dallas starts on the Vikings' 47 after a punt early in the overtime period. Staubach scores seven plays later on a four-yard run at 6:14.

Sept. 26, 1977—Cleveland 30, New England 27, at Cleveland; Browns win toss. Sipe throws a 22-yard pass to Logan at Patriots' 19. Cockroft kicks 35-yard field goal at 4:45.

Oct. 16, 1977—Minnesota 22, Chicago 16, at Minnesota; Bears win toss. Parsons punts 53 yards to Vikings' 18. Minnesota drives to Bears' 11. On a first-and-10, Vikings fake a field goal and holder Krause hits Voigt with a touchdown pass at 6:45.

Oct. 30, 1977—Cincinnati 13, Houston 10, at Cincinnati; Bengals win toss. Bahr kicks a 22-yard field goal at 5:51.

Nov. 13, 1977—San Francisco 10, New Orleans 7, at New Orleans; Saints win toss. Saints fail to move ball and Blanchard punts to 49ers' 41. Wersching kicks a 33-yard field goal at 6:33.

Dec. 18, 1977—Chicago 12, New York Giants 9, at East Rutherford, N.J.; Giants win toss. The ball changes hands eight times before Thomas kicks a 28-yard field goal at 14:51.

Sept. 10, 1978—Cleveland 13, Cincinnati 10, at Cleveland; Browns win toss. Collins returns kickoff 41 yards to the Browns' 47. Cockroft kicks 27-yard field goal at 4:30.

Sept. 11, 1978—Minnesota 12, Denver 9, at Minnesota; Vikings win toss. Danmeier kicks 44-yard field goal at 2:56.

Sept. 24, 1978—Pittsburgh 15, Cleveland 9, at Pittsburgh; Steelers win toss. Cunningham scores on a 37-yard "gadget" pass from Bradshaw at 3:43. Steelers start winning drive on their 21.

Sept. 24, 1978—Denver 23, Kansas City 17, at Kansas City; Denver wins toss. Dilts punts to Kansas City. Chiefs advance to the Denver 40 where Reed fails to make first down on fourth-and-one situation. Broncos march downfield. Preston scores two-yard touchdown at 10:28.

Oct. 1, 1978—Oakland 25, Chicago 19, at Chicago; Chicago wins toss. Both teams punt on first possession. On Chicago's second offensive series, Colzie intercepts Avellini's pass and returns it to the Bears' 3 yard line. Three plays later, Whittington runs two yards for a touchdown at 5:19.

Oct. 15, 1978—Dallas 24, St. Louis 21, at St. Louis; Cowboys win toss. Dallas drives from its 23 into field goal range. Septien kicks 27-yard field goal at 3:28.

Oct. 29, 1978—Denver 20, Seattle 17, at Seattle; Broncos win toss. Ball changes hands four times before Turner kicks 18-yard field goal at 12:59.

Nov. 12, 1978—San Diego 29, Kansas City 23, at San Diego; Chiefs win toss. Fouts hits Jefferson for decisive 14-yard touchdown pass on the last play (15:00) of overtime period.

Nov. 12, 1978—Washington 16, New York Giants 13, at Washington; Redskins win toss. Moseley kicks winning 45-yard field goal at 8:32 after missing first down field goal attempt of 35 yards at 4:50 of overtime.

Nov. 26, 1978—Green Bay 10, Minnesota 10, at Green Bay; Packers win toss. Both teams have possession of the ball four times.

Dec. 9, 1978—Cleveland 37, New York Jets 34, at Cleveland; Browns win toss. Cockroft kicks 22-yard field goal at 3:07.

Sept. 2, 1979—Atlanta 40, New Orleans 34, at New Orleans; Falcons win toss. Bartkowski's pass intercepted by Myers and returned to Falcons' 46. Erxleben punts to Falcons' 4. James punts to Chandler on Saints' 43. Erxleben punts and Ryckman returns to Falcons' 28. James punts and Chandler returns to Saints' 36. Erxleben retrieves punt snap on Saints' 1 and attempts pass. Mayberry intercepts and returns six yards for touchdown at 8:22.

Sept. 2, 1979—Cleveland 25, New York Jets 22, at New York; Jets win toss. Leahy's 43-yard field goal attempt goes wide right at 4:41. Evans's punt blocked by Dykes, recovered by Newton. Ramsey punts into end zone for touchback. Evans punts and Harper returns to Jets' 24. Robinson's pass intercepted by Davis and returned 33 yards to Jets' 31. Cockroft kicks 27-yard field goal at 14:45.

Sept. 3, 1979—Pittsburgh 16, New England 13, at Foxboro; Patriots win toss. Hare punts to Swann at Steelers' 31. Bahr kicks 41-yard field goal at 5:10.

Sept. 9, 1979—Tampa Bay 29, Baltimore 26, at Baltimore; Colts win toss. Landry fumbles, recovered by Kollar at Colts' 14. O'Donoghue kicks 31-yard, first-down field goal at 1:41.

Sept. 15, 1979—Denver 20, Atlanta 17, at Atlanta; Broncos win toss. Broncos march 65 yards to Falcons' 7. Turner kicks 24-yard field goal at 6:15.

Sept. 23, 1979—Houston 30, Cincinnati 27, at Cincinnati; Oilers win toss. Parsley punts and Lusby returns to Bengals' 33. Bahr's 32-yard field goal attempt wide right at 8:05. Parsley punt downed on Bengals' 5. McInally punts and Ellender returns to Bengals' 42. Fritsch's third down, 29-yard field goal attempt hits left upright and bounces through at 14:28.

Sept. 23, 1979—Minnesota 27, Green Bay 21, at Minnesota; Vikings win toss. Kramer throws 50-yard touchdown pass to Rashad at 3:18.

Oct. 28, 1979—Houston 27, New York Jets 24, at Houston; Oilers win toss. Oilers march 58 yards to Jets 18. Fritsch kicks 35-yard field goal at 5:10.

Nov. 18, 1979—Cleveland 30, Miami 24, at Cleveland; Browns win toss. Sipe passes 39-yards to Rucker for touchdown at 1:59.

Nov. 25, 1979—Pittsburgh 33, Cleveland 30, at Pittsburgh; Browns win toss. Sipe's pass intercepted by Blount on Steelers' 4. Bradshaw pass intercepted by Bolton on Browns' 12. Evans punts and Bell returns to Steelers' 17. Bahr kicks 37-yard field goal at 14:51.

Nov. 25, 1979—Buffalo 16, New England 13, at Foxboro; Patriots win toss. Hare punt downed on Bills' 38. Jackson punts and Morgan returns to Patriots' 20. Grogan's pass intercepted by Haslett and returned to Bills' 42. Ferguson's 51-yard pass to Butler sets up Nick Mike-Mayer's 29-yard field goal at 9:15.

Dec. 2, 1979—Los Angeles 27, Minnesota 21, at Los Angeles; Rams win toss. Clark punts and Miller returns to Vikings' 25. Kramer's pass intercepted by Brown and returned to Rams' 40. Cromwell, holding for 22-yard field goal attempt, runs around left end untouched for winning score at 6:53.

Sept. 7, 1980—Green Bay 12, Chicago 6, at Green Bay; Bears win toss. Parsons punts and Nixon returns 16 yards. Five plays later, Marcol returns own blocked field goal attempt 24 yards for touchdown at 6:00.

Sept. 14, 1980—San Diego 30, Oakland 24, at San Diego; Raiders win toss. Pastorini's first-down pass intercepted by Edwards. Millen intercepts Fouts's first-down pass and returns to San Diego 46. Bahr's 50-yard field goal attempt partially blocked by Williams and recovered on Chargers' 32. Eight plays later, Fouts throws 24-yard touchdown pass to Jefferson at 8:09.

Sept. 14, 1980—San Francisco 24, St. Louis 21, at San Francisco; Cardinals win toss. Swider punts and Robinson returns to 49ers' 32. San Francisco drives 52 yards to St. Louis 16, where Wersching kicks 33-yard field goal at 4:12.

Oct. 12, 1980—Green Bay 14, Tampa Bay 14, at Tampa Bay; Packers win toss. Teams trade punts twice. Lee returns second Tampa Bay punt to Green Bay 42. Dickey completes three passes to Buccaneers 18, where Birney's 36-yard field goal attempt is wide right as time expires.

Nov. 9, 1980—Atlanta 33, St. Louis 27; at St. Louis. Falcons win toss. Strong runs 21 yards for touchdown at 4:20.

Nov. 20, 1980—San Diego 27, Miami 24, at Miami; Chargers win toss. Partridge punts into end zone, Dolphins take over on their own 20. Woodley's pass for Nathan intercepted by Lowe and returned 28 yards to Dolphins 12. Benirschke kicks 28-yard field goal at 7:14.

Nov. 23, 1980—New York Jets 31, Houston 28, at New York; Jets win toss. Leahy kicks 38-yard field goal at 3:58.

Nov. 27, 1980—Chicago 23, Detroit 17, at Detroit; Bears win toss. Williams returns kickoff 95 yards for touchdown at :21.

Dec. 7, 1980—Buffalo 10, Los Angeles 7, at Buffalo; Rams win toss. Corral punts and Hooks returns to Bills' 34. Ferguson's 30-yard pass to Lewis sets up Mike-Mayer's 30-yard field goal at 5:14.

Dec. 7, 1980—San Francisco 38, New Orleans 35, at San Francisco; Saints win toss. Erxleben's punt downed by Hardy on 49ers' 27. Wersching kicks 36-yard field goal at 7:40.

Dec. 8, 1980—Miami 16, New England 13, at Miami; Dolphins win toss. Von Schamann kicks 23-yard field goal at 3:20.

Dec. 14, 1980—Cincinnati 17, Chicago 14, at Chicago; Bengals win toss. Breech kicks 28-yard field goal at 4:23.

Dec. 21, 1980—Los Angeles 20, Atlanta 17, at Los Angeles; Rams win toss. Corral's punt downed at Rams' 37. James punts into end zone for touchback. Corral's punt downed on Falcons' 17. Bartkowski fumbles when hit by Harris, recovered by Delaney. Corral kicks 23-yard field goal on first play of possession at 7:00.

Postseason

Dec. 28, 1958—Baltimore 23, New York Giants 17, at New York; Giants win toss. Maynard returns kickoff to Giants' 20. Chandler punts and Taseff returns one yard to Colts' 20. Colts win at 8:15 on a one-yard run by Ameche.

Dec. 23, 1962—Dallas Texans 20, Houston Oilers 17, at Houston; Texans win toss and kick off. Jancik returns kickoff to Oilers' 33. Norton punts and Jackson makes fair catch on Texans' 22. Wilson punts and Jancik makes fair catch on Oilers' 45. Robinson intercepts Blanda's pass and returns 13 yards to Oilers' 47. Wilson's punt rolls dead at Oilers' 12. Hull intercepts Blanda's pass and returns 23 yards to midfield. Texans win at 17:54 on a 25-yard field goal by Brooker.

Dec. 26, 1965—Green Bay 13, Baltimore 10, at Green Bay; Packers win toss. Moore returns kickoff to Packers' 22. Chandler punts and Haymond returns nine yards to Colts' 41. Gilburg punts and Wood makes fair catch at Packers' 21. Chandler punts and Haymond returns one yard to Colts' 41. Michaels misses 47-yard field goal. Packers win at 13:39 on a 25-yard field goal by Don Chandler.

Dec. 25, 1971—Miami 27, Kansas City 24, at Kansas City; Chiefs win toss. Podolak, after a lateral from Buchanan, returns kickoff to Chiefs' 46. Stenerud's 42-yard field goal is blocked. Seiple punts and Podolak makes fair catch at Chiefs' 17. Wilson punts and Scott returns 18 yards to Dolphins' 39. Yepremian misses 52-yard field goal. Scott intercepts Dawson's pass and returns 13 yards to Dolphins' 46. Seiple punts and Podolak loses one yard to Chiefs' 15. Wilson punts and Scott makes fair catch on Dolphins' 30. Dolphins win at 22:40 on a 37-yard field goal by Yepremian.

Dec. 24, 1977—Oakland 37, Baltimore 31, at Baltimore; Baltimore wins toss. The Raiders start on their 42 following a punt late in the first overtime. Stabler's 19-yard pass to Branch puts Raiders' at the Colts' 26. On the second play of the second overtime, Stabler hits Casper with a 10-yard touchdown pass at 15:43.

1980 NFL Standings

American Football Conference

Eastern Division

	W	L	T	Pct.	Pts.	OP
Buffalo	11	5	0	.688	320	260
New England	10	6	0	.625	441	325
Miami	8	8	0	.500	266	305
Baltimore	7	9	0	.438	355	387
N.Y. Jets	4	12	0	.250	302	395

Central Division

	W	L	T	Pct.	Pts.	OP
Cleveland	11	5	0	.688	357	310
Houston*	11	5	0	.688	295	251
Pittsburgh	9	7	0	.563	352	313
Cincinnati	6	10	0	.375	244	312

Western Division

	W	L	T	Pct.	Pts.	OP
San Diego	11	5	0	.688	418	327
Oakland*	11	5	0	.688	364	306
Kansas City	8	8	0	.500	319	336
Denver	8	8	0	.500	310	323
Seattle	4	12	0	.250	291	408

*AFC Wild Card Qualifiers

National Football Conference

Eastern Division

	W	L	T	Pct.	Pts.	OP
Philadelphia	12	4	0	.750	384	222
Dallas*	12	4	0	.750	454	311
Washington	6	10	0	.375	261	293
St. Louis	5	11	0	.313	299	350
N.Y. Giants	4	12	0	.250	249	425

Central Division

	W	L	T	Pct.	Pts.	OP
Minnesota	9	7	0	.563	317	308
Detroit	9	7	0	.563	334	272
Chicago	7	9	0	.438	304	264
Tampa Bay	5	10	1	.344	271	341
Green Bay	5	10	1	.344	231	371

Western Division

	W	L	T	Pct.	Pts.	OP
Atlanta	12	4	0	.750	405	272
Los Angeles*	11	5	0	.688	424	289
San Francisco	6	10	0	.375	320	415
New Orleans	1	15	0	.063	291	487

*NFC Wild Card Qualifiers

Postseason Results
(Home Team in capitals)

Sunday, December 28
AFC First Round Playoff: OAKLAND 27, Houston 7
NFC First Round Playoff: DALLAS 34, Los Angeles 13

Saturday, January 3
AFC Divisional Playoff: SAN DIEGO 20, Buffalo 14
NFC Divisional Playoff: PHILADELPHIA 31, Minnesota 16

Sunday, January 4
AFC Divisional Playoff: Oakland 14, CLEVELAND 12
NFC Divisional Playoff: DALLAS 30, ATLANTA 27

Sunday, January 11
AFC Championship Game: Oakland 34, SAN DIEGO 27
NFC Championship Game: PHILADELPHIA 20, Dallas 7

Sunday, January 25
Super Bowl XV: Oakland 27, Philadelphia 10

Sunday, February 1
AFC-NFC Pro Bowl: NFC 21, AFC 7

1980 Week by Week

Attendances as they appear in the following, and in the club-by-club sections starting on page 44, are turnstile counts and not paid attendance. Paid attendance totals are on page 36.

FIRST WEEK SUMMARY

The National Football League inaugurated its sixty-first season with aerial displays and scoring fireworks. The 28 teams combined to score 575 points, and were on an opening-day weekend. The Broncos' Fred Steinfort kicked field goals of 43 and 44 yards before Jaworski finished the Eagles' scoring with an 11-yard touchdown to John Spagnola. The Eagles' defense recorded five sacks, two by defensive end Dennis Harrison.

SUNDAY, SEPTEMBER 7

Minnesota 24, Atlanta 23 — At Metropolitan Stadium, attendance 44,773. Rick Danmeier's 27-yard field goal with 25 seconds left in the game gave Minnesota a victory over Atlanta. The Falcons took a 23-21 lead with 3:17 left in the game on Tim Mazzetti's 23-yard field goal. Vikings quarterback Tommy Kramer (30 of 42 for 395 yards and three touchdowns) completed six passes in driving Minnesota 69 yards and three touchdowns in the Vikings' triumph over Atlanta; and Ahmad Rashad was the game's leading receiver with 11 catches for 160 yards.

Atlanta	6	7	0	10	—23
Minnesota	7	7	0	10	—24

Atl—Cain 3 run (kick failed)
Minn—S. White 24 pass from Kramer (Danmeier kick)
Minn—Senser 4 pass from Kramer (Danmeier kick)
Atl—Tucker 4 pass from Bartkowski (Mazzetti kick)
Atl—Jenkins 46 pass from Bartkowski (Mazzetti kick)
Atl—A. Jackson 19 pass from Bartkowski (Mazzetti kick)
Minn—FG Mazzetti 23
Minn—FG Danmeier 27

Baltimore 17, New York Jets 14 — At Shea Stadium, attendance 50,777. Steve Mike-Mayer's 46-yard field goal was the difference in Baltimore's win over the New York Jets. New York tied the score 14-14 in the third quarter when rookie safety Darrol Ray returned a fumble 75 yards for a touchdown. Midway through the fourth quarter, Baltimore drove 52 yards in 17 plays to set up the winning field goal. The Colts' Bert Jones celebrated his twenty-ninth birthday by completing 24 of 42 passes for 257 yards. He also passed for a first touchdown on a 12-yard run in the second quarter. Baltimore's defense shut down the Jets' passing attack by intercepting four passes.

Baltimore	0	7	7	3	—17
New York Jets	0	7	0	7	—14

Balt—Jones 12 run (Mike-Mayer kick)
Balt—Franklin 1 run (Mike-Mayer kick)
NYJ—Todd 3 run (Leahy kick)
NYJ—Ray 75 fumble recovery return (Leahy kick)
Balt—FG Mike-Mayer 46

Green Bay 12, Chicago 6 — At Lambeau Field, attendance 54,381. Chester Marcol's 25-yard return of a blocked field goal gave Green Bay an overtime victory against Chicago. Four minutes into the overtime period Green Bay's Lynn Dickey hit James Lofton with a 32-yard pass to put the ball on Chicago's 18 yard line. Chicago then blocked the ensuing field goal attempt, but the ball bounced back to Marcol, who took it up the left sideline for the winning score. In addition to his touchdown run, Marcol kicked field goals of 41 and 46 yards. The Packers' defense intercepted three passes and recovered a fumble.

Chicago	3	0	3	0	0	—6
Green Bay	0	3	0	3	6	—12

Chi—FG Thomas 42
GB—FG Marcol 41
Chi—FG Thomas 34
GB—FG Marcol 46
GB—Marcol 25 blocked field goal return

New England 34, Cleveland 17 — At Schaefer Stadium, attendance 49,222. New England scored on its first four possessions of the second half to defeat Cleveland. The Patriots took a 20-3 third quarter lead when Steve Grogan (17 of 26 for 277 yards and three touchdowns), and Stanley Morgan combined on a 67-yard touchdown pass. Don Calhoun's two-yard touchdown run, and New England's Harold Jackson caught four passes for 77 yards and one touchdown to increase his career reception total to 501.

Cleveland	3	0	0	14	—17
New England	0	3	10	7	—34

NE—FG Smith 35
NE—Jackson 10 pass from Grogan (Smith kick)
Cle—FG Cockroft 25
NE—Morgan 67 pass from Grogan (Smith kick)
NE—Calhoun 2 run (Smith kick)
Cle—Hasselbeck 17 pass from Sipe (Cockroft kick)
NE—Logan 10 run (Smith kick)
Cle—Wright 11 pass from Sipe (Cockroft kick)

Philadelphia 27, Denver 6 — At Veterans Stadium, attendance 70,307. Ron Jaworski threw two touchdown passes to lead Philadelphia past Denver. Jaworski (18 of 28 for 281 yards) helped Philadelphia build a 20-0 halftime lead with touchdown passes of 56 yards to Harold Carmichael and 16 yards to Scott Fitzkee.

Denver	0	0	6	0	—6
Philadelphia	7	13	0	7	—27

Phil—Carmichael 56 pass from Jaworski (Franklin kick)
Phil—Fitzkee 16 pass from Jaworski (Franklin kick)
Phil—FG Franklin 17
Phil—FG Franklin 32
Den—FG Steinfort 44
Den—FG Steinfort 43
Phil—Spagnola 11 pass from Jaworski (Franklin kick)

Detroit 41, Los Angeles 20 — At Anaheim Stadium, attendance 64,892. Billy Sims rushed for 153 yards on 22 carries and scored three touchdowns as Detroit surprised Los Angeles. With the score tied 20-20 in the third quarter Lions quarterback Gary Danielson hit Sims with a 60-yard pass that set up a 15-yard touchdown run by Dexter Bussey. Detroit sealed the victory in the final quarter on touchdown runs of 41 yards by Sims and 4 yards by Horace King. Bussey joined Sims in going over the 100-yard rushing mark, gaining 111 yards on 14 carries.

Detroit	10	7	10	14	—41
Los Angeles	0	13	7	0	—20

LA—D. Hill 98 kickoff return (kick blocked)
Det—FG Murray 52
LA—Bryant 1 run (Corral kick)
LA—Peacock 1 run (Corral kick)
Det—Sims 1 run (Murray kick)
Det—Bussey 15 run (Murray kick)
Det—FG Murray 38
Det—Sims 41 run (Murray kick)
Det—King 4 run (Murray kick)

Buffalo 17, Miami 7 — At Rich Stadium, attendance 79,598. Joe Ferguson connected with Roosevelt Leaks on a four-yard scoring pass and rookie running back Joe Cribbs added an insurance touchdown with 2:02 left to play as the Bills ended their NFL-record 20-game losing streak to the Dolphins. Isiah Robertson's 39-yard interception return set up a one-yard scoring plunge by Cribbs, who set a club record for running backs with nine receptions for 71 yards. Safety Jeff Nixon's three interceptions and fumble recovery led the Bills' defense, which limited Miami to 110 net yards passing.

Miami	0	0	0	7	—7
Buffalo	7	7	3	0	—17

Buff—Leaks 4 pass from Ferguson (Mike-Mayer kick)
Mia—Nathan 4 run (von Schamann kick)
Buff—FG Mike-Mayer 40
Buff—Cribbs 1 run (Mike-Mayer kick)

Pittsburgh 31, Houston 17 — At Three Rivers Stadium, attendance 54,386. Terry Bradshaw threw two touchdown passes and ran for another as Pittsburgh defeated Central Division rival Houston. With the score tied 17-17 in the fourth quarter, Bradshaw capped a 10-play, 80-yard scoring drive with a one-yard scoring run. Three minutes later, John Stallworth grabbed a 50-yard touchdown pass from Bradshaw to insure the Steelers victory. Pittsburgh's Franco Harris gained 46 yards on 20 carries to move into third place on the NFL's all-time rushing list.

Houston	0	17	0	0	—17
Pittsburgh	0	17	0	14	—31

Pitt—Thornton 29 pass from Bradshaw (Bahr kick)
Pitt—Harris 1 run (Bahr kick)
Hou—Campbell 1 run (Fritsch kick)
Pitt—FG Bahr 27
Hou—Johnson 57 pass from Campbell (Fritsch kick)
Pitt—Bradshaw 1 run (Bahr kick)
Pitt—Stallworth 50 pass from Bradshaw (Bahr kick)

New York Giants 41, St. Louis 35 — At Busch Memorial Stadium, attendance 49,122. Phil Simms threw five touchdown passes—four to wide receiver Earnest Gray—to lead the Giants to their first victory in St. Louis since 1972. Trailing 21-17, New York rallied on Simms's 58-yard scoring toss to Johnny Perkins. Mark Haynes's interception return set up a 42-yard Simms-to-Gray scoring pass 66 seconds later. Gray caught nine passes for 174 yards and a club record four touchdowns (10, 20, 37, and 42 yards).

New York Giants	7	7	17	10	—41
St. Louis	7	14	0	14	—35

StL—Morris 5 run (Little kick)
NYG—Gray 10 pass from Simms (Danelo kick)
StL—Morris 5 run (Little kick)
NYG—Gray 20 pass from Simms (Danelo kick)
StL—Anderson 24 run (Little kick)
NYG—Perkins 58 pass from Simms (Danelo kick)
NYG—Gray 42 pass from Simms (Danelo kick)
StL—Marsh 7 pass from Hart (Little kick)
NYG—Gray 37 pass from Simms (Danelo kick)
StL—Tilley 42 pass from Hart (Little kick)
NYG—FG Danelo 33

Oakland 27, Kansas City 14—At Arrowhead, attendance 54,269. Dan Pastorini made his Raiders debut, passing for 317 yards and touchdowns of 16 and 32 yards to Bob Chandler. With the score tied 7-7 at the half, Oakland countered a Kansas City blitz with a 55-yard pass from Pastorini to Arthur Whittington, which set up Mark van Eeghen's two-yard scoring plunge. Chandler caught five passes to reach the 300-reception career mark and Chris Bahr kicked field goals of 39 and 41 yards in his first game with the Raiders.

Oakland	7	0	14	6	—27
Kansas City	7	0	0	7	—14

KC —McKnight 7 run (Lowery kick)
Oak—Chandler 16 pass from Pastorini (Bahr kick)
Oak—van Eeghen 1 run (Bahr kick)
Oak—Chandler 32 pass from Pastorini (Bahr kick)
Oak—FG Bahr 41
KC —Samuels 4 pass from Fuller (Lowery kick)
Oak—FG Bahr 39

San Diego 34, Seattle 13—At Kingdome, attendance 62,042. Dan Fouts passed for four touchdowns, including three in the second period, to pace the Chargers' third consecutive opening-day victory over the Seahawks. John Cappelletti, making his Chargers debut, rushed for over 100 yards (112) for the first time since November 12, 1978. John Jefferson had 103 yards on six receptions.

San Diego	3	21	7	3	—34
Seattle	3	0	3	7	—13

Sea—FG Herrera 46
SD —FG Benirschke 41
SD —McCrary 1 pass from Fouts (Benirschke kick)
SD —Joiner 19 pass from Fouts (Benirschke kick)
SD —Jefferson 10 pass from Fouts (Benirschke kick)
Sea—FG Herrera 28
SD —Jefferson 23 pass from Fouts (Benirschke kick)
Sea—McCullum 36 pass from Zorn (Herrera kick)
SD —FG Benirschke 29

San Francisco 26, New Orleans 23—At Louisiana Superdome, attendance 58,621. Ray Wersching kicked a 38-yard field goal with 3:46 remaining to give the 49ers their first opening day victory in four years. Rookie Earl Cooper led the 49ers' offensive attack, rushing for 77 yards and two touchdowns on 17 carries. Steve DeBerg completed 21 of 29 passes for 223 yards. Cooper had 10 receptions for 71 yards and Paul Hofer added 114 yards and a 27-yard touchdown. The Saints tied the game with a 38-yard field goal in the fourth quarter, but Russell Erxleben missed a 34-yarder on the final play of the game that would have sent the game into overtime.

San Francisco	0	14	6	6	—26
New Orleans	0	7	6	10	—23

NO—Galbreath 1 run (Erxleben kick)
SF —Cooper 1 run (Wersching kick)
SF —Cooper 6 run (Wersching kick)
SF —Hofer 27 pass from DeBerg (kick blocked)
NO—Muncie 7 (run failed)
SF —FG Wersching 37
NO—Chandler 49 pass from Manning (Erxleben kick)
NO—FG Erxleben 37
SF —FG Wersching 38

Tampa Bay 17, Cincinnati 12—At Riverfront Stadium, attendance 55,551. Doug Williams converted a key mistake by the Bengals into a 15-yard scoring pass to Jimmie Giles with 1:47 left, and linebacker David Lewis intercepted a desperation pass in the waning moments to preserve the victory. Bengals punter Pat McInally fumbled a snap to give the Buccaneers possession on the Cincinnati 5-yard line. Williams connected with Giles on the following play. Randy Crowder's 12 tackles led the Tampa Bay defense, which limited the Bengals to 128 yards total offense.

Tampa Bay	0	10	0	7	—17
Cincinnati	3	0	2	7	—12

Cin—FG Sunter 35
TB —FG Yepremian 19
TB —Giles 32 pass from Williams (Yepremian kick)
Cin—Safety, Blanchard ran out of end zone
Cin—Ross 3 pass from Thompson (Sunter kick)
TB —Giles 15 pass from Williams (Yepremian kick)

MONDAY, SEPTEMBER 8

Dallas 17, Washington 3—At Robert F. Kennedy stadium, attendance 55,045. Danny White, replacing the retired Roger Staubach at quarterback, directed scoring drives of 59 and 80 yards as the Cowboys won their sixteenth straight season opener. Tony Dorsett's six-yard touchdown run opened the Dallas scoring. Ron Springs added an insurance touchdown with a four-yard run in the fourth quarter. Safety Charlie Waters recorded his thirty-fourth career interception to lead the Dallas defense, which allowed only 58 yards rushing.

Dallas	7	3	0	7	—17
Washington	0	0	0	3	— 3

Dall —Dorsett 6 run (Septien kick)
Dall —FG Septien 19
Wash—FG Moseley 45
Dall —Springs 4 run (Septien kick)

SECOND WEEK SUMMARY

Several rookies led their teams to victories at Detroit and New England. Ed Murray kicked field goals of 23, 32, 39, 42, and 43 yards and Billy Sims added two touchdowns (a one-yard run and an 87-yard pass) in the Lions' 29-7 win over Green Bay. Tight end Junior Miller caught eight passes for 117 yards and two scores in Atlanta's win over New England. Safety Jeff Nixon sped 50 yards with his fourth interception of the young season to help Buffalo defeat the New York Jets on O.J. Simpson day in Rich Stadium. Denver safety Bill Thompson set an NFL record with his fourth career fumble return for a touchdown to climax the Broncos first ever regular season win over Dallas. Don Shula's resourcefullness evened Miami's record at 1-1. The Dolphins were down 16-7 with 6:21 to play, Shula called for an onside punt and that triggered a 10-point outburst that led to a 17-16 win. John Jefferson's 76-yard touchdown reception capped San Diego's overtime victory over Oakland. Walter Payton and Wilbert Montgomery exploded for big days. Payton rushed for 183 yards, including a career-best 69-yard scoring run, against New Orleans, and Montgomery registered 169 yards, and a 72-yard touchdown run, against Minnesota.

THURSDAY, SEPTEMBER 11

Tampa Bay 10, Los Angeles 9—At Tampa Stadium, attendance 66,576. Doug Williams scored the game's only touchdown from one yard out with 57 seconds left, lifting the Buccaneers to their second straight win. The game was a defensive battle for better than three quarters. Los Angeles limited Tampa Bay to 183 total yards, but Tampa Bay intercepted four of Vince Ferragamo's passes to halt drives. A pass interference penalty gave the Buccaneers the ball at the Rams' 11 yard line. Two plays later, Williams scored the winning touchdown.

Los Angeles	0	3	3	3	— 9
Tampa Bay	0	3	0	7	— 10

LA—FG Corral 43
TB—FG Yepremian 43
LA—FG Corral 32
LA—FG Corral 27
TB—Williams 1 run (Yepremian kick)

SUNDAY, SEPTEMBER 14

Atlanta 37, New England 21—At Schaefer Stadium, attendance 48,321. Steve Bartkowski fired three touchdown passes, and William Andrews rushed for 124 yards as Atlanta recorded its first win. With the score tied 14-14, Bartkowski found rookie Junior Miller with scoring tosses of 12 and 22 yards for a 28-21 halftime lead. Andrews's one-yard touchdown plunge preceded Wallace Francis's 28-yard touchdown reception. Tim Mazzetti connected on field goals of 26, 27, and 39 yards in the second half.

Atlanta	14	14	3	6	— 37
New England	7	14	0	0	— 21

NE—Hasselbeck 9 pass from Grogan (Smith kick)
Atl —Andrews 1 run (Mazzetti kick)
Atl —Francis 28 pass from Bartkowski (Mazzetti kick)
NE—Calhoun 1 run (Smith kick)
Atl —Miller 12 pass from Bartkowski (Mazzetti kick)
Atl —Miller 22 pass from Bartkowski (Mazzetti kick)
NE—Morgan 25 pass from Grogan (Smith kick)
Atl —FG Mazzetti 26
Atl —FG Mazzetti 27
Atl —FG Mazzetti 39

Miami 17, Cincinnati 16—At Orange Bowl, attendance 38,322. Bill Barnett's blocked punt set up Uwe von Schamann's 39-yard field goal with 1:55 remaining to cap the Dolphins' comeback. Miami trailed 14-0 in the final quarter when Don Strock found Nat Moore with a 15-yard scoring pass. A safety by the Bengals, which increased their lead to 16-7, proved to be the game's turning point. On the ensuing play, Miami coach Don Shula ordered an onside kick, which was recovered by the Dolphins' Jeff Allen. Miami went on to score (Nick Giaquinto recovered Duriel Harris's fumble in the end zone), narrowing the margin to 16-14. Barnett's defensive play then set the stage for von Schamann's game winner.

Cincinnati	0	7	7	2	— 16
Miami	0	0	0	17	— 17

Cin —Bass 5 pass from Thompson (Sunter kick)
Cin —Johnson 2 run (Sunter kick)
Mia—Moore 15 pass from Strock (von Schamann kick)
Cin —Safety, Williams tackled Howell in end zone
Mia—Giaquinto fumble recovery in end zone
(von Schamann kick)
Mia—FG von Schamann 39

Denver 41, Dallas 20—At Mile High Stadium, attendance 74,919. Matt Robinson scored on runs of one and three yards, and for the fourth time in his career safety Bill Thompson returned a fumble for a touchdown, an NFL record, to lead the Broncos. After building a 24-10 halftime lead, Robinson passed 52 yards to Steve Watson to set up Otis Armstrong's three-yard scoring plunge. Three plays into Dallas's next possession, Tim Foley's 36-yard interception return set up Jim Jensen's four-yard touchdown. Fred Steinfort kicked a 55-yard field goal to cap the scoring for the winners.

Dallas	0	10	3	7	— 20
Denver	7	17	14	3	— 41

Den—Robinson 1 run (Steinfort kick)
Den—FG Steinfort 46
Den—Robinson 3 run (Steinfort kick)
Dall—Hill 36 pass from White (Septien kick)
Den—Thompson 32 fumble recovery return (Steinfort kick)
Dall—FG Septien 30
Dall—FG Septien 37
Den—Armstrong 3 run (Steinfort kick)
Den—Jensen 4 run (Steinfort kick)
Dall—Hill 22 pass from White (Septien kick)
Den—FG Steinfort 55

Detroit 29, Green Bay 7—At Milwaukee County Stadium, attendance 53,099. Two rookies accounted for all the points in the Lions' 29-7 win. Billy Sims rushed 20 times for 134 yards and a touchdown and caught two passes for 94 yards, including an 87-yard score. Kicker Ed Murray kicked five field goals and added two extra points. Quarterback Gary Danielson completed 11 of 17 passes for 246 yards in directing the Lions' offense to 459 total yards. The defense limited the Packers to 59 yards rushing and 242 overall.

Detroit	3	13	6	7	— 29
Green Bay	0	7	0	0	— 7

Det—FG Murray 32
Det—FG Murray 39
GB —Ivery 5 run (Marcol kick)
Det—Sims 1 run (Murray kick)
Det—FG Murray 43
Det—FG Murray 42
Det—FG Murray 23
Det—Sims 87 pass from Danielson (Murray kick)

Chicago 22, New Orleans 3—At Soldier Field, attendance 62,523. Walter Payton rushed for 183 yards on 18 carries, including a 69-yard run—longest of his career—leading the Bears to their first win. Chicago broke a 3-3 tie when Mike Phipps passed 56 yards to rookie tight end Robert Fisher for a touchdown. The Bears' Alan Page tied an NFL mark with his third career safety when he tackled Archie Manning in the end zone for one of the Bears' six sacks on the day.

New Orleans	3	0	0	0	— 3
Chicago	10	3	2	7	— 22

Chi—FG Thomas 37
NO—FG Erxleben 26
Chi—Fisher 56 pass from Phipps (Thomas kick)
Chi—Safety Page tackled Manning in end zone
Chi—Payton 69 run (Thomas kick)

Buffalo 20, New York Jets 10—At Rich Stadium, attendance 65,315. Rookie safety Jeff Nixon ran 50 yards with an interception to provide the clinching touchdown in the Bills' 20-10 victory. Joe Ferguson riddled the Jets' secondary, completing 18 of 29 passes for 207 yards, including a 48-yarder to Reuben Gant that set up Joe Cribbs's one-yard score. The victory overshadowed the effort of the Jets' Clark Gaines, who rushed for 94 yards on 14 carries and caught 12 passes for 91 yards and New York's lone touchdown.

New York Jets	3	0	0	7	— 10
Buffalo	0	10	10	0	— 20

NYJ—FG Leahy 44
Buff—Cribbs 1 run (Mike-Mayer kick)
Buff—FG Mike-Mayer 47
Buff—FG Mike-Mayer 38
Buff—Nixon 50 interception return (Mike-Mayer kick)
NYJ—Gaines 11 pass from Todd (Leahy kick)

San Diego 30, Oakland 24—At San Diego Stadium, attendance 51,943. Dan Fouts threw a 24-yard scoring pass to John Jefferson 8:09 into overtime to climax the Chargers' comeback. Jim Plunkett sent the game into overtime when he hit Ray Chester on an 18-yard touchdown pass with 33 seconds left to play. Fouts passed for 387 yards including a 25-yard touchdown pass to Kellen Winslow. He was intercepted four times in the third quarter. Clarence Williams ran four yards with the go-ahead score before Plunkett engineered the tying drive to force the extra period.

Oakland	3	7	7	7	0	— 24
San Diego	3	7	0	14	6	— 30

SD —FG Benirschke 52
Oak—FG Bahr 35
SD —Jefferson 4 pass from Fouts (Benirschke kick)
Oak—Branch 48 pass from Pastorini (Bahr kick)
Oak—Jones 11 fumble recovery return (Bahr kick)
SD —Winslow 25 pass from Fouts (Benirschke kick)
SD —C. Williams 4 run (Benirschke kick)
Oak—Chester 18 pass from Plunkett (Bahr kick)
SD —Jefferson 24 pass from Fouts (no PAT atttempted)

Philadelphia 42, Minnesota 7—At Metropolitan Stadium, attendance 46,460. Ron Jaworski completed 20 of 26 passes for 234 yards and Wilbert Montgomery rushed for 169 yards and two touchdowns as the Eagles crushed the Vikings. Jaworski completed 11 of 12 passes in the second half and had touchdown strikes of 45 yards to Scott Fitzkee and 13 yards to Harold Carmichael. Montgomery's 72-yard first-quarter scoring run was the longest of his career and touched off the Eagles' 529-yard offensive onslaught. Running mate Leroy Harris added a pair of touchdowns. The Eagles' defense limited Minnesota to 32 yards rushing.

Philadelphia	14	0	14	14	— 42
Minnesota	0	7	0	0	— 7

Phil —Harris 2 run (Franklin kick)
Phil —Montgomery 72 run (Franklin kick)
Minn—Rashad 16 pass from Kramer (Danmeier kick)
Phil —Harris 4 run (Franklin kick)
Phil —Montgomery 1 run (Franklin kick)
Phil —Fitzkee 45 pass from Jaworski (Franklin kick)
Phil —Carmichael 13 pass from Jaworski (Franklin kick)

Pittsburgh 20, Baltimore 17—At Memorial Stadium, attendance 54,914. Terry Bradshaw connected with Jim Smith on a 24-yard scoring pass in the fourth quarter and Donnie Shell intercepted a pass with 3:30 remaining to preserve the Steelers' second victory. Baltimore scored 10 points in the third quarter to open a 17-13 advantage. The Steelers' game-winning drive, which covered 49 yards, was kept alive by a 22-yard reception of a deflected pass by Calvin Sweeney. The ball was intended for Lynn Swann.

Pittsburgh	3	10	0	7	— 20
Baltimore	0	7	10	0	— 17

Pitt —FG Bahr 25
Pitt —FG Bahr 29
Balt —Shiver 34 interception return (Mike-Mayer kick)
Pitt —Harris 10 pass from Bradshaw (Bahr kick)
Balt —Butler 15 pass from Jones (Mike-Mayer kick)
Balt —FG Mike-Mayer 20
Pitt —Smith 24 pass from Bradshaw (Bahr kick)

San Francisco 24, St. Louis 21—At Candlestick Park, attendance 49,999. Ray Wersching kicked a 33-yard field goal with 4:12 elapsed in overtime to cap the 49ers' victory. Paul Hofer, who rushed for 89 yards and caught nine passes for 135 yards, tied the game on a 26-yard touchdown run with 58 seconds remaining in regulation play. Steve DeBerg drove San Francisco 52 yards to the St. Louis 16 on the 49ers' first overtime possession. Wersching followed with the winning kick.

St. Louis	0	0	14	7	0	— 21
San Francisco	0	7	0	14	3	— 24

SF —Hofer 19 pass from DeBerg (Wersching kick)
StL—Brown 13 pass from Hart (Little kick)
StL—Marsh 5 pass from Hart (Little kick)

SF —Cooper 9 pass from DeBerg (Wersching kick)
StL—Harrell 5 run (Little kick)
SF —Hofer 26 run (Wersching kick)
SF —FG Wersching 33

Seattle 17, Kansas City 16—At Arrowhead, attendance 42,403. Jim Zorn passed for two touchdowns and Efren Herrera added a field goal as the Seahawks withstood the Chiefs' second-half rally and held on for their first win. Zorn found Sam McCullum (12 yards) and Sherman Smith (7 yards) with first-half scoring passes and sustained a Seattle drive the final 4:56 of the game after Kansas City had whittled the Seahawks lead to one point on three field goals by Nick Lowery (23, 50, and 57 yards). Lowery became only the fourth kicker in NFL history to kick two field goals of 50 or more yards in the same game.

Seattle	7	10	0	0	— 17
Kansas City	0	7	6	3	— 16

Sea—McCullum 12 pass from Zorn (Herrera kick)
Sea—FG Herrera 19
Sea—Smith 7 pass from Zorn (Herrera kick)
KC —Marshall 1 pass from Fuller (Lowery kick)
KC —FG Lowery 50
KC —FG Lowery 23
KC —FG Lowery 57

Washington 23, New York Giants 21—At Giants Stadium, attendance 73,343. Mark Moseley kicked a 45-yard field goal with 1:55 remaining to provide the Redskins with the victory. Lemar Parrish notched his second interception of the game with one minute left to ensure the win. New York took the lead 21-20 with 5:40 to play on Phil Simms's 35-yard touchdown pass to Tom Mullady. Joe Theismann responded, directing the 51-yard, nine-play drive that set up Moseley's game-winner. Dave Jennings's five punts in the game gave him a career total of 527, surpassing the previous club record of 525 set by Don Chandler.

Washington	6	14	0	3	— 23
New York Giants	0	14	0	7	— 21

Wash—Harmon 20 pass from Theismann (kick blocked)
NYG —Hogan 1 run (Danelo kick)
Wash—Theismann 37 run (Moseley kick)
NYG —Garrett 32 pass from Simms (Danelo kick)
Wash—Jackson 2 run (Moseley kick)
NYG —Mullady 35 pass from Simms (Danelo kick)
Wash—FG Moseley 45

MONDAY, SEPTEMBER 15

Houston 16, Cleveland 7—At Cleveland Stadium, attendance 80,243. Ken Stabler completed 23 of 28 passes (82.1 percent) to lead the Houston attack, which controlled the ball for 42:20. Earl Campbell ran for 106 yards and Tim Wilson scored the Oilers' only touchdown, a two-yard plunge in the third quarter. Toni Fritsch added field goals of 17, 25 and 29 yards. The Oilers' defense held the Browns to 181 total yards.

Houston	0	3	7	6	— 16
Cleveland	0	7	0	0	— 7

Cle —Hill 3 pass from Sipe (Cockroft kick)
Hou—FG Fritsch 25
Hou—Wilson 2 run (Fritsch kick)
Hou—FG Fritsch 29
Hou—FG Fritsch 17

THIRD WEEK SUMMARY

The quarterbacks stole the spotlight in the NFL's third weekend of the 1980 season, and San Francisco, Detroit, Buffalo, San Diego, and Philadelphia remained undefeated. The 49ers beat the New York Jets 37-27, although Jets quarterback Richard Todd completed an NFL-record 42 passes. Joe Ferguson became Buffalo's all-time passing leader in the Bills' 35-26 victory over New Orleans. Detroit downed St. Louis 20-7 but couldn't stop Jim Hart from becoming the NFL's seventh passer to throw for over 30,000 yards (30,070). Atlanta's Steve Bartkowski set a club record with 332 yards passing, while Seattle's Jim Zorn threw for 312 yards. However, both teams fell victim to fourth quarter comebacks as Miami beat Atlanta 20-17, and New England outscored Seattle 37-31. Oakland's Kenny King was the week's leading rusher with 136 yards on 25 carries as the Raiders downed Washington 24-21.

SUNDAY, SEPTEMBER 21

Houston 21, Baltimore 16—At Astrodome, attendance 47,878. Earl Campbell and Rob Carpenter both scored on one-yard touchdown runs as Houston beat Baltimore. Campbell gave Houston a 7-0 first-quarter lead but left the game when he reinjured a groin muscle. Carpenter then came on to gain 114 yards on 24 carries and score Houston's final touchdown midway through the third quarter. Oilers quarterback Ken Stabler (18 of 21 for 219 yards) accounted for Houston's other touchdown with a three-yard pass to Rich Caster.

Baltimore	0	9	0	7	— 16
Houston	7	7	7	0	— 21

Hou—Campbell 1 run (Fritsch kick)
Balt—FG Mike-Mayer 30
Balt—FG Mike-Mayer 23
Hou—Caster 3 pass from Stabler (Fritsch kick)
Balt—FG Mike-Mayer 29
Hou—Carpenter 1 run (Fritsch kick)
Balt—Washington 18 pass from B. Jones (Mike-Mayer kick)

Buffalo 35, New Orleans 26—At Louisiana Superdome, attendance 65,551. Joe Ferguson threw three touchdown passes to lead Buffalo by New Orleans. Ferguson completed 22 of 31 passes for 295 yards and became the Bills' career passing leader with 15,250 yards. Jerry Butler caught five of Ferguson's passes for 133 yards, and Frank Lewis grabbed six for 82 yards and two touchdowns. Archie Manning paced the Saints' attack, completing 24 of 34 passes for 285 yards and two touchdowns.

Buffalo	7	7	7	14	— 35
New Orleans	0	19	0	7	— 26

Buff—Lewis 12 pass from Ferguson (Mike-Mayer kick)
NO —Muncie 1 run (Ricardo kick)
Buff—Cribbs 12 run (Mike-Mayer kick)
NO —Harris 44 pass from Manning (kick blocked)
NO —FG Ricardo 45
NO —FG Ricardo 47
Buff—Lewis 18 pass from Ferguson (Mike-Mayer kick)
Buff—Brammer 2 pass from Ferguson (Mike-Mayer kick)
Buff—Cribbs 7 run (Mike-Mayer kick)
NO —Harris 15 pass from Manning (Ricardo kick)

Los Angeles 51, Green Bay 21—At Anaheim Stadium, attendance 63,850. Two interception returns for touchdowns highlighted a 37-point second quarter as Los Angeles upended Green Bay. With Los Angeles leading 17-7 in the second quarter, rookie safety Johnnie Johnson returned an interception 99 yards (a club record) for a touchdown. Rod Perry completed the Rams' second quarter scoring by returning an interception 83 yards. Rams quarterback Vince Ferragamo completed 15 of 19 passes for 202 yards and three touchdowns. The Los Angeles defense accounted for seven sacks and five interceptions.

Green Bay	0	7	0	14	— 21
Los Angeles	7	37	7	0	— 51

LA —Waddy 33 pass from Ferragamo (Corral kick)
LA —FG Corral 29
LA —Bryant 4 run (Corral kick)
GB—Ivery 46 pass from Dickey (Marcol kick)
LA —Johnson 99 interception return (Corral kick)
LA —Peacock 1 run (Corral kick)
LA —Miller 29 pass from Ferragamo (Corral kick)
LA —Perry 83 interception return (kick failed)
LA —Dennard 15 pass from Ferragamo (Corral kick)
GB—Huckleby 1 run (Marcol kick)
GB—Ellis 1 run (Marcol kick)

Cleveland 20, Kansas City 13—At Cleveland Stadium, attendance 63,614. Charles White ran for one touchdown and caught a pass for another as Cleveland defeated Kansas City. White negated two of Nick Lowery's field goals with a two-yard touchdown run that gave Cleveland a 7-6 halftime lead. In the third quarter, Brian Sipe (23 of 36 for 295 yards and two touchdowns) broke a 13-13 tie with a 31-yard touchdown pass to White, who was the game's leading rusher (59 yards on 15 carries) and receiver (seven receptions for 100 yards).

Kansas City	0	6	7	0	— 13
Cleveland	0	7	13	0	— 20

KC—FG Lowery 38
KC—FG Lowery 22
Cle—White 2 run (Cockroft kick)
Cle—Wright 12 pass from Sipe (kick blocked)
KC—Samuels 16 pass from Fuller (Lowery kick)
Cle—White 31 pass from Sipe (Cockroft kick)

Miami 20, Atlanta 17—At Atlanta-Fulton County Stadium, attendance 55,479. Uwe von Schamann's 27-yard field goal with 32 seconds left in the game provided the Dolphins' winning points. Miami trailed 17-3 before Bob Griese came off the bench to throw two fourth-quarter touchdown passes that tied the game. With 2:10 left to play, Tim Mazzetti's 50-yard field goal attempt was blocked by Dolphins defensive tackle Bob Baumhower. Griese then completed a 33-yard pass to Nat Moore to set up the winning field goal.

Miami	3	0	0	17	— 20
Atlanta	0	7	7	3	— 17

Mia—FG von Schamann 28
Atl —Jackson 6 pass from Bartkowski (Mazzetti kick)
Atl —Miller 7 pass from Bartkowski (Mazzetti kick)
Atl —FG Mazzetti 37
Mia—Hardy 1 pass from Griese (von Schamann kick)
Mia—Lee 4 pass from Griese (von Schamann kick)
Mia—FG von Schamann 27

Minnesota 34, Chicago 14—At Soldier Field, attendance 59,983. Ted Brown scored twice as Minnesota beat Chicago. In addition to his touchdowns, Brown gained 113 yards on 22 carries to become the first Viking since 1978 to rush for over 100 yards in a game. Minnesota's defense scored one touchdown on Tom Hannon's 41-yard interception return and set up another with an interception by Matt Blair. Bears quarterback Vince Evans accounted for both Chicago touchdowns with a one-yard run and a 27-yard pass to Rickey Watts.

Minnesota	14	7	7	6	— 34
Chicago	0	0	0	14	— 14

Minn—Rashad 76 pass from Kramer (Danmeier kick)
Minn—Hannon 41 interception return (Danmeier kick)
Minn—Brown 55 run (Danmeier kick)
Minn—Brown 1 run (Danmeier kick)
Chi —Evans 1 run (Thomas kick)
Chi —Watts 89 pass from Evans (Thomas kick)
Minn—Miller 27 run (kick failed)

New England 37, Seattle 31—At Kingdome, attendance 61,035. The Patriots rallied late in the game and scored their winning touchdown when Steve Grogan and Don Hasselbeck combined on a 16-yard touchdown pass with 2:52 left. Seattle took a 31-30 fourth-quarter lead when Jim Zorn (20 of 36 for 312 yards and four touchdowns) threw a 21-yard touchdown pass to Sam McCullum. New England took the ensuing kickoff and drove 68 yards in 12 plays for the winning score. Cornerback Ray Clayborn secured the victory with an interception at the Seattle 49-yard line with 2:24 left in the game.

New England	3	17	7	10	— 37
Seattle	3	14	0	14	— 31

NE —FG Smith 19
Sea—FG Herrera 33
Sea—Largent 20 pass from Zorn (Herrera kick)
NE —Morgan 68 pass from Grogan (Smith kick)
NE —Morgan 40 pass from Grogan (Smith kick)
Sea—McCullum 22 pass from Zorn (Herrera kick)
NE —FG Smith 30
NE —Ivory 20 run (Smith kick)
Sea—Largent 31 pass from Zorn (Herrera kick)
NE —FG Smith 29
Sea—McCullum 21 pass from Zorn (Herrera kick)
NE —Hasselbeck 16 pass from Grogan (Smith kick)

Cincinnati 30, Pittsburgh 28—At Riverfront Stadium, attendance 52,490. Ian Sunter's 21-yard field goal with 2:25 left in the game boosted Cincinnati over Pittsburgh. The Bengals trailed 28-20 with six minutes left to play when quarterback Jack Thompson fired a 22-yard touchdown pass to Don Bass. Pittsburgh fumbled the ensuing kickoff and Rick Razzano recovered to set up Sunter's winning kick. The Steelers had one more chance for victory, but Matt Bahr's 51-yard field goal went wide as time expired. The Bengals' defense forced six turnovers, including Ray Griffin's 28-yard interception return for a touchdown.

Pittsburgh	0	14	7	7	— 28
Cincinnati	10	3	0	17	— 30

Cin—R. Griffin 28 interception return (Sunter kick)
Cin—FG Sunter 27
Pitt—Smith 45 pass from Bradshaw (Bahr kick)
Pitt—Swann 14 pass from Bradshaw (Bahr kick)
Cin—FG Sunter 42
Pitt—Swann 68 pass from Bradshaw (Bahr kick)
Cin—Curtis 18 pass from Thompson (Sunter kick)
Pitt—Hawthorne 4 run (Bahr kick)
Cin—Bass 22 pass from Thompson (Sunter kick)
Cin—FG 21 Sunter

Detroit 20, St. Louis 7—At Pontiac Silverdome, attendance 80,027. Detroit rookies Billy Sims and Eddie Murray combined to make their regular season home debuts successful as Detroit downed St. Louis. Sims remained the NFL's leading rusher, gaining 95 yards on 25 carries and scoring one touchdown. Murray kicked field goals of 25 and 34 yards to remain tied with Sims for the NFL scoring lead. Cardinals quarterback Jim Hart hit 22 of 36 passes for 275 yards and one touchdown to move his career passing yardage past the 30,000-yard mark. The Lions' defense recorded five sacks, a fumble recovery, and an interception.

St. Louis	0	7	0	0	— 7
Detroit	0	10	0	10	— 20

Det—FG Murray 25
Det—King 13 pass from Danielson (Murray kick)
StL—Gray 63 pass from Hart (Little kick)
Det—Sims 13 run (Murray kick)
Det—FG Murray 34

San Diego 30, Denver 13—At Mile High Stadium, attendance 74,970. San Diego's alert defense intercepted six passes to lead the Chargers to their first victory in Denver since 1966. Glen Edwards intercepted two passes, returning one 68 yards for a touchdown. San Diego's two other touchdowns were set up by Fred Dean's fumble recovery and Woodrow Lowe's interception. Rolf Benirschke kicked three field goals, including a club record 53-yarder.

San Diego	3	24	3	0	— 30
Denver	3	3	7	0	— 13

SD —FG Benirschke 53
Den—FG Steinfort 51
SD —Cappelletti 1 run (Benirschke kick)
Den—FG Steinfort 46
SD —Joiner 22 pass from Fouts (Benirschke kick)
SD —Edwards 68 interception return (Benirschke kick)
SD —FG Benirschke 32
SD —FG Benirschke 42
Den—Moses 15 pass Morton (Steinfort kick)

San Francisco 37, New York Jets 27—At Shea Stadium, attendance 50,608. Joe Montana and Steve DeBerg each threw two touchdown passes as San Francisco outscored the New York Jets. DeBerg completed 17 of 23 passes for 181 yards; Montana hit 4 of 6 passes for 60 yards and ran five yards for a touchdown. Jets quarterback Richard Todd set an NFL record for completions, hitting 42 of 60 passes for 447 yards and three touchdowns. Running back Clark Gaines caught a club record 17 passes, one short of the NFL record, for 160 yards.

San Francisco	14	10	6	7	— 37
New York Jets	0	3	3	21	— 27

SF —Young 15 pass from DeBerg (Wersching kick)
SF —Montana 5 run (Wersching kick)
SF —Clark 20 pass from Montana (Wersching kick)
SF —FG Wersching 25
NYJ—FG Leahy 49
NYJ—FG Leahy 35
SF —Clark 7 pass from Montana (kick failed)
NYJ—Gaffney 15 pass from Todd (Leahy kick)
SF —Solomon 32 pass from DeBerg (Wersching kick)
NYJ—Harper 9 pass from Todd (Leahy kick)
NYJ—Darby 13 pass from Todd (Leahy kick)

Dallas 28, Tampa Bay 17—At Texas Stadium, attendance 62,750. Danny White threw three touchdown passes as Dallas came from behind to beat Tampa Bay. Trailing 17-7, Dallas started its comeback with 46 seconds left in the first half when White hit tight end Billy Joe DuPree with a nine-yard touchdown pass. In the third quarter, fullback Robert Newhouse's two-yard touchdown run put Dallas ahead 21-17. A nine-yard touchdown pass from White to DuPree, in the fourth quarter completed the Cowboys' comeback. Tampa Bay set a club record with 442 yards total offense.

Tampa Bay	7	10	0	0	— 17
Dallas	7	7	7	7	— 28

Dall—Johnson 28 pass from D. White (Septien kick)
TB —Williams 11 run (Yepremian kick)
TB —FG Yepremian 22
TB —Giles 49 pass from Williams (Yepremian kick)
Dall—DuPree 9 pass from D. White (Septien kick)
Dall—Newhouse 2 run (Septien kick)
Dall—DuPree 9 pass from D. White (Septien kick)

Oakland 24, Washington 21—At Oakland-Alameda County Coliseum, attendance 45,163. Dan Pastorini passed for two touchdowns, and Arthur Whittington scored on a 42-yard touchdown run, as Oakland defeated Washington. Pastorini completed 17 of 33 passes for 176 yards and two touchdowns, which gave him a career total of 101 scoring passes. Kenny King led the Raiders' ground attack, gaining 136 yards on 25 carries, while Whittington chipped in with 48 yards on 8 carries. The Redskins' defense chalked up five sacks and intercepted three passes, two by safety Tony Peters.

Washington	0	7	7	7	— 21
Oakland	3	7	7	7	— 24

Oak —FG Bahr 21
Oak —Casper 20 pass from Pastorini (Bahr kick)
Wash—Walker 15 pass from Theismann (Moseley kick)
Oak —Whittington 42 run (Bahr kick)
Wash—Theismann 4 run (Moseley kick)
Oak —Chandler 5 pass from Pastorini (Bahr kick)
Wash—Thompson 3 pass from Theismann (Moseley kick)

MONDAY, SEPTEMBER 22

Philadelphia 35, New York Giants 3—At Veterans Stadium, attendance 70,767. Ron Jaworski fired three touchdown passes to lead Philadelphia over the New York Giants. Trailing 3-0, Philadelphia came back when Jaworski hit Wilbert Montgomery with a three-yard scoring pass to complete a six-play, 62-yard drive. Philadelphia increased its lead to 21-3 just before halftime by driving 80 yards in five plays with Leroy Harris scoring on a two-yard touchdown run. In the second half, Jaworski combined with Charlie Smith on a 12-yard touchdown pass. Montgomery completed the Eagles' scoring with a one-yard touchdown run.

New York Giants	3	0	0	0	— 3
Philadelphia	7	14	7	7	— 35

NYG —FG Danelo 50
Phil —Montgomery 3 pass from Jaworski (Franklin kick)
Phil —Carmichael 22 pass from Jaworski (Franklin kick)
Phil —Harris 2 run (Franklin kick)
Phil —Smith 12 pass from Jaworski (Franklin kick)
Phil —Montgomery 1 run (Franklin kick)

FOURTH WEEK SUMMARY

Three teams kept perfect records intact, but two others dropped from the undefeated ranks. Buffalo controlled the ball for over 41 minutes in its 24-7 domination of Oakland. San Diego capitalized on Kansas City turnovers and scored three touchdowns in seven plays. Ray Oldham, claimed on waivers from the Giants in preseason, intercepted two passes, returning one 29 yards for a score, as Detroit defeated Minnesota. Despite Steve DeBerg's 93-yard scoring pass to Freddie Solomon and a 14-point fourth-quarter, San Francisco suffered its first loss, 20-17 to Atlanta. Jim Hanifan claimed his first NFL head coaching victory as St. Louis dropped Philadelphia from its undefeated perch 24-14. Miami clinched its third comeback win in as many weeks as Bob Griese, who was replacing David Woodley, directed the Dolphins' to three fourth-period touchdowns in a 21-16 win over New Orleans. New England avenged a humiliating 45-10 loss to Denver in 1979 by defeating the Broncos 23-14 on Monday night.

SUNDAY, SEPTEMBER 28

Atlanta 20, San Francisco 17—At Candlestick Park, attendance 56,518. Alfred Jackson and Lynn Cain scored fourth quarter touchdowns as the Falcons sent the 49ers to their first defeat. The game was a battle of field goals until the fourth quarter, when the teams combined to score four touchdowns. Atlanta built a 20-3 lead on Steve Bartkowski's 10-yard pass to Jackson and Cain's two-yard run. Steve DeBerg, who completed a club record 32 of 51 passes for 345 yards, rallied the 49ers. He threw a club record 93-yard touchdown bomb to Freddie Solomon and a 27-yard scoring toss to Earl Cooper with 1:28 remaining.

Atlanta	3	0	3	14	— 20
San Francisco	0	3	0	14	— 17

Atl—FG Mazzetti 40
SF—FG Wersching 47
Atl—FG Mazzetti 23
Atl—Jackson 10 pass from Bartkowski (Mazzetti kick)
Atl—Cain 2 run (Mazzetti kick)
SF—Solomon 93 pass from DeBerg (Wersching kick)
SF—Cooper 27 pass from DeBerg (Wersching kick)

Pittsburgh 38, Chicago 3—At Three Rivers Stadium, attendance 53,987. Terry Bradshaw passed for four touchdowns, including strikes of 21, 23, and 29 yards to Jim Smith, to lead the Steelers. Cliff Stoudt made his first NFL appearance, replacing Bradshaw in the third period, and directed an 80-yard, 11-play drive that ended with a nine-yard touchdown pass to Franco Harris. Mike Wagner intercepted three passes. Pittsburgh's defense held Walter Payton to 60 yards rushing.

Chicago	3	0	0	0	— 3
Pittsburgh	7	17	7	7	— 38

Chi—FG Thomas 28
Pitt—Smith 21 pass from Bradshaw (Bahr kick)
Pitt—FG Bahr 20
Pitt—Smith 29 pass from Bradshaw (Bahr kick)
Pitt—Smith 23 pass from Bradshaw (Bahr kick)
Pitt—Cunningham 2 pass from Bradshaw (Bahr kick)
Pitt—Harris 9 pass from Stoudt (Bahr kick)

Cleveland 34, Tampa Bay 27—At Tampa Stadium, attendance 65,540. Brian Sipe passed for three touchdowns, including two to Calvin Hill, and completed a club record 13 consecutive passes as the Browns evened their record at 2-2. Sipe (22 of 32 for 318 yards) connected with Hill on a three-yard touchdown pass to give the Browns a 17-13 halftime lead. In the fourth period a 43-yard bomb from Sipe to Hill clinched the victory. Charles White (eight-yard run) and Rickey Feacher (13-yard pass) also had touchdowns. Don Cockroft rounded out the scoring with 35- and 36-yard field goals. Tampa Bay's bid for a tying touchdown failed as time ran out with the Buccaneers on the Browns' 30-yard line.

Cleveland	0	17	7	10	— 34
Tampa Bay	6	7	0	14	— 27

TB —FG Yepremian 37
TB —FG Yepremian 35
Cle—FG Cockroft 35
TB —Jones 41 pass from Williams (Yepremian kick)
Cle—White 8 run (Cockroft kick)
Cle—Hill 3 pass from Sipe (Cockroft kick)
Cle—Feacher 13 pass from Sipe (Cockroft kick)
Cle—Hill 43 pass from Sipe (Cockroft kick)
TB —Jones 3 pass from Williams (Yepremian kick)
Cle—FG Cockroft 36
TB —Eckwood 7 pass from Williams (Yepremian kick)

Dallas 28, Green Bay 7—At Milwaukee County Stadium, attendance 54,776. Danny White directed scoring drives of 70, 70, 90, and 48 yards and completed 16 of 20 passes for 217 yards to lead the Cowboys. White's 48-yard run from punt formation set up Tony Dorsett's one-yard plunge in the first quarter. Robert Newhouse added a one-yard touchdown run just before halftime for a 14-7 lead. Doug Cosbie's five-yard touchdown reception ended a 90-yard drive in the third quarter that increased the lead to 21-7. Steve Wilson's fourth quarter interception set up Drew Pearson's 20-yard touchdown reception.

Dallas	7	7	7	7	— 28
Green Bay	0	7	0	0	— 7

Dall—Dorsett 1 run (Septien kick)
GB —Atkins 6 run (Marcol kick)
Dall—Newhouse 1 run (Septien kick)
Dall—Cosbie 5 pass from White (Septien kick)
Dall—Pearson 20 pass from White (Septien kick)

Houston 13, Cincinnati 10—At Riverfront Stadium, attendance 50,413. Carl Roaches's 68-yard punt return set up Toni Fritsch's 29-yard field goal with 5:33 remaining to key the Oilers' comeback win. With Earl Campbell sidelined because of a groin injury, Houston relied on the passing of Ken Stabler (26 of 34 for 241 yards) to rebound from a 10-7 halftime deficit. Fritsch's 27-yard field goal early in the final quarter tied the game. Jack Tatum's interception with 1:01 left clinched the victory.

Houston	0	7	0	6	— 13
Cincinnati	7	3	0	0	— 10

Cin —Bass 12 pass from Thompson (Sunter kick)
Cin —FG Sunter 26
Hou—Coleman 1 run (Fritsch kick)
Hou—FG Fritsch 27
Hou—FG Fritsch 29

Los Angeles 28, N.Y. Giants 7—At Giants Stadium, attendance 73,414. Elvis Peacock scored three touchdowns, and Vince Ferragamo completed 14 of 18 passes for 215 yards, as the Rams evened their record at 2-2. Pat Thomas recovered a fumble, and Nolan Cromwell returned an interception 17 yards, setting up Peacock's first two touchdowns. Ferragamo added a 14-yard scoring pass to Walt Arnold to give Los Angeles a 21-0 lead at the half. The Rams' defense smothered the Giants' offense until the final play of the game, when rookie Scott Brunner hit Johnny Perkins with a 19-yard touchdown pass to avoid the shutout.

Los Angeles	14	7	7	0	— 28
New York Giants	0	0	0	7	— 7

LA —Peacock 1 run (Corral kick)
LA —Peacock 1 run (Corral kick)
LA —Arnold 14 pass from Ferragamo (Corral kick)
LA —Peacock 4 run (Corral kick)
NYG—Perkins 19 pass from Brunner (Danelo kick)

Detroit 27, Minnesota 7—At Pontiac Silverdome, attendance 80,219. Gary Danielson threw a pair of touchdown passes and Billy Sims rushed for 157 yards as the Lions recorded their fourth straight win. The Lions broke a 7-7 halftime tie, scoring 20 points in the second half. Ed Murray's 36-yard field goal gave Detroit a 10-7 lead at the end of the three quarters. In the fourth quarter, Danielson finished a 12-play, 80-yard drive with a five-yard touchdown pass to Freddie Scott. On the Vikings' next offensive play, the Lions' Ray Oldham returned an interception 29 yards for a touchdown. Detroit intercepted five passes and limited Minnesota to 59 yards rushing.

Minnesota	0	7	0	0	— 7
Detroit	7	0	3	17	— 27

Det —Hill 3 pass from Danielson (Murray kick)
Minn—Rashad 40 pass from Kramer (Danmeier kick)
Det —FG Murray 36
Det —Scott 5 pass from Danielson (Murray kick)
Det —Oldham 29 interception return (Murray kick)
Det —FG Murray 24

Miami 21, New Orleans 16—At Orange Bowl, attendance 40, 946. Bob Griese led the Dolphins' fourth-quarter rally, which was capped by Delvin Williams' six-yard touchdown run with 2:36 left. Griese, replacing rookie David Woodley, started Miami's comeback with a 12-play, 91-yard drive that ended on Steve Howell's one-yard plunge. The Saints' lead was cut to 16-14 by an 82-yard march. Miami scored its second touchdown on Griese's five-yard touchdown pass to Ron Lee. A 26-yard pass to Tony Nathan who had seven receptions for 118 yards, set up Williams's winning score.

New Orleans	0	9	7	0	— 16
Miami	0	0	0	21	— 21

NO—FG Ricardo 34
NO—FG Ricardo 36
NO—FG Ricardo 39
NO—Harris 25 pass from Manning (Ricardo kick)
Mia—Howell 1 run (von Schamann kick)
Mia—Lee 5 pass from Griese (von Schamann kick)
Mia—Williams 6 run (von Schamann kick)

Baltimore 35, New York Jets 21—At Memorial Stadium, attendance 33,373. Bert Jones threw for three touchdowns as the Colts evened their record at 2-2. Jones completed 18 of 25 passes for 275 yards, including touchdowns of 14 yards to Don McCauley, 19 yards to Randy Burke, and 5 yards to Roger Carr. Joe Washington opened the Colts' scoring with a five-yard touchdown run. McCauley's touchdown followed Larry Braziel's 60-yard interception return in the second quarter. Baltimore rolled up 447 yards in total offense; New York managed 336 yards.

New York Jets	0	14	0	7	— 21
Baltimore	7	14	7	7	— 35

Balt—Washington 5 run (Mike-Mayer kick)
Balt—McCauley 14 pass from B. Jones (Mike-Mayer kick)
NYJ—Long 5 run (Leahy kick)
NYJ—Gaines 10 pass from Todd (Leahy kick)
Balt—Burke 19 pass from B. Jones (Mike-Mayer kick)
Balt—Dickey 3 run (Mike-Mayer kick)
NYJ—Long 5 run (Leahy kick)
Balt—Carr 5 pass from B. Jones (Mike-Mayer kick)

Buffalo 24, Oakland 7—At Rich Stadium, attendance 77,259. Rookie Joe Cribbs scored on a one-yard run and a 21-play pass from Joe Ferguson (17 of 22 for 175 yards) to lead the Bills. Ferguson directed an 81-yard scoring drive on the Bills' first possession. Rod Kush's fumble recovery on the Oakland 16 set up Cribbs's first score. Buffalo's offense controlled the ball for 41:07. Its defense allowed only 70 yards rushing (179 overall), intercepted two passes, and recovered three fumbles.

Oakland	0	0	7	0	— 7
Buffalo	7	10	0	7	— 24

Buff—Brown 4 run (Mike-Mayer kick)
Buff—Cribbs 1 run (Mike-Mayer kick)
Buff—FG Mike-Mayer 30
Oak—Hayes 48 interception return (Bahr kick)
Buff—Cribbs 21 pass from Ferguson (Mike-Mayer kick)

St. Louis 24, Philadelphia 14—At Busch Memorial Stadium, attendance 49,079. Ottis Anderson rushed for 151 yards and touchdowns of 14 and 37 yards as the Cardinals posted their first win of the season. Carl Allen returned an interception 70 yards for a touchdown, and Steve Little kicked a 31-yard field goal to give St. Louis a 10-7 halftime edge. Anderson gained 98 yards in the second half. His touchdown runs ended drives of 67 and 65 yards. It was the Eagles' first loss of the season.

Philadelphia	0	7	0	7	— 14
St. Louis	7	3	7	7	— 24

StL —Allen 70 interception return (Little kick)
Phil—Jaworski 1 run (Franklin kick)
StL —FG Little 31
StL —Anderson 14 run (Little kick)
StL —Anderson 37 run (Little kick)
Phil—Krepfle 9 pass from Jaworski (Franklin kick)

San Diego 24, Kansas City 7—At Arrowhead, attendance 45,161. Dan Fouts connected with Kellen Winslow on second quarter scoring passes of 15 and 16 yards, and John Cappelletti scored on a three-yard run, as the Chargers rolled to their fourth straight win. San Diego capitalized on Kansas City turnovers to score three first-half touchdowns in a span of seven plays. Louie Kelcher recovered a fumble to set up Cappelletti's touchdown, and Hal Stringert's 26-yard fumble return led to Fouts's first scoring pass to Winslow. Fred Dean had three of the Chargers' five quarterback sacks.

San Diego	7	14	3	0	— 24
Kansas City	0	7	0	0	— 7

SD—Cappelletti 3 run (Benirschke kick)
KC—McKnight 1 run (Lowery kick)
SD—Winslow 15 pass from Fouts (Benirschke kick)
SD—Winslow 16 pass from Fouts (Benirschke kick)
SD—FG Benirschke 32

Seattle 14, Washington 0—At Robert F. Kennedy Stadium, attendance 55,045. Jim Zorn and Dan Doornink ran for touchdowns and the Seahawks' defense shut out the Redskins as Seattle recorded its second victory. Zorn closed out an 80-yard, 13-play drive in the second quarter with a 21-yard quarterback draw. Doornink added an eight-yard touchdown with 1:56 remaining in the game. Jim Jodat rushed for 117 yards, the first 100-yard game of his career. Dave Brown had two interceptions to lead the Seahawks' defense, which limited Washington to 78 yards rushing.

Seattle	0	7	0	7	— 14
Washington	0	0	0	0	— 0

Sea—Zorn 21 run (Herrera kick)
Sea—Doornink 8 run (Herrera kick)

MONDAY, SEPTEMBER 29

New England 23, Denver 14—At Schaefer Stadium, attendance 60,153. Steve Grogan and Stanley Morgan provided the offensive fireworks—a 45-yard touchdown pass in the third quarter—but the real story was the New England defense, which limited Denver to a total of 170 yards and only 52 in the second half. The touchdown pass from Grogan to Morgan came after Denver's Otis Armstrong had scored on an eight-yard run to give the Broncos a 14-10 lead. The Patriots' John Smith kicked field goals of 19, 26, and 36 yards.

Denver	7	0	7	0	— 14
New England	3	7	7	6	— 23

Den—Moses 17 pass from Robinson (Steinfort kick)
NE —FG Smith 26
NE —Ferguson 2 run (Smith kick)
Den—Armstrong 8 run (Steinfort kick)
NE —Morgan 45 pass from Grogan (Smith kick)
NE —FG Smith 19
NE —FG Smith 36

FIFTH WEEK SUMMARY

After five weeks the NFL's lone undefeated team was Buffalo. The Bills needed two fourth-quarter touchdowns to remain unbeaten and hand San Diego its first setback. Atlanta converted three turnovers into touchdowns and handed Detroit its first loss. Walter Payton gained 133 yards to become the NFL's seventh all-time rusher and led Chicago to its first victory. Kansas City chalked up its initial win of 1980 by building a 31-0 lead on the way to a 31-17 victory over Oakland. Franco Harris scored his 74th career rushing touchdown, tying him for third on the NFL's all-time touchdown list as Pittsburgh defeated Minnesota. Philadelphia's Harold Carmichael became the NFL's 18th all-time receiver during the Eagles victory over Washington. Miami's Bob Griese became the 14th NFL quarterback to top 25,000 career passing yards, but Baltimore topped Miami.

SUNDAY, OCTOBER 5

Baltimore 30, Miami 17—At Orange Bowl, attendance 50,631. Bert Jones passed for three touchdowns and ran for another as Baltimore downed Miami. Jones capped an 80-yard drive with a one-yard pass to Curtis Dickey in the third quarter. Baltimore went ahead on its next possession when Jones and Roger Carr combined on an eight-yard pass that capped a 10-play, 71-yard drive. Four minutes later, Colts' linebacker Barry Krauss recovered a fumble to set up Jones's nine-yard touchdown run. Bob Griese completed 21 of 37 passes for 272 yards and became the fourteenth player in NFL history to top 25,000 career passing yards.

Baltimore	10	0	7	13	— 30
Miami	3	14	0	0	— 17

Balt—Carr 25 pass from B. Jones (Mike-Mayer kick)
Balt—FG Mike-Mayer 45
Mia—FG von Schamann 24
Mia—Giaquinto 15 pass from Griese (von Schamann kick)
Mia—Harris 4 pass from Griese (von Schamann kick)
Balt—Dickey 1 pass from B. Jones (Mike-Mayer kick)
Balt—Carr 8 pass from B. Jones (Mike-Mayer kick)
Balt—B. Jones 9 run (kick blocked)

Buffalo 26, San Diego 24—At San Diego Stadium, attendance 51,982. Buffalo needed two fourth-quarter touchdowns to score a come-from-behind victory over San Diego and remain undefeated. With San Diego leading 24-12, Chargers' punter Rick Partridge, fumbled a high snap from center and Buffalo gained possession at the Chargers' 13 yard line. Four plays later, Joe Ferguson hit tight end Mark Brammer with a nine-yard scoring pass. On San Diego's next possession, Bills' linebacker Jim Haslett intercepted Dan Fouts's pass and returned it 17 yards to the Chargers' 21. Buffalo took the lead five plays later on Joe Cribbs's three-yard touchdown run. The win gave Buffalo its best start since 1964.

Buffalo	3	9	0	14	— 26
San Diego	7	10	7	0	— 24

Buff—FG Mike-Mayer 48
SD —Winslow 4 pass from Fouts (Benirschke kick)
SD —Jefferson 5 pass from Fouts (Benirschke kick)
Buff—FG Mike-Mayer 29
Buff—Sanford recovered block punt in end zone (kick failed)
SD —FG Benirschke 29
SD —C. Williams 3 run (Benirschke kick)
Buff—Brammer 9 pass from Ferguson (Mike-Mayer kick)
Buff—Cribbs 3 run (Mike-Mayer kick)

Green Bay 14, Cincinnati 9—At Lambeau Field, attendance 55,006. Lynn Dickey threw two touchdown passes to lead Green Bay over Cincinnati. The Bengals' Ian Sunter ticked two of his three field goals early in the first quarter to give Cincinnati a 6-0 lead. Green Bay came back late in the same period with a 70-yard scoring march, ending with Dickey hitting James Lofton with a 15-yard touchdown pass. Dickey's eight-yard touchdown pass to Steve Atkins in the second quarter capped a 14-play, 92-yard drive that built the Packers' halftime advantage to 14-6. Dickey completed 18 of 26 passes for 203 yards. James Lofton caught eight passes for 114 yards.

Cincinnati	6	0	0	3	— 9
Green Bay	7	7	0	0	— 14

Cin—FG Sunter 20
Cin—FG Sunter 34
GB—Lofton 15 pass from Dickey (Marcol kick)
GB—Atkins 8 pass from Dickey (Marcol kick)
Cin—FG Sunter 31

Denver 19, Cleveland 16—At Cleveland Stadium, attendance 81,065. Fred Steinfort's fourth field goal of the game was Denver's margin of victory over Cleveland. The Browns went ahead 10-6 in the second quarter when Brian Sipe and Reggie Rucker combined on a 40-yard touchdown pass. Denver regained the lead when linebacker Randy Gradishar returned an interception 93 yards for a touchdown to give the Broncos a 13-10 edge. Cleveland came back to tie twice more before Denver drove 41 yards in 10 plays to set up Steinfort's winning 19-yard field goal with 5:50 left. Cleveland had a chance to send the game into overtime with 2:32 left in regulation, but Don Cockroft's 54-yard field goal attempt fell short.

Denver	3	10	3	3	— 19
Cleveland	3	10	3	0	— 16

Den—FG Steinfort 18
Cle —FG Cockroft 24
Den—FG Steinfort 47
Cle —Rucker 40 pass from Sipe (Cockroft kick)
Den—Gradishar 93 interception return (Steinfort kick)
Cle —FG Cockroft 45
Den—FG Steinfort 41
Cle —FG Cockroft 40
Den—FG Steinfort 19

Atlanta 43, Detroit 28—At Atlanta-Fulton County Stadium, attendance 57,652. Atlanta capitalized on Detroit turnovers and handed the Lions their first defeat of the season. Frank Reed gave Atlanta a 7-3 first-quarter lead when he returned a blocked punt 16 yards for a touchdown. Three plays later, the Falcons upped the lead to 14-3 when linebacker Buddy Curry scooped up Gary Danielson's fumble and returned it 30 yards for a touchdown. Atlanta built a 32-6 lead before Danielson (23 of 36 for 348 yards) closed the gap with three fourth-quarter touchdown passes. The Lions' Walt Williams' third-quarter interception ended Steve Bartkowski's streak of consecutive passes without being intercepted at 118.

Detroit	3	3	0	22	— 28
Atlanta	17	17	2	7	— 43

Det—FG Murray 43
Atl —Reed 16 blocked punt return (Mazzetti kick)
Atl —Curry 30 fumble recovery return (Mazzetti kick)
Atl —FG Mazzetti 26
Atl —Jenkins 43 pass from Bartkowski (Mazzetti kick)
Atl —Williams 42 fumble recovery return (Mazzetti kick)
Atl —FG Mazzetti 33
Det—FG Murray 32
Atl —Safety, Williams tackled Danielson in end zone
Det—Scott 43 pass from Danielson (Murray kick)
Atl —Andrews 11 run (Mazzetti kick)
Det—L. Thompson 79 pass from Danielson (Murray kick)
Det—Scott 6 pass from Danielson (kick failed)
Det—Safety, Cole tackled R. Smith in end zone

Kansas City 31, Oakland 17—At Oakland-Alameda County Coliseum, attendance 40,153. Linebackers Gary Spani and Whitney Paul each returned fumbles for touchdowns as Kansas City defeated Oakland. The fumble returns of 16 yards by Spani and 32 yards by Paul helped Kansas City build a 31-3 halftime lead. The Chiefs' defense also intercepted five passes and recorded six sacks. Jim Plunkett (20 of 52 for 238 yards) replaced Dan Pastorini, who suffered a broken leg in the first quarter, and threw two touchdown passes. The victory enabled Kansas City to snap a four-game losing streak.

Kansas City	14	17	0	0	— 31
Oakland	0	3	0	14	— 17

KC —Spani 16 fumble recovery return (Lowery kick)
KC —McKnight 2 run (Lowery kick)
KC —FG Lowery 35
KC —Morgado 1 run (Lowery kick)
KC —Paul 32 fumble recovery return (Lowery kick)
Oak—FG Bahr 39
Oak—Branch 10 pass from Plunkett (Bahr kick)
Oak—Chandler 6 pass from Plunkett (Bahr kick)

New England 21, New York Jets 11—At Shea Stadium, attendance 53,603. Mike Haynes's 65-yard touchdown return of a blocked field goal sparked New England past the Jets. Trailing 7-6 with 2:21 left in the first half, New York attempted a 49-yard field goal that was blocked by linebacker Steve Nelson and recovered by John Zamberlin. Zamberlin lateraled to Haynes, who went a club-record 65 yards for the touchdown. New England opened the second half by driving 78 yards in 12 plays with Matt Cavanaugh hitting Harold Jackson with a 37-yard touchdown pass.

New England	7	7	7	0	— 21
New York Jets	6	0	0	5	— 11

NE —Calhoun 1 run (Smith kick)
NYJ—Gaines 16 pass from Todd (kick failed)
NE —Haynes 65 blocked field goal return (Smith kick)
NE —Jackson 37 pass from Cavanaugh (Smith kick)
NYJ—FG Leahy 40
NYJ—Safety, Cavanaugh ran out of end zone

Dallas 24, New York Giants 3—At Texas Stadium, attendance 59,126. Danny White threw two touchdown passes as Dallas downed the Giants. White (22 of 33 for 266 yards) gave Dallas a 10-0 second quarter lead with a 46-yard scoring pass to Tony Hill. Dallas took a 17-0 halftime advantage after driving 86 yards in less than two minutes. White's 29-yard pass to Butch Johnson ended the drive. Defensive tackle John Dutton scored the Cowboys' final touchdown in the fourth quarter on a 38-yard interception return. The victory enabled Dallas to remain tied with Philadelphia for first place in the NFC Eastern Division.

New York Giants	0	0	0	3	— 3
Dallas	3	14	0	7	— 24

Dall —FG Septien 38
Dall —Hill 46 pass from D. White (Septien kick)
Dall —Johnson 29 pass from D. White (Septien kick)
NYG—FG Danelo 51
Dall —Dutton 38 interception return (Septien kick)

Pittsburgh 23, Minnesota 17—At Metropolitan Stadium, attendance 47,583. Terry Bradshaw ran two yards for one touchdown and threw 21 yards to Calvin Sweeney for another, as Pittsburgh defeated Minnesota. Vikings quarterback Tommy Kramer brought Minnesota back from a 23-3 deficit with a 21-yard touchdown pass to Sammy White and a four-yard scoring run. Pittsburgh's defense stiffened late in the fourth quarter, intercepting two passes inside their own 40 yard line.

Pittsburgh	6	10	7	0	— 23
Minnesota	3	0	0	14	— 17

Pitt —Sweeney 21 pass from Bradshaw (kick failed)
Minn—FG Danmeier 35
Pitt —Harris 4 run (Bahr kick)
Pitt —FG Bahr 28
Pitt —Bradshaw 2 run (Bahr kick)
Minn—S. White 21 pass from Kramer (Danmeier kick)
Minn—Kramer 4 run (Danmeier kick)

St. Louis 40, New Orleans 7—At Louisiana Superdome, attendance 45,388. Ottis Anderson and Wayne Morris each ran for over 100 yards to lead St. Louis over New Orleans. Anderson was the game's leading rusher with 126 yards on 22 carries. He also caught three passes for 18 yards. Morris scored three touchdowns (a pair of two-yard runs and a one-yard plunge) and gained 102 yards on 22 carries. The Cardinals' offense gained a total of 433 yards and accumulated 23 first downs rushing. The Cardinals' defense held New Orleans to 80 yards and three first downs.

St. Louis	7	20	3	10	— 40
New Orleans	0	0	7	0	— 7

StL—Morris 2 run (Little kick)
StL—Morris 2 run (Little kick)
StL—Tilley 7 pass from Hart (kick blocked)
StL—Morris 1 run (Little kick)
StL—FG Little 25
NO—Price 19 blocked punt return (Ricardo kick)
StL—FG Little 36
StL—Harrell 11 run (Little kick)

Los Angeles 48, San Francisco 26—At Anaheim Stadium, attendance 62,188. Vince Ferragamo threw four touchdown passes as Los Angeles outscored San Francisco. Ferragamo completed 20 of 27 passes for 304 yards in leading the Rams, who rolled up a season-high 462 yards total offense. Elvis Peacock was the game's leading rusher with 114 yards on 18 carries. Cullen Bryant was the Rams' top receiver with six receptions for 78 yards. San Francisco's Paul Hofer remained the NFL's leading receiver after catching nine passes for 91 yards. The Rams' victory extended their winning streak to three and enabled them to move into a tie for the NFC Western Division lead.

San Francisco	0	14	6	6	— 26
Los Angeles	17	17	7	7	— 48

LA—Bryant 20 pass from Ferragamo (Corral kick)
LA—FG Corral 28
LA—Youngblood 33 interception return (Corral kick)
LA—FG Corral 35
SF—Clark 14 pass from DeBerg (Wersching kick)
LA—Miller 35 pass from Ferragamo (Corral kick)
LA—Cromwell 24 interception return (Corral kick)
SF—Cooper 1 run (Wersching kick)
SF—Clark 5 pass from Montana (kick failed)
LA—Peacock 8 pass from Ferragamo (Corral kick)
SF—Solomon 38 pass from Montana (kick blocked)
LA—Miller 8 pass from Ferragamo (Corral kick)

Seattle 26, Houston 7—At Astrodome, attendance 46,860. Seattle scored 17 points in just over three minutes of the second quarter on the way to surprising Houston. Jim Zorn started the scoring outburst by hitting Sam McCullum with a 22-yard touchdown pass. On the ensuing kickoff, safety Vic Minor recovered a fumble to set up a 32-yard field goal by Efren Herrera. Seattle's final touchdown of the second quarter came on a 24-yard pass from Zorn to McCullum. Herrera set a club record by kicking four field goals. The Seahawks' defense intercepted five passes, the most in their history.

Seattle	3	20	3	0	— 26
Houston	0	0	0	7	— 7

Sea—FG Herrera 32
Sea—McCullum 22 pass from Zorn (Herrera kick)
Sea—FG Herrera 33
Sea—McCullum 24 pass from Zorn (Herrera kick)
Sea—FG Herrera 50
Sea—FG Herrera 44
Hou—Barber 22 pass from Stabler (Fritsch kick)

Philadelphia 24, Washington 14—At Veterans Stadium, attendance 69,044. Ron Jaworski threw for two touchdowns and Wilbert Montgomery ran for another as Philadelphia downed Washington. With the score tied 7-7, Eagles' rookie cornerback Roynell Young intercepted a pass and returned it 26 yards to the Redskins' 17 yard line. Five plays later Montgomery swept three yards around right end to give Philadelphia a 14-7 lead. Philadelphia went ahead 21-7 with 30 seconds left in the first half when Jaworski and Harold Carmichael combined on a six-yard scoring pass. Carmichael had four receptions for 63 yards and moved into eighteenth place on the NFL's all-time pass receiving list (431).

Washington	7	0	0	7	— 14
Philadelphia	7	14	3	0	— 24

Wash—Thompson 54 pass from Theismann (Moseley kick)
Phil —Harris 51 pass from Jaworski (Franklin kick)
Phil —Montgomery 3 run (Franklin kick)
Phil —Carmichael 6 pass from Jaworski (Franklin kick)
Phil —FG Franklin 39
Wash—Claitt 10 run (Moseley kick)

MONDAY, OCTOBER 6

Chicago 23, Tampa Bay 0—At Soldier Field, attendance 61,350. Bob Thomas kicked three field goals and Mike Phipps ran for two touchdowns as Chicago shut out Tampa Bay. Chicago took a 10-0 third-quarter lead on Phipps's five-yard run, his first rushing touchdown since 1974. After two field goals by Thomas, Alan Page intercepted a pass and returned it 10 yards to the Buccaneers' 1 yard line to set up Phipps's second touchdown run. Walter Payton, who was held to 11 yards in the first half, came on to rush for 133 yards on 28 carries. Payton became the Bears' all-time combined offense leader with 9,492 yards and moved into seventh on the NFL's all-time rushing list.

Tampa Bay	0	0	0	0	— 0
Chicago	0	3	10	10	— 23

Chi—FG Thomas 30
Chi—Phipps 5 run (Thomas kick)
Chi—FG Thomas 44
Chi—FG Thomas29
Chi—Phipps 1 run (Thomas kick)

SIXTH WEEK SUMMARY

The New York Jets broke into the win column with a 14-7 win over Atlanta, while Buffalo bacame the last team to plummet from the undefeated ranks, dropping a 17-12 decision to the Colts in rain-soaked and windswept Rich Stadium. New England shut out Miami to gain a share of the AFC East lead with Buffalo. It was the Dolphins' first shut out loss since November, 1970. A blocked extra point proved the difference in the Cincinnati's 17-16 victory over Pittsburgh. It was the first time in Cincinnati history that the Bengals had swept a season series from the Steelers. Oakland snapped a two-game losing streak, defeating San Diego 38-24. Jim Plunkett made his first start in three seasons and led the Raiders' attack, completing 11 of 14 passes for 164 yards. Dallas and Philadelphia both won to remain tied in the NFC East. The Eagles defeated the New York Giants 31-16. Danny White directed scoring drives on 9 of the Cowboys' first 11 possessions, including four touchdown passes, in leading Dallas's win over San Francisco. The "Battle of the Bays" (Tampa Bay and Green Bay) produced the NFL's first tie game since Green Bay and Minnesota struggled to a 10-10 deadlock in 1978. Lynn Dickey set team records (35 of 51 for 418 yards) in becoming the first NFC passer to throw for over 400 yards since James Harris (Los Angeles) in 1976. The NFL set weekly marks for tickets sold (898,268) and in-house attendance (875,866).

SUNDAY, OCTOBER 12

Baltimore 17, Buffalo 12—At Rich Stadium, attendance 73,634. Bert Jones capitalized on poor punting in rainy windswept Rich Stadium, directing the Colts to 17 first-half points and victory over the previously unbeaten Bills. Short punts set up Jones's 38-yard touchdown strike to Mike Siani and Steve Mike-Mayer's 21-yard field goal. Don McCauley's one-yard run shortly before halftime ended the Colts' scoring for the day. Roosevelt Leaks's one-yard touchdown run climaxed a 94-yard drive, and Nick Mike-Mayer added two field goals, but Kim Anderson's interception in the end zone blunted Buffalo's final threat.

Baltimore	10	7	0	0	— 17
Buffalo	0	9	0	3	— 12

Balt—Siani 38 pass from Jones (S. Mike-Mayer kick)
Balt—FG S. Mike-Mayer 21
Buff—Leaks 1 run (kick failed)
Balt—McCauley 1 run (S. Mike-Mayer kick)
Buff—FG N. Mike-Mayer 49
Buff—FG N. Mike-Mayer 20

Minnesota 13, Chicago 7—At Metropolitan Stadium, attendance 46,751. Dennis Johnson's fumble recovery set up Ted Brown's one-yard touchdown run with 11:13 left to complete the Vikings' comeback. Rick Danmeier connected on field goals of 35 and 37 yards in the first and third quarters. Johnson's recovery at the Bears' 20 came when Fred McNeil jarred the ball loose from Chicago quarterback Mike Phipps. John Turner tied a club record, intercepting three of Phipps's passes, and Nate Wright added a fourth interception; Minnesota evened its record at 3-3.

Chicago	0	0	7	0	— 7
Minnesota	3	0	3	7	— 13

Minn—FG Danmeier 35
Minn—FG Danmeier 37
Chi —Earl 3 pass from Phipps (Thomas kick)
Minn—Brown 1 run (Danmeier kick)

Cincinnati 17, Pittsburgh 16—At Three Rivers Stadium, attendance 53,668. Cincinnati jumped to a 17-0 lead on touchdowns by Charles Alexander (1-yard run) and Pete Johnson (28-yard pass) and Ian Sunter's 24-yard field goal. The Bengals withstood Pittsburgh's second-half rally, sweeping the season series for the first time. Nose tackle Mike White's blocked conversion attempt in the third period proved to be the difference. The Steelers almost rallied to win, but Matt Bahr was wide on a 39-yard field goal attempt with four seconds left.

Cincinnati	10	7	0	0	— 17
Pittsburgh	0	0	16	0	— 16

Cin—Alexander 1 run (Sunter kick)
Cin—FG Sunter 24
Cin—Johnson 28 pass from Anderson (Sunter kick)
Pitt—Davis 1 run (kick blocked)
Pitt—Smith 13 pass from Bradshaw (Bahr kick)
Pitt—FG Bahr 35

Cleveland 27, Seattle 3—At Kingdome, attendance 61,366. Mike Pruitt rushed for 116 yards, including first and fourth period touchdown carries of 2 and 22 yards, to lead the Browns' victory. Brian Sipe directed Cleveland's 387-yard offense, completing a 91-yard drive with a 39-yard touchdown pass to Keith Wright and setting up Charles White's 3-yard scoring run with a 44-yard pass to Ozzie Newsome. Jim Zorn completed 15 consecutive passes and was 23 of 29 overall, but he was sacked five times by the Browns' defense.

Cleveland	7	6	7	7	— 27
Seattle	0	3	0	0	— 3

Cle —M. Pruitt 2 run (Cockroft kick)
Sea—FG Herrera 29
Cle —Wright 39 pass from Sipe (kick blocked)
Cle —White 3 run (Cockroft kick)
Cle —M. Pruitt 22 run (Cockroft kick)

Green Bay 14, Tampa Bay 14—At Tampa Stadium, attendance 64,854. The Packers and Buccaneers played the NFL's first tie game since November 26, 1978, when the Packers and Vikings fought to a 10-10 deadlock. Lynn Dickey directed Green Bay's 569-yard attack, setting team records with 35 completions in 51 attempts for 418 yards, but his Tampa Bay counterpart Doug Williams ran five yards for a touchdown with 4:50 remaining to send the game into overtime. Packers placekicker Tom Birney missed a 24-yard field goal with 1:09 left in regulation time and a 36-yard attempt with five seconds remaining in overtime.

Green Bay	7	7	0	0	0	— 14
Tampa Bay	0	7	0	7	0	— 14

GB—Middleton 3 run (Birney kick)
TB —Wood 55 interception return (Yepremian kick)
GB—Coffman 6 pass from Dickey (Birney kick)
TB —Williams 5 run (Yepremian kick)

Kansas City 21, Houston 20—At Arrowhead Stadium, attendance 75,048. Steve Fuller scrambled 38 yards for a touchdown with 2:51 remaining to lead the Chiefs' comeback. Kansas City trailed 10-0 at the half but scored twice during a 1:33 third period span on Fuller's 31-yard touchdown strike to Henry Marshall and Gary Spanl's 47-yard interception return. The victory overshadowed the efforts of Houston's Earl Campbell, who carried the ball a club record 38 times for 178 yards.

Houston	3	7	3	7	— 20
Kansas City	0	0	14	7	— 21

Hou—FG Fritsch 41
Hou—Campbell 3 run (Fritsch kick)
KC —Marshall 31 pass from Fuller (Lowery kick)
KC —Spani 47 interception return (Lowery kick)
Hou—FG Fritsch 46
Hou—Barber 26 pass from Stabler (Fritsch kick)
KC —Fuller 38 run (Lowery kick)

Los Angeles 21, St. Louis 13—At Busch Memorial Stadium, attendance 50,230. Vince Ferragamo ran for one touchdown and threw for another, and CullenBryant rushed for 115 yards, as the Rams retained a one-game lead in the NFC West. Los Angeles's 14-0 halftime lead was the result of Ferragamo's touchdown pass to Willie Miller and the quarterback's own four-yard scoring run. Mike Guman's clinching six-yard score in the fourth quater was set up by Jack Reynold's 20-yard interception return.

Los Angeles	0	14	0	7	— 21
St. Louis	0	0	7	6	— 13

LA —Miller 9 pass from Ferragamo (Corral kick)
LA —Ferragamo 4 run (Corral kick)
StL —Harrell 2 run (Little kick)
LA —Guman 6 run (Corral kick)
StL —Marsh 22 pass from Hart (kick blocked)

New England 34, Miami 0—At Schaefer Stadium, attendance 60,777. Steve Grogan and Matt Cavanaugh each threw one touchdown pass as the Patriots became the first team to hold the Dolphins scoreless since November 1, 1970. In the first half, Don Calhoun scored on a one-yard run and Grogan found Harold Jackson with a 33-yard touchdown pass. Cavanaugh lighted a 17-point fourth quarter outburst, firing a 12-yard touchdown pass to Russ Francis. New England held Miami to a club-low 88 total yards (27 passing) and eight first downs. The Patriots' defense also intercepted four passes.

Miami	0	0	0	0	— 0
New England	10	7	0	17	— 34

NE —FG Smith 30
NE —Calhoun 1 run (Smith kick)
NE —Jackson 33 pass from grogan (Smith kick)
NE —Francis 12 pass from Cavanaugh (Smith kick)
NE —FG Smith 36
NE —Clark 14 run (Smith kick)

Detroit 24, New Orleans 13—At Pontiac Silverdome, attendance 78,147. Billy Sims ran for two fourth quarter touchdowns to lead the Lions' victory. Rick Kane's 62-yard kickoff return set up Sims's nine-yard score two plays later, breaking a 10-10 tie. Benny Ricardo's second field goal narrowed Detroit's lead to 17-13, but Gary Danielson scrambled 31 yards to the New Orleans 12-yard line. From there, a pass interference penalty in the end zone gave the Lions first and goal at the 1. With 2:55 remaining. Sims somersaulted in for the clinching score.

New Orleans	0	3	7	3	— 13
Detroit	0	3	7	14	— 24

NO —FG Ricardo 46
Det —FG Murray 31
Det —Scott 48 run (Murray kick)
NO —Chandler 4 pass from Manning (Ricardo kick)
Det —Sims 9 run (Murray kick)
NO —FG Ricardo 22
Det —Sims 1 run (Murray kick)

New York Jets 14, Atlanta 7—At Atlanta-Fulton County Stadium, attendance 57,458. Kevin Long's one-yard touchdown run with 1:38 remaining propelled the Jets to their first win. New York took the early lead on Scott Dierking's one-yard plunge in the first quarter, and the Jets' defense kept the Falcons from penetrating the 30 yard line until early in the fourth quarter. Atlanta's Lynn Cain ran one yard for the tying touchdown with 12:49 left. Long carried 25 times to 100 yards, the first Jet this season to reach 100 in a single game.

New York Jets	7	0	0	7	— 14
Atlanta	0	0	0	7	— 7

NYJ—Dierking 1 run (Leahy kick)
Atl —Cain 1 run (Mazzetti kick)
NYJ—Long 1 run (Leahy kick)

Philadelphia 31, New York Giants 16—At Giants Stadium, attendance 71,051. Louie Giammona ran for two touchdowns in the second half to lead the Eagles' comeback victory. Philadelphia overcame New York's 16-3 halftime lead on Giammona's one-yard burst and Perry Harrington's 19-yard touchdown run. Giammona (three-yard run) and Keith Krepfle (six-yard pass) added fourth period touchdowns, and the Eagles' defense held the Giants to 161 total yards offense (82 rushing, 79 passing).

Philadelphia	0	3	14	14	— 31
New York Giants	7	9	0	0	— 16

NYG—Simms 1 run (Danelo kick)
NYG—Perkins 15 pass from Simms (kick failed)
Phil —FG Framklin 41
NYG—FG Danelo 42
Phil —Giammona 1 run (Franklin kick)
Phil —Harrington 19 run (Franklin kick)
Phil —Giammona 3 run (Franklin kick)
Phil —Krepfle 6 pass from Jaworski (Franklin kick)

Oakland 38, San Diego 24—At Oakland-Alameda County Coliseum, attendance 44,826. Fourth quarter touchdowns by Kenny King and Todd Christensen helped the Raiders snap a two-game losing streak. San Diego came from a 24-10 deficit and tied the game at 24-24. Then King ran 89 yards for a touchdown and Christensen recovered the ensuing kickoff in the end zone. Oakland quarterback Jim Plunkett, making his first start in three seasons, completed 11 of 14 passes for 164 yards, including a 43-yard scoring pass to Cliff Branch. King opened the scoring with a 31-yard touchdown jaunt, and his later scoring run was the longest in Oakland history.

San Diego	7	3	7	7	— 24
Oakland	7	10	7	14	— 38

Oak—King 31 run (Bahr kick)
SD —Cappelletti 5 run (Benirschke kick)
Oak—FG Bahr 42
SD —FG Benirschke 25
Oak—Branch 43 pass from Plunkett (Bahr kick)
Oak—van Eeghen 3 run (Bahr kick)
SD —Jefferson 25 pass from Fouts (Benirschke kick)
SD —Fouts 1 run (Benirschke kick)
Oak—King 89 run (Bahr kick)
Oak—Christensen recovered fumble in end zone (Bahr kick)

Dallas 59, San Francisco 14—At Texas Stadium, attendance 63,399. Danny White threw a carrer-high four touchdown passes, three to Drew Pearson (16, 22 and 17 yards) as the Cowboys recorded their fifth victory. Dallas scored on 9 of its first 11 possessions, taking a 38-7 halftime lead. Ron Springs (one-yard run) and Tony Dorsett (two-yard run) added to Pearson's touchdowns. The Cowboys' defense had five interceptions and five fumble recoveries and held the 49ers to 147 yards passing and 225 overall.

San Francisco	0	7	0	7	— 14
Dallas	14	24	14	7	— 59

Dall—D. Pearson 16 pass from D. White (Septien kick)
Dall—FG Septien 26
Dall—D. Pearson 22 pass from D. White (Septien kick)
SF —Clark 52 pass from DeBerg (Wersching kick)
Dall—Dorsett 2 run (Septien kick)
Dall—D. Pearson 17 pass from D. White (Septien kick)
Dall—DuPree 9 pass from D. White (Septien kick)
Dall—Springs 20 run (Septien kick)
Dall—Newhouse 3 run (Septien kick)
SF —Clark 19 pass from DeBerg (Wersching kick)

MONDAY, OCTOBER 13

Denver 20, Washington 17—At Mile High Stadium, attendance 74,657. Craig Morton and Rick Upchurch combined on a 32-yard touchdown pass with 3:08 remaining to climax the Broncos' second straight victory. Otis Armstrong rushed for 107 yards, including an eight-yard touchdown run, and Fred Steinfort added two field goals, including a club-record 57-yarder. Washington took a 17-13 lead with 7:30 remaining on Joe Theismann's one-yard scoring pass to Art Monk, but Denver followed with the decisive 79-yard drive. With 13 seconds remaining, Mark Moseley's 52-yard field goal attempt was wide.

Washington	3	0	7	7	— 17
Denver	7	3	3	7	— 20

Den —Armstrong 8 run (Steinfort kick)
Wash—FG Moseley 23
Den —FG Steinfort 57
Wash—Jackson 55 run (Moseley kick)
Den —FG Steinfort 23
Wash—Monk 1 pass from Theismann (Moseley kick)
Den —Upchurch 32 pass from Morton (Steinfort kick)

SEVENTH WEEK SUMMARY

After seven weeks, three of the AFC Central Division's four teams were tied for first place. Oakland outscored Pittsburgh 45-34, enabling Houston and Cleveland to grab a share of the lead with the defending Super Bowl Champions. Houston beat Tampa Bay 20-14 with Earl Campbell's 203 yards rushing on 33 carries. Cleveland needed a 46-yard touchdown pass from Brian Sipe to Dave Logan to defeat Green Bay 26-21. In the AFC East, New England moved into sole possession of first place, beating Baltimore 37-21, while Miami downed Buffalo 17-14. In the NFC East, Philadelphia wrestled the lead from Dallas by Beating the Cowboys 17-10. In the NFC West, Atlanta quarterback Steve Bartkowski threw four touchdown passes to lead the Falcons past New Orleans 41-14. Los Angeles quarterback Vince Ferragamo matched Bartkowski with four touchdown passes of his own as the Rams beat San Francisco and remained one game ahead of the Falcons.

SUNDAY, OCTOBER 19

Atlanta 41, New Orleans 14—At Louisiana Superdome, attendance 62,651. Steve Bartkowski fired four touchdown passes as Atlanta defeated New Orleans. Trailing 14-13 at halftime, the Falcons came back with three touchdowns in the third quarter. Linebacker Joel Williams set up two of those with interceptions. Bartkowski completed 16 of 28 passes for 202 yards. His four touchdown passes brought his career total to 60, a club record. Saints quarterback Archie Manning completed 23 of 32 passes for 323 yards and two touchdowns. Wes Chandler was the game's leading receiver with eight receptions for 14o yards and one touchdown.

Atlanta	7	6	21	7	— 41
New Orleans	7	7	0	0	— 14

NO—Chandler 18 pass from Manning (Ricardo kick)
Atl —Miller 11 pass from Bartkowski (Mazzetti kick)
NO—Galbreath 15 pass from Manning (Ricardo kick)
Atl —Francis 24 pass from Bartkowski (kick failed)
Atl —Jenkins 49 pass from Bartkowski (Mazzetti kick)
Atl —Cain 1 run (Mazzetti kick)
Atl —Miller 4 pass from Bartkowski (Mazzetti kick)
Atl —Andrews 13 run (Mazzetti kick)

Miami 17, Buffalo 14—At Orange Bowl, attendance 41,636. Miami's defense recovered three fumbles, setting up two touchdowns and a field goal. In the first quarter safety Don Bessillieu picked up Joe Cribbs's fumble and returned it 44 yards to give Miami a 7-0 lead. Glen Blackwood recovered a second quarter fumble on the Buffalo 27, and eight plays later David Woodley hit Nat Moore with a three-yard touchdown pass. Blackwood's second fumble recovery, late in the third quarter, set up Uwe von Schamann's 23-yard field goal, giving Miami a 17-7 lead. Fullback Terry Robiskie led the Dolphin offense, gaining 84 yards on 18 carries.

Buffalo	0	0	7	7	— 14
Miami	7	7	3	0	— 17

Mia—Bessillieu 44 fumble recovery return (von Schamann kick)
Mia—Moore 3 pass from Woodley (von Schamann kick)
Buff—Cribbs 2 run (Mike-Mayer kick)
Mia—FG von Schamann 23
Buff—Butler 7 pass from Ferguson (Mike-Mayer kick)

Philadelphia 17, Dallas 10—At Veterans Stadium, attendance

70,696. Ron Jaworski threw two touchdown passes to lead Philadelphia past Dallas and into sole possession of first place in the NFC East. With six minutes left, Eagles middle guard Charlie Johnson intercepted a deflected pass at the Dallas 20. Two plays later, Jaworski hit Charlie Smith with a 15-yard touchdown pass, giving Philadelphia a 17-10 lead. The Cowboys took the ensuing kickoff and drove 52 yards to the Philadelphia eight. But on fourth down, with 45 seconds left, rookie cornerback Roynell Young batted down a pass in the end zone, preserving the Eagles' victory.

Dallas	7	3	0	0	— 10
Philadelphia	0	10	0	7	— 17

Dall—Hegman fumble recovery in end zone (Septien kick)
Phil—FG Franklin 35
Phil—Carmichael 5 pass from Jaworski (Franklin kick)
Dall—FG Septien 33
Phil—Smith 15 pass from Jaworski (Franklin kick)

Chicago 24, Detroit 7—At Soldier Field, attendance 58,508. Vince Evans threw for one touchdown and ran for another to lead Chicago over Detroit. Evans took advantage of Jim Osborne's fumble recovery, scoring on a one-yard touchdown run to give Chicago a 7-0 first quarter lead. In the third quarter, with Chicago leading 10-0, Evans hit James Scott with a 59-yard pass to set up Roland Harper's four-yard touchdown run. Evans and Scott teamed again in the final quarter on a 64-yard touchdown pass. Evans completed five of eight passes for 172 yards; Walter Payton ran 27 times for 101 yards.

Detroit	0	0	0	7	— 7
Chicago	7	3	7	7	— 24

Chi—Evans 1 run (Thomas kick)
Chi—FG Thomas 18
Chi—Harper 4 run (Thomas kick)
Det—L. Thompson 34 pass from Danielson (Murray kick)
Chi—Scott 64 pass from Evans (Thomas kick)

Cleveland 26, Green Bay 21—At Cleveland Stadium, attendance 75,548. Brian Sipe's 46-yard touchdown pass to Dave Logan with 16 seconds left in the game enabled Cleveland to defeat Green Bay. Trailing 21-20, Cleveland started the winning drive on its own 13-yard line with 1:53 left in the game. Sipe completed two passes and ran twice to move the ball to the Green Bay 46 with 25 seconds left. Sipe then lofted a pass to Logan, who outjumped a Green Bay defender, and ran 19 yards for the winning score. Sipe completed 24 of 39 passes for 391 yards and two touchdowns.

Green Bay	0	0	14	7	— 21
Cleveland	0	10	3	13	— 26

Cle—FG Cockroft 40
Cle—M. Pruitt 1 run (Cockroft kick)
Cle—FG Cockroft 42
GB—Dickey 7 run (Birney kick)
GB—Ellis 1 run (Birney kick)
GB—Lofton 26 pass from Dickey (Birney kick)
Cle—Newsome 19 pass from Sipe (Cockroft kick)
Cle—Logan 46 pass from Sipe (kick failed)

Kansas City 23, Denver 17—At Mile High Stadium, attendance 74,459. Steve Fuller fired two touchdown passes, and Nick Lowery kicked three field goals, as Kansas City beat Denver. Kansas City took a 20-17 lead on the final play of the third quarter when Fuller hit Henry Marshall with a 46-yard touchdown pass. Lowery's 34-yard fourth quarter field goal completed a 14-play drive that consumed eight minutes and narrowed the Broncos' changes. Craig Morton accounted for both Denver scores with touchdown passes of 14 yards to Rick Upchurch and 6 yards to Riley Odoms.

Kansas City	3	10	7	3	— 23
Denver	7	7	3	0	— 17

KC —FG Lowery 37
Den—Upchurch 14 pass from Morton (Steinfort kick)
Den—Odoms 6 pass from Morton (Steinfort kick)
KC —FG Lowery 39
KC —Dixon 26 pass from Fuller (Lowery kick)
Den—FG Steinfort 41
KC —Marshall 46 pass from Fuller (Lowery kick)
KC —FG Lowery 34

Los Angeles 31, San Francisco 17—At Candlestick Park, attendance 55,360. Vince Ferragamo completed four touchdown passes to four different receivers as Los Angeles defeated San Francisco. Ferragamo staked Los Angeles to a 14-3 halftime lead with touchdown passes of 17 yards to Cullen Bryant and 24 yards to Drew Hill. In the second half, Ferragamo struck with a 13-yard scoring pass to Willie Miller and one of 40 yards to Preston Dennard. Ferragamo completed 18 of 27 passes for 291 yards to remain the NFL's leading passer. The Rams' victory extended their winning streak to five and preserved their one-game lead in the NFC West.

Los Angeles	0	14	10	7	— 31
San Francisco	0	3	0	14	— 17

SF—FG Wersching 39
LA—Bryant 17 pass from Ferragamo (Corral kick)
LA—D. Hill 24 pass from Ferragamo (Corral kick)
LA—FG Corral 47
LA—Miller 13 pass from Ferragamo (Corral kick)
SF—Young 2 pass from Montana (Wersching kick)
LA—Dennard 40 pass from Ferragamo (Corral kick)
SF—Solomon 3 pass from Montana (Wersching kick)

Cincinnati 14, Minnesota 0—At Riverfront Stadium, attandance 44,487. Cincinnati's defense limited Minnesota to 168 yards, and the Bengals became the first team since 1973 to shut out the Vikings. Pete Johnson led the Bengals' ground attack with 26 carries for 115 yards, including a two-yard touchdown run. Cincinnati quarterback Ken Anderson completed 21 of 28 passes for 270 yards, including a 55-yard touchdown toss to Don Bass. In his 13-year coaching career at Minnesota, Bud Grant has been shut out twice, both times by Cincinnati.

Minnesota	0	0	0	0	— 0
Cincinnati	7	0	0	7	— 14

Cin—Johnson 2 run (Sunter kick)
Cin—Bass 55 pass from Anderson (Sunter kick)

New England 37, Baltimore 21—At Memorial Stadium, attendance 53,924. Horace Ivory returned a kickoff 98 yards for a touchdown, and John Smith kicked three field goals, as New England beat Baltimore. After Baltimore's Bert Jones hit Reese McCall with an eight-yard touchdown pass, Ivory took the ensuing kickoff 98 yards, giving New England a 24-21 third quarter lead. Steve Grogan (15 of 24 for 264 yards) completed the 100th touchdown pass of his career when he hit Harold Jackson with a 37-yard strike in the first quarter. The victory was the Patriots' fifth straight and gave them sole possession of first place in the AFC East.

New England	7	3	17	10	— 37
Baltimore	7	7	7	0	— 21

NE —Jackson 37 pass from Grogan (Smith kick)
Balt—Franklin 1 run (Mike-Mayer kick)
NE —FG Smith 27
Balt—McCauley 3 pass from B. Jones (Mike-Mayer kick)
NE —Calhoun 19 run (Smith kick)
Balt—McCall 8 pass from B. Jones (Mike-Mayer kick)
NE —Ivory 98 kickoff return (Smith kick)
NE —FG Smith 29
NE —FG Smith 37
NE —Foreman 1 run (Smith kick)

San Diego 44, New York Giants 7—At San Diego Stadium, attendance 50,397. San Diego's offense gained 567 yards as the Chargers upended the New York Giants. Quarterback Dan Fouts led the Chargers' attack completing 26 of 41 passes for a club record 444 yards and three touchdowns. Three San Diego receivers went over the 100-yard mark. Charlie Joiner had ten receptions for 171 yards, John Jefferson had five for 107 yards, and tight end Kellen Winslow caught six for 102 yards. Charger Chuck Muncie led the ground attack with nine carries for 56 yards and one touchdown.

New York Giants	0	0	7	0	— 7
San Diego	0	21	7	16	— 44

SD —Cappelletti 1 run (Benirschke kick)
SD —Jefferson 39 pass from Fouts (Benirschke kick)
SD —Joiner 11 pass from Fouts (Benirschke kick)
NYG—Taylor 1 run (Danelo kick)
SD —Cappelletti 1 run (Benirschke kick)
SD —Floyd 31 pass from Fouts (kick failed)
SD —FG Benirschke 50
SD —Muncie 5 run (Benirschke kick)

Washington 23, St. Louis 0—At Robert Kennedy Stadium, attendance 55,045. Joe Theismann threw two touchdown passes, and Jeris White intercepted two passes as Washington shut out St. Louis. Before three minutes had elapsed, Theismann (21 of 31 for 307 yards) gave Washington a 7-0 lead, hitting Clarence Harmon with a four-yard touchdown pass. In the second quarter, Theismann's 36-yard touchdown toss to Ricky Thompson gave Washington a 16-0 lead. The Redskins' final score came 23 seconds before halftime on Harmon's 20-yard touchdown run, set up by White's first interception. His second came in the third quarter, in his own end zone, to preserve the Redskins' shutout.

St. Louis	0	0	0	0	— 0
Washington	10	13	0	0	— 23

Wash—Harmon 4 pass from Theismann (Moseley kick)
Wash—FG Moseley 30
Wash—Thompson 36 pass from Theismann (kick failed)
Wash—Harmon 20 run (Moseley kick)

Seattle 27, New York Jets 17—At Shea Stadium, attendance 52,496. Jessie Green returned a blocked punt 32 yards for a touchdown to help Seattle defeat the New York Jets. Training 14-3 in the third quarter, Seahawks wide receiver Sam McCullum blocked a punt, and Green returned the loose ball. Seattle took a 20-17 lead in the fourth quarter, driving 88 yards with Jim Jodat scoring on a two-yard touchdown run. Jodat's second scoring run came one minute later, following Keith Simpson's interception. In addition to blocking the punt, McCullum was the game's leading receiver with five catches for 107 yards.

Seattle	3	0	7	17	— 27
New York Jets	0	7	7	3	— 17

Sea—FG Herrera 48
NYJ—Shuler 4 pass from Todd (Leahy kick)
NYJ—Dierking 20 pass from Todd (Leahy kick)
Sea—J. Green 32 blocked punt return (Herrera kick)
NYJ—FG Leahy 22
Sea—FG Herrera 23
Sea—Jodat 2 run (Herrera kick)
Sea—Jodat 1 run (Herrera kick)

Houston 20, Tampa Bay 14—At Astrodome, attendance 48,167. Using tight ends Mike Barber and Dave Casper simultaneously, Houston gained 467 yards in total offense and controlled the ball for 39 minutes. Earl Campbell rushed for 203 yards on 33 carries to become the AFC's leading rusher. Oilers quarterback Ken Stabler completed 19 of 26 passes for 242 yards and one touchdown.

Tampa Bay	0	7	0	7	— 14
Houston	3	10	7	0	— 20

Hou—FG Fritsch 21
Hou—FG Fritsch 33
Hou—Barber 17 pass from Stabler (Fritsch kick)
TB —Jones 17 pass from Williams (Yepremian kick)
Hou—Carpenter 10 run(Fritsch kick)
TB —Brown 80 fumble recovery (Yepremian kick)

MONDAY, OCTOBER 20

Oakland 45, Pittsburgh 34—At Three Rivers Stadium, attendance 53,940. After Jim Plunkett completed three long touchdown passes to lead the Raiders. Plunkett (13 of 21 for 247 yards) hit Morris Bradshaw for a 45-yard score, Jim Smith scored on a 13-yard pass, leaving the Raiders ahead 28-24 at halftime. On Oakland's next possession in the third quarter, Plunkett and Cliff Branch combined on a 56-yard touchdown pass. The Raiders clinched the victory in the fourth quarter when Plunkett threw 34 yards to Branch. The 79 points scored by the two teams was the highest total ever for a Monday night game.

Oakland	7	21	7	10	— 45
Pittsburgh	10	14	10	0	— 34

Pitt —Smith 19 pass from T. Bradshaw (M. Bahr kick)
Pitt —FG M. Bahr 18
Oak—King 27 run (C. Bahr kick)
Pitt —Hawthorne 1 run (M. Bahr kick)
Oak—van Eeghen 1 run (C. Bahr kick)
Oak—Martin 34 fumble recovery (C. Bahr kick)
Oak—M. Bradshaw 45 pass from Plunkett (C. Bahr kick)
Pitt —Smith 13 pass from Stoudt (M. Bahr kick)
Oak—Branch 56 pass from Plunkett (C. Bahr kick)
Pitt —Bell 36 pass from T. Bradshaw (M. Bahr kick)
Pitt —FG M. Bahr 32
Oak—Branch 34 pass from Plunkett (C. Bahr kick)
Oak—FG C. Bahr 36

EIGHTH WEEK SUMMARY

There were ties in four of the six divisions at the halfway point of the 1980 season. Buffalo seized a share of the lead in the AFC East by defeating New England as Joe Cribbs rushed for 118 yards. Cleveland kept pace with the Oilers in the AFC Central Division with a one-point victory over Pittsburgh. Brian Sipe completed a club-record 28 passes in 46 attempts for 349 yards in the win. Houston's Earl Campbell became only the second running back (O. J. Simpson was the other) to gain over 200 yards in consecutive games rushing. He had 202 yards in the Oilers' 23-3 romp over Cincinnati. Oakland gained a share of the AFC West lead by defeating Seattle on three Jim Plunkett-to-Bob Chandler touchdown passes. Two runs by Danny White from punt formation kept key drives alive as Dallas downed San Diego. Atlanta captured its first season meeting with the Rams to deadlock for the NFC West lead. Philadelphia maintained the top record in the NFL (7-1), capitalizing on Tony Franklin's 18-yard field goal to defeat Chicago. Mark Moseley kicked five field goals in the Redskins' win over New Orleans. The St. Louis defense registered 12 quarterback sacks to headline a victory over Baltimore.

SUNDAY, OCTOBER 26

Philadelphia 17, Chicago 14—At Veterans Stadium, attendance 68,752. Louie Giammona's 27-yard halfback option pass to Keith Krepfle helped set up Tony Franklin's decisive 18-yard field goal with 2:02 left. Philadelphia jumped to a 14-0 lead on a pair of touchdown passes by Ron Jaworski. Chicago had tied the score in the third quarter on a one-yard plunge by Roland Harper and a three-yard run by Vince Evans. After Franklin's field goal, the Bears moved into scoring position with three seconds left in the game, but Bob Thomas's 47-yard field goal attempt fell short.

Chicago	0	0	14	0	— 14
Philadelphia	7	0	7	3	— 17

Phil—Campfield 2 pass from Jaworski (Franklin kick)
Phil—Giammona 2 pass from Jaworski (Franklin kick)
Chi —Harper 1 run (Thomas kick)
Chi —Evans 3 run (Thomas kick)
Phil—FG Franklin 18

Houston 23, Cincinnati 3—At Astrodome, attendance 49,189. Earl Campbell broke a 3-3 tie with touchdown runs of 55 and 3 yards, sandwiched around a field goal, and became the second player in NFL history to rush for 200 or more yards in successive games. Campbell's 202 yards (he had 203 yards the week before) matched the feat achieved twice by O.J. Simpson in 1973 and 1976. Toni Fritsch contributed field goals of 33, 46, and 30 yards. In the first half, the Houston defense stopped four drives in its own territory, one at the Oilers' 5 yard line.

Cincinnati	3	0	0	0	— 3
Houston	0	3	10	10	— 23

Cin —FG Sunter 23
Hou—FG Fritsch 33
Hou—Campbell 55 run (Fritsch kick)
Hou—FG Fritsch 46
Hou—Campbell 3 run (Fritsch kick)
Hou—FG Fritsch 30

Denver 14, New York Giants 9—At Giants Stadium, attendance 67,598. Otis Armstrong rushed for 106 yards on 25 carries, including a decisive two-yard touchdown plunge, to lead the Broncos' comeback victory. The Giants held a 9-7 halftime lead on Joe Danelo's field goals of 28, 28, and 45 yards. Jim Jensen scored Denver's first touchdown on a one-yard run, and Bill Thompson's 36-yard interception return helped set up Armstrong's winning score.

Denver	0	7	7	0	— 14
New York Giants	3	6	0	0	— 9

NYG—FG Danelo 28
Den —Jensen 1 run (Steinfort kick)
NYG—FG Danelo 28
NYG—FG Danelo 45
Den —Armstrong 2 run (Steinfort kick)

Kansas City 20, Detroit 17—At Arrowhead, attendance 59,391. Nick Lowery connected on a 40-yard field goal with 1:14 remaining, and the Chiefs picked up their fourth straight victory. Kansas City survived the performance of Billy Sims, who rushed for 155 yards.

Detroit	0	3	7	7	— 17
Kansas City	0	10	0	10	— 20

KC—FG Lowery 52
KC—Williams 3 pass from Fuller (Lowery kick)
Det—FG Murray 20
Det—Sims 45 run (Murray kick)
KC—Fuller 1 run (Lowery kick)
Det—Sims 1 run (Murray kick)
KC—FG Lowery 40

Atlanta 13, Los Angeles 10—At Atlanta-Fulton County Stadium, attendance 57,401. Steve Bartkowski converted a fourth-and-11 situation into a 54-yard touchdown pass to Alfred Jackson with 1:15 remaining to move the Falcons into a tie with the Rams atop the

NFC West. Rolland Lawrence's 37-yard interception return set up Bartkowski's seven-yard touchdown pass to Jackson and gave Atlanta a 6-3 halftime edge. Los Angeles jumped ahead on Vince Ferragamo's 74-yard touchdown bomb to Drew Hill. The Rams nearly sent the game into overtime with one second remaining, but Frank Corral's 55-yard field goal attempt fell short.

Los Angeles	0	3	7	0	— 10
Atlanta	6	0	0	7	— 13

Atl—Jackson 7 pass from Bartkowski (kick failed)
LA— FG Corral 23
LA—Hill 74 pass from Ferragamo (Corral kick)
Atl—Jackson 54 pass from Bartkowski (Mazzetti kick)

Green Bay 16, Minnesota 3—At Lambeau Field, attendance 55,361. Lynn Dickey fired fourth quarter touchdown passes of 4 and 12 yards to tight ends Bill Larson and Paul Coffman as the Packers beat the Vikings in Green Bay for the first time since 1965. Larson's touchdown reception broke a 3-3 tie, and Green Bay clinched the victory with 7:01 left when Coffman beat Fred McNeill over the middle. Rick Danmeier's 47-yard field goal avoided the shutout for Minnesota.

Minnesota	0	0	3	0	— 3
Green Bay	0	0	3	13	— 16

GB —FG Birney 36
Minn—FG Danmeier 47
GB —Larson 4 pass from Dickey (Birney kick)
GB —Coffman 12 pass from Dickey (kick failed)

Buffalo 31, New England 13—At Rich Stadium, attendance 75,092. Joe Ferguson threw second quarter scoring passes of 14 and 12 yards to Frank Lewis, and the Bills moved into a first place tie with the Patriots in the AFC East. Lewis's first scoring catch put Buffalo ahead to stay with 5:42 remaining in the half. Joe Cribbs rushed for 118 yards and scored on runs of 16 and 5 yards to put the game out of reach. New England was unable to convert any of its 11 third down situations and was held to 39 yards rushing, 148 overall, by the Bills' defense.

New England	3	0	10	0	— 13
Buffalo	0	14	0	17	— 31

NE —FG Smith 41
Buff—Lewis 14 pass from Ferguson (Mike-Mayer kick)
Buff—Lewis 12 pass from Ferguson (Mike-Mayer kick)
NE —Francis 26 pass from Grogan (Smith kick)
NE —FG Smith 32
Buff—FG Mike-Mayer 23
Buff—Cribbs 16 run (Mike-Mayer kick)
Buff—Cribbs 5 run (Mike-Mayer kick)

Washington 22, New Orleans 14—At Robert F. Kennedy Stadium attendance 51,375. Mark Moseley kicked a career-high five field goals to help lead the Redskins to their third win. Moseley connected from 52, 50, 38, 35, and 28 yards. In the third quarter, the first of Rich Milot's two interceptions set up Joe Theismann's 26-yard touchdown pass to Ricky Thompson. The Washington defense held New Orleans to 83 net yards passing and sacked Archie Manning five times.

New Orleans	0	7	0	7	— 14
Washington	3	6	10	3	— 22

Wash—FG Moseley 50
Wash—FG Moseley 28
Wash—FG Moseley 35
NO —Rogers 10 run (Ricardo kick)
Wash—FG Moseley 52
Wash—Thompson 26 pass from Theismann (Moseley kick)
Wash—FG Moseley 38
NO —Childs 2 pass from Manning (Ricardo kick)

Cleveland 27, Pittsburgh 26—At Cleveland Stadium, attendance 79,095. Brian Sipe fired four touchdown passes, including a clinching 18-yarder to Ozzie Newsome with 5:38 remaining. It was the Steelers' third straight defeat. Pittsburgh led almost the entire game, but Sipe, who completed 28 or 46 for 349 yards, brought the Browns back with touchdown passes of six and seven yards to Greg Pruitt, Cliff Stoudt, making his first NFL start, threw for 310 yards, but Chris Bahr's missed conversion attempt following Sidney Thornton's two-yard touchdown run proved to be the difference.

Pittsburgh	10	3	13	0	— 26
Cleveland	0	7	7	13	— 27

Pitt—Hawthorne 1 run (Bahr kick)
Pitt—FG Bahr 27
Cle—Hill 5 pass from Sipe (Cockroft kick)
Pitt—FG Bahr 22
Pitt—Hawthorne 2 run (Bahr kick)
Cle—G. Pruitt 6 pass from Sipe (Cockroft kick)
Pitt—Thornton 2 run (kick failed)
Cle—G. Pruitt 7 pass from Sipe (kick failed)
Cle—Newsome 18 pass from Sipe (Cockroft kick)

St. Louis 17, Baltimore 10—At Memorial Stadium, attendance 33,506. St. Louis built a 17-0 lead on Ottis Anderson's four-yard run, Pat Tilley's 10-yard touchdown catch, and Neil O'Donoghue's 30-yard field goal. Mel Gray caught seven passes for 101 yards. The Cardinals' defense tied an NFL record, sacking Bert Jones 12 times. In the first half, the Colts were held to 36 yards on 35 plays.

St. Louis	7	0	10	0	— 17
Baltimore	0	0	0	10	— 10

StL —Anderson 4 run (O'Donoghue kick)
StL —Tilley 10 pass from Hart (O'Donoghue kick)
StL —FG O'Donoghue 30
Balt—FG Mike-Mayer 35
Balt—Carr 9 pass from B. Jones (Mike-Mayer kick)

Dallas 42, San Diego 31—At Texas Stadium, attendance 60,639. Cowboys rookie Timmy Newsome scored a pair of one-yard touchdowns, igniting a 21-point third quarter explosion. Dallas trailed 24-14 at halftime, but Newsome scored on the Cowboys' first two possessions of the second half, the latter after Danny White kept a 60-yard drive alive with a 12-yard dash from punt formation. White completed 22 of 34 passes for 260 yards and three touchdowns to Butch Johnson, Jay Saldi, and Billy Joe DuPree. The Cowboys dominated the second half, controlling the ball for 23 minutes, and the defense forced turnovers on six consecutive San Diego drives (three fumbles, three interceptions).

San Diego	3	21	0	7	— 31
Dallas	7	7	21	7	— 42

SD —FG Benirschke 45
Dall—Spring 4 run (Septien kick)
SD —Jefferson 58 pass from Fouts (Benirschke kick)
SD —Lowe 16 interception return (Benirschke kick)
Dall—Johnson 17 pass from D. White (Septien kick)
SD —Winslow 9 pass from Fouts (Benirschke kick)
Dall—Newsome 1 run (Septien kick)
Dall—Newsome 1 run (Septien kick)
Dall—Saldi 12 pass from D. White (Septien kick)
Dall—DuPree 9 pass from D. White (Septien kick)
SD —Winslow 3 pass from Fouts (Benirschke kick)

Oakland 33, Seattle 14—At Oakland-Alameda County Coliseum, attendance 50,185. Jim Plunkett threw three second-half touchdown passes to Bob Chandler, and Matt Bahr kicked four field goals, as the Raiders broke a four-game losing streak to the Seahawks. Oakland led 6-0 at the half on Bahr's field goals of 34 and 38 yards before Plunkett threw touchdown passes of 5, 12, and 23 yards to Chandler, Jim Zorn passed for 282 yards, including a 67-yard touchdown bomb to Steve Largent, but was sacked six times and was intercepted twice by the Raiders' defense.

Seattle	0	0	0	14	— 14
Oakland	3	3	10	17	— 33

Oak—FG Bahr 34
Oak—FG Bahr 38
Oak—FG Bahr 30
Oak—Chandler 5 pass from Plunkett (Bahr kick)
Oak—Chandler 12 pass from Plunkett (Bahr kick)
Sea—McCutcheon 1 run (Herrera kick)
Oak—Chandler 23 pass from Plunkett (Bahr kick)
Sea—Largent 67 pass from Zorn (Herrera kick)
Oak—FG Bahr 25

Tampa Bay 24, San Francisco 23—At Candlestick Park, attendance 51,925. Garo Yepremian kicked a 30-yard field goal with 47 seconds left to secure the Buccaneers' victory. The 49ers had moved in front 23-21 with 8:08 remaining on Ray Wersching's third field goal of the day, an 18-yarder. The 49ers earlier had a 45-yard touchdown pass to Lenvil Elliott. The Buccaneers responded with a two-yard scoring run by quarterback Doug Williams, set up by Mike Washington's 14-yard interception return. Freddie Solomon had opened the scoring by returning a punt 53 yards for a touchdown.

Tampa Bay	7	0	14	3	— 24
San Francisco	7	6	7	3	— 23

SF—Solomon 53 punt return (Wersching kick)
TB—Eckwood 2 run (Yepremian kick)
SF—FG Wersching 38
SF—FG Wersching 40
TB—Eckwood 35 run (Yepremian kick)
SF—Elliot 45 pass from Montana (Wersching kick)
TB—Williams 2 run (Yepremian kick)
SF—FG Wersching 18
TB—FG Yepremian 30

MONDAY, OCTOBER 27

New York Jets 17, Miami 14—At Shea Stadium, attendance 53,046. Richard Todd and Scott Dierking scored second quarter touchdowns, and Pat Leahy kicked a 48-yard field goal with 6:31 left to ensure the Jets' victory. New York held a 14-0 halftime lead on Dierking's one-yard run, which completed a 99-yard drive and Todd's 16-yard scramble for a score. Tony Nathan scored twice for the Dolphins in the final minute of the game, on an 11-yard pass from David Woodley and a one-yard plunge.

Miami	0	0	0	14	— 14
New York Jets	0	14	0	3	— 17

NYJ—Dierking 1 run (Leahy kick)
NYJ—Todd 16 run (Leahy kick)
NYJ—FG Leahy 48
Mia —Nathan 11 pass from Woodley (von Schamann kick)
Mia —Nathan 1 run (von Schamann kick)

NINTH WEEK SUMMARY

The NFC's top two teams needed late touchdown passes to emerge victorious in week nine. Ron Jaworski's five-yard touchdown pass to Billy Campfield gave Philadelphia a 27-20 victory over Seattle. Dallas stayed one game behind Philadelphia in the NFC East when Danny White hit Tony Hill with a 28-yard touchdown pass with 45 seconds left, giving the Cowboys a 27-24 victory over St. Louis. Cleveland and Houston remained tied for first place in the AFC Central. Earl Campbell regained the NFL rushing lead in Houston's 20-16 victory over Denver, and Brian Sipe set a club record for career passing yards in the Browns' 27-21 triumph over Chicago. Vince Ferragamo threw five touchdown passes as Los Angeles beat New Orleans 45-31, but Atlanta remained tied with Rams in the NFC West by beating Buffalo 30-14. In the AFC West San Diego and Oakland shared the lead. Oakland needed a strong defensive performance to defeat Miami 16-10, while Dan Diego used three interceptions by Pete Shaw to turn back Cincinnati 31-14. Tampa Bay's Garo Yepremian kicked three field goals becoming the ninth player in NFL history with a career total over 200.

SUNDAY, NOVEMBER 2

Atlanta 30, Buffalo 14—At Rich Stadium, attendance 57,959. Atlanta scored ten points in the final 41 seconds of the first half and went on to beat Buffalo. With his team trailing 14-0, Atlanta safety Tom Pridemore returned a blocked field goal 18 yards to help set up Tim Mazzetti's 28-yard field goal. There were 22 seconds left in the first half when Falcon linebacker Al Richardson returned an interception 20 yards to the Bills' 16-yard line. On the next play Steve Bartkowski hit Junior Miller with a touchdown pass, cutting the Bills' halftime lead to 14-10. In the second half Lynn Cain closed scoring drives of 72 and 15 yards with one-yard touchdown runs. Between Cain's two scores, Mazzetti kicked field goals of 50 and 44 yards.

Atlanta	0	10	10	10	— 30
Buffalo	7	7	0	0	— 14

Buff—Lewis 11 pass from Ferguson (Mike-Mayer kick)
Buff—Cribbs 13 run (Mike Mayer kick)
Atl —FG Mazzetti
Atl —Miller 16 pass from Bartkowski (Mazzetti kick)
Atl —Cain 1 run (Mazzetti kick)
Atl —FG Mazzetti 50
Atl —FG Mazzetti 44
Atl —Cain 1 run (Mazzetti kick)

Baltimore 31, Kansas City 24—At Arrowhead, attendance 52,283. Curtis Dickey ran for two touchdowns, both in the third quarter, enabling Baltimore to defeat Kansas City. Bert Jones completed a 47-yard pass to Reese McCall, setting up two-yard touchdown run by Dickey that moved Baltimore ahead 21-17. Kansas City then drove 80 yards in three plays, Horace Belton scoring on a three-yard touchdown run to put the Chiefs ahead 24-21. Baltimore regained the lead with 1:38 left in the third quarter, when Dickey went 51 yards for a touchdown. The Colts' defense recorded ten sacks; their offense permitted none.

Baltimore	7	7	14	3	— 31
Kansas City	3	14	7	0	— 24

KC —FG Lowery 27
Balt—McCall 18 pass from B. Jones (Mike-Mayer kick)
Balt—McCauley 7 pass from B. Jones (Mike-Mayer kick)
KC —Belton 8 run (Lowery kick)
KC —Fuller 7 run (Lowery kick)
Balt—Dickey 2 run (Mike-Mayer kick)
KC —Belton 3 run (Lowery kick)
Balt—Dickey 51 run (Mike-Mayer kick)
Balt—FG Mike-Mayer 21

Dallas 27, St. Louis 24—At Busch Memorial Stadium, attendance 50,701. Danny White's 28-yard touchdown pass to Tony Hill with 45 seconds left to play enabled Dallas to defeat St. Louis. Early in the fourth quarter, Dallas safety Dennis Thuman returned an interception 78 yards for a touchdown, putting Dallas on top 20-17. With 9:07 left to play, Jim Hart hit Mel Gray with a 34-yard touchdown pass and the Cardinals led 24-20. The Cowboys' winning drive started with 1:52 left to play and covered 69 yards in six plays. Both quarterbacks threw for 258 yards. White completed 23 of 38 passes, Hart 12 of 24.

Dallas	0	10	3	14	— 27
St. Louis	7	3	7	7	— 24

StL —Morris 1 run (O'Donoghue kick)
Dall—Dorsett 4 run (Septien kick)
Dall—FG Septien 28
StL —FG O'Donoghue 42
StL —Tilley 42 pass from Hart (O'Donoghue kick)
Dall—FG Septien 32
Dall—Thurmond 78 interception return (Septien kick)
StL —Gray 34 pass from Hart (O'Donoghue kick)
Dall—Hill 28 pass from D. White (Septien kick)

Pittsburgh 22, Green Bay 20—At Three Rivers Stadium attendance 52,165. Pittsburgh took a 22-14 lead with five minutes to play, when Terry Bradshaw hit Rocky Bleier with a four-yard touchdown pass. Green Bay came back, driving 84 yards in 12 plays, with Lynn Dickey and Aundra Thompson combining on a 14-yard touchdown pass. The Steelers then recovered the Packers' onside kick and ran out the reamining 45 seconds. In the second quarter, Steelers wide receiver Lynn Swann caught a seven-yard touchdown pass, tying Buddy Dial's club record for career touchdown receptions with 46.

Green Bay	7	7	0	6	— 20
Pittsburgh	2	7	6	7	— 22

Pitt—Safety, ball snapped out of end zone
GB—Ellis 7 pass from Dickey (Birney kick)
Pitt—Swann 7 pass from Bradshaw (Bahr kick)
GB—Ellis 69 pass from Dickey (Birney kick)
Pitt—FG Bahr 27
Pitt—FG Bahr 18
Pitt—Bleier 4 pass from Bradshaw (Bahr kick)
GB—Thompson 14 pass from Dickey (kick blocked)

Houston 20, Denver 18—At Mile High Stadium, attendance 74,717. Earl Campbell rushed for two touchdowns as Houston defeated Denver. Broncos kicker Fred Steinfort provided Denver with a 9-7 halftime lead by kicking field goals of 45, 20, and 28 yards. In the third quarter, Campbell's second touchdown, a nine-yard run, concluded a 78-yard drive and gave Houston a 13-9 lead. The Oilers' clinching touchdown came in the fourth quarter, when Rob Carpenter scored on a two-yard run that completed a 14-play, 75-yard drive. Campbell gained 157 yards on 36 carries.

Houston	0	7	6	7	— 20
Denver	6	3	0	7	— 16

Den—FG Steinfort 45
Den—FG Steinfort 20
Hou—Campbell 1 run (Fritsch kick)
Den—FG Steinfort 28
Hou—Campbell 9 run (kick blocked)
Hou—Carpenter 2 run (Fritsch kick)
Den—Jensen 8 pass from Morton (Steinfort kick)

Oakland 16, Miami 10—At Oakland-Alameda County Coliseum, attendance 46,378. Oakland combined Jim Plunkett's two touchdown passes with a stingy second half defense. Plunkett (16 of 26 for 157 yards) completed a 17-yard touchdown pass to Bob Chandler that gave Oakland a 16-3 halftime lead. In the third quarter, Dolphin safety Glen Blackwood recovered a fumble to set up Terry Robiskie's two-yard touchdown run, cutting Oakland's lead to 16-10. The Raiders' defense then stiffened, holding Miami to one first down over the final 22 minutes.

Miami	0	3	7	0	— 10
Oakland	6	10	0	0	— 16

Oak—Chester 13 pass from Plunkett (kick failed)
Mia —FG von Schamann 35
Oak—FG Bahr 48
Oak—Chandler 17 pass from Plunkett (Bahr kick)
Mia —Robiskie 2 run (von Schamann kick)

Minnesota 39, Washington 14—At Robert F. Kennedy Stadium, attendance 52,060. Keith Nord's 70-yard kickoff return highlighted a 23-point first half. Steve Dils, making his first NFL start, threw two touchdown passes to give Minnesota a 14-0 second quarter lead. Vikings defensive end Randy Holloway scored a safety by sacking Joe Theismann in the Redskins' end zone. Nord then returned the ensuing free kick for a touchdown, giving Minnesota a 23-0 lead. Clarence Harmon accounted for both Washington touchdowns with a one-yard run and a one-yard reception.

Minnesota	7	16	7	9	— 39
Washington	0	7	7	0	— 14

Minn —Young 5 pass from Dils (Danmeier kick)
Minn —Senser 2 pass from Dils (Danmeier kick)
Minn —Safety, Holloway tackled Theismann in end zone
Minn —Nord 70 kickoff return (Danmeier kick)
Wash—Harmon 1 pass from Theismann (Moseley kick)
Wash—Harmon 1 run (Moseley kick)
Minn —Young 3 run (Danmeier kick)
Minn —FG Danmeier 31
Minn —FG Danmeier 27
Minn —FG Danmeier 35

Los Angeles 45, New Orleans 31—At Anaheim Stadium, attendance 59,909. Vince Ferragamo threw five touchdown passes to lead Los Angeles past New Orleans. Ferragamo (15 of 26 for 270 yards) completed four of his five touchdown passes in the first half, enabling Los Angeles to take a 31-17 halftime lead. Elvis Peacock led the Rams' running back with 92 yards on 14 carries and caught a 59-yard touchdown pass. Saints quarterback Archie Manning led the New Orleans offense, completing 24 of 48 passes for 263 yards and three touchdowns. The victory enabled Los Angeles to remain tied with Atlanta for first place in the NFC West.

New Orleans	0	7	17	7	— 31
Los Angeles	24	7	7	7	— 45

LA —FG Corral 27
LA —Waddy 38 pass from Ferragamo (Corral kick)
LA —Waddy 9 pass from Ferragamo (Corral kick)
LA —Peacock 59 pass from Ferragamo (Corral kick)
LA —Miller 7 pass from Ferragamo (Corral kick)
NO—Rogers 2 pass from Manning (Ricardo kick)
LA —Moore 19 pass from Ferragamo (Corral kick)
NO—Harris 12 pass from Manning (Ricardo kick)
NO—Reese 34 fumble recovery return (Ricardo kick)
NO—FG Ricardo 36
LA —Guman 3 run (Corral kick)
NO—Childs 3 pass from Manning (Ricardo kick)

Tampa Bay 30, New York Giants 13—At Tampa Stadium, attendance 68,256. Ricky Bell scored two touchdowns and rushed for over 100 yards to lead Tampa Bay. Tampa Bay took a 23-0 halftime lead, scoring 13 points in the final 48 seconds of the half. Garo Yepremian kicked three field goals and became the ninth NFL player to kick over 200. Bell gained a total of 130 yards on 26 carries. The Buccaneers' offense had 379 total yards including a club record 244 yards rushing.

New York Giants	0	0	6	7	— 13
Tampa Bay	7	16	0	7	— 30

TB —Bell 21 run (Yepremian kick)
TB —FG Yepremian 22
TB —FG Yepremian 37
TB —Schumann 25 pass from Williams (Yepremian kick)
TB —FG Yepremian 35
NYG—Shirk 8 pass from Simms (kick failed)
TB —Bell 1 run (Yepremian kick)
NYG—Heater 1 run (Danelo kick)

New England 34, New York Jets 21—At Schaefer Stadium, attendance 60,834. New England scored 24 points in the game's first 16 minutes and hung on to beat the New York Jets. The Patriots took a 7-0 lead when Steve Grogan hit Russ Francis with a 33-yard touchdown pass. Five plays later Roland James returned a punt 75 yards for a touchdown, increasing New England's lead to 14-0. The lead became 24-0 on the second play of the second quarter, when Grogan completed a nine-yard touchdown pass to Stanley Morgan. The victory enabled New England to move into first place in the AFC East.

New York Jets	0	14	0	7	— 21
New England	17	14	3	0	— 34

NE —Francis 33 pass from Grogan (Smith kick)
NE —James 75 punt return (Smith kick)
NE —FG Smith 21
NE —Morgan 9 pass from Grogan (Smith kick)
NYJ—Barkum 27 pass from Todd (Leahy kick)
NYJ—Harper 18 pass from Todd (Leahy kick)
NE —Ivory 1 run (Smith kick)
NE —FG Smith 27
NYJ—Long 3 run (Leahy kick)

Philadelphia 27, Seattle 20—At Kingdome, attendance 61,047. Ron Jaworski completed a five-yard touchdown pass to Billy Campfield, with 2:43 left to play, enabling Philadelphia to down Seattle. Dan Doornink's nine-yard touchdown run put Seattle ahead 20-17 with 11:40 left to play. Philadelphia then controlled the ball for the next nine minutes, marching 84 yards in 15 plays for the go-ahead touchdown. The Eagles defense held Seattle on downs, setting up Tony Franklin's 25-yard field goal with 1:30 left to play. Harold Carmichael's three receptions gave him 31 for the season and made 1980 the eighth consecutive season in which he has caught 30 or more passes.

Philadelphia	0	7	10	10	— 27
Seattle	6	0	7	7	— 20

Sea—FG Herrera 21
Sea—FG Herrera 31
Phil—Campfield 1 run (Franklin kick)
Sea—Largent 27 pass from Zorn (Herrera kick)
Phil—Smith 15 pass from Jaworski (Franklin kick)
Phil—FG Franklin 39
Sea—Doornink 9 run (Herrera kick)
Phil—Campfield 5 pass from Jaworski (Franklin kick)
Phil—FG Franklin 25

San Diego 31, Cincinnati 14—At Riverfront Stadium, attendance 46,406. Dan Fouts completed three touchdown passes as San Diego beat Cincinnati. Fouts (22 of 41 for 270 yards) hit Kellen Winslow with an 11-yard touchdown pass late in the second quarter to give the Chargers a 17-7 halftime lead. In the third quarter, Fouts boosted the Chargers' lead to 31-7 with touchdown passes of 9 and 16 yards to John Jefferson. Winslow was the game's leading receiver with nine receptions for 153 yards, San Diego's Mike Thomas was the game's top rusher with 71 yards on 16 carries. San Diego safety Pete Shaw tied a club record, intercepting three passes.

San Diego	10	7	14	0	— 31
Cincinnati	0	7	0	7	— 14

SD —Thomas 7 run (Benirschke kick)
SD —FG Benrischke 40
SD —Winslow 11 pass from Fouts (Benirschke kick)
Cin—Bass 11 pass from Anderson (Sunter kick)
SD —Jefferson 9 pass from Fouts (Benirschke kick)
SD —Jefferson 16 pass from Fouts (Benirschke kick)
Cin—Turner 15 pass from Thompson (Sunter kick)

Detroit 17, San Francisco 13—At Pontiac Silverdome, attendance 78,845. Gary Danielson's eight-yard touchdown run with 3:42 left to play enabled Detroit to defeat San Francisco. Danielson's run concluded a nine-play, 72-yard drive, wiping out a 13-10 San Francisco lead. The 49ers then drove 73 yards to the Lions' 11-yard line before Detroit's defense stopped them. Billy Sims rushed 17 times for 37 yards to maintain his NFC rushing lead and break the Lions' rookie rushing record. Sims also was the game's leading receiver with 11 receptions for 96 yards.

San Francisco	7	0	3	3	— 13
Detroit	7	3	0	7	— 17

Det—Sims 41 pass from Danielson (Murray kick)
SF —Owens 101 kickoff return (Wersching kick)
Det—FG Murray 32
SF —FG Wersching 36
SF —FG Wersching 39
Det—Danielson 8 run (Murray kick)

MONDAY, NOVEMBER 3

Cleveland 27, Chicago 21—At Cleveland Stadium, attendance 83,224. Mike Pruitt ran for two touchdowns in the fourth quarter as Cleveland beat Chicago. Pruitt's 1-yard touchdown run ended a 12-play, 84-yard drive to extend Cleveland's lead to 20-7. Vince Evans hit Brian Bashnagel with a 17-yard TD pass, with 4:45 to play, tightening the score to 20-14. Pruitt then clinched the Browns victory with a 56-yard touchdown run, giving him 129 yards on 27 carries. Brian Sipe completed 23 of 39 passes for 298 yards and one touchdown to break Otto Graham's club record for career passing yardage.

Chicago	0	0	7	14	— 21
Cleveland	3	7	3	14	— 27

Cle—FG Cockroft 23
Cle—Rucker 4 pass from Sipe (Cockroft kick)
Cle—FG Cockroft 42
Chi—Evans 7 run (Thomas kick)
Cle—M. Pruitt 1 run (Cockroft kick)
Chi—Baschnagel 17 pass from Evans (Thomas kick)
Cle—M. Pruitt 56 run (Cockroft kick)
Chi—Earl 6 pass from Evans (Thomas kick)

TENTH WEEK SUMMARY

Buffalo regained a share of the lead in the AFC East by defeating the New York Jets in the final six seconds of the game. Joe Ferguson's 31-yard touchdown pass to Frank Lewis climaxed the win. Cleveland collected its sixth straight win, defeating Baltimore. The victory helped the Browns maintain a share of the AFC Central lead. Steve Fuller drove Kansas City 91 yards in the closing minutes to give the Chiefs a 31-30 victory over Seattle. Atlanta beat St. Louis in overtime to take sole possession of first place in the NFC West. Ray Strong bolted 21-yards for the winning touchdown 4:42 into overtime. Dallas's Tony Dorsett led all rushers this week with 183 yards and two touchdowns; for the first time, however, the Cowboys did not win when he topped the 100-yard rushing mark. The Giants' Joe Danelo kicked a 27-yard field goal with 1:07 left to give New York the 38-35 win. Green Bay used all-pro wide-receiver James Lofton as a fifth defensive back in its 23-16 win over San Francisco. Teams combined to score 732 points—a record for a 14-game weekend.

SUNDAY, NOVEMBER 9

Atlanta 33, St. Louis 27—At Busch Memorial Stadium, attendance 48,662. Ray Strong dashed 21-yards for a touchdown with 4:42 elapsed in overtime to climax Atlanta's comeback victory. The Falcons trailed 24-6 at the half, but Steve Bartkowski, who set single-game club records by completing 31 of 47 for 378 yards, moved Atlanta into striking distance in the second half. Bartkowski rifled a 27-yard touchdown pass to Wallace Francis to narrow the deficit to 27-20 after Lynn Cain had scored from five yards out. Cain tied the game with 8:4 left, carrying 10 yards for the touchdown. The Falcons' five interceptions included Al Richardson's fifth of the season, which ended the Cardinals' final scoring threat at the Atlanta 18-yard line with 50 seconds left in regulation time.

Atlanta	3	3	14	7	6	— 33
St. Louis	17	7	3	0	0	— 27

StL—Combs 38 pass from Hart (O'Donoghue kick)
Atl —FG Mazzetti 42
StL—Tilley 50 pass from Hart (O'Donoghue kick)
StL—FG O'Donoghue 34
Atl —FG Mazzetti 44
StL—Anderson 8 run (O'Donoghue kick)
Atl —Cain 5 run (Mazzetti kick)
StL—FG O'Donoghue 37
Atl —Francis 27 pass from Bartkowski (Mazzetti kick)
Atl —Cain 10 run (Mazzetti kick)
Atl —Strong 21 run (no PAT attempt)

Buffalo 31, New York Jets 24—At Shea Stadium, attendance 45,677. Joe Ferguson threw a 31-yard touchdown pass to Frank Lewis with six seconds left to give the Bills a 31-24 victory. The game seemed headed for overtime until Joe Cribbs returned Chuck Ramsey's punt 15 yards to the Jets' 47-yard line with 19 seconds left. Ferguson, who threw first-half touchdowns of six and three yards to Mark Brammer, set up the decisive score with a 16-yard pass to the rookie tight end. That gave the Bills a first down at the Jets 31-yard line with 12 seconds to go. The victory moved Buffalo into a first place tie with New England in the AFC East.

Buffalo	10	7	7	7	— 31
New York Jets	0	10	0	14	— 24

Buff—Brammer 6 pass from Ferguson (Mike-Mayer kick)
Buff—FG Mike-Mayer 30
Buff—Brammer 3 pass from Ferguson (Mike-mayer kick)
NYJ—Todd 1 run (Leahy kick)
NYJ—FG Leahy 33
Buff—Leaks 1 run (Mike-Mayer kick)
NYJ—Gaffney 9 pass from Todd (Leahy kick)
NYJ—Dierking 2 run (Leahy kick)
Buff—Lewis 31 pass from Fergsuon (Mike-Mayer kick)

Oakland 28, Cincinnati 17—At Oakland-Alameda County Coliseum, attendance 44,132. Jim Plunkett's four-yard scoring run with 5:28 remaining helped Oakland take sole possession of first place in the AFC West. Touchdown runs by Mark van Eeghen and Kenny King gave the Raiders a 14-10 halftime lead, and Arthur Whittington opened the second half by returning the kickoff 90 yards for a score. Cincinnati narrowed the margin to 21-17 on Jack Thompson's 20-yard touchdown pass to Don Bass. The Bengals could have gone ahead on their next possession, but Rod Martin's interception set up Oakland's clinching 49-yard scoring drive.

Cincinnati	3	7	0	7	— 17
Oakland	0	14	7	7	— 28

Cin —FG Sunter 29
Oak—van Eeghen 2 run (Bahr kick)
Cin —Ross 1 pass from Anderson (Sunter kick)
Oak—King 8 run (Bahr kick)
Oak—Whittington 90 kickoff return (Bahr kick)
Cin —Bass 20 pass from Thompson (Sunter kick)
Oak—Plunkett 4 run (Bahr kick)

Cleveland 28, Baltimore 27—At Memorial Stadium, attendance 45,369. Brian Sipe threw for two touchdowns and Charles White scored twice on five yard runs to pace the Browns' win. Sipe, the AFC's leading passer, completed 22 of 29 passes for 212 yards. He directed the Cleveland offense to touchdowns on three of its first four possessions. White's touchdowns and Sipe's 39-yard scoring pass to Dave Logan gave the Browns a 21-6 halftime edge. Greg Pruitt's final period 12-yard touchdown reception finished the Browns scoring. Bert Jones narrowed the score to 28-27 passing two yards to Reese McCall and five yards to Don McCauley for touchdowns. Cleveland covered Baltimore's onside kick with 19 seconds left to preserve the victory.

Cleveland	14	7	0	7	— 28
Baltimore	0	6	7	14	— 27

Cle —White 5 run (Cockroft kick)
Cle —Logan 39 pass from Sipe (Cockroft kick)
Balt—McCall 23 pass from B. Jones (kick failed)
Balt—Dickey 5 run (Mike-Mayer kick)
Cle —G. Pruitt 12 pass from Sipe (Cockroft kick)
Balt—McCall 2 pass from B. Jones (Mike-Mayer kick)
Balt—McCauley 5 pass from B. Jones (Mike-Mayer kick)

New York Giants 38, Dallas 35—At Giants Stadium, attendance 68,343. Phil Simms' 40-yard gadget pass to Mike Friede set up Joe Danelo's 27-yard field goal with 1:07 left, as the Giants broke an eight game losing streak. Simms threw first-half touchdown passes of 25 yards to Earnest Gray and 4 yards to George Martin for a 28-21 halftime lead. Dallas rallied on Tony Dorsett's NFC season-high 183 yard rushing including his 13-yard touchdown gallop. Simms fired a 20-yard touchdown strike to Tom Mullady on the Giants' next possession to tie the game. Gary Woolford's interception at the New York 12-yard line ended the Cowboys' final threat with 19 seconds left.

Dallas	7	14	14	0	— 35
New York Giants	7	21	0	10	— 38

NYG—Gray 25 pass from Simms (Danelo kick)
Dall —Dorsett 1 run (Septien kick)
NYG—Heater 1 run (Danelo kick)
Dall —Newhouse 1 run (Septien kick)
NYG—Martin 4 pass from Simms (Danelo kick)
NYG—Perry 1 run (Danelo kick)
Dall —Springs 58 pass from D. White (Septien kick)
Dall —Newhouse 29 run (Septien kick)
Dall —Dorsett 13 run (Septien kick)
NYG—Mullady 20 pass from Simms (Danelo kick)
NYG—FG Danelo 27

Denver 20, San Diego 13—At San Diego Stadium, attendance 51,435. Larry Brunson's 53-yard kickoff return set up Rob Lytle's three-yard touchdown run to erase a 6-0 San Diego lead. Denver evened its record at 5-5. Fred Steinfort kicked field goals of 28 and 42 yards and Dave Preston scored on a four-yard run to complete the Broncos' scoring. The Chargers' lone touchdown came on a three-yard pass from Dan Fouts to John Jefferson with 1:26 remaining. Chuck Muncie recorded his first 100-yard game as a Charger, rushig 23 times for 115 yards.

Denver	0	7	6	7	— 20
San Diego	0	6	0	7	— 13

SD —FG Benirschke 30
SD —FG Benirschke 34
Den—Lytle 3 run (Steinfort kick)
Den—FG Steinfort 28
Den—FG Steinfort 42
Den—D. Preston 4 run (Steinfort kick)
SD —Jefferson 3 pass from Fouts (Benirschke kick)

Minnesota 34, Detroit 0—At Metropolitan Stadium, attendance 46,264. Tommy Kramer threw for 295 yards and two touchdowns, and safety Kurt Knoff returned an interception 67 yards for a touchdown, as Minnesota scored its first shutout victory since November 9, 1975. Kramer hit Ted Brown with a 67-yard touchdown bomb and Rickey Young on a 22-yard scoring pass while backup Steve Dils completed the scoring with a 58-yard scoring toss to Joe Senser. The defense held Billy Sims to a season-low 21 yards rushing and sacked Gary Danielson eight times.

Detroit	0	0	0	0	— 0
Minnesota	0	10	14	10	— 34

Minn—FG Danmeier 27
Minn—Brown 67 pass from Kramer (Danmeier kick)
Minn—Knoff 67 interception return (Danmeier kick)
Minn—Young 22 pass from Kramer (Danmeier kick)
Minn—FG Danmeier 23
Minn—Senser 58 pass from Dils (Danmeier kick)

Kansas City 31, Seattle 30—At Kingdome, attendance 58,976. Arnold Morgado's one-yard plunge with 40 seconds remaining climaxed a 91-yard drive and helped the Chiefs post a 31-30 comeback victory. Steve Fuller directed the decisive 11-play drive, completing six of seven for 82 yards. Kansas City's five interceptions included Frank Manumaleuga's 22-yard touchdown return.

Kansas City	3	0	7	21	— 31
Seattle	0	17	6	7	— 30

KC —FG Lowery 42
Sea —Brinson 22 run (Herrera kick)
Sea —FG Herrera 39
Sea —Doornick 4 pass from Zorn (Herrera kick)
KC —Reed 12 pass from Fuller (Lowery kick)
Sea —FG Herrera 31
Sea —FG Herrera 33
KC —Marshall 11 pass from Fuller (Lowery kick)
KC —Manumaleuga 22 interception return (Lowery kick)
Sea —Jodat 2 run (Herrera kick)
KC —Morgado 1 run (Lowery kick)

Miami 35, Los Angeles 14—At Anaheim Stadium, attendance 62,198. Rookie David Woodley passed for three touchdowns and ran for two more and Delvin Williams added 151 yards rushing to lead the Dolphins' 441-yard offensive attack. Woodley fired touchdown passes to Tony Nathan, Nat Moore, and Bruce Hardy and scored on runs of 6 and 10 yards. Williams's effort was his first 100-yard game since November 12, 1978 against Buffalo. The loss dropped Los Angeles to second place in the NFC West, one game behind division leader Atlanta.

Miami	7	14	7	7	— 35
Los Angeles	0	7	0	7	— 14

Mia—Nathan 31 pass from Woodley (von Schamann kick)
Mia—Woodley 6 run (von Schamann kick)
LA —J. Thomas recovered blocked punt in end zone (Corral kick)
Mia—Moore 6 pass from Woodley (von Schamann kick)
Mia—Woodley 10 run (von Schamann kick)
LA —Hicks 32 pass from Ferragamo (Corral kick)
Mia—Hardy 2 pass from Woodley (von Schamann kick)

Philadelphia 34, New Orleans 21—At Louisiana Superdome, attendance 44,340. Ron Jaworski threw touchdown passes of 10, 6, and 25 yards to Harold Carmichael, and Tony Franklin kicked two field goals to lead the Eagles. Jaworski completed 21 of 32 passes for 323 yards, including nine for 13 yards to Charles Smith, who had his second straight 100-yard game. Carmichael's performance marked the first time in his 10-year career that he had caught three touchdown passes in a single game. Mike Hogan's two-yard touchdown run with five minutes left concluded Philadelphia's scoring.

Philadelphia	0	17	7	10	— 34
New Orleans	7	7	7	0	— 21

NO—Williams 24 pass from Manning (Ricardo kick)
Phil—Carmichael 10 pass from Jaworski (Franklin kick)
NO —Chandler 17 pass from Manning (Ricardo kick)
Phil—FG Franklin 32
Phil—Carmichael 6 pass from Jaworski (Franklin kick)
Phil—Carmichael 25 pass from Jaworski (Franklin kick)
NO —Williams 8 pass from Manning (Ricardo kick)
Phil—FG Franklin 30
Phil—Hogan 2 run (Franklin kick)

Pittsburgh 24, Tampa Bay 21—At Tampa Stadium, attendance 71,636. Pittsburgh capitalized on first half turnovers to score all its points. The Steelers held Tampa Bay to one touchdown in the second half to defeat the Buccaneers. Mike Wagner's fumble recovery set up Chris Bahr's 48-yard field goal. Two minutes later Dennis Winston recovered a blocked punt in the end zone for a touchdown and a 10-0 lead. Sidney Thornton ran one-yard for a touchdown, and Terry Bradshaw's 20-yard scoring pass to Lynn Swann concluded the Steelers scoring. Swann's forty-third career touchdown reception broke Buddy Dial's club record.

Pittsburgh	10	14	0	0	— 24
Tampa Bay	7	7	7	0	— 21

Pitt —FG Bahr 48
Pitt—Winston recovered blocked punt in end zone (Bahr kick)
TB—House 26 pass from Williams (Yepremian kick)
Pitt—Thornton 1 run (Bahr kick)
TB—Giles 12 pass from Williams (Yepremian)
Pitt—Swann 20 pass from Bradshaw (Bahr kick)
TB—Bell 8 pass from Williams (Yepremian kick)

Green Bay 23, San Francisco 16—At Milwaukee County Stadium, attendance 54,475. Gerry Ellis's eight-yard touchdown run broke a 13-13 tie, and Johnnie Gray recovered a fumble to preserve the Packers' win. Gray's 30-yard fumble return set up Tom Birney's third field goal, a 32-yarder with 2:16 left. Lynn Dickey set up Ellis's go-ahead touchdown with a 37-yard pass to James Lofton, who caught eight passes for 146 yards. Lofton filled in at safety in Green Bay's prevent defense.

San Francisco	13	0	0	3	— 16
Green Bay	0	13	0	10	— 23

SF —Solomon 20 pass from DeBerg (kick blocked)
SF —Elliott 1 run (Wersching kick)
GB—FG Birney 50
GB—Middleton 1 run (Birney kick)
GB—FG Birney 39
GB—Ellis 8 run (Birney kick)
SF —FG Wersching 24
GB—FG Birney 32

Chicago 35, Washington 21—At Soldier Field, attendance 57,159. Vince Evans passed for three touchdowns and Walter Payton rushed for 107 yards as the Bears jumped to a 35-0 halftime lead and coasted to victory. Payton opened the scoring on a 50-yard touchdown burst and later took a swing pass from Evans and darted 54 yards for another score. Evans combined with James Scott on touchdown passes of 40 and 12 yards, and Gary Campbell's interception set up Roland Harper's two-yard touchdown plunge.

Washington	0	0	14	7	— 21
Chicago	21	14	0	0	— 35

Chi —Payton 50 run (Thomas kick)
Chi —Scott 40 pass from Evans (Thomas kick)
Chi —Harper 2 run (Thomas kick)
Chi —Payton 54 pass from Evans (Thomas kick)
Chi —Scott 12 pass from Evans (Thomas kick)
Wash—Claitt 3 pass from Theismann (Moseley kick)
Wash—Theismann 7 run (Moseley kick)
Wash—Thompson 16 pass from Theismann (Moseley kick)

MONDAY, NOVEMBER 10

Houston 38, New England 34—At Astrodome, attendance 51,524. Ken Stabler completed 15 of 17 passes for 258 yards, including touchdowns to Mike Barber, Dave Casper, and Mike Renfro. Earl Campbell rushed for 130 yards and two touchdowns. Steve Grogan rallied the Patriots from a 24-6 halftime deficit. Don Calhoun's one-yard touchdown plunge preceded Grogan's scoring pass to Harold Jackson and two to Russ Francis. Mosi Tatupu recovered an onside kick with 1:09 left, but Greg Stemrick's interception in the end zone with 35 seconds left ended the Patriots' final threat.

New England	0	6	14	14	— 34
Houston	3	21	0	14	— 38

Hou—FG Fritsch 45
NE —FG Smith 26
Hou—Barber 79 pass from Stabler (Fritsch kick)
NE —FG Smith 44
Hou—Casper 4 pass from Stabler (Fritsch kick)
Hou—Campbell 3 run (Fritsch kick)
NE —Calhoun 1 run (Smith kick)
NE —Jackson 39 pass from Grogan (Smith kick)
Hou—Campbell 7 run (Fritsch kick)
NE —Francis 21 pass from Grogan (Smith kick)
Hou—Renfro 16 pass from Stabler (Fritsch kick)
NE —Francis 15 pass from Grogan (Fritsch kick)

ELEVENTH WEEK SUMMARY

Trick plays and strong defensive efforts highlighted week 11 in the NFL. Houston took sole possession of first place in the AFC Central Division by beating Chicago 10-6. The Oilers faked a field goal with Gifford Nielson shoveling a pass to Tim Wilson, who went eight yards for the game's lone touchdown. A flea-flicker helped Los Angeles edge New England 17-14. After receiving a handoff, Cullen Bryant lateraled to Vince Ferragamo, who hit Preston Dennard with a 44-yard pass to set up the Rams' winning touchdown. Buffalo moved past the Patriots into first place in the AFC Eastern Division shutting out Cincinnati 14-0. Philadelphia also recorded a shutout over Washington 24-0 and retained the best record in the NFL. Billy Sims set a single season rushing record for Detroit, but Baltimore didn't allow him to cross the goal line and beat the Lions 10-9. The offensive fireworks for the week were set off in Minnesota where the Vikings defeated Tampa Bay 38-30. The two offenses together gained 1,023 yards, which is the seventh highest in NFL history.

SUNDAY, NOVEMBER 16

Baltimore 10, Detroit 9—At Pontiac Silverdome, attendance 77,677. Curtis Dickey scored on a one-yard run as Baltimore edged Detroit. Baltimore received the opening kickoff and drove 70 yards in 11 plays to produce the day's lone touchdown. On the last play of the first half Steve Mike-Mayer kicked a 43-yard field goal, giving the Colts a 10-0 halftime lead. Billy Sims gained 126 yards on 30 carries and helped set up Eddie Murray's field goals of 47, 24, and 46 yards. Sims went over the 1000-yard mark (1,043) and set a Lions single season rushing record.

Baltimore	7	3	0	0	— 10
Detroit	0	0	3	6	— 9

Balt—Dickey 1 run (Mike-Mayer kick)
Balt—FG Mike-Mayer 43
Det —FG Murray 47
Det —FG Murray 24
Det —FG Murray 46

Buffalo 14, Cincinnati 0—At Riverfront Stadium, attendance 40,836. Buffalo shut out Cincinnati and took sole possession of first place in the AFC Eastern Division. Buffalo took a 7-0 halftime lead when Joe Ferguson hit Jerry Butler with a 16-yard touchdown pass. Roland Hooks's five-yard touchdown run capped a 16-play, 12-minute drive giving the Bills a 14-0 lead with 2:55 left to play. Offensive guard Reggie McKenzie set a club record by playing in his 127th consecutive game. Buffalo's defense held Cincinnati to 213 total yards in recording its first shutout since 1978.

Buffalo	0	7	0	7	— 14
Cincinnati	0	0	0	0	— 0

Buff—Butler 16 pass from Ferguson (Mike-Mayer kick)
Buff—Hooks 5 run (Mike-Mayer kick)

Pittsburgh 16, Cleveland 13—At Three Rivers Stadium, attendance 54,563. Terry Bradshaw's three-yard touchdown pass to Lynn Swann with 11 seconds left in the game lifted Pittsburgh past Cleveland. Leading 13-7 with two minutes to play, Browns punter Johnny Evans took an intentional safety. The ensuing free kick gave Pittsburgh possession on its own 46 yard line with 1:44 left remaining. Bradshaw then completed passes of 24 yards to Theo Bell and 23 yards to Lynn Swann to help set up the winning score. Franco Harris gained 40 yards on 15 carries to become the third player in NFL history to rush over 9,000 yards with 9,030.

Cleveland	0	13	0	0	— 13
Pittsburgh	0	7	0	9	— 16

Pitt —Smith 10 pass from Bradshaw (Bahr kick)
Cle —Newsome 4 pass from Sipe (kick failed)
Cle —Logan 15 pass from Sipe (Cockroft kick)
Pitt —Safety, Toews tackled Evans in end zone
Pitt —Swann 3 pass from Bradshaw (Bahr kick)

New York Giants 27, Green Bay 21—At Giants Stadium, attendance 72,368. Phil Simms completed three touchdown passes to Earnest Gray as New York defeated Green Bay. New York took a 7-0 lead on its first offensive play when Simms hit Gray with a 50-yard touchdown pass. With two minutes left in the first half, Simms and Gray combined on a 20-yard touchdown pass to give New York a 14-7 halftime lead. The Giants extended their lead to 21-7 in the third quarter when Simms culminated an eight-play, 51-yard drive with a four-yard touchdown pass to Gray. Simms completed 17 of 33 passes for 322 yards, and Gray had six receptions for 119 yards. Gerry Ellis accounted for two Packers' touchdowns with a two-yard run and a four-yard pass reception.

Green Bay	0	7	7	7	— 21
New York Giants	7	7	7	6	— 27

NYG—Gray 50 pass from Simms (Danelo kick)
GB —Ellis 2 run (Birney kick)
NYG—Gray 20 pass from Simms (Danelo kick)
NYG—Gray 4 pass from Simms (Danelo kick)
GB —Ellis 4 pass from Dickey (Birney kick)
NYG—FG Danelo 24
GB —Lofton 8 pass from Dickey (Birney kick)
NYG—FG Danelo 32

Houston 10, Chicago 6—At Soldier Field, attendance 53,390. Tim Wilson scored on an eight-yard touchdown pass off a fake field goal as Houston beat Chicago. With 14 seconds left in the first half, Houston lined up for a 25-yard field goal. At the snap, holder Gifford Nielsen shoveled a pass to Wilson who ran eight yards up the middle for the touchdown. Earl Campbell was Houston's offensive leader, rushing for 206 yards on 31 carries.

Houston	0	7	3	0	— 10
Chicago	0	6	0	0	— 6

Chi —FG Thomas 27
Chi —FG Thomas 22
Hou—Wilson 8 pass from Nielsen (Fritsch kick)
Hou—FG Fritsch 29

San Diego 20, Kansas City 7—At San Diego Stadium, attendance 50,248. San Diego needed two second half touchdowns to defeat Kansas City. Mike Thomas climaxed an 80-yard drive with a seven-yard run to give the Chargers a 13-7 lead in the third quarter. San Diego's final touchdown came with 6:21 left to play when Clarence Williams scored on an eight-yard run to finish a 59-yard march. Thomas led all rushers with 109 yards on 27 carries and scored two touchdowns.

Kansas City	7	0	0	0	— 7
San Diego	0	6	7	7	— 20

KC —Fuller 4 run (Lowery kick)
SD —Thomas 4 run (kick failed)
SD —Thomas 7 run (Benirschke kick)
SD —C. Williams 8 run (Benirschke kick)

Los Angeles 17, New England 14—At Schaefer Stadium, attendance 60,609. A flea-flicker set up Elvis Peacock's one-yard touchdown run enabling Los Angeles to defeat New England. After receiving a handoff, Cullen Bryant lateraled back to Vince Ferragamo, who hit Preston Dennard with a 44-yard pass to the Patriots' three-yard line. Three plays later Peacock scored to give the Rams a 17-14 lead with 1:58 left in the third quarter. The Los Angeles defense intercepted two passes and recovered three rumbles. Steve Grogan accounted for both New England scores with a 35-yard pass to Don Hasselback and a one-yard touchdown run.

Los Angeles	7	0	10	0	— 17
New England	0	14	0	0	— 14

LA —Hicks 10 pass from Ferragamo (Corral kick)
NE —Hasselbeck 35 pass from Grogan (Smith kick)
NE —Grogan 1 run (Smith kick)
LA —FG Corral 29
LA —Peacock 1 run (Corral kick)

Atlanta 31, New Orleans 13—At Atlanta-Fulton County Stadium, attendance 53,871. Steve Bartkowski passed for three touchdowns and ran for another to lead Atlanta by New Orleans. Bartkowski's one-yard touchdown run and 47-yard touchdown pass to Alfred Jackson helped Atlanta build a 17-7 lead entering the fourth quarter. In the final 7:30, Bartkowski hit Wallace Francis with a 5-yard pass and Junior Miller with a 10-yard scoring strike. Bartkowski completed 13 of 24 passes for 195 yards, and Lynn Cain led all rushers with 93 yards on 18 carries.

New Orleans	7	0	0	6	— 13
Atlanta	3	7	7	14	— 31

NO—Chandler 26 pass from Manning (Ricardo kick)
Atl —FG Mazzetti 19

Atl —Jackson 47 pass from Bartkowski (Mazzetti kick)
Atl —Bartkowski 1 run (Mazzetti kick)
Atl —Francis 5 pass from Bartkowski (Mazzetti kick)
Atl —Miller 10 pass from Bartkowski (Mazzetti kick)
NO—Galbreath 3 pass from Scott (kick failed)

Denver 31, New York Jets 24—At Mile High Stadium, attendance 72,114. Craig Morton's 13-yard touchdown pass to Rick Upchurch in the fourth quarter led Denver past New York. New York tied the score 24-24 with 9:24 left to play on Scott Dierking's one-yard touchdown run. Denver came back on its next possession, driving 58 yards to score the go-ahead touchdown on Morton's pass to Upchurch with 5:24 left to play. Morton completed 27 of 39 passes for 306 yards, including two touchdowns, marking his first 300-yard passing game since 1970. Jets rookie wide receiver Johnny "Lam" Jones caught five passes for 103 yards and scored his first NFL touchdown.

New York Jets	7	10	0	7	— 24
Denver	3	7	7	14	— 31

Den —FG Steinfort 30
NYJ—Walker 36 pass from Todd (Leahy kick)
NYJ—FG Leahy 23
NYJ—J. Jones 31 pass from Todd (Leahy kick)
Den —Odoms 22 pass from Morton (Steinfort kick)
Den —Preston 3 run (Steinfort kick)
Den —Keyworth 1 run (Steinfort kick)
NYJ—Dierking 1 run (Leahy kick)
Den —Upchurch 13 pass from Morton (Steinfort kick)

Philadelphia 24, Washington 0—At Robert F. Kennedy Stadium, attendance 51,897. Philadelphia's defense forced five turnovers and shut out Washington. Philadelphia was leading 7-0 midway through the first quarter when Eagles cornerback Richard Blackmore intercepted a Redskins' pass. Four minutes later Ron Jaworski hit John Spagnola with a 14-yard touchdown pass. In the third quarter Eagles linebacker Jerry Robinson returned a fumble 59 yards for a touchdown to give Philadelphia a 24-0 lead.

Philadelphia	14	3	7	0	— 24
Washington	0	0	0	0	— 0

Phil—Krepfle 8 pass from Jaworski (Franklin kick)
Phil—Spagnola 14 pass from Jaworski (Franklin kick)
Phil—FG Franklin 38
Phil—Robinson 59 fumble recovery return (Franklin kick)

Dallas 31, St. Louis 21—At Texas Stadium, attendance 52,567. Danny White tossed three touchdown passes to lead Dallas over St. Louis. In the third quarter White (20 of 36 for 296 yards) hit Drew Pearson with a 14-yard touchdown pass to put Dallas ahead 24-21. In the fourth quarter Tony Dorsett (26 carries for 122 yards) scored the Cowboys' final touchdown on an 11-yard run. Pearson's three catches for 42 yards enabled him to become the Cowboys' all-time leading receiver with 366 receptions.

St. Louis	14	7	0	0	— 21
Dallas	7	10	7	7	— 31

StL —Anderson 51 run (O'Donoghue kick)
StL —Gray 69 pass from Hart (O'Donoghue kick)
Dall—P. Pearson 18 pass from D. White (Septien kick)
Dall—FG Septien 23
StL —Tilley 60 pass from Hart (O'Donoghue kick)
Dall—Hill 58 pass from D. White. (Septien kick)
Dall—D. Pearson 14 pass from D. White (Septien kick)
Dall—Dorsett 11 run (Septien kick)

Miami 17, San Francisco 13—At Orange Bowl, attendance 45,135. David Woodley threw two touchdown passes to lead Miami past San Francisco. Woodley gave Miami a 10-7 halftime lead with a 15-yard touchdown pass to Nat Moore. In the third quarter after recovering a Dolphins fumble, San Francisco went ahead 13-10 on a one-yard touchdown pass from Steve DeBerg to Freddie Solomon. Woodley then drove Miami 80 yards in nine plays, hitting Tony Nathan with an eight-yard touchdown pass to give Miami a 17-13 lead. DeBerg completed 15 straight passes, falling two short of the NFL record.

San Francisco	7	0	6	0	— 13
Miami	3	7	7	0	— 17

Mia—FG von Schamann 21
SF —Cooper 1 run (Wersching kick)
Mia—Moore 15 pass from Woodley (von Schamann kick)
SF —Solomon 1 pass from DeBerg (kick failed)
Mia—Nathan 8 pass from Woodley (von Schamann kick)

Minnesota 38, Tampa Bay 30—At Metropolitan Stadium, attendance 46,032. Ted Brown ran for two touchdowns and Tommy Kramer passed for two as Minnesota outscored Tampa Bay. Kramer (24 of 37 for 324 yards) completed both his touchdown passes in the first quarter, giving Minnesota a 14-6 lead. Brown (15 carries for 73 yards) scored touchdowns in the second and third quarters to help clinch Minnesota's victory. Buccaneers quarterback Doug Williams completed 30 of 55 passes for 486 yards, the fourth highest total in NFL history.

Tampa Bay	6	7	10	7	— 30
Minnesota	14	10	7	7	— 38

Minn—S. White 27 pass from Kramer (Danmeier kick)
TB —House 19 pass from Williams (kick blocked)
Minn—Senser 12 pass from Kramer (Danmeier kick)
TB —House 49 pass from Williams (Yepremian kick)
Minn—Brown 3 run (Danmeier kick)
Minn—FG Danmeier 19
TB —T. Davis 9 pass from Williams (Yepremian kick)
Minn—Brown 7 run (Danmeier kick)
TB —FG Yepremian 32
Minn—Young 1 run (Danmeier kick)
TB —Hagins 29 pass from Williams (Yepremian kick)

MONDAY, NOVEMBER 17

Oakland 19, Seattle 17—At Kingdome, attendance 60,480. Chris Bahr's 28-yard field goal with 56 seconds left to play lifted Oakland over Seattle. Early in the fourth quarter Raiders linebacker Ted Hendricks blocked a punt that rolled through the end zone for a safety. Jim Plunkett hit Derrick Ramsey with a 58-yard pass, setting up Mark van Eeghan's one-yard scoring run with 8:30 remaining. Oakland's winning score culminated a 51-yard drive that started after an interception by Lester Hayes. The Raiders extended their winning streak to six and kept their one-game lead in the AFC Western Division.

Oakland	0	0	7	12	— 19
Seattle	0	7	7	3	— 17

Sea—McCutcheon 1 run (Herrera kick)
Sea—Doornink 8 pass from Zorn (Herrera kick)
Oak—Whittington 10 run (Bahr kick)
Sea—FG Herrera 37
Oak—Safety, Hendricks blocked punt out of end zone
Oak—van Eeghen 1 run (Bahr kick)
Oak—FG Bahr 28

TWELFTH WEEK SUMMARY

With four weeks remaining in the season, Philadelphia became the first team to clinch at least a wild card playoff berth. The Eagles ran their record to 11-1 when Wilbert Montgomery scored from three yards out to cap a 10-7 victory over the Raiders. Dallas survived a scare from Washington to remain two games back in the NFC East. Defensive tackle Larry Cole went 43 yards with an interception to score the winning touchdown in the fourth quarter. It was Cole's fourth career touchdown—all against the Redskins. Detroit and Atlanta both maintained one game leads in the NFC Central and West Divisions, respectively. New England kept pace with Buffalo in the AFC East. The Bills defeated the Steelers 28-13 while the Patriots humbled Baltimore 47-21 despite the absence of quarterback Steve Grogan, who suffered a knee injury that forced him to sit out the game after 78 consecutive starts. Cleveland gained a share of the AFC Central lead, defeating Cincinnati 31-7. Houston dropped a 31-28 overtime decision to the New York Jets despite Ken Stabler's 388-yard passing performance. San Diego moved into a first-place deadlock with Oakland in the AFC West by defeating Miami in overtime. Woodrow Lowe picked off David Woodley's pass to set up Rolf Benirschke's 28-yard winning field goal.

THURSDAY, NOVEMBER 20

San Diego 27, Miami 24—At Orange Bowl, attendance 63,013. Woodrow Lowe's 28-yard interception return set up Rolf Benirschke's 28-yard field goal with 7:14 elapsed in overtime as San Diego moved into a first-place tie with Oakland in the AFC West. Dan Fouts threw touchdown passes of four yards to Clarence Williams, seven yards to Charlie Joiner, and six yards to John Jefferson to give the Chargers a 24-17 edge. Delvin Williams's one-yard touchdown dive with 1:21 remaining sent the game into overtime. It was San Diego's second overtime win of the season.

San Diego	7	10	7	0	3	— 27
Miami	7	10	0	7	0	— 24

Mia—Robiskie 6 run (von Schamann kick)
SD —C. Williams 4 pass from Fouts (Benirschke kick)
SD —FG Benirschke 37
Mia—Nathan 7 pass from Woodley (von Schamann kick)
SD —Joiner 7 pass from Fouts (Benirschke kick)
Mia—FG von Schamann 48
SD —Jefferson 6 pass from Fouts (Benirschke kick)
Mia—D. Williams 1 run (von Schamann kick)
SD —FG Benirschke 28

SUNDAY, NOVEMBER 23

New England 47, Baltimore 21—At Schaefer Stadium, attendance 61,297. Rick Sanford and Allan Clark returned fumbled kickoffs 22 and 15 yards respectively for touchdowns and Rod Shoate returned an interception 42 yards for a score as the Patriots ended a two-game losing streak. Don Calhoun, (106 yards rushing and two touchdowns) and Vagas Ferguson (100 yards rushing) became the first pair of Patriots ever to rush for 100-or-more yards in the same game. Matt Cavanaugh made his first NFL start, and John Smith kicked two field goals and five PATs to score over 100 points (103) for the second straight year.

Baltimore	0	0	7	14	— 21
New England	7	3	10	27	— 47

NE —Calhoun 1 run (Smith kick)
NE —FG Smith 22
NE —Shoate 42 interception return (Smith kick)
Balt—Washington 23 pass from Landry (Mike-Mayer kick)
NE —FG Smith 35
NE —Sanford 22 fumble recovery return (Smith kick)
Balt—Dickey 28 run (Mike-Mayer kick)
NE —Pennywell 9 pass from Cavanaugh (kick failed)
Balt—Dickey 1 run (Mike-Mayer kick)
NE —Calhoun 3 run (Smith kick)
NE —Clark 15 fumble recovery return (Smith kick)

Atlanta 28, Chicago 17—At Atlanta Fulton-County Stadium, attendance 49,156. Steve Bartkowski threw three touchdown passes, including two to Alfred Jenkins, as the Falcons gained another comeback victory. Bartkowski and Jenkins combined for a 7-yard touchdown in the second quarter and a 42-yard score early in the final period that gave the Falcons a 21-17 lead. Ken Johnson's 56-yard punt return set up Bartkowski's nine-yard scoring toss to William Andrews, which clinched the victory for leaders of the NFC West.

Chicago	7	3	7	0	— 17
Atlanta	0	14	0	14	— 28

Chi—Payton 1 run (Thomas kick)
Chi—FG Thomas 41
Atl —Jenkins 7 pass from Bartkowski (Mazzetti kick)
Atl —Andrews 4 run (Mazzetti kick)
Chi—Evans 1 run (Thomas kick)
Atl —Jenkins 42 pass from Bartkowski (Mazzetti kick)
Atl —Andrews 9 pass from Bartkowski (Mazzetti kick)

Cleveland 31, Cincinnati 7—At Cleveland Stadium, attendance 79,253. Brian Sipe threw touchdown passes to four different receivers as Cleveland moved into a first-place tie with Houston in the AFC Central Division. Sipe, who completed 27 of 36 passes for 310 yards, directed the Browns to a 14-7 halftime lead with scoring passes of 16 yards to Reggie Rucker and 5 yards to Calvin Hill, his 100th career touchdown reception. Greg Pruitt (2 yards) and Rickey Feacher (55 yards) caught scoring passes from Sipe in the third quarter.

Cincinnati	7	0	0	0	— 7
Cleveland	0	14	14	3	— 31

Cin—Alexander 6 run (Vitiello kick)
Cle—Rucker 16 pass from Sipe (Cockroft kick)
Cle—Hill 5 pass from Sipe (Cockroft kick)
Cle—G. Pruitt 2 pass from Sipe (Cockroft kick)
Cle—Feacher 55 pass from Sipe (Cockroft kick)
Cle—FG Cockroft 31

Detroit 24, Tampa Bay 10—At Tampa Stadium, attendance 64,976. The Lions' league-leading rushing attack accounted for all three of their touchdowns as Detroit moved into a one-game lead in the NFC Central Division. Gary Danielson contributed to the balanced offense by completing 22 of 29 passes for 157 yards. The Lions overcame Tampa Bay's 10-0 lead on an 11-yard end-around touchdown by Ray Williams and a 21-yard score by Billy Sims that was set up by Ray Oldham's fumble recovery on the Bucs' 36 yard line. Dexter Bussey scored the other Lions' touchdown on a five-yard run.

Detroit	0	14	3	7	— 24
Tampa Bay	3	7	0	0	— 10

TB —FG Yepremian 24
TB —Jones 12 pass from D. Williams (Yepremian kick)
Det—R. Williams 11 run (Murray kick)
Det—Sims 21 run (Murray kick)
Det—FG Murray 33
Det—Bussey 5 run (Murray kick)

Green Bay 25, Minnesota 13—At Metropolitan Stadium, attendance 47,234. Eddie Lee Ivery rushed for 145 yards and Gerry Ellis ran for 101 as the Packers beat the Vikings twice in one season for the first time since 1965. Ellis's one-yard plunge and Aundra Thompson's 35-yard touchdown catch from Lynn Dickey gave Green Bay a 16-6 lead in the third quarter. Minnesota's Ted Brown cut the margin to three points with a five-yard touchdown run. Ivery raced 38 yards for a touchdown with 56 seconds left to clinch the Packers' first road victory of the year.

Green Bay	0	10	6	9	— 25
Minnesota	0	6	7	0	— 13

GB —Ellis 1 run (Birney kick)
Minn—FG Danmeier 22
GB —FG Birney 24
Minn—FG Danmeier 23
GB —Thompson 35 pass from Dickey (kick failed)
Minn—Brown 5 run (Danmeier kick)
GB —FG Birney 33
GB —Ivery 38 run (kick blocked)

New York Jets 31, Houston 28—At Shea Stadium, attendance 52,358. Pat Leahy's 38-yard field goal with 3:58 elapsed in overtime helped the Jets snap a three-game losing streak and dropped the Oilers into a first-place tie with the Browns in the AFC Central Division. New York capitalized on Houston's turnovers to take a 21-0 halftime lead on Ken Schroy's 82-yard interception return and one-yard runs by Richard Todd and Kevin Long. Houston came back in the fourth period as Ken Stabler threw four touchdown passes, including a five-yard toss to Richard Caster with 1:31 left to tie the game 28-28. Stabler achieved personal highs for attempts (51), completions (33), and passing yards (388).

Houston	0	0	0	28	0	— 28
New York Jets	14	7	0	7	3	— 31

NYJ—Schroy 82 interception return (Leahy kick)
NYJ—Todd 1 run (Leahy kick)
NYJ—Long 1 run (Leahy kick)
Hou—Barber 5 pass from Stabler (Thompson kick)
Hou—Johnson 6 pass from Stabler (Thompson kick)
Hou—Caster 68 pass from Stabler (Thompson kick)
NYJ—Harper 45 pass from Todd (Leahy kick)
Hou—Caster 5 pass from Stabler (Thompson kick)
NYJ—FG Leahy 38

Kansas City 21, St. Louis 13—At Busch Memorial Stadium, attendance 42,871. J. T. Smith's 75-yard punt return for a touchdown late in the fourth quarter clinched Kansas City's interconference victory. The Chiefs went ahead for the first time with 6:31 remaining in the game on a two-yard touchdown pass from Steve Fuller to Arnold Morgado. Ed Beckman recovered a fumbled point by St. Louis to set up the play. The Cardinals led 10-0 at the half on Neil O'Donoghue's 40-yard field goal and Ottis Anderson's two-yard touchdown plunge. Anderson finished with 107 yards on 16 carries.

Kansas City	0	0	7	14	— 21
St. Louis	10	0	3	0	— 13

StL—FG O'Donoghue 40
StL—Anderson 2 run (O'Donoghue kick)
KC—Morgado 1 run (Lowery kick)
StL—FG O'Donoghue 43
KC—Morgado 2 pass from Fuller (Lowery kick)
KC—Smith 75 punt return (Lowery kick)

San Francisco 12, New York Giants 0—At Candlestick Park, attendance 38,574. The 49ers' defense sacked Phil Simms 10 times, once for a safety, and rookie Earl Cooper gained 170 yards (86 rushing, 84 receiving) as San Francisco snapped an eight-game losing streak. All of the 49ers' scoring came in the second period. Joe Montana threw a 66-yard touchdown bomb to Cooper, Jim Stuckey caught Simms in the end zone for a safety, and Ray Wersching kicked a 43-yard field goal. It was the 49ers' first shut out since Oct. 23, 1976, when they blanked the Falcons 15-0.

New York Giants	0	0	0	0	— 0
San Francisco	0	12	0	0	— 12

SF —Cooper 66 pass from Montana (Wersching kick)
SF —Safety, Stuckey tackled Simms in end zone.
SF —FG Wersching 43

Philadelphia 10, Oakland 7—At Veterans Stadium, attendance 68,535. Wilbert Montgomery's three-yard touchdown run with 2:56 left rallied the Eagles to their eighth straight victory and snapped Oakland's six-game winning streak. Tony Franklin's 51-yard field goal in the third period opened the scoring. Jim Plunkett hit Cliff Branch on an 86-yard touchdown bomb with 12:23 left in the game to give the Raiders a 7-3 lead. Ron Jaworski directed Philadelphia's decisive drive, passing to Leroy Harris (43 yards) and Harold Carmichael (12 yards) to set up Montgomery's winning run. The Eagles sacked Plunkett eight times. Philadelphia maintained its two-game lead in the NFC East while Oakland dropped into a first place tie with San Diego in the AFC West.

Oakland	0	0	0	7	— 7
Philadelphia	0	0	3	7	— 10

Phil —FG Franklin 51
Oak—Branch 86 pass from Plunkett (Bahr kick)
Phil —Montgomery 3 run (Franklin kick)

Buffalo 28, Pittsburgh 13—At Rich Stadium, attendance 79,659. Joe Ferguson threw three touchdown passes, two of them in the first half to Jerry Butler, and Joe Cribbs rushed for 110 yards as the Bills maintained a one-game lead in the AFC East. Butler's first touchdown reception tied the score 7-7 after Franco Harris put Pittsburgh in front with his 75th career rushing touchdown, third best in NFL history. In the second period Butler scored on a 10-yard catch, and the Steelers narrowed the Bills' lead to four points on Matt Bahr's 36-yard field goal. Curtis Brown raced 34 yards for a touchdown in the third period to end a 92-yard march, and Ferguson's two-yard touchdown pass to Reuben Gant early in the fourth quarter ensured the victory.

Pittsburgh	7	3	0	3	— 13
Buffalo	7	7	7	7	— 28

Pitt —Harris 2 run (Bahr kick)
Buff—Butler 29 pass from Ferguson (Mike-Mayer kick)
Buff—Butler 10 pass from Ferguson (Mike-Mayer kick)
Pitt —FG Bahr 36
Buff—Brown 34 run (Mike-Mayer kick)
Buff—Gant 2 pass from Ferguson (Mike-Mayer kick)
Pitt —FG Bahr 42

Denver 36, Seattle 20—At Mile High Stadium, attendance 73,274. Craig Morton threw for two touchdowns and ran for another to lead the Broncos to their third straight victory. Morton hit Riley Odoms with a two-yard scoring toss, ran one yard for a touchdown, and completed a 27-yard touchdown pass to Haven Moses to give Denver a 27-13 lead in the fourth quarter. Defensive tackle Don Latimer returned an interception 15 yards for a score and Rulon Jones tackled Jim Zorn in the end zone for a safety as the defense accounted for the rest of Denver's points.

Seattle	0	10	0	10	— 20
Denver	7	10	3	16	— 36

Den—Odoms 2 pass from Morton (Steinfort kick)
Sea—FG Herrera 21
Sea—Lewis 75 punt return (Herrera kick)
Den—FG Steinfort 24
Den—Morton 1 run (Steinfort kick)
Den—FG Steinfort 33
Sea—FG Herrera 20
Den—Moses 27 pass from Morton (Steinfort kick)
Den—Latimer 15 interception return (Steinfort kick)
Den—Safety, Jones tackled Zorn in end zone
Sea—McCutcheon 5 pass from Adkins (Herrera kick)

Dallas 14, Washington 10—At Texas Stadium, attendance 58,809. Defensive tackle Larry Cole rambled 43 yards with an interception for his fourth career touchdown against the Redskins. Randy White set up Cole's winning score when he hit Mike Kruczek just as he was releasing the ball. Tony Dorsett gave Dallas an early edge with a three-yard touchdown run. Washington took a 10-7 lead on a 34-yard field goal by Mark Moseley and an eight yard touchdown run by Wilbur Jackson; who gained 128 yards on 21 carries. The stingy Cowboys' defense did not allow a Washington first down until the second quarter and held the Redskins to 38 net yards passing.

Washington	0	3	0	7	— 10
Dallas	7	0	0	7	— 14

Dall —Dorsett 3 run (Septien kick)
Wash—FG Moseley 34
Wash—Jackson 8 run (Moseley kick)
Dall —Cole 43 interception return (Septien kick)

MONDAY, NOVEMBER 24

Los Angeles 27, New Orleans 7—At Louisiana Superdome, attendance 53,448. Preston Dennard caught two touchdown passes and the Rams' defense allowed the Saints beyond midfield only twice as Los Angeles remained one game behind Atlanta in the NFC West. Dennard's second-quarter touchdowns came on a 31-yard option pass from Mike Guman and 16-yard throw from Vince Ferragamo. Elvis Peacock added a one-yard run. Two interceptions by Nolan Cromwell set up Frank Corral's 23 and 19-yard field goals. Jimmy Rogers's 88-yard kickoff return led to Bobby Scott's 15-yard scoring pass to Henry Childs for the Saints' only touchdown.

Los Angeles	0	14	3	10	— 27
New Orleans	0	0	0	7	— 7

LA —Dennard 31 pass from Guman (Corral kick)
LA —Dennard 16 pass from Ferragamo (Corral kick)
LA —FG Corral 23
LA —Peacock 1 run (Corral kick)
LA —FG Corral 19
NO—Childs 15 pass from Scott (Ricardo kick)

THIRTEENTH WEEK SUMMARY

Cleveland took a giant step toward securing a playoff spot with a 17-14 win over Houston in the Astrodome. The Browns were led by reserve running back Cleo Miller, who gained 69 yards on eight carries and scored two touchdowns. Pittsburgh remained tied with Houston for second place at 8-5 in the AFC Central with a 23-10 victory over Miami. Oakland and San Diego remained deadlocked in the AFC West with victories over Denver and Philadelphia, respectively. New England missed an opportunity to gain a tie with Buffalo (28-24 losers to Baltimore) when Patriots quarterback Steve Grogan was intercepted six times by San Francisco, who prevailed 21-17. Los Angeles running back Elvis Peacock gained 152 yards to lead the Rams over the New York Jets 38-13. The win keeps the Rams' NFC West title hopes alive. They remain one game behind Atlanta, who topped Washington 10-6.

THURSDAY, NOVEMBER 27 (THANKSGIVING DAY)

Chicago 23, Detroit 17—At Pontiac Silverdome, attendance 75,397. Dave Williams became the first player ever to return a kickoff in overtime for a touchdown when he raced 95 yards. The Bears trailed 17-3 entering the fourth quarter before quarterback Vince Evans completed a 20-yard touchdown pass to Bob Fisher. Evans tied the game on the final play of the fourth quarter with a four-yard touchdown run that climaxed a 14-play, 94-yard drive. Walter Payton gained 123 yards on 18 carries to go over the 1,000-yard mark (1,122) for the fifth straight season.

Chicago	0	3	0	14	6	— 23
Detroit	3	7	7	0	0	— 17

Det —FG Murray 34
Det —Sims 47 pass from Danielson (Murray kick)
Chi —FG Thomas 24
Det —Danielson 1 run (Murray kick)
Chi —Fisher 20 pass from Evans (Thomas kick)
Chi —Evans 4 run (Thomas kick)
Chi —Williams 95 kickoff return

Dallas 51, Seattle 7—At Texas Stadium, attendance 57,540. The Dallas defense forced seven turnovers to spur the Cowboys over Seattle. Mike Hegman intercepted two passes and Bob Breunig picked off another to lead the Cowboys' defense that also recovered four fumbles and recorded six sacks. Tony Dorsett paced the offense with 107 yards on 24 carries, including two touchdowns. Dorsett set a club record with the 18th 100-yard game of his career.

Seattle	0	0	0	7	— 7
Dallas	9	21	0	21	— 51

Dall —Hill 18 pass from D. White (Septien kick)
Dall —Safety, Zorn intentionally grounded pass from end zone
Dall —DuPree 14 pass from D. White (Septien kick)
Dall —Springs 3 run (Septien kick)
Dall —Newhouse 3 run (Septien kick)
Dall —Dorsett 1 run (Septien kick)
Dall —Dorsett 1 run (Septien kick)
Dall —DuPree 12 pass from Carano (Septien kick)
Sea—Essink 2 pass from Zorn (Herrera kick)

SUNDAY, NOVEMBER 30

Baltimore 28, Buffalo 24—At Memorial Stadium, attendance 36,184. Curtis Dickey ran for two touchdowns to lead Baltimore. In the third quarter the Colts broke a 14-14 tie on Dickey's 18-yard scoring run that culminated a 79-yard drive. Dickey's second touchdown, a three-yard run with 1:56 left to play, was set up by Ricky Jones's fumble recovery. Buffalo's Joe Ferguson made the score 28-24 on a seven-yard touchdown pass to Jerry Butler with 44 seconds left.

Buffalo	7	7	3	7	— 24
Baltimore	0	14	7	7	— 28

Buff—Cribbs 2 run (N. Mike-Mayer kick)
Buff—Jessie 12 pass from Ferguson (N. Mike-Mayer kick)
Balt—Landry 6 run (S. Mike-Mayer kick)
Balt—R. Butler 8 pass from Landry (S. Mike-Mayer kick)
Balt—Dickey 18 run (S. Mike-Mayer kick)
Buff—FG N. Mike-Mayer 40
Balt—Dickey 3 run (S. Mike-Mayer kick)
Buff—Butler 7 pass from Ferguson (N. Mike-Mayer kick)

Cincinnati 20, Kansas City 6—At Arrowhead, attendance 41,594. Pete Johnson's 57-yard touchdown run in the fourth quarter climaxed Cincinnati's victory. Midway through the fourth quarter, Jack Thompson hit Dan Ross with a one-yard touchdown pass to give the Bengals a 13-3 lead. Nick Lowery's second field goal, a 40-yarder with 4:55 left to play, made the score 13-6 before Johnson's touchdown run clinched the Bengals' victory. Johnson gained 112 yards on 17 carries to lead all rushers.

Cincinnati	7	0	0	13	— 20
Kansas City	0	3	0	3	— 6

Cin—McInally 4 pass from Anderson (Breech kick)
KC—FG Lowery 26
Cin—Ross 1 pass from Thompson (kick failed)
KC—FG Lowery 40
Cin—Johnson 57 run (Breech kick)

Cleveland 17, Houston 14—At Astrodome, attendance 51,514. Cleo Miller scored two touchdowns and set up the winning field goal as Cleveland took over first place in the AFC Central. A fumble recovery and an interception led to Miller's touchdown runs of six and one yards that gave Cleveland a 14-7 halftime lead. In the third quarter, Miller broke away for a 50-yard run that set up Don Cockroft's 25-yard field goal. Miller gained 69 yards on eight carries, and Earl Campbell led all rushers with 109 yards on 27 carries.

Cleveland	7	7	3	0	— 17
Houston	0	7	7	0	— 14

Cle —Miller 6 run (Cockroft kick)
Cle —Miller 1 run (Cockroft kick)
Hou—Campbell 1 run (Fritsch kick)
Cle —FG Cockroft 25
Hou—Casper 30 pass from Stabler (Fritsch kick)

Pittsburgh 23, Miami 10—At Three Rivers Stadium, attendance 51,384. Franco Harris ran nine yards for a touchdown that clinched Pittsburgh's victory. Early in the fourth quarter with Pittsburgh leading 16-10, Jack Ham recovered a fumble on the Steelers' two yard line. Pittsburgh's offense then marched 98 yards in 15 plays, climaxed by Harris's touchdown run. Harris led all rushers with 116 yards on 28 carries. Steelers wide receiver Theo Bell caught four passes for a career-high 173 yards.

Miami	0	3	0	7	— 10
Pittsburgh	0	13	3	7	— 23

Pitt —FG Bahr 32
Pitt —Swann 30 pass from Bradshaw (Bahr kick)
Mia—FG von Schamann 42
Pitt —FG Bahr 33
Pitt —FG Bahr 30
Mia—Moore 31 pass from Woodley (von Schamann kick)
Pitt —Harris 9 run (Bahr kick)

Minnesota 23, New Orleans 20—At Louisiana Superdome, attendance 30,936. Minnesota held a 23-0 lead and withstood New Orleans' rally in Dick Stanfel's first game as the Saints' interim head coach. With 11 minutes left in the third quarter, Doug Paschal ran 10 yards for a touchdown, giving Minnesota a 23-0 advantage. In the next 15 minutes, Archie Manning (19 of 31 for 248 yards) threw three touchdown passes to cut the Vikings' lead to 23-20. With 33 seconds left, Minnesota linebacker Matt Blair blocked a 25-yard field goal attempt to preserve the victory which tied Minnesota with Detroit for first place in the NFC Central Division.

Minnesota	3	13	7	0	— 23
New Orleans	0	0	13	7	— 20

Minn—FG Danmeier 28
Minn—S. White 17 pass from Kramer (kick failed)
Minn—Brown 1 run (Danmeier kick)
Minn—Paschal 10 run (Danmeier kick)
NO —Childs 9 pass from Manning (kick failed)
NO —Wilson 23 pass from Manning (Ricardo kick)
NO —Childs 27 pass from Manning (Ricardo kick)

San Francisco 21, New England 17—At Candlestick Park, attendance 45,254. Three of San Francisco's six interceptions (a club record) set up touchdowns in the 49ers' upset of New England. Joe Montana threw a touchdown pass in each of the first three quarters to give San Francisco a 21-3 lead. Mosi Tatupu brought New England back with two touchdown runs to cut the 49ers' lead to 21-17 in the fourth quarter. New England's final scoring chance was thwarted by Keena Turner's interception. Ricky Churchman led the 49ers with two interceptions.

New England	0	3	7	7	— 17
San Francisco	7	7	7	0	— 21

SF —Solomon 8 pass from Montana (Wersching kick)
NE—FG Smith 42
SF —Cooper 15 pass from Montana (Wersching kick)
SF —Ramson 2 pass from Montana (Wersching kick)
NE—Tatupu 2 run (Smith kick)
NE—Tatupu 1 run (Smith kick)

Los Angeles 38, New York Jets 13—At Anaheim Stadium, attendance 59,743. Vince Ferragamo fired four touchdown passes to lead Los Angeles. Ferragamo (22 of 36 for 284 yards) threw three of his four touchdown tosses in the first half, giving the Rams a 24-13 halftime lead. Elvis Peacock led the Rams' running attack with 152 yards on 19 carries, and Billy Waddy caught a game-high six passes for 98 yards and one touchdown. The Rams' offense gained a season-high 510 yards. The defense held the Jets to 224 yards and recorded six sacks.

New York Jets	0	13	0	0	— 13
Los Angeles	10	14	0	14	— 38

LA —Bryant 12 pass from Ferragamo (Corral kick)
LA —FG Corral 25
NYJ—FG Leahy 22
NYJ—FG Leahy 40
LA —Waddy 44 pass from Ferragamo (Corral kick)
NYJ—Jones 35 pass from Todd (Leahy kick)
LA —Miller 15 pass from Ferragamo (Corral kick)
LA —Guman 4 run (Corral kick)
LA —Miller 19 pass from Ferragamo (Corral kick)

San Diego 22, Philadelphia 21—At San Diego Stadium, attendance 51,567. Dan Fouts and Kellen Winslow combined for two touchdown passes to lead San Diego. Fouts (20 of 28 for 342 yards) hit Winslow with touchdown passes of 14 and 17 yards to help the Chargers build a 19-0 lead at halftime. Philadelphia came back to make the score 22-21 with 2:50 left to play when Ron Jaworski completed an 11-yard touchdown pass to Wilbert Montgomery. San Diego's John Jefferson caught eight passes for 164 yards to become the first NFL player ever to amass 1,000 yards receiving in each of his first three seasons.

Philadelphia	0	0	7	14	— 21
San Diego	9	10	0	3	— 22

SD —Winslow 14 pass from Fouts (kick failed)
SD —FG Benirschke 34
SD —Winslow 17 pass from Fouts (Benirschke kick)
SD —FG Benirschke 45
Phil—Montgomery 1 run (Franklin kick)
SD — FG Benirschke 42
Phil—Krepfle 16 pass from Jaworski (Franklin kick)
Phil—Montgomery 11 pass from Jaworski (Franklin kick)

St. Louis 23, New York Giants 7—At Giants Stadium, attendance 65,852. Ottis Anderson ran for two touchdowns and went over the 1,000-yard mark for the second straight season. Anderson gained 168 yards on 31 carries to push his season total to 1,123 yards. Ken Stone intercepted two passes, and the Cardinals held New York to 189 total yards. The victory snapped St. Louis' four-game losing streak.

St. Louis	7	0	6	10	— 23
New York Giants	0	0	0	7	— 7

StL —Anderson 6 run (O'Donoghue kick)
StL —FG O'Donoghue 43
StL —FG O'Donoghue 41
NYG—Heater 10 run (Danelo kick)

StL —FG O'Donoghue 23
StL —Anderson 18 run (O'Donoghue kick)

Tampa Bay 20, Green Bay 17—At Milwaukee County Stadium, attendance 54,225. Johnny Davis ran one yard for the winning touchdown with 1:58 left. The Packers took a 17-13 lead, early in the fourth quarter when Lynn Dickey completed a 16-yard touchdown pass to Paul Coffman. Just before the two-minute warning, Buccaneers quarterback Doug Williams and Kevin House combined on a 44-yard pass to the Green Bay one yard line. On the next play Davis scored to give Tampa Bay a 20-17 lead. Green Bay missed a chance to send the game into overtime with 17 seconds left to play when Jan Stenerud's 45-yard field goal attempt drifted wide to the left.

Tampa Bay	10	0	3	7	— 20
Green Bay	0	3	0	14	— 17

TB —FG Yepremian 39
TB —Hagins 17 pass from Williams (Yepremian kick)
GB—FG Stenerud 40
TB —FG Yepremian 20
GB—Ivery 1 run (Stenerud kick)
GB—Coffman 16 pass from Dickey (Stenerud kick)
TB —J. Davis 1 run (Yepremian kick)

Atlanta 10, Washington 6—At Atlanta-Fulton County Stadium, attendance 55,665. After being shut out in the first half, Atlanta marched 64 yards for a touchdown on its first possession of the third quarter. Steve Bartkowski's 14-yard touchdown pass to Alfred Jenkins completed the drive as the Falcons came from behind to win for the ninth time in 10 victories. Atlanta increased its lead to 10-3 with less than six minutes to play on Tim Mazzetti's 23-yard field goal. Mark Moseley accounted for all of the Redskins' points with field goals of 51 and 46 yards. Atlanta's William Andrews gained 111 yards on 24 carries to set a club season record with 1,024 yards.

Washington	0	3	0	3	— 6
Atlanta	0	0	7	3	— 10

Wash—FG Moseley 51
Atl —Jenkins 14 pass from Bartkowski (Mazzetti kick)
Atl —FG Mazzetti 23
Wash—FG Moseley 46

MONDAY, DECEMBER 1

Oakland 9, Denver 3—At Oakland-Alameda County Coliseum, attendance 51,593. Jim Plunkett's eight-yard touchdown run in the third quarter provided the margin of difference in Oakland's victory over Denver. In the first quarter Fred Steinfort's 41-yard field goal finished a 60-yard drive and gave Denver a 3-0 advantage. Oakland took a 6-3 lead on its first possession of the second half when Plunkett finished a 77-yard drive with his touchdown run. The Raiders' defense forced six turnovers and in the second half limited Denver to only two first downs.

Denver	3	0	0	0	— 3
Oakland	0	0	6	3	— 9

Den—FG Steinfort 41
Oak—Plunkett 8 run (kick failed)
Oak—FG Bahr 44

FOURTEENTH WEEK SUMMARY

After 14 weeks of play, three NFC teams (Atlanta, Dallas, Philadelphia), had reserved playoff appearances, while no AFC team was yet guaranteed a postseason berth. In the AFC East, Buffalo and New England were involved in overtime games with differing results. The Bills notched their first 10-win season since 1965 when Nick Mike-Mayer kicked a 30-yard field goal with 5:14 elapsed in overtime to defeat Los Angeles 10-7. The Patriots dropped two games behind the Bills, losing to Miami 16-13 as Uwe von Schamann kicked a 23-yard field goal after 3:20 of overtime. Brian Sipe completed a club-record 30 of 41 passes for 340 yards to help Cleveland register a 17-14 victory over the New York Jets and maintain a one-game edge in the AFC Central. AFC West co-leaders Oakland and San Diego both lost to NFC East foes. Dallas notched a playoff berth, dropping the Raiders 19-13 while Washington ended a five-game losing streak in defeating the Chargers 40-17. Atlanta opened a two-game lead in the NFC West with a 20-17 victory over Philadelphia. The defeat dropped the Eagles into a tie with Dallas in the NFC East. Both have 11-3 marks. Walter Payton rushed for 130 yards and three touchdowns in Chicago's 61-7 rout of Green Bay.

THURSDAY, DECEMBER 4

Houston 6, Pittsburgh 0—At Astrodome, attendance 53,960. Toni Fritsch kicked field goals of 37 and 33 yards in the second half, and the Houston defense forced five turnovers. The Steelers were shut out for the first time since September 29, 1974. Fritsch's first field goal was set up by Ken Stabler's 23-yard pass to Mike Renfro and his second one by Gregg Bingham's fumble recovery. Mike Reinfeldt's interception in the end zone in the third quarter halted the Steelers' only serious scoring threat. The win kept Houston one game behind Cleveland in the AFC Central.

Pittsburgh	0	0	0	0	— 0
Houston	0	0	3	3	— 6

Hou—FG Fritsch 37
Hou—FG Fritsch 33

SUNDAY, DECEMBER 7

Atlanta 20, Philadelphia 17—At Veterans Stadium, attendance 70,205. Tim Mazzetti kicked a 37-yard field goal with seven seconds remaining to give the Falcons another comeback win. Mazzetti's 26-yard field goal gave Atlanta an early edge, but Ron Jaworski connected with Harold Carmichael on a 22-yard touchdown pass and Louie Giammona lofted a 15-yard option pass to John Spagnola for another score that put the Eagles ahead 14-3. Steve Bartkowski helped Atlanta regain the lead with touchdown passes of 11 yards to Wallace Francis and 12 yards to Lynn Cain. Tony Franklin's 40-yard field goal early in the fourth quarter tied the game 17-17. Atlanta started its final drive from its own 8 yard line with 1:05 remaining.

Atlanta	3	7	7	3	— 20
Philadelphia	0	14	0	3	— 17

Atl —FG Mazzetti 26
Phil—Carmichael 22 pass from Jaworski (Franklin kick)
Phil—Spagnola 15 pass from Giammona (Franklin kick)
Atl —Francis 11 pass from Bartkowski (Mazzetti kick)
Atl —Cain 12 pass from Bartkowski (Mazzetti kick)
Phil—FG Franklin 40
Atl —FG Mazzetti 37

Cincinnati 34, Baltimore 33—At Riverfront Stadium, attendance 35,651. Jim Breech's 21-yard field goal with 12 seconds left climaxed a 77-yard drive to give the Bengals the victory after Baltimore had rallied from a 25-point deficit to take the lead. Cincinnati held a 31-6 lead in the third quarter on two touchdown runs by Pete Johnson, Ken Anderson' 67-yard scoring bomb to Isaac Curtis, and Jack Thompson's 17-yard touchdown pass to Dan Ross. In the fourth quarter Bert Jones directed the Colts to 27 points, but a missed extra point proved the difference.

Baltimore	0	6	0	27	— 33
Cincinnati	7	17	7	3	— 34

Cin —Johnson 5 run (Breech kick)
Cin —Johnson 1 run (Breech kick)
Cin —Curtis 67 pass from Anderson (Breech kick)
Balt—FG Mike-Mayer 41
Cin —FG Breech 32
Balt—FG Mike-Mayer 37
Cin —Ross 17 pass from Thompson (Breech kick)
Balt—Sims 2 run (Mike-Mayer kick)
Balt—Burke 16 pass from B. Jones (kick failed)
Balt—Dickey 1 run (Mike-Mayer kick)
Balt—Dickey 22 pass from B. Jones (Mike-Mayer kick)
Cin —FG Breech 21

Dallas 19, Oakland 13—At Oakland-Alameda County Stadium, attendance 53,194. Aaron Mitchell's interception in the end zone with 1:44 left ensured the victory as Dallas clinched a playoff spot for the 14th time in the last 15 years. Oakland scored on its first possession when Jim Plunkett hit Raymond Chester with a six-yard scoring pass. Tony Dorsett followed with a 20-yard touchdown sprint to tie the game, and Dallas went on to take a 16-10 lead at halftime. Dorsett, who rushed for 97 yards to give him 1,034 for the season, became the first player in NFL history to surpass 1,000 yards rushing in each of his first four seasons. The win moved Dallas into a tie for first place with Philadelphia in the NFC East.

Dallas	7	9	3	0	— 19
Oakland	7	3	3	0	— 13

Oak—Chester 6 pass from Plunkett (Bahr kick)
Dall—Dorsett 20 run (Septien kick)
Dall—FG Septien 52
Dall—Springs 2 run (kick failed)
Oak—FG Bahr 22
Dall—FG Septien 34
Oak—FG Bahr 38

Kansas City 31, Denver 14—At Arrowhead, attendance 40,237. Bill Kenney, making his first start of the season, completed 12 of 18 passes for 142 yards, including touchdown passes of 33 yards to J. T. Smith and 8 yards to Bubba Garcia. Kansas City capitalized on three Denver turnovers to score 28 points in the second quarter.

Denver	0	0	7	7	— 14
Kansas City	0	28	0	3	— 31

KC —Smith 33 pass from Kenney (Lowery kick)
KC —Morgado 1 run (Lowery kick)
KC —Howard 3 fumble recovery return (Lowery kick)
KC —Garcia 8 pass from Kenney (Lowery kick)
Den—Odoms 22 pass from Morton (Steinfort kick)
Den—Moses 4 pass from Morton (Steinfort kick)
KC —FG Lowery 20

St. Louis 24, Detroit 23—At Busch Memorial Stadium, attendance 46,966. Roy Green's 57-yard punt return for a touchdown with 3:40 remaining helped clinch the Cardinals' comeback win. Jim Hart threw touchdown passes of six yards to Doug Marsh and three yards to Wayne Morris to give St. Louis an early 14-3 edge. Detroit rallied to take a 23-14 lead on two field goals by Eddie Murray, Billy Sims' one-yard touchdown run, and Leonard Thompson's 37-yard touchdown reception.

Detroit	0	13	10	0	— 23
St. Louis	7	7	0	10	— 24

StL —Marsh 6 pass from Hart (O'Donoghue kick)
Det —FG Murray 40
StL —Morris 3 pass from Hart (O'Donoghue kick)
Det —Sims 1 run (Murray kick)
Det —FG Murray 24
Det —FG Murray 26
Det —Thompson 37 pass from Danielson (Murray kick)
StL —FG O'Donoghue 25
StL —Green 57 punt return (O'Donoghue kick)

Chicago 61, Green Bay 7—At Soldier Field, attendance 57,176. Walter Payton ran for three touchdowns and Vince Evans passed for three more as the Bears scored the most points in an NFL game since Atlanta beat New Orleans 62-7 on Sept. 16, 1973. Evans directed Chicago to 594 total yards. He completed 18 of 22 passes for 316 yards, including touchdown passes to Brian Baschnagel, Robin Earl, and Rickey Watts. Evans's long pass completions set up Payton's scoring runs of 1, 3, and 14 yards. Payton rushed for 130 yards to pass Larry Csonka among the NFL's career rushing leaders, moving into sixth place with 8,178 yards.

Green Bay	0	7	0	0	— 7
Chicago	0	28	13	20	— 61

Chi—Payton 1 run (Thomas kick)
Chi—Payton 3 run (Thomas kick)
Chi—Harper 1 run (Thomas kick)
GB—Lofton 15 pass from Dickey (Stenerud kick)
Chi—Baschnagel 4 pass from Evans (Thomas kick)
Chi—Earl 9 pass from Evans (kick blocked)
Chi—Watts 53 pass from Evans (Thomas kick)
Chi—Payton 14 run (Thomas kick)
Chi—Walterscheid 36 interception return (Thomas kick)
Chi—McClendon 1 run (kick failed)

Buffalo 10, Los Angeles 7—At Rich Stadium, attendance 77,133. Nick Mike-Mayer kicked a 30-yard field goal with 5:14 elapsed in overtime to give the Bills their first 10-victory season since 1965. Joe Ferguson's 30-yard pass to Frank Lewis set up the winning score. Joe Cribbs rushed for 83 yards to become the fourth Buffalo player ever to gain 1,000 yards in a season. The victory gave the first place Bills a two-game edge in the AFC East while the Rams dropped two games behind the NFC West leader, Atlanta.

Los Angeles	0	0	7	0	0	— 7
Buffalo	0	0	7	0	3	— 10

Buff—Freeman 47 interception return (Mike-Mayer kick)
LA —Guman 3 run (Cromwell run)
Buff—FG Mike-Mayer 30

Minnesota 21, Tampa Bay 10—At Tampa Stadium, attendance 65,649. Tommy Kramer, who completed 22 of 31 passes for 264 yards, rallied the Vikings from a 10-0 halftime deficit. Ted Brown's one-yard touchdown run culminated an 80-yard drive, and Kramer's 17-yard scoring toss to Sammy White climaxed a 66-yard march as the Vikings took a 14-10 lead. Fred McNeil's fumble recovery on the Minnesota 12 yard line with 5:09 left ended Tampa Bay's final threat. The victory moved the Vikings into sole possession of first place in the NFC Central Division.

Minnesota	0	0	7	14	— 21
Tampa Bay	3	7	0	0	— 10

TB —FG Yepremian 27
TB —House 30 pass from Williams (Yepremian kick)
Minn—Brown 1 run (Danmeier kick)
Minn—S. White 17 pass from Kramer (Danmeier kick)
Minn—Young 3 run (Danmeier kick)

San Francisco 38, New Orleans 35—At Candlestick Park, attendance 37,949. The 49ers overcame a 35-7 halftime deficit to win with 7:40 elapsed in overtime on Ray Wersching's 36-yard field goal. Joe Montana led San Francisco's comeback with a 71-yard touchdown bomb to Dwight Clark, a 14-yard scoring pass to Freddie Solomon, and a one-yard touchdown plunge. Lenvil Elliott's seven-yard scoring run with 1:50 left sent the game into overtime.

New Orleans	14	21	0	0	0	— 35
San Francisco	0	7	14	14	3	— 38

NO—Harris 33 pass from Manning (Ricardo kick)
NO—Childs 21 pass from Manning (Ricardo kick)
NO—Holmes 1 run (Ricardo kick)
SF —Solomon 57 punt return (Wersching kick)
NO—Holmes 1 run (Ricardo kick)
NO—Harris 41 pass from Manning (Ricardo kick)
SF —Montana 1 run (Wersching kick)
SF —Clark 71 pass from Montana (Wersching kick)
SF —Solomon 14 pass from Montana (Wersching kick)
SF —Elliott 7 run (Wersching kick)
SF —FG Wersching 36

New York Giants 27, Seattle 21—At Kingdome, attendance 51,617. Billy Taylor raced 30 yards for the winning touchdown on a fourth-and-one situation with 1:57 left. New York took a 13-0 lead on two field goals by Joe Danelo and Scott Brunner's 48-yard touchdown pass to Earnest Gray. Brunner added a 50-yard scoring bomb to Gray before Seattle took the lead 21-20 on Jim Zorn's 34-yard touchdown toss to Steve Largent with 7:59 remaining.

New York Giants	3	10	0	14	— 27
Seattle	0	7	7	7	— 21

NYG—FG Danelo 43
NYG—FG Danelo 32
NYG—Gray 48 pass from Brunner (Danelo kick)
Sea —Doornink 1 run (Herrera kick)
Sea —Jodat 1 run (Herrera kick)
NYG—Gray 50 pass from Brunner (Danelo kick)
Sea —Largent 34 pass from Zorn (Herrera kick)
NYG—Taylor 30 run (Danelo kick)

Cleveland 17, New York Jets 14—At Cleveland Stadium, attendance 78,454. Brian Sipe completed a club-record 30 of 41 passes for 340 yards including a five-yard touchdown pass to Greg Pruitt with 9:27 remaining as the Browns kept a one-game lead in the AFC Central. Cleveland jumped to 10-0 lead on Don Cockroft's 34-yard field goal and Mike Pruitt's nine-yard scoring run. The Jets came back to take a 14-10 advantage on Richard Todd's touchdown passes to Johnny "Lam" Jones and Mickey Shuler.

New York Jets	0	0	7	7	— 14
Cleveland	0	3	7	7	— 17

Cle —FG Cockroft 34
Cle —M. Pruitt 9 run (Cockroft kick)
NYJ—J. Jones 39 pass from Todd (Leahy kick)
NYJ—Shuler 5 pass from Todd (Leahy kick)
Cle —G. Pruitt 5 pass from Sipe (Cockroft kick)

Washington 40, San Diego 17—At Robert F. Kennedy Stadium, attendance 48,556. Joe Lavender returned one of his three interceptions 51 yards for a score, and Mark Moseley kicked field goals of 28, 45, 46, and 46 yards as the Redskins ended a five-game losing streak. Joe Theismann completed a personal-high 26 of 37 for 269 yards and two touchdowns. Clarence Harmon set a club record with 12 receptions (118 yards). Washington's defense intercepted five passes and recovered two fumbles.

San Diego	7	3	0	7	— 17
Washington	14	6	6	14	— 40

Wash—Lavender 51 interception return (Moseley kick)
Wash—Jackson 18 pass from Theismann (Moseley kick)
SD —McCrary 28 pass from Fouts (Benirschke kick)
Wash—FG Moseley 28
SD —FG Benirschke 26
Wash—FG Moseley 45
Wash—FG Moseley 46
Wash—FG Moseley 46

SD —Bauer 2 run (Benirschke kick)
Wash—Forte 4 pass from Theismann (Moseley kick)
Wash—Forte 3 run (Moseley kick)

MONDAY, DECEMBER 8

Miami 16, New England 13—At Orange Bowl, attendance 63,282. Uwe von Schamann's 23-yard field goal with 3:20 elapsed in overtime gave Miami a comeback victory. David Woodley completed 15 of 24 for 192 yards, including a 54-yard bomb to Duriel Harris that set up the winning field goal. Russ Francis's diving 38-yard touchdown grab gave the Patriots a 13-6 lead with 12:55 remaining. Miami tied the score when Woodley completed a 10-play, 78-yard drive with an eight-yard touchdown pass which deflected off the hands of tight end Joe Rose to Nat Moore. Bob Baumhower sent the game into overtime by blocking John Smith's 35-yard field goal attempt with three seconds left.

New England	0	6	0	7	0	— 13
Miami	0	0	6	7	3	— 16

NE —FG Smith 23
NE —FG Smith 33
Mia—FG von Schamann 27
Mia—FG Von Schamann 24
NE —Francis 38 pass from Cavanaugh (Smith kick)
Mia—Moore 8 pass from Woodley (von Schamann kick)
Mia—FG von Schamann 23

FIFTEENTH WEEK SUMMARY

The two remaining NFC playoff spots were filled in week 15. Minnesota's last-second victory over Cleveland makes the Vikings NFC Central champions for the seventh time in the last eight years. Tommy Kramer's desperation pass to Ahmad Rashad as time ran out clinched the division. Los Angeles secured a wild card spot with a 38-14 defeat of Dallas. Houston's 22-3 win over Green Bay now means that the Oilers and Cleveland are tied with 10-5 records. If the Browns win next week against Cincinnati, they take the title. If Houston wins and Cleveland loses, the Oilers are champions. Oakland and San Diego remained tied at 10-5 in the AFC West and New England closed to one game behind Buffalo after the Patriots beat the Bills 24-2. New Orleans broke its 14-game losing streak with 21-20 win over the New York Jets.

SATURDAY, DECEMBER 13

Washington 16, New York Giants 13—At Robert F. Kennedy Stadium, attendance 44,443. Bobby Hammond caught a seven-yard touchdown pass from Joe Theismann with 39 seconds left to give the Redskins the victory. Hammond, cut from the Giants twice in 1979, ran for 47 yards on nine carries and caught three passes while only playing in the second half. Joe Danelo hit on a 39-yard field goal that put the Giants on top 13-10 in the fourth quarter. The Redskins marched 48 yards in the final two minutes for the winning score.

New York Giants	0	10	0	3	— 13
Washington	0	0	7	9	— 16

NYG —FG Danelo 48
NYG —Taylor 1 run (Danelo kick)
Wash—FG Moseley 40
NYG —FG Danelo 39
Wash—Hammond 7 pass from Theismann (kick blocked)

San Diego 21, Seattle 14—At San Diego Stadium, attendance 49,980. Dan Fouts threw a 19-yard touchdown pass to John Jefferson and Chuck Muncie ran for two scores as the Chargers handed Seattle its eighth straight defeat. Seattle's final score came on a two-yard pass from Jim Zorn to Steve Largent after time had expired. Fouts set NFL season records for most 300-yard games (seven) and most yards passing (4,407).

Seattle	0	0	7	7	— 14
San Diego	0	21	0	0	— 21

SD —Muncie 1 run (Benirschke kick)
SD —Muncie 10 run (Benirschke kick)
SD —Jefferson 19 pass from Fouts (Benirschke kick)
Sea—Jodat 15 run (Herrera kick)
Sea—Largent 2 pass from Zorn (Herrera kick)

SUNDAY, DECEMBER 14

New England 24, Buffalo 2—At Schaefer Stadium, attendance 63,292. Led by a strong defense and Matt Cavanaugh's passing, the Patriots crushed the division-leading Bills and kept their playoff chances alive. The New England defense recorded eight quarterback sacks and held Buffalo to just 154 total yards. Cavanaugh tossed scoring passes of 5 yards to Russ Francis and 13 yards to Andy Johnson. Vagas Ferguson, who scored on a nine-yard run, finished the day with 81 yards, which gave him 736 for the season, a Patriots rookie rushing record. Bills quarterback Joe Ferguson sprained his ankle and left the game after just six minutes of play.

Buffalo	0	0	2	0	— 2
New England	7	7	7	3	— 24

NE —Ferguson 9 run (Smith kick)
NE —Francis 5 pass from Cavanaugh (Smith kick)
NE —Johnson 13 pass from Cavanaugh (Smith kick)
Buff—Safety, Hubach tackled in end zone
NE —FG Smith 27

Cincinnati 17, Chicago 14—At Soldier Field, attendance 48,808. The Bengals, after winning the coin toss, marched 62 yards on a drive that culminated with Jim Breech's 28-yard field goal to defeat Chicago with 4:23 gone into the overtime period. Cincinnati forced the overtime period when Louis Breeden's third interception of the day, a Bengals record, came in the end zone with nine seconds left in regulation play. Fullback Pete Johnson gained 134 yards for the Bengals on 28 carries and scored a one-yard touchdown. Alan Page tied an NFL record when he recovered Jack Thompson's fumble in the end zone, the third such recovery of Page's career.

Cincinnati	7	7	0	0	3	— 17
Chicago	0	7	0	7	0	— 14

Cin —Johnson 1 run (Breech kick)
Cin —Curtis 7 pass from Thompson (Breech kick)
Chi —Page recovered fumble in end zone (Thomas kick)
Cin —FG Breech 28

Minnesota 28, Cleveland 23—At Metropolitan Stadium, attendance 42,202. Tommy Kramer's desperation pass with no time left on the clock was tipped by Browns' safety Thom Darden into the hands of Ahmad Rashad for the 46-yard game-winning score as the Vikings captured their eleventh NFC Central Division title in 14 years. The Vikings who scored two touchdowns in the final 1:35 of play, went 80 yards in 23 seconds (with no time outs) for the final score. Kramer's 12-yard touchdown pass to Rashad with 1:35 left brought Minnesota to within one point of Cleveland. Kramer set Vikings' single-game records with 38 completions (in 49 attempts) and 456 yards passing.

Cleveland	7	6	3	7	— 23
Minnesota	0	0	9	19	— 28

Cle —Hill 18 pass from Sipe (Cockroft kick)
Cle —Sipe 2 run (kick failed)
Minn—Senser 31 pass from Kramer (kick failed)
Cle —FG Cockroft 32
Minn—FG Danmeier 24
Cle —C. Miller 1 run (Cockroft kick)
Minn—Brown 7 pass from Kramer (kick blocked)
Minn—Rashad 12 pass from Kramer (Danmeier kick)
Minn—Rashad 46 pass from Kramer (kick blocked)

Houston 22, Green Bay 3—At Lambeau Field, attendance 53,201. Earl Campbell ran for 181 yards and scored two touchdowns as Houston ground down the Packers. Campbell, who increased his league-leading rushing total to 1,731 yards, surpassed his previous season high of 1,697 yards, set in 1979, and assured himself of his third straight NFL rushing title. Ex-Packer Chester Marcol, signed the day before the game to replace injured Toni Fritsch, kicked a 27-yard field goal. Linebacker John Corker scored on a 43-yard run following Lynn Dickey's fumble with four seconds left in the game.

Houston	6	3	0	13	— 22
Green Bay	0	3	0	0	— 3

Hou—Campbell 1 run (kick failed)
GB —FG Stenerud 27
Hou—FG Marcol 27
Hou—Campbell 24 run (Marcol kick)
Hou—Corker 43 fumble recovery return (kick failed)

Pittsburgh 21, Kansas City 16—At Three Rivers Stadium, attendance 50,013. Rocky Bleier, playing in his last game at Three Rivers Stadium, ran for the winning 11-yard touchdown with 6:08 left to keep the Steelers' playoff hopes alive. Bleier's score capped off a 14-point fourth quarter for the Steelers. Terry Bradshaw produced the first score of the period on a 13-yard pass to Theo Bell.

Kansas City	0	3	13	0	— 16
Pittsburgh	7	0	0	14	— 21

Pitt—Swann 9 pass from Bradshaw (Bahr kick)
KC —FG Lowery 36
KC —Hadnot 3 run (Lowery kick)
KC —FG Lowery 22
KC —FG Lowery 50
Pitt—Bell 13 pass from Bradshaw (Bahr kick)
Pitt—Bleier 11 run (Bahr kick)

Miami 24, Baltimore 14—At Memorial Stadium, attendance 30,564. David Woodley threw three touchdown passes that enabled Miami to defeat Baltimore in windy Memorial Stadium. Woodley completed only 9 of 29 passes for 143 yards, but a 19-yard touchdown pass to Woody Bennett, a 37-yard touchdown pass to Jimmy Cefalo, and a 26-yard scoring pass to Nat Moore gave Miami the victory.

Miami	7	7	0	10	— 24
Baltimore	7	0	7	0	— 14

Balt—Dickey 38 run (Mike-Mayer kick)
Mia —Bennett 19 pass from Woodley (von Schamann kick)
Mia —Cefalo 37 pass from Woodley (von Schamann kick)
Balt—McCall 16 pass from Jones (Mike-Mayer kick)
Mia —FG von Schamann 34
Mia —Moore 26 pass from Woodley (von Schamann kick)

New Orleans 21, New York Jets 20—At Shea Stadium, attendance 38,077. Tony Galbreath scored two fourth-quarter touchdowns as the Saints, winless in 14 games, gained their first victory of the season. Galbreath's winning score came with 4:49 left, capping a 10-play, 73-yard drive. Jets quarterback Richard Todd's 31-yard touchdown run with 9:39 left enabled the New Yorkers to take a 20-14 lead. It was Saints' interim coach Dick Stanfel's first win in three tries after replacing Dick Nolan on November 25.

New Orleans	7	0	0	14	— 21
New York Jets	0	13	0	7	— 20

NO —Holmes 14 pass from Manning (Ricardo kick)
NYJ—Long 1 run (Leahy kick)
NYJ—FG Leahy 27
NYJ—FG Leahy 47
NO —Galbreath 1 run (Ricardo kick)
NYJ—Todd 31 run (Leahy kick)
NO —Galbreath 1 run (Ricardo kick

Oakland 24, Denver 21—At Mile High Stadium, attendance 73,974. The Raiders' ability to capitalize on Denver mistakes kept their playoff hopes alive. Oakland converted three of Denver's four turnovers into scores. Safety Burgess Owens returned an interception 58 yards for a first quarter score. The Raiders got a touchdown and a field goal following fumble recoveries in the second quarter. Jim Plunkett threw two touchdown passes to Bob Chandler. Denver quarterbacks Craig Morton and Matt Robinson combined for 431 yards passing.

Oakland	7	10	0	7	— 24
Denver	0	7	7	7	— 21

Oak—Owens 58 interception return (Bahr kick)
Den—Preston 2 run (Steinfort kick)
Oak—FG Bahr 44
Oak—Chandler 11 pass from Plunkett (Bahr kick)
Den—Odoms 12 pass from Morton (Steinfort kick)
Oak—Chandler 38 pass from Plunkett (Bahr kick)
Den—Preston 9 run (Steinfort kick)

Philadelphia 17, St. Louis 3—At Veterans Stadium, attendance 68,969. Linebacker Jerry Robinson came up with two big plays in the second half to ignite the Eagles' victory. The first was a recovered fumble that led to a nine-yard touchdown run by Wilbert Montgomery, and the second a pass rush that set up an interception and led to Tony Franklin's field goal in the fourth quarter. The Eagles' defense held the Cardinals to a net offense of 125 yards and limited Ottis Anderson to 37 yards rushing.

St. Louis	0	0	0	3	— 3
Philadelphia	0	0	7	10	— 17

Phil—Montgomery 9 run (Franklin kick)
Phil—FG Franklin 19
StL —FG O'Donoghue 25
Phil—Giammona 1 run (Franklin kick)

Atlanta 35, San Francisco 10—At Atlanta-Fulton County Stadium, attendance 55,767. Quarterback Steve Bartkowski passed for three second-half touchdowns in leading the Falcons to their ninth straight victory and the NFC Western Division title, ending the seven-year reign held by the Los Angeles Rams. Wide receiver Wallace Francis caught two of Bartkowski's touchdown passes, including one of 81 yards, and had 148 yards for the day on four catches. The Falcons were deep in San Francisco territory four times, but only scored once, on a Bartkowski quarterback sneak.

San Francisco	0	3	0	7	— 10
Atlanta	7	0	14	14	— 35

Atl —Bartkowski 1 run (Mazzetti kick)
SF—FG Wersching 41
Atl —Miller 11 pass from Bartkowski (Mazzetti kick)
Atl —Francis 81 pass from Bartkowski (Mazzetti kick)
Atl —Francis 12 pass from Bartkowski (Mazzetti kick)
Atl —Richardson recovered fumble in end zone (Mazzetti kick)
SF—Clark 13 pass from Montana (Wersching kick)

Detroit 27, Tampa Bay 14—At Pontiac Silverdome, attendance 77,098. Rookie Ray Williams's 91-yard kickoff return with 8:32 left was the clinching score that enabled Detroit to keep its playoff hopes alive. The Lions, having been beaten on a kickoff return and a punt return in their two previous games, also benefited on an early one-yard touchdown run by rookie running back Billy Sims that set a club-record 15 touchdowns in one season. However, Tampa Bay held Sims to 16 yards on 12 attempts. Rookie placekicker Ed Murray set a club record with his twenty-fifth and twenty-sixth field goals.

Tampa Bay	7	0	0	7	— 14
Detroit	7	7	3	10	— 27

TB —Logan 60 fumble recovery return (Yepremian kick)
Det—Sims 1 run (Murray kick)
Det—R. Williams 22 pass from Danielson (Murray kick)
Det—FG Murray 24
Det—FG Murray 25
TB —House 32 pass from Williams (Yepremian kick)
Det—R. Williams 91 kickoff return (Murray kick)

MONDAY, DECEMBER 15

Los Angeles 38, Dallas 14—At Anaheim Stadium, attendance 65,154. Vince Ferragamo threw three touchdown passes in a Monday night battle between playoff-contending teams. Ferragamo, who completed 15 of 25 passes for 275 yards, threw scoring passes of 40 yards to Billy Waddy, 34 to Preston Dennard, and 1 yard to Victor Hicks as the Rams took a commanding 38-0 lead. Rams rookie running back Jewerl Thomas carried 16 times for 147 yards, including a 34-yard second period touchdown run.

Dallas	0	0	0	14	— 14
Los Angeles	7	21	10	0	— 38

LA —Bryant 4 run (Corral kick)
LA —J. Thomas 34 run (Corral kick)
LA —Waddy 40 pass from Ferragamo (Corral kick)
LA —Dennard 34 pass from Ferragamo (Corral kick)
LA —FG Corral 27
LA —Hicks 1 pass from Ferragamo (Corral kick)
Dall—T. Hill 36 pass from D. White (Septien kick)
Dall—B. Johnson 17 pass from Carano (Septien kick)

SIXTEENTH WEEK SUMMARY

San Diego defeated Pittsburgh 26-17 to win the AFC West title. Dan Fouts threw for 308 yards, raising his NFL single-season passing record to 4,715 yards. The Chargers established an NFL team mark gaining 6,410 yards in 1980, surpassing the record of 6,288 set by the 1961 Houston Oilers. Don Cockroft's 22-yard field goal with 1:25 left provided the winning margin in Cleveland's 27-24 win over Cincinnati. The victory clinched the AFC Central Division championship for the Browns, who gained the title over Houston on the basis of a better conference record. Brian Sipe was the NFL's leading passer with a rating of 91.9 and became only the third quarterback in league history to pass for more than 4,000 yards in a single season (4,132). Buffalo captured the AFC East title and its first playoff appearance since 1974 by downing San Francisco 18-13. In the NFC East, Dallas assured itself of the home field advantage in next week's wild card matchup against Los Angeles. The Rams ended the regular season in winning fashion, defeating Atlanta in overtime 20-17. Earl Campbell picked up 203 yards and a touchdown in the Oilers' victory over the Vikings to bring his season total to 1,934 yards. It was Campbell's third rushing title in as many years and left him only 69 yards shy of O. J. Simpson's NFL single-season mark of 2,003, which was set in 1973.

SATURDAY, DECEMBER 20

Chicago 14, Tampa Bay 13—At Tampa Stadium, attendance 55,298. Vince Evans scored two touchdowns to highlight the Bears' comeback win. Otis Wilson's interception and Lenny Walterscheid's fumble recovery set up Evans's touchdowns, which gave Chicago a 14-10 edge. Al Harris deflected Garo Yepremian's 32-yard field goal attempt in the closing seconds to ensure the Bears's seventh victory. Walter Payton ran for 130 yards to tie O.J. Simpson's mark of 42 career 100-yard rushing games.

Chicago	0	7	7	0	— 14
Tampa Bay	10	0	3	0	— 13

TB —Jones 33 pass from D. Williams (Yepremian kick)
TB —FG Yepremian 27
Chi—Evans 6 run (Thomas kick)
Chi—Evans 1 run (Thomas kick)
TB —FG Yepremian 26

New York Jets 24, Miami 17—At Orange Bowl, attendance 41,854. Richard Todd's pinpoint passing (12 of 19 for 172 yards) helped set up two one-yard plunges by Scott Dierking and rookie safety Darrol Ray returned an interception 71 yards for a touchdown to propel the Jets past the Dolphins. Todd broke Joe Namath's 1967 club-record of 258 completions, finishing the season with 264. Donald Dykes intercepted David Woodley's pass in the end zone with 1:19 remaining to clinch the victory. NBC televised the game nationally without commentators.

New York Jets	7	7	7	3	— 24
Miami	10	0	0	7	— 17

Mia —FG von Schamann 21
NYJ—Dierking 1 run (Leahy kick)
Mia —Harris 16 pass from Woodley (von Schamann kick)
NYJ—Dierking 1 run (Leahy kick)
NYJ—Ray 71 interception return (Leahy kick)
Mia —Woodley 1 run (von Schamann kick)
NYJ—FG Leahy 35

SUNDAY, DECEMBER 21

Los Angeles 20, Atlanta 17—At Anaheim Stadium, attendance 62,469. Frank Corral, who earlier had missed three field goal attempts, kicked a 23-yarder seven minutes into overtime as Los Angeles defeated Atlanta in the battle of NFC West powers. Corral's 47-yard field goal attempt with seconds remaining in regulation time was blocked by Kenny Johnson. In overtime, the Rams' Joe Harris sacked quarterback Steve Bartkowski and jarred the ball loose. Jeff Delaney recovered for Los Angeles at the 6. Corral then kicked his game-winner. The Falcons had tied the score on Tim Mazzetti's 18-yard field goal with 3:41 left, after the Rams stopped three straight running plays from the 1.

Atlanta	7	7	0	3	0	— 17
Los Angeles	3	0	14	0	3	— 20

Atl—Jackson 13 pass from Bartkowski (Mazzetti kick)
LA—FG Corral 26
Atl—J. Miller 9 pass from Bartkowski (Mazzetti kick)
LA—J. Thomas 37 run (Corral kick)
LA—Dennard 17 pass from Ferragamo (Corral kick)
Atl—FG Mazzetti 18
LA—FG Corral 23

Buffalo 18, San Francisco 13—At Candlestick Park, attendance 37,476. Buffalo won its first division title since 1966. Nick Mike-Mayer's 25-yard field goal snapped a 13-13 tie in the third quarter. The Bills went ahead 18-13 when a poor snap on a punting attempt resulted in a Buffalo safety. Rookie running back Joe Cribbs burst 48 yards on his first carry to key a 76-yard scoring drive as Buffalo took a quick 6-0 lead.

Buffalo	6	7	5	0	— 18
San Francisco	6	0	7	0	— 13

Buff—Butler 10 pass from Ferguson (kick failed)
SF —Cooper 4 run (kick failed)
Buff—Brown 4 run (Mike-Mayer kick)
SF —Ramson 2 pass from Montana (Wersching kick)
Buff—FG Mike-Mayer 25
Buff—Safety, Miller tackled in end zone

Cleveland 27, Cincinnati 24—At Riverfront Stadium, attendance 50,058. Brian Sipe, the NFL's top-rated passer, threw three touchdown passes and Don Cockroft kicked a game-winning 22-yard field goal with 1:25 left as the Browns won the AFC Central Division championship. Sipe's three touchdowns gave him 30 for the season, a new Browns' record. His 308 yards gave him 4,132 for the year to join Joe Namath and Dan Fouts as the only quarterbacks to reach the 4,000-yard plateau. Against the Bengals, Sipe threw scoring passes of 42-yards to Reggie Rucker and 35 and 34 yards to Ricky Feacher.

Cleveland	0	10	14	3	— 27
Cincinnati	3	7	14	0	— 24

Cin—FG Breech 42
Cin—Thompson 13 run (Breech kick)
Cle—Rucker 42 pass from Sipe (Cockroft kick)
Cle—FG Cockroft 26
Cin—R. Griffin 52 pass interception return (Breech kick)
Cle—Feacher 35 pass from Sipe (Cockroft kick)
Cle—Feacher 34 pass from Sipe (Cockroft kick)
Cin—McInally 59 pass from Thompson (Breech kick)
Cle—FG Cockroft 22

Denver 25, Seattle 17—At Kingdome, attendance 51,853. Matt Robinson, making his seventh start of the season, passed for one touchdown and ran for another, and Fred Steinfort kicked field goals of 34, 38, 53, and 55 yards to help the Broncos even their season record at 8-8. Robinson hit Riley Odoms with an 18-yard scoring pass and capped Denver's 19-0 halftime lead with a one-yard quarterback sneak in the second quarter. The Seahawks made the final score close with two touchdowns in the last six minutes.

Denver	10	9	6	0	— 25
Seattle	0	0	3	14	— 17

Den—FG Steinfort 53
Den—Odoms 18 pass from Robinson (Steinfort kick)
Den—Robinson 1 run (kick failed)
Den—FG Steinfort 55
Sea—FG Herrera 47
Den—FG Steinfort 34
Den—FG Steinfort 38
Sea—McCutcheon 2 run (Herrera kick)
Sea—Jodat 9 pass from Zorn (Herrera kick)

Detroit 24, Green Bay 3—At Silverdome, attendance 75,111. Gary Danielson completed 17 of 26 passes for 219 yards and one touchdown to help the Lions defeat the Packers. Danielson climaxed a 70-yard scoring drive with an eight-yard pass to Freddie Scott. Billy Sims (one-yard) and Dexter Bussey (eight-yards) added second-half touchdown runs as Detroit ran its record to 9-7, the Lions' first winning season since 1972.

Green Bay	0	0	3	0	— 3
Detroit	0	10	0	14	— 24

Det—Scott 8 pass from Danielson (Murray kick)
Det—FG Murray 41
GB—FG Stenerud 33
Det—Sims 1 run (Murray kick)
Det—Bussey 8 run (Murray kick)

Kansas City 38, Baltimore 28—At Memorial Stadium, attendance 16, 941. Bill Kenney threw three touchdown passes, including two in the second half, to help lift the Chiefs to a 38-28 victory over the Colts. Kenney teamed with Henry Marshall on scoring strikes of 23 and 75 yards to eclipse a 28-21 Baltimore halftime lead. A pair of first quarter touchdowns by J.T. Smith (37-yard pass, 53-yard punt return) and a one-yard plunge by James Hadnot staked Kansas City to a 21-0 advantage before Bert Jones fired three second-period touchdown passes and Marvin Sims scored from two yards out to give the Colts the lead.

Kansas City	21	0	7	10	— 38
Baltimore	0	28	0	0	— 28

KC —Hadnot 1 run (Lowery kick)
KC —Smith 37 pass from Kenney (Lowery kick)
KC —Smith 53 punt return (Lowery kick)
Balt—Washington 20 pass from Jones (Mike-Mayer kick)
Balt—Carr 5 pass from Jones (Mike-Mayer kick)
Balt—Sims 2 run (Mike-Mayer kick)
Balt—Burke 14 pass from Jones (Mike-Mayer kick)
KC —Marshall 23 pass from Kenney (Lowery kick)
KC —FG Lowery 39
KC —Marshall 75 pass from Kenney (Lowery kick)

Houston 20, Minnesota 16—At Astrodome, attendance 51,064. Earl Campbell, who clinched his third consecutive NFL rushing title by gaining 203 yards in 29 carries, scored the winning three-yard touchdown with 1:58 left and earned the Oilers a wild-card playoff berth for the third straight year. Campbell set an NFL record with his fourth 200-yard game of the season and finished the year with 1,934 yards, only 69 short of O.J. Simpson's 1973 record of 2,003 yards. Tommy Kramer hit 26 of 53 passes for 266 yards to set a Vikings season record of 3,582 yards, erasing the mark of 3,468 set by Fran Tarkenton in 1978.

Minnesota	6	7	0	3	— 16
Houston	3	0	10	7	— 20

Minn—Senser 3 pass from Kramer (kick failed)
Hou —FG Fritsch 23
Minn—Senser 3 pass from Kramer (Danmeier kick)
Hou —Casper 7 pass from Stabler (Fritsch kick)
Hou —FG Fritsch 31
Minn—FG Danmeier 38
Hou —Campbell 3 run (Fritsch kick)

New England 38, New Orleans 27—At Louisiana Superdome, attendance 38,277. Matt Cavanaugh threw three touchdown passes and Don Calhoun rushed for 113 yards and one touchdown to lead the Patriots over the Saints. Cavanaugh rallied New England from a 10-3 deficit, hitting Russ Francis (39 yards) and Andy Johnson (11 and 6 yards) with scoring passes. Calhoun scampered 22 yards for a touchdown in the fourth quarter after New Orleans took a 27-24 lead. Mosi Tatupu added a four-yard touchdown run with 1:38 left to ensure the Patriots victory.

New England	3	14	7	14	— 38
New Orleans	10	3	7	7	— 27

NO—Rogers 23 pass from Holmes (Ricardo kick)
NO—FG Ricardo 30
NE —FG Smith 22
NE —Francis 39 pass from Cavanaugh (Smith kick)
NE —Johnson 11 pass from Cavanaugh (Smith kick)
NO—FG Ricardo 38
NE —Johnson 6 pass from Cavanaugh (Smith kick)
NO—Wilson 1 run (Ricardo kick)
NO—Chandler 23 pass from Manning (Ricardo kick)
NE —Calhoun 22 run (Smith kick)
NE —Tatupu 4 run (Smith kick)

Oakland 33, New York Giants 17—At Giants Stadium, attendance 61,287. A swarming Oakland defense forced five turnovers and sacked Giants quarterback Scott Brunner five times. Jim Plunkett completed 12 of 22 passes for 164 yards and had touchdown throws of 31 yards to Cliff Branch and 37 yards to Raymond Chester. The final Oakland score came when Derrick Jensen streaked 33 yards untouched with an onside kick with 16 seconds left in the game.

Oakland	10	10	7	6	— 33
New York Giants	0	10	0	7	— 17

Oak —FG Bahr 41
Oak —Whittington 7 run (Bahr kick)
NYG—FG Danelo 47
Oak —Branch 31 pass from Plunkett (Bahr kick)
Oak —FG Bahr 38
NYG—Perry 11 pass from Brunner (Danelo kick)
Oak —Chester 37 pass from Plunkett (Bahr kick)
NYG—Taylor 1 run (Danelo kick)
Oak —Jensen 33 kickoff return (kick failed)

Dallas 35, Philadelphia 27—At Texas Stadium, attendance 62,548. Danny White threw four touchdown passes and scored on a one-yard run to power Dallas to victory. The Cowboys had to win by 25 points or better, according to the NFL tie-breaking formula, to capture the NFC Eastern Division title. White keyed Dallas to leads of 21-0 at halftime and 35-10 in the third quarter, before the Eagles rallied to clinch the division title. Harold Carmichael's NFL record streak of games in which he had at least one pass reception was snapped at 127.

Philadelphia	0	0	10	17	— 27
Dallas	7	14	7	7	— 35

Dall—D. White 1 run (Septien kick)
Dall—Hill 36 pass from D. White (Septien kick)
Dall—P. Pearson 9 pass from D. White (Septien kick)
Phil—Giammona 1 run (Franklin kick)
Dall—D. Pearson 11 pass from D. White (Septien kick)
Phil—FG Franklin 29
Dall—Dupree 15 pass from D. White (Septien kick)
Phil—Parker 30 pass from Jaworski (Franklin kick)
Phil—FG Franklin 19
Phil—Montgomery 6 run (Franklin kick)

Washington 31, St. Louis 7—At Busch Memorial Stadium, attendance 35,942. Joe Theismann fired three touchdown passes, including two to rookie Art Monk, as the Redskins capped the season with their third straight win. Washington exploded for 21 points in the second quarter as Theismann connected with Monk on a 54-yard bomb and found Clarence Harmon with a 15-yard scoring toss after Harmon had opened the scoring with a one-yard plunge. Theismann extended the Redskins' lead with a two-yard touchdown pass to Monk and Mark Moseley converted a 34-yard field goal for a 31-0 edge. Theotis Brown's four-yard touchdown run with 7:36 remaining averted the shutout.

Washington	0	21	3	7	— 31
St. Louis	0	0	0	7	— 7

Wash—Harmon 1 run (Moseley kick)
Wash—Monk 54 pass from Theismann (Moseley kick)
Wash—Harmon 15 pass from Theismann (Moseley kick)
Wash—FG Moseley 34
Wash—Monk 2 pass from Theismann (Moseley kick)
StL —Brown 4 run (O'Donoghue kick)

MONDAY, DECEMBER 22

San Diego 26, Pittsburgh 17—At San Diego Stadium, attendance 51,785. Rolf Benirschke kicked four field goals as the Chargers defeated Pittsburgh in the season's final regular season game to capture the AFC Western Division title. In a duel between two passing quarterbacks, the Chargers' Don Fouts completed 21 of 37 passes for 308 yards while Terry Bradshaw hit on 16 of 32 aerials for 272 yards. It was the first time since the 1971 season that the Steelers failed to reach the playoffs.

Pittsburgh	0	3	7	7	— 17
San Diego	3	6	10	7	— 26

SD —FG Benirschke 33
Pitt—FG Bahr 32
SD —FG Benirschke 26
SD —FG Benirschke 26
SD — Fouts 1 run (Benirschke kick)
Pitt—Thornton 2 run (Bahr kick)
SD —FG Benirschke 33
SD —Muncie 10 run (Benirschke kick)
Pitt—Cunningham 16 pass from Bradshaw (Bahr kick)

SEVENTEENTH WEEK

SUNDAY, DECEMBER 28, 1980
AFC FIRST-ROUND PLAYOFF GAME

Oakland 27, Houston 7—At Oakland Coliseum, attendance 52,762. The Raiders, ending a two-year absence from postseason play, advanced to the divisional playoffs by shutting out the Oilers over the final three quarters. Oakland converted Earl Campbell's fumble on the first play of the game into Chris Bahr's 47-yard field goal. Campbell came back to score on a one-yard plunge to give Houston a 7-3 lead. Jim Plunkett's one-yard touchdown pass to Todd Christensen early in the second quarter put the Raiders ahead to stay 10-7. Plunkett added another touchdown when he caught the Oilers in a man-to-man defense and lofted a 44-yard pass to Arthur Whittington on the first play of the final period. Kenny King's 31-yard run set up Bahr's 37-yard field goal that gave Oakland a 20-7 edge. Lester Hayes added 2 interceptions to his NFL-leading regular season total of 13. He picked off Ken Stabler's pass in the end zone to end a third-period scoring threat and his final-quarter 20-yard interception return capped the Raiders' scoring. The Oakland defense sacked Stabler, its former all-pro quarterback, seven times for 65 yards. Ray Guy's 51.1 punting average kept the Oilers in poor field position all day.

Houston	7	0	0	0	— 7
Oakland	3	7	0	17	— 27

Oak—FG Bahr 47
Hou—Campbell 1 run (Fritsch kick)
Oak—Christensen 1 pass from Plunkett (Bahr kick)
Oak—Whittington 44 pass from Plunkett (Bahr kick)
Oak—FG Bahr 37
Oak—Hayes 20 interception return (Bahr kick)

SUNDAY, DECEMBER 28, 1980
NFC FIRST-ROUND PLAYOFF GAME

Dallas 34, Los Angeles 13—At Texas Stadium, attendance 64,533. The NFC wild card matchup found Rams and Cowboys tied 13-13 at halftime, but Dallas scored the first three times it had the ball in the second half. Quarterback Danny White threw three touchdowns, while completing 12 of 25 passes for 190 yards. Tony Dorsett set a club playoff record for rushing with 160 yards on 22 carries Drew Pearson caught four passes for 60 yards, including an 11-yard touchdown.

Los Angeles	6	7	0	0	— 13
Dallas	3	10	14	7	— 34

Dall—FG Septien 28
LA —Thomas 1 run (kick blocked)
Dall—FG Septien 29

LA —Dennard 21 pass from Ferragamo (Corral kick)
Dall—Dorsett 12 run (Septien kick)
Dall—Dorsett 10 pass from White (Septien kick)
Dall—Johnson 35 pass from White (Septien kick)
Dall—D. Pearson 11 pass from White (Septien kick)

EIGHTEENTH WEEK

SATURDAY, JANUARY 3, 1981
AFC DIVISIONAL PLAYOFF

San Diego 20, Buffalo 14—At San Diego Stadium, attendance 52,028. Dan Fouts fired a 50-yard touchdown pass to wide receiver Ron Smith with 2:08 remaining to lift San Diego over Buffalo and send the Chargers into the AFC Championship Game. San Diego had to come from behind to give Don Coryell his first playoff victory in four attempts as an NFL coach. Trailing 14-3 at halftime, Fouts hit Charlie Joiner with a nine-yard touchdown pass on the Chargers' first possession of the second half to cap a 70-yard, four-play drive. Rolf Benirschke added a 22-yard field goal to slice the Bills' lead to 14-13 with 51 seconds gone in the final period. Fouts, who completed 22 of 37 passes for 314 yards, directed a 397-yard attack, while the Chargers' defense limited the Bills to 244 yards. San Diego wide receiver John Jefferson led all receivers with seven receptions for 102 yards. Chuck Muncie rushed 18 times for 80 yards and had six catches for 53. The Chargers intercepted Buffalo quarterback Joe Ferguson three times, including two by safety Glen Edwards. The loss eliminated the AFC East champion Bills, who were making their first playoff appearance since 1974.

Buffalo	0	14	0	0	— 14
San Diego	3	0	7	10	— 20

SD —FG Benirschke 22
Buff—Leaks 1 run (Mike-Mayer kick)
Buff—Lewis 9 pass from Ferguson (Mike-Mayer kick)
SD —Joiner 9 pass from Fouts (Benirschke kick)
SD —FG Benirschke 22
SD —Smith 50 pass from Fouts (Benirschke kick)

SATURDAY, JANUARY 3, 1981
NFC DIVISIONAL PLAYOFF

Philadelphia 31, Minnesota 16—At Veterans Stadium, attendance 68,434. The NFC Eastern champion Eagles rallied for 24 second-half points to defeat NFC Central titlist Minnesota 31-16. The Vikings, who had lost only three fumbles during the regular season, lost an equal number during the last two periods against Philadelphia. Minnesota had a 14-0 lead when the Eagles completed a 13-play, 85-yard scoring drive with Ron Jaworski's nine-yard touchdown pass to Harold Carmichael with one minute remaining in the first half. Philadelphia's second-half opening drive covered 66 yards in eight plays as Wilbert Montgomery (26 carries for 74 yards, two touchdowns) scored on an eight-yard draw play. Minnesota went ahead 16-14 when Jaworski was tackled in his own end zone for a safety. However, Eagles linebacker Reggie Wilkes recovered a Vikings' punt return fumble to set up an 18-yard, four-play scoring drive with Montgomery's subsequent five-yard run putting Philadelphia on top to stay. Jaworski finished the day 17 for 38 for 190 yards and one touchdown. Philadelphia's five interceptions were by Roynell Young and Herman Edwards (two each), and Frank LeMaster.

Minnesota	7	7	2	0	— 16
Philadelphia	0	7	14	10	— 31

Minn—S. White 30 pass from Kramer (Danmeier kick)
Minn—Brown 1 run (Danmeier kick)
Phil —Carmichael 9 pass from Jaworski (Franklin kick)
Phil —Montgomery 8 run (Franklin kick)
Minn—Safety, Jaworski tackled in end zone by Martin and Blair
Phil —Montgomery 5 run (Franklin kick)
Phil —FG Franklin 33
Phil —Harrington 2 run (Franklin kick)

SUNDAY, JANUARY 4, 1981
AFC DIVISIONAL PLAYOFF

Oakland 14, Cleveland 12—At Cleveland Stadium, attendance 77,655. Safety Mike Davis saved the victory for Oakland when he intercepted Brian Sipe's pass with 41 seconds remaining to wipe out a Cleveland scoring threat. Davis picked off a pass intended for tightend Ozzie Newsome in the Raiders' end zone after Cleveland had marched from its own 14 to the Oakland 13. The victory moved the Raiders into their first AFC Championship Game since 1977, when they lost to Denver 20-17. Oakland came from behind twice against the Browns in a game that was played in one-degree weather. Mark van Eeghen's 1-yard touchdown run with 9:22 remaining put the Raiders ahead to stay after a pair of 30-yard field goals by Don Cockroft gave the Browns a 12-7 advantage entering the final period. Van Eeghen also scored from one yard out with 18 seconds left in the second period to provide the Raiders with a 7-6 halftime lead. Van Eeghen's first score capped a 64-yard, 14-play drive, while the latter completed an 80-yard, 12-play drive. In addition to Davis's key interception, Lester Hayes stole two passes to bring his regular and postseason total to 17. Jim Plunkett, who completed 14 of 30 passes for 149 yards, directed the Raiders to their eleventh win in 13 games since he became a starter in the sixth game of the season.

Oakland	0	7	0	7	— 14
Cleveland	0	6	6	0	— 12

Cle —Bolton 42 interception return (kick failed)
Oak—van Eeghen 1 run (Bahr kick)
Cle —FG Cockroft 30
Cle —FG Cockroft 30
Oak—van Eeghen 1 run (Bahr kick)

SUNDAY, JANUARY 4, 1981
NFC DIVISIONAL PLAYOFF

Dallas 30, Atlanta 27—At Atlanta-Fulton County Stadium, attendance 60,022. Drew Pearson's 23-yard touchdown catch with 42 seconds remaining gave wild card entry Dallas a 30-27 victory over Western champion Atlanta and advanced the Cowboys to the NFC title game. The Falcons held a 24-10 lead heading into the fourth period, but Dallas scored 20 final-quarter points to Atlanta's 3. The Cowboys' defense, which allowed 255 first-half yards, yielded only 94 in the second half. Danny White completed 25 of 39 passes for 322 yards and three touchdowns. Drew Pearson caught five for 90 yards and two scores, including a 14-yarder from White with 3:04 to go.

Dallas	3	7	0	20	— 30
Atlanta	10	7	7	3	— 27

Atl —FG Mazzetti 38
Atl —Jenkins 60 pass from Bartkowski (Mazzetti kick)
Dall—FG Septien 38
Dall—DuPree 5 pass from White (Septien kick)
Atl —Cain 1 run (Mazzetti kick)
Atl —Andrews 12 pass from Bartkowski (Mazzetti kick)
Dall—Newhouse 1 run (Septien kick)
Atl —FG Mazzetti 34
Dall—D. Pearson 14 pass from White (Septien kick)
Dall—D. Pearson 23 pass from White (Septien kick)

NINETEENTH WEEK

SUNDAY, JANUARY 11, 1981
AFC CHAMPIONSHIP GAME

Oakland 34, San Diego 27—At San Diego Stadium, San Diego, California, attendance 52,438. Jim Plunkett completed 14 of 18 passes for 261 yards and two touchdowns to lead Oakland to a 34-27 victory over San Diego in the 1980 AFC Championship Game and send the Raiders into Super Bowl XV against NFC Champion Philadelphia at the Louisiana Superdome in New Orleans on Sunday, January 25, 1981. Oakland would be making its third appearance in a Super Bowl. The Raiders lost to Green Bay 33-14 in Super Bowl II and won the NFL championship in Super Bowl XI by defeating Minnesota 32-14. The Raiders are the second wild card team to enter a Super Bowl, following Dallas, which was the NFC wild card in 1975 and went on to win the NFC title, but lost to AFC Champion Pittsburgh 21-17 in Super Bowl X. The Raiders gained Super Bowl XV by defeating Houston 27-7 at Oakland in the first round of the AFC playoffs, then went to Cleveland and edged the Browns 14-12 in freezing temperatures in the divisional playoffs before outscoring San Diego for the AFC title. Plunkett's touchdown passes covered 65 yards to Raymond Chester and 21 yards to Kenny King. The Plunkett-to-Chester touchdown came on the first pass of the game with an assist by King as the ball ricocheted off the latter's hands at the Oakland 40 and flew through the air to midfield where Chester grabbed it and raced for the game's first score. San Diego tied the count at 7-7 on Dan Fouts's 48-yard pass to Charlie Joiner midway through the first period, but Oakland came back for two more touchdowns—a five-yard Plunkett run and the King reception—to take a 21-7 lead. Mark van Eeghen's three-yard run lifted the Oakland advantage to 28-7. San Diego pulled within 28-24 in the third period, but a pair of field goals by Chris Bahr gave Oakland the winning edge.

Oakland	21	7	3	3	— 34
San Diego	7	7	10	3	— 27

Oak—Chester 65 pass from Plunkett (Bahr kick)
SD —Joiner 48 pass from Fouts (Benirschke kick)
Oak—Plunkett 5 run (Bahr kick)
Oak—King 21 pass from Plunkett (Bahr kick)
Oak—van Eeghen 3 run (Bahr kick)
SD —Joiner 8 pass from Fouts (Benirschke kick)
SD —FG Benirschke 26
SD —Muncie 6 run (Benirschke kick)
Oak—FG Bahr 27
Oak—FG Bahr 33
SD —FG Benirschke 27

SUNDAY, JANUARY 11, 1981
NFC CHAMPIONSHIP GAME

Philadelphia 20, Dallas 7—At Veterans Stadium, Philadelphia, attendance 70,696. The Eagles, spurred by Wilbert Montgomery's 194-yard rushing effort, gained their first NFC championship by defeating wild card entry Dallas 20-7. Montgomery's 194 yards on 26 carries were 3 yards shy of breaking former Eagle Steve Van Buren's NFC Championship Game rushing record of 196 yards set in 1949 (Philadelphia vs. Los Angeles). Montgomery's 42-yard first possession touchdown gave Philadelphia an early lead, although the Cowboys tied the game on Tony Dorsett's three-yard run 9:10 into the second quarter. Carl Hairston's sack of Danny White and the subsequent fumble recovery by Dennis Harrison preceded Tony Franklin's 26-yard field goal with 7:18 elapsed in the third quarter. On Dallas's following series, Jerry Robinson recovered a Cowboy's fumble at the Eagles' 40 and returned it to the Dallas 38. Leroy Harris's nine-yard run six plays later gave Philadelphia a 17-7 advantage. The Eagles' final score came on a 12-play, 62-yard drive capped by Franklin's 20-yard field goal with 2:10 left in the game. Eagles quarterback Ron Jaworski completed 9 of 29 passes for 91 yards. Rodney Parker paced all receivers with four catches for 31 yards.

Dallas	0	7	0	0	— 7
Philadelphia	7	0	10	3	— 20

Phil—Montgomery 42 run (Franklin kick)
Dall—Dorsett 3 run (Septien kick)
Phil—FG Franklin 26
Phil—Harris 9 run (Franklin kick)
Phil—FG Franklin 20

TWENTIETH WEEK

SUPER BOWL XV
SUNDAY, JANUARY 25, 1981
NEW ORLEANS, LOUISIANA

Oakland 27, Philadelphia 10—At Louisiana Superdome, New Orleans, attendance 75,500. Jim Plunkett threw three touchdown passes, including an 80-yarder to Kenny King, as the Raiders became the first wild card team to win the Super Bowl. Plunkett's touchdown bomb to King—the longest play in Super Bowl history—gave Oakland a decisive 14-0 lead with nine seconds left in the first period. Linebacker Rod Martin had set up Oakland's first touchdown, a two-yard reception by Cliff Branch, with a 16-yard interception return to the Eagles' 32 yard line. The Eagles never recovered from that early deficit, managing only Tony Franklin's field goal (30 yards) and an eight-yard touchdown pass from Ron Jaworski to Keith Krepfle the rest of the game. Plunkett, who became a starter in the sixth game of the season, completed 13 of 21 passes for 261 yards and was named the game's most valuable player. Oakland won 9 of 11 games with Plunkett starting, but that was good enough only for second place in the AFC West, although they tied the division winner, San Diego, with an 11-5 record. The Raiders, who had previously won Super Bowl XI over Minnesota, had to win three playoff games to get to the championship game. Oakland defeated Houston 27-7 at home followed by road victories over Cleveland, 14-12, and San Diego, 34-27. Oakland's Mark van Eeghen was the game's leading rusher with 80 yards on 19 carries. Philadelphia's Wilbert Montgomery led all receivers with six receptions for 91 yards, followed by Branch with five for 67 and Harold Carmichael of Philadelphia with five for 83. Martin finished the game with three interceptions, a Super Bowl record.

Oakland	14	0	10	3	— 27
Philadelphia	0	3	0	7	— 10

Oak—Branch 2 pass from Plunkett (Bahr kick)
Oak—King 80 pass from Plunkett (Bahr kick)
Phil —FG Franklin 30
Oak—Branch 29 pass from Plunkett (Bahr kick)
Oak—FG Bahr 46
Phil —Krepfle 8 pass from Jaworski (Franklin kick)
Oak—FG Bahr 35

TWENTY-FIRST WEEK

AFC-NFC PRO BOWL
SUNDAY, FEBRUARY 1, 1981
HONOLULU, HAWAII

NFC 21, AFC 7—At Aloha Stadium, Honolulu, Hawaii, attendance 50,360. Ed Murray kicked four field goals and Steve Bartkowski fired a 55-yard scoring pass to Alfred Jenkins to lead the NFC to its fourth straight victory over the AFC. The NFC has a 7-4 edge in the series. Murray who was named the game's most valuable player, missed tying Garo Yepremian's Pro Bowl record of five field goals when a 37-yard attempt hit the cross bar with 22 seconds remaining. The AFC's only score came on a nine-yard pass from Brian Sipe to Stanley Morgan in the second period. Bartkowski completed 9 of 21 passes for 173 yards, while Sipe connected on 10 of 15 for 142 yards. Ottis Anderson led all rushers with 70 yards on 10 carries. Earl Campbell was limited to 24 on 8 attempts.

AFC	0	7	0	0	— 7
NFC	3	6	0	12	— 21

NFC—FG Murray 31
AFC—Morgan 9 pass from Sipe (Smith kick)
NFC—FG Murray 31
NFC—FG Murray 34
NFC—Jenkins 55 pass from Bartkowski (Murray kick)
NFC—FG Murray 36
NFC—Safety, AFC holding in end zone

1980 Professional Football Awards

	NFL	AFC	NFC

Professional Football Writers Association

	NFL	AFC	NFC
Most Valuable Player	Brian Sipe		
Rookie of the Year	Billy Sims		
Coach of the Year		Chuck Knox	Leeman Bennett

Associated Press

	NFL
Most Valuable Player	Brian Sipe
Offensive Player of the Year	Earl Campbell
Defensive Player of the Year	Lester Hayes
Rookie of the Year—Offense	Billy Sims
Rookie of the Year—Defense	Al Richardson
	Buddy Curry
Coach of the Year	Chuck Knox

United Press International

	AFC	NFC
Player of the Year	Brian Sipe	Ron Jaworski
Rookie of the Year	Joe Cribbs	Billy Sims
Coach of the Year	Sam Rutigliano	Leeman Bennett

Newspaper Enterprise Association

	NFL
Jim Thorpe Trophy—Most Valuable Player	Earl Campbell
Bert Bell Trophy—Rookie of the Year	Billy Sims
George Halas Trophy—Defensive Player of the Year	Lester Hayes

The Sporting News

	NFL
Player of the Year	Brian Sipe
Rookie of the Year	Billy Sims

Pro Football Weekly

	NFL
Offensive Most Valuable Player	Brian Sipe
Defensive Most Valuable Player	Lester Hayes
Offensive Rookie of the Year	Billy Sims
Defensive Rookie of the Year	Buddy Curry
Comeback Player of the Year	Jim Plunkett
Coach of the Year	Chuck Knox

Football Digest

	NFL
Player of the Year	Brian Sipe
Offensive Rookie of the Year	Billy Sims
Defensive Rookie of the Year	Buddy Curry
Coach of the Year	Chuck Knox

Football News

	AFC	NFC
Coach of the Year	Chuck Knox	Leeman Bennett
Man of the Year	Leonard Tose	

AFC-NFC Pro Bowl

	NFL
Player of the Game	Ed Murray

Maxwell Club

	NFL
Player of the Year	Ron Jaworski

Past Super Bowl Most Valuable Players
(Selected by Sport Magazine)

SB I	Bart Starr, Green Bay
SB II	Bart Starr, Green Bay
SB III	Joe Namath, N.Y. Jets
SB IV	Len Dawson, Kansas City
SB V	Chuck Howley, Dallas
SB VI	Roger Staubach, Dallas
SB VII	Jake Scott, Miami
SB VIII	Larry Csonka, Miami
SB IX	Franco Harris, Pittsburgh
SB X	Lynn Swann, Pittsburgh
SB XI	Fred Biletnikoff, Oakland
SB XII	Randy White and Harvey Martin, Dallas
SB XIII	Terry Bradshaw, Pittsburgh
SB XIV	Terry Bradshaw, Pittsburgh
SB XV	Jim Plunkett, Oakland

Ten Best Rushing Performances, 1980

	Attempts	Yards	TDs
1. Earl Campbell, Houston vs. Chicago, November 16	31	206	0
2. Earl Campbell, Houston vs. Tampa Bay, October 19	33	203	0
3. Earl Campbell, Houston vs. Minnesota, December 21	29	203	1
4. Earl Campbell, Houston vs. Cincinnati, October 26	27	202	2
5. Walter Payton, Chicago vs. New Orleans, September 14	18	183	1
6. Tony Dorsett, Dallas vs. New York Giants, November 9	24	183	2
7. Earl Campbell, Houston vs. Green Bay, December 14	36	181	2
8. Earl Campbell, Houston vs. Kansas City, October 12	38	178	1
9. Wilbert Montgomery, Philadelphia vs. Minnesota, September 14	20	169	2
10. Ottis Anderson, St. Louis vs. New York Giants, November 30	31	168	2

100-Yard Rushing Performances, 1980

First Week
Billy Sims, Detroit — 153 yards vs. Los Angeles
Lynn Cain, Atlanta — 123 yards vs. Minnesota
John Cappelletti, San Diego — 112 yards vs. Seattle
Dexter Bussey, Detroit — 111 yards vs. Los Angeles

Second Week
Walter Payton, Chicago — 183 yards vs. New Orleans
Wilbert Montgomery, Philadelphia — 169 yards vs. Minnesota
Billy Sims, Detroit — 134 yards vs. Green Bay
William Andrews, Atlanta — 124 yards vs. New England
Earl Campbell, Houston — 106 yards vs. Cleveland

Third Week
Kenny King, Oakland — 136 yards vs. Washington
Rob Carpenter, Houston — 114 yards vs. Baltimore
Ted Brown, Minnesota — 113 yards vs. Chicago
Tony Dorsett, Dallas — 100 yards vs. Tampa Bay

Fourth Week
Billy Sims, Detroit — 157 yards vs. Minnesota
Ottis Anderson, St. Louis — 151 yards vs. Philadelphia
Jim Jodat, Seattle — 117 yards vs. Washington

Fifth Week
Walter Payton, Chicago — 133 yards vs. Tampa Bay
Ottis Anderson, St. Louis — 126 yards vs. New Orleans
Elvis Peacock, Los Angeles — 114 yards vs. San Francisco
Lynn Cain, Atlanta — 102 yards vs. Detroit
Franco Harris, Pittsburgh — 102 yards vs. Minnesota
Wayne Morris, St. Louis — 102 yards vs. New Orleans

Sixth Week
Earl Campbell, Houston — 178 yards vs. Kansas City
Kenny King, Oakland — 138 yards vs. San Diego
Mike Pruitt, Cleveland — 116 yards vs. Seattle
Cullen Bryant, Los Angeles — 115 yards vs. St. Louis
Otis Armstrong, Denver — 107 yards vs. Washington
Wilbur Jackson, Washington — 104 yards vs. Denver
Walter Payton, Chicago — 102 yards vs. Minnesota
Kevin Long, N.Y. Jets — 100 yards vs. Atlanta

Seventh Week
Earl Campbell, Houston — 203 yards vs. Tampa Bay
Pete Johnson, Cincinnati — 115 yards vs. Minnesota
Walter Payton, Chicago — 101 yards vs. Detroit

Eighth Week
Earl Campbell, Houston — 202 yards vs. Cincinnati
Billy Sims, Detroit — 155 yards vs. Kansas City
Joe Cribbs, Buffalo — 118 yards vs. New England
Jimmy Rogers, New Orleans — 114 yards vs. Washington
William Andrews, Atlanta — 111 yards vs. Los Angeles
Otis Armstrong, Denver — 106 yards vs. N.Y. Giants

Ninth Week
Earl Campbell, Houston — 157 yards vs. Denver
Rickey Bell, Tampa Bay — 130 yards vs. N.Y. Giants
Mike Pruitt, Cleveland — 129 yards vs. Chicago

Tenth Week
Tony Dorsett, Dallas — 183 yards vs. N.Y. Giants
Delvin Williams, Miami — 151 yards vs. Los Angeles
Earl Campbell, Houston — 130 yards vs. New England
William Andrews, Atlanta — 115 yards vs. St. Louis
Chuck Muncie, San Diego — 115 yards vs. Denver
Walter Payton, Chicago — 107 yards vs. Washington
Mike Pruitt, Cleveland — 103 yards vs. Baltimore

Eleventh Week
Earl Campbell, Houston — 206 yards vs. Chicago
Billy Sims, Detroit — 126 yards vs. Baltimore
Tony Dorsett, Dallas — 122 yards vs. St. Louis
Mike Thomas, San Diego — 109 yards vs. Kansas City
Ottis Anderson, St. Louis — 100 yards vs. Dallas

Twelfth Week
Eddie Lee Ivery, Green Bay — 145 yards vs. Minnesota
Wilbur Jackson, Washington — 128 yards vs. Dallas
Joe Cribbs, Buffalo — 110 yards vs. Pittsburgh
Ottis Anderson, St. Louis — 107 yards vs. Kansas City
Don Calhoun, New England — 106 yards vs. Baltimore
Curtis Dickey, Baltimore — 102 yards vs. New England
Gerry Ellis, Green Bay — 101 yards vs. Minnesota
Vagas Ferguson, New England — 100 yards vs. Pittsburgh

Thirteenth Week
Ottis Anderson, St. Louis — 168 yards vs. N.Y. Giants
Elvis Peacock, Los Angeles — 152 yards vs. N.Y. Jets
Walter Payton, Chicago — 123 yards vs. Detroit
Franco Harris, Pittsburgh — 116 yards vs. Miami
Pete Johnson, Cincinnati — 112 yards vs. Kansas City
William Andrews, Atlanta — 111 yards vs. Washington
Earl Campbell, Houston — 109 yards vs. Cleveland
Tony Dorsett, Dallas — 107 yards vs. Seattle

Fourteenth Week
Walter Payton, Chicago — 130 yards vs. Green Bay
Lenvill Elliot, San Francisco — 125 yards vs. New Orleans
Pete Johnson, Cincinnati — 118 yards vs. Baltimore
Billy Taylor, N.Y. Giants — 103 yards vs. Seattle
William Andrews, Atlanta — 101 yards vs. Philadelphia

Fifteenth Week
Earl Campbell, Houston — 181 yards vs. Green Bay
Jewerl Thomas, Los Angeles — 147 yards vs. Dallas
Pete Johnson, Cincinnati — 134 yards vs. Chicago
Tom Newton, N.Y. Jets — 117 yards vs. New Orleans
William Andrews, Atlanta — 105 yards vs. San Francisco

Sixteenth Week
Earl Campbell, Houston — 203 yards vs. Minnesota
Jewerl Thomas, Los Angeles — 144 yards vs. Atlanta
Bobby Hammond, Washington — 135 yards vs. St. Louis
Walter Payton, Chicago — 130 yards vs. Tampa Bay
Joe Cribbs, Buffalo — 128 yards vs. San Francisco
Ottis Anderson, St. Louis — 122 yards vs. Washington
Chuck Muncie, San Diego — 115 yards vs. Pittsburgh
Mark van Eeghen, Oakland — 115 yards vs. N.Y. Giants
Don Calhoun, New England — 113 yards vs. New Orleans

Times 100 or More
Campbell 10; Payton 8; Anderson 6; Sims 5; Andrews, Cain, Dorsett, and Johnson 4; Cribbs and M. Pruitt 3; Armstrong, Cain, Calhoun, Harris, Jackson, King, Muncie, Peacock, and Thomas 2.

Ten Best Passing Yardage Performances, 1980

	Att.	Comp.	Yards	TD
1. Doug Williams, Tampa Bay vs. Minnesota, November 16	55	30	486	4
2. Tommy Kramer, Minnesota vs. Cleveland, December 14	49	38	456	4
3. Richard Todd, N.Y. Jets vs. San Francisco, September 21	59	42	447	3
4. Dan Fouts, San Diego vs. New York Giants, October 19	41	26	444	3
5. Lynn Dickey, Green Bay vs. Tampa Bay, October 12	51	35	418	1
6. Tommy Kramer, Minnesota vs. Atlanta September 7	42	30	395	3
7. Brian Sipe, Cleveland vs. Green Bay, October 19	39	24	391	2
8. Dan Fouts, San Diego vs. Oakland, October 12	39	23	388	1
9. Ken Stabler, Houston vs. New York Jets, November 23	51	33	388	4
10. Dan Fouts, San Diego vs. Oakland, September 14	44	29	387	3

300-Yard Passing Performances

First Week
Tommy Kramer, Minnesota — 395 yards vs. Atlanta
Jim Hart, St. Louis — 322 yards vs. N.Y. Giants
Dan Pastorini, Oakland — 317 yards vs. Kansas City
Archie Manning, New Orleans — 314 yards vs. San Francisco

Second Week
Dan Fouts, San Diego — 387 yards vs. Oakland

Third Week
Richard Todd, N.Y. Jets — 447 yards vs. San Francisco
Steve Bartkowski, Atlanta — 332 yards vs. Miami
Jim Zorn, Seattle — 312 yards vs. New England

Fourth Week
Steve DeBerg, San Francisco — 345 yards vs. Atlanta
Doug Williams, Tampa Bay — 343 yards vs. Cleveland
Brian Sipe, Cleveland — 318 yards vs. Tampa Bay

Fifth Week
Gary Danielson, Detroit — 348 yards vs. Atlanta
Vince Ferragamo, Los Angeles — 304 yards vs. San Francisco

Sixth Week
Lynn Dickey, Green Bay — 418 yards vs. Tampa Bay
Dan Fouts, San Diego — 388 yards vs. Oakland
Archie Manning, New Orleans — 314 yards vs. Detroit

Seventh Week
Dan Fouts, San Diego — 444 yards vs. N.Y. Giants
Brian Sipe, Cleveland — 391 yards vs. Green Bay
Archie Manning, New Orleans — 323 yards vs. Atlanta
Joe Theismann, Washington — 307 yards vs. St. Louis

Eighth Week
Dan Fouts, San Diego — 371 yards vs. Dallas
Brian Sipe, Cleveland — 349 yards vs. Pittsburgh
Cliff Stoudt, Pittsburgh — 310 yards vs. Cleveland

Ninth Week
NONE

Tenth Week
Steve Bartkowski, Atlanta — 378 yards vs. St. Louis
Steve Grogan, New England — 374 yards vs. Houston
Dan Fouts, San Diego — 363 yards vs. Denver
Phil Simms, N.Y. Giants — 351 yards vs. Seattle
Jim Hart, St. Louis — 344 yards vs. Dallas
Ron Jaworski, Philadelphia — 323 yards vs. New Orleans
Archie Manning, New Orleans — 306 yards vs. Philadelphia
Joe Theismann, New Orleans — 306 yards vs. Chicago
Doug Williams, Tampa Bay — 302 yards vs. Pittsburgh

Eleventh Week
Doug Williams, Tampa Bay — 486 yards vs. Minnesota
Lynn Dickey, Green Bay — 331 yards vs. N.Y. Giants
Tommy Kramer, Minnesota — 324 yards vs. Tampa Bay
Phil Simms, N.Y. Giants — 322 yards vs. Green Bay
Craig Morton, Denver — 306 yards vs. N.Y. Jets

Twelfth Week
Ken Stabler, Houston — 388 yards vs. N.Y. Jets
Brian Sipe, Cleveland — 310 yards vs. Cincinnati

Thirteenth Week
Dan Fouts, San Diego — 342 yards vs. Philadelphia

Fourteenth Week
Archie Manning, New Orleans — 377 yards vs. San Francisco
Brian Sipe, Cleveland — 340 yards vs. N.Y. Jets
Vince Evans, Chicago — 316 yards vs. Green Bay

Fifteenth Week
Tommy Kramer, Minnesota — 456 yards vs. Cleveland
Gary Danielson, Detroit — 360 yards vs. Tampa Bay
Craig Morton, Denver — 339 yards vs. Seattle
Lynn Dickey, Green Bay — 309 yards vs. Houston

Sixteenth Week
Doug Williams, Tampa Bay — 350 yards vs. Chicago
Ron Jaworski, Philadelphia — 331 yards vs. Dallas
Bill Kenney, Kansas City — 316 yards vs. Baltimore
Dan Fouts, San Diego — 308 yards vs. Pittsburgh
Brian Sipe, Cleveland — 308 yards vs. Cincinnati
Archie Manning, New Orleans — 301 yards vs. New England

> **Times 300 or More**
> Fouts 8; Sipe and Manning 6; Williams 4; Dickey and Kramer 3; Jaworski, Morton, Danielson, Theismann, Hart, and Bartkowski 2.

Ten Best Receiving Yardage Performances, 1980

	No.	Yards	TD
1. Isaac Curtis, Cincinnati vs. Baltimore, December 7	7	176	1
2. Henry Marshall, Kansas City vs. Baltimore, December 21	9	176	2
3. James Lofton, Green Bay vs. New York Giants, November 16	8	175	1
4. Earnest Gray, New York Giants vs. St. Louis, September 7	9	174	4
5. Theo Bell, Pittsburgh vs. Miami, November 30	4	173	0
6. Charlie Joiner, San Diego vs. New York Giants, October 19	10	171	1
7. Kellen Winslow, San Diego vs. Pittsburgh, December 22	10	171	0
8. John Jefferson, San Diego vs. Philadelphia, November 30	8	164	0
9. Ahmad Rashad, Minnesota vs. Atlanta, September 7	11	160	0
10. Clark Gaines, N.Y. Jets vs. San Francisco, September 21	17	160	0

100-Yard Receiving Performances, 1980
(Number in parentheses is receptions.)

First Week
Earnest Gray, New York Giants — 174 yards (9) vs. St. Louis
Ahmad Rashad, Minnesota — 160 yards (11) vs. Atlanta
Harold Carmichael, Philadelphia — 135 yards (3) vs. Denver
John Stallworth, Pittsburgh — 135 yards (5) vs. Houston
Paul Hofer, San Francisco — 125 yards (5) vs. New Orleans
John Jefferson, San Diego — 114 yards (7) vs. Seattle
Larry Hardy, New Orleans — 103 yards (6) vs. San Francisco
Stanley Morgan, New England — 102 yards (3) vs. Cleveland

Second Week
Paul Hofer, San Francisco — 135 yards (9) vs. St. Louis
Kellen Winslow, San Diego — 132 yards (9) vs. Oakland
Tony Hill, Dallas — 117 yards (5) vs. Denver
Junior Miller, Atlanta — 110 yards (6) vs. New England
John Jefferson, San Diego — 108 yards (6) vs. Oakland
Roger Carr, Baltimore — 108 yards (6) vs. Pittsburgh

Eleventh Week
James Lofton, Green Bay — 175 yards (8) vs. New York Giants
Lynn Swann, Pittsburgh — 138 yards (9) vs. Cleveland
Tony Hill, Dallas — 126 yards (7) vs. St. Louis
Gordon Jones, Tampa Bay — 121 Yards (7) vs. Minnesota
Sammy White, Minnesota — 120 yards (6) vs. Tampa Bay
Earnest Gray, New York Giants — 119 yards (6) vs. Green Bay
Mike Friede, New York Giants — 108 yards (6) vs. Green Bay
Johnnie Jones, New York Jets — 103 yards (5) vs. Denver

Twelfth Week
Cliff Branch, Oakland — 125 yards (4) vs. Philadelphia
Henry Marshall, Kansas City — 117 yards (7) vs. St. Louis
Tony Nathan, Miami — 102 yards (7) vs. San Diego

Thirteenth Week
Theo Bell, Pittsburgh — 173 yards (4) vs. Miami
John Jefferson, San Diego — 164 yards (8) vs. Philadelphia
Dave Casper, Houston — 150 yards (6) vs. Cleveland
Stanley Morgan, New England — 142 yards (4) vs. San Francisco
James Scott, Chicago — 106 yards (6) vs. Detroit

Fourteenth Week
Isaac Curtis, Cincinnati — 176 yards (7) vs. Baltimore
Dwight Clark, San Francisco — 155 yards (6) vs. New Orleans
Henry Childs, New Orleans — 144 yards (8) vs. San Francisco
Steve Largent, Seattle — 139 yards (8) vs. New York Giants
Roger Carr, Baltimore — 133 yards (7) vs. Cincinnati
Rickey Watts, Chicago — 126 yards (4) vs. Green Bay
Clarence Harmon, Washington — 118 yards (12) vs. San Diego
Earnest Gray, New York Giants — 114 yards (3) vs. Seattle
James Lofton, Green Bay — 111 yards (6) vs. Chicago
Reggie Rucker, Cleveland — 108 yards (5) vs. New York Jets

Fifteenth Week
Wallace Francis, Atlanta — 148 yards (4) vs. San Francisco
Ahmad Rashad, Minnesota — 142 yards (9) vs. Cleveland
Haven Moses, Denver — 141 yards (6) vs. Oakland
Charlie Smith, Philadelphia — 134 yards (7) vs. St. Louis
Riley Odoms, Denver — 128 yards (8) vs. Oakland
Billy Waddy, Los Angeles — 124 yards (5) vs. Dallas
Tony Hill, Dallas — 121 yards (6) vs. Los Angeles
John Jefferson, San Diego — 113 yards (8) vs. Seattle
Leonard Thompson, Detroit — 106 yards (5) vs. Tampa Bay

Sixteenth Week
Henry Marshall, Kansas City — 176 yards (9) vs. Baltimore
Kellen Winslow, San Diego — 171 yards (10) vs. Pittsburgh
Kevin House, Tampa Bay — 138 yards (3) vs. Chicago
J.T. Smith, Kansas City — 129 yards (7) vs. Baltimore
Theo Bell, Pittsburgh — 127 yards (5) vs. San Diego
Dave Casper, Houston — 120 yards (7) vs. Minnesota
Tony Hill, Dallas — 110 yards (4) vs. Philadelphia

Times 100 or More
Jefferson 7; Winslow and Lofton 5; T. Hill, Bell, and Largent 4; Marshall, C. Smith, Gray, Carr, Morgan, Chandler, Joiner, and Tilley 3; Casper, Thompson, Moses, Rashad, Watts, Clark, Scott, Nathan, Branch, Friede, Jones, Swann, Soloman, Giles, Pearson, Butler, D. Hill, J. Smith, Carmichael, and Hofer 2.

Third Week
Clark Gaines, New York Jets — 160 yards (17) vs. San Francisco
Alfred Jenkins, Atlanta — 136 yards (4) vs. Miami
Jerry Butler, Buffalo — 133 yards (5) vs. New Orleans
Pat Tilley, St. Louis — 128 yards (10) vs. Detroit
Steve Largent, Seattle — 127 yards (6) vs. New England
Stanley Morgan, New England — 108 yards (2) vs. Seattle
Jimmie Giles, Tampa Bay — 105 yards (4) vs. Minnesota
Rickey Watts, Chicago — 104 yards (2) vs. Minnesota
Haven Moses, Denver — 103 yards (5) vs. San Diego
Charles White, Cleveland — 100 yards (7) vs. Kansas City

Fourth Week
Freddie Solomon, San Francisco — 132 yards (5) vs. Atlanta
Jim Smith, Pittsburgh — 131 yards (6) vs. Chicago
Tony Nathan, Miami — 118 yards (7) vs. New Orleans
Drew Hill, Los Angeles — 109 yards (2) vs. New York Giants
Harold Carmichael, Philadelphia — 108 yards (5) vs. St. Louis
Gordon Jones, Tampa Bay — 106 yards (7) vs. Cleveland
Jerry Eckwood, Tampa Bay — 101 yards (10) vs. Cleveland

Fifth Week
Leonard Thompson, Detroit — 129 yards (3) vs. Atlanta
James Lofton, Green Bay — 114 yards (8) vs. Cincinnati
Freddie Scott, Detroit — 107 yards (5) vs. Atlanta
Lynn Swann, Pittsburgh — 107 yards (6) vs. Minnesota

Sixth Week
Dwight Clark, San Francisco — 148 yards (8) vs. Dallas
Charlie Joiner, San Diego — 135 yards (8) vs. Oakland
Eddie Lee Ivery, Green Bay — 128 yards (11) vs. Tampa Bay
John Jefferson, San Diego — 114 yards (5) vs. Oakland
Paul Coffman, Green Bay — 109 yards (9) vs. Tampa Bay
Wes Chandler, New Orleans — 106 yards (6) vs. Detroit
Aundra Thompson, Green Bay — 102 yards (7) vs. Tampa Bay

Seventh Week
Charlie Joiner, San Diego — 171 yards (10) vs. N.Y. Giants
Wes Chandler, New Orleans — 140 yards (8) vs. Atlanta
James Scott, Chicago — 140 yards (3) vs. Detroit
James Lofton, Green Bay — 136 yards (8) vs. Cleveland
Harold Jackson, New England — 127 yards (6) vs. Baltimore
Cliff Branch, Oakland — 123 yards (5) vs. Pittsburgh
Theo Bell, Pittsburgh — 114 yards (4) vs. Oakland
Don Bass, Cincinnati — 110 yards (7) vs. Minnesota
John Jefferson, San Diego — 107 yards (5) vs. New York Giants
Sam McCullum, Seattle — 107 yards (5) vs. New York Jets
Drew Pearson, Dallas — 107 yards (8) vs. Philadelphia
Henry Marshall, Kansas City — 103 yards (6) vs. Denver
Jim Smith, Pittsburgh — 102 yards (6) vs. Oakland
Kellen Winslow, San Diego — 102 yards (6) vs. New York Giants

Eighth Week
John Jefferson, San Diego — 160 yards (8) vs. Dallas
Steve Largent, Seattle — 142 yards (4) vs. Oakland
Dave Logan, Cleveland — 131 yards (8) vs. Pittsburgh
Theo Bell, Pittsburgh — 125 yards (4) vs. Cleveland
Roger Carr, Baltimore — 120 yards (9) vs. St. Louis
Drew Hill, Los Angeles — 117 yards (3) vs. Atlanta
Kellen Winslow, San Diego — 110 yards (5) vs. Dallas
Mel Gray, St. Louis — 101 yards (5) vs. Baltimore

Ninth Week
Kellen Winslow, San Diego — 153 yards (9) vs. Cincinnati
Pat Tilley, St. Louis — 145 yards (5) vs. Dallas
Jerry Butler, Buffalo — 122 yards (9) vs. Atlanta
Charlie Smith, Philadelphia — 109 yards (5) vs. Seattle
Gerry Ellis, Green Bay — 106 yards (7) vs. Pittsburgh
Drew Pearson, Dallas — 103 yards (9) vs. St. Louis
Steve Largent, Seattle — 101 yards (6) vs. Philadelphia

Tenth Week
James Lofton, Green Bay — 146 yards (8) vs. San Francisco
Ted Brown, Minnesota — 140 yards (9) vs. Detroit
Wes Chandler, New Orleans — 139 yards (9) vs. Philadelphia
Mike Friede, New York Giants — 137 yards (7) vs. Dallas
Charlie Smith, Philadelphia — 137 yards (9) vs. New Orleans
Jimmie Giles, Tampa Bay — 128 yards (9) vs. Pittsburgh
Charlie Joiner, San Diego — 127 yards (9) vs. Denver
Art Monk, Washington — 124 yards (8) vs. Chicago
Pat Tilley, St. Louis — 120 yards (6) vs. Atlanta
Ike Harris, New Orleans — 119 yards (4) vs. Philadelphia
Mike Barber, Houston — 105 yards (3) vs. New England
Freddie Solomon, San Francisco — 104 yards (5) vs. Green Bay

1981 American Football Conference

Baltimore Colts

American Football Conference
Eastern Division

Team Colors: Royal Blue and White

P.O. Box 2000
Owings Mills, Maryland 21117
Telephone: (301) 356-9600

Club Officials

President-Treasurer: Robert Irsay
Executive Vice President-General Manager:
  Richard Szymanski
Vice President: Harriet Irsay
Vice President-General Counsel: Michael G. Chernoff
Assistant General Manager: Ernie Accorsi
Controller: Elizabeth H. Moses
Director of Player Personnel: Fred Schubach
College Scout: Bob Terpening
Public Relations Director: Walt Gutowski
Assistant Director of Public Relations: Marge Blatt
Marketing Coordinator: Marty Goldman
Promotions Director: Lenny Moore
Special Consultant: Johnny Unitas
Administrative Assistant: Greg Gladyslewski
Ticket Manager: Bill Roberts
Assistant Ticket Manager: Carol Martin
Trainer Emeritus: Ed Block
Head Trainer: John Kasik
Assistant Trainer: John Lopez
Equipment Manager: Rex Patterson

Stadium: Memorial Stadium • **Capacity:** 60,714
  33rd and Ellerslie Streets
  Baltimore, Maryland 21218

Playing Surface: Grass
Training Camp: Goucher College
  Towson, Maryland 21204

1981 SCHEDULE

Preseason

Aug. 8	at New Orleans	7:00
Aug. 15	at New York Giants	8:00
Aug. 22	**Washington**	8:00
Aug. 28	at Seattle	7:30

Regular Season

Sept. 6	at New England	1:00
Sept. 13	**Buffalo**	2:00
Sept. 20	at Denver	2:00
Sept. 27	**Miami**	2:00
Oct. 4	at Buffalo	1:00
Oct. 11	**Cincinnati**	2:00
Oct. 18	**San Diego**	2:00
Oct. 25	at Cleveland	1:00
Nov. 1	at Miami	1:00
Nov. 8	**New York Jets**	4:00
Nov. 15	at Philadelphia	1:00
Nov. 22	**St. Louis**	2:00
Nov. 29	at New York Jets	1:00
Dec. 6	**Dallas**	2:00
Dec. 13	at Washington	1:00
Dec. 20	**New England**	2:00

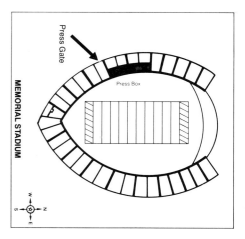

MEMORIAL STADIUM

Press Gate

Press Box

1980 TEAM STATISTICS

	Baltimore	Opp.
Total First Downs	327	338
Rushing	128	140
Passing	174	164
Penalty	25	34
Third Down Efficiency	106/223	100/213
Third Down Percentage	47.5	46.9
Total Net Yards	5206	5546
Total Offensive Plays	1056	1080
Avg. Gain per Play	4.9	5.1
Avg. Gain per Game	325.4	346.6
Net Yards Rushing	2078	2210
Total Rushing Plays	527	574
Avg. Gain per Rush	3.9	3.9
Avg. Gain Rushing per Game	129.9	138.1
Net Yards Passing	3128	3336
Gross Yards Passing	3409	3576
Attempts/Completions	493/272	476/260
Percent Completed	55.2	54.6
Had Intercepted	24	17
Avg. Net Passing per Game	195.5	208.5
Punts/Avg.	84/38.1	72/39.7
Punt Returns/Avg.	26/7.2	49/7.3
Kickoff Returns/Avg.	67/20.6	54/19.7
Interceptions/Avg. Ret.	17/18.2	24/15.8
Penalties/Yards	104/914	98/775
Fumbles/Ball Lost	23/13	32/17
Total Points	355	387
Avg. Points per Game	22.2	24.2
Touchdowns	46	47
Rushing	20	20
Passing	25	21
Returns and Recoveries	1	6
Field Goals	12/23	20/30
Conversions	43/46	45/47
Safeties	0	0

1980 TEAM RECORD

Preseason (2-2)

Baltimore		Opponents
3	Washington	13
17	Green Bay	3
37	New York Giants	20
35	Atlanta	51
92		87

Regular Season (7-9)

Baltimore		Opponents	Att.
17	New York Jets	14	50,777
17	*Pittsburgh	20	54,914
16	Houston	21	47,878
35	*New York Jets	21	33,373
30	Miami	17	50,631
17	Buffalo	12	73,634
21	*New England	37	53,924
10	*St. Louis	17	33,506
31	Kansas City	24	52,383
27	*Cleveland	28	45,369
10	Detroit	9	77,307
21	New England	47	60,994
28	*Buffalo	24	36,184
33	Cincinnati	34	35,651
14	*Miami	24	30,564
28	*Kansas City	38	16,941
355		387	754,030

*Home Game

Score by Periods

	1	2	3	4	OT	Total
Baltimore	55	115	80	105	—	355
Opponents	93	112	85	97	—	387

Attendance

Home 304,775   Away 449,255   Total 754,030
Single game home record, 60,763 (12-24-77)
Single season home record, 418,292 (1968)

1980 INDIVIDUAL STATISTICS

Rushing

	Att	Yds	Avg	LG	TD
Dickey	176	800	4.5	51t	11
Washington	144	502	3.5	17	1
Franklin	83	264	3.2	21	2
Sims	54	186	3.4	13	2
B. Jones	27	175	6.5	19	2
McCauley	35	133	3.8	12	1
Landry	7	26	3.7	14	0
Carr	1	-8	-8.0	-8	0
Baltimore	527	2078	3.9	51t	20
Opponents	574	2210	3.9	27	20

Field Goal Success

Distance	1-19	20-29	30-39	40-49	50 Over
Made-Att.	0-0	5-6	3-8	4-7	0-2

Passing

	Att	Comp	Pct	Yds	TD	Int	LG	Tkld	Rate
B. Jones	446	248	55.6	3134	23	21	51t	34/262	75.5
Landry	47	24	51.1	275	2	3	17	2/19	56.7
Baltimore	493	272	55.2	3409	25	24	51t	36/281	73.5
Opponents	476	260	54.6	3576	21	17	27	30/240	—

Receiving

	No	Yds	Avg	LG	TD
Carr	61	924	15.1	43	5
Washington	51	494	9.7	33	3
Butler	34	574	16.9	42	3
McCauley	34	313	9.2	19	4
Dickey	25	204	8.2	32	2
McCall	18	322	17.9	47	5
Burke	14	185	13.2	19t	3
Franklin	14	112	8.0	16	1
Siani	9	174	19.3	38t	0
Sims	9	64	7.1	13	0
DeRoo	2	34	17.0	18	0
Garry	1	9	9.0	9	0
Baltimore	272	3409	12.5	47	25
Opponents	260	3576	13.8	77	21

Interceptions

	No	Yds	Avg	LG	TD
Laird	5	71	14.2	18	0
Glasgow	4	65	16.3	29	0
Braziel	2	87	43.5	60	0
Anderson	2	35	17.5	18	0
Shiver	1	34	34.0	34t	1
Woods	1	13	13.0	13	0
Ehrmann	1	5	5.0	5	0
Blackwood	1	0	0.0	0	0
Baltimore	17	310	18.2	60	1
Opponents	24	378	15.8	44	1

Punting

	No	Yds	Avg	LG	In 20
Bragg	82	3203	39.1	59	22
Baltimore	84	3203	38.1	59	22
Opponents	72	2860	39.7	66	12

Punt Returns

	No	FC	Yds	Avg	LG	TD
Glasgow	23	15	187	8.1	20	0
Anderson	3	0	1	0.3	1	0
Baltimore	26	15	188	7.2	20	0
Opponents	49	13	357	7.3	56	1

Kickoff Returns

	No	Yds	Avg	LG	TD
Glasgow	33	743	22.5	44	0
Anderson	20	386	19.3	35	0
Dickey	4	86	21.5	28	0
Garry	3	55	18.3	24	0
Blackwood	2	41	20.5	25	0
LaPointe	1	18	18.0	18	0
McCauley	1	18	18.0	18	0
Hart	1	17	17.0	17	0
Sims	1	10	10.0	10	0
Foote	1	9	9.0	9	0
Baltimore	67	1383	20.6	44	0
Opponents	54	1062	19.7	98t	1

Scoring

	TD	TD R	TD P	TD Rt	PAT	FG	TP
Mike-Mayer					43/46	12/23	79
Dickey	13	11	2	0			78
Carr	5	0	5	0			30
McCall	5	0	5	0			30
McCauley	5	1	4	0			30
Washington	4	1	3	0			24
Burke	3	0	3	0			18
Butler	2	0	2	0			12
Franklin	2	2	0	0			12
B. Jones	2	2	0	0			12
Sims	2	2	0	0			12
Landry	1	1	0	0			6
Shiver	1	0	0	1			6
Siani	1	1	0	0			6
Baltimore	46	20	25	1	43/46	12/23	355
Opponents	47	20	21	6	45/47	20/30	387

BALTIMORE RECORD HOLDERS

Individual Records—Single Season

Category	Name	Performance
Rushing (Yds.)	Lydell Mitchell, 1976	1200
Passing (Pct.)	Bert Jones, 1976	60.3
Passing (Yds.)	Johnny Unitas, 1963	3481
Passing (TDs)	Johnny Unitas, 1959	32
Receiving (No.)	Joe Washington, 1979	82
Receiving (Yds.)	Raymond Berry, 1960	1298
Interceptions	Tom Keane, 1953	11
Punting (Avg.)	David Lee, 1966	45.6
Punt Ret. (Avg.)	Wendall Harris, 1964	12.6
Kickoff Ret. (Avg.)	Jim Duncan, 1970	35.4
Field Goals	Jim Martin, 1963	24
Touchdowns (Tot.)	Lenny Moore, 1964	20
Points	Lenny Moore, 1964	120

Team Records—Single Game

Category	Opponent, Date	Performance
Offense		
First Downs	vs. NYJ, 12/15/74	33
Total Points	vs. Buff, 12/12/76	58
Touchdowns	vs. LA, 11/25/56	8
	vs. GB, 11/2/58	8
Total Net Yards	vs. Atl, 11/12/67	595
Net Yards Rushing	vs. GB, 10/28/56	318
Net Yards Passing	vs. Minn, 12/16/62	451
Rushing Attempts	vs. SF, 11/22/59	60
Passing Attempts	vs. NYJ, 12/15/74	54
Interceptions by	vs. Chi Bears, 10/2/60	7
Defense		
Net Yards Allowed	vs. Det, 11/6/54	69
Net Rushing Yards Allowed	vs. Buff, 10/10/71	4
Net Passing Yards Allowed	vs. TB, 10/3/74	13

FIRST PLAYERS SELECTED

Year	Player, College, Position
1968	John Williams, Minnesota, G
1969	Eddie Hinton, Oklahoma, WR
1970	Norman Bulaich, TCU, RB
1971	Leonard Dunlap, North Texas State, DB
1972	Tom Drougas, Oregon, T
1973	Bert Jones, LSU, QB
1974	John Dutton, Nebraska, DE
1975	Ken Huff, North Carolina, G
1976	Ken Novak, Purdue, DT
1977	Randy Burke, Kentucky, WR
1978	Reese McCall, Auburn, TE
1979	Barry Krauss, Alabama, LB
1980	Curtis Dickey, Texas A&M, RB
1981	Randy McMillan, Pittsburgh, RB

COLTS COACHING HISTORY (220-170-6)

1953	Keith Molesworth	3-9-0
1954-62	Weeb Ewbank	60-53-1
1963-69	Don Shula	73-25-4
1970-72	Don McCafferty*	26-11-1
1972	John Sandusky	4-5-0
1973-74	Howard Schnellenberger**	4-13-0
1974	Joe Thomas	2-9-0
1975-79	Ted Marchibroda	41-36-0
1980	Mike McCormack	7-9-0

*Released after five games in 1972
**Released after three games in 1974

BALTIMORE COLTS 1981 VETERAN ROSTER

No.	Name	Pos.	Ht.	Wt.	NFL Exp.	Birth-date	Birthplace	College	Residence	Games in '80
26	Anderson, Kim	CB	5-11	182	2	7/19/57	Pasadena, Calif.	Arizona State	Los Angeles, Calif.	16
41	Bailey, Mark	RB	6-4	237	4	12/13/54	Lynwood, Calif.	Long Beach State	Long Beach, Calif.	0*
63	Barnes, Mike	DT	6-6	251	9	12/24/50	Pittsburgh, Pa.	Miami	Monkton, Md.	16
44	Blackwood, Lyle	S	6-1	188	9	5/2/51	San Antonio, Tex.	Texas Christian	Austin, Tex.	16
4	†Bragg, Mike	P	5-11	186	14	9/26/46	Richmond, Va.	Richmond	Fairfax, Va.	11
47	Braziel, Larry	CB	6-0	195	4	9/25/54	Fort Worth, Tex.	Southern California	Randallstown, Md.	16
84	†Burke, Randy	WR	6-2	190	4	5/26/55	Miami, Fla.	Kentucky	Sparks, Md.	15
80	Butler, Ray	WR	6-3	190	2	6/28/56	Sweeny, Tex.	Southern California	Bay City, Tex.	10
81	Carr, Roger	WR	6-2	193	8	7/1/52	Seminole, Okla.	Louisiana Tech	Cotton Valley, La.	16
72	†Cook, Fred	DE	6-4	252	8	4/15/52	Pascagoula, Miss.	Southern Mississippi	Pascagoula, Miss.	16
87	DeRoo, Brian	WR	6-3	190	3	4/25/56	Redlands, Calif.	Redlands	Redlands, Calif.	0*
27	Dickey, Curtis	RB	6-0	201	2	11/27/56	Madisonville, Tex.	Texas A&M	Bryan, Tex.	16
35	Dixon, Zachary	RB	6-0	200	3	3/5/56	Dorchester, Mass.	Temple	Westville, N.J.	6*
53	Donaldson, Ray	C	6-3	252	2	5/18/58	Rome, Ga.	Georgia	Rome, Ga.	16
76	Ehrmann, Joe	DT	6-4	252	9	3/29/49	Buffalo, N.Y.	Syracuse	Cockeysville, Md.	0*
73	Fernandes, Ron	DE	6-5	256	4	9/11/51	Toronto, Can.	Eastern Michigan	Hampstead, Md.	0*
79	Fields, Greg	DE	6-7	262	3	1/23/55	San Francisco, Calif.	Grambling	San Francisco, Calif.	16
66	Foote, Chris	C	6-3	250	2	12/2/56	Louisville, Ky.	Southern California	Laguna Hills, Calif.	16
38	Franklin, Cleveland	FB	6-1	212	4	4/24/55	Brenham, Tex.	Baylor	Columbia, Md.	13
29	Garry, Ben	RB	6-0	223	3	2/11/56	Hazelhurst, Miss.	Southern Mississippi	Pascagoula, Miss.	3
25	Glasgow, Nesby	S-KR	5-10	185	3	4/15/57	Los Angeles, Calif.	Washington	Redmond, Wash.	16
69	Griffin, Wade	T	6-5	245	5	8/7/54	Winona, Miss.	Mississippi	Winona, Miss.	16
68	Hart, Jeff	T	6-5	265	5	9/10/53	Portland, Ore.	Oregon State	Beaverton, Ore.	16
42	Hatchett, Derrick	CB	5-11	180	2	8/14/58	Bryan, Tex.	Texas	San Antonio, Tex.	16
58	Heimkreiter, Steve	LB	6-2	226	2	6/9/57	Cincinnati, Ohio	Notre Dame	Cincinnati, Ohio	15
62	Huff, Ken	G	6-4	258	7	2/21/53	Hutchinson, Kan.	North Carolina	Glen Arm, Md.	16
90	Johnson, Gary Don	DT	6-4	263	2	6/28/56	Tyler, Tex.	Baylor	Tyler, Tex.	0*
7	Jones, Bert	QB	6-3	209	9	9/7/51	Ruston, La.	Louisiana State	Ruston, La.	15
51	Jones, Ricky	LB	6-1	215	5	3/9/55	Birmingham, Ala.	Tuskegee	Birmingham, Ala.	12
55	Krauss, Barry	LB	6-3	238	3	3/17/57	Pompano Beach, Fla.	Alabama	Birmingham, Ala.	16
40	Laird, Bruce	S	6-1	194	10	5/23/50	Lowell, Mass.	American International	Towson, Md.	15
11	Landry, Greg	QB	6-4	210	14	12/18/46	Nashua, N.H.	Massachusetts	Baltimore, Md.	16
86	McCall, Reese	TE	6-7	235	4	6/15/56	Bessemer, Ala.	Auburn	Randallstown, Md.	16
23	McCauley, Don	RB	6-1	211	11	5/12/49	Garden City, N.Y.	North Carolina	Huntington Bay, N.Y.	16
57	McCreary, Loaird	TE	6-5	235	5	3/15/53	Crawford, Ga.	Tennessee State	Atlanta, Ga.	0*
57	Mendenhall, Ken	C	6-3	238	11	8/11/48	Enid, Okla.	Oklahoma	Enid, Okla.	16
5	Mike-Mayer, Steve	K	6-0	180	7	8/8/47	Budapest, Hungary	Maryland	San Jose, Calif.	16
88	Orvis, Herb	DT	6-4	255	10	10/17/46	Petoskey, Mich.	Colorado	Charlotte, N.C.	16
71	Ozdowski, Mike	DE	6-5	247	4	9/24/55	Parma, Ohio	Virginia	Reisterstown, Md.	15
37	Pinkney, Reggie	S	5-11	187	8	5/27/55	St. Louis, Mo.	East Carolina	Fayetteville, N.C.	16
61	Pratt, Robert	G	6-4	243	8	5/25/51	Richmond, Va.	North Carolina	Richmond, Va.	16
54	Shiver, Sanders	LB	6-2	228	6	2/14/55	Glasden, S.C.	Carson-Newman	Baltimore, Md.	16
56	Simonini, Ed	LB	6-0	206	6	2/24/55	Portsmouth, Va.	Texas A&M	Baltimore, Md.	14
39	Sims, Marvin	FB	6-4	237	2	6/18/57	Columbus, Ga.	Clemson	Phenix City, Ala.	16
52	Smith, Ed	LB	6-2	217	2	5/18/57	Knoxville, Tenn.	Vanderbilt	Signal Mountain, Tenn.	16
59	Woods, Mike	LB	6-2	237	3	1/1/54	Cleveland, Ohio	Cincinnati	Shaker Heights, Ohio	13

*Bailey and Fernandez missed '80 season due to injuries; Dixon played 5 games with Philadelphia, 1 with Baltimore; Johnson active for 3 games but did not play. McCreary last active with N.Y. Giants in '79.

†Option playout; subject to developments.

Traded—Running back Joe Washington to Washington.

Retired—George Kunz, 10-year tackle, 9 games in '80.

Also played with Colts in '80—TE Mack Alston (13 games), DT Jim Krahl (2), TE Ron LaPointe (2), TE Bob Raba (3), WR Mike Siani (10), G Bob Van Duyne (7).

BALTIMORE COLTS 1981 FIRST-YEAR ROSTER

Name	Pos.	Ht.	Wt.	Birth-date	Birthplace	College	Residence	How Acq.
Ariri, Obed	K	5-9	162	4/7/56	Oiverri, Nigeria	Clemson	Pendleton, S.C.	D7
Bowers, Jerry	RB	5-11	205	5/18/58	Lexington, Ky.	Indiana	Chapin, S.C.	FA
Bryant, Trent	CB	5-9	180	8/14/59	Clark City, Ark.	Arkansas	Arkadelphia, Ark.	D10a
Byrd, Eugene (1)	WR	6-0	184	6/7/57	East St. Louis, Ill.	Michigan State	East St. Louis, Ill.	FA
Clemons, Wayne	S	6-1	195	3/19/56	Baltimore, Md.	Salisbury State	Baltimore, Md.	FA
Dark, Frank (1)	CB-S	6-0	180	12/30/53	Richmond, Va.	Virginia Union	Richmond, Va.	FA
Diaz, Arnie	G	6-2	266	12/28/58	Havana, Cuba	Tulane	Tampa, Fla.	FA
Foley, Tim (1)	T	6-6	260	5/30/58	Cincinnati, Ohio	Notre Dame	Cincinnati, Ohio	D2a (80)
Garrett, Mike (1)	P	6-2	182	6/13/57	Atlanta, Ga.	Georgia	Tallapoosa, Ga.	FA
Geathers, Eddie	CB-S	6-1	186	12/9/58	Myrtle Beach, S.C.	Clemson	Myrtle Beach, S.C.	FA
Gerken, Gregg	LB	6-5	238	4/30/59	Denver, Colo.	North Arizona	Denver, Colo.	D10
Gooch, Tim	DE	6-2	241	10/4/58	Corinth, Miss.	Kentucky	Hawesville, Ky.	D9
Green, Bubba	DT	6-4	278	9/30/57	Cape May, N.J.	North Carolina State	Woodbine, N.J.	D6
Hartwig, Dan (1)	QB	6-4	215	1/19/57	Berkeley, Calif.	California-Lutheran	Walnut Creek, Calif.	FA
McMillan, Randy	FB	6-1	226	12/17/58	Havre de Grace, Md.	Pittsburgh	Jarrettsville, Md.	D1
Moore, Jimmy (1)	G	6-4	271	1/28/57	Pittsburgh, Pa.	Ohio State	Reisterstown, Md.	D6 (79)
Newhall, Forrest (1)	TE	6-3	235	4/9/58	Norfolk, Va.	Virginia	Virginia Beach, Va.	FA
Ordonez, Ish	K	5-6	157	7/11/59	Mexico City, Mex.	Arkansas	Carson, Calif.	FA
Pierce, Kurt	G	6-2	263	1/24/59	Washington, D.C.	Virginia	Rockville, Md.	FA
Powell, Delbert	WR	5-11	188	2/24/58	Elizabeth City, N.C.	North Carolina	Carrboro, N.C.	FA
Scoggins, Eric	LB	6-3	215	1/23/59	Inglewood, Calif.	Southern California	Inglewood, Calif.	D12
Sherwin, Tim	TE	6-5	235	5/4/58	Watervliet, N.Y.	Boston College	Watervliet, N.Y.	D4
Shula, Dave	WR	5-11	183	3/12/59	Lexington, Ky.	Dartmouth	Miami Lakes, Fla.	FA
Sims, Dave	P	6-3	220	2/2/59	Albany, Ga.	Clemson	Jonesboro, Ga.	FA
Sitton, Ken	S	6-3	200	8/24/58	Marshall, Tex.	Oklahoma	Marshall, Tex.	D8
Smith, Holden	WR	6-2	190	11/5/58	San Jose, Calif.	California	Los Gatos, Calif.	D11
Snodgrass, Richard (1)	K	6-0	180	12/9/56	Pittsburgh, Pa.	Slippery Rock State	Butler, Pa.	FA
Stepney, Sam (1)	LB	6-2	230	5/18/57	Plainfield, N.J.	Boston University	Kansas City, Mo.	D8a
Taylor, Hosea	DT	6-5	265	12/3/58	Longview, Tex.	Houston	Hattiesburg, Miss.	D1a
Thompson, Donnell	DT	6-5	257	10/27/58	Lumberton, N.C.	North Carolina	Lumberton, N.C.	D3
Van Divier, Randy	T	6-5	276	6/5/58	Anaheim, Calif.	Washington	Mercer Island, Wash.	FA
Venuto, Jay	QB	6-1	195	2/5/58	Salem, N.J.	Wake Forest	Salem, N.J.	FA
Wilkerson, Daryl (1)	DT	6-4	260	9/25/58	Houston, Tex.	Houston	Fort Ord, Calif.	FA

Players who report to an NFL team for the first time are designated on rosters as rookies (R). If a player reported to an NFL training camp in a previous year but was not on the active squad for three or more regular season or postseason games, he is listed on the first-year roster and designated by a (1). Thereafter, a player who is on the active squad for three or more regular season games is credited with an additional year of playing experience.

COACHING STAFF

Head Coach, Mike McCormack

Pro Career: Named seventh head coach in club's history on January 18, 1980. Starts second season as Colts head coach after compiling 7-9 mark last year. Began pro coaching career in 1964 as Washington Redskins offensive line coach. He remained there until 1972 when he became head coach of the Philadelphia Eagles, where he compiled a 16-25-1 record in three seasons, including a 7-7 mark in 1974. Following his stay in Philadelphia, joined the Cincinnati Bengals staff as offensive line coach in 1975 and served in that position until taking over the Baltimore Colts. Was number-one draft pick of the Colts (then New York Yanks) in 1951. Was involved in 15-player trade in 1954 that sent him to Cleveland Browns, where he played for nine seasons. He played middle guard before switching to tackle in 1955. Earned Pro Bowl honors four times and played in three NFL championship games (1954, 1955, and 1957). Career record: 23-34-1.

Background: Played guard and tackle at Kansas from 1948-50. Earned all Big-Seven honors and was captain of the West squad in 1951 East-West All Star game. Attended De La Salle High School in Kansas City. Spent 1952-53 in the army.

Personal: Born June 21, 1930 in Chicago, Ill. Mike and his wife, Ann, live in Baltimore and have four children—Molly, Colleen, Mike, and Timothy.

ASSISTANT COACHES

Dick Bielski, receivers; born September 7, 1932, Baltimore, lives in Timonium, Md. Fullback-kicker Maryland 1951, 1956-59, Tennessee 1954-55, Detroit 1960-64 (head coach). Tulane 1965. Pro coach: Dallas Cowboys 1960-61, Baltimore Colts 1962-63. Pro coach: Baltimore Colts 1964-72, Washington Redskins 1973-76, rejoined Colts 1977.

George Boutselis, special teams-tight ends; born March 16, 1940, Harrisburg, Pa., lives in Baltimore. Quarterback North Carolina 1959-62. No pro playing experience. College coach: North Carolina 1963-66, Cincinnati 1967-68, Maryland 1969-71, Iowa State 1972, Virginia 1973. Pro coach: Charlotte Hornets (WFL) 1974, Colts since 1975.

John Idzik, offensive backfield; born June 25, 1928, Philadelphia, Pa., lives in Baltimore. Back Maryland 1947-51. No pro playing experience. College coach: Maryland 1951, 1956-59, Tennessee 1954-55, Detroit 1960-64 (head coach). Tulane 1965. Pro coach: Miami Dolphins 1966-69, Baltimore Colts 1970-72, Philadelphia Eagles 1973-76, New York Jets 1977-79, rejoined Colts in 1980.

Ed Khayat, defensive line; born September 14, 1935, Moss Point, Miss., lives in Hunt Valley, Md. Lineman Millsaps 1953, Perkinston JC 1954, Tulane 1955-56. Pro lineman Washington Redskins 1957, 1962-63, Philadelphia Eagles 1958-61, 1964-65, Boston Patriots, 1966. Pro coach: New Orleans Saints 1967-70, Philadelphia Eagles 1971-72 (head coach), Detroit Lions 1973-74, Atlanta Falcons 1975-76, fifth year with Colts.

Clyde Powers, special assignments; born August 19, 1951, Pascagoula, Miss., lives in Baltimore. Safety Oklahoma 1971-73. Pro defensive back N.Y. Giants 1974-77, Kansas City Chiefs 1978. Pro coach: Joined Colts in 1980.

John Symank, defensive backs; born August 31, 1935, La Grange, Tex., lives in Baltimore. Back Florida 1955-56. Pro defensive back Green Bay Packers 1957-62, St. Louis Cardinals 1963. College coach: Tulane 1964, Virginia 1965, Northern Arizona 1969-70, Texas-Arlington 1971-73. Pro coach: Atlanta Falcons 1966-68, New York Giants 1974-78, third year with Colts.

Chuck Weber, defensive coordinator-linebackers; born March 26, 1930, Philadelphia, lives in Baltimore. Linebacker West Chester State 1949-53. Pro linebacker Cleveland Browns 1955-56, Chicago Cardinals 1956-58, Philadelphia Eagles 1959-61. Pro coach: Boston Patriots 1964-67, San Diego Chargers 1968-69, Cincinnati Bengals 1970-75, St. Louis Cardinals 1976-77, Cleveland Browns 1978-79, second year with Colts.

Ray Wietecha, offensive line; born November 4, 1928, East Chicago, Ind., lives in Baltimore. Center Northwestern 1948-50. Pro center New York Giants 1953-62. Pro coach: Los Angeles Rams 1963-64, Green Bay Packers 1970-75, St. Louis Cardinals 1976-77, New York Giants 1972-76, Buffalo Bills 1977, second year with Colts.

NOTES

Buffalo Bills

**American Football Conference
Eastern Division**

Team Colors: Scarlet Red,
Royal Blue, and White

One Bills Drive
Orchard Park, New York 14127
Telephone: (716) 648-1800

Club Officials
President: Ralph C. Wilson, Jr.
Vice President in Charge of Administration:
Stew Barber
Vice President: Patrick J. McGroder, Jr.
Vice President in Charge of Football Operations-
Head Coach: Chuck Knox
Director of College Scouting: Norm Pollom
Director of Pro Scouting: Doug Hafner
Vice President-Public Relations: L. Budd Thalman
Ticket Director: Jim Cipriano
Assistant Public Relations Director: Mike Shaw
Trainers: Ed Abramoski, Bud Tice
Equipment Manager: Chuck Ziober

Stadium: Rich Stadium • **Capacity:** 80,020
One Bills Drive
Orchard Park, New York 14127

Playing Surface: AstroTurf

Training Camp: Fredonia State University College
Fredonia, New York 14063

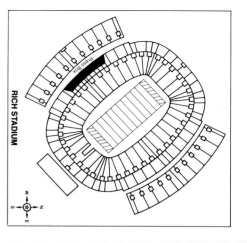

RICH STADIUM

1981 SCHEDULE

Preseason

Aug. 8	**Detroit**	6:00
Aug. 15	**Cleveland**	6:00
Aug. 22	at Cleveland	7:30
Aug. 28	at San Diego	6:00

Regular Season

Sept. 6	**New York Jets**	4:00
Sept. 13	at Baltimore	2:00
Sept. 17	**Philadelphia** (Thursday)	8:30
Sept. 27	at Cincinnati	1:00
Oct. 4	**Baltimore**	9:00
Oct. 12	**Miami** (Monday)	9:00
Oct. 18	at New York Jets	1:00
Oct. 25	**Denver**	1:00
Nov. 1	**Cleveland**	1:00
Nov. 9	at Dallas (Monday)	8:00
Nov. 15	at St. Louis	12:00
Nov. 22	**New England**	1:00
Nov. 29	**Washington**	1:00
Dec. 6	at San Diego	1:00
Dec. 13	at New England	1:00
Dec. 19	at Miami (Saturday)	4:00

1980 TEAM STATISTICS

	Buffalo	Opp.
Total First Downs	317	251
Rushing	134	109
Passing	157	120
Penalty	26	22
Third Down Efficiency	127/240	91/217
Third Down Percentage	52.9	41.9
Total Net Yards	4972	4101
Total Offensive Plays	1084	952
Avg. Gain per Play	4.6	4.3
Avg. Gain per Game	310.8	256.3
Net Yards Rushing	2222	1819
Total Rushing Plays	603	486
Avg. Gain per Rush	3.7	3.7
Avg. Gain Rushing per Game	138.9	113.7
Lost Attempting to Pass	20/186	33/279
Gross Yards Passing	2936	2561
Attempts/Completions	461/262	433/240
Percent Completed	56.8	55.4
Had Intercepted	19	24
Net Passing per Game	171.9	142.6
Punts/Avg.	74/38.2	82/39.3
Punt Returns/Avg.	39/6.6	34/6.0
Kickoff Returns/Avg.	47/17.6	52/20.2
Interceptions/Avg. Ret.	24/13.9	19/10.2
Penalties/Yards	90/731	97/805
Fumbles/Ball Lost	36/22	37/20
Total Points	320	260
Avg. Points per Game	20.0	16.3
Touchdowns	40	31
Rushing	17	14
Passing	20	15
Returns and Recoveries	3	2
Field Goals	13/23	15/20
Conversions	37/40	29/31
Safeties	2	0

1980 TEAM RECORD

Preseason (1-3)

Buffalo		Opponents
9	Philadelphia	24
17	Detroit	24
35	Green Bay	0
7	Houston	24
47		72

Regular Season (11-5)

Buffalo		Opponents	Att.
17	*Miami	7	79,598
20	New York Jets	10	65,315
35	New Orleans	26	51,154
24	*Oakland	7	77,259
26	San Diego	24	51,982
12	*Baltimore	17	73,634
14	Miami	17	41,636
31	*New England	13	75,092
14	*Atlanta	30	57,959
31	New York Jets	24	45,677
28	Cincinnati	0	40,836
24	*Pittsburgh	13	79,659
10	Baltimore	28	36,184
10	*Los Angeles (OT)	7	77,133
24	New England	24	58,324
18	San Francisco	13	37,476
320		260	948,918

*Home Game   (OT) Overtime

Score by Periods

Buffalo	54	104	55	104	3	— 320
Opponents	50	87	72	51	0	— 260

Attendance

Home 585,649   Away 363,269   Total 948,918
Single game home record, 79,791 (9-16-74)
Single season home record, 585,647 (1980)

1980 INDIVIDUAL STATISTICS

Rushing

	Att	Yds	Avg	LG	TD
Cribbs	306	1185	3.9	48	11
Brown	153	559	3.7	34t	3
Leaks	67	219	3.3	15	2
Hooks	25	118	4.7	25	1
Ferguson	31	65	2.1	15	0
Miller	12	35	2.9	6	0
Manucci	3	29	9.7	17	0
Butler	1	18	18.0	18	0
Brammer	1	8	8.0	8	0
Humm	1	5	5.0	5	0
Jessie	1	-9	-9.0	-9	0
Cater	2	-10	-5.0	-1	0
Buffalo	603	2222	3.7	48	17
Opponents	486	1819	3.7	47	14

Field Goal Success

Distance	1-19	20-29	30-39	40-49	50 Over
Made-Att.	0-0	4-4	4-9	5-9	0-1

Passing

	Att	Comp	Pct	Yds	TD	Int	Tkld	Rate
Ferguson	439	251	57.2	2805	20	18	13/129	74.6
Humm	14	4	28.6	39	0	1	2/9	10.0
Cater	1	1	100.0	0	0	0	0/0	—
Cribbs	1	1	100.0	13	0	0	0/0	—
Manucci	6	5	83.3	64	0	0	5/48	73.2
Buffalo	461	262	56.8	2936	20	19	20/186	
Opponents	433	240	55.4	2561	15	24	33/279	

Receiving

	No	Yds	Avg	LG	TD
Butler	57	832	14.6	69	6
Cribbs	52	415	8.0	21t	1
Lewis	40	648	16.2	31t	6
Brown	27	137	5.1	20	0
Brammer	26	283	10.9	36	4
Hooks	23	179	7.8	26	0
Gant	12	181	15.1	48	1
Leaks	8	57	7.1	18	0
Piccone	7	82	11.7	18	0
Jessie	4	56	14.0	20	1
Fergerson	3	41	13.7	19	0
Miller	3	25	8.3	15	0
Buffalo	262	2936	11.2	69	20
Opponents	240	2561	10.7	56	15

Interceptions

	No	Yds	Avg	LG	TD
Freeman	7	107	15.3	47t	1
Nixon	5	81	16.2	50t	0
Simpson	4	36	9.0	14	0
Romes	2	41	20.5	30	0
Robertson	2	39	19.5	39	0
Haslett	2	30	15.0	17	0
Clark	1	0	0.0	0	0
White	1	0	0.0	0	0
Buffalo	24	334	13.9	50t	2
Opponents	19	193	10.2	48t	1

Punting

	No	Yds	Avg	In 20	LG
Cater	73	2828	38.7	12	61
Buffalo	74	2828	38.2	12	61
Opponents	82	3226	39.3	21	61

Punt Returns

	No	FC	Yds	Avg	LG	TD
Cribbs	29	7	154	5.3	16	0
Hooks	8	2	90	11.3	17	0
Piccone	2	3	15	7.5	8	0
Buffalo	39	12	259	6.6	17	0
Opponents	34	6	204	6.0	21	0

Kickoff Returns

	No	Yds	Avg	LG	TD
Miller	16	303	18.9	43	0
Brown	10	181	18.1	25	0
Owens	8	157	19.6	29	0
Hooks	7	109	15.6	35	0
Keating	3	38	12.7	16	0
Cribbs	2	39	19.5	20	0
Vogler	1	0	0.0	0	0
Buffalo	47	827	17.6	43	0
Opponents	52	1051	20.2	44	0

Scoring

	TD	TD R	TD P	TD Rt	PAT	FG	TP
Mike-Mayer					37/39	13/23	76
Cribbs	12	11	1	0			72
Butler	6	0	6	0			36
Lewis	6	0	6	0			36
Brammer	4	0	4	0			24
Brown	3	3	0	0			18
Leaks	3	2	1	0			18
Freeman	1	0	0	1			6
Gant	1	0	1	0			6
Hooks	1	1	0	0			6
Jessie	1	0	1	0			6
Nixon	1	0	0	1			6
Sanford	1	0	0	1			6
Johnson					(Safety)		2
Simpson					(Safety)		2
Buffalo	40	17	20	3	37/40	13/23	320
Opponents	31	14	15	2	29/31	15/20	260

BUFFALO RECORD HOLDERS

Individual Records—Single Season

Category	Name	Performance
Rushing (Yds.)	O.J. Simpson, 1973	2003
Passing (Pct.)	Joe Ferguson, 1980	57.2
Passing (Yds.)	Joe Ferguson, 1979	3572
Passing (TDs)	Joe Ferguson, 1975	25
Receiving (No.)	Bill Miller, 1963	69
Receiving (Yds.)	Elbert Dubenion, 1964	1139
Interceptions	Billy Atkins, 1961	10
	Tom Janik, 1967	10
Punting (Avg.)	Billy Atkins, 1961	44.5
Punt Ret. (Avg.)	Keith Moody, 1977	13.1
Kickoff Ret. (Avg.)	Ed Rutkowski, 1963	30.2
Field Goals	Pete Gogolak, 1965	28
Touchdowns (Tot.)	O.J. Simpson, 1975	23
Points	O.J. Simpson, 1975	138

Team Records—Single Game

Category	Opponent, Date	Performance
Offense		
First Downs	vs. Den, 10/5/75	29
Total Points	vs. Mia, 9/18/66	58
Touchdowns	vs. Mia, 9/18/66	8
Total Net Yards	vs. Hou, 10/11/65	565
Net Yards Rushing	vs. NYG, 11/26/78	366
Net Yards Passing	vs. Hou, 10/11/65	405
Rushing Attempts	vs. KC, 10/29/73	65
Passing Attempts	vs. Bos, 11/15/64	53
Interceptions by	vs. Bos, 12/9/67	6
	vs. LA Chargers, 11/20/60	6
	vs. Den, 11/19/61	6
	vs. Hou, 9/9/62	6
Defense		
Net Yards Allowed	vs. KC, 10/29/73	104
Net Rushing Yards Allowed	vs. LA Chargers, 11/20/60	11
Net Passing Yards Allowed	vs. Balt, 10/13/74	1

FIRST PLAYERS SELECTED

Year	Player, College, Position
1969	O.J. Simpson, So. California, RB
1970	Al Cowlings, So. California, DE
1971	J.D. Hill, Arizona State, WR
1972	Walt Patulski, Notre Dame, DE
1973	Paul Seymour, Michigan, TE
1974	Reuben Gant, Oklahoma State, TE
1975	Tom Ruud, Nebraska, LB
1976	Mario Clark, Oregon, DB
1977	Phil Dokes, Oklahoma State, DT (2)
1978	Terry Miller, Oklahoma State, RB
1979	Tom Cousineau, Ohio State, LB
1980	Jim Ritcher, North Carolina State, C
1981	Booker Moore, Penn State, RB

BILLS COACHING HISTORY
(129-169-8)

1962-65	Lou Saban	38-19-3
1966-68	Joe Collier*	13-17-1
1968	Harvey Johnson	1-10-1
1969-70	John Rauch	7-20-1
1971	Harvey Johnson	1-13-0
1972-76	Lou Saban**	32-28-1
1976-77	Jim Ringo	3-20-0
1978-80	Chuck Knox	23-26-0

*Released after two games in 1968
**Resigned after five games in 1976

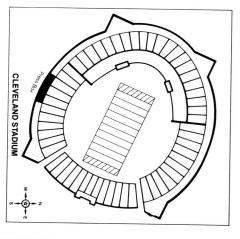

CLEVELAND STADIUM

Cleveland Browns

American Football Conference
Central Division

Team Colors: Seal Brown,
Orange, and White

Tower B
Cleveland Stadium
Cleveland, Ohio 44114
Telephone: (216) 696-5555

Club Officials

President: Arthur B. Modell
Assistant to the President: Paul Warfield
Vice President and General Counsel: James N. Bailey
Vice President-Director of Public Relations: Nate Wallack
Treasurer-Controller: Gordon Helms
Director of Player Personnel: Bill Davis
Draft Coordinator: Tommy Prothro
Director of Operations: Denny Lynch
Director of Publicity: Kevin Byrne
Director of Programs and Promotions: John Minco
Director of Pro Scouting: Alan Webb
Director of College Scouting: Mike Nixon
Special Scouts: Ben Bedini, Chuck Garcia, Bill Long,
Tim Miner, Al Satterfield
Film Coordinator: Ed Ulinski
Ticket Director: Bill Breit
Trainer: Leo Murphy
Equipment Manager: Charles Cusick

Stadium: Cleveland Stadium • **Capacity:** 80,322
West 3rd Street
Cleveland, Ohio 44114

Playing Surface: Grass
Training Camp: Kent State University
Kent, Ohio 44242

1981 SCHEDULE

Preseason

Aug. 1	vs. Atlanta at Canton, Ohio (HOF)	3:30
Aug. 8	**Pittsburgh**	7:30
Aug. 15	at Buffalo	6:00
Aug. 22	**Buffalo**	7:30
Aug. 29	at Green Bay	7:00

Regular Season

Sept. 7	**San Diego** (Monday)	9:00
Sept. 13	**Houston**	1:00
Sept. 20	at Cincinnati	1:00
Sept. 27	**Atlanta**	1:00
Oct. 4	at Los Angeles	1:00
Oct. 11	at Pittsburgh	1:00
Oct. 18	**New Orleans**	1:00
Oct. 25	**Baltimore**	1:00
Nov. 1	at Buffalo	1:00
Nov. 8	at Denver	2:00
Nov. 15	at San Francisco	1:00
Nov. 22	**Pittsburgh**	1:00
Nov. 29	**Cincinnati**	1:00
Dec. 3	at Houston (Thursday)	8:00
Dec. 12	**New York Jets** (Saturday)	12:30
Dec. 20	at Seattle	1:00

Scoring

	TD	TD R	TD P	TD Rt	PAT	FG	TP
Cockroft					39/44	16/26	87
Hill	6	0	6	0			36
M. Pruitt	6	6	0	0			36
White	6	5	1	0			36
G. Pruitt	5	0	5	0			30
Feacher	4	0	4	0			24
Logan	4	0	4	0			24
Rucker	4	0	4	0			24
Miller	3	3	0	0			18
Newsome	3	0	3	0			18
Wright	3	0	3	0			18
Sipe	1	1	0	0			6
Cleveland	45	15	30	0	39/45	16/26	357
Opponents	37	12	23	2	32/37	18/29	310

1980 INDIVIDUAL STATISTICS

Rushing

	Att	Yds	Avg	LG	TD
M. Pruitt	249	1034	4.2	56t	6
White	86	279	3.2	16	5
Miller	28	139	5.0	50	3
G. Pruitt	40	117	2.9	19	1
Sipe	20	55	2.8	24	0
D. Hall	2	26	13.0	19	0
Newsome	2	13	6.5	9	0
Hill	1	11	11.0	11	0
Adams	2	7	3.5	15	0
McDonald	3	-2	-0.7	0	0
Evans	3	-6	-2.0	0	0
Cleveland	436	1673	3.8	56t	15
Opponents	485	1761	3.6	32	12

Field Goal Success

Distance	1-19	20-29	30-39	40-49	50 Over
Made-Att.	0-0	6-7	5-7	5-9	0-3

Passing

	Att	Comp	Pct	Yds	TD	Int	LG	Tkld	Rate
Sipe	554	337	60.8	4132	30	14	56t	23/217	91.4
Cleveland	554	337	60.8	4132	30	14	56t	23/217	91.4
Opponents	536	336	62.7	4089	23	22	32	32/224	—

Receiving

	No	Yds	Avg	LG	TD
M. Pruitt	63	471	7.5	28	0
Rucker	52	768	14.8	45	4
Logan	51	822	16.1	65	4
Newsome	51	594	11.6	44	3
G. Pruitt	50	444	8.9	43	5
Hill	27	383	14.2	50	6
White	17	153	9.0	31t	1
Feacher	10	244	24.4	55t	4
Adams	8	165	20.6	39	0
Wright	3	62	20.7	39t	3
Oden	3	18	6.0	7	0
Miller	2	8	4.0	8	0
Cleveland	337	4132	12.3	65	30
Opponents	336	4089	12.2	72	23

Interceptions

	No	Yds	Avg	LG	TD
Bolton	6	62	10.3	28	0
Burrell	5	51	10.2	29	0
Darden	2	42	21.0	23	0
R. L. Jackson	2	15	7.5	9	0
Scott	2	14	7.0	9	0
C. Hall	2	3	1.5	3	0
Davis	1	70	70.0	53	1
Matthews	1	6	6.0	6	0
Johnson	1	3	3.0	3	0
Cleveland	22	266	12.1	53	0
Opponents	14	270	19.3	93t	2

Punting

	No	Yds	Avg	LG	In 20	TD
Evans	66	2530	38.3	56	12	0
Cleveland	66	2530	38.3	56	12	0
Opponents	63	2356	37.4	62	23	0

Punt Returns

	No	FC	Yds	Avg	LG	TD
Wright	29	4	129	4.4	15	0
D. Hall	6	3	41	6.8	14	0
Cleveland	35	7	170	4.9	15	0
Opponents	38	6	245	6.4	15	0

Kickoff Returns

	No	Yds	Avg	LG	TD
Wright	25	576	23.0	50	0
D. Hall	32	691	21.6	40	0
Miller	2	22	11.0	13	0
White	1	20	20.0	20	0
Flint	1	0	0.0	0	0
R. E. Jackson	1	0	0.0	0	0
Darden	1	-1	-1.0	-1	0
Cleveland	63	1308	20.8	50	0
Opponents	71	1018	14.3	31	0

CLEVELAND RECORD HOLDERS

Individual Records—Single Season

Category	Name	Performance
Rushing (Yds.)	Jim Brown, 1963	1863
Passing (Pct.)	Otto Graham, 1953	64.7
Passing (Yds.)	Brian Sipe, 1980	4132
Passing (TDs)	Brian Sipe, 1980	30
Receiving (No.)	Mike Pruitt, 1980	63
Receiving (Yds.)	Paul Warfield, 1968	1067
Interceptions	Thom Darden, 1978	10
Punting (Avg.)	Gary Collins, 1965	46.7
Punt Ret. (Avg.)	Leroy Kelly, 1965	15.6
Kickoff Ret. (Avg.)	Bo Scott, 1969	28.9
Field Goals	Lou Groza, 1953	23
Touchdowns (Tot.)	Jim Brown, 1965	21
Points	Jim Brown, 1965	126

Team Records—Single Game

Category	Opponent, Date	Performance
Offense		
First Downs	vs. KC, 10/30/77	34
Total Points	vs. NYG, 12/6/53	62
	vs. Wash, 11/7/54	62
Touchdowns	vs. NYG, 12/6/53	8
	vs. Wash, 11/7/54	8
Total Net Yards	vs. Chi Bears, 11/25/51	550
Net Yards Rushing	vs. Pitt, 10/29/50	338
Net Yards Passing	vs. Pitt, 10/4/52	401
Rushing Attempts	vs. SF, 10/2/55	60
Passing Attempts	vs. Pitt, 10/4/52	49
Interceptions by	vs. Chi Bears, 12/11/60	7
Defense		
Net Yards Allowed	vs. Wash, 11/7/54	64
Net Rushing Yards Allowed	vs. NYG, 11/28/54	4
Net Passing Yards Allowed	vs. Phil, 11/18/56	3

FIRST PLAYERS SELECTED

Year	Player, College, Position
1964	Paul Warfield, Ohio State, WR
1965	Walter Johnson, Cal State-L.A., DT (2)
1966	Milt Morin, Massachusetts, TE
1967	Bob Matheson, Duke, LB
1968	Marvin Upshaw, Trinity, Tex., DT-DE
1969	Ron Johnson, Michigan, RB
1970	Mike Phipps, Purdue, QB
1971	Clarence Scott, Kansas State, CB
1972	Thom Darden, Michigan, DB
1973	Steve Holden, Arizona State, WR
1974	Billy Corbett, Johnson C. Smith, T (2)
1975	Mack Mitchell, Houston, DE
1976	Mike Pruitt, Purdue, RB
1977	Robert Jackson, Texas A&M, LB
1978	Clay Matthews, Southern California, LB
1979	Willis Adams, Houston, WR
1980	Charles White, Southern California, RB
1981	Hanford Dixon, Southern Mississippi, DB

BROWNS COACHING HISTORY
(270-158-9)

1950-62	Paul Brown	115-49-5
1963-70	Blanton Collier	79-38-2
1971-74	Nick Skorich	30-26-2
1975-77	Forrest Gregg*	18-23-0
1977	Dick Modzelewski	0-1-0
1978-80	Sam Rutigliano	28-21-0

*Released after 13 games in 1977

1980 TEAM STATISTICS

	Cleveland	Opp.
Total First Downs	336	340
Rushing	102	105
Passing	207	197
Penalty	27	38
Third Down Efficiency	98/207	105/220
Third Down Percentage	47.3	47.7
Total Net Yards	5588	5626
Total Offensive Plays	1013	1053
Avg. Gain per Play	5.5	5.3
Avg. Gain per Game	349.3	351.6
Net Yards Rushing	1673	1761
Total Rushing Plays	436	485
Avg. Gain per Rush	3.8	3.6
Avg. Gain Rushing per Game	104.6	110.1
Net Yards Passing	3915	3865
Lost Attempting to Pass	23/217	32/224
Gross Yards Passing	4132	4089
Attempts/Completions	554/337	536/336
Percent Completed	60.8	62.7
Had Intercepted	14	22
Avg. Net Passing per Game	244.7	241.6
Punts/Avg.	66/38.3	63/37.4
Kickoff Returns/Avg.	35/4.9	38/6.4
Interceptions/Avg. Ret.	63/20.8	71/14.3
Penalties/Yards	117/1042	96/766
Fumbles/Ball Lost	24/14	23/10
Total Points	357	310
Avg. Points per Game	22.3	19.4
Touchdowns	45	37
Rushing	15	12
Passing	30	23
Returns and Recoveries	0	2
Field Goals	16/26	18/29
Conversions	39/45	32/37
Safeties	0	1

1980 TEAM RECORD

Preseason (1-3)

Cleveland		Opponents
0	Kansas City	42
3	Washington	12
33	Chicago	31
16	Minnesota	38
52		123

Regular Season (11-5)

Cleveland		Opponents	Att.
17	New England	34	49,222
7	*Houston	16	79,438
20	*Kansas City	13	63,614
34	Tampa Bay	27	65,540
16	*Denver	19	81,065
27	Seattle	3	61,366
26	Green Bay	21	75,540
27	*Pittsburgh	26	79,095
27	*Chicago	21	83,224
28	Baltimore	27	45,369
13	Pittsburgh	16	54,563
31	*Cincinnati	7	79,253
17	Houston	14	51,514
17	*New York Jets	14	78,454
23	Minnesota	28	42,202
27	Cincinnati	24	50,058
357		310	1,039,517

*Home Game

Score by Periods

Cleveland	41	134	84	98	—	357
Opponents	32	69	109	100	—	310

Attendance

Home 619,683   Away 419,834   Total 1,039,517

Single game home record, 85,703 (9-21-70)
Single season home record, 619,683 (1980)

CLEVELAND BROWNS 1981 VETERAN ROSTER

No.	Name	Pos.	Ht.	Wt.	NFL Exp.	Birth-date	Birthplace	College	Residence	Games in '80
80	Adams, Willis	WR	6-2	194	3	8/22/56	Houston, Tex.	Houston	Houston, Tex.	16
77	Alzado, Lyle	DE	6-3	250	11	4/3/49	Brooklyn, N.Y.	Yankton	Brentwood, Calif.	16
52	Ambrose, Dick	LB	6-0	228	7	1/17/53	New Rochelle, N.Y.	Virginia	North Ridgeville, Ohio	16
24	Beamon, Autry	S	6-1	190	7	4/16/50	Terrell, Tex.	East Texas State	Seattle, Wash.	13
28	Bolton, Ron	CB	6-2	170	10	11/22/50	Petersburg, Va.	Norfolk State	Cleveland, Ohio	16
91	Bradley, Henry	DT	6-2	260	3	9/4/53	St. Joseph, La.	Alcorn State	San Diego, Calif.	16
49	Burrell, Clinton	S	6-1	192	3	9/4/56	Franklin, La.	Louisiana State	Berea, Ohio	16
12	Cockroft, Don	K	6-1	195	14	2/6/45	Cheyenne, Wyo.	Adams State	Lake George, Colo.	16
53	Cowher, Bill	LB	6-3	225	2	5/8/57	Pittsburgh, Pa.	North Carolina State	Berea, Ohio	16
93	Crews, Ron	DT	6-1	256	2	10/9/56	Springfield, Ill.	Nevada-Las Vegas	Columbia, Mo.	15
27	Darden, Thom	S	6-3	193	10	8/28/50	Sandusky, Ohio	Michigan	Beachwood, Ohio	16
21	Davis, Oliver	CB	6-2	205	5	8/29/54	Columbus, Ohio	Tennessee State	Bedford Heights, Ohio	16
64	DeLamielleure, Joe	G	6-3	245	9	3/16/51	Detroit, Mich.	Michigan State	Birmingham, Mich.	16
54	DeLeone, Tom	C	6-2	248	10	7/30/50	Kent, Ohio	Ohio State	Medina, Ohio	16
73	Dieken, Doug	T	6-5	252	11	2/12/49	Streator, Ill.	Illinois	Bay Village, Ohio	16
83	Feacher, Rickey	WR	5-10	174	6	9/2/54	Crystal River, Fla.	Mississippi Valley	Warrensville Heights, Ohio	15
20	Flint, Judson	CB	6-0	201	2	7/9/59	Judson, Pa.	Memphis State	Farrell, Pa.	16
94	Franks, Elvis	DE	6-4	238	2	1/2/57	San Antonio, Tex.	Morgan State	Beachwood, Ohio	16
86	Fulton, Dan	WR	6-2	186	3	2/11/54	Baltimore, Md.	Nebraska-Omaha	Omaha, Neb.	0*
50	Goode, Don	LB	6-2	230	12	12/6/51	Charlotte, N.C.	Kansas	Houston, Tex.	15
59	Hall, Charlie	LB	6-3	235	11	2/12/48	Houston, Tex.	Houston	Yoakum, Tex.	14
26	Hall, Dino	RB-KR	5-7	165	3	8/13/50	Scranton, Pa.	Glassboro State	Fayetteville, N.Y.	16
90	Harris, Marshall	DE	6-6	261	2	3/16/51	Atlantic City, N.J.	Texas Christian	Pleasantville, N.J.	14
35	†Hill, Calvin	RB	6-4	227	12	1/2/47	Baltimore, Md.	Yale	Parma, Ohio	0*
68	Jackson, Robert E.	G	6-5	260	6	6/21/53	San Antonio, Tex.	Duke	Reston, Va.	16
56	Jackson, Robert L.	LB	6-1	230	5	12/2/55	Houston, Tex.	Texas A&M	Bay Village, Ohio	2
10	Jacobs, Dave	K	5-7	155	2	6/21/57	Scranton, Pa.	Syracuse	Warrensville Heights, Ohio	0*
48	Johnson, Lawrence	CB	6-1	204	3	7/15/57	Gary, Ind.	Wisconsin	Gary, Ind.	16
85	Logan, Dave	WR	6-3	216	6	7/30/54	Fargo, N.D.	Colorado	Lakewood, Colo.	16
57	Matthews, Clay	LB	6-4	230	4	3/15/56	Palo Alto, Calif.	Southern California	Los Angeles, Calif.	16
16	McDonald, Paul	QB	6-2	185	2	2/23/58	Montebello, Calif.	Southern California	Covina, Calif.	6
30	Miller, Cleo	FB	5-11	214	7	4/1/53	Pine Bluff, Ark.	Arkansas-Pine Bluff	Pine Bluff, Ark.	14
71	Miller, Matt	T	6-6	270	4	8/7/54	Durango, Colo.	Colorado	Durango, Colo.	0*
42	‡Miller, Terry	RB	5-10	196	3	9/5/52	Columbus, Colo.	Oklahoma State	Yukon, Okla.	0*
55	Mohring, John	LB	6-3	230	2	3/15/56	Glen Cove, N.Y.	C.W. Post	Locust Valley, N.Y.	2
82	Newsome, Ozzie	TE	6-2	232	4	3/16/56	Muscle Shoals, Ala.	Alabama	Tuscaloosa, Ala.	16
84	Oden, McDonald	TE	6-4	228	2	11/14/56	Franklin, Tenn.	Tennessee State	Spring Hill, Tenn.	16
58	Odom, Cliff	LB	6-2	220	2	8/15/58	Beaumont, Tex.	Texas-Arlington	Beaumont, Tex.	16
69	Patten, Joel	T	6-6	240	2	2/7/58	Augsberg, Germany	Duke	Fairfax, Va.	8
34	Pruitt, Greg	RB	5-10	190	9	8/18/51	Houston, Tex.	Oklahoma	Shaker Heights, Ohio	6
43	Pruitt, Mike	FB	6-0	225	6	4/3/54	Chicago, Ill.	Purdue	Westlake, Ohio	16
63	Risien, Cody	T	6-7	255	3	3/22/57	Bryan, Tex.	Texas A&M	Houston, Tex.	16
33	Rucker, Reggie	WR	6-2	190	12	9/21/47	Washington, D.C.	Boston University	Beachwood, Ohio	16
22	Scott, Clarence	CB	6-0	190	11	4/9/49	Atlanta, Ga.	Kansas State	Decatur, Ga.	16
65	Sheppard, Henry	T	6-6	263	6	11/12/52	Cuero, Tex.	Southern Methodist	Cuero, Tex.	16
72	Sherk, Jerry	DT	6-4	250	12	7/7/48	Grants Pass, Ore.	Oklahoma State	Medina, Ohio	1
79	Sipe, Brian	QB	6-1	195	8	8/8/49	San Diego, Calif.	San Diego State	Encinitas, Calif.	16
17	Sullivan, Gerry	C-T	6-4	250	8	1/15/52	Oak Park, Ill.	Illinois	Berea, Ohio	16
87	Weathers, Curtis	LB	6-4	220	3	9/16/56	Memphis, Tenn.	Mississippi	Missoula, Mont.	16
25	White, Charles	RB	5-10	183	2	1/22/58	Los Angeles, Calif.	Southern California	Laguna Niguel, Calif.	14
89	Wright, Keith	WR-KR	5-9	175	4	1/30/56	Mercedes, Tex.	Memphis State	Tyler, Tex.	12

*Fulton last active with Buffalo in '79; Jacobs last active with N.Y. Jets in '79; M. Miller missed '80 season due to injury.

†Option playout; subject to developments.

‡Browns traded for T. Miller (Buffalo).

Traded—Punter Johnny Evans to Buffalo.

Also played with Browns in '80—DE Jerry Wilkinson (7 games).

COACHING STAFF

Head Coach, Sam Rutigliano

Pro Career: Starts his fourth season as an NFL head coach after guiding the Browns to a 11-5 record last year and their first AFC Central title since 1971. Pro assistant for 11 years before taking over at Cleveland. Was receivers coach with the Denver Broncos 1967-70, offensive coordinator with the New England Patriots 1971-72 and receivers coach in 1973, defensive backfield coach with the New York Jets 1974-75, and receivers coach for the New Orleans Saints for two years prior to his present assignment with the Browns. Career record: 28-21.

Background: Played end at Tulsa from 1954-56. Earned master's degree at Columbia University. Coached on the college level at Connecticut 1964-65 and Maryland 1966.

Personal: Born July 1, 1932, Brooklyn, N.Y. Sam and his wife, Barbara, live in Cleveland and have three children — Paul, Alison, and Kerry.

ASSISTANT COACHES

Dave Adolph, linebackers; born June 6, 1937, Akron, Ohio, lives in Bath, Ohio. Guard-linebacker Akron University 1955-58. No pro playing experience. College coach: Akron 1963-64, Connecticut 1965-68, Kentucky 1969-72, Illinois 1973-76, Ohio State 1977-78. Pro coach: Third year with Browns.

Jim Garrett, offensive backfield; born June 19, 1930, Rutherford, N.J., lives in Cleveland Heights. Running back Utah State 1949-52. Pro running back Philadelphia Eagles 1954, British Columbia Lions (CFL) 1955, New York Giants 1956, Ottawa Rough Riders (CFL) 1957. College coach: Coast Guard 1957-58, Lehigh 1959, Susquehanna 1960-66 (head coach). Pro coach: New York Giants 1970-73, Houston Texans (WFL) 1974 (head coach). New Orleans Saints 1976-77, fourth year with Browns.

Len Fontes, defensive backfield; born March 8, 1938, New Bedford, Mass., lives in Cleveland. Defensive back Ohio State 1958-59. No pro playing experience. College coach: Eastern Michigan 1968, Dayton 1969-72, Navy 1973-76, Miami 1977-79. Pro coach: Second year with Browns.

Paul Hackett, quarterbacks; born July 5, 1947, Burlington, Vt., lives in Strongsville, Ohio. Quarterback Cal-Davis 1965-68. No pro playing experience. College coach: Cal-Davis 1970-71, California 1972-75, Southern California 1976-80. Pro coach: First year with Browns.

Rod Humenuik, offensive line; born June 17, 1938, Detroit, Mich., lives in Brecksville, Ohio. Guard Southern California 1956-58. Pro guard Winnipeg Blue Bombers (CFL) 1960-62. College coach: Fullerton Junior College 1964-65, Southern California 1966-70, Cal State-Northridge 1971-72 (head coach). Pro coach: Toronto Argonauts (CFL) 1973-74, Browns since 1975.

Rich Kotite, receivers; born October 13, 1942, Brooklyn, N.Y., lives in Berea, Ohio. End Wagner 1963-65. Pro tight end New York Giants 1967, 1969-72, Pittsburgh Steelers 1968. College coach: Tennessee-Chattanooga 1973-76. Pro coach: New Orleans Saints 1977, fourth year with Browns.

John Petercuskie, special teams; born January 31, 1925, Old Forge, Pa., lives in Strongsville, Ohio. Guard East Stroudsburg State 1947-49. No pro playing experience. College coach: Dartmouth 1966-68, Boston College 1969-72, Princeton 1973-77. Pro coach: Fourth year with Browns.

Tom Pratt, defensive line; born June 21, 1935, Edgerton, Wis., lives in Medina, Ohio. Linebacker Miami 1954-56. No pro playing experience. College coach: Miami 1957-59, Southern Mississippi 1960-62. Pro coach: Kansas City Chiefs 1963-77, New Orleans Saints 1978-80, first year with Browns.

Marty Schottenheimer, defensive coordinator; born September 23, 1943, Canonsburg, Pa., lives in Strongsville, Ohio. Linebacker Pittsburgh 1962-65. Pro linebacker Buffalo Bills 1965-68, Boston Patriots 1969-70. Pro coach: Portland Storm (WFL) 1974, New York Giants 1975-77, Detroit Lions 1978-79, second year with Browns.

CLEVELAND BROWNS 1981 FIRST-YEAR ROSTER

Name	Pos.	Ht.	Wt.	Birth-date	Birthplace	College	Residence	How Acq.
Bennett, Tom	RB	5-11	194	7/23/58	Endicott, N.Y.	C. W. Post	Endicott, N.Y.	FA
Bloch, Raymond	T	6-7	255	2/6/59	Lackawanna, N.Y.	Ohio University	Trenton, Mich.	FA
Bond, Hubie	TE	6-3	238	4/27/59	Neptune, N.J.	Montclair State	Asbury Park, N.J.	FA
Booze, David	WR	6-2	190	1/9/58	St. Petersburg, Fla.	Eastern Kentucky	St. Petersburg, Fla.	FA
Bushak, Andy	LB	6-4	230	6/24/54	Cleveland, Ohio	Navy	Parma, Ohio	FA
Byrom, Bruce	C	6-4	240	6/21/59	McKees Rocks, Pa.	Maryland	McKees Rocks, Pa.	FA
Cain, Stan	FB	6-3	258	7/13/55	Dothan, Ala.	Alabama	Columbia, S.C.	D5
Cox, Steve	P-K	6-4	195	5/11/58	Shreveport, La.	Arkansas	Charleston, Ark.	D1
Dixon, Hanford	CB	5-11	182	12/15/58	Mobile, Ala.	Southern Mississippi	Theodore, Ala.	D1
Foster, Henry	RB	6-0	200	8/3/58	Birmingham, Ala.	Tennessee State	Birmingham, Ala.	D11
Friday, Larry	S	6-4	205	1/23/58	Jackson, Miss.	Mississippi State	Jackson, Miss.	D11
Haynes, Lee	WR	6-3	190	2/21/58	Warren, Ohio	Tennessee State	Dallas, Tex.	FA
Hicks, Tyrone	WR-KR	5-11	175	2/17/57	Warren, Ohio	Ohio State	Warren, Ohio	FA
Jackson, Marcus (1)	DT	6-2	261	6/8/57	Lima, Ohio	Purdue	Lima, Ohio	D12 ('80)
Johnson, Billy	FB	6-0	260	3/29/57	Newcaton, Va.	North Carolina	Newcaton, Va.	D7
Johnson, Ed	LB	6-1	210	2/3/59	Albany, Ga.	Louisville	Albany, Ga.	D7
Knight, Tom	CB	5-9	180	2/14/58	Chicago, Ill.	Hawaii	Mt. Clemons, Mich.	FA
Locklin, Ray (1)	FB	6-2	235	9/12/57	Rockdale, Tex.	New Mexico State	Rockdale, Tex.	FA
McGill, Kevin	T	6-7	262	3/17/58	Portland, Ore.	Oregon	Portland, Ore.	D12
McKnight, Dennis	C	6-2	260	9/12/59	Dallas, Tex.	Drake	Des Moines, Iowa	FA
Mills, Sam	LB	5-10	225	6/3/59	Neptune, N.J.	Montclair State	Long Branch, N.J.	FA
Moorer, Kevin	TE	6-2	213	2/2/56	New Haven, Conn.	New Haven	New Haven, Conn.	FA
Phillips, Anthony (1)	WR	5-10	170	2/20/57	Atlanta, Ga.	Morris Brown	Atlanta, Ga.	FA
Prater, Dean	DT	6-5	245	9/29/58	Altus, Okla.	Oklahoma State	Vernon, Tex.	D10
Puhalski, John	TE	6-1	230	9/8/58	Trenton, N.J.	Trenton State	Trenton, N.J.	FA
Restic, Joe (1)	S	6-3	205	8/23/57	Providence, R.I.	Notre Dame	Milford, Mass.	FA
Roarke, Ken	C	6-3	243	2/17/59	Middlesboro, Ky.	Kentucky	Middlesboro, Ky.	FA
Robinson, Ken	WR-KR	5-10	185	3/5/59	Hogansville, Ga.	Louisville	Hogansville, Ga.	FA
Robinson, Mike	DE	6-4	260	8/19/56	Cleveland, Ohio	Arizona	Cleveland, Ohio	D4
Savage, Lawrence (1)	LB	6-2	225	6/18/57	Connellsville, Pa.	Michigan State	Niles, Ohio	D9
Schleusener, Randy	G	6-6	248	10/23/57	Ft. Collins, Colo.	Nebraska	Lincoln, Neb.	D9
Simmons, Ron	DT	6-0	245	5/15/59	Warner Robins, Ga.	Florida State	Warner Robins, Ga.	D6
Stracina, Bob	K	6-4	218	3/10/57	Montreal, Canada	Acadia, Canada	Mississauga, Ont.	FA
Sybeldon, Steve (1)	T	6-5	260	1/26/56	Milwaukee, Wis.	North Dakota	Green Bay, Wis.	FA
Taylor, Anthony	WR	6-3	216	5/16/57	Glen Ridge, N.J.	Tennessee	Verona, N.J.	FA
Woodward, Doug (1)	QB	6-3	200	9/12/58	Peekskill, N.Y.	Pace	Peeksville, N.Y.	FA
Yepremian, Berj (1)	K	5-6	165	8/25/55	Larnoca, Cyprus	Miami	Miami, Fla.	FA

Players who report to an NFL team for the first time are designated on rosters as rookies (R). If a player reported to an NFL training camp in a previous year but was not on the active squad for three or more regular season or postseason games, he is listed on the first-year roster and designated by a (1). Thereafter, a player who is on the active squad for three or more regular season games is credited with an additional year of playing experience.

NOTES

DENVER BRONCOS 1981 VETERAN ROSTER

No.	Name	Pos.	Ht.	Wt.	NFL Exp.	Birth-date	Birthplace	College	Residence	Games in '80
54	Bishop, Keith	C	6-3	260	2	3/10/57	San Diego, Calif.	Baylor	Englewood, Colo.	16
77	Boyd, Greg	DE	6-6	280	4	9/15/53	Merced, Calif.	San Diego State	Santa Barbara, Calif.	16
52	Bracelin, Greg	LB	6-1	218	2	4/16/57	Lawrence, Kan.	California	Aurora, Colo.	12
82	Brunson, Larry	WR-KR	5-11	180	8	8/11/49	Little Rock, Ark.	Colorado	Aurora, Colo.	12
64	Bryan, Bill	C	6-2	244	5	6/21/55	Burlington, N.C.	Duke	Englewood, Colo.	13
35	Canada, Larry	RB	6-2	226	3	12/16/54	Chicago, Ill.	Wisconsin	Burlington, N.C.	16
68	Carter, Rubin	NT	6-0	253	7	12/12/52	Pompano Beach, Fla.	Miami	Aurora, Colo.	0*
79	Chavous, Barney	DE	6-3	245	9	3/22/51	Aiken, S.C.	South Carolina State	Aurora, Colo.	16
73	Clark, Kelvin	T	6-3	245	3	1/30/56	Odessa, Tex.	Nebraska	Englewood, Colo.	16
85	Egloff, Ron	TE	6-5	227	5	10/3/55	Plymouth, Mich.	Wisconsin	Aurora, Colo.	14
56	Evans, Larry	LB	6-2	220	6	7/11/53	Mountrose, Miss.	Mississippi College	Aurora, Colo.	16
43	†Foley, Steve	CB	6-2	190	6	11/11/53	New Orleans, La.	Tulane	New Orleans, La.	16
62	Glassic, Tom	G	6-3	250	6	4/17/54	Elizabeth, N.J.	Virginia	Littleton, Colo.	13
53	Gradishar, Randy	LB	6-3	231	8	3/3/52	Warren, Ohio	Ohio State	Littleton, Colo.	16
31	Harden, Mike	S	6-0	188	2	2/16/58	Memphis, Tenn.	Michigan	Highland Park, Mich.	16
27	Harvey, Maurice	S	5-10	190	3	1/14/56	Cincinnati, Ohio	Ball State	Denver, Colo.	15
60	Howard, Paul	G	6-3	260	8	9/12/50	San Jose, Calif.	Brigham Young	Denver, Colo.	16
65	†Hyde, Glenn	T	6-3	252	6	3/14/51	Boston, Mass.	Pittsburgh	Redding, Calif.	14
57	Jackson, Tom	LB	5-11	228	9	4/4/51	Cleveland, Ohio	Louisville	Denver, Colo.	16
30	†Jensen, Jim	RB	6-3	230	5	11/28/53	Waterloo, Iowa	Iowa	Englewood, Colo.	14
75	Jones, Rulon	DE	6-6	260	2	3/25/58	Salt Lake City, Utah	Utah State	Thornton, Colo.	14
32	Keyworth, Jon	RB	6-3	230	8	12/15/50	San Diego, Calif.	Colorado	Englewood, Colo.	10
16	Knapple, Jeff	QB	6-2	200	2	8/27/56	Werzberg, W. Germany	Northern Colorado	Boulder, Colo.	2
22	Kyle, Aaron	CB	5-11	185	6	4/6/54	Detroit, Mich.	Wyoming	Denver, Colo.	10
67	Land, Melvin	LB	6-0	240	6	11/30/55	Youngstown, Ohio	Colorado State	Denver, Colo.	3*
72	Latimer, Don	NT	6-2	253	4	3/1/55	Ft. Pierce, Fla.	Miami	Campbell, Ohio	14
76	Long, Kenneth	T	6-4	260	2	7/24/53	Pittsburgh, Pa.	Purdue	Ravenna, Ohio	0*
41	Lytle, Rob	RB	6-1	195	5	11/12/54	Fremont, Ohio	Michigan	Englewood, Colo.	16
66	Manor, Brison	DE	6-4	248	5	8/10/52	Bridgeton, N.J.	Arkansas	Northern Little Rock, Ark.	16
55	Merrill, Mark	LB	6-4	220	5	11/15/55	St. Paul, Minn.	Minnesota	New Brighton, Minn.	0*
71	Minor, Claudie	T	6-4	275	8	4/21/51	Pomona, Calif.	San Diego State	Englewood, Colo.	15
86	Moorehead, Emery	WR	6-2	210	5	3/22/54	Evanston, Ill.	Colorado	Broomfield, Colo.	16
7	†Morton, Craig	QB	6-4	211	17	2/5/43	Flint, Mich.	California	Englewood, Colo.	12
25	Moses, Haven	WR	6-2	201	14	7/27/46	Los Angeles, Calif.	San Diego State	Englewood, Colo.	15
58	Naine, Rob	LB	6-4	220	5	3/24/54	Redding, Calif.	Oregon State	Denver, Colo.	15
89	Odoms, Riley	TE	6-3	245	4	3/1/50	Corpus Christi, Tex.	Houston	Houston, Tex.	16
50	Preston, Dave	RB	5-10	212	3	5/18/57	Camden, N.J.	William & Mary	Bellmawr, N.J.	16
63	Prestridge, Luke	P	6-4	250	2	9/29/58	Nashville, Tenn.	Baylor	Littleton, Colo.	15
83	†Reed, Tony	RB	5-10	195	4	5/29/55	Dayton, Ohio	Colorado	Nashville, Tenn.	0*
45	Robinson, Matt	QB	6-2	197	5	1/27/56	Houston, Tex.	Georgia	Englewood, Colo.	15
19	Rucker, Conrad	TE	6-3	235	5	9/17/56	Tuskegee, Ala.	Southern	Overland Park, Kan.	16
17	Ryan, Jim	LB	6-1	196	3	3/30/55	San Francisco, Calif.	Boston College	Denver, Colo.	16
88	Short, Laval	NT	6-3	245	4	6/28/55	Farmington, Mich.	Colorado	Englewood, Colo.	14
46	Smith, John	WR	6-0	175	2	11/3/56	Cincinnati, Ohio	Tennessee State	Houston, Tex.	2*
11	Smith, Perry	CB	6-1	190	9	3/29/51	Greer City, S.C.	Colorado State	Englewood, Colo.	16
86	Steinfort, Fred	K	5-11	180	6	11/3/52	Wetter/Ruhr, W. Germany	Boston College	Englewood, Colo.	12
70	Studdard, Dave	T	6-4	255	3	11/22/55	San Antonio, Tex.	Texas	Denver, Colo.	16
51	†Swenson, Bob	LB	6-3	225	7	7/1/53	Stockton, Calif.	California	Evergreen, Colo.	0*
36	Thompson, Arland	C	6-3	265	2	9/9/57	Lockney, Tex.	Baylor	Denver, Colo.	2
61	Thompson, Bill	S	6-1	197	13	10/10/46	Greenville, S.C.	Maryland State	Englewood, Colo.	16
80	Upchurch, Rick	WR	5-10	176	7	5/20/52	Toledo, Ohio	Minnesota	Lakewood, Colo.	16
81	Watson, Steve	WR	6-4	192	3	5/28/57	Baltimore, Md.	Temple	Englewood, Colo.	16
87	Wright, Jim	TE	6-3	240	6	9/1/56	Fort Hood, Tex.	Texas Christian	Newark, Del.	1
20	Wright, Louis	CB	6-2	200	7	1/31/53	Gilmer, Tex.	San Jose State	Bakersfield, Calif.	15

*Canada and Swenson missed '80 season due to injuries; Land played 3 games with San Francisco in '80; Long last active with Detroit in '76; Merrill last active with Chicago in '79;
Rucker played 2 games with Tampa Bay in '80; John Smith last active with Cleveland in '79.

†Option playout; subject to developments.

‡Broncos traded for Reed (Kansas City).

Retired—Otis Armstrong, 8-year running back, 9 games.

Also played with Broncos in '80—CB Bernard Jackson (4 games), TE Bill Larson (2), RB Lawrence McCutcheon (6), RB Ben Norman (3), LB Art Smith (2).

COACHING STAFF

Head Coach, Dan Reeves

Pro Career: Became ninth head coach in Broncos history on Feb. 28, 1981 after spending entire pro career as both player and coach with Cowboys. He joined the Cowboys as a free agent running back in 1965 and became a member of the coaching staff in 1970 when he undertook the dual role of player-coach for two seasons. Was Cowboys offensive backfield coach from 1972-76 and became offensive coordinator in 1977. Was an all-purpose running back during his eight seasons as a player, rushing for 1,990 yards and catching 129 passes for 1,693.

Background: Quarterback at South Carolina from 1962-64 and was inducted into the school's Hall of Fame in 1978.

Personal: Born January 19, 1944, Rome, Ga. Dan and his wife Pam live in Denver and have three children—Dana, Laura and Lee.

ASSISTANT COACHES

Joe Collier, defensive coordinator; born June 7, 1932, Rock Island, Ill. No pro playing experience. End Northwestern 1950-53. College coach: Western Illinois 1957-59. Pro coach: Boston Patriots 1960-62, Buffalo Bills 1963-68 (head coach 1966-68), Broncos since 1969.

Jerry Frei, offensive line; born June 3, 1924, Brooklyn, Wis., lives in Denver. Guard Wisconsin 1946-47. No pro playing experience. College coach: Willamette 1952-54, Oregon 1955-71 (head coach 1967-71). Pro coach: Denver Broncos 1972-75, Tampa Bay Buccaneers 1976-77, Chicago Bears 1978-80, rejoined Broncos in 1981.

Rod Dowhower, receivers; born April 15, 1943, Ord, Neb., lives in Denver. Quarterback San Diego State 1963-64. No pro playing experience. College coach: San Diego State 1968-72, UCLA 1974-75, Boise State 1976, Stanford 1977-79 (head coach 1979). Pro coach: St. Louis Cardinals 1973, second year with Broncos.

Stan Jones, defensive line; born November 24, 1931, Altoona, Pa., lives in Denver. Tackle Maryland 1950-53. Pro lineman Chicago Bears 1954-65, Washington Redskins 1966. Pro coach: Denver Broncos 1967-71, Buffalo Bills 1972-75, rejoined Broncos in 1976.

Charlie Lee, running backs; born February 28, 1945, Liberty, Mo., lives in Denver. Running back Northern Arizona 1966-67. No pro playing experience. College coach: Northwest Missouri State 1973, Arizona 1974-76, Texas 1977-80. First year with Broncos.

Richie McCabe, defensive secondary; born March 12, 1934, Pittsburgh, lives in Denver. Back Pittsburgh 1951-54. Pro defensive back Pittsburgh Steelers 1955-58, Washington Redskins 1959, Buffalo Bills 1960. College coach: Carnegie Tech 1964-65. Pro coach: Buffalo Bills 1966-68, 1976-77, Oakland Raiders 1969-70, Cleveland Browns 1971-75, fourth year with Broncos.

Nick Nicolau, special assistant; born May 5, 1933, New York, N.Y., lives in Denver. Running back Southern Connecticut 1957-59. No pro playing experience. College coach: Southern Connecticut 1960, Springfield 1961, Bridgeport 1962-69 (head coach 1965-69), Massachusetts 1970, Connecticut 1971-72, Kentucky 1973-75, Kent State 1976. Pro coach: Hamilton Tiger Cats (CFL) 1977, Montreal Alouettes 1978-79, New Orleans Saints 1980, first year with Broncos.

Fran Polsfoot, tight ends; born April 19, 1927, Montesano, Wash., lives in Denver. End Washington State 1946-49. Pro end Chicago Cardinals 1950-52, Washington Redskins 1953. College coach: Wisconsin State 1954-61. Pro coach: St. Louis Cardinals 1962-67, Houston Oilers 1968-71, 1975-76, Cleveland Browns 1971-74, fifth year with Broncos.

Bob Zeman, linebackers; born February 22, 1937, Wheaton, Ill., lives in Denver. Fullback-halfback Wisconsin 1957-59. Pro defensive back Los Angeles-San Diego Chargers 1960-61, 1965-66, Denver Broncos 1962-63. College coach: Northwestern 1968-69, Wisconsin 1970. Pro coach: Oakland Raiders 1971-77, fourth year with Broncos.

DENVER BRONCOS 1981 FIRST-YEAR ROSTER

Name	Pos.	Ht.	Wt.	Birth-date	Birthplace	College	Residence	How Acq.
Allen, Carl	C	6-3	254	4/26/58	San Jose, Calif.	Long Beach State	San Jose, Calif.	FA
Allen, Tom (1)	DE	6-5	250	7/26/58	Phoenix, Ariz.	Arizona State	Phoenix, Ariz.	FA
Arnold, Anthony	WR	5-11	176	12/18/58	Athens, Ga.	Georgia	Athens, Ga.	FA
Blacken, Ron	WR	5-10	191	12/6/57	Arlington, Wash.	Washington	Arlington, Wash.	FA
Bramble, Bobbie	RB	5-9	175	6/12/59	Brooklyn, N.Y.	American Int'l.	Brooklyn, N.Y.	FA
Brown, Clay	TE	6-2	223	9/20/58	Los Angeles, Calif.	Brigham Young	Los Angeles, Calif.	D2
Busick, Steve	LB	6-4	227	12/10/58	Los Angeles, Calif.	Southern California	Los Angeles, Calif.	D7
Davis, Tom (1)	C	6-2	245	7/31/55	Omaha, Neb.	Nebraska	Denver, Colo.	FA
Dennison, Rick (1)	LB	6-3	210	6/22/58	Kalispel, Mont.	Colorado State	Kalispel, Mont.	FA
Drake, Perry	LB	6-2	225	5/18/57	Salt Lake City, Utah	Utah State	Salt Lake City, Utah	FA
Dunn, Dennis	RB	6-1	188	1/11/57	Aurora, Colo.	Montana State	Aurora, Colorado	FA
Foster, Greg	WR	6-2	217	2/15/59	St. Louis, Mo.	Illinois	St. Louis, Mo.	FA
Gibbons, Tom	S	6-0	188	3/8/59	Pennsacola, Fla.	Notre Dame	Pennsacola, Fla.	FA
Greene, Ron	RB	6-0	211	8/4/57	Denver, Colo.	Cal State-Hayward	Denver, Colo.	FA
Hankerd, John	LB	6-3	238	8/2/59	Jackson, Mich.	Notre Dame	Jackson, Mich.	D12
Harris, Mackel (1)	RB	5-11	185	10/9/57	Americus, Ga.	Georgia Tech	Americus, Ga.	FA
Hay, Bernard	NT	6-1	243	6/30/59	Palm Beach, Fla.	Michigan State	Lansing, Mich.	FA
Herrmann, Mark	QB	6-4	184	1/8/59	Cincinnati, Ohio	Purdue	Cincinnati, Ohio	D4
Hipp, Jeff	S	6-2	194	1/30/58	Columbia, S.C.	Georgia	Columbia, S.C.	FA
Hogan, Hoskin (1)	QB	6-1	179	10/24/57	Los Angeles, Calif.	Ft. Hays State	Compton, Calif.	FA
Kessler, Scott	CB-S	6-0	194	6/15/57	Harvey, N.D.	Pacific Lutheran	Lodi, Calif.	FA
Lanier, Ken	T	6-3	269	7/8/59	Columbus, Ohio	Florida State	Columbus, Ohio	D5
Lewis, Alvin	RB	5-11	185	8/25/59	Detroit, Mich.	Colorado State	Detroit, Mich.	D6
Liggins, David	CB	5-11	209	4/9/58	Freemont, Ohio	Arizona	Freemont, Ohio	FA
Lindsay, Tony	RB	5-6	179	4/25/58	Denver, Colo.	Utah	Denver, Colo.	D4
Manns, Eric	LB	6-2	214	12/18/58	South Bend, Ind.	Wayne State	South Bend, Ind.	FA
McClung, William	C	6-3	245	5/4/56	Bristol, Va.	Carson-Newman	Bristol, Va.	FA
Nolan, Mike	S	5-10	171	3/7/59	Baltimore, Md.	Oregon	Woodside, Ore.	FA
Nunn, Greg	RB	6-1	185	1/14/58	Boston, Mass.	Winston-Salem	Boston, Mass.	FA
Olsen, Rusty	DE	6-3	251	6/18/59	West Covina, Calif.	Washington	Spokane, Wash.	D9
Ondra, Todd	LB	6-2	213	3/25/59	Belleville, Ill.	Memphis State	Belleville, Ill.	FA
Parros, Rick (1)	RB	5-11	200	6/14/58	Brooklyn, N.Y.	Utah State	Aurora, Colo.	D4 ('80)
Price, Harry (1)	WR	6-0	184	3/1/56	Lafayette, La.	McNeese State	Lafayette, La.	FA
Reddick, Kevin	CB-S	6-0	195	8/23/56	Topeka, Kan.	Cal. State-Fullerton	Omaha, Neb.	FA
Roberts, Richard	TE	6-2	238	10/22/57	Akron, Ohio	Arizona State	Akron, Ohio	FA
Robinson, Mandel	RB	6-1	215	4/1/58	Byrd Park, England	Wyoming	Syracuse, N.Y.	D12a
Ros, Frank	LB	6-0	215	3/1/59	Barcelona, Spain	Georgia	Greenville, S.C.	FA
Roskopf, Don	NT	6-1	245	3/27/59	South Bend, Ind.	Howard Payne	Prescott, Ariz.	FA
Schremp, Tom (t)	DE-DT	6-4	255	12/18/57	Milwaukee, Wis.	Wisconsin	Antigo, Wis.	Trade
Scott, Davis	WR	5-10	173	1/29/59	Antigo, Wis.	Texas A&M	Jasper, Tex.	FA
Sella, Chris (1)	FB-LB	5-11	215	9/22/55	Jasper, Tex.	S.W. Missouri State	Greenville, Mo.	FA
Sivek, Karl	RB	6-1	238	5/5/57	Greenville, Mo.	Lafayette	Belle Vernon, Pa.	FA
Smith, Dennis	S	6-3	200	2/3/59	Santa Monica, Calif.	Southern California	Santa Monica, Calif.	D4 (80)
Smith, F. Joey	TE	6-3	228	6/24/58	Nashville, Tenn.	Vanderbilt	Nashville, Tenn.	FA
Snowden, George	T	6-3	233	10/24/59	Washington, D.C.	Sheppard	Rockville, Md.	FA
Stiggers, Gary	WR	5-9	181	12/15/58	Commerce, Tex.	Arkansas	Fort Worth, Tex.	FA
Steward, Edward	LB	5-11	234	1/13/58	Long Branch, N.J.	Rutgers	Long Branch, N.J.	FA
Trimble, Steve	CB-S	5-10	181	5/11/58	Cumberland, Md.	Maryland	Cumberland, Md.	FA
Walker, Pat	WR	6-3	180	3/13/59	Winter Haven, Fla.	Miami	Auburndale, Fla.	FA
White, Roy	LB	6-3	230	8/14/58	Greenville, Miss.	Lane College	Greenville, Miss.	FA
Wilkinson, Sherman	CB	6-1	180	9/12/57	Opp, Ala.	Troy State	Opp, Ala.	FA
Wright, Michael	LB	6-4	220	12/17/57	Denver, Colo.	Claremont	Denver, Colo.	FA

Players who report to an NFL team for the first time are designated on rosters as rookies (R). If a player reported to an NFL training camp in a previous year but was not on the active squad for three or more regular season or postseason games, he is listed on the first-year roster and designated by a (1). Thereafter, a player who is on the active squad for three or more regular season games is credited with an additional year of playing experience.

t-Broncos traded for Schremp (N.Y. Jets).

NOTES

Houston Oilers

**American Football Conference
Central Division**

Team Colors: Scarlet, Columbia Blue, and White

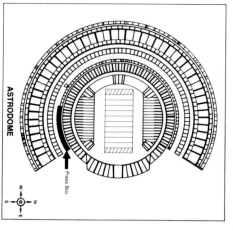

ASTRODOME

**Box 1516
Houston, Texas 77001
Telephone: (713) 797-9911**

Club Officials
President: K. S. (Bud) Adams, Jr.
Executive Vice President-General Manager: Ladd K. Herzeg
Assistant General Manager: Mike Holovak
Vice President Marketing/Public Relations: Mike McClure
Manager of Media Services: Bob Hyde
Business Manager: Lewis Mangum
Ticket Manager: Rick Nichols
Head Trainer: Jerry Meins
Assistant Trainers: Bruce McCrary, Joel Krekelberg
Equipment Manager: Ed Temple
Stadium: Astrodome • **Capacity:** 50,452
Loop 610, Kirby and Fannin Streets
Houston, Texas 77202
Playing Surface: AstroTurf
Training Camp: Angelo State University
San Angelo, Texas 76901

1981 SCHEDULE

Preseason

Aug. 6	**Philadelphia**		7:00
Aug. 15	at New Orleans		7:00
Aug. 22	at Tampa Bay		7:00
Aug. 29	at Dallas		8:00

Regular Season

Sept. 6	at Los Angeles		1:00
Sept. 13	at Cleveland		1:00
Sept. 20	**Miami**		12:00
Sept. 27	at New York Jets		1:00
Oct. 4	**Cincinnati**		1:00
Oct. 11	**Seattle**		1:00
Oct. 18	at New England		1:00
Oct. 26	at Pittsburgh (Monday)		9:00
Nov. 1	at Cincinnati		1:00
Nov. 8	**Oakland**		12:00
Nov. 15	at Kansas City		12:00
Nov. 22	**New Orleans**		12:00
Nov. 29	**Atlanta**		3:00
Dec. 3	**Cleveland** (Thursday)		8:00
Dec. 13	at San Francisco		1:00
Dec. 20	**Pittsburgh**		3:00

1980 TEAM STATISTICS

	Houston	Opp.
Total First Downs	329	259
Rushing	155	94
Passing	152	147
Penalty	22	18
Third Down Efficiency	92/211	76/211
Third Down Percentage	43.6	36.0
Total Net Yards	5642	4612
Total Offensive Plays	1063	932
Avg. Gain per Play	5.3	4.9
Avg. Gain per Game	352.6	288.3
Net Yards Rushing	2635	1811
Total Rushing Plays	573	444
Avg. Gain per Rush	4.6	4.1
Avg. Gain Rushing per Game	164.7	113.2
Net Yards Passing	3007	2801
Lost Attempting to Pass	27/264	34/252
Gross Yards Passing	3271	3053
Attempts/Completions	463/296	454/246
Percent Completed	63.9	54.2
Had Intercepted	28	26
Avg. Net Passing per Game	187.9	175.1
Punts/Avg.	67/40.7	78/40.9
Punt Returns/Avg.	48/8.0	40/9.9
Kickoff Returns/Avg.	53/18.5	68/18.6
Interceptions/Avg. Ret.	26/12.0	28/15.1
Penalties/Yards	101/838	101/763
Fumbles/Ball Lost	33/19	22/13
Total Points	295	251
Avg. Points per Game	18.4	15.7
Touchdowns	34	27
Rushing	18	8
Passing	15	16
Returns and Recoveries	1	3
Field Goals	20/25	21/29
Conversions	31/34	26/27
Safeties	0	0

1980 TEAM RECORD

Preseason (2-2)

Houston		Opponents
7	Tampa Bay	21
20	New Orleans	17
13	Dallas	20
24	*Buffalo	7
64		65

Regular Season (11-5)

Houston		Opponents	Att.
17	Pittsburgh	31	54,386
16	Cleveland	7	79,438
21	*Baltimore	16	47,878
13	Cincinnati	10	50,413
7	*Seattle	26	46,860
20	Kansas City	21	75,048
20	*Tampa Bay	14	48,167
23	*Cincinnati	3	49,189
20	Denver	16	74,717
38	*New England	34	51,524
10	Chicago	6	59,390
28	New York Jets (OT)	31	52,358
14	*Cleveland	17	51,514
6	*Pittsburgh	0	53,960
22	Green Bay	3	53,168
20	*Minnesota	16	51,064
295		251	899,074

*Home Game   (OT) Overtime

Score by Periods

	1	2	3	4	OT	Total
Houston	25	82	80	108	0	295
Opponents	63	85	34	66	3	251

Attendance

Home 400,156   Away 498,918   Total 899,074
Single game home record, 55,293 (12-10-79)
Single season home record, 400,156 (1980)

1980 INDIVIDUAL STATISTICS

Rushing

	Att	Yds	Avg	LG	TD
Campbell	373	1934	5.2	55t	13
Carpenter	97	359	3.7	46	3
T. Wilson	66	257	3.9	15	1
Coleman	14	82	5.9	27	1
Renfro	1	12	12.0	12	0
Casper	2	8	4.0	6	0
Clark	1	3	3.0	3	0
Barber	1	1	1.0	1	0
Johnson	2	1	0.5	4	0
Nielsen	1	0	0.0	0	0
Stabler	15	-22	-1.5		0
Houston	573	2635	4.6	55t	18
Opponents	444	1811	4.1	58	8

Field Goal Success

Distance	1-19	20-29	30-39	40-49	50 Over
Made-Att.	1-1	8-10	7-8	4-6	0-0

Passing

	Att	Comp	Pct	Yds	TD	Int	LG	Tkld	Rate
Stabler	457	293	64.1	3202	13	28	79t	27/264	68.6
Campbell	2	1	50.0	57	1	0	57t	0/0	—
Nielsen	4	2	50.0	12	1	0	12	0/0	—
Houston	463	296	63.9	3271	15	28	79t	27/264	
Opponents	454	246	54.2	3053	16	26	50t	34/252	70.4

Receiving

	No	Yds	Avg	LG	TD
Barber	59	712	12.1	79t	5
Carpenter	43	346	8.0	25	0
Renfro	35	459	13.1	42	3
Casper	34	526	15.5	43	3
Johnson	31	343	11.1	57t	2
T. Wilson	30	170	5.7	13	1
Caster	27	341	12.6	68t	3
Coleman	16	168	10.5	27	0
Campbell	11	47	4.3	10	0
Burrough	4	91	22.8	54	0
Groth	4	47	11.8	18	0
Smith	2	21	10.5	13	0
Houston	296	3271	11.1	79t	15
Opponents	246	3053	12.4	50t	16

Interceptions

	No	Yds	Avg	LG	TD
Tatum	7	100	14.3	35	0
Perry	5	85	17.0	42	0
Reinfeldt	4	36	9.0	23	0
Stemrick	4	25	6.3	15	0
Brazile	2	38	19.0	33	0
J. Wilson	2	26	13.0	26	0
Henderson	1	3	3.0	3	0
Hartwig	1				0
Houston	26	313	12.0	42	0
Opponents	28	424	15.1	82t	2

Punting

	No	Yds	Avg	In 20	LG
Parsley	67	2727	40.7	19	57
Houston	67	2727	40.7	19	57
Opponents	78	3193	40.9	15	57

Punt Returns

	No	FC	Yds	Avg	LG	TD
Roaches	47	6	384	8.2	68	0
Groth	1	0	0	0.0	0	0
Bingham	0	2	0	—	0	0
Houston	48	8	384	8.0	68	0
Opponents	40	9	394	9.9	50	0

Kickoff Returns

	No	Yds	Avg	LG	TD
Roaches	37	746	20.2	46	0
Groth	12	216	18.0	27	0
Barber	1	12	12.0	12	0
Carpenter	1	7	7.0	7	0
Bingham	1	0	0.0	0	0
Smith	1				0
Houston	53	981	18.5	46	0
Opponents	68	1265	18.6	63	0

Scoring

	TD	TD R	TD P	TD Rt	PAT	FG	TP
Fritsch					26/27	19/24	83
Campbell	13	13	0	0			78
Barber	5	0	5	0			30
Carpenter	3	3	0	0			18
Casper	3	0	3	0			18
Caster	3	0	3	0			18
Johnson	2	0	2	0			12
T. Wilson	2	1	1	0			12
Coleman	1	1	0	0			6
Corker	1	0	0	1			6
Renfro	1	0	1	0			6
Marcol					1/3	1/1	4
Thompson					4/4		4
Houston	34	18	15	1	31/34	20/25	295
Opponents	27	8	16	3	26/27	21/29	251

HOUSTON RECORD HOLDERS

Individual Records—Single Season

Category	Name	Performance
Rushing (Yds.)	Earl Campbell, 1980	1934
Passing (Pct.)	Ken Stabler, 1980	64.1
Passing (Yds.)	George Blanda, 1961	3330
Passing (TDs)	George Blanda, 1961	36
Receiving (No.)	Charlie Hennigan, 1964	101
Receiving (Yds.)	Charlie Hennigan, 1961	1746
Interceptions	Freddy Glick, 1963	12
	Mike Reinfeldt, 1979	12
Punting (Avg.)	Jim Norton, 1965	44.2
Punt Ret. (Avg.)	Larry Carwell, 1967	17.1
Kickoff Ret. (Avg.)	Billy Cannon, 1960	33.2
Field Goals	Toni Fritsch, 1979	21
Touchdowns (Tot.)	Earl Campbell, 1979	19
Points	George Blanda, 1960	115

Team Records—Single Game

Category	Opponent, Date	Performance
Offense		
First Downs	vs. SD, 9/12/64	28
	vs. Den, 9/3/66	28
	vs. Cle, 11/5/78	28
	vs. NY Jets, 11/23/80	28
Total Points	vs. NY Titans, 10/14/62	56
Touchdowns	vs. NY Titans, 10/14/62	8
Total Net Yards	vs. Den, 11/5/61	582
Net Yards Rushing	vs. Mia, 12/2/67	279
Net Yards Passing	vs. Den, 10/29/61	464
Rushing Attempts	vs. SD, 9/28/75	56
Passing Attempts	vs. Buff, 11/1/64	68
Interceptions by	vs. Den, 12/2/62	8
Defense		
Net Yards Allowed	vs. Pitt, 12/9/73	83
Net Rushing Yards Allowed	vs. Bos, 11/25/60	-14
Net Passing Yards Allowed	vs. Cin, 10/13/71	-52

FIRST PLAYERS SELECTED

Year	Player, College, Position
1970	Doug Wilkerson, N. Carolina Central, G
1971	Dan Pastorini, Santa Clara, QB
1972	Greg Sampson, Stanford, DE
1973	John Matuszak, Tampa, DE
1974	Steve Manstedt, Nebraska, LB (4)
1975	Robert Brazile, Jackson State, LB
1976	Mike Barber, Louisiana Tech, TE (2)
1977	Morris Towns, Missouri, T
1978	Earl Campbell, Texas, RB
1979	Mike Stensrud, Iowa State, DE (2)
1980	Angelo Fields, Michigan State, T (2)
1981	Michael Holston, Morgan State, WR (3)

OILERS COACHING HISTORY

(147-159-6)

1960-61	Lou Rymkus*	12-7-1
1961	Wally Lemm	10-2-0
1962-63	Frank (Pop) Ivy	17-12-0
1964	Sammy Baugh	4-10-0
1965	Hugh Taylor	4-10-0
1966-70	Wally Lemm	28-38-4
1971	Ed Hughes	4-9-1
1972-73	Bill Peterson**	1-18-0
1973-74	Sid Gillman	8-15-0
1975-80	O.A. (Bum) Phillips	59-38-0

*Released after five games in 1961
**Released after five games in 1973

HOUSTON OILERS 1981 VETERAN ROSTER

No.	Name	Pos.	Ht.	Wt.	NFL Exp.	Birth-date	Birthplace	College	Residence	Games in '80
39	Armstrong, Adger	RB	6-0	210	2	6/21/57	Houston, Tex.	Texas A&M	Houston, Tex.	16
75	Baker, Jesse	DE	6-5	265	3	7/10/57	Conyers, Ga.	Jacksonville State	Houston, Tex.	16
86	Barber, Mike	TE	6-3	225	5	6/4/53	White Oak, Tex.	Louisiana Tech	Missouri City, Tex.	16
65	Bethea, Elvin	DE	6-2	255	14	3/1/46	Trenton, N.J.	North Carolina A&T	Houston, Tex.	14
54	Bingham, Gregg	LB	6-1	230	9	3/13/51	Chicago, Ill.	Purdue	Houston, Tex.	16
10	Bradshaw, Craig	QB	6-5	215	2	8/14/57	Shreveport, La.	Utah State	Missouri City, Tex.	2
52	Brazile, Robert	LB	6-4	238	7	2/7/53	Pineland, Ala.	Jackson State	Houston, Tex.	16
00	Burrough, Ken	WR	6-3	210	12	7/14/48	Jacksonville, Fla.	Texas Southern	Houston, Tex.	16
34	Campbell, Earl	RB	5-11	224	4	3/29/55	Tyler, Tex.	Texas	Houston, Tex.	15
26	Carpenter, Rob	RB	6-1	230	5	4/20/55	Lancaster, Ohio	Miami, Ohio	Houston, Tex.	15
58	Carter, David	G-C	6-2	245	5	11/27/53	Vincennes, Ind.	Western Kentucky	Missouri City, Tex.	16
87	Casper, Dave	TE	6-4	230	8	9/26/51	Chilton, Wis.	Notre Dame	Sugarland, Tex.	16*
88	Caster, Rich	TE	6-5	230	12	11/16/48	Mobile, Ala.	Jackson State	Houston, Tex.	16
42	†Clark, Boobie	RB	6-2	245	9	11/8/50	Jacksonville, Fla.	Bethune-Cookman	Houston, Tex.	6
47	Coleman, Ronnie	RB	5-11	198	8	7/9/51	Jasper, Ala.	Alabama A&M	Houston, Tex.	14
57	Corker, John	LB	6-5	240	2	12/29/58	Miami, Fla.	Oklahoma State	Houston, Tex.	14
66	Davidson, Greg	C	6-2	250	2	4/24/58	Independence, Iowa	North Texas State	Houston, Tex.	0*
69	Dorris, Andy	DE	6-4	240	9	9/15/51	Bellaire, Ohio	New Mexico State	Conroe, Tex.	14
77	Fields, Angelo	G	6-6	330	2	1/9/49	Washington, D.C.	Michigan State	Houston, Tex.	16
60	Fisher, Ed	G	6-3	250	3	11/3/56	Stockton, Calif.	Arizona State	Missouri City, Tex.	16
16	Fritsch, Toni	K	5-7	180	10	7/10/45	Vienna, Austria	No College	Houston, Tex.	16
	Gibbons, Mike	T	6-4	262	3	1/23/51	Lewisville, Ark.	SW Oklahoma State	Dallas, Tex.	0*
74	Gray, Leon	T	6-3	260	9	11/15/51	Olive Branch, Miss.	Jackson State	Houston, Tex.	15
81	Groth, Jeff	WR	5-10	172	3	7/2/57	Makato, Minn.	Bowling Green	Houston, Tex.	16
36	Hartwig, Carter	CB	6-0	205	3	2/2/56	Culver City, Calif.	Southern California	Houston, Tex.	16
18	Hayman, Conway	T-G	6-3	270	9	1/9/49	Newark, Del.	Delaware	Houston, Tex.	16
70	Hunt, Daryl	LB	6-3	220	3	11/9/49	Odessa, Tex.	Oklahoma	Houston, Tex.	14
50	Jefferson, Charles	S-CB	6-3	178	5	9/22/53	New Orleans, La.	McNeese State	Houston, Tex.	0*
21	Kennard, Ken	DT	6-2	245	4	10/4/54	Fort Worth, Tex.	Angelo State	Decatur, Ala.	16
71	Marshall, Charles	DE	6-4	245	3	1/6/55	Dallas, Tex.	Texas A&M	Dallas, Tex.	16
55	Mauck, Carl	C	6-4	250	12	7/7/47	McLeansboro, Ill.	Southern Illinois	Houston, Tex.	16
	Mitchell, Mack	DE	6-8	262	5	8/16/52	Dallas, Tex.	Houston	Houston, Tex.	0*
14	Nielsen, Gifford	QB	6-4	205	4	10/25/54	Provo, Utah	Brigham Young	Houston, Tex.	16
32	Parsley, Cliff	P	6-1	211	5	12/26/54	Baraboo, Wis.	Oklahoma State	Houston, Tex.	16
64	Perry, Vernon	S	6-2	211	3	9/22/53	Jackson, Miss.	Jackson State	Houston, Tex.	16
	Posey, David	K	5-11	167	3	4/1/56	Painesville, Ohio	Florida	Boca Raton, Fla.	0*
	†Reinfeldt, Mike	S	6-2	192	6	4/27/55	Milwaukee, Wis.	Wisconsin-Milwaukee	Houston, Tex.	16
37	Reihner, George	G	6-4	263	6	5/6/53	Pittsburgh, Pa.	Penn State	Houston, Tex.	0*
	†Renfro, Mike	WR	6-0	184	4	6/19/55	Fort Worth, Tex.	Texas Christian	Fort Worth, Tex.	15
82	Roaches, Carl	WR-KR	5-8	165	2	10/2/53	Houston, Tex.	Texas A&M	Houston, Tex.	16
	Schumacher, John	G	6-3	275	6	9/23/55	Salem, Ore.	Southern California	Missouri City, Tex.	0*
85	Smith, Tim	WR	6-2	192	2	3/20/57	Tucson, Ariz.	Nebraska	Stafford, Tex.	16
12	Stabler, Ken	QB	6-3	210	12	12/25/45	Foley, Ala.	Alabama	Houston, Tex.	15
27	Stemrick, Greg	CB	5-11	185	7	10/25/51	Cincinnati, Ohio	Colorado State	Houston, Tex.	16
67	Stensrud, Mike	DE	6-5	280	3	2/19/56	Lake Mills, Iowa	Iowa State	Clear Lake, Tex.	16
53	†Stringer, Art	LB	6-2	223	3	1/30/54	Troy, Ala.	Ball State	Houston, Tex.	8
51	†Thompson, Ted	LB	6-1	220	7	1/17/53	Atlanta, Tex.	Southern Methodist	Houston, Tex.	16
76	†Towns, Morris	T-G	6-2	275	5	1/10/51	St. Louis, Mo.	Missouri	Missouri City, Tex.	16
59	Washington, Ted	LB	6-4	245	9	2/16/48	Tampa, Fla.	Mississippi Valley	Houston, Tex.	15
33	Wilson, J.C.	CB	6-2	177	5	3/11/56	Cincinnati, Ohio	Pittsburgh	Houston, Tex.	16
45	Wilson, Tim	RB	6-0	220	5	1/14/55	New Castle, Del.	Maryland	Tuskegee, Ala.	16
79	Young, Bob	G	6-3	279	16	9/3/42	Marshall, Tex.	Howard Payne	St. Charles, Mo.	15

*Casper played 6 games with Oakland, 10 with Houston; Gibbons last active with N.Y. Giants in '77; Jefferson, Reihner, Schumacher missed '80 season due to injuries; Posey last active with New England in '78; Marshall last active with N.Y. Jets in '77; Mitchell last active with Cincinnati in '79.

†Option playout; subject to developments.

Also played with Oilers in '80—DT Curley Culp (10 games), Charlie Davis (1), LB Sammy Green (2), LB Thomas Henderson (7), WR Billy Johnson (16), K Chester Marcol (1), WR Guido Merkens (3), S Jack Tatum (16).

HOUSTON OILERS 1981 FIRST-YEAR ROSTER

Name	Pos.	Ht.	Wt.	Birth-date	Birthplace	College	Residence	How Acq.
Bailey, Harold (1)	WR	6-2	195	4/2/57	Houston	Oklahoma State	Houston, Tex.	D8 ('80)
Barley, Ben	G	6-0	270	8/25/58	San Antonio, Tex.	Angelo State	San Angelo, Tex.	FA
Campbell, Joe	MG	5-11	265	9/15/58	Cuero, Tex.	Baylor	Cuero, Tex.	FA
Capece, Bill	K	5-7	170	4/1/59	Miami, Fla.	Florida State	Tallahassee, Fla.	D12
Eyre, Nick	T	6-5	276	6/16/59	Las Vegas, Nev.	Brigham Young	Las Vegas, Nev.	D4
Fowler, Delbert	LB	6-2	214	5/4/58	Cleveland, Ohio	West Virginia	Cleveland, Ohio	D5
Harper, Tommy	DE	6-5	241	9/1/56	Jasper, Tex.	North Texas State	Beaumont, Tex.	FA
Holden, James	CB-S	5-10	180	7/17/56	Denver, Colo.	Southern Colorado	Aurora, Colo.	FA
Holm, Jeffrey	DE	6-4	240	12/8/59	Fort Worth, Tex.	SW Louisiana	Nederland, Tex.	FA
Holston, Michael	WR	6-3	183	1/8/58	Washington, D.C.	Morgan State	Seatpleasant, Md.	D3
Jaco, Bill (1)	T	6-5	270	2/24/57	Toledo, Ohio	Ohio State	Houston, Tex.	FA
Jennings, Curtis	G-T	6-6	270	11/30/56	Baytown, Tex.	Texas A&M	Baytown, Tex.	FA
Johnson, Gregory	RB	5-10	185	7/27/56	New Orleans, La.	Texas Southern	Baton Rouge, La.	D10
Jones, Larry	RB	5-10	184	9/16/59	Barstow, Calif.	Colorado State	Fort Collins, Colo.	D6
Kay, Bill	CB-S	6-2	194	1/10/60	Detroit, Mich.	Purdue	Melrose Park, Ill.	D6
Locklear, Mike	TE	6-3	225	5/7/58	Mobile, Ala.	Auburn	Auburn, Ala.	FA
Mask, Alfred	TE	6-4	205	10/23/58	Crockett, Tex.	Lamar	Crockett, Tex.	FA
Mathews, Claude	T	6-2	254	1/15/58	Phoenix City, Ala.	Auburn	Auburn, Ala.	D11
Miller, Paul	WR	5-10	180	4/26/58	Houston, Tex.	Angelo State	Houston, Tex.	FA
Monk, Kelly	C	6-3	246	8/28/58	Bay City, Tex.	SW Texas State	San Marcos, Tex.	FA
Neal, Taliferro	LB	6-1	216	6/16/55	San Antonio, Tex.	Tarleton State	San Antonio, Tex.	D8
Riley, Avon	LB	6-3	213	2/10/58	Savannah, Ga.	UCLA	Los Angeles, Calif.	D9
Skaugstad, Daryle (1)	DT	6-5	260	4/8/57	Seattle, Wash.	California	Seattle, Wash.	D2b (80)
Smith, Rodney	WR-KR	5-9	169	5/15/59	Mandeville, La.	SW Louisiana	Lafayette, La.	FA
Theriot, Press	P	6-0	170	7/1/59	Port Arthur, Tex.	West Texas State	Canyon, Tex.	FA
Thomaselli, Rich	RB	6-1	195	2/26/57	Fallansbee, W. Va.	W. Va. Wesleyan	Houston, Tex.	D8
Tullis, Willie	WR	5-11	190	4/5/58	Newville, Ala.	Troy State	Troy, Ala.	D7
Walker, George	TE	6-4	230	3/23/57	Sugar Land, Tex.	Houston	Missouri City, Tex.	FA
Washington, Don	CB-S	6-0	181	1/28/58	Galveston, Tex.	Texas A&I	Galveston, Tex.	FA
Williams, Brett	LB	6-2	225	5/23/58	Norfolk, Va.	Austin Peay	Millington, Tenn.	FA
Williams, Ralph	T	6-3	250	3/27/58	Monroe, La.	Southern	West Monroe, La.	FA
Woodard, George (1)	RB	6-0	250	9/11/55	Bay City, Tex.	Texas A&M	Bay City, Tex.	FA
Young, Thomas	CB-S	5-11	175	5/2/59	Houston, Tex.	Baylor	Houston, Tex.	FA

Players who report to an NFL team for the first time are designated on rosters as rookies (R). If a player reported to an NFL training camp in a previous year but was not on the active squad for three or more regular season or postseason games, he is listed on the first-year roster and designated by a (1). Thereafter, a player who is on the active squad for three or more regular season games is credited with an additional year of playing experience.

COACHING STAFF

Head Coach, Ed Biles

Pro Career: Named head coach on January 2, 1981. Joined Oilers in 1974 as defensive backfield coach under Sid Gillman. Helped transform NFL's 26th ranked team in terms of points allowed (448) in '73 to 5th place ranking in 75 (226). Became defensive coordinator in 1975. Broke into pro coaching ranks as an assistant coach with New Orleans in 1969 before joining the New York Jets in 1971. No pro playing experience.

Background: Quarterback at Miami, Ohio 1949-52. College assistant coach at Xavier, Ohio 1957-60; head coach 1961-68.

Personal: Born October 18, 1931, Cincinnati, Ohio. Ed and his wife, Jackie live in Missouri City, Tex., and have four children—Jim, Jay, Mike, and Sharon.

ASSISTANT COACHES

Andy Bourgeois, receivers; born March 29, 1938, New Orleans, lives in Missouri City, Tex. Defensive back Louisiana State 1958-60. No pro playing experience. College coach: Tulane 1970, Texas Christian 1971-72. Pro coach: Oilers since 1973.

Ray Callahan, offensive line; born April 28, 1933, Lebanon, Ky., lives in Houston. Guard-linebacker Kentucky 1952-56. No pro playing experience. College coach: Kentucky 1963-67, Cincinnati 1967-72 (head coach 1969-72). Pro coach: Baltimore Colts 1973, Florida Blazers (WFL) 1974. Chicago Bears 1975-77, first year with Oilers.

Joe Galat, defensive line: born April 22, 1939, Cresson, Pa., lives in Houston. Linebacker Miami, Ohio 1959-61. No pro playing experience. College coach: Miami, Ohio 1964-68, Yale 1969-72, Kentucky 1973, Youngstown State 1976. Pro coach: Denver Broncos 1972-77, fourth year with Oilers.

Bob Gambold, defensive backfield; born February 5, 1929, Longview, Wash., lives in Houston. Quarterback Washington State 1948-51. Pro back Chicago Cardinals 1953, Philadelphia Eagles 1954. College coach: Everett JC 1955, Oregon State 1961-62, Stanford 1963-71. Pro coach: Denver Broncos 1972-77, fourth year with Oilers.

Dick Nolan, defensive coordinator; born March 26, 1932, Pittsburgh, Pa. Offensive-defensive halfback Maryland 1951-53. Pro defensive back New York Giants 1954-57, 1959-61, St. Louis 1958. Dallas player-coach 1962. Pro coach: Dallas Cowboys 1963-67, San Francisco 49ers 1968-75 (head coach), New Orleans Saints 1977-80 (head coach), first year with Oilers.

Elijah Pitts, running backs; born February 3, 1938, Mayflower, Ark., lives in Houston. Back Philander Smith 1957-60. Pro running back Green Bay 1961-69, 1971, Los Angeles Rams 1970, New Orleans Saints 1970. Pro coach: Los Angeles Rams 1974-77, Buffalo Bills 1978-80, first year with Oilers.

Dick Selcer, linebackers; born August 22, 1937, Cincinnati, Ohio, lives in Houston. Running back Notre Dame 1955-58. No pro playing experience. College coach: Xavier, Ohio 1962-64, 1970-71 (head coach), Cincinnati 1965-66, Brown 1967-69, Wisconsin 1972-74, Kansas State 1975-77, Southwestern Louisiana 1978-80. Pro coach: First year with Oilers.

Jim Shofner, offensive coordinator; born December 18, 1935, Grapevine, Tex., lives in Houston. Running back Texas Christian 1955-57. Pro defensive back Cleveland Browns 1958-63. College coach: Texas Christian 1964-66, 1974-76 (head coach). Pro coach: San Francisco 49ers 1967-73, 1977, Cleveland Browns 1978-80, first year with Oilers.

NOTES

Kansas City Chiefs

American Football Conference
Western Division

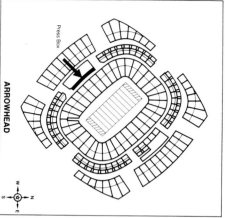

ARROWHEAD

Press Box

Team Colors: Red and Gold

One Arrowhead Drive
Kansas City, Missouri 64129
Telephone: (816) 924-9300

Club Officials

Owner: Lamar Hunt
President: Jack Steadman
Vice President and General Manager: Jim Schaaf
Director of Player Personnel: Les Miller
Director of Pro Personnel: Ron Waller
Treasurer: Roger Peyton
Secretary: Jim Seigfried
Stadium Manager: Bob Wachter
Ticket Manager: Joe Mazza
Public Relations Director: Bob Sprenger
Assistant Director of Public Relations: Doug Kelly
Promotions Director: Russ Cline
Director of Sales: David Smith
Trainer: Wayne Rudy
Assistant Trainer: Dave Kendall
Equipment Manager: Bobby Yarborough

Stadium: Arrowhead Stadium • **Capacity:** 78,067
One Arrowhead Drive
Kansas City, Missouri 64129
Playing Surface: Tartan Turf
Training Camp: William Jewell College
Liberty, Missouri 64068

1981 SCHEDULE

Preseason

Aug. 7	at Washington		7:30
Aug. 15	**Chicago**		7:35
Aug. 22	**St. Louis**		7:35
Aug. 28	at Miami		8:00

Regular Season

Sept. 6	at Pittsburgh		1:00
Sept. 13	**Tampa Bay**		12:00
Sept. 20	**San Diego**		1:00
Sept. 27	at Seattle		1:00
Oct. 4	at New England		1:00
Oct. 11	**Oakland**		3:00
Oct. 18	**Denver**		3:00
Oct. 25	at Oakland		3:00
Nov. 1	at San Diego		1:00
Nov. 8	**Chicago**		1:00
Nov. 15	**Houston**		1:00
Nov. 22	**Seattle**		1:00
Nov. 26	at Detroit (Thanksgiving)		12:30
Dec. 6	at Denver		2:00
Dec. 13	**Miami**		1:00
Dec. 20	at Minnesota		12:00

1980 TEAM STATISTICS

	Kansas City	Opp.
Total First Downs	270	328
Rushing	130	136
Passing	122	179
Penalty	18	13
Third Down Efficiency	93/230	109/236
Third Down Percentage	40.4	46.2
Total Net Yards	4321	5315
Total Offensive Plays	1010	1096
Avg. Gain per Play	4.3	4.8
Avg. Gain per Game	270.1	332.2
Net Yards Rushing	1873	2206
Total Rushing Plays	552	536
Avg. Gain per Rush	3.4	4.1
Avg. Gain Rushing per Game	117.1	137.9
Net Yards Passing	2448	3109
Lost Attempting to Pass	57/421	37/284
Gross Yards Passing	2869	3393
Attempts/Completions	401/237	523/278
Percent Completed	59.1	53.2
Had Intercepted	14	28
Punts/Avg.	85/39.0	66/42.2
Punt Returns/Avg.	40/14.5	44/6.6
Kickoff Returns/Avg.	62/20.1	61/20.5
Interceptions/Avg. Ret.	28/13.0	14/9.3
Penalties/Yards	74/591	82/617
Fumbles/Ball Lost	42/16	26/15
Total Points	319	336
Avg. Points per Game	19.9	21.0
Touchdowns	37	42
Rushing	15	17
Passing	15	25
Returns and Recoveries	7	0
Field Goals	20/26	15/30
Conversions	37/37	39/42
Safeties	0	0

1980 TEAM RECORD

Preseason (3-1)

Kansas City		Opponents
42	Cleveland	0
24	Minnesota	10
20	St. Louis	10
21	San Francisco	31
107		51

Regular Season (8-8)

Kansas City		Opponents	Att.
14	*Oakland	27	54,269
16	*Seattle	17	42,403
13	Cleveland	20	63,614
7	*San Diego	24	45,161
31	Oakland	17	40,153
21	*Houston	20	75,048
23	Denver	17	74,459
20	*Detroit	17	59,391
24	*Baltimore	31	52,383
31	Seattle	30	58,976
7	San Diego	20	50,248
21	St. Louis	13	42,871
6	*Cincinnati	20	41,594
31	*Denver	14	40,237
16	Pittsburgh	21	50,013
38	Baltimore	28	16,941
319		336	807,761

*Home Game

Score by Periods

Kansas City	58	105	75	81	— 319
Opponents	62	109	80	85	— 336

Attendance

Home 410,486   Away 397,275   Total 807,761

Single game home record, 82,094 (11-5-72)
Single season home record, 509,291 (1972)

1980 INDIVIDUAL STATISTICS

Rushing

	Att	Yds	Avg	LG	TD
McKnight	206	693	3.4	25	3
Fuller	60	274	4.6	38t	4
Belton	68	273	4.0	14	2
Hadnot	76	244	3.2	11	2
Reed	68	180	2.6	24	0
Morgado	47	120	2.6	11	4
Carson	2	41	20.5	37	0
Gant	9	32	3.6	11	0
Marshall	3	22	7.3	9	0
Kenney	8	8	1.0	4	0
Clements	2	0	0.0	0	0
Grupp	3	-14	-4.7	0	0
Kansas City	552	1873	3.4	38t	15
Opponents	536	2206	4.1	57t	17

Field Goal Success

Distance	1-19	20-29	30-39	40-49	50 Over
Made-Att.	0-0	6-6	7-9	3-4	4-7

Passing

	Att	Comp	Pct	Yds	TD	Int	LG	Tkd	Rate
Fuller	320	193	60.3	2250	10	12	75t	49/348	76.1
Kenney	69	37	53.6	542	5	2	77	5/43	91.4
Clements	12	7	58.3	77	0	0	77	3/30	77.4
Kansas City	401	237	59.1	2869	15	14	77	57/421	78.9
Opponents	523	278	53.2	3393	25	28	63	37/284	

Receiving

	No	Yds	Avg	LG	TD
Marshall	47	799	17.0	75t	6
J. Smith	46	655	14.2	77	2
Reed	44	422	9.6	34	0
McKnight	38	320	8.4	26	0
Hadnot	15	97	6.5	18	0
Gant	9	68	7.6	33	0
Samuels	8	110	13.8	34	2
Dixon	7	115	16.4	32	1
Belton	5	94	18.8	55	0
Carson	5	68	13.6	32	0
Morgado	5	27	5.4	10	0
Rome	3	58	19.3	33	0
Garcia	3	27	9.0	10	1
Williams	1	6		6	0
Kansas City	237	2869	12.1	77	15
Opponents	278	3393	12.2	63	25

Interceptions

	No	Yds	Avg	LG	TD
Barbaro	10	163	16.3	39	0
Harris	7	54	7.7	41	0
Manumaleuga	3	44	14.7	22t	1
Christopher	2	25	12.5	25	0
Green	2	25	12.5	25	0
Spani	1	47	47.0	47t	1
Dombroski	1	6	6.0	6	0
Mangiero	1	0	0.0	0	0
Paul	1	0	0.0	0	0
Kansas City	28	364	13.0	47t	2
Opponents	14	130	9.3	42	0

Punting

	No	Yds	Avg	In 20	LG
Grupp	84	3317	39.5	23	57
Kansas City	85	3317	39.0	23	57
Opponents	66	2788	42.2	9	63

Punt Returns

	No	FC	Yds	Avg	LG	TD
J. Smith	40	8	581	14.5	75t	2
Kansas City	40	8	581	14.5	75t	2
Opponents	44	11	289	6.6	31	0

Kickoff Returns

	No	Yds	Avg	LG	TD
Carson	40	917	22.9	47	0
Belton	6	110	18.3	35	0
Williams	4	79	19.8	28	0
Gant	3	44	14.7	23	0
Beckman	3	38	12.7	18	0
Budde	3	28	9.3	15	0
Morgado	2	33	16.5	22	0
Dixon	1	0	0.0	0	0
Kansas City	62	1249	20.1	47	0
Opponents	61	1253	20.5	50	0

Scoring

	TD R	TD P	TD Rt	PAT	FG	TP
Lowery				37/37	20/26	97
Marshall		6				36
Morgado	4		1			30
Fuller	4					24
J. Smith		2	2			24
McKnight	3					18
Belton	2					12
Hadnot	2					12
Samuels		2				12
Spani			2			12
Dixon		1				6
Garcia		1				6
Howard		1				6
Manumaleuga			1			6
Paul			1			6
Reed		1				6
Williams		1				6
Kansas City	15	15	7	37/37	20/26	319
Opponents	17	25	0	39/42	15/30	336

KANSAS CITY RECORD HOLDERS

Individual Records—Single Season

Category	Name	Performance
Rushing (Yds.)	Mike Garrett, 1967	1087
Passing (Pct.)	Len Dawson, 1975	66.5
Passing (Yds.)	Len Dawson, 1964	2879
Passing (TDs)	Len Dawson, 1964	30
Receiving (No.)	Chris Burford, 1962	68
Receiving (Yds.)	Otis Taylor, 1966	1297
Interceptions	Emmitt Thomas, 1974	12
Punting (Avg.)	Jerrel Wilson, 1965	46.1
Punt Ret. (Avg.)	Abner Haynes, 1960	15.4
Kickoff Ret. (Avg.)	Dave Grayson, 1962	29.7
Field Goals	Jan Stenerud, 1968, 1970	30
Touchdowns (Tot.)	Abner Haynes, 1962	19
Points	Jan Stenerud, 1968	129

Team Records—Single Game

Category	Opponent, Date	Performance
Offense		
First Downs	vs. Hou, 10/24/65	32
Total Points	vs. Den, 9/7/63	59
Touchdowns	vs. Den, 9/7/63	8
Total Net Yards	vs. Den, 10/23/66	615
Net Yards Rushing	vs. Hou, 10/1/61	398
Net Yards Passing	vs. Den, 10/23/66	435
Rushing Attempts	vs. Cin, 9/3/78	69
Passing Attempts	vs. Buff, 10/13/63	46
Interceptions by	vs. SD, 12/8/68	7
Defense		
Net Yards Allowed	vs. Hou, 10/12/69	91
Net Rushing Yards Allowed	vs. Hou, 12/4/60	-27
Net Passing Yards Allowed	vs. NYJ, 11/7/71	9

FIRST PLAYERS SELECTED

Year	Player, College, Position
1964	Pete Beathard, So. California, QB
1965	Gale Sayers, Kansas, RB
1966	Aaron Brown, Minnesota, DE
1967	Gene Trosch, Miami, DE-DT
1968	Mo Moorman, Texas A&M, G
1969	Jim Marsalis, Tennessee State, CB
1970	Sid Smith, So. California, T
1971	Elmo Wright, Houston, WR
1972	Jeff Kinney, Nebraska, RB
1973	Gary Butler, Rice, TE (2)
1974	Woody Green, Arizona State, RB
1975	Elmore Stephens, Kentucky, TE (2)
1976	Rod Walters, Iowa, G
1977	Gary Green, Baylor, DB
1978	Art Still, Kentucky, DE
1979	Mike Bell, Colorado State, DE
1980	Brad Budde, Southern California, G
1981	Willie Scott, South Carolina, TE

CHIEFS COACHING HISTORY

Dallas Texans 1960-62
(160-138-10)

1960-74	Hank Stram	129-79-10
1975-77	Paul Wiggin*	11-24-0
1977	Tom Bettis	1-6-0
1978-80	Marv Levy	19-29-0

*Released after seven games in 1977

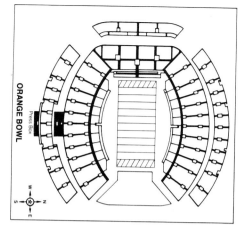

ORANGE BOWL

Miami Dolphins

American Football Conference
Eastern Division

Team Colors: Aqua and Orange
3550 Biscayne Boulevard
Miami, Florida 33137
Telephone: (305) 576-1000

Club Officials
President: Joseph Robbie
Vice President-General Manager: J. Michael Robbie
Vice President-Head Coach: Don Shula
Director of Finance: Bob Brodhead
Vice President: Joe Thomas
Director of Player Personnel: Chuck Connor
Assistant Director of Player Personnel: Charley Winner
Director of Pro Personnel: Steve Crosby
Director of Public Relations: Bob Kearney
Publicity Director: Charlie Callahan
Ticket Director: Ross R. Paul
Controller: Howard Rieman
Trainers: Bob Lundy, Junior Wade
Equipment Manager: Danny Dowe

Stadium: Orange Bowl • **Capacity:** 75,459
1501 N.W. Third Street
Miami, Florida 33125
Playing Surface: Grass (PAT)
Training Camp: 16400-D NW 32nd Avenue
Miami, Florida 33054

1981 SCHEDULE

Preseason
Aug. 8	at Minnesota	8:00
Aug. 15	**Denver**	8:00
Aug. 22	at Detroit	7:00
Aug. 28	**Kansas City**	8:00

Regular Season
Sept. 6	at St. Louis	12:00
Sept. 10	**Pittsburgh** (Thursday)	8:30
Sept. 20	at Houston	12:00
Sept. 27	at Baltimore	2:00
Oct. 4	**New York Jets**	4:00
Oct. 12	at Buffalo (Monday)	9:00
Oct. 18	**Washington**	4:00
Oct. 25	at Dallas	3:00
Nov. 1	**Baltimore**	1:00
Nov. 8	at New England	1:00
Nov. 15	**Oakland**	4:00
Nov. 22	at New York Jets	4:00
Nov. 30	**Philadelphia** (Monday)	9:00
Dec. 6	**New England**	1:00
Dec. 13	at Kansas City	1:00
Dec. 19	**Buffalo** (Saturday)	4:00

72

1980 TEAM STATISTICS

	Miami	Opp.
Total First Downs	284	309
Rushing	107	107
Passing	149	185
Penalty	28	17
Third Down Efficiency	90/232	115/239
Third Down Percentage	38.8	48.1
Total Net Yards	4564	5224
Total Offensive Plays	1015	1062
Avg. Gain per Play	4.5	4.9
Avg. Gain per Game	285.3	326.5
Net Yards Rushing	1876	2018
Total Rushing Plays	492	530
Avg. Gain per Rush	3.8	3.8
Avg. Gain Rushing per Game	117.3	126.1
Net Yards Passing	2688	3206
Lost Attempting to Pass	31/265	27/233
Gross Yards Passing	2953	3439
Attempts/Completions	492/267	505/290
Percent Completed	54.3	57.4
Had Intercepted	26	28
Avg. Net Passing per Game	168.0	200.4
Punts/Avg.	79/41.5	72/37.3
Punt Returns/Avg.	32/6.7	42/8.1
Kickoff Returns/Avg.	61/20.2	53/22.8
Interceptions/Avg. Ret.	28/7.1	26/14.8
Penalties/Yards	74/567	108/923
Fumbles/Ball Lost	33/16	31/17
Total Points	266	305
Avg. Points per Game	16.6	19.1
Touchdowns	32	36
Rushing	9	13
Passing	21	21
Returns and Recoveries	2	2
Field Goals	14/23	18/25
Conversions	32/32	33/36
Safeties	0	1

1980 TEAM RECORD

Preseason (3-1)

Miami		Opponents
17	Detroit	7
24	Seattle	7
10	Minnesota	17
20	New Orleans	0
71		31

Regular Season (8-8)

Miami		Opponents	Att.
7	Buffalo	17	79,598
17	*Cincinnati	16	38,322
20	Atlanta	17	55,479
21	*New Orleans	16	40,946
17	*Baltimore	30	50,631
0	New England	34	41,636
17	*Buffalo	14	53,046
14	New York Jets	17	46,378
10	Oakland	16	62,198
35	Los Angeles	14	45,135
17	*San Francisco	13	63,013
24	*San Diego (OT)	27	51,384
10	Pittsburgh	23	63,292
16	*New England (OT)	13	30,564
24	Baltimore	14	41,854
17	New York Jets	24	
266		305	Total 823,853

*Home Game   (OT) Overtime

Score by Periods

	1	2	3	4	OT		Total
Miami	47	65	37	114	3	—	266
Opponents	54	100	65	83	3	—	305

Attendance

Home 384,829   Away 439,024   Total 823,853

Single game home record, 78,939 (1-2-72)
Single season home record, 557,881 (1972)

1980 INDIVIDUAL STATISTICS

Rushing

	Att	Yds	Avg	LG	TD
Williams	187	671	3.6	65	2
Nathan	60	327	5.5	18	1
Robiskie	78	250	3.2	36	2
Woodley	55	214	3.9	17	3
Howell	60	206	3.4	23	1
Bennett	43	187	4.3	19	0
Giaquinto	5	16	3.2	5	0
Testerman	1	5	5.0	5	0
Moore	1	3	3.0	3	0
Griese	1	0	0.0	0	0
Strock	1	-3	-3.0	-3	0
Miami	492	1876	3.8	65	9
Opponents	530	2018	3.8	53	13

Field Goal Success

Distance	1-19	20-29	30-39	40-49	50 Over
Made-Att.	0-0	9-10	3-5	2-5	0-3

Passing

	Att	Comp	Pct	Yds	TD	Int	LG	Tkld	Rate
Woodley	327	176	53.8	1850	14	17	65	17/127	63.2
Griese	100	61	61.0	790	6	4	58	9/89	89.2
Strock	62	30	48.4	313	1	5	49	5/49	35.1
Moore	1	0	0.0	0	0	0	—	0/0	—
Nathan	1	0	0.0	0	0	0	—	0/0	—
Williams	1	0	0.0	0	0	0	—	0/0	—
Miami	492	267	54.3	2953	21	26	65	31/265	64.6
Opponents	505	290	57.4	3439	21	28	61	27/233	

Receiving

	No	Yds	Avg	LG	TD
Nathan	57	588	10.3	61	5
Moore	47	564	12.0	33	7
Harris	33	583	17.7	54	2
Williams	31	207	6.7	19	0
Giaquinto	24	192	8.0	25	1
Hardy	19	159	8.4	19	2
Rose	13	149	11.5	50	0
Robiskie	13	60	4.6	15	0
Cefalo	11	199	18.1	52	1
Lee	7	83	11.9	41	2
Howell	5	38	7.6	13	0
Bailey	4	105	26.3	39	0
Bennett	3	26	8.7	19t	1
Miami	267	2953	11.1	61	21
Opponents	290	3439	11.9	61	21

Interceptions

	No	Yds	Avg	LG	TD
Small	7	46	6.6	22	0
McNeal	5	17	3.4	15	0
Bessillieu	4	13	3.3	12	0
Taylor	3	55	18.3	44	0
Rhone	3	33	11.0	12	0
Blackwood	3	0	0.0	0	0
Ortega	1	17	17.0	13	0
Gordon	1	11	11.0	11	0
Bokamper	1	6	6.0	6	0
Miami	28	198	7.1	44	0
Opponents	26	386	14.8	71t	1

Punting

	No	Yds	Avg	In 20	LG
Roberts	77	3279	42.6	18	71
Miami	79	3279	41.5	18	71
Opponents	72	2684	37.3	18	69

Punt Returns

	No	FC	Yds	Avg	LG	TD
Nathan	23	11	178	7.7	30	0
Giaquinto	7	1	35	5.0	15	0
Blackwood	1	3	0	0.0	0	0
Bessillieu	1	8	0	0.0	0	0
Miami	32	23	213	6.7	30	0
Opponents	42	9	339	8.1	52	0

Kickoff Returns

	No	Yds	Avg	LG	TD
Bessillieu	40	890	22.3	87	0
Giaquinto	9	146	16.2	22	0
Nathan	5	102	20.4	31	0
Harris	5	89	17.8	22	0
Barnett	1	7	7.0	7	0
Allen	1	0	0.0	0	0
Miami	61	1234	20.2	87	0
Opponents	53	1210	22.8	52	0

Scoring

	TD R	TD P	TD Rt	PAT	FG	TP
von Schamann	0	0	0	32/32	14/23	74
Moore	0	7	0			42
Nathan	1	5	0			36
Woodley	3	0	0			18
Giaquinto	0	1	1			12
Hardy	0	2	0			12
Harris	0	2	0			12
Lee	0	2	0			12
Robiskie	2	0	0			12
Williams	2	0	0			12
Bennett	0	1	0			6
Cefalo	0	1	0			6
Howell	1	0	0			6
Bessillieu	0	0	1			6
Miami	9	21	2	32/32	14/23	266
Opponents	13	21	2	33/36	18/25	305

MIAMI RECORD HOLDERS

Individual Records—Single Season

Category	Name	Performance
Rushing (Yds.)	Delvin Williams, 1978	1258
Passing (Pct.)	Bob Griese, 1978	63.0
Passing (Yds.)	Bob Griese, 1968	2473
Passing (TDs)	Bob Griese, 1977	22
Receiving (No.)	Jack Clancy, 1967	67
Receiving (Yds.)	Paul Warfield, 1971	996
Interceptions	Dick Westmoreland, 1967	10
Punting (Avg.)	George Roberts, 1980	42.6
Punt Ret. (Avg.)	Freddie Solomon, 1975	12.3
Kickoff Ret. (Avg.)	Duriel Harris, 1976	32.9
Field Goals	Garo Yepremian, 1971	28
Touchdowns (Tot.)	Nat Moore, 1977	13
	Larry Csonka, 1979	13
Points	Garo Yepremian, 1971	117

Team Records—Single Game

Category	Opponent, Date	Performance
Offense		
First Downs	vs. StL, 11/24/77	34
Total Points	vs. StL, 11/24/77	55
Touchdowns	vs. StL, 11/24/77	8
Total Net Yards	vs. StL, 11/24/77	503
Net Yards Rushing	vs. Balt, 11/11/73	315
Net Yards Passing	vs. Hou, 11/20/78	327
Rushing Attempts	vs. GB, 10/5/75	58
Passing Attempts	vs. NE, 11/27/66	52
Interceptions by	vs. Pitt, 12/3/73	6
	vs. NYJ, 10/19/75	6
	vs. Balt, 9/10/78	6
Defense		
Net Yards Allowed	vs. Buff, 10/21/73	76
Net Rushing Yards Allowed	vs. Wash, 10/13/74	26
Net Passing Yards Allowed	vs. Buff, 10/21/73	1

FIRST PLAYERS SELECTED

Year	Player, College, Position
1966	Rick Norton, Kentucky, QB
1967	Bob Griese, Purdue, QB
1968	Larry Csonka, Syracuse, RB
1969	Bill Stanfill, Georgia, DE
1970	Jim Mandich, Michigan, TE (2)
1971	Otto Stowe, Iowa State, WR (2)
1972	Mike Kadish, Notre Dame, DT
1973	Chuck Bradley, Oregon, C (2)
1974	Donald Reese, Jackson State, DE
1975	Darryl Carlton, Tampa, T
1976	Larry Gordon, Arizona State, LB
1977	A.J. Duhe, Louisiana State, DT
1978	Guy Benjamin, Stanford, QB (2)
1979	Jon Giesler, Michigan, T
1980	Don McNeal, Alabama, DB
1981	David Overstreet, Oklahoma, RB

DOLPHINS COACHING HISTORY

(135-92-3)

1966-69	George Wilson	15-39-2
1970-80	Don Shula	120-53-1

MIAMI DOLPHINS 1981 VETERAN ROSTER

No.	Name	Pos.	Ht.	Wt.	NFL Exp.	Birth-date	Birthplace	College	Residence	Games in '80
43	Allen, Jeff	CB	5-11	185	2	7/18/57	Richmond, Ind.	Cal-Davis	Rancho Cordova, Calif.	16
88	Bailey, Elmer	WR	6-0	195	2	12/13/57	Evanston, Ill.	Minnesota	Pembroke Pines, Fla.	14
78	Barisich, Carl	NT	6-4	255	9	7/12/51	Jersey City, N.J.	Princeton	Medina, Ohio	15
70	Barnett, Bill	DE	6-4	255	2	5/10/56	St. Paul, Minn.	Nebraska	Lincoln, Neb.	16
73	Baumhower, Bob	NT	6-5	260	5	8/4/55	Portsmouth, Va.	Alabama	Fort Lauderdale, Fla.	16
44	Beaudoin, Doug	S	6-1	190	6	5/15/54	Dickinson, N.D.	Minnesota	Foxboro, Mass.	10
34	Bennett, Woody	FB	6-2	222	3	3/24/55	York, Pa.	Miami	York, Pa.	12*
46	Bessillieu, Don	S	6-1	200	5	5/4/56	Fort Benning, Ga.	Georgia Tech	Atlanta, Ga.	16
75	Betters, Doug	DE	6-7	260	4	6/11/56	Lincoln, Neb.	Nevada-Reno	Pembroke Pines, Fla.	16
47	Blackwood, Glenn	S	6-1	183	3	2/23/57	San Antonio, Tex.	Texas	Kenner, La.	16
58	Bokamper, Kim	LB	6-6	247	5	9/25/54	San Diego, Calif.	San Jose State	Plantation, Fla.	16
59	†Brudzinski, Bob	LB	6-4	229	5	1/1/55	Fremont, Ohio	Ohio State	Long Beach, Calif.	16
81	Cefalo, Jimmy	WR	5-11	188	4	10/5/56	Pittston, Pa.	Penn State	Pittston, Pa.	9
83	†Den Herder, Vern	DE	6-6	252	11	11/28/48	Lemars, Iowa	Central College, Iowa	Sioux Center, Iowa	16
63	Dennard, Mark	C	6-1	252	3	11/2/55	Bay City, Tex.	Texas A&M	Bryan, Tex.	16
61	Dornbrook, Thom	G-C	6-2	256	2	12/1/56	Pittsburgh, Pa.	Kentucky	Pittsburgh, Pa.	4
77	Duhe, A.J.	DE-LB	6-4	252	5	11/27/55	New Orleans, La.	Louisiana State	Fort Lauderdale, Fla.	16
35	Giaquinto, Nick	RB	5-11	204	3	4/4/55	Bridgeport, Conn.	Connecticut	Fort Lauderdale, Fla.	16
79	Giesler, Jon	DE	6-4	260	3	12/23/56	Toledo, Ohio	Michigan	Pembroke Pines, Fla.	16
50	Gordon, Larry	LB	6-4	230	6	7/8/54	Monroe, La.	Arizona State	Phoenix, Ariz.	15
74	Green, Cleveland	T	6-3	265	3	9/11/57	Tallahassee, Fla.	Southern	Miami, Fla.	10
84	Hardy, Bruce	TE	6-4	230	4	6/1/56	Murray, Utah	Arizona State	West Jordan, Utah	16
82	Harris, Duriel	WR	5-11	184	6	11/27/54	Port Arthur, Tex.	New Mexico State	Miami, Fla.	16
36	Henderson, Thomas	LB	6-2	220	7	3/1/53	Austin, Tex.	Langston	Garland, Tex.	7*
33	Howell, Steve	FB	6-2	235	3	12/24/56	Woodbury, N.Y.	Baylor	Waxahachie, Tex.	16
28	Johnson, Ken	CB	6-2	192	2	11/27/56	Corsicana, Tex.	Miami	Miami, Fla.	0*
40	Kozlowski, Mike	S	5-9	195	2	2/24/56	Newark, N.J.	Colorado	Miami, Fla.	0*
67	Kuechenberg, Bob	G-T	6-2	265	12	10/14/47	Gary, Ind.	Notre Dame	Miami Beach, Fla.	13
68	Laakso, Eric	T-G	6-4	265	4	5/19/55	New York, N.Y.	Tulane	Pembroke Pines, Fla.	16
86	Lee, Ronnie	TE	6-2	235	3	12/18/56	Pine Bluff, Ark.	Baylor	Pembroke Pines, Fla.	16
28	McNeal, Don	CB	6-0	192	2	1/14/57	Atmore, Ala.	Alabama	Miami, Fla.	16
89	Moore, Nat	WR	5-11	184	8	9/19/51	Miami, Fla.	Florida	Miami, Fla.	16
29	Moriarty, Pat	RB	6-0	195	2	5/6/58	Cleveland, Ohio	Georgia Tech	University Heights, Ohio	0*
31	Moser, Rick	RB	6-0	210	4	8/20/53	Scarsdale, N.Y.	Rhode Island	Marina del Rey, Calif.	16
82	Murphy, Mike	LB	6-0	206	2	7/5/53	St. Louis, Mo.	Southwest Missouri State	St. Louis, Mo.	0*
22	Nathan, Tony	RB-KR	6-0	222	3	12/14/56	Birmingham, Ala.	Alabama	Birmingham, Ala.	16
64	Newman, Ed	G	6-2	255	9	6/4/51	Woodmere, N.Y.	Duke	Miami, Fla.	16
54	Ortega, Ralph	LB	6-2	225	6	11/29/56	Havana, Cuba	Florida	Miami, Fla.	12
55	Rhone, Earnest	LB	6-2	225	6	12/24/56	Ogden, Ark.	Henderson State	Miami, Fla.	16
4	Roberts, George	P	6-0	184	4	11/27/56	Lynchburg, Va.	Virginia Tech	Miami, Fla.	16
38	Robiskie, Terry	WR	6-0	210	5	11/12/54	New Orleans, La.	Louisiana State	Miami Lakes, Fla.	16
80	Rose, Joe	TE	6-3	225	2	6/24/57	Marysville, Calif.	California	Williams, Calif.	8
52	Shull, Steve	LB	6-1	218	2	3/27/58	Philadelphia, Pa.	William & Mary	Atlanta, Ga.	16
48	Small, Gerald	CB	6-1	192	4	8/10/56	Washington, N.C.	San Jose State	San Francisco, Calif.	16
57	Stephenson, Dwight	C	6-2	255	2	11/20/57	Murfreesboro, N.C.	Alabama	Hampton, Va.	16
10	†Strock, Don	QB	6-5	220	8	11/27/50	Pottstown, Pa.	Virginia Tech	Miami Lakes, Fla.	16
45	Taylor, Ed	CB	6-0	175	7	5/13/53	Memphis, Tenn.	Memphis State	Memphis, Tenn.	16
60	Toews, Jeff	G	6-2	220	3	11/4/57	San Jose, Calif.	Washington	Miami Springs, Fla.	16
56	†Towle, Steve	LB	6-3	230	7	10/23/53	Kansas City, Kan.	Kansas	Pembroke Pines, Fla.	7
5	von Schamann, Uwe	K	6-0	188	3	4/23/58	West Berlin, Germany	Oklahoma	Norman, Okla.	16
24	Williams, Delvin	RB	6-0	200	8	4/17/51	Houston, Tex.	Kansas	Los Altos Hills, Calif.	15
16	Woodley, David	QB	6-2	196	2	10/25/58	Shreveport, La.	Louisiana State	Shreveport, La.	13

*Bennett played 8 games with N.Y. Jets, 4 with Miami in '80; Henderson played 7 games with Houston in '80; Johnson last active with N.Y. Giants in '79; Kozlowski missed '80 season due to injury; Moriarty last active with Cleveland in '79; Murphy last active with Houston in '79.

†Option playout; subject to developments.

†-Dolphins traded for Brudzinski (Los Angeles).

Retired—Tim Foley, 10-year safety, 7 games in 1980; Bob Griese, 15-year quarterback, 5 games in 1980; Larry Little, 14-year tackle, 5 games in 1980; Bob Matheson, 13-year linebacker, 0 games in 1980.

Also played with Dolphins in '80—S Billy Cesare (2 games), LB Rusty Chambers (16), RB Don Testerman (5), G Rod Walters (1).

COACHING STAFF

Head Coach, Don Shula

Pro Career: Starts nineteenth season as NFL head coach, twelfth at Miami where he has guided Dolphins to playoffs seven times including 17-0 Super Bowl VII champs in 1972. Has highest winning percentage (.708) among active NFL coaches. Captured back-to-back NFL championships, defeating Washington 14-7 in Super Bowl VII and Minnesota 24-7 in Super Bowl VIII. Lost to Dallas 24-3 in Super Bowl VI. Is a part-owner and vice-president of the Dolphins. Started his pro playing career with Cleveland as defensive back in 1951. After two seasons with Browns, spent 1953-56 with Washington Redskins. Joined Detroit Lions as defensive coach in 1960 and was named head coach of the Colts in 1963. Baltimore had a 13-1 record in 1968 and captured NFL championship before losing to New York Jets in Super Bowl III. Career record: 193-78-5.

Background: Outstanding offensive player at John Carroll University in Cleveland before becoming defensive specialist as a pro. His alma mater gave him doctorate in humanities, May, 1973. Served as assistant coach at Virginia in 1958 and at Kentucky in 1959.

Personal: Born January 4, 1930, in Painesville, Ohio. Don and his wife, Dorothy, live in Miami Lakes and have five children—David, Donna, Sharon, Annie, and Mike.

ASSISTANT COACHES

Bill Arnsparger, assistant head coach-defense; born December 16, 1926, Paris, Ky., lives in Miami. Tackle Miami, Ohio 1946-49. No pro playing experience. College coach: Miami, Ohio 1950, Ohio State 1951-53, Kentucky 1954-61, Tulane 1962-63. Pro coach: Baltimore Colts 1964-69, Miami Dolphins 1970-74, New York Giants 1974-76 (head coach), rejoined Dolphins 1976.

Steve Crosby, special teams; born July 3, 1950, Pawnee Rock, Kan., lives in Miami. Running back Fort Hays (Kan.) College 1971-73. Pro running back New York Giants 1974-76. Pro coach: Dolphins since 1977.

Wally English, quarterbacks, receivers, passing game; born June 28, 1939, Louisville, Ky., lives in Miami. Quarterback Louisville 1957-59. No pro playing experience. College coach: Kentucky 1965-68, Virginia Tech 1971-72, Nebraska 1973, Brigham Young 1978, Pittsburgh 1979-80. Pro coach: Detroit Lions 1974-77, joined Dolphins 1981.

Tom Keane, defensive backfield-punters; born September 7, 1926, Bellaire, Ohio, lives in Miami. Back Ohio State 1944, West Virginia 1946-47. Pro Back Los Angeles Rams 1948-51, Dallas Texans 1952, Baltimore Colts 1953-54, Chicago Cardinals 1957. Pro coach: Calgary Stampeders (CFL) 1960, Wheeling (UFL) 1961-64, Pittsburgh Steelers 1965, Dolphins since 1966.

John Sandusky, offensive line-running game; born December 28, 1925, Philadelphia, lives in Miami. Tackle Villanova 1946-49. Pro tackle Cleveland Browns 1950-55, Green Bay Packers 1956. College coach: Villanova 1956-58. Pro coach: Baltimore Colts 1959-72 (head coach 1972), Philadelphia Eagles 1973-75, Dolphins since 1976.

Mike Scarry, defensive line-run defense; born February 1, 1920, Duquesne, Pa., lives in Miami. Center Waynesburg 1939-41. Pro center Cleveland Rams 1944-45, Cleveland Browns (AAFC) 1946-47. College coach: Western Reserve 1948-49, Santa Clara 1950-52, Loras 1953, Washington State 1954-55, Cincinnati 1956-62, Waynesburgh 1963-65. Pro coach: Washington Redskins 1966-68, Dolphins since 1970.

Carl Taseff, offensive backfield-special teams; born September 28, 1928, Cleveland, lives in Key Biscayne, Fla. Back John Carroll 1947-50. Pro defensive back Cleveland Browns 1951, Baltimore Colts 1953-61, Philadelphia Eagles 1961, Buffalo Bills 1962. Pro coach: Boston Patriots 1964, Detroit Lions 1965-68, Dolphins since 1970.

MIAMI DOLPHINS 1981 FIRST-YEAR ROSTER

Name	Pos.	Ht.	Wt.	Birth-date	Birthplace	College	Residence	How Acq.
Alford, John	DT	6-2	277	1/30/57	Dillon, S.C.	South Carolina State	Dillon, S.C.	D12
Buonamici, Nick (1)	DT	6-2	170	1/12/56	Bethpage, N.Y.	Ohio State	Brentwood, N.Y.	FA
Cowell, Vince	G	6-2	250	11/14/58	Borger, Tex.	Alabama	Snellville, Ga.	FA
Daum, Mike	T	6-6	256	10/25/58	Kenosha, Wis.	Cal Poly-SLO	Kenosha, Wis.	D7
Doehla, George (1)	LB	6-3	227	10/24/56	Fort Wayne, Ind.	Indiana	Fort Wayne, Ind.	FA
Driscoll, Phil (1)	DE	6-5	265	8/21/57	Kewanuee, Ill.	Mankato State	Blue Earth, Minn.	D11 ('80)
Folsom, Steve	TE	6-4	230	3/21/58	Los Angeles, Calif.	Utah	Downey, Calif.	D10
Franklin, Andra	FB	5-10	225	8/22/59	Anniston, Ala.	Nebraska	Anniston, Ala.	D2
Greene, Sam	WR	6-1	192	1/28/59	Los Angeles, Calif.	Nevada-Las Vegas	Santa Barbara, Calif.	D4
Groves, Tim	S	6-1	192	2/18/59	Sumter, S.C.	Florida	Orlando, Fla.	FA
Hartig, Junior	LB	6-2	218	1/17/59	Hobbs, N.M.	Fort Hays State	Ellinwood, Kan.	FA
Huggins, Gerald (1)	LB	6-1	224	10/22/57	Orangeburg, S.C.	Morgan State	Brooklyn, N.Y.	FA
Hunter, Ivory Joe (1)	CB-S	5-11	185	7/8/57	Tallahassee, Fla.	Florida State	Tallahassee, Fla.	FA
Jacobs, Chris	S	6-1	180	9/8/58	Macon, Ga.	Kentucky	Coral Gables, Fla.	FA
Jensen, Jim	QB	6-4	212	11/14/58	Abington, Pa.	Boston University	Warrington, Pa.	D11
Judson, William	CB	6-1	181	3/26/59	Detroit, Mich.	South Carolina State	Atlanta, Ga.	D8
Moore, Mack	DE	6-3	255	3/4/59	Monroe, La.	Texas A&M	Ferriday, La.	D6
Murphy, Mike (1)	LB	6-2	225	1/14/57	St. Louis, Mo.	SW Missouri State	St. Louis, Mo.	FA
Noonan, John	WR	6-1	190	12/11/58	Painesville, Ohio	Nebraska	Omaha, Neb.	D9
Orosz, Tom	P	6-1	204	9/26/59	Evanston, Ill.	Ohio State	Fairport Harbor, Ohio	FA
Pokorney, Jim	G	6-3	242	2/21/59	Hermitage, Ark.	Miami	Boca Raton, Fla.	FA
Poole, Ken	DE	6-3	251	10/20/58	Bradford, Pa.	Northeast Louisiana	Hermitage, Ark.	D5
Potter, Steve (1)	LB	6-3	235	11/6/57	Pittsburgh, Pa.	Virginia	Erie, Pa.	FA
Rasp, Bob (1)	LB	6-4	225	4/27/58	N. Tonawanda, N.Y.	Lafayette	McKeesport, Pa.	FA
Rusin, Stan (1)	LB	6-4	230	12/9/56	N. Tonawanda, N.Y.	Mesa JC, Colo.	N. Tonawanda, N.Y.	FA
Sewell, Don (1)	T	6-5	252	12/17/56	Starke, Fla.	Georgia Tech	Marietta, Ga.	FA
Smyth, Seamus	K	5-9	180	2/3/55	Dublin, Ireland	Delta State	Jacksonville, Fla.	D5
Thomas, Rodell	LB	6-1	227	8/2/58	Quincy, Fla.	Alabama State	Quincy, Fla.	D6
Vigorito, Tommy	RB	5-11	197	10/23/59	Passaic, N.J.	Virginia	Wayne, N.J.	D5
Walker, Fulton	CB	5-11	193	4/30/58	Martinsburg, W. Va.	West Virginia	Martinsburg, W. Va.	D6
Webb, Ray	CB	6-3	245	6/29/59	Paris, Tex.	North Lamar JC, Tex.	Arlington, Tex.	FA
Woods, Pete (1)	QB	6-4	215	11/29/55	St. Louis, Mo.	Missouri	Denver, Colo.	FA
Wright, Brad	QB	6-3	209	5/15/59	Odessa, Tex.	New Mexico	Midland, Tex.	D4

Players who report to an NFL team for the first time are designated on rosters as rookies (R). If a player reported to an NFL training camp in a previous year but was not on the active squad for three or more regular season or postseason games, he is listed on the first-year roster and designated by a (1). Thereafter, a player who is on the active squad for three or more regular season games is credited with an additional year of playing experience.

NOTES

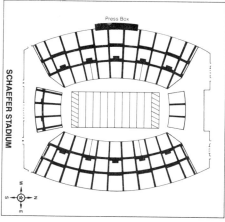

SCHAEFER STADIUM

Press Box

New England Patriots

American Football Conference
Eastern Division

Team Colors: Red, Blue, and White

Schaefer Stadium
Route 1
Foxboro, Massachusetts 02035
Telephone: (617) 543-7911, 262-1776

Club Officials

President: William H. Sullivan, Jr.
Executive Vice President: Charles W. Sullivan
General Manager: Frank (Bucko) Kilroy
Assistant General Manager: Patrick J. Sullivan
Director of Player Development: Dick Steinberg
Executive Director of Player Personnel:
    Darryl Stingley
Director, Marketing: Miceal Chamberlain
Director of Media Relations: Tom Hoffman
Director, Pro Scouting: Bill McPeak
Director, Public Affairs: Claudia Smith
Personnel Scouts: George Blackburn, Joe Mendes
    Bob Teahan
Ticket Manager: Kevin Fitzgerald
Assistant Director, Media Relations: Dave Wintergrass
Assistant Director, Pro Scouting: Tom Yewcic
Trainer: Tom Healion
Equipment Manager: George Luongo
Stadium: Schaefer Stadium • **Capacity:** 61,297
    Route 1
    Foxboro, Massachusetts 02035
Playing Surface: Super Turf
Training Camp: Bryant College
    Smithfield, Rhode Island 02917

1981 SCHEDULE

Preseason

Aug. 10	at Los Angeles		8:00
Aug. 15	at Tampa Bay		7:00
Aug. 22	**Oakland**		2:00
Aug. 30	**Washington**		12:30

Regular Season

Sept. 6	**Baltimore**		1:00
Sept. 13	at Philadelphia		1:00
Sept. 21	**Dallas** (Monday)		9:00
Sept. 27	at Pittsburgh		1:00
Oct. 4	**Kansas City**		1:00
Oct. 11	at New York Jets		1:00
Oct. 18	**Houston**		1:00
Oct. 25	at Washington		1:00
Nov. 1	at Oakland		1:00
Nov. 8	**Miami**		1:00
Nov. 15	**New York Jets**		1:00
Nov. 22	at Buffalo		1:00
Nov. 29	**St. Louis**		1:00
Dec. 6	at Miami		1:00
Dec. 13	**Buffalo**		1:00
Dec. 20	at Baltimore		2:00

1980 TEAM STATISTICS

	New England	Opp.
Total First Downs	319	270
Rushing	139	118
Passing	154	141
Penalty	26	11
Third Down Efficiency	98/210	79/214
Third Down Percentage	46.7	36.9
Total Net Yards	5435	4762
Total Offensive Plays	1026	984
Avg. Gain per Play	5.3	4.8
Avg. Gain per Game	339.7	297.6
Net Yards Rushing	2240	1876
Total Rushing Plays	588	482
Avg. Gain per Rush	3.8	3.9
Avg. Gain Rushing per Game	140.0	117.3
Net Yards Passing	3195	2886
Lost Attempting to Pass	25/200	44/346
Gross Yards Passing	3395	3232
Attempts/Completions	413/240	458/266
Percent Completed	58.1	58.1
Had Intercepted	27	24
Avg. Net Passing per Game	199.7	180.4
Punts/Avg.	63/38.0	92/41.0
Punt Returns/Avg.	60/8.6	28/8.5
Kickoff Returns/Avg.	56/22.9	89/18.5
Interceptions/Avg. Ret.	24/12.0	27/13.7
Penalties/Yards	79/696	92/833
Fumbles/Ball Lost	19/9	31/10
Total Points	441	325
Avg. Points per Game	27.6	20.3
Touchdowns	52	40
Rushing	19	12
Passing	27	28
Returns and Recoveries	6	0
Field Goals	26/34	14/20
Conversions	51/52	39/40
Safeties	0	2

1980 TEAM RECORD

Preseason (1-3)

New England		Opponents
35	Los Angeles	31
29	Oakland	31
17	Philadelphia	23
23	Seattle	30
104		115

Regular Season (10-6)

New England		Opponents	Att.
34	*Cleveland	17	49,222
21	*Atlanta	37	48,321
37	Seattle	31	61,035
23	*Denver	14	59,602
21	New York Jets	11	53,603
34	*Miami	0	60,377
37	Baltimore	21	53,924
13	Buffalo	31	75,092
34	*New York Jets	21	60,834
34	Houston	38	51,524
14	*Los Angeles	17	60,609
47	*Baltimore	21	60,994
17	San Francisco	21	45,254
13	*Miami (OT)	16	63,292
24	*Buffalo	2	58,324
38	New Orleans	27	38,277
441		325	900,284

*Home Game   (OT) Overtime

Score by Periods

New England	77	132	110	122	0	—	441
Opponents	64	97	56	105	3	—	325

Attendance

Home 458,283   Away 442,001   Total 900,284
Single game home record, 61,457 (12-5-71)
Single season home record, 475,081 (1978)

1980 INDIVIDUAL STATISTICS

Rushing

	Att	Yds	Avg	LG	TD
Ferguson	211	818	3.9	44	2
Calhoun	200	787	3.9	22t	9
Grogan	30	112	3.7	19	1
Ivory	42	111	2.6	20t	0
Cavanaugh	19	97	5.1	22	2
Tatupu	33	97	2.9	11	0
Foreman	23	63	2.7	7	3
Clark	9	56	6.2	7	1
Jackson	5	37	7.4	15	0
Morgan	5	36	9.0	16	0
Johnson	4	26	2.4	11	0
Hubach	11	0	0.0	0	0
New England	588	2240	3.8	44	19
Opponents	482	1876	3.9	33	12

Field Goal Success

Distance	1-19	20-29	30-39	40-49	50 Over
Made-Att.	2-2	11-11	10-14	3-7	0-0

Passing

	Att	Comp	Pct	Yds	TD	Int	LG	Tkld	Rate
Grogan	306	175	57.2	2475	18	22	71	17/138	73.1
Cavanaugh	105	63	60.0	885	9	5	39t	8/62	95.9
Jackson	2	2	100.0	35	0	0		0/0	
N. England	413	240	58.1	3395	27	27	71	25/200	79.3
Opponents	458	266	58.1	3232	28	24	79t	44/346	

Receiving

	No	Yds	Avg	LG	TD
Morgan	45	991	22.0	71	6
Francis	41	664	16.2	39t	8
Jackson	35	737	21.1	40	5
Calhoun	27	129	4.8	12	0
Johnson	24	259	10.8	22	2
Ferguson	22	173	7.9	18	0
Foreman	14	99	7.1	18	0
Ivory	12	95	7.9	19	0
Hasselbeck	8	130	16.3	35t	4
Westbrook	4	60	15.0	21	0
Pennywell	4	31	7.8	16	1
Tatupu	4	27	6.8	11	0
New England	240	3395	14.1	71	27
Opponents	266	3232	12.2	79t	28

Interceptions

	No	Yds	Avg	LG	TD
Clayborn	5	87	17.4	29	0
Fox	4	41	10.3	23	0
James	4	32	8.0	19	0
Shoate	3	50	16.7	42t	1
Nelson	3	37	12.3	33	0
Hawkins	2	5	2.5	5	0
Haynes	1	31	31.0	31	0
Matthews	1	0	0.0	0	0
Sanford	1	5	5.0	5	0
New England	24	288	12.0	42t	1
Opponents	27	369	13.7	80	0

Punting

	No	Yds	Avg	LG	In 20
Hubach	63	2392	38.0	69	12
New England	63	2392	38.0	69	12
Opponents	92	3775	41.0	66	14

Punt Returns

	No	FC	Yds	Avg	LG	TD
James	33	3	331	10.0	75t	1
Haynes	17	2	140	8.2	35	0
Brown	10	1	42	4.2	14	0
New England	60	6	513	8.6	75t	1
Opponents	28	13	237	8.5	25	0

Kickoff Returns

	No	Yds	Avg	LG	TD
Ivory	36	992	27.6	98t	1
Brown	9	156	17.3	26	0
Currier	6	98	16.3	26	0
Clark	3	21	7.0	13	0
Westbrook	1	14	14.0	14	0
Pennywell	1	0	0.0	0	0
New England	56	1281	22.9	98t	1
Opponents	89	1649	18.5	35	0

Scoring

	TD	TD R	TD P	TD Rt	PAT	FG	TP
Smith	0				51/51	26/34	129
Calhoun	9	9					54
Francis	8		8				48
Morgan	6		6				36
Jackson	5		5				30
Hasselbeck	4		4				24
Ivory	3			1			18
Johnson	3		3				18
Tatupu	2	2					12
Clark	2	1					12
Ferguson	2	2					12
Foreman	2	2					12
Grogan	1	1					6
Haynes	1			1			6
James	1			1			6
Pennywell	1		1				6
Sanford	1			1			6
Shoate	1			1			6
New England	52	19	27	6	51/52	26/34	441
Opponents	40	12	28	0	39/40	14/20	325

NEW ENGLAND RECORD HOLDERS

Individual Records—Single Season

Category	Name	Performance
Rushing (Yds.)	Jim Nance, 1966	1458
Passing (Pct.)	Matt Cavanaugh, 1980	60.0
Passing (Yds.)	Babe Parilli, 1964	3465
Passing (TDs)	Babe Parilli, 1964	31
Receiving (No.)	Reggie Rucker, 1973	53
Receiving (Yds.)	Harold Jackson, 1979	1013
Interceptions	Ron Hall, 1964	11
Punting (Avg.)	Tom Janik, 1969	41.5
Punt Ret. (Avg.)	Mack Herron, 1974	14.8
Kickoff Ret. (Avg.)	Raymond Clayborn, 1977	31.0
Field Goals	John Smith, 1980	26
Touchdowns (Tot.)	Steve Grogan, 1976	13
	Stanley Morgan, 1979	13
Points	Gino Cappelletti, 1964	155

Team Records—Single Game

Category	Opponent, Date	Performance
Offense		
First Downs	vs. Hou, 12/11/66	31
Total Points	vs. NYJ, 9/9/79	56
Touchdowns	vs. NYJ, 10/29/78	8
	vs. NYJ, 9/9/79	8
Total Net Yards	vs. NYJ, 9/9/79	597
Net Yards Rushing	vs. Den, 11/28/76	332
Net Yards Passing	vs. Oak, 10/16/64	405
Rushing Attempts	vs. Den, 11/28/76	62
Passing Attempts	vs. Hou, 9/19/65	50
	vs. NYJ, 11/14/65	50
Interceptions by	vs. NYJ, 11/21/76	7
Defense		
Net Yards Allowed	vs. Balt, 10/23/77	86
Net Rushing Yards Allowed	vs. SD, 12/17/61	2
Net Passing Yards Allowed	vs. NYJ, 10/14/73	0

FIRST PLAYERS SELECTED

Year	Player, College, Position
1975	Russ Francis, Oregon, TE
1976	Mike Haynes, Arizona State, DB
1977	Raymond Clayborn, Texas, DB
1978	Bob Cryder, Alabama, G
1979	Rick Sanford, South Carolina, DB
1980	Roland James, Tennessee, DB
1981	Brian Holloway, Stanford, T

PATRIOTS COACHING HISTORY

Boston 1960-70
(140-155-9)

1960-61	Lou Saban*	7-12-0
1961-68	Mike Holovak	53-47-9
1969-70	Clive Rush**	5-18-0
1970-72	John Mazur***	9-19-0
1972	Phil Bengtson	1-4-0
1973-78	Chuck Fairbanks	46-42-0
1979-80	Ron Erhardt	19-13-0

*Released after five games in 1961
**Released after nine games in 1970
***Released after nine games in 1972

NEW ENGLAND PATRIOTS 1981 VETERAN ROSTER

No.	Name	Pos.	Ht.	Wt.	NFL Exp.	Birth-date	Birthplace	College	Residence	Games in '80
85	Adams, Julius	DE	6-4	263	10	4/26/48	Macon, Ga.	Texas Southern	Macon, Ga.	16
64	Bishop, Richard	NT-DE	6-1	260	6	3/23/50	Cleveland, Ohio	Louisville	Miami, Fla.	13
58	Brock, Pete	C	6-5	260	6	7/14/54	Portland, Ore.	Colorado	Norfolk, Mass.	16
87	Brown, Preston	WR-KR	5-10	184	2	3/2/58	Nashville, Tenn.	Vanderbilt	Nashville, Tenn.	5
63	Buben, Mark	DE	6-3	260	2	4/29/57	Geneva, N.Y.	Tufts	Foxboro, Mass.	0*
44	Calhoun, Don	RB	6-0	212	8	3/23/57	Muskogee, Okla.	Kansas State	Wichita, Kan.	16
12	Cavanaugh, Matt	QB	6-1	210	4	10/27/56	Youngstown, Ohio	Pittsburgh	Foxboro, Mass.	16
35	Clark, Allan	RB	5-10	186	3	6/8/57	Grand Rapids, Minn.	Northern Arizona	Attleboro, Mass.	11
26	Clayborn, Ray	CB	6-1	190	5	1/2/55	Ft. Worth, Tex.	Texas	Ft. Worth, Tex.	16
55	†Costict, Ray	LB	6-0	218	4	1/26/53	Moss Point, Miss.	Mississippi State	Moss Point, Miss.	0*
75	Cryder, Bob	G	6-4	265	4	3/19/55	East St. Louis, Ill.	Alabama	O'Fallon, Ill.	16
28	Currier, Bill	S	6-0	195	5	1/5/55	Glen Burnie, Md.	South Carolina	Missouri City, Tex.	16
43	Ferguson, Vagas	RB	6-1	194	2	3/6/57	Richmond, Ind.	Notre Dame	Attleboro, Mass.	16
22	Foreman, Chuck	RB	6-2	212	9	10/26/50	Frederick, Md.	Miami	Frederick, Md.	0*
48	Fox, Tim	S	5-11	190	6	11/1/53	Canton, Ohio	Ohio	Foxboro, Mass.	16
81	Francis, Russ	TE	6-6	235	6	4/3/53	Seattle, Wash.	Oregon	Norfolk, Mass.	15
51	Golic, Bob	LB	6-2	240	2	10/26/57	Cleveland, Ohio	Notre Dame	Parma, Ohio	16
14	Grogan, Steve	QB	6-4	208	7	7/24/53	Ottawa, Kan.	Kansas State	Foxboro, Mass.	16
71	†Hamilton, Ray	NT	6-1	245	9	1/20/51	Omaha, Neb.	Oklahoma	Ft. Worth, Tex.	12
73	Hannah, John	G	6-2	265	9	4/4/51	Canton, Ga.	Alabama	Honolulu, Hawaii	16
80	†Hasselbeck, Don	TE	6-7	245	5	4/1/55	Cincinnati, Ohio	Colorado	Willowick, Ohio	15
59	Hawkins, Mike	LB	6-2	232	4	11/29/55	Bay City, Tex.	Texas A&I	Sharon, Mass.	16
40	Haynes, Mike	CB	6-2	195	6	7/1/53	Denison, Tex.	Arizona State	Sharon, Mass.	13
6	Hubach, Mike	P	5-10	185	2	1/26/58	Cleveland, Ohio	Kansas	Crossville, Ala.	11
23	†Ivory, Horace	RB	5-10	212	6	8/8/54	Ft. Worth, Tex.	Oklahoma	Norfolk, Mass.	14
29	Jackson, Harold	WR	5-10	175	14	1/6/46	Hattiesburg, Miss.	Jackson State	Bay City, Tex.	16
38	James, Roland	CB-S	6-2	189	2	2/2/58	Jamestown, Ohio	Tennessee	Norfolk, Mass.	16
32	Johnson, Andy	RB	6-0	204	7	10/18/52	Athens, Ga.	Georgia	South Attleboro, Mass.	16
74	Jordan, Shelby	T	6-7	260	6	1/23/52	St. Louis, Mo.	Washington, Mo.	Canton, Mass.	16
52	†King, Steve	LB	6-4	230	9	6/10/51	Quinton, Okla.	Tulsa	Nonwood, Mass.	6
67	Lenkaitis, Bill	C	6-4	235	14	6/30/46	Cleveland, Ohio	Penn State	Fayetteville, N.C.	16
53	Matthews, Bill	LB	6-2	235	4	3/12/56	Santa Monica, Calif.	South Dakota State	Norton, Mass.	16
70	McDougald, Doug	DE	6-4	235	2	2/6/57	Fayetteville, N.C.	Virginia Tech	South Attleboro, Mass.	8
78	McGee, Tony	DE	6-4	271	11	1/18/49	Battle Creek, Mich.	Bishop	Smithfield, R.I.	11
50	McGrew, Larry	LB	6-4	250	2	7/23/57	Berkeley, Calif.	Southern California	Los Angeles, Calif.	0*
66	McMichael, Steve	NT	6-4	231	2	10/17/57	Freer, Tex.	Texas	Willington, Calif.	6
86	Morgan, Stanley	WR	5-11	180	5	2/17/55	Easley, S.C.	Tennessee	Oak Hill, Tex.	16
57	Nelson, Steve	LB	6-1	230	8	4/26/51	Farmington, Minn.	North Dakota State	Plainville, Mass.	16
17	†Owen, Tom	QB	6-1	194	8	9/1/52	Shreveport, La.	Wichita State	Norfolk, Mass.	6
88	Pennywell, Carlos	WR	6-2	180	4	3/18/56	Crowley, La.	Grambling	Shreveport, La.	11
77	Puetz, Garry	T	6-4	265	8	3/14/52	Elmhurst, Ill.	Valparaiso	Wichita, Kan.	0*
25	Sanford, Rick	S	6-1	192	3	1/9/57	Rock Hill, S.C.	South Carolina	Tampa, Fla.	16
56	Schindler, Steve	G	6-3	250	6	7/24/54	Caldwell, N.J.	Boston College	Foxboro, Mass.	0*
1	†Shoate, Rod	LB	6-1	215	6	4/26/53	Spiro, Okla.	Oklahoma	Denver, Colo.	16
30	Smith, John	K	6-0	185	8	12/30/49	Leafield, Eng.	Southampton, Eng.	Norfolk, Mass.	16
83	Stewart, Jimmy	CB	5-11	194	5	10/15/54	St. Louis, Mo.	Tulsa	Norfolk, Mass.	16
62	Tatupu, Mosi	RB	6-0	229	4	11/1/52	Pago Pago, Amer. Samoa	Southern California	San Diego, Calif.	16
54	Westbrook, Don	WR	5-10	184	6	4/26/55	Reno, Nev.	Nebraska	Quincy, Mass.	16
	Wheeler, Dwight	T	6-3	255	3	11/1/52	Memphis, Tenn.	Tennessee State	Nashville, Tenn.	14
	Zamberlin, John	LB	6-2	232	3	2/13/56	Tacoma, Wash.	Pacific Lutheran	Tacoma, Wash.	16

*Buben, Costict, Schindler, and Stewart missed '80 season due to injuries; Owen active for 7 games but did not play.

†Option playout; subject to developments.

Traded—Guard Sam Adams to New Orleans, defensive end Mel Lunsford to Cincinnati.

Also played with Patriots in '80—S Prentice McCray (3 games).

COACHING STAFF

Head Coach, Ron Erhardt

Pro Career: Starts third season as NFL head coach. Directed Patriots to 10-6 record last year. He joined Patriots staff in 1973 as an offensive backfield coach and added the responsibility of offensive coordinator in 1977. Under his direction in 1978, the Patriots established an NFL rushing record with 3,165 yards and led the league in total offense with 5,965 yards. No pro playing experience. Career record: 19-13.

Background: Quarterback at Jamestown (North Dakota) College, where he won all-conference honors during his senior year in 1953. Also lettered in baseball and basketball. Spent three years in the military service (1953-55). Started his college coaching career in 1963 at North Dakota State as defensive line coach. Was elevated to head coaching position in 1966 until he resigned in March 1973 to join the Parrtriots. Posted 59-6-1 collegiate record.

Personal: Born February 27, 1932, in Mandan, N.D. He and his wife, Anita, live in Medfield, Mass. They have four children—Jan, Rob, Jimmy, and Jill.

ASSISTANT COACHES

Raymond Berry, receivers; born February 27, 1933, Corpus Christi, Tex., lives in Foxboro, Mass. End Southern Methodist 1953-54. Pro end Baltimore Colts 1955-67. College coach: Arkansas 1970-72. Pro coach: Dallas Cowboys 1968-69, Detroit Lions 1973-75, Cleveland Browns 1976-77, fourth year with Patriots.

Gino Cappelletti, special teams; born March 26, 1934, Keewatin, Minn., lives in Foxboro, Mass. Quarterback Minnesota 1952-55. Pro wide receiver-kicker Boston/New England Patriots 1960-70. Pro coach: Joined Patriots in 1979.

Bobby Grier, offensive backfield; born November 10, 1942, Detroit, Mich., lives in Holliston, Mass. Running back Iowa 1961-63. No pro playing experience. College coach: Eastern Michigan 1974-77, Boston College 1978-80. Pro coach: Joined Patriots in 1981.

Rick Lantz, linebackers; born January 4, 1938, New Britain, Conn., lives in Foxboro. Linebacker Central Connecticut State College 1960-62. No pro playing experience. College coach: Boston University 1964, 1966-67, Rhode Island 1968, Buffalo University 1971-76, Navy 1971-76, Miami 1977-80. Pro coach: Joined Patriots in 1981.

Babe Parilli, quarterbacks; born May 7, 1930, Rochester, Pa., lives in Foxboro. N.J., lives in Foxboro. Quarterback Kentucky 1948-51. Pro quarterback Green Bay Packers 1952-53, 1957-58, Cleveland Browns 1956, Ottawa Rough Riders (CFL) 1959, Oakland Raiders 1960, Boston Patriots 1960-67, New York Jets 1968-69. Pro coach: Pittsburgh Steelers 1971-73, New York Stars (WFL) 1974 (head coach), Chicago Wind (WFL) 1975 (head coach), Denver Broncos 1977-79, first year with Patriots.

Jim Ringo, offensive coordinator-offensive line; born November 21, 1932, Orange, N.J., lives in Foxboro. Mass. Center-linebacker Syracuse 1949-52. Pro center Green Bay Packers 1953-63, Philadelphia Eagles 1964-67. Pro coach: Chicago Bears 1969-71, Buffalo Bills 1972-77 (head coach 1976-77), second year with Patriots.

Dick Roach, defensive backs; born August 23, 1932, Rapid City, S.D. lives in Foxboro. Defensive back Black Hills College. No pro playing experience. College coach: Montana State 1966-69, Oregon State 1970, Wyoming 1971-72, Fresno State 1973, Washington State 1974-75, Pro Coach: Montreal Alouettes (CFL) 1976-77, Kansas City Chiefs 1978-80, joined Patriots in 1981.

Fritz Shurmur, defensive coordinator-defensive line; born July 15, 1932, Riverview, Mich., lives in Foxboro. Center-linebacker Albion 1950-53. No pro playing experience. College coach: Albion 1954-61, Wyoming 1962-74 (head coach 1971-74). Pro coach: Detroit Lions 1975-77, fourth year with Patriots.

NEW ENGLAND PATRIOTS 1981 FIRST-YEAR ROSTER

Name	Pos.	Ht.	Wt.	Birth-date	Birthplace	College	Residence	How Acq.
Beard, Reggie (1)	WR	6-2	217	4/22/55	Elizabeth, N.J.	Cheney State, Pa.	Roselle, N.J.	FA
Blackmon, Don	LB	6-3	235	3/14/58	Pompano Beach, Fla.	Tulsa	Ft. Lauderdale, Fla.	D4
Brooks, Stanley	WR	5-11	185	5/29/55	Groesheck, Tex.	No College	Thornton, Tex.	FA
Buckley, Brian	QB	6-2	205	2/9/58	Salem, Mass.	Harvard	Marblehead, Mass.	D11
Burke, Bill	RB	5-10	200	4/16/58	Holyoke, Mass.	American Int'l.	Southampton, Mass.	FA
Bush, Mike	WR	6-1	188	4/14/58	Hollywood, Calif.	Cal Poly-SLO	San Luis Obispo, Calif.	FA
Camarillo, Rich	P	5-11	189	11/29/59	Whittier, Calif.	Washington	Pico Rivera, Calif.	FA
Cassidy, Charles	T	6-3	264	12/26/53	Syracuse, N.Y.	Mansfield State, Pa.	Syracuse, N.Y.	FA
Clark, Steve	DE	6-5	258	10/29/59	Chattanooga, Tenn.	Kansas State	Manhattan, Kan.	D5
Collins, Tony	RB	5-11	202	5/27/59	Sanford, Fla.	East Carolina	Penn Yan, N.Y.	D2
Compton, Russ	G	6-2	240	3/25/55	Boise, Idaho	Indiana	Bonita Springs, Fla.	FA
Cook, Charles	DE	6-3	255	5/13/59	Gainesville, Fla.	Miami	Gainesville, Fla.	FA
Crissy, Cris	CB-KR	5-11	195	2/3/59	Penn Yan, N.Y.	Princeton	Penn Yan, N.Y.	D12
Davidson, Chy*	WR	5-10	167	5/9/59	Brooklyn, N.Y.	Rhode Island	Kingston, R.I.	D11
Dawson, Lin	TE	6-3	235	6/24/59	Norfolk, Va.	North Carolina State	Kinston, N.C.	D8
Eccleston, Reggie	WR	5-11	185	6/26/58	LaGrange, Ga.	Connecticut	New London, Conn.	FA
Foster, Steve	G	6-3	252	11/20/58	Oklahoma City, Okla.	Springfield	Somerset, N.J.	FA
Golden, Tim	LB	6-2	220	11/15/59	Pahokee, Fla.	Florida	Ft. Lauderdale, Fla.	FA
Holloway, Brian	T	6-7	273	7/25/59	Omaha, Neb.	Stanford	Potomac, Md.	D1
Hopkins, Bobby	G	6-0	260	6/8/57	Baltimore, Md.	Gardner Webb	Ft. Pierce, Fla.	FA
Johnson, Craig	RB	6-1	200	9/26/59	Viborg, S.D.	Nebraska	Lincoln, Neb.	FA
Kempf, Florian	K	5-9	164	5/25/56	Philadelphia, Pa.	Pennsylvania	Philadelphia, Pa.	FA
Klein, John	WR	6-1	185	2/10/59	Brooklyn, N.Y.	Central Conn. State	West Islip, N.Y.	FA
Lyon, William (1)	NT	6-2	247	6/9/57	Beverly, Mass.	American Int'l.	Springfield, Mass.	FA
Manning, Bob	CB-S	6-2	180	4/3/59	Newton, Mass.	Massachusetts	Newton, Mass.	FA
McCarty, Colin	NT	6-2	263	5/22/58	Pittsburgh, Pa.	Temple	Berwyn, Pa.	FA
Naber, Ken	P-K	6-3	180	2/24/59	Cincinnati, Ohio	Stanford	Kenwood, Ohio	D8a
Pinkston, Arnie (1)	CB-S	6-0	172	8/2/58	New London, Conn.	Yale	Oakdale, Conn.	FA
Quinn, John (1)	S	6-1	203	9/24/57	Pittsfield, Mass.	Springfield	Pittsfield, Mass.	FA
Regan, Bob	T	6-4	258	4/3/59	New York, N.Y.	Yale	Floral Park, N.Y.	FA
Rill, Jim	C	6-5	252	10/7/58	Boston, Mass.	Dartmouth	Hanover, N.H.	FA
Ross, Mark (1)	P	5-10	175	11/2/57	Caldwell, Kan.	Northeast Oklahoma	Tahlequah, Okla.	FA
Ross, Tim	LB	6-5	216	12/27/58	Toledo, Ohio	Bowling Green	Toledo, Ohio	FA
Sidor, Tony	TE	6-4	233	1/31/59	Cleveland, Ohio	Syracuse	Pittsford, N.Y.	FA
Stevens, Kyle	RB	5-8	180	7/13/58	Loma Linda, Calif.	Washington	Seattle, Wash.	FA
Tate, Ronald	RB	6-1	212	7/12/58	Philadelphia, Pa.	N. Carolina Central	Berlin, Md.	D8a
Tautolo, John	G	6-1	260	5/29/59	Long Beach, Calif.	UCLA	Bellflower, Calif.	FA
Toler, Ken	WR	6-2	195	4/9/59	Greenville, Miss.	Mississippi	Jackson, Miss.	D7
Villela, Rich	RB	5-11	197	1/18/59	Martins Ferry, Ohio	Brown	Canton, Ohio	FA
Walker, Lea (1)	RB	6-3	228	11/10/56	Dublin, Ga.	Texas Southern	Houston, Tex.	FA
Webb, John	CB-S	6-1	184	9/23/57	Saxe, Va.	Connecticut	Bridgeport, Conn.	FA
Wilson, Darrell	CB-S	5-11	180	7/28/58	Camden, N.J.	Connecticut	Pennsauken, N.J.	FA
Wooten, Ron	G	6-4	257	6/28/59	Barnstable, Mass.	North Carolina	Kinston, N.C.	D6
Wright, Edward	WR	5-11	174	1/27/58	Brooklyn, N.Y.	Wake Forest	Brooklyn, N.Y.	FA
Wright, Gary	TE	6-3	235	4/8/57	Bennington, Vt.	American Int'l.	Springfield, Mass.	FA

*Selected in 1981 supplemental draft.

Players who report to an NFL team for the first time are designated on rosters as rookies (R). If a player reported to an NFL training camp in a previous year but was not on the active squad for three or more regular season or postseason games, he is listed on the first-year roster and designated by a (1). Thereafter, a player who is on the active squad for three or more regular season games is credited with an additional year of playing experience.

NOTES

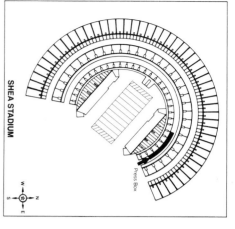

SHEA STADIUM

Press Box

New York Jets

American Football Conference
Eastern Division

Team Colors: Kelly Green and White
598 Madison Avenue
New York, New York 10022
Telephone: (212) 421-6600

Club Officials

Chairman of the Board: Leon Hess
President-Chief Operating Officer: Jim Kensil
Secretary and Administrative Manager: Steve Gutman
Director of Public Relations: Frank Ramos
Assistant Director of Public Relations: Ron Cohen
Director of Facilities Operation: Tim Davey
Traveling Secretary: Mike Kensil
Ticket Manager: Bob Parente
Director of Player Personnel: Mike Hickey
Pro Personnel Director: Jim Royer
Talent Scouts: Joe Collins, Don Grammer, Sid Hall,
   Carroll Huntress, Marv Sunderland
Film Director: Jim Pons
Trainer: Bob Reese
Assistant Trainer: Pepper Burruss
Equipment Manager: Bill Hampton

Stadium: Shea Stadium • **Capacity:** 60,372
   Flushing, New York 11368
Playing Surface: Grass
Training Center: 1000 Fulton Avenue
   Hempstead, Long Island,
   New York 11550
   516-538-6600

1981 SCHEDULE

Preseason

Aug. 7	at Denver	....	7:30
Aug. 15	at Atlanta	....	7:00
Aug. 22	at New York Giants	....	8:00
Aug. 29	**Philadelphia** (Giants Stadium)	......	8:00

Regular Season

Sept. 6	at Buffalo	....	4:00
Sept. 13	**Cincinnati**	....	4:00
Sept. 20	at Pittsburgh	....	1:00
Sept. 27	**Houston**	....	1:00
Oct. 4	at Miami	....	4:00
Oct. 11	**New England**	....	1:00
Oct. 18	**Buffalo**	....	1:00
Oct. 25	**Seattle**	....	4:00
Nov. 1	at New York Giants	....	1:00
Nov. 8	at Baltimore	....	4:00
Nov. 15	at New England	....	1:00
Nov. 22	**Miami**	....	1:00
Nov. 29	**Baltimore**	....	4:00
Dec. 6	at Seattle	....	1:00
Dec. 12	at Cleveland (Saturday)	....	12:30
Dec. 20	**Green Bay**	....	1:00

1980 TEAM STATISTICS

	New York Jets	Opp.
Total First Downs	289	348
Rushing	124	127
Passing	146	198
Penalty	19	23
Third Down Efficiency	86/202	106/220
Third Down Percentage	42.6	48.2
Total Net Yards	4882	5615
Total Offensive Plays	993	1080
Avg. Gain per Play	4.9	5.2
Avg. Gain per Game	305.1	350.9
Net Yards Rushing	1873	1951
Total Rushing Plays	470	508
Avg. Gain per Rush	4.0	3.8
Avg. Gain Rushing per Game	117.1	121.9
Net Yards Passing	3009	3664
Lost Attempting to Pass	42/326	28/235
Gross Yards Passing	3335	3899
Attempts/Completions	481/265	544/337
Percent Completed	55.1	61.9
Had Intercepted	30	23
Avg. Net Passing per Game	188.1	229.0
Punts/Avg.	74/41.8	63/39.9
Punt Returns/Avg.	33/8.2	46/8.0
Kickoff Returns/Avg.	74/20.1	54/22.4
Interceptions/Avg. Ret.	23/12.7	30/13.6
Penalties/Yards	103/767	90/872
Fumbles/Ball Lost	27/11	26/9
Total Points	302	395
Avg. Points per Game	18.9	24.7
Touchdowns	37	51
Rushing	17	20
Passing	17	27
Returns and Recoveries	3	4
Field Goals	14/22	13/24
Conversions	36/37	50/51
Safeties	1	0

1980 TEAM RECORD

Preseason (2-2)

New York Jets		Opponents
9	Chicago	21
13	Philadelphia	28
20	Pittsburgh	13
32	New York Giants	7
74		69

Regular Season (4-12)

New York Jets		Att.
14	*Baltimore	17
10	Buffalo	20
27	*San Francisco	37
21	Baltimore	35
11	*New England	21
14	Atlanta	7
17	*Seattle	27
17	*Miami	14
21	New England	34
24	*Buffalo	31
31	*Houston (OT)	28
13	Los Angeles	38
14	Cleveland	17
24	*New Orleans	21
24	Miami	17
302		395

*Home Game   (OT) Overtime

Score by Periods

New York Jets	44	112	38	105	3	— 302
Opponents	88	93	68	146	0	— 395

Attendance

Home 396,642   Away 469,773   Total 866,415

Single game home record, 63,962 (11-5-72)
Single season home record, 441,099 (1971)

1980 INDIVIDUAL STATISTICS

Rushing

	Att	Yds	Avg	LG	TD
Dierking	156	567	3.6	15	6
Long	115	355	3.1	18	6
Todd	49	330	6.7	31t	5
Newton	59	299	5.1	23	0
Gaines	36	174	4.8	15	0
Harper	45	126	2.8	22	0
Darby	1	15	15.0	15	0
Bennett	3	13	4.3	6	0
J. Jones	2	5	2.5	7	0
Batton	3	4	1.3	3	0
Ramsey	1	-15	-15.0	-15	0
New York Jets	470	1873	4.0	31t	17
Opponents	508	1951	3.8	36	20

Field Goal Success

Distance	1-19	20-29	30-39	40-49	50 Over
Made-Att.	0-0	4-4	4-9	6-8	0-1

Passing

	Att	Comp	Pct	Yds	TD	Int	LG	Tkld	Rate
Todd	479	264	55.1	3329	17	30	52	42/326	62.4
Ramsey				6	0	0	16t	0/0	
N.Y. Jets	481	265	55.1	3335	17	30	55	42/326	62.7
Opponents	544	337	61.9	3899	27	23		28/235	

Receiving

	No	Yds	Avg	LG	TD
Harper	50	634	12.7	52	3
Gaines	36	310	8.6	16t	3
J. Jones	25	482	19.3	55	3
Gaffney	24	397	16.5	36	2
Shuler	22	226	10.3	26	2
Newton	20	144	7.2	18	0
Long	20	137	6.9	16	0
Dierking	19	138	7.3	22	1
Walker	18	376	20.9	47	1
B. Jones	14	193	13.8	25	1
Barkum	13	244	18.8	28	1
Darby	3	48	16.0	20	1
Lewis	1	6	6.0	6	0
New York Jets	265	3335	12.6	55	17
Opponents	337	3899	11.6	68t	27

Interceptions

	No	Yds	Avg	LG	TD
Schroy	8	91	11.4	82t	1
Ray	6	132	22.0	71t	1
Dykes	5	1	0.2	1	0
Crosby	2	47	23.5	42	0
Buttle	1	15	15.0	15	0
Jackson	1	7	7.0	7	0
New York Jets	23	293	12.7	82t	2
Opponents	30	408	13.6	60	1

Punting

	No	Yds	Avg	LG	In 20
Ramsey	73	3096	42.4	59	15
New York Jets	74	3096	41.8	59	15
Opponents	63	2512	39.9	53	13

Punt Returns

	No	FC	Yds	Avg	LG	TD
Harper	28	7	242	8.6	24	0
Schroy	4	0	27	6.8	15	0
B. Jones	1	0	0	0.0	0	0
New York Jets	33	8	269	8.2	24	0
Opponents	46	7	369	8.0	75t	1

Kickoff Returns

	No	Yds	Avg	LG	TD
Harper	49	1070	21.8	35	0
Darby	7	139	19.9	30	0
Bennett	6	88	14.7	26	0
J. Jones	4	67	16.8	19	0
B. Jones	2	50	25.0	29	0
Shuler	2	25	12.5	25	0
Bingham	1	19	19.0	19	0
Schroy	1	17	17.0	10	0
Carter	1	12	12.0	12	0
Winkel	1	4	4.0	4	0
New York Jets	74	1491	20.1	35	0
Opponents	54	1207	22.4	47	0

Scoring

	TD R	TD P	TD Rt	PAT	FG	TP
Leahy				36/36	14/22	78
Dierking	6	1	0			42
Long	6					36
Todd	5					30
Gaines		3				18
Harper		3				18
J. Jones		3				18
Gaffney		2				12
Ray			2			12
Shuler		2				12
Barkum		1				6
Darby		1				6
Schroy			1			6
Walker		1				6
Team						(Safety) 2
N.Y. Jets	17	17	3	36/37	14/22	302
Opponents	20	27	4	50/51	13/24	395

NEW YORK JETS RECORD HOLDERS

Individual Records—Single Season

Category	Name	Performance
Rushing (Yds.)	John Riggins, 1975	1005
Passing (Pct.)	Richard Todd, 1980	55.1
Passing (Yds.)	Joe Namath, 1967	4007
Passing (TDs)	Al Dorow, 1960	26
	Joe Namath, 1967	26
Receiving (No.)	George Sauer, 1967	75
Receiving (Yds.)	Don Maynard, 1967	1434
Interceptions	Dainard Paulson, 1964	12
Punting (Avg.)	Curley Johnson, 1965	45.3
Punt Ret. (Avg.)	Dick Christy, 1961	21.3
Kickoff Ret. (Avg.)	Leon Burton, 1960	28.7
Field Goals	Jim Turner, 1968	34
Touchdowns (Tot.)	Art Powell, 1960	14
	Don Maynard, 1965	14
	Emerson Boozer, 1972	14
Points	Jim Turner, 1968	145

Team Records—Single Game

Category Offense	Opponent, Date	Performance
First Downs	vs. Cle, 9/21/70	31
Total Points	vs. Hou, 9/18/66	52
Touchdowns	vs. Hou, 9/18/66	7
Total Net Yards	vs. Balt, 9/24/72	573
Net Yards Rushing	vs. NE, 10/15/72	333
Net Yards Passing	vs. NE, 10/24/72	490
Rushing Attempts	vs. NE, 10/14/73	58
Passing Attempts	vs. Den, 12/3/67	62
Interceptions by	vs. Balt, 9/23/73	8

Defense	Opponent, Date	Performance
Net Yards Allowed	vs. Bos, 11/22/70	80
Net Rushing Yards Allowed	vs. Oak, 10/10/64	17
Net Passing Yards Allowed	vs. Buff, 9/29/74	0

FIRST PLAYERS SELECTED

Year	Player, College, Position
1970	Steve Tannen, Florida, CB
1971	John Riggins, Kansas, RB
1972	Jerome Barkum, Jackson State, WR
1973	Burgess Owens, Miami, DB
1974	Carl Barzilauskas, Indiana, DT
1975	Anthony Davis, So. California, RB (2)
1976	Richard Todd, Alabama, QB
1977	Marvin Powell, Southern California, T
1978	Chris Ward, Ohio State, T
1979	Marty Lyons, Alabama, DE
1980	Johnny (Lam) Jones, Texas, WR
1981	Freeman McNeil, UCLA, RB

JETS COACHING HISTORY

New York Titans 1960-62 (129-168-6)

1963-73	Weeb Ewbank	74-77-6
1974-75	Charley Winner*	9-14-0
1975	Ken Shipp	1-4-0
1976	Lou Holtz**	3-10-0
1976	Mike Holovak	0-1-0
1977-80	Walt Michaels	23-39-0

*Released after nine games in 1975
**Resigned after 13 games in 1976

NEW YORK JETS 1981 VETERAN ROSTER

No.	Name	Pos.	Ht.	Wt.	NFL Exp.	Birth-date	Birthplace	College	Residence	Games in '80
60	Alexander, Dan	G	6-4	255	5	6/17/55	Houston, Tex.	Louisiana State	Houston, Tex.	16
83	Barkum, Jerome	TE	6-4	225	10	7/18/50	Gulfport, Miss.	Jackson State	Gulfport, Miss.	16
30	Batton, Bobby	RB	5-11	190	2	3/17/57	Yazoo City, Miss.	Nevada-Las Vegas	San Francisco, Calif.	8
64	Bingham, Guy	C-T-G	6-3	255	2	2/25/58	Koizumi Gumma Ken, Jap.	Montana	Aberdeen, Wash.	16
54	Blinka, Stan	LB	6-2	230	3	4/29/57	Columbus, Ohio	Sam Houston State	Huntsville, Tex.	16
51	Buttle, Greg	LB	6-3	232	6	2/20/54	Atlantic City, N.J.	Penn State	Point Lookout, N.Y.	16
55	Crosby, Ron	LB	6-3	222	4	3/2/55	McKeesport, Pa.	Penn State	Venetia, Pa.	14
68	Cunningham, Eric	G	6-3	257	3	3/16/57	Akron, Ohio	Penn State	Akron, Ohio	6
84	Darby, Paul	WR	5-10	192	3	10/22/56	Austin, Tex.	Southwest Texas State	Austin, Tex.	8
25	Dierking, Scott	RB	5-10	215	5	5/24/55	Great Lakes, Ill.	Purdue	West Chicago, Ill.	16
26	Dykes, Donald	CB	5-11	180	5	8/24/55	Independence, La.	Southeast Louisiana	Hammond, La.	16
65	Fields, Joe	C	6-2	253	7	11/14/53	Woodbury, N.J.	Widener	Woodbury Heights, N.J.	16
81	Gaffney, Derrick	WR	6-1	180	6	5/24/55	Jacksonville, Fla.	Florida	Jacksonville, Fla.	16
21	Gaines, Clark	RB	6-1	209	5	2/1/54	Elberton, Ga.	Wake Forest	Scottsdale, Ariz.	13
99	Gastineau, Mark	DE	6-5	280	3	11/20/56	Ardmore, Okla.	East Central, Okla.	Lathrup Village, Mich.	13
90	Godfrey, Chris	G	6-3	250	2	5/17/58	Detroit, Mich.	Michigan	Englewood, N.J.	5
42	Harper, Bruce	RB-KR	5-8	177	5	6/20/55	Englewood, N.J.	Kutztown State	Hampton, Va.	6
47	Holmes, Jerry	CB-S	6-2	175	2	12/22/57	Newport News, Va.	West Virginia	Westbury, N.Y.	15
40	Jackson, Bobby	CB	5-10	185	4	1/20/57	Albany, Ga.	Florida State	Blacksburg, Va.	12
27	Johnson, Jesse	CB-S	6-3	190	5	8/23/57	Fort Collins, Colo.	Colorado	Cheyenne, Wyo.	15
89	Jones, Bobby	WR	5-11	180	3	12/23/56	Sharon, Pa.	No College	Brookfield, Ohio	15
80	Jones, Johnny "Lam"	WR	5-11	180	2	4/4/58	Lawton, Okla.	Texas	Austin, Tex.	16
73	Klecko, Joe	DT-DE	6-3	265	5	10/15/53	Chester, Pa.	Temple	West Chester, Pa.	16
5	Leahy, Pat	K	6-0	195	8	3/19/51	St. Louis, Mo.	St. Louis	St. Louis, Mo.	16
24	Lewis, Kenny	RB	6-0	190	2	10/2/57	Danville, Va.	Virginia Tech	Bellaire, Ohio	16
33	Long, Kevin	FB	6-1	218	5	1/20/57	Clinton, S.C.	South Carolina	Columbia, S.C.	15
29	Lynn, Johnny	CB	6-0	190	2	12/19/56	Los Angeles, Calif.	UCLA	Altadena, Calif.	0*
93	Lyons, Marty	DT	6-5	260	3	1/15/57	Tokoma Park, Md.	Alabama	Freeport, N.Y.	16
53	McKibben, Mike	LB	6-3	228	2	9/3/56	Mt. Carmel, Ill.	Kent State	Davis, Calif.	9
56	Mehl, Lance	LB	6-3	230	2	2/14/58	Bellaire, Ohio	Penn State	Long Beach, N.Y.	15
44	Newton, Tom	FB	6-0	213	5	3/8/54	Carmel, Calif.	California	Bellaire, Ohio	8
11	Penrose, Craig	QB	6-3	212	6	2/24/52	Woodland, Calif.	San Diego State	Long Beach, Calif.	0*
79	Powell, Marvin	T	6-5	268	5	8/30/55	Fort Bragg, N.C.	Southern California		16
15	Ramsey, Chuck	P	6-2	189	5	7/25/53	Rock Hill, S.C.	Wake Forest	Knoxville, Tenn.	16
66	Rasmussen, Randy	G	6-2	255	15	5/10/45	St. Paul, Neb.	Kearney State	Elmsford, N.Y.	8
28	Ray, Darrol	S	6-1	200	2	6/25/58	San Francisco, Calif.	Oklahoma	Norman, Okla.	16
92	Roberts, Wesley	DE	6-4	260	2	8/1/57	Dodge City, Kan.	Texas Christian	Amarillo, Tex.	5
61	Roman, John	T	6-4	260	6	8/31/52	Ventnor, N.J.	Idaho State	New York, N.Y.	16
10	Ryan, Pat	QB	6-3	205	4	9/16/55	Hutchinson, Kan.	Tennessee	Knoxville, Tenn.	14
74	Salaam, Abdul	DT	6-3	265	6	2/12/53	New Brockton, Ala.	Kent State	Cincinnati, Ohio	16
48	Schroy, Ken	S	6-2	196	6	9/22/52	Valley Forge, Pa.	Maryland	Roslyn Heights, N.Y.	16
82	Shuler, Mickey	TE	6-3	235	4	8/21/56	Harrisburg, Pa.	Penn State	Enola, Pa.	14
50	Sullivan, John	LB	6-1	225	3	10/1/56	Amityville, N.Y.	Illinois	Point Lookout, N.Y.	9
14	Todd, Richard	QB	6-2	203	6	11/19/53	Birmingham, Ala.	Alabama	Mobile, Ala.	16
70	Waldemore, Stan	G	6-4	250	5	2/20/55	Newark, N.J.	Nebraska	Nutley, N.J.	16
85	Walker, Wesley	WR	6-0	175	5	5/26/55	San Bernardino, Calif.	California	Dix Hills, N.Y.	10
72	Ward, Chris	T	6-3	270	4	12/16/55	Cleveland, Ohio	Ohio State	Dix Hills, N.Y.	14
71	Winkel, Bob	DT	6-4	255	3	10/23/55	Paducah, Ky.	Kentucky	Lexington, Ky.	16

*Lynn missed '80 season due to injury; Penrose active for 16 games but did not play.

Also played with Jets in '80 — RB Woody Bennett (10 games), S Steve Carpenter (3), WR Gerald Carter (3), CB Saladin Martin (3), S Tim Moresco (11), DE Lawrence Pillers (3), S Shafer Suggs (4).

COACHING STAFF

Head Coach, Walt Michaels

Pro Career: Starts fifth season as NFL head coach. Led Jets to an 8-8 mark in 1978 and 1979. Pro linebacker, drafted by Cleveland Browns in 1951 but traded to Green Bay and played 1951 season with Packers. Reacquired by Browns in 1952, with whom he stayed with until his retirement following 1961 season. Member of Cleveland's 1954 and 1955 NFL champions and named all-pro 1957-60. Started pro coaching career as defensive line coach with Oakland Raiders in 1962 before moving to Jets from 1963 to 1972. Joined Philadelphia Eagles staff in 1973 as defensive line coach until 1975, returning to Jets in 1976 as defensive co-ordinator. Career record: 23-39.

Background: Fullback at Washington and Lee from 1947 through 1950, averaged 5.5 yards per carry. Earned B.A. in psychology and education.

Personal: Born October 16, 1929 in Swoyersville, Pa., Walt and his wife, Betty, live in Islip, N.Y., and have four children—Mary Ann, Walter, Mark, and Paul.

ASSISTANT COACHES

Bill Baird, defensive backs; born March 1, 1939, Lindsay, Calif., lives in New York City. Defensive back San Francisco State 1959-61. Pro defensive back New York Jets 1963-69. College coach: Stanford 1970, Fresno State 1973-75, 1979, Pacific 1980. Pro coach: First year with Jets.

Ralph Baker, linebackers; born August 25, 1942, Lewiston, Pa., lives in New York. Linebacker Penn State 1961-63. Pro linebacker New York Jets 1964-74. Pro coach: Second year with Jets.

Bob Fry, offensive line; born November 11, 1930, Cincinnati, Ohio, lives in Islip, N.Y. Tackle Kentucky 1949-52. Pro tackle Los Angeles Rams 1953-59, Dallas Cowboys 1960-64. Pro coach: Atlanta Falcons 1966-68, Pittsburgh Steelers 1969-73, Jets since 1974.

Joe Gardi, defensive coordinator; born March 2, 1929, Newark, N.J., lives in Sayville, N.Y. Offensive-defensive tackle Maryland 1956-59. No pro playing experience. College coach: Maryland 1970-74. Pro coach: Philadelphia Bell (WFL) 1974-75 (interim head coach one game in 1975), Portland Thunder (WFL) 1975 (head coach), Jets since 1976.

Bob Ledbetter, running backs; born September 24, 1934, Tupelo, Miss., lives in East Northport, N.Y. Tackle Mississippi Industrial 1957-59. No pro playing experience. College coach: Southern Illinois 1969-71, Norfolk State 1972-73 (head coach), Grambling 1976. Pro coach: Baltimore Colts 1973-75, Washington Redskins 1976-77, San Francisco 49ers 1978 (head coach 10 games), third year with Jets.

Pete McCulley, receivers; born November 29, 1931, Franklin, Miss., lives in Garden City, N.Y. Quarterback Louisiana Tech 1954-56. No pro playing experience. College coach: Stephen F. Austin 1959, Houston 1960-61, Baylor 1963-69, Navy 1970-72. Pro coach: Baltimore Colts 1973-75, Washington Redskins 1976-77, San Francisco 49ers 1978 (head coach 10 games), third year with Jets.

Larry Pasquale, special teams; born April 21, 1941, New York, N.Y., lives in New York City. Quarterback Bridgeport 1961-63. No pro playing experience. College coach: Slippery Rock State 1967, Boston University 1968, Navy 1969-70, Massachusetts 1971-75, Idaho State 1976. Pro coach: Montreal Alouettes (CFL) 1977-78, Detroit Lions 1979, second year with Jets.

Dan Sekanovich, defensive line; born July 27, 1933, Hazleton, Pa., lives in Sayville, N.Y. Defensive end Tennessee 1951-53. Pro defensive end Montreal Alouettes (CFL) 1955. College coach: Connecticut 1964-67, Pittsburgh 1968, Kentucky 1971-72. Pro coach: Montreal Alouettes 1973-76, fifth year with Jets.

Joe Walton, offensive coordinator-quarterbacks; born December 15, 1935, Beaver Falls, Pa., lives in New York City, End Pittsburgh 1953-56. Pro end Washington 1957-60, N.Y. Giants 1961-63. Pro coach: New York Giants 1969-73, Washington Redskins 1974-80, first year with Jets.

NEW YORK JETS 1981 FIRST-YEAR ROSTER

Name	Pos.	Ht.	Wt.	Birth-date	Birthplace	College	Residence	How Acq.
Augustyniak, Mike (1)	RB	5-11	225	7/17/56	Ft. Wayne, Ind.	Purdue	Leo, Ind.	FA
Barber, Marion	RB	6-3	230	12/6/59	Ft. Lauderdale, Fla.	Minnesota	Detroit, Mich.	D2
Barilla, Mickey (1)	K	6-0	184	3/27/58	Steubenville, Ohio	Nevada-Las Vegas	Las Vegas, Nev.	FA
Barnes, Steve (1)	CB-S	6-0	195	2/18/57	Galveston, Tex.	Texas Christian	Alvin, Tex.	FA
Benjamin, William	LB	6-2	228	9/14/58	Indianapolis, Ind.	San Jose State	Indianapolis, Ind.	FA
Benson, Todd	LB	6-2	222	12/6/59	Altoona, Pa.	Maryland	Altoona, Pa.	FA
Blackwell, Ted	RB	5-11	190	10/25/58	Virginia, Minn.	Rutgers	Summit, N.J.	FA
Blanshan, Alan (1)	T	6-5	270	11/3/57	Mankato, Minn.	Minnesota	Minneapolis, Minn.	FA
Boermeester, Peter (1)	K	5-10	200	10/8/56	Holland, Netherlands	UCLA	Harbor City, Calif.	FA
Brewington, Mike (1)	LB	6-3	226	12/4/57	Greenville, N.C.	East Carolina	Greenville, N.C.	FA
Carter, Walter (1)	DT	6-4	241	12/19/57	Richmond, Va.	Florida State	Richmond, Va.	FA
Cernansky, Dan (1)	LB	6-1	220	4/17/57	Toronto, Ohio	Waynesburg	Toronto, Ohio	FA
Clausen, Kent	LB	6-4	233	12/6/57	Watertown, S.D.	Montana	Missoula, Mont.	FA
Clay, Dexter (1)	WR	6-4	194	6/12/56	Vernon, Tex.	Jacksonville	Houston, Tex.	D11
Clayton, Ralph (1)	RB	6-3	222	9/29/58	Detroit, Mich.	Michigan	Detroit, Mich.	D2a(80)
Cotton, Tim (1)	WR	6-0	190	11/29/54	Houston, Tex.	Xavier, Ohio	Missouri City, Tex.	FA
DeLoach, Ralph (1)	DE	6-5	254	1/13/57	Sacramento, Calif.	California	Sacramento, Calif.	FA
England, Gary	G	6-4	257	9/28/57	Salt Lake City, Utah	Nebraska	Lincoln, Neb.	FA
Fanz, Scott	G	6-3	259	12/7/57	Berea, Ohio	Maryland	College Park, Md.	FA
Faulkner, Mike (1)	DT	6-2	248	5/21/57	Baltimore, Md.	Virginia Tech	Oxon Hill, Md.	FA
Gall, Ed	DT	6-4	265	4/25/58	Allentown, Pa.	Maryland	Egypt, Pa.	D11
Grossart, Kyle (1)	QB	6-4	210	1/19/55	Chico, Calif.	Oregon State	Oakland, Calif.	FA
Harris, Mike (1)	WR	5-11	184	5/3/59	Los Angeles, Calif.	Purdue	Cerritos, Calif.	FA
Henderson, Carlos (1)	CB	6-2	209	5/11/55	River Rough, Mich.	Marquette	Brown Deer, Wis.	FA
Hubert, Wes (1)	C	6-3	265	11/7/57	Houston, Tex.	Texas	Houston, Tex.	FA
Jones, Homer	RB-KR	5-10	200	8/1/59	Silver Springs, Md.	Brigham Young	Orem, Utah	FA
Jones, Lloyd	WR	6-3	185	1/7/58	Detroit, Mich.	Brigham Young	Pomona, Calif.	D8
Larry, Admiral Dewey	CB	5-11	190	9/1/58	New Orleans, La.	Nevada-Las Vegas	Omaha, Neb.	D9
Lewandoski, Frank (1)	LB	6-1	233	2/12/58	Muskegon, Mich.	Northern Illinois	Rockford, Ill.	FA
Massey, Alan	T	6-3	260	7/22/58	Monroe, La.	Mississippi State	Jackson, Miss.	D1
McNeil, Freeman	RB	5-11	220	4/22/59	Jackson, Miss.	UCLA	Los Angeles, Calif.	D1
Misko, John (1)	P	6-5	200	10/1/54	Highland Park, Mich.	Oregon State	Porterville, Calif.	FA
Moeller, Mike	T	6-5	280	2/2/59	Cleveland, Ohio	Drake	Florissant, Mo.	D12
Moon, Tim (1)	TE	6-3	215	8/5/57	Oak Ridge, Tenn.	Virginia	Virginia Beach, Va.	FA
Moyer, Steve	T	6-7	271	9/29/58	San Diego, Calif.	Southern California	Los Angeles, Calif.	FA
Neil, Kenny	DE-DT	6-4	250	1/8/59	Cincinnati, Ohio	Iowa State	Cincinnati, Ohio	D7
Nitti, John	RB	6-1	208	12/22/58	Brooklyn, N.Y.	Yale	Westbury, N.Y.	FA
Pellegrini, Joe	C	6-4	252	4/8/57	Boston, Mass.	Harvard	Hingham, Mass.	FA
Perillo, Joe	LB	6-2	228	6/26/57	Brooklyn, N.Y.	Nassau C.C.	Central Islip, N.Y.	FA
Rudolph, Ben	DT-DE	6-5	255	8/29/57	Evergreen, Ala.	Long Beach State	Daphene, Ala.	D3
Sanders, Danny (1)	QB	6-4	203	5/14/55	Oak Ridge, Tenn.	Carson-Newman	Oak Ridge, Tenn.	FA
Schulze, Jim	G	6-3	241	3/22/57	Massillon, Ohio	Lehigh	Marietta, Ga.	FA
Semall, Bruce	TE	6-3	244	1/6/58	Cleveland, Ohio	Syracuse	Maple Heights, Ohio	FA
Sisco, Lance (1)	TE	6-2	224	4/7/57	Montclair, N.J.	William Paterson, N.J.	Fairfield, N.J.	FA
Sohn, Kurt (1)	WR-KR	5-11	180	6/26/57	Ithaca, N.Y.	Fordham	Huntington, N.Y.	FA
Springs, Kirk (1)	CB-S	6-0	192	8/16/58	Cincinnati, Ohio	Miami, Ohio	Cincinnati, Ohio	FA
Stephens, Steve (1)	TE	6-3	232	3/4/57	Tampa, Fla.	Oklahoma State	Tampa, Florida	FA
Streeter, Mark (1)	CB-S	6-0	191	3/22/57	Massillon, Ohio	Arizona	Scottsdale, Ariz.	FA
Washington, Al	LB	6-3	235	9/25/58	Erie, Pa.	Ohio State	Cleveland, Ohio	D4
Wetzel, Marty	LB	6-3	235	1/6/58	New Orleans, La.	Tulane	New Orleans, La.	D10
Wojtowicz, John	G	6-4	251	1/29/59	New Castle, Pa.	Penn State	New Castle, Pa.	FA
Wooding, John	LB	6-2	230	4/4/59	Philadelphia, Pa.	Brown	Erdenheim, Pa.	D6

Players who report to an NFL team for the first time are designated on rosters as rookies (R). If a player reported to an NFL training camp in a previous year but was not on the active squad for three or more regular season or postseason games, he is listed on the first-year roster and designated by a (1). Thereafter, a player who is on the active squad for three or more regular season games is credited with an additional year of playing experience.

NOTES

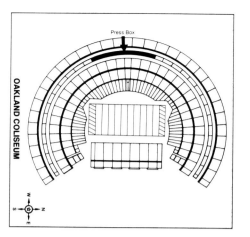

OAKLAND COLISEUM

Press Box

Oakland Raiders

American Football Conference
Western Division

Team Colors: Silver and Black

7850 Edgewater Drive
Oakland, California 94621
Telephone: (415) 562-5900

Club Officials

General Partners: Al Davis, E. W. McGah
Managing General Partner: Al Davis
Executive Assistant: Al LoCasale
Special Projects: John Madden
Player Personnel Operations: Ron Wolf
Player Personnel: Dan Conners, Tom Grimes,
 Kent McCloughan
Business Manager: Ken LaRue
Publications Director: Bill Glazier
Ticket Manager: George Glace
Controller: Steve Ballard
Trainers: George Anderson, H. Rod Martin
Equipment Manager: Richard Romanski
Film Coordinator: Max Friedman
Computer Operations: John Otten
Administrative Assistants: Ken Bishop, Phil Camicia,
 Pete Eiges

Stadium: Oakland-Alameda County Coliseum •
 Capacity: 54,616
 Hegenberger Road and
 Nimitz Freeway
 Oakland, California 94621

Playing Surface: Grass
Training Camp: El Rancho Tropicana
 Santa Rosa, California 95401

1981 SCHEDULE

Preseason

Aug. 8	**Atlanta**	6:00
Aug. 15	vs. Green Bay (Milwaukee)	7:00
Aug. 22	at New England	2:00
Aug. 29	**San Francisco**	6:00

Regular Season

Sept. 6	at Denver	2:00
Sept. 14	at Minnesota (Monday)	8:00
Sept. 20	**Seattle**	1:00
Sept. 27	at Detroit	1:00
Oct. 4	**Denver**	1:00
Oct. 11	at Kansas City	3:00
Oct. 18	**Tampa Bay**	1:00
Oct. 25	**Kansas City**	1:00
Nov. 1	**New England**	1:00
Nov. 8	at Houston	12:00
Nov. 15	at Miami	1:00
Nov. 22	**San Diego**	1:00
Nov. 29	at Seattle	1:00
Dec. 7	**Pittsburgh** (Monday)	6:00
Dec. 13	**Chicago**	1:00
Dec. 21	at San Diego (Monday)	6:00

1980 TEAM STATISTICS

	Oakland	Opp.
Total First Downs	281	319
Rushing	108	108
Passing	149	181
Penalty	24	30
Third Down Efficiency	92/243	80/220
Third Down Percentage	37.9	36.4
Total Net Yards	5045	5038
Total Offensive Plays	1044	1079
Avg. Gain per Play	4.8	4.7
Avg. Gain per Game	315.3	314.9
Net Yards Rushing	2146	1726
Total Rushing Plays	541	501
Avg. Gain per Rush	4.0	3.4
Avg. Gain Rushing per Game	134.1	107.9
Net Yards Passing	2899	3312
Gross Yards Passing	3294	3731
Attempts/Completions	456/235	524/296
Percent Completed	51.5	56.5
Had Intercepted	24	35
Avg. Net Passing per Game	181.2	207.0
Punts/Avg.	71/43.6	87/38.9
Punt Returns/Avg.	49/8.6	34/7.9
Kickoff Returns/Avg.	62/19.0	66/19.9
Interceptions/Avg. Ret.	35/14.3	24/6.4
Penalties/Yards	98/929	102/922
Fumbles/Ball Lost	38/20	34/17
Total Points	364	306
Avg. Points per Game	22.8	19.1
Touchdowns	44	38
Rushing	14	14
Passing	23	17
Returns and Recoveries	7	2
Field Goals	19/37	14/24
Conversions	41/44	36/37
Safeties	1	0

1980 TEAM RECORD

Preseason (2-2)

Oakland		Opponents
14	San Francisco	33
31	New England	29
17	Washington	34
24	Philadelphia	23
86		119

Regular Season (11-5)

Oakland		Opponents	Att.
27	Kansas City	14	54,269
24	San Diego (OT)	30	51,943
24	*Washington	21	45,163
7	Buffalo	24	77,257
17	*Kansas City	31	40,153
38	*San Diego	24	44,826
45	Pittsburgh	34	53,940
33	*Seattle	14	50,185
16	*Miami	10	46,378
28	*Cincinnati	17	44,132
19	Seattle	17	60,480
7	Philadelphia	10	68,585
9	*Denver	3	51,583
13	*Dallas	19	53,194
24	Denver	21	73,274
33	New York Giants	17	61,287
364		306	876,649

*Home Game   OT (Overtime)

Score by Periods

					OT	Total
Oakland	60	98	89	117	0	— 364
Opponents	61	101	51	87	6	— 306

Attendance

Home 375,614   Away 501,035   Total 876,649
Single game home record,
74,121 (9-12-73 at Berkeley)
54,843 (12-11-72 at Oakland)
Single season home record, 423,838 (1979)

1980 INDIVIDUAL STATISTICS

Rushing

	Att	Yds	Avg	LG	TD
van Eeghen	222	838	3.8	34	5
King	172	761	4.4	89t	4
Whittington	91	299	3.3	42t	2
Plunkett	28	141	5.0	17	2
Guy	3	38	12.7	24	0
Jensen	14	30	2.1	4	0
Pastorini	4	24	6.0	10	0
Matthews	5	11	2.2	5	0
Wilson	1	3	3.0	3	0
Branch	1	1	1.0	1	0
Oakland	541	2146	4.0	89t	14
Opponents	501	1726	3.4	37	19

Field Goal Success

Distance	1-19	20-29	30-39	40-49	50 Over
Made-Att.	0-0	4-6	9-12	6-13	0-6

Passing

	Att	Comp	Pct	Yds	TD	Int	Tkld	Rate
Plunkett	320	165	51.6	2299	18	16	36/285	72.8
Pastorini	130	66	50.8	932	5	7	10/103	61.1
Guy	1	1	100.0	32	0	0	0/0	—
Wilson	5	3	60.0	31	0	0	0/0	—
Christensen	0	0	0.0	0	0	0	1/7	—
Oakland	456	235	51.5	3294	23	24	47/395	69.7
Opponents	524	296	56.5	3731	17	35	54/419	—

Receiving

	No	Yds	Avg	LG	TD
Chandler	49	786	16.0	56	10
Branch	44	858	19.5	86t	7
van Eeghen	29	259	8.9	37	0
Chester	28	366	13.1	47	4
Casper	22	270	12.3	35	1
King	22	145	6.6	18	0
Whittington	19	205	10.8	55	0
Jensen	7	87	12.4	32	0
Bradshaw	6	132	22.0	45t	1
Ramsey	5	117	23.4	58	0
Matthews	3	33	11.0	20	0
Martini	1	36	36.0	36	0
Oakland	235	3294	14.0	86t	23
Opponents	296	3731	12.6	67t	17

Interceptions

	No	Yds	Avg	LG	TD
Hayes	13	273	21.0	62	1
M. Davis	3	88	29.3	49	0
Owens	3	59	19.7	58t	1
McKinney	3	22	7.3	22	0
Hendricks	3	10	3.3	5	0
O'Steen	3	10	3.3	14	0
Millen	2	17	8.5	9	0
Martin	2	15	7.5	15	0
McClanahan	1	7	7.0	7	0
Jackson	1	0	0.0	0	0
Nelson	1	0	0.0	0	0
Oakland	35	501	14.3	62	2
Opponents	24	153	6.4	37	0

Punting

	No	Yds	Avg	LG	In 20
Guy	71	3099	43.6	66	18
Oakland	71	3099	43.6	66	18
Opponents	87	3382	38.9	71	13

Punt Returns

	No	FC	Yds	Avg	LG	TD
Matthews	48	7	421	8.8	34	0
McKinney	1	0	0	0.0	0	0
Oakland	49	7	421	8.6	34	0
Opponents	34	6	268	7.9	20	0

Kickoff Returns

	No	Yds	Avg	LG	TD
Matthews	29	585	20.2	45	0
Whittington	21	392	18.7	90t	1
Moody	8	150	18.8	39	0
Jensen	1	33	33.0	33t	1
Christensen	1	10	10.0	10	0
Ramsey	1	10	10.0	10	0
Hayes	1	0	0.0	0	0
Oakland	62	1180	19.0	90t	2
Opponents	66	1315	19.9	54	0

Scoring

	TD R	TD P	TD Rt	PAT	FG	TP
Bahr	0	0	0	41/44	19/37	98
Chandler	0	10	0			60
Branch	0	7	0			42
van Eeghen	5	0	0			30
Chester	0	4	0			24
King	4	0	0			24
Whittington	2	0	1			24
Plunkett	2	0	0			12
Bradshaw	0	1	0			6
Casper	0	1	0			6
Christensen	0	0	1			6
Hayes	0	0	1			6
Jensen	0	0	1			6
Jones	0	0	1			6
Martin	0	0	1			6
Owens	0	0	1			6
Hendricks			(Safety)			2
Oakland	14	23	7	41/44	19/37	364
Opponents	19	17	2	36/37	14/24	306

OAKLAND RECORD HOLDERS

Individual Records—Single Season

Category	Name	Performance
Rushing (Yds.)	Mark van Eeghen, 1977	1273
Passing (Pct.)	Ken Stabler, 1976	66.7
Passing (Yds.)	Ken Stabler, 1979	3615
Passing (TDs.)	Daryle Lamonica, 1969	34
Receiving (No.)	Art Powell, 1964	76
Receiving (Yds.)	Art Powell, 1964	1361
Interceptions	Lester Hayes, 1980	13
Punting (Avg.)	Ray Guy, 1973	45.3
Punt Ret. (Avg.)	Claude Gibson, 1964	14.4
Kickoff Ret. (Avg.)	Harold Hart, 1975	30.5
Field Goals	George Blanda, 1973	23
Touchdowns (Tot.)	Art Powell, 1963	16
	Pete Banaszak, 1975	16
Points	George Blanda, 1968	117

Team Records—Single Game

Category	Opponent, Date	Performance
Offense		
First Downs	vs. NO, 11/9/75	34
Total Points	vs. Hou, 12/22/63	52
Touchdowns	vs. NYJ, 10/20/63	7
	vs. Hou, 12/22/63	7
	vs. TB, 11/28/76	7
Total Net Yards	vs. Den, 10/25/64	637
Net Yards Rushing	vs. GB, 9/17/78	348
Net Yards Passing	vs. KC, 11/3/68	469
Rushing Attempts	vs. Buff, 11/28/77	64
Passing Attempts	vs. KC, 10/5/80	60
Interceptions by	vs. Hou, 9/7/63	6
	vs. LA, 10/29/72	6
Defense		
Net Yards Allowed	vs. Hou, 10/9/72	89
Net Rushing Yards Allowed	vs. Den, 10/22/72	13
Net Passing Yards Allowed	vs. SD, 10/5/75	-22

FIRST PLAYERS SELECTED

Year	Player, College, Position
1971	Jack Tatum, Ohio State, S
1972	Mike Siani, Villanova, WR
1973	Ray Guy, So. Mississippi, K-P
1974	Henry Lawrence, Florida A&M, T
1975	Neal Colzie, Ohio State, DB
1976	Charles Philyaw, Texas Southern, DT (2)
1977	Mike Davis, Colorado, DB (2)
1978	Dave Browning, Washington, DE (2)
1979	Willie Jones, Florida State, DE (2)
1980	Marc Wilson, Brigham Young, QB
1981	Ted Watts, Texas Tech, DB

RAIDERS COACHING HISTORY

(203-110-11)

Eddie Erdelatz*	1960-61	6-10-0
Marty Feldman**	1961-62	2-15-0
Red Conkright	1962	1-8-0
Al Davis	1963-65	23-16-3
John Rauch	1966-68	35-10-1
John Madden	1969-78	112-39-7
Tom Flores	1979-80	24-12-0

*Released after two games in 1961
**Released after five games in 1962

Pittsburgh Steelers

American Football Conference
Central Division

Team Colors: Black and Gold
Three Rivers Stadium
300 Stadium Circle
Pittsburgh, Pennsylvania 15212
Telephone: (412) 323-1200

Club Officials

Chairman of the Board: Arthur J. Rooney, Sr.
President: Daniel M. Rooney
Vice President: John R. McGinley
Vice President: Arthur J. Rooney, Jr.
Controller: Dennis P. Thimons
Traveling Secretary: Jim Boston
Director of Public Relations: Ed Kiely
Publicity Director: Joe Gordon
Assistant Publicity Director: John Evenson
Director of Player Personnel: Dick Haley
Assistant Director of Player Personnel:
 William Nunn, Jr.
Talent Scout-West Coast: Bob Schmitz
Pro Talent Scout: Tom Modrak
College Talent Scout: Joe Krupa
Director of Ticket Sales: Geraldine R. Glenn
Trainer: Ralph Berlin
Equipment Manager: Anthony Parisi

Stadium: Three Rivers Stadium • **Capacity:** 54,000
 300 Stadium Circle
 Pittsburgh, Pennsylvania 15212
Playing Surface: Tartan Turf
Training Camp: St. Vincent College
 Latrobe, Pennsylvania 15650

1981 SCHEDULE

Preseason

Aug. 8	at Cleveland	7:30
Aug. 15	at Philadelphia	6:00
Aug. 22	at Dallas	8:00
Aug. 29	**New York Giants**	6:00

Regular Season

Sept. 6	**Kansas City**	1:00
Sept. 10	at Miami (Thursday)	8:30
Sept. 20	**New York Jets**	1:00
Sept. 27	**New England**	1:00
Oct. 4	at New Orleans	1:00
Oct. 11	**Cleveland**	1:00
Oct. 18	at Cincinnati	1:00
Oct. 26	**Houston** (Monday)	9:00
Nov. 1	**San Francisco**	1:00
Nov. 8	at Seattle	1:00
Nov. 15	at Atlanta	1:00
Nov. 22	at Cleveland	1:00
Nov. 29	**Los Angeles**	1:00
Dec. 7	at Oakland (Monday) . . .	6:00
Dec. 13	**Cincinnati**	1:00
Dec. 20	at Houston	3:00

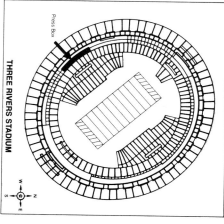

THREE RIVERS STADIUM

Press Box

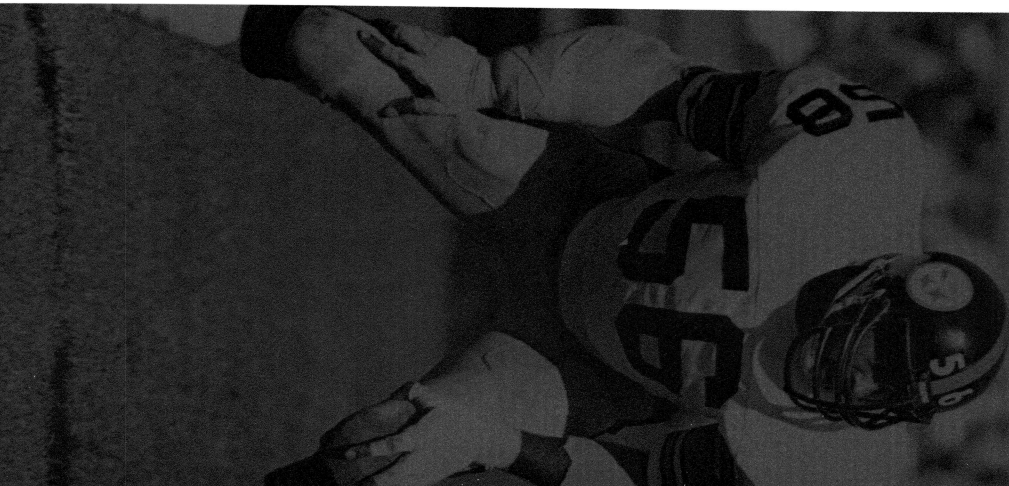

1980 TEAM STATISTICS

	Pittsburgh	Opp.
Total First Downs	308	302
Rushing	111	101
Passing	177	171
Penalty	20	30
Third Down Efficiency	101/224	94/232
Third Down Percentage	45.1	40.5
Total Net Yards	5554	5134
Total Offensive Plays	1033	1036
Avg. Gain per Play	5.4	5.0
Avg. Gain per Game	347.1	320.9
Net Yards Rushing	1986	1762
Total Rushing Plays	512	486
Avg. Gain per Game	124.1	110.1
Avg. Gain per Rush	3.9	3.6
Net Yards Passing	3568	3372
Lost Attempting to Pass	37/264	18/145
Gross Yards Passing	3832	3517
Attempts/Completions	484/250	532/280
Percent Completed	51.7	52.6
Had Intercepted	24	26
Avg. Net Passing per Game	223.0	210.8
Punts/Avg.	66/40.2	73/40.7
Punt Returns/Avg.	45/8.7	34/6.4
Kickoff Returns/Avg.	65/20.8	68/19.7
Interceptions/Avg. Ret.	26/10.0	24/9.4
Penalties/Yards	111/933	93/806
Fumbles/Ball Lost	38/18	23/14
Total Points	352	313
Avg. Points per Game	22.0	19.6
Touchdowns	42	37
Rushing	15	9
Passing	26	25
Returns and Recoveries	1	3
Field Goals	19/28	19/29
Conversions	39/42	34/37
Safeties	2	0

1980 TEAM RECORD

Preseason (3-1)

Pittsburgh		Opponents
13	New York Giants	0
17	Atlanta	14
13	New York Jets	20
31	Dallas	44
74		78

Regular Season (9-7)

Pittsburgh		Opponents	Att.
31	*Houston	17	54,386
20	Baltimore	17	54,914
28	Cincinnati	30	52,490
38	*Chicago	3	53,987
23	Minnesota	17	47,583
16	*Cincinnati	17	53,668
34	Oakland	45	53,940
26	Cleveland	27	79,095
22	*Green Bay	20	52,165
24	Tampa Bay	21	71,636
16	*Cleveland	13	54,563
13	Buffalo	28	79,659
23	*Miami	10	51,384
0	Houston	6	53,960
21	*Kansas City	16	50,013
17	San Diego	26	51,785
352		313	915,228

*Home Game

Score by Periods

Pittsburgh	79	115	76	82	—	352
Opponents	57	91	81	84	—	313

Attendance

Home 424,106   Away 491,122   Total 915,228

Single game home record, 54,563 (11-16-80)
Single season home record, 424,106 (1980)

1980 INDIVIDUAL STATISTICS

Rushing

	Att	Yds	Avg	LG	TD
Harris	208	789	3.8	26	4
Bleier	78	340	4.4	19	1
Thornton	78	325	4.2	28	3
Hawthorne	63	226	3.6	15	4
Davis	33	132	4.0	12	1
Bradshaw	36	111	3.1	18	2
Stoudt	9	35	3.9	13	0
Colquitt	1	17	17.0	17	0
Pollard	4	16	4.0	12	0
Smith	1	-1	-1.0	-1	0
Swann	1	-4	-4.0	-4	0
Pittsburgh	512	1986	3.9	28	15
Opponents	486	1762	3.6	37	9

Field Goal Success

Distance	1-19	20-29	30-39	40-49	50 Over
Made-Att.	2-2	8-9	7-10	2-6	0-1

Passing

	Att	Comp	Pct	Yds	TD	Int	LG	Tkld	Rate
Bradshaw	424	218	51.4	3339	24	22	68t	33/245	75.1
Stoudt	60	32	53.3	493	2	2	45t	4/19	78.0
Pittsburgh	484	250	51.7	3832	26	24	72	37/264	75.3
Opponents	532	280	52.6	3517	25	26	69t	18/145	—

Receiving

	No	Yds	Avg	LG	TD
Swann	44	710	16.1	68t	7
Smith	37	711	19.2	45t	9
Harris	30	196	6.5	31	2
Bell	29	748	25.8	72	2
Grossman	23	293	12.7	35	0
Bleier	21	174	8.3	17	1
Cunningham	18	232	12.9	35	2
Thornton	15	131	8.7	29t	1
Sweeney	12	158	13.2	34	1
Hawthorne	12	282	23.5	33	0
Stallworth	9	197	21.9	50t	1
Pittsburgh	250	3832	15.3	72	26
Opponents	280	3517	12.6	69t	25

Interceptions

	No	Yds	Avg	LG	TD
Shell	7	135	19.3	67	0
Wagner	6	27	4.5	17	0
Blount	4	28	7.0	17	0
Ham	2	16	8.0	15	0
Lambert	2	0	0.0	0	0
Thomas	2	0	0.0	0	0
Cole	1	34	34.0	34	0
Johnson	1	19	19.0	19	0
Woodruff	1	0	0.0	0	0
Pittsburgh	26	260	10.0	67	0
Opponents	24	226	9.4	36	2

Punting

	No	Yds	Avg	LG	In 20
Colquitt	61	2483	40.7	54	13
Bradshaw	5	173	34.6	44	0
Pittsburgh	66	2656	40.2	54	13
Opponents	73	2970	40.7	61	19

Punt Returns

	No	FC	Yds	Avg	LG	TD
Bell	34	6	339	10.0	27	0
Smith	7	0	28	4.0	11	0
Cobb	3	0	19	6.3	13	0
Pollard	1	0	5	5.0	5	0
Pittsburgh	45	6	391	8.7	27	0
Opponents	34	8	217	6.4	33	0

Kickoff Returns

	No	Yds	Avg	LG	TD
Pollard	22	494	22.5	34	0
Anderson	14	379	27.1	63	0
Hawthorne	9	169	18.8	36	0
Davis	9	160	17.8	24	0
Bell	3	50	16.7	21	0
Sweeney	3	42	14.0	25	0
Cobb	1	19	19.0	19	0
Thornton	1	15	15.0	15	0
Winston	1	13	13.0	13	0
Blount	1	9	9.0	9	0
Valentine	1	0	0.0	0	0
Pittsburgh	65	1350	20.8	63	0
Opponents	68	1339	19.7	41	0

Scoring

	TD R	TD P	TD Rt	PAT	FG	TP
Bahr				39/42	19/28	96
Smith	0	9	0			54
Swann	0	7	0			42
Harris	4	2	0			36
Hawthorne	4	0	0			24
Thornton	3	1	0			24
Bell	0	2	0			12
Bleier	1	1	0			12
Bradshaw	2	0	0			12
Cunningham	0	2	0			12
Davis	1	0	0			6
Stallworth	0	1	0			6
Sweeney	0	1	0			6
Winston	0	0	1			6
Toews			(Safety)			2
Team			(Safety)			2
Pittsburgh	15	26	1	39/42	19/28	352
Opponents	9	25	3	34/37	19/29	313

PITTSBURGH RECORD HOLDERS

Individual Records—Single Season

Category	Name	Performance
Rushing (Yds.)	Franco Harris, 1975	1246
Passing (Pct.)	Terry Bradshaw, 1975	57.7
Passing (Yds.)	Terry Bradshaw, 1979	3724
Passing (TDs)	Terry Bradshaw, 1978	28
Receiving (No.)	John Stallworth, 1979	70
Receiving (Yds.)	Buddy Dial, 1963	1295
Interceptions	Mel Blount, 1975	11
Punting (Avg.)	Bobby Joe Green, 1961	47.0
Punt Ret. (Avg.)	Art Jones, 1941	16.6
Kickoff Ret. (Avg.)	Lynn Chandnois, 1952	35.2
Field Goals	Roy Gerela, 1973	29
Touchdowns (Tot.)	Franco Harris, 1976	14
Points	Roy Gerela, 1973	123

Team Records—Single Game

Category	Opponent, Date	Performance
Offense		
First Downs	vs. Cle, 11/25/79	36
Total Points	vs. NYG, 11/30/52	63
Touchdowns	vs. NYG, 11/30/52	9
Total Net Yards	vs. Cle, 12/13/58	683
Net Yards Rushing	vs. Cle, 10/7/79	361
Net Yards Passing	vs. Chi Cards, 12/13/58	409
Rushing Attempts	vs. Bos, 10/3/50	80
Passing Attempts	vs. Chi Cards, 12/13/58	52
Interceptions by	vs. NYG, 11/30/52	7
Defense		
Net Yards Allowed	vs. Hou, 12/9/73	83
Net Rushing Yards Allowed	vs. Brooklyn, 10/2/43	-33
Net Passing Yards Allowed	vs. Wash, 11/27/55	-32

FIRST PLAYERS SELECTED

Year	Player, College, Position
1975	Dave Brown, Michigan, DB
1976	Bennie Cunningham, Clemson, TE
1977	Robin Cole, New Mexico, LB
1978	Ron Johnson, Eastern Michigan, DB
1979	Greg Hawthorne, Baylor, RB
1980	Mark Malone, Arizona State, QB
1981	Keith Gary, Oklahoma, DE

STEELERS COACHING HISTORY (284-323-20)

1933	Forrest (Jap) Douds	3-6-2
1934	Luby DiMelo	2-10-0
1935-36	Joe Bach	10-14-0
1937-39	Johnny Blood (McNally)	6-19-0
1939-40	Walter Kiesling	3-13-3
1941	Bert Bell	0-2-0
	Aldo (Buff) Donelli	0-5-0
1941-44	Walter Kiesling*	13-20-2
1945	Jim Leonard	2-8-0
1946-47	Jock Sutherland	13-10-1
1948-51	Johnny Michelosen	20-26-2
1952-53	Joe Bach	11-13-0
1954-56	Walter Kiesling	14-22-0
1957-64	Raymond (Buddy) Parker	51-47-6
1965	Mike Nixon	2-12-0
1966-68	Bill Austin	11-28-3
1969-80	Chuck Noll	123-68-1

*Co-Coach in Philadelphia-Pittsburgh merger in 1943 and in Chicago Cardinal-Pittsburgh merger in 1944.

PITTSBURGH STEELERS 1981 VETERAN ROSTER

No.	Name	Pos.	Ht.	Wt.	NFL Exp.	Birth-date	Birthplace	College	Residence	Games in '80
30	Anderson, Larry	CB	5-11	177	4	9/25/56	Monroe, La.	Louisiana Tech	West Monroe, La.	4
9	Bahr, Matt	K	5-10	165	3	7/6/56	Philadelphia, Pa.	Penn State	Pittsburgh, Pa.	16
76	Banaszak, John	DE	6-3	244	7	8/24/50	Cleveland, Ohio	Eastern Michigan	Pittsburgh, Pa.	16
65	Beasley, Tom	DT-DE	6-5	253	4	8/11/54	Norfolk, Va.	Virginia Tech	Prosperity, Pa.	12
83	Bell, Theo	WR	5-11	180	5	12/21/53	Bakersfield, Calif.	Arizona	Pittsburgh, Pa.	15
47	Blount, Mel	CB	6-3	205	12	4/10/48	Vidalia, Ga.	Southern	Slidell, La.	14
12	Bradshaw, Terry	QB	6-3	215	12	9/2/48	Shreveport, La.	Louisiana Tech	Grand Cane, La.	15
79	Brown, Larry	T	6-4	265	11	6/16/49	Jacksonville, Fla.	Kansas	Pittsburgh, Pa.	16
56	Cole, Robin	LB	6-2	220	5	9/11/55	Compton, Calif.	New Mexico	Pittsburgh, Pa.	16
5	Colquitt, Craig	P	6-2	182	4	6/9/54	Knoxville, Tenn.	Tennessee	Knoxville, Tenn.	14
77	Courson, Steve	G	6-1	260	4	10/1/55	Philadelphia, Pa.	South Carolina	Columbia, S.C.	16
89	Cunningham, Bennie	TE	6-5	247	6	12/23/54	Laurens, S.C.	Clemson	Seneca, S.C.	8
45	Davis, Russell	RB	6-1	215	2	9/15/56	Millen, Ga.	Michigan	Woodbridge, Va.	15
57	Davis, Sam	G	6-1	255	14	7/4/44	Ocilla, Ga.	Allen University	Pittsburgh, Pa.	0*
67	Dunn, Gary	DT	6-3	247	6	12/25/50	Miami, Fla.	Miami	Miami, Fla.	16
64	Furness, Steve	DT-DE	6-4	255	10	9/24/54	Providence, R.I.	Rhode Island	Pittsburgh, Pa.	16
75	Greene, Joe	DT	6-4	260	13	9/24/46	Temple, Tex.	North Texas State	Duncanville, Tex.	15
84	Greenwood, L.C.	DE	6-6	250	13	9/8/46	Canton, Miss.	Arkansas AM&N	Pittsburgh, Pa.	13
68	Grossman, Randy	TE	6-1	225	8	9/20/52	Philadelphia, Pa.	Temple	Pittsburgh, Pa.	15
59	Ham, Jack	LB	6-1	225	11	12/23/48	Johnstown, Pa.	Penn State	Pittsburgh, Pa.	16
32	Harris, Franco	RB	6-2	225	10	3/7/50	Fort Dix, N.J.	Penn State	Pittsburgh, Pa.	16
27	Hawthorne, Greg	RB	6-3	225	3	9/5/56	Fort Worth, Tex.	Baylor	Fort Worth, Tex.	16
62	Ilkin, Tunch	T	6-3	253	2	9/23/57	Istanbul, Turkey	Indiana State	Highland Park, Ill.	10
29	Johnson, Ron	CB	5-10	200	4	6/8/56	Detroit, Mich.	Eastern Michigan	Detroit, Mich.	7
55	Kolb, Jon	T	6-2	262	13	8/30/47	Ponca City, Okla.	Oklahoma State	Pittsburgh, Pa.	14
58	Lambert, Jack	LB	6-4	220	8	7/8/52	Mantua, Ohio	Kent State	Pittsburgh, Pa.	16
16	Malone, Mark	QB	6-4	223	2	11/22/58	El Cajon, Calif.	Arizona State	El Cajon, Calif.	16
61	McGriff, Tyrone	G	6-0	267	2	1/13/58	Vero Beach, Fla.	Florida A&M	Gifford, Fla.	16
41	Moriarty, Tom	S	6-0	180	5	4/7/53	Lima, Ohio	Bowling Green	South Euclid, Ohio	16
66	Petersen, Ted	C-T	6-5	244	5	6/29/54	Kankakee, Ill.	Eastern Illinois	Pittsburgh, Pa.	16
44	Pinney, Ray	G-T-C	6-4	240	5		Seattle, Wash.	Washington	Seattle, Wash.	16
74	Pollard, Frank	RB	5-10	210	2	6/15/57	Meridian, Tex.	Baylor	Meridian, Tex.	4
31	Shell, Donnie	S	5-11	190	8	8/26/52	Whitmire, S.C.	South Carolina State	Columbia, S.C.	16
86	Smith, Jim	WR-KR	6-2	205	5	7/20/55	Blue Island, Ill.	Michigan	Ypsilanti, Mich.	16
82	Stallworth, John	WR	6-2	183	8	7/15/52	Tuscaloosa, Ala.	Alabama A&M	Huntsville, Ala.	3
18	Stoudt, Cliff	QB	6-4	218	5	3/27/55	Oberlin, Ohio	Youngstown State	Pittsburgh, Pa.	12
88	†Swann, Lynn	WR	6-0	180	8	3/7/52	Alcoa, Tenn.	Southern California	Marina del Rey, Calif.	13
85	Sweeney, Calvin	WR	6-2	180	2	1/12/55	Riverside, Calif.	Southern California	Santa Monica, Calif.	6
24	Thomas, J.T.	S-CB	6-2	196	9	4/22/51	Macon, Ga.	Florida State	Pittsburgh, Pa.	14
38	Thornton, Sidney	RB	5-11	230	5	9/2/54	Baton Rouge, La.	Northwest Louisiana	Baton Rouge, La.	16
51	Toews, Loren	LB	6-3	222	11	11/3/51	Dinuba, Calif.	California	Pittsburgh, Pa.	16
54	Valentine, Zack	LB	6-2	220	3	5/29/57	Edenton, N.C.	East Carolina	Edenton, N.C.	16
52	Webster, Mike	C	6-1	250	8	3/18/52	Tomahawk, Wis.	Wisconsin	Pittsburgh, Pa.	16
53	Winston, Dennis	LB	6-0	228	5	10/25/55	Marianna, Ariz.	Arkansas	Fayetteville, Ariz.	16
73	Wolfley, Craig	G	6-1	258	2	5/19/58	Buffalo, N.Y.	Syracuse	Orchard Park, N.Y.	14
49	Woodruff, Dwayne	CB-S	5-11	189	3	2/18/57	Bowling Green, Ky.	Louisville	Louisville, Ky.	16

* S. Davis missed '80 season due to injury.

† Option playout; subject to developments.

Retired—Rocky Bleier, 12-year running back, 16 games in '80. Mike Wagner, 10-year safety, 15 games. Dwight White, 10-year defensive end, 7 games.

Also played with Steelers in '80—S Marvin Cobb (6 games).

COACHING STAFF

Head Coach, Chuck Noll

Pro Career: Became first NFL coach to win four Super Bowls when Steelers defeated Los Angeles 31-19 in Super Bowl XIV. Has guided Steelers into postseason play eight of last nine years. Led Steelers to consecutive NFL championships twice (1974-75, 1978-79). Has 3rd-highest won-lost percentage among active coaches (.643) and ranks tenth among the NFL's all-time winningest coaches with a career record of 123-68-1. Played pro ball as guard-linebacker for Cleveland Browns from 1953-59. At age 27, he started coaching career as defensive coach with Los Angeles (San Diego) Chargers in 1960. Left after 1965 season to become Don Shula's defensive backfield assistant in Baltimore. Remained with Colts until taking over Pittsburgh reins as head coach in 1969.

Background: Was an all-state star at Benedictine High in Cleveland. Captained the University of Dayton team, playing both tackle and linebacker. He was drafted by the Browns in 1953.

Personal: Born in Cleveland on January 5, 1932. He and wife, Marianne, live in Pittsburgh and have one son—Chris.

ASSISTANT COACHES

Rollie Dotsch, offensive line; born February 14, 1933, Escanaba, Mich., lives in Pittsburgh. Guard Michigan State 1952-54. No pro playing experience. College coach: Northern Michigan 1958-60, Colorado 1961, Missouri 1962-65, Northern Michigan 1966-70 (head coach). Pro coach: Green Bay Packers 1971-74, New England Patriots 1975-76, Detroit Lions 1977, fourth year with Steelers.

Tony Dungy, defensive assistant; born October 6, 1955, Jackson, Mich., lives in Pittsburgh. Defensive back Minnesota 1973-76. Pro safety Pittsburgh Steelers 1977-78, San Francisco 49ers 1979. College coach: Minnesota 1980. Pro coach: First year with Steelers.

Dick Hoak, offensive backfield; born December 8, 1939, Jeannette, Pa., lives in Greenburg, Pa. Halfback-quarterback Penn State 1958-60. Pro running back Pittsburgh Steelers 1961-70. Pro coach: Steelers since 1972.

George Perles, assistant head coach-defensive line; born July 16, 1934, Detroit, lives in Pittsburgh. Tackle Michigan State 1958. No pro playing experience. College coach: Dayton 1965-66, Michigan State 1967-71. Pro coach: Steelers since 1972.

Tom Moore, receivers; born November 7, 1938, Owatonna, Minn., lives in Pittsburgh. Quarterback Iowa 1957-60. No pro playing experience. College coach: Iowa 1961-62, Dayton 1965-68, Wake Forest 1969, Georgia Tech 1970-71, Minnesota 1972-73, 1975-76. Pro coach: New York Stars (WFL) 1974, fifth year with Steelers.

Paul Uram, conditioning; born May 14, 1926, Butler, Pa., lives in Pittsburgh. Quarterback Slippery Rock 1945-46. No pro playing experience. Pro coach: Steelers since 1973.

Dick Walker, defensive backfield; born January 21, 1933, Cleveland, Ohio. lives in Pittsburgh. Center-linebacker John Carroll 1953-55. No pro playing experience. College coach: Toledo 1967-68, Ohio State 1969-76. Pro coach: New England Patriots 1977, fourth year with Steelers.

Woody Widenhofer, defensive coordinator; born January 20, 1943, Butler, Pa., lives in Pittsburgh. Linebacker Missouri 1961-64. No pro playing experience. College coach: Michigan State 1969-70, Eastern Michigan 1971, Minnesota 1972. Pro coach: Steelers since 1973.

PITTSBURGH STEELERS 1981 FIRST-YEAR ROSTER

Name	Pos.	Ht.	Wt.	Birth-date	Birthplace	College	Residence	How Acq.
Bolden, Nelson	RB	6-1	225	11/23/59	Toledo, Ohio	Findlay, Ohio	Toledo, Ohio	FA
Brown, Keith (1)	S	5-11	204	7/24/57	St. Louis, Mo.	Minnesota	St. Louis, Mo.	FA
Bruton, Charles	S-CB	5-11	192	10/19/58	Nacagdoches, Tex.	Southern Methodist	Nacagdoches, Tex.	FA
Bullock, Plummer	DE	6-3	250	3/7/54	Manson, N.C.	Virginia Union	Richmond, Va.	FA
Bunche, Curtis (1)	DE	6-5	243	8/4/55	Crystal River, Fla.	Albany State	Brookeville, Fla.	FA
Carifa, Tony	S	5-11	190	2/7/59	Columbus, Ohio	Ohio University	Columbus, Ohio	FA
Cockrell, Ray	TE	6-3	230	10/2/58	Killeen, Tex.	Baylor	Killeen, Tex.	FA
Coffey, Larry	RB	5-10	195	6/7/59	Daytona Beach, Fla.	W. Va. Wesleyan	Deerfield Beach, Fla.	FA
Collier, Willie	WR	5-10	172	6/17/58	Cordele, Ga.	Pittsburgh	Cordele, Ga.	FA
Cowins, James	WR	6-1	195	10/3/58	St. Louis, Mo.	Oklahoma State	St. Louis, Mo.	FA
Cugliari, Joe	DT	6-3	270	12/4/58	Buenos Aires, Arg.	Indiana, Pa.	Churchill, Pa.	FA
Danenhauer, Bill	C	6-3	250	12/1/57	Baltimore, Md.	Nebraska-Omaha	Omaha, Neb.	D3
Dombrowski, Mike	TE	6-3	225	9/18/59	Buffalo, N.Y.	Pittsburgh	Cheektowaga, N.Y.	FA
Donnalley, Rick	C-G	6-2	247	12/11/58	Wilmington, Del.	North Carolina	Raleigh, N.C.	FA
Dudash, Bill (1)	DT	6-4	258	4/18/58	Cleveland, Ohio	Kent State	Kent, Ohio	FA
Fedell, Steve	LB	6-2	238	12/19/57	Pittsburgh, Pa.	Pittsburgh	Pittsburgh, Pa.	D2 ('80)
Ferranti, Jim (1)	WR	5-9	160	10/30/57	Youngstown, Ohio	Youngstown State	Youngstown, Ohio	FA
Finn, Jeff	TE	6-4	238	11/16/58	Grand Island, Neb.	Nebraska	Grand Island, Neb.	FA
Goodman, John (1)	DE	6-6	250	11/21/58	Oklahoma City, Okla.	Oklahoma	Garland, Tex.	FA
Hawkins, Artrell	WR	5-9	176	10/19/56	Johnstown, Pa.	Pittsburgh	Johnstown, Pa.	FA
Henderson, Curtis	WR	5-10	190	8/4/58	Woonsocket, R.I.	Morgan State	Baltimore, Md.	D6
Hinkle, Bryan	LB	6-1	214	6/4/59	Long Beach, Calif.	Oregon	Silverdale, Wash.	D9
Hunter, James	T	6-4	226	9/13/57	Haskell, Okla.	Southern California	Los Angeles, Calif.	FA
Hurley, Bill (1)	S-CB	5-11	195	5/16/57	Depew, N.Y.	Syracuse	Depew, N.Y.	D4 ('80)
Isaac, Ricky	DE	6-3	240	12/15/58	Pittsburgh, Tex.	Northeast Louisiana	Pittsburgh, Tex.	FA
Kohrs, Bob (1)	LB	6-3	224	11/8/58	Phoenix, Ariz.	Arizona State	Phoenix, Ariz.	D2a ('80)
Little, David	LB	6-1	220	1/3/59	Miami, Fla.	Florida	Miami, Fla.	D7
Martin, Ricky	WR	6-2	201	10/27/58	Los Angeles, Calif.	New Mexico	Los Angeles, Calif.	D5
Martin, Robbie	WR	5-8	181	12/3/58	Los Angeles, Calif.	Cal Poly-SLO	Orange, Calif.	D4
Mayock, Mike	S	6-2	210	8/14/58	Wynnewood, Pa.	Boston College	Chestnut Hill, Mass.	D10
Najarian, Mal (1)	RB	5-11	188	4/28/58	Cranston, R.I.	Boston University	Cranston, R.I.	FA
Natale, Mike (1)	LB	6-2	226	9/20/58	Greensburgh, Pa.	Marshall	Irwin, Pa.	FA
Noel, Dana	S-CB	5-10	180	8/26/58	Chicago, Ill.	Minnesota	Wheaton, Ill.	FA
Phillips, Rudy	G	6-3	226	2/25/58	Dallas, Tex.	North Texas State	Dallas, Tex.	FA
Prince, Alvis	DT	6-4	250	9/16/58	Terrell, Tex.	Prairie View A&M	Houston, Tex.	FA
Quarles, Donald	LB	6-2	220	6/8/57	Columbia, S.C.	Johnson C. Smith	Columbia, S.C.	FA
Riley, David (1)	RB	6-0	205	6/30/56	Northfork, W. Va.	West Virginia	Northfork, W. Va.	FA
Robson, Robby	RB	6-0	175	11/4/58	Wheeling W. Va.	Youngstown State	Wellsburg, W. Va.	FA
Taylor, Harold (1)	DT	6-3	255	8/12/57	Chicago, Ill.	Mississippi Valley St.	Richmond, Calif.	FA
Trocano, Rick	QB-S	6-0	188	4/4/59	Cleveland, Ohio	Pittsburgh	Brooklyn, Ohio	D11
Trout, David	K	5-6	165	11/12/57	Mt. Pleasant, Pa.	Pittsburgh	Mt. Pleasant, Pa.	FA
Walton, Ted (1)	CB-S	5-10	195	8/11/57	Bridgeport, Conn.	Connecticut	Bridgeport, Conn.	D8 ('80)
Washington, Anthony	CB	6-1	204	2/4/58	San Francisco, Calif.	Fresno State	Fresno, Calif.	D2
Wilson, Frank	RB-TE	6-2	233	10/11/58	Austin, Tex.	Rice	Austin, Tex.	D8

Players who report to an NFL team for the first time are designated on rosters as rookies (R). If a player reported to an NFL training camp in a previous year but was not on the active squad for three or more regular season or postseason games, he is listed on the first-year roster and designated by a (1). Thereafter, a player who is on the active squad for three or more regular season games is credited with an additional year of playing experience.

NOTES

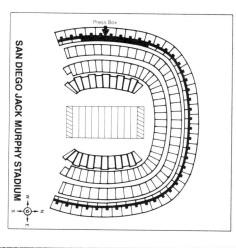

SAN DIEGO JACK MURPHY STADIUM

San Diego Chargers

American Football Conference
Western Division

Team Colors: Blue, Gold, and White

San Diego Jack Murphy Stadium
P.O. Box 20666
San Diego, California 92120
Telephone: (714) 280-2111

Club Officials
President: Eugene V. Klein
General Manager: John R. Sanders
Assistant General Manager: Paul (Tank) Younger
Assistant to the President: Jack Teele
Chief Scout: Aubrey (Red) Phillips
Director of Public Relations: Rick Smith
Business Manager: Pat Curran
Director of Advertising-Promotions: Rich Israel
Ticket Manager: Gary McCauley
Assistant Public Relations Director: Rodney Knox
Controller: Frances Beede
Trainer: Ric McDonald
Equipment Manager: Sid Brooks

Stadium: San Diego Jack Murphy Stadium •
Capacity: 52,675
9449 Friars Road
San Diego, California 92108
Playing Surface: Grass
Training Camp: University of California-San Diego
La Jolla, California 92037

1981 SCHEDULE
Preseason

Aug. 8	**St. Louis**	6:00
Aug. 15	at San Francisco	6:00
Aug. 21	**Los Angeles**	6:00
Aug. 28	**Buffalo**	6:00

Regular Season

Sept. 7	at Cleveland (Monday)		9:00
Sept. 13	**Detroit**		1:00
Sept. 20	at Kansas City		1:00
Sept. 27	at Denver		2:00
Oct. 4	**Seattle**		1:00
Oct. 11	**Minnesota**		1:00
Oct. 18	at Baltimore		2:00
Oct. 25	at Chicago		3:00
Nov. 1	**Kansas City**		1:00
Nov. 8	**Cincinnati**		1:00
Nov. 16	at Seattle (Monday)		6:00
Nov. 22	at Oakland		1:00
Nov. 29	**Denver**		1:00
Dec. 6	**Buffalo**		1:00
Dec. 13	at Tampa Bay		1:00
Dec. 21	**Oakland** (Monday)		6:00

1980 TEAM STATISTICS

	San Diego	Opp.
Total First Downs	372	284
Rushing	106	101
Passing	244	156
Penalty	22	27
Third Down Efficiency	97/210	95/248
Third Down Percentage	46.2	38.3
Total Net Yards	6410	4691
Total Offensive Plays	1135	1057
Avg. Gain per Play	5.6	4.4
Avg. Gain per Game	400.6	293.2
Net Yards Rushing	1879	1842
Total Rushing Plays	509	478
Avg. Gain per Rush	3.7	3.9
Avg. Gain Rushing per Game	117.4	115.1
Net Yards Passing	4531	2849
Lost Attempting to Pass	32/210	60/475
Gross Yards Passing	4741	3324
Attempts/Completions	594/350	519/300
Percent Completed	58.9	57.8
Had Intercepted	26	20
Avg. Net Passing per Game	283.2	178.1
Punts/Avg.	61/38.5	86/40.4
Punt Returns/Avg.	41/8.2	43/8.3
Kickoff Returns/Avg.	62/18.3	75/21.6
Interceptions/Avg. Ret.	20/13.5	26/16.1
Penalties/Yards	109/912	104/880
Fumbles/Ball Lost	40/22	39/18
Total Points	418	327
Avg. Points per Game	26.1	20.4
Touchdowns	50	40
Rushing	18	18
Passing	30	18
Returns and Recoveries	2	4
Field Goals	24/36	16/34
Conversions	46/49	39/40
Safeties	0	0

1980 TEAM RECORD

Preseason (1-3-1)

San Diego		Opponents
0	Green Bay	13
17	Minnesota	27
14	San Francisco	17
17	Atlanta	9
17	Los Angeles	34
65		87

Regular Season (11-5)

San Diego		Opponents
34	Seattle	13
30	*Oakland (OT)	24
30	Denver	13
24	Kansas City	7
24	*Buffalo	26
24	Oakland	38
44	*New York Giants	7
31	Dallas	42
31	Cincinnati	14
13	*Denver	20
20	*Kansas City	7
27	Miami (OT)	24
22	*Philadelphia	21
17	Washington	40
21	*Seattle	14
26	*Pittsburgh	17
418		327

*Home Game   (OT) Overtime

Score by Periods

San Diego	69	190	72	78	9	—	418
Opponents	54	76	85	112	0	—	327

Attendance

Home 409,530   Away 450,972   Total 860,502
Single game home record, 54,611 (12-31-72)
Single season home record, 409,530 (1980)

1980 INDIVIDUAL STATISTICS

Rushing

	Att	Yds	Avg	LG	TD
Muncie	135	659	4.9	53	4
Thomas	118	484	4.1	18	3
Cappelletti	101	364	3.6	46	5
C. Williams	97	258	2.7	13	3
Russell	8	41	5.1	7	0
Bauer	10	34	3.4	7	1
Jefferson	1	16	16.0	16	0
Fouts	23	15	0.7	9	0
Woods	4	10	2.5	5	0
Luther	3	5	1.7	9	0
Fuller	2	0	0.0	0	0
Partridge	3	0	0.0	0	0
Harrington	4	−7	−1.8	−1	0
San Diego	509	1879	3.7	53	18
Opponents	478	1842	3.9	89t	18

Field Goal Success

Distance	1-19	20-29	30-39	40-49	50 Over
Made-Att.	0-0	7-8	8-12	6-10	3-6

Passing

	Att	Comp	Pct	Yds	TD	Int	Tkld	Rate
Fouts	589	348	59.1	4715	30	24	32/210	84.6
Luther	3	2	66.7	26	0	1	0/0	—
Thomas	2	0		0	0	0	0/0	—
San Diego	594	350	58.9	4741	30	26	32/210	83.1
Opponents	519	300	57.8	3324	18	20	60/475	—

Receiving

	No	Yds	Avg	LG	TD
Winslow	89	1290	14.5	65	9
Jefferson	82	1340	16.3	65t	13
Joiner	71	1132	15.9	51	4
Thomas	29	218	7.5	27	0
C. Williams	26	230	8.8	26	1
Muncie	24	234	9.8	19	0
Cappelletti	13	112	8.6	12	1
McCrary	11	106	9.6	28t	0
Smith	4	48	12.0	24	1
Floyd	1	31	31.0	31t	1
San Diego	350	4741	13.5	65	30
Opponents	300	3324	11.1	61	18

Interceptions

	No	Yds	Avg	LG	TD
Edwards	5	122	24.4	68t	1
Shaw	4	50	12.5	25	0
Lowe	3	72	24.0	28	1
Buchanon	2	13	6.5	7	0
Laslavic	2	11	5.5	11	0
Kelcher	1	2	2.0	2	0
Stringert	1	0	0.0	0	0
Thrift	1	0	0.0	0	0
M. Williams	1	0	0.0	0	0
San Diego	20	270	13.5	68t	2
Opponents	26	419	16.1	51t	1

Punting

	No	Yds	Avg	In 20	LG	TD
Partridge	60	2347	39.1	10	55	0
San Diego	61	2347	38.5		55	0
Opponents	86	3471	40.4		62	0

Punt Returns

	No	FC	Yds	Avg	LG	TD
Fuller	30	12	298	9.9	31	0
Shaw	5	0	20	4.0	8	0
Edwards	4	1	17	4.3	8	0
Floyd	1	0	0	0.0	0	0
Horn	1	0	0	0.0	0	0
San Diego	41	13	335	8.2	31	0
Opponents	43	5	359	8.3	42	0

Kickoff Returns

	No	Yds	Avg	LG	TD
Muncie	16	344	21.5	44	0
Fuller	15	289	19.3	30	0
Smith	10	186	18.6	27	0
Jackson	9	149	16.6	32	0
Duncan	5	85	17.0	22	0
Bauer	2	37	18.5	23	0
Laslavic	2	26	13.0	21	0
Russell	1	19	19.0	19	0
Cappelletti	1	0	0.0	0	0
Jefferson	1	0	0.0	0	0
San Diego	62	1135	18.3	44	0
Opponents	75	1617	21.6	53	0

Scoring

	TD	TD R	TD P	TD Rt	PAT	FG	TP
Benirschke					46/48	24/36	118
Jefferson	13	0	13	0			78
Winslow	9	0	9	0			54
Cappelletti	5	5	0	0			30
Joiner	4	0	4	0			24
Muncie	4	4	0	0			24
C. Williams	4	3	1	0			24
Thomas	3	3	0	0			18
Fouts	2	2	0	0			12
McCrary	2	0	2	0			12
Bauer	1	1	0	0			6
Edwards	1	0	0	1			6
Floyd	1	0	1	0			6
Lowe	1	0	0	1			6
San Diego	50	18	30	2	46/49	24/36	418
Opponents	40	18	18	4	39/40	16/34	327

SAN DIEGO RECORD HOLDERS

Individual Records—Single Season

Category	Name	Performance
Rushing (Yds.)	Don Woods, 1974	1162
Passing (Pct.)	Dan Fouts, 1979	62.6
Passing (Yds.)	Dan Fouts, 1980	4715
Passing (TDs)	Dan Fouts, 1980	30
Receiving (No.)	Kellen Winslow, 1980	89
Receiving (Yds.)	Lance Alworth, 1965	1602
Interceptions	Charlie McNeil, 1961	9
Punting (Avg.)	Dennis Partee, 1969	44.6
Punt Ret. (Avg.)	Keith Lincoln, 1961	21.4
Kickoff Ret. (Avg.)	Speedy Duncan, 1964	34.4
Field Goals	Rolf Benirschke, 1980	24
Touchdowns (Tot.)	Lance Alworth, 1964	15
Points	Rolf Benirschke, 1980	118

Team Records—Single Game

Category	Opponent, Date	Performance
Offense		
First Downs	vs. Oak, 11/27/60	31
	vs. NO, 12/9/79	31
	vs. NYG, 10/19/80	31
Total Points	vs. Den, 12/22/63	58
Touchdowns	Six times; most recent,	
	vs. NYJ, 10/31/71	7
Total Net Yards	vs. Den, 10/20/68	581
Net Yards Rushing	vs. NYJ, 10/13/63	287
Net Yards Passing	vs. NYG, 10/19/80	456
Rushing Attempts	vs. Oak, 11/20/77	58
Passing Attempts	vs. Oak, 12/16/68	53
Interceptions by	Six times; most recent,	
	vs. Den, 9/21/80	6
Defense		
Net Yards Allowed	vs. Oak, 10/22/61	58
Net Rushing Yards Allowed	vs. Oak, 10/22/61	2
Net Passing Yards Allowed	vs. Cin, 12/8/70	0

FIRST PLAYERS SELECTED

Year	Player, College, Position	
1971	Leon Burns, Cal State-Long Beach, RB	
1972	Pete Lazetich, Stanford, DE (2)	
1973	Johnny Rodgers, Nebraska, WR	
1974	Bo Matthews, Colorado, RB	
1975	Gary Johnson, Grambling, DT	
1976	Joe Washington, Oklahoma, RB	
1977	Bob Rush, Memphis State, C	
1978	John Jefferson, Arizona State, WR	
1979	Kellen Winslow, Missouri, TE	
1980	Ed Luther, San Jose State, QB (4)	
1981	James Brooks, Auburn, RB	

CHARGERS COACHING HISTORY

Los Angeles 1960 (157-140-11)

1960-69	Sid Gillman*	83-51-6
1969-70	Charlie Waller	9-7-3
1971	Sid Gillman**	4-6-0
1971-73	Harland Svare***	7-17-2
1973	Ron Waller	1-5-0
1974-78	Tommy Prothro****	21-39-0
1978-80	Don Coryell	32-15-0

*Retired after nine games in 1969
**Released after 10 games in 1971
***Resigned after eight games in 1973
****Resigned after four games in 1978

SAN DIEGO CHARGERS 1981 VETERAN ROSTER

No.	Name	Pos.	Ht.	Wt.	NFL Exp.	Birth-date	Birthplace	College	Residence	Games in '80
60	Audick, Dan	T-G	6-3	253	4	11/15/54	San Bernardino, Calif.	Hawaii	San Diego, Calif.	15
37	Bauer, Hank	RB	5-11	200	5	7/15/54	Scottsbluff, Neb.	California-Lutheran	San Diego, Calif.	16
6	Benirschke, Rolf	K	6-1	175	5	2/7/55	Boston, Mass.	California-Davis	La Jolla, Calif.	16
82	Brooks, Billy	WR	6-3	202	4	8/20/53	Houston, Tex.	Oklahoma	Houston, Tex.	0*
28	Buchanon, Willie	CB	6-0	185	10	11/4/50	Oceanside, Calif.	San Diego State	San Diego, Calif.	16
25	†Cappelletti, John	RB	6-1	220	7	8/9/52	Philadelphia, Pa.	Penn State	Westminster, Calif.	10
71	Dean, Fred	DE	6-2	230	7	2/28/52	Arcadia, La.	Louisiana Tech	San Diego, Calif.	16
73	DeJurnett, Charles	DT	6-4	260	6	6/17/52	Picyun, Miss.	San Jose State	San Diego, Calif.	15
48	Dove, Jerome	CB	6-2	193	6	10/3/53	Newport News, Va.	Colorado State	San Diego, Calif.	14
47	Duncan, Frank	S	6-1	188	3	11/6/56	San Francisco, Calif.	San Jose State	Daly City, Calif.	16
27	Edwards, Glen	S	6-0	183	11	7/31/47	St. Petersburg, Fla.	Florida A&M	San Diego, Calif.	16
86	Floyd, John	WR	6-1	195	3	9/10/56	Big Sandy, Tex.	Northeast Louisiana	San Diego, Calif.	15
14	Fouts, Dan	QB	6-3	210	9	6/10/51	San Francisco, Calif.	Oregon	San Diego, Calif.	16
42	Fuller, Mike	S	5-9	182	7	4/7/53	Jackson, Miss.	Auburn	Carlsbad, Calif.	16
34	Harrington, LaRue	RB	6-0	210	2	6/28/57	Norfolk, Va.	Norfolk State	Portsmouth, Va.	4
12	Harris, James	QB	6-3	221	12	7/20/47	Monroe, La.	Grambling	Los Angeles, Calif.	0*
55	Horn, Bob	LB	6-4	230	6	2/6/54	Salem, Ore.	Oregon State	San Diego, Calif.	16
26	†Jackson, Bernard	S	6-0	180	10	9/24/50	Inglewood, Calif.	Washington State	Englewood, Colo	8*
83	Jefferson, John	WR	6-1	198	4	2/3/56	Dallas, Tex.	Arizona State	San Diego, Calif.	16
79	Johnson, Gary	DT	6-3	252	7	8/31/53	Shreveport, La.	Grambling	San Diego, Calif.	16
18	Joiner, Charlie	WR	5-11	183	13	10/14/47	Many, La.	Grambling	Houston, Tex.	16
68	Jones, Leroy	DE	6-8	260	6	9/29/50	Greenwood, Miss.	Norfolk State	San Diego, Calif.	16
74	Kelcher, Louie	DT	6-5	282	6	8/23/53	Beaumont, Tex.	Southern Methodist	San Diego, Calif.	15
57	King, Linden	LB	6-4	230	4	6/28/55	Memphis, Tenn.	Colorado State	Encinitas, Calif.	15
54	Laslavic, Jim	LB	6-2	236	8	10/24/51	Pittsburgh, Pa.	Penn State	El Cajon, Calif.	5
69	Lee, John	DE	6-2	210	8	2/17/53	Fort Monmouth, N.J.	California	Birmingham, Mich.	16
64	Loewen, Chuck	G-T	6-3	259	2	1/23/57	Mountain Lake, Minn.	South Dakota State	San Diego, Calif.	11
51	Lowe, Woodrow	LB	6-0	227	6	6/9/54	Columbus, Ga.	Alabama	Tempe, Ariz.	16
11	Luther, Ed	QB	6-2	206	2	1/2/57	Gardena, Calif.	San Jose State	Seal Beach, Calif.	6
62	Macek, Don	C-G	6-2	253	6	7/2/54	Manchester, N.H.	Boston College	La Mirada, Calif.	16
58	McCrary, Gregg	TE	6-2	235	6	3/24/52	Griffin, Ga.	Clark, Ga.	Decatur, Ga.	4
88	McGee, Carl	LB	6-2	228	2	7/15/56	Cincinnati, Ohio	Duke	Cincinnati, Ohio	6
46	Muncie, Chuck	RB	6-3	228	6	3/17/53	Uniontown, Pa.	California	Kenner, La.	15*
75	Nicholson, Jim	T	6-6	275	7	8/26/49	Orange, Calif.	Michigan State	Irvine, Calif.	0*
44	Partridge, Rick	P	6-1	175	3	8/23/53	Vicksburg, Miss.	Utah	Ewa Beach, Hawaii	16
17	Perretta, Ralph	G-C	6-1	251	7	1/10/53	Rockville Center, N.Y.	Purdue	San Diego, Calif.	16
53	Perry, Scott	CB	6-0	180	6	3/11/54	Wilton, Conn.	Williams	Miamiville, Ohio	12
32	Preston, Ray	LB	6-0	218	6	11/20/56	Lakeland, Fla.	Syracuse	San Diego, Calif.	16
52	Rush, Bob	C	6-5	264	5	1/21/56	Los Angeles, Calif.	Memphis State	Los Angeles, Calif.	16
56	Russell, Booker	RB	6-2	235	4	1/25/56	Lawrence, Mass.	Southwest Texas	Belton, Tex.	15
41	Shaw, Pete	S	5-10	178	5	2/28/56	Santa Monica, Calif.	Northwestern	Germantown, Tenn.	10
66	Shields, Billy	T	6-8	275	7	7/7/53	Belton, Tex.	Georgia Tech	San Diego, Calif.	16
22	Smith, Ron	WR	6-0	185	4	5/3/56	Newark, N.J.	Nevada-Las Vegas	San Diego, Calif.	5
84	Steptoe, Jack	WR	6-1	180	2	1/25/56	Honolulu, Hawaii	Hawaii	Pearl City, Hawaii	10
20	Stringer, Hal	T	5-11	182	7	7/17/53	Greenville, Tex.	East Central Oklahoma	Greenville, Tex.	0*
70	Thomas, Mike	RB	5-11	190	2	12/17/46	Dallas, Tex.	Nevada-Las Vegas	La Mesa, Calif.	15
67	Thrift, Cliff	LB	6-2	232	2	4/4/47	Kansas City, Mo.	East Central Oklahoma	La Mesa, Calif.	10
63	Washington, Russ	T	6-7	288	14	11/20/45	Fayetteville, N.C.	Missouri	San Diego, Calif.	16
40	White, Ed	G	6-2	271	13	3/27/47	Oakley, Calif.	California	Carlsbad, Calif.	16
29	Wilkerson, Doug	G	6-3	262	12	3/27/47	Gloucester, Mass.	North Carolina Central	San Diego, Calif.	16
80	Williams, Clarence	RB	5-10	195	5	1/25/55	New Orleans, La.	South Carolina	San Diego, Calif.	13
16	†Williams, Jeff	T	6-4	255	4	4/15/55	Gloucester, Mass.	Rhode Island	Gloucester, Mass.	14
72	Williams, Mike	CB	5-10	179	7	11/22/53	St. Louis, Mo.	Louisiana State	Spring Valley, Calif.	15
49	Winslow, Kellen	TE	6-5	252	3	11/5/57	St. Louis, Mo.	Missouri	San Diego, Calif.	16
3	Wood, Mike	K	5-11	199	3	9/3/54	Madison, Fla.	Southeast Missouri	Kirkwood, Mo.	1
13	Wright, Nate	CB	5-11	180	13	12/21/47	San Diego, Calif.	San Diego State	San Diego, Calif.	16*

*Brooks and Nicholson missed '80 season due to injuries; Harris active for 16 games but did not play; Jackson played 4 games with Denver, 4 with San Diego; Muncie played 4 games with New Orleans, 11 with San Diego; Steptoe last active with San Francisco in '78; Wright played 16 games with Minnesota.

†Option playout; subject to developments.

‡Chargers traded for J. Williams (Washington).

Traded—Defensive end Wilbur Young to Washington.

Also played with Chargers in '80—RB Don Woods (2 games).

COACHING STAFF

Head Coach, Don Coryell

Pro Career: Guided Chargers to an 11-5 mark and second straight AFC West title last season. Became head coach of the Chargers after fourth game of 1978 season and led them to eight wins in final 12 games. Has 32-15 record at San Diego. Before coming to Chargers, was St. Louis Cardinals' head coach for five seasons, compiling a 42-29-1 record and leading Cardinals to the NFC East titles in 1974-75. Career record: 74-44-1.

Background: Played defensive back for University of Washington 1947-49. Assistant coach Punahou Academy, Honolulu, 1951. Head coach Farrington High School, Honolulu, 1952. Head coach University of British Columbia 1953-54. Head coach, Fort Ord, California, army team 1956. Head coach Whittier College 1957-59 (23-5-1). Offensive backfield coach Southern California 1960. Head coach San Diego State 1961-72 (104-19-2).

Personal: Born October 17, 1924 in Seattle, Washington. Graduated from Lincoln High School, Seattle, in 1943. Served in United States Army 1943-46, released as first lieutenant. Don and his wife, Aliisa, live in San Diego and have two children —Mike and Mindy.

ASSISTANT COACHES

Marv Braden, special assistant; born January 25, 1938, Kansas City, Mo., lives in La Mesa, Calif. Linebacker Southwest Missouri State 1956-59. No pro playing experience. College coach: Northeast Missouri State 1967-68 (head coach), U.S. International 1969-72. Iowa State 1973. Southern Methodist 1974-75. Michigan State 1976. Pro coach: Denver Broncos 1977-80, joined Chargers in 1981.

Earnel Durden, offensive backs; born January 24, 1937, Los Angeles, lives in Carrollton, Mo., Guard UCLA 1953-54. No pro playing experience. College coach: Compton JC 1966-67, Long Beach State 1968, UCLA 1969-70. Pro coach: Los Angeles Rams 1971-72, Houston Oilers 1973, Chargers since 1974.

Dave Levy, offensive line; born October 25, 1932, Carrollton, Mo., lives in Solana Beach, Calif. Guard UCLA 1953-54. No pro playing experience. College coach: UCLA 1954, Long Beach City College 1955, Southern California 1960-75. Pro coach: Second year with Chargers.

Jack Pardee, Assistant head coach-defense; born April 19, 1936, Exira, Iowa, lives in San Diego. Linebacker Texas A&M 1954-56. Pro linebacker Los Angeles Rams 1957-64, 1966-70. Washington Redskins 1971-72. Pro coach: Washington Redskins 1973, 1978-80, Florida Blazers (WFL) 1974 (head coach), Chicago Bears (head coach) 1975-77, first year with Chargers.

Jerry Smith, defensive line; born September 9, 1930, Dayton, Ohio, lives in San Diego. Linebacker Wisconsin 1948-51. Pro linebacker San Francisco 49ers 1952-53, Green Bay Packers 1956. College coach: Dayton 1959. Pro coach: Boston Patriots 1960-61, Buffalo Bills 1962-68, New Orleans Saints 1969-70, Denver Broncos 1971, Houston Oilers 1972, Cleveland Browns 1973, Baltimore Colts 1974-76, fifth year with Chargers.

Jim Wagstaff, defensive backfield; born June 12, 1936, American Falls, Idaho, lives in San Diego. Back Idaho State 1954-58. Pro defensive back Chicago Cardinals 1959. Buffalo Bills 1960-61. College coach: Boise State 1969-72. Pro coach: Los Angeles Rams 1973-77, New England Patriots 1978-80, first year with Chargers.

Larrye Weaver, offensive coordinator; born November 17, 1931, Monte Vista, Colo., lives in San Diego. A graduate of Adams State 1961. No pro playing experience. College coach: Hancock JC 1962-65, Cal Poly (SLO) 1966, San Diego State 1967-75. Pro coach: San Diego Chargers 1976, rejoined Chargers in 1978.

Ernie Zampese, receivers; born March 12, 1936, Santa Barbara, Calif., lives in San Diego. Halfback Southern California 1956-58. No pro playing experience. College coach: North Dakota State 1964-66, Arizona 1967-68, UCLA 1969-70. Pro coach: Los Angeles Rams 1971-72, New England Patriots 1973-76, fifth year with Chargers.

SAN DIEGO CHARGERS 1981 FIRST-YEAR ROSTER

Name	Pos.	Ht.	Wt.	Birth-date	Birthplace	College	Residence	How Acq.
Allbritton, Norm (1)	CB-S	6-0	187	3/8/55	Rock Island, Ill.	Iowa Wesleyan	Rock Island, Ill.	FA
Banks, Douglas	RB	6-0	216	10/26/57	New Bern, N.C.	East Carolina	Maysville, N.C.	FA
Bradley, Carlos	LB	6-0	221	4/27/60	Philadelphia, Pa.	Wake Forest	Philadelphia, Pa.	D11a
Brooks, James	RB	5-9	180	12/28/58	Warner Robins, Ga.	Auburn	Warner Robins, Ga.	D1
Charles, Stacy	WR	5-10	184	8/15/58	Daytona Beach, Fla.	Bethune-Cookman	Daytona Beach, Fla.	D12
Claphan, Sammy (1)	T	6-6	275	10/10/56	Tahlequah, Okla.	Oklahoma	Norman, Okla.	FA
Cobbs, Ervin	CB-S	5-11	190	8/3/58	San Diego, Calif.	Long Beach State	San Diego, Calif.	FA
Cook, Arthur (1)	LB	6-3	219	8/24/58	Richmond, Va.	Morgan State	Baltimore, Md.	FA
Duckworth, Bobby	WR	6-4	198	11/27/58	Crossett, Ark.	Arkansas	Hamburg, Ark.	D6a
Ferguson, Keith	LB	6-5	231	4/3/59	Miami, Fla.	Ohio State	Miami, Fla.	D5
Gissinger, Andrew	T	6-4	271	7/4/59	Barberton, Ohio	Syracuse	Parma, Ohio	D6
Gossett, Jeff (1)	P	6-2	195	1/25/59	Charleston, Ill.	Eastern Illinois	Charleston, Ill.	FA
Gregor, Bob (1)	CB	6-2	187	2/10/57	Riverside, Calif.	Washington State	Irvine, Calif.	D4 ('80)
Henderson, Wyatt (1)	WR	5-10	180	11/10/56	Bakersfield, Calif.	Fresno State	Los Angeles, Calif.	FA
Hendrix, Brad (1)	G	6-4	245	3/17/57	Birmingham, Ala.	North Alabama	San Diego, Calif.	FA
Holohan, Peter	TE	6-4	226	7/25/59	Albany, N.Y.	Notre Dame	Liverpool, N.Y.	FA
Howell, Stanley (1)	RB	6-1	190	11/5/57	Guntersville, Ala.	Mississippi State	Guntersville, Ala.	FA
Lawrence, Amos	RB	5-11	181	1/9/58	Norfolk, Va.	North Carolina	Norfolk, Va.	D4
Leverett, Bennie (1)	RB	6-2	210	5/13/56	Polk County, Fla.	Bethune-Cookman	Holly Hills, Fla.	FA
Mullins, William*	WR	6-1	195	2/1/58	Los Angeles, Calif.	Southern California	Los Angeles, Calif.	D9 ('80)
Parham, Robert	FB	6-0	218	1/17/58	Atlanta, Ga.	Grambling	Atlanta, Ga.	D10
Peot, Richard (1)	P	6-2	190	11/11/55	Green Bay, Wis.	Wisconsin	Green Bay, Wis.	FA
Petrzelka, Matt	T	6-6	254	12/31/58	Cedar Rapids, Iowa	Iowa	Cedar Rapids, Iowa	D11
Phillips, Irvin	CB	6-1	192	1/23/60	Leesburg, Fla.	Arkansas	Russelville, Ark.	D3
Preston, Rob (1)	QB	6-4	210	7/9/57	The Dalles, Ore.	Southern California	Vista, Calif.	FA
Quintela, Michael (1)	CB-S	6-1	190	6/9/57	Port Arthur, Tex.	Louisiana State	Port Arthur, Tex.	FA
Rajisch, Robert	P	6-3	170	12/15/56	Youngstown, Ohio	Miami	Phoenix, Ariz.	FA
Sievers, Eric	TE	6-4	234	11/19/57	Urbana, Ill.	Maryland	Arlington, Va.	D4a
Tisby, Dexter (1)	RB	5-9	185	6/8/57	Los Angeles, Calif.	San Jose State	Los Angeles, Calif.	FA
Whitman, Steve (1)	FB	6-3	231	6/27/57	Birmingham, Ala.	Alabama	Tuscaloosa, Ala.	D9 ('80)
Wickham, Andre (1)	LB	6-2	220	8/1/58	Richmond, Va.	Morgan State	Baltimore, Md.	FA

*Selected in 1980 Supplemental Draft.

Players who report to an NFL team for the first time are designated on rosters as rookies (R). If a player reported to an NFL training camp in a previous year but was not on the active squad for three or more regular season or postseason games, he is listed on the first-year roster and designated by a (1). Thereafter, a player who is on the active squad for three or more regular season games is credited with an additional year of playing experience.

NOTES

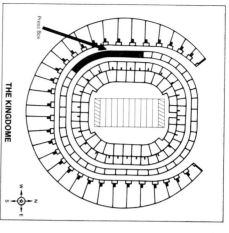

THE KINGDOME

Press Box

Seattle Seahawks

American Football Conference
Western Division

Team Colors: Blue, Green, and Silver
5305 Lake Washington Boulevard
Kirkland, Washington 98033
Telephone: (206) 827-9777

Club Officials
Majority Ownership: Elmer J. Nordstrom, Representative
Managing General Partner: Herman Sarkowsky
General Manager: John Thompson
Assistant General Manager: Mark Duncan
Director of Public Relations: Don H. Andersen
Publicity Director: Gary Wright
Director of Player Personnel: Dick Mansperger
Director of Pro Scouting: Chuck Allen
Business Manager: Bob Anderson
Ticket Manager: Chuck Velte
Assistant to the General Manager: Mike Keller
Trainers: Bruce Scott, Jim Whitesel
Equipment Managers: Walt Loeffler, Terry Sinclair

Stadium: Kingdome • **Capacity** • 64,757
201 South King Street
Seattle, Washington 98104
Playing Surface: AstroTurf
Training Camp: Eastern Washington University
Cheney, Washington 99004

1981 SCHEDULE

Preseason

Aug. 5	**San Francisco**	7:30
Aug. 14	**St. Louis**	7:30
Aug. 22	at San Francisco	6:00
Aug. 28	**Baltimore**	7:30

Regular Season

Sept. 6	at Cincinnati	1:00
Sept. 13	**Denver**	1:00
Sept. 20	at Oakland	1:00
Sept. 27	**Kansas City**	1:00
Oct. 4	at San Diego	1:00
Oct. 11	at Houston	1:00
Oct. 18	**New York Giants**	1:00
Oct. 25	at New York Jets	4:00
Nov. 1	at Green Bay	1:00
Nov. 8	**Pittsburgh**	1:00
Nov. 16	**San Diego** (Monday)	6:00
Nov. 22	at Kansas City	6:00
Nov. 29	**Oakland**	1:00
Dec. 6	**New York Jets**	1:00
Dec. 13	at Denver	2:00
Dec. 20	**Cleveland**	1:00

1980 TEAM STATISTICS

	Seattle	Opp.
Total First Downs	302	301
Rushing	114	129
Passing	166	147
Penalty	22	25
Third Down Efficiency	85/230	110/235
Third Down Percentage	37.0	46.8
Total Net Yards	4879	5177
Total Offensive Plays	1024	1038
Avg. Gain per Play	4.8	5.0
Avg. Gain per Game	304.9	323.6
Net Yards Rushing	1783	2067
Total Rushing Plays	456	550
Avg. Gain per Rush	3.9	3.8
Avg. Gain Rushing per Game	111.4	129.2
Net Yards Passing	3096	3110
Lost Attempting to Pass	51/398	26/170
Gross Yards Passing	3494	3280
Attempts/Completions	517/287	462/267
Percent Completed	55.5	57.8
Had Intercepted	23	23
Avg. Net Passing per Game	193.5	194.4
Punts/Avg.	70/40.4	66/40.2
Punt Returns/Avg.	41/8.5	42/11.3
Kickoff Returns/Avg.	73/20.4	64/19.1
Interceptions/Avg. Ret.	23/4.1	23/7.4
Penalties/Yards	109/901	103/876
Fumbles/Ball Lost	38/15	33/11
Total Points	291	408
Avg. Points per Game	18.2	25.5
Touchdowns	33	47
Rushing	13	17
Passing	18	28
Returns and Recoveries	2	2
Field Goals	20/31	25/33
Conversions	33/33	45/47
Safeties	0	3

1980 TEAM RECORD

Preseason (3-1)

Seattle		Opponents
14	Atlanta	10
7	Miami	24
10	San Francisco	7
30	New England	23
61		64

Regular Season (4-12)

Seattle		Opponents
13	*San Diego	34
17	Kansas City	16
31	*New England	37
14	Washington	0
26	Houston	7
3	*Cleveland	27
27	New York Jets	17
14	Oakland	33
20	*Philadelphia	27
30	*Kansas City	31
17	*Oakland	19
20	Denver	36
7	Dallas	51
21	*New York Giants	27
14	San Diego	21
17	*Denver	25
291		408

*Home Game

Score by Periods

	1	2	3	4	OT	Total
Seattle	25	95	50	121	—	291
Opponents	48	139	77	144	—	408

Attendance

Home 468,416   Away 426,001   Total 894,417
Single game home record, 62,948 (10-29-78)
Single season home record, 487,881 (1979)

1980 INDIVIDUAL STATISTICS

Rushing

	Att	Yds	Avg	LG	TD
Jodat	155	632	4.1	26	5
Doornink	100	344	3.4	22	3
Zorn	44	214	4.9	25	1
McCutcheon	40	202	5.1	32	3
Moore	60	202	3.4	20	0
Smith	23	94	4.1	23	0
Brinson	16	57	3.6	22t	1
Adkins	6	18	3.0	12	0
Hunter	9	14	1.6	7	0
Walsh	2	4	2.0	2	0
Largent	1	2	2.0	2	0
Seattle	456	1783	3.9	32	13
Opponents	550	2067	3.8	46	17

Field Goal Success

Distance	1-19	20-29	30-39	40-49	50 Over
Made-Att.	1-1	6-6	8-9	4-10	1-5

Passing

	Att	Comp	Pct	Yds	TD	Int	Tkld	Rate
Zorn	488	276	56.6	3346	17	20	44/341	72.4
Adkins	23	10	43.5	136	1	3	6/51	37.7
Krieg							1/6	—
McCutcheon	2	1	50.0	12	0	0	0/0	—
Weaver	2	0	0.0	0	0	0	0/0	—
Seattle	517	287	55.5	3494	18	23	51/398	69.8
Opponents	462	267	57.8	3280	28	23	26/170	—

Receiving

	No	Yds	Avg	LG	TD
Largent	66	1064	16.1	67t	6
McCullum	62	874	14.1	58	6
Sawyer	36	410	11.4	32	0
Doornink	31	237	7.6	16	2
Jodat	26	190	7.3	14	1
Moore	25	231	9.2	34	0
Raible	16	232	14.5	40	0
McCutcheon	8	64	8.0	17	1
Smith	6	72	12.0	19t	1
Je. Green	4	47	11.8	19	0
Hunter	3	40	13.3	18	0
Bell	1	13	13.0	13	0
Brinson	1	9	9.0	9	0
Herrera	1	9	9.0	9	0
Essink	1	2	2.0	2t	1
Seattle	287	3494	12.2	67t	18
Opponents	267	3280	12.3	68t	28

Interceptions

	No	Yds	Avg	LG	TD
Brown	6	32	5.3	24	0
Harris	6	28	4.7	15	0
Simpson	3	15	5.0	10	0
Butler	2	11	5.5	9	0
Jackson	2	9	4.5	9	0
Justin	1	0	0.0	0	0
Minor	1	0	0.0	0	0
Norman	1	0	0.0	0	0
Webster	1	0	0.0	0	0
Seattle	23	95	4.1	24	0
Opponents	23	170	7.4	25	2

Punting

	No	Yds	Avg	In 20	LG	TD
Weaver	67	2798	41.8	14	62	1
Herrera	1	29	29.0	1	29	0
Seattle	70	2827	40.4	15	62	1
Opponents	66	2652	40.2	20	60	0

Punt Returns

	No	FC	Yds	Avg	LG	TD
Lewis	41	9	349	8.5	75t	1
Seattle	41	9	349	8.5	75t	1
Opponents	42	9	476	11.3	36	0

Kickoff Returns

	No	Yds	Avg	LG	TD
Lewis	25	585	23.4	54	0
Webster	21	406	19.3	34	0
Je. Green	15	274	18.3	30	0
Hunter	11	213	19.4	40	0
Moore	1	11	11.0	11	0
Seattle	73	1489	20.4	54	0
Opponents	64	1223	19.1	46	0

Scoring

	TD	TD R	TD P	TD Rt	PAT	FG	TP
Herrera					33/33	20/31	93
Jodat	6	5	1	0			36
Largent	6	0	6	0			36
McCullum	6	0	6	0			36
Doornink	5	3	2	0			30
McCutcheon	4	3	1	0			24
Brinson	1	1	0	0			6
Essink	1	0	0	1			6
Je. Green	1	0	0	1			6
Lewis	1	0	0	1			6
Smith	1	0	1	0			6
Zorn	1	1	0	0			6
Seattle	33	13	18	2	33/33	20/31	291
Opponents	47	17	28	2	45/47	25/33	408

SEATTLE RECORD HOLDERS

Individual Records—Single Season

Category	Name	Performance
Rushing (Yds.)	Sherman Smith, 1978	805
Passing (Pct.)	Jim Zorn, 1980	56.6
Passing (Yds.)	Jim Zorn, 1979	3661
Passing (TDs)	Jim Zorn, 1979	20
Receiving (No.)	Steve Largent, 1978	71
Receiving (Yds.)	Steve Largent, 1979	1237
Interceptions	Autry Beamon, 1977	6
Interceptions	Dave Brown, 1980	6
Interceptions	John Harris, 1980	6
Punting (Avg.)	Herman Weaver, 1980	41.8
Punt Ret. (Avg.)	Will Lewis, 1980	8.5
Kickoff Ret. (Avg.)	Al Hunter, 1978	24.1
Field Goals	Efren Herrera, 1980	20
Touchdowns (Tot.)	David Sims, 1978	15
Touchdowns (Tot.)	Sherman Smith, 1979	15
Points	Efren Herrera, 1979	100

Team Records—Single Game

Category	Opponent, Date	Performance
Offense		
First Downs	vs. Buff, 10/30/77	30
Total Points	vs. Buff, 10/30/77	56
Touchdowns	vs. Buff, 10/30/77	8
Total Net Yards	vs. Buff, 10/30/77	559
Net Yards Rushing	vs. Wash, 9/28/80	235
Net Yards Passing	vs. NO, 11/18/79	391
Rushing Attempts	vs. KC, 12/11/77	47
Passing Attempts	vs. Wash, 9/28/80	47
Interceptions by	vs. Phil, 12/12/76	49
	vs. Hou, 10/5/80	5
Defense		
Net Yards Allowed	vs. NYJ, 11/13/77	124
Net Rushing Yards Allowed	vs. Oak, 10/22/78	70
Net Passing Yards Allowed	vs. KC, 9/30/79	15

FIRST PLAYERS SELECTED

Year	Player, College, Position
1976	Steve Niehaus, Notre Dame, DT
1977	Steve August, Tulsa, G
1978	Keith Simpson, Memphis State, DB
1979	Manu Tuiasosopo, UCLA, DT
1980	Jacob Green, Texas A&M, DE
1981	Ken Easley, UCLA, DB

SEAHAWKS COACHING HISTORY
(29-47-0)

1976-80	Jack Patera	29-47-0

SEATTLE SEAHAWKS 1981 VETERAN ROSTER

No.	Name	Pos.	Ht.	Wt.	NFL Exp.	Birth-date	Birthplace	College	Residence	Games in '80
12	Adkins, Sam	QB	6-2	214	5	5/21/55	Van Nuys, Calif.	Wichita State	Woodinville, Wash.	4
63	†Anderson, Fred	DE	6-4	235	3	10/30/54	Toppenish, Wash.	Prairie View	Kirkland, Wash.	7
76	August, Steve	T	6-5	254	5	9/4/54	Jeannette, Pa.	Tulsa	Redmond, Wash.	16
58	Beeson, Terry	LB	6-3	235	5	9/19/55	Coffeyville, Kan.	Kansas	Bothell, Wash.	16
82	Bell, Mark	TE	6-4	235	3	8/30/57	Wichita, Kan.	Colorado State	Wichita, Kan.	0*
68	Boyd, Dennis	T	6-6	255	4	1/5/55	Washington, D.C.	Oregon State	Kirkland, Wash.	16
36	Brinson, Larry	RB	6-0	214	5	6/6/54	Opalocka, Fla.	Florida	Gainesville, Fla.	7
22	Brown, Dave	CB	6-2	190	7	1/16/53	Akron, Ohio	Michigan	Woodinville, Wash.	16
72	Bullard, Louis	T	6-6	265	4	5/6/56	DeSoto, Miss.	Jackson State	Woodinville, Wash.	8
53	Butler, Keith	LB	6-4	225	4	5/16/56	Anniston, Ala.	Memphis State	Bothell, Wash.	16
67	Cooke, Bill	DT	6-5	250	7	2/26/51	Lowell, Mass.	Massachusetts	Bellevue, Wash.	16
57	Cronan, Peter	LB	6-2	238	4	1/13/55	Bourne, Mass.	Boston College	Bellevue, Wash.	0*
62	Dion, Terry	DE	6-6	254	2	11/22/57	Shelton, Wash.	Oregon	Auburn, Wash.	9
33	Doornink, Dan	FB	6-3	210	4	2/1/56	Wapato, Wash.	Washington State	Kirkland, Wash.	15
25	†Dufek, Don	S	6-0	195	5	4/28/54	Ann Arbor, Mich.	Michigan	Bellevue, Wash.	8
64	Essink, Ron	T	6-6	246	2	7/30/58	Zeeland, Mich.	Grand Valley State	Zeeland, Mich.	16
79	Green, Jacob	DE	6-3	247	2	1/21/57	Pasadena, Tex.	Texas A&M	Houston, Tex.	14
77	Gregory, Bill	DE	6-5	260	11	12/14/49	Galveston, Tex.	Wisconsin	Bellevue, Wash.	14
75	Hardy, Robert	DT	6-2	250	3	7/3/56	Tulsa, Okla.	Jackson State	Bellevue, Wash.	16
44	Harris, John	S	6-2	200	4	6/13/56	Ft. Benning, Ga.	Arizona State	Woodinville, Wash.	16
1	Herrera, Efren	K	5-9	190	7	7/30/51	Guadalajara, Mex.	UCLA	Bellevue, Wash.	16
73	Hines, Andre	T	6-6	275	2	2/28/58	Oakland, Calif.	Stanford	Issaquah, Wash.	1
24	Hunter, Al	RB	5-11	195	5	2/21/55	Greenville, N.C.	Notre Dame	Redmond, Wash.	9
55	Jackson, Michael	LB	6-1	220	3	7/15/57	Pasco, Wash.	Washington	Redmond, Wash.	16
26	Justin, Kerry	CB	5-11	175	4	5/3/55	New Orleans, La.	Oregon State	Kirkland, Wash.	16
43	Jodat, Jim	FB	6-1	213	5	3/3/54	Milwaukee, Wis.	Carthage	Bellevue, Wash.	15
17	Krieg, Dave	QB	6-1	185	2	10/20/58	Iola, Wis.	Milton, Wis.	Rothschild, Wis.	15*
52	Kuehn, Art	C	6-3	255	6	2/21/53	Victoria, B.C.	UCLA	Kirkland, Wash.	16
80	Largent, Steve	WR	5-11	184	6	9/28/54	Tulsa, Okla.	Tulsa	Woodinville, Wash.	16
41	Lewis, Will	CB	5-9	185	2	1/16/58	Quakertown, Pa.	Millersville State	Bellevue, Wash.	16
61	†Lynch, Tom	G	6-5	260	5	5/24/55	Chicago, Ill.	Boston College	Kirkland, Wash.	0*
84	McCullum, Sam	WR	6-2	190	8	11/30/52	McComb, Miss.	Montana State	Kirkland, Wash.	16
30	†McCutcheon, Lawrence	RB	6-1	205	10	6/2/50	Plainview, Tex.	Colorado State	Huntington Beach, Calif.	15*
21	Minor, Vic	S	6-0	198	2	8/16/49	Shreveport, La.	Northeast Louisiana	Bellevue, Wash.	9
32	Moore, Jeff	RB	6-0	195	3	8/20/56	Kosciusko, Miss.	Jackson State	Kosciusko, Miss.	14
16	Myer, Steve	QB	6-2	200	5	7/17/54	Covina, Calif.	New Mexico	Redmond, Wash.	0*
78	†Newton, Bob	G	6-5	260	11	11/28/50	Pomona, Calif.	Nebraska	Woodinville, Wash.	16
54	Norman, Joe	LB	6-1	220	3	10/15/56	Millersburg, Ohio	Indiana	Bellevue, Wash.	16
88	Peets, Brian	TE	6-4	225	5	11/15/56	Stockton, Calif.	Pacific	Redmond, Wash.	16
83	Raible, Steve	WR	6-2	195	6	6/2/54	Louisville, Ky.	Georgia Tech	Kirkland, Wash.	16
59	Rennaker, Terry	LB	6-2	225	2	5/1/58	Newport, R.I.	Stanford	Bothell, Wash.	15
81	†Sawyer, John	TE	6-2	230	6	7/26/53	Baker, La.	Southern Mississippi	Woodinville, Wash.	15
70	†Sevy, Jeff	T	6-5	260	7	10/24/52	Palo Alto, Calif.	California	Monte Vista, Calif.	16
42	Simpson, Keith	S	6-1	195	6	3/9/56	Memphis, Tenn.	Memphis State	Woodinville, Wash.	16
47	Smith, Sherman	RB	6-4	225	6	11/1/54	Youngstown, Ohio	Miami, Ohio	Kirkland, Wash.	15
74	Tuiasosopo, Manu	DT	6-3	252	3	8/30/57	Los Angeles, Calif.	UCLA	Woodinville, Wash.	16
56	Walker, Tim	LB	6-1	230	2	5/12/58	Hartford, Conn.	Savannah State	Woodinville, Wash.	3
34	Walsh, Jim	FB	5-11	220	2	12/17/56	Burlingame, Calif.	San Jose State	Belmont, Calif.	16
18	†Weaver, Herman	P	6-4	210	12	11/17/48	Villa Rica, Ga.	Tennessee	Warner Robins, Ga.	16
5	West, Jeff	P	6-2	210	12	4/6/53	Ravenna, Ohio	Cincinnati	Carlsbad, Calif.	0*
51	Yarno, John	C	6-5	251	5	12/17/54	Spokane, Wash.	Idaho	Redmond, Wash.	15
10	Zorn, Jim	QB	6-2	200	6	5/10/53	Whittier, Calif.	Cal Poly-Pomona	Mercer Island, Wash.	16

*Boyd, Cronan, Myer, Peets missed '80 season due to injuries; McCutcheon played 7 games with Denver, 8 with Seattle; West last active with San Diego in '79.

†Option playout; subject to developments.

Also played with Seahawks in '80 — WR Jessie Green (11 games), CB Cornell Webster (8).

COACHING STAFF

Head Coach, Jack Patera

Pro Career: Starts sixth season as head coach at Seattle. Piloted Seahawks to identical 9-7 records in 1978 and 1979. The 1978 record was best ever by a third year expansion team. Spent 13 years as a pro assistant prior to being named Seattle head coach, coaching the defensive line with Los Angeles Rams 1963-66, New York Giants 1967-68, and Minnesota Vikings 1969-75. Pro guard with Baltimore Colts 1955-57, middle guard Chicago Cardinals 1958-59, and linebacker Dallas Cowboys 1960-61. Pro record: 29-47.

Background: Played for University of Oregon 1951-54 (All Pacific Coast Conference 1954). East-West Shrine game, Hula Bowl, College All-Star Game.

Personal: Born August 1, 1933, Bismarck, N.D. Jack and his wife, Susan, live on Mercer Island, Wash., with their four children—Beth, John, Mary, and Michael.

ASSISTANT COACHES

Jack Christiansen, defensive backfield; born December 20, 1928, Sublett, Kan., lives in Seattle. Defensive halfback Colorado State 1948-50. Pro defensive back Detroit Lions 1951-58. College coach: Stanford 1968-76 (head coach 1972-76). Pro coach: San Francisco 49ers 1959-67 (head coach 1963-67), Kansas City Chiefs 1977, fourth year with Seahawks.

Andy MacDonald, running backs; born January 2, 1930, Flint, Mich., lives in Bellevue, Wash. Quarterback Central Michigan 1950-51. No pro playing experience. College coach: Iowa 1961-64, Northern Arizona 1965-68, Tulsa 1969, Colorado State 1970-71, Michigan State 1973-75. Pro coach: Seahawks since 1976.

Jim Mora, defensive line; born May 24, 1935, Los Angeles, Calif., lives in Seattle. End Occidental 1954-56. No pro playing experience. College coach: Occidental 1960-66 (head coach 1964-66), Stanford 1967, Colorado 1968-73, UCLA 1974, Washington 1975-77. Pro coach: Fourth year with Seahawks.

Howard Mudd, offensive line; born February 10, 1942, Midland, Mich., lives in Seattle. Guard Hillsdale 1961-64. Pro guard San Francisco 49ers 1965-69, Chicago Bears 1970-71. College coach: California 1972-73. Pro coach: San Diego Chargers 1974-76, San Francisco 49ers 1977, fourth year with Seahawks.

Jerry Rhome, offensive coach/quarterbacks-receivers; born March 6, 1942, Dallas, Tex., lives in Seattle. Quarterback Southern Methodist 1960-61, Tulsa 1963-64. Pro quarterback Dallas Cowboys 1965-68, Cleveland Browns 1969, Houston Oilers 1970, Los Angeles Rams 1971-72. College coach: Tulsa 1973-75. Pro coach: Seahawks since 1976.

Jackie Simpson, defensive coach-linebackers; born August 20, 1937, Corinth, Miss., lives in Seattle. Guard-linebacker Mississippi 1954-57. Pro linebacker Montreal Alouettes (CFL) 1958-61, Denver Broncos 1961, Oakland Raiders 1962-64, Winnipeg Bombers (CFL) 1965. Pro coach: San Diego Chargers 1967-71, 1974-80, Houston Oilers 1972, St. Louis Cardinals 1973, first year with Seahawks.

Rusty Tillman, special teams; born February 27, 1948, Beloit, Wis., lives in Seattle. Linebacker Northern Arizona 1967-69. Pro linebacker Washington Redskins 1970-77. Pro coach: Third year with Seahawks.

SEATTLE SEAHAWKS 1981 FIRST-YEAR ROSTER

Name	Pos.	Ht.	Wt.	Birth-date	Birthplace	College	Residence	How Acq.
Allen, Mike (1)	WR	6-3	190	6/5/56	Soap Lake, Wash.	Washington State	Bellevue, Wash.	FA
Alvarez, Wilson	K	6-0	165	3/22/57	Santa Cruz, Bolivia	Southeast Louisiana	Hammond, La.	FA
Anthony, Benny	TE	6-7	226	8/3/58	Bainbridge, Ga.	Auburn	Bainbridge, Ga.	FA
Babb, Mike	P	6-2	170	3/21/59	Eugene, Ore.	Oregon	Eugene, Ore.	FA
Bailey, Edwin	G	6-4	255	5/15/59	Savannah, Ga.	South Carolina State	Savannah, Ga.	D5
Baker, Kim	LB	6-3	219	8/25/58	Miller, S.D.	Nebraska	Lincoln, Neb.	FA
Bayle, David	TE	6-4	221	2/16/59	New Orleans, La.	Washington	San Marino, Calif.	FA
Bednarek, Jeff	DT	6-4	252	6/12/58	Trenton, Mich.	Pacific	Bloomingdale, Wash.	D12
Boomhower, Dan	RB	6-2	220	8/19/59	Spokane, Wash.	Kearney State	Cheyenne, Wyo.	FA
Boschma, Dave	RB	6-0	190	1/16/60	Lemon Grove, Calif.	Linfield	Hillsboro, Ore.	FA
Buono, Chris	S	6-0	185	11/6/59	Massapequa, N.Y.	Furman	Orlando, Fla.	FA
Chauza, Bob	T	6-6	255	6/16/59	Axtell, Kan.	NW Missouri State	Maryville, Mo.	FA
Collins, Mickey	RB	5-10	185	5/14/59	Okmulgee, Okla.	Wichita State	Tulsa, Okla.	FA
Cosgrove, Jack (1)	C	6-3	245	6/22/58	Stockton, Calif.	Pacific	Bellevue, Wash.	D8 ('80)
Danenhauer, Bob	LB	6-2	215	10/9/59	Concordia, Kan.	Nebraska-Omaha	Omaha, Neb.	FA
Dawson, Ken	RB	6-1	194	2/2/58	Brunswick, Ga.	Savannah State	Brunswick, Ga.	D10
Dedrick, Thomas	DT	6-6	238	9/6/58	Tuscaloosa, Ala.	Morris Brown	Soayerville, Ala.	FA
Dudley, Steve (1)	WR	6-1	185	2/5/57	Biloxi, Miss.	Eastern Oregon	Santa Barbara, Calif.	FA
Dugan, Bill	G	6-4	271	6/5/59	Hornell, N.Y.	Penn State	Hornell, N.Y.	D3
Durham, Steve	DE	6-5	258	10/11/58	Greer, S.C.	Clemson	Greer, S.C.	D6
Easley, Kenny	S	6-3	206	1/15/59	Chesapeake, Va.	UCLA	Chesapeake, Va.	D1
Elion, Kolas	WR	5-11	196	1/10/58	Memphis, Tenn.	Middle Tennessee	Memphis, Tenn.	FA
Ena, Tali (1)	RB	6-0	192	12/25/57	American Samoa	Washington State	San Francisco, Calif.	D11 ('80)
Fenn, Bill	RB	6-0	195	5/13/57	Orlando, Fla.	Illinois State	Eatonville, Fla.	FA
Flones, Brian	LB	6-1	228	9/1/59	Mt. Vernon, Wash.	Washington State	Sedro Woolley, Wash.	FA
Gaines, Greg	S	6-3	202	10/16/58	Martinsville, Va.	Tennessee	Old Hickory, Tenn.	FA
Goss, Wilbert	LB	6-3	225	8/19/57	Bainbridge, Ga.	Lincoln	Riviera Beach, Fla.	FA
Graham, Andy	K	6-0	185	9/30/58	Wadsworth, Ohio	Akron	Wadsworth, Ohio	FA
Griffiths, Steve	LB	6-5	231	12/24/59	Utica, N.Y.	Penn State	Utica, N.Y.	FA
Hinton, Heyward	LB	5-11	196	1/28/59	Columbia, S.C.	Presbyterian	Columbia, S.C.	FA
Hughes, David	FB	6-0	220	6/1/59	Honolulu, Hawaii	Boise State	Kailua, Hawaii	D2
Jacobs, Daniel (1)	DE	6-6	265	4/24/58	Durham, N.C.	Winston-Salem State	Durham, N.C.	D5b ('80)
Johns, Paul	WR	5-11	170	11/14/58	Waco, Tex.	Tulsa	Wichita Falls, Tex.	FA
Johnson, Gary	P	5-11	190	2/8/58	Harrodsburg, Ky.	Kentucky State	Lexington, Ky.	FA
Johnson, Greg	S	6-1	188	10/10/58	Houston, Tex.	Oklahoma State	Houston, Tex.	FA
Johnson, Ron	WR	6-3	180	9/21/58	Monterey, Calif.	Long Beach State	Monterey, Calif.	D7
King, Leroy (1)	FB	6-2	215	3/11/57	Weimer, Tex.	Texas	Weimer, Tex.	FA
Kirk, Danny	LB	6-3	230	12/12/58	Marlin, Tex.	East Texas State	Marlin, Tex.	FA
Lane, Eric	RB	6-0	195	1/6/59	Oakland, Calif.	Brigham Young	Hayward, Calif.	D8
Laubenthal, Al	WR	5-11	180	3/18/59	Lima, Ohio	Dayton	Ottawa, Ohio	FA
Lewis, Glenn	RB	6-1	210	10/28/57	Minneapolis, Minn.	Minnesota	Edina, Minn.	FA
Mathews, Jamey	G	6-2	251	5/19/59	Des Moines, Iowa	Oregon	Boulder, Colo.	D11
Matthews, Jim	WR	6-3	185	9/15/58	Portland, Ore.	Brigham Young	Provo, Utah	D4
McGrath, Mark (1)	WR	5-11	175	12/17/57	Washington, D.C.	Montana State	Washington, D.C.	FA
Miller, Gary	DT	6-3	265	2/15/58	San Diego, Calif.	Dubuque	Seattle, Wash.	FA
Mollica, Dave	TE	6-2	220	9/21/59	Fresno, Calif.	Fresno State	Fresno, Calif.	FA
Newman, Don	S	6-1	187	5/26/59	Newport Beach, Calif.	Pacific	Costa Mesa, Calif.	FA
Olander, Lance	RB	6-0	195	11/22/57	New Orleans, La.	Notre Dame	New Orleans, La.	FA
Phillips, Scott	WR	6-0	204	5/19/59	Des Moines, Iowa	Colorado	Boulder, Colo.	FA
Postell, Jeffrey	WR	6-2	185	11/18/58	Washington, D.C.	Brigham Young	Provo, Utah	FA
Rowell, Gene	DT	6-3	267	11/11/58	Memphis, Tenn.	Morehouse	Washington, D.C.	FA
Scambray, Scott	TE	6-2	243	11/12/58	San Diego, Calif.	Virginia Union	Fennimore, Wis.	FA
Scovill, Brad	TE	6-3	230	12/6/58	Cincinnati, Ohio	Penn State	Fresno, Calif.	D7a
Stone, Jim	RB	6-0	198	2/2/59	New Orleans, La.	Notre Dame	Reading, Pa.	D9
Sydney, Harry	FB	6-1	215	6/26/59	New Orleans, La.	Kansas	Renton, Wash.	FA
Sykes, Greg	T	6-6	243	10/30/58	Petersburg, Va.	Washington State	Fayetteville, N.C.	FA
Thompson, Ken	WR	6-2	175	12/6/58	Snyder, Tex.	Utah State	Los Angeles, Calif.	FA
Tice, Mike	QB	6-7	235	2/2/59	Bayshore, N.Y.	Maryland	East Islip, N.Y.	FA
Umphrey, Woody	P	6-0	176	10/5/58	Kankakee, Ill.	Alabama	Barrington, Ill.	FA
Whatley, Jim	WR	6-0	172	5/7/59	Birmingham, Ala.	Washington State	Tuscaloosa, Ala.	D9
Wells, Joe	LB	6-2	230	4/26/59	Phoenix, Ariz.	Southern Utah	Cedar City, Utah	FA

Players who report to an NFL team for the first time are designated on rosters as rookies (R). If a player reported to an NFL training camp in a previous year but was not on the active squad for three or more regular season or postseason games, he is listed on the first-year roster and designated by a (1). Thereafter, a player who is on the active squad for three or more regular season games is credited with an additional year of playing experience.

NOTES

1981 National Football Conference

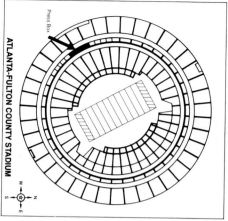

ATLANTA-FULTON COUNTY STADIUM

Press Box

Atlanta Falcons

National Football Conference
Western Division

Team Colors: Red, Black, White, and Silver

Suwanee Road at I-85
Suwanee, Georgia 30174
Telephone: (404) 588-1111

Club Officials

Chairman of the Board: Rankin M. Smith, Sr.
President: Rankin Smith, Jr.
General Manager: Eddie LeBaron
Assistant General Manager: Curt Mosher
Director of Player Personnel: Tom Braatz
Director of Pro Personnel: Bill Jobko
Scouts: Bob Cegelski, John Jelacic, Bob Riggle, Bill Striegel
Ticket Manager: Bill Brokaw
Assistant Ticket Manager: Ken Grantham
Public Relations Director: Charlie Dayton
Head Trainer: Jerry Rhea
Assistant Trainer: J.L. Shoop
Equipment Manager: Whitey Zimmerman
Assistant Equipment Manager: Horace Daniel

Stadium: Atlanta-Fulton County Stadium •
Capacity: 60,748
521 Capitol Avenue, S.W.
Atlanta, Georgia 30312

Playing Surface: Grass

Training Camp: Suwanee Road at I-85
Suwanee, Georgia 30174

1981 SCHEDULE

Preseason

Aug. 1	vs. Cleveland at Canton, OH (HOF)	3:30
Aug. 8	at Oakland	6:00
Aug. 15	**New York Jets**	7:00
Aug. 22	at Minnesota	8:00
Aug. 28	**Tampa Bay**	8:30

Regular Season

Sept. 6	**New Orleans**	1:00
Sept. 13	at Green Bay	12:00
Sept. 20	**San Francisco**	1:00
Sept. 27	at Cleveland	1:00
Oct. 5	at Philadelphia (Monday)	9:00
Oct. 11	**Los Angeles**	1:00
Oct. 18	**St. Louis**	1:00
Oct. 25	**New York Giants**	1:00
Nov. 1	at New Orleans	12:00
Nov. 8	at San Francisco	1:00
Nov. 15	**Pittsburgh**	1:00
Nov. 23	**Minnesota** (Monday)	9:00
Nov. 29	at Houston	3:00
Dec. 6	at Tampa Bay	4:00
Dec. 14	at Los Angeles (Monday)	6:00
Dec. 20	**Cincinnati**	1:00

1980 TEAM STATISTICS

	Atlanta	Opp.
Total First Downs	336	298
Rushing	145	100
Passing	166	175
Penalty	25	23
Third Down Efficiency	87/222	91/235
Third Down Percentage	39.2	38.7
Total Net Yards	5649	5264
Total Offensive Plays	1061	1051
Avg. Gain per Play	5.3	5.0
Avg. Gain per Game	353.1	329.0
Net Yards Rushing	2405	1670
Total Rushing Plays	559	441
Avg. Gain per Rush	4.3	3.8
Avg. Gain Rushing per Game	150.3	104.4
Net Yards Passing	3244	3594
Lost Attempting to Pass	35/324	46/396
Gross Yards Passing	3568	3990
Attempts/Completions	467/259	564/333
Percent Completed	55.5	59.0
Had Intercepted	17	26
Avg. Net Passing per Game	202.8	224.6
Punts/Avg.	79/39.1	85/41.3
Punt Returns/Avg.	53/10.1	36/6.7
Kickoff Returns/Avg.	53/18.1	73/21.6
Interceptions/Avg. Ret.	26/12.0	17/8.4
Penalties/Yards	91/861	101/919
Fumbles/Ball Lost	32/9	33/16
Total Points	405	272
Avg. Points per Game	25.3	17.0
Touchdowns	50	32
Rushing	15	8
Passing	31	24
Returns and Recoveries	4	0
Field Goals	19/27	16/25
Conversions	46/49	30/32
Safeties	1	1

1980 TEAM RECORD

Preseason (1-3)

Atlanta		Opponents	
10	Seattle	14	
14	Pittsburgh	17	
9	San Diego	17	
51	Baltimore	35	
84		83	

Regular Season (12-4)

Atlanta		Opponents	Att.
23	Minnesota	24	44,773
37	New England	21	48,321
17	*Miami	20	55,479
20	San Francisco	17	56,518
43	*Detroit	28	57,652
7	*New York Jets	14	57,458
41	New Orleans	14	62,651
13	*Los Angeles	10	57,401
30	Buffalo	14	57,959
33	St. Louis (OT)	27	48,662
31	*New Orleans	13	53,871
28	*Chicago	17	49,164
10	*Washington	6	55,665
20	Philadelphia	17	70,205
35	*San Francisco	10	55,767
17	Los Angeles (OT)	20	62,469
405		272	894,015

*Home Game   (OT) Overtime

Score by Periods

Atlanta	76	92	102	129	6	— 405
Opponents	75	74	38	82	3	— 272

Attendance

Home 442,457   Away 451,558   Total 894,015
Single game home record, 59,257 (10-30-77)
Single season home record, 442,457 (1980)

1980 INDIVIDUAL STATISTICS

Rushing

	Att	Yds	Avg	LG	TD
Andrews	265	1308	4.9	33	4
Cain	235	914	3.9	37	8
Mayberry	18	88	4.9	24	0
Strong	6	42	7.0	21t	1
Bartkowski	25	35	1.4	11	2
James	1	13	13.0	13	0
Anderson	6	5	0.8	8	0
Francis	1	2	2.0	2	0
J. Miller	2	-2	-1.0	0	0
Atlanta	559	2405	4.3	37	15
Opponents	441	1670	3.8	40	8

Field Goal Success

Distance	1-19	20-29	30-39	40-49	50 Over
Made-Att.	2-2	8-8	4-7	4-8	1-2

Passing

	Att	Comp	Pct	Yds	TD	Int	LG	Tkld	Rate
Bartkowski	463	257	55.5	3544	31	16	33	35/324	88.0
James	1	0	0.0	0	0	1	0	0/0	—
Moroski	3	2	66.7	24	0	0	24	0/0	87.2
Atlanta	467	259	55.5	3568	31	17	33	35/324	—
Opponents	564	333	59.0	3990	24	26	40	46/396	—

Receiving

	No	Yds	Avg	LG	TD
Jenkins	57	1026	18.0	57	6
Francis	54	862	16.0	81t	1
Andrews	51	456	8.9	26	1
J. Miller	46	584	12.7	36	9
Cain	24	223	9.3	30	1
Jackson	23	412	17.9	54t	7
Mayberry	3	1	0.3	6	0
Mikeska	1	4	4.0	4	0
Atlanta	259	3568	13.8	81t	31
Opponents	333	3990	12.0	93t	24

Interceptions

	No	Yds	Avg	LG	TD
Richardson	7	139	19.9	52	0
Johnson	4	49	12.3	33	0
Lawrence	3	37	12.3	37	0
Curry	3	13	4.3	9	0
Williams	2	55	27.5	32	0
Glazebrook	2	6	3.0	6	0
Pridemore	2	2	1.0	2	0
Laughlin	1	7	7.0	7	0
Yeates	1	5	5.0	5	0
Jones	1	0	0.0	0	0
Atlanta	26	313	12.0	52	0
Opponents	17	143	8.4	30	0

Punting

	No	Yds	Avg	In 20	LG	TD
James	79	3087	39.1	25	59	
Atlanta	79	3087	39.1	25	59	
Opponents	85	3512	41.3	15	65	

Punt Returns

	No	FC	Yds	Avg	LG	TD
Johnson	23	5	281	12.2	56	0
R. Smith	27	4	262	9.7	25	0
Lawrence	3	0	-7	-2.3		0
Glazebrook	0	1	0	—		0
Atlanta	53	10	536	10.1	56	0
Opponents	36	18	240	6.7	64	0

Kickoff Returns

	No	Yds	Avg	LG	TD
R. Smith	25	512	20.5	35	0
Strong	10	168	16.8	31	0
Anderson	7	97	13.9	23	0
Jackson	3	70	23.3	36	0
M. Smith	3	58	19.3	26	0
Pridemore	3	39	13.0	20	0
Fields	1	11	11.0	11	0
Daykin	1	3	3.0	3	0
Atlanta	53	958	18.1	36	0
Opponents	73	1579	21.6	87	0

Scoring

	TD R	TD P	TD Rt	PAT	FG	TP
Mazzetti				46/49	19/27	103
Cain	9	8	1			54
J. Miller	0	9	0			54
Francis	7	0	0			42
Jackson	0	7	0			42
Jenkins	6	6	0			36
Andrews	5	4	1			30
Bartkowski	2	2	0			12
Williams	1	0	1			8
				(Safety)		
Curry	1	0	0			6
Reed	1	0	0			6
Richardson	1	0	1			6
Strong	1	0	0			6
Atlanta	50	15	31	4	46/49	19/27	405
Opponents	32	8	24	0	30/32	16/25	272

ATLANTA RECORD HOLDERS

Individual Records—Single Season

Category	Name	Performance
Rushing (Yds.)	William Andrews, 1980	1308
Passing (Pct.)	Bob Berry, 1971	60.2
Passing (Yds.)	Steve Bartkowski, 1980	3544
Passing (TDs)	Steve Bartkowski, 1980	31
Receiving (No.)	Wallace Francis, 1979	74
Receiving (Yds.)	Alfred Jenkins, 1980	1025
Interceptions	Rolland Lawrence, 1975	9
Punting (Avg.)	Billy Lothridge, 1968	44.3
Punt Ret. (Avg.)	Gerald Tinker, 1974	13.9
Kickoff Ret. (Avg.)	Dennis Pearson, 1978	26.5
Field Goals	Nick Mike-Mayer, 1973	26
Touchdowns (Tot.)	Eddie Ray, 1973	11
Points	Nick Mike-Mayer, 1973	112

Team Records—Single Game

Category	Opponent, Date	Performance
Offense		
First Downs	vs. NO, 9/2/79	35
Total Points	vs. NO, 9/16/73	62
Touchdowns	vs. NO, 9/16/73	8
Total Net Yards	vs. StL, 11/9/80	563
Net Yards Rushing	vs. LA, 10/1/72	297
Net Yards Passing	vs. SF, 12/14/75	362
Rushing Attempts	vs. TB, 11/27/77	58
Passing Attempts	vs. StL, 11/9/80	47
Interceptions by	vs. LA, 10/1/72	6
Defense		
Net Yards Allowed	vs. TB, 11/27/77	78
Net Rushing Yards Allowed	vs. NO, 10/19/80	36
Net Passing Yards Allowed	vs. StL, 12/9/73	9

FIRST PLAYERS SELECTED

Year	Player, College, Position
1966	Tommy Nobis, Texas, LB
1967	Leo Carroll, San Diego State, DE (2)
1968	Claude Humphrey, Tennessee State, DE
1969	George Kunz, Notre Dame, T
1970	John Small, Citadel, LB
1971	Joe Profit, N. E. Louisiana, RB
1972	Clarence Ellis, Notre Dame, DB
1973	Greg Marx, Notre Dame, DT (2)
1974	Gerald Tinker, Kent State, WR (2)
1975	Steve Bartkowski, California, QB
1976	Bubba Bean, Texas A&M, RB
1977	Warren Bryant, Kentucky, T
1978	Mike Kenn, Michigan, T
1979	Don Smith, Miami, DE
1980	Junior Miller, Nebraska, TE
1981	Bobby Butler, Florida State, DB

FALCONS COACHING HISTORY

(85-130-4)

1966-68	Norb Hecker*	4-26-1
1968-74	Norm Van Brocklin**	37-49-3
1974-76	Marion Campbell***	6-19-0
1976	Pat Peppler	3-6-0
1977-80	Leeman Bennett	35-30-0

*Released after three games in 1968
**Released after eight games in 1974
***Released after five games in 1976

ATLANTA FALCONS 1981 VETERAN ROSTER

No.	Name	Pos.	Ht.	Wt.	NFL Exp.	Birth-date	Birthplace	College	Residence	Games in '80
33	Anderson, Anthony	RB	6-0	197	3	9/26/56	Wilmington, Del.	Temple	Wilmington, Del.	16
31	Andrews, William	RB	6-0	200	3	12/25/55	Thomasville, Ga.	Auburn	Norcross, Ga.	16
10	Bartkowski, Steve	QB	6-4	213	7	11/12/52	Des Moines, Iowa	California	Cumming, Ga.	16
44	Bean, Bubba	RB	5-11	195	4	1/26/54	Kirbyville, Tex.	Texas A&M	Kirbyville, Tex.	0*
66	Bryant, Warren	T	6-6	270	5	11/11/55	Miami, Tex.	Kentucky	Roswell, Ga.	16
38	Byas, Rick	CB	5-9	180	8	10/10/50	Detroit, Mich.	Wayne State	Detroit, Mich.	15
21	Cain, Lynn	RB	6-1	205	3	10/16/55	Los Angeles, Calif.	Southern California	Atlanta, Ga.	16
53	Correal, Chuck	C	6-3	247	3	5/17/56	Uniontown, Pa.	Penn. State	Norcross, Ga.	16
50	Curry, Buddy	LB	6-3	221	2	6/4/58	Danville, Va.	North Carolina	Danville, Va.	16
55	Daykin, Tony	LB	6-1	215	2	5/13/55	Taipei, Taiwan	Georgia Tech	Roswell, Ga.	16
32	Easterling, Ray	S	6-0	192	8	9/3/49	Richmond, Va.	Richmond	Richmond, Va.	0*
74	Faumuina, Wilson	DT	6-5	275	5	8/11/54	San Francisco, Calif.	San Jose State	Los Angeles, Calif.	14
77	Fields, Edgar	DT	6-2	255	5	3/10/54	Austin, Tex.	Texas A&M	Roswell, Ga.	14
9	Fortner, Larry	QB	6-4	212	2	12/24/55	Lorain, Ohio	Miami, Ohio	Lorain, Ohio	0*
89	Francis, Wallace	WR	5-11	190	9	11/7/51	Franklin, La.	Arkansas-Pine Bluff	Marietta, Ga.	16
36	Glazebrook, Bob	S	6-1	200	4	3/7/56	Fresno, Calif.	Florida	Clovis, Calif.	16
63	Herman, Chuck	G	6-3	250	2	10/7/58	Little Rock, Ark.	Arkansas	Little Rock, Ark.	2
64	Howell, Pat	G	6-5	253	3	3/12/57	Fresno, Calif.	Southern California	Austin, Tex.	16
85	Jackson, Alfred	WR	5-11	176	4	8/3/55	Cameron, Tex.	Texas	Clovis, Calif.	5
6	James, John	P	6-3	200	10	1/21/49	Panama City, Fla.	Florida	Gainesville, Fla.	16
84	Jenkins, Alfred	WR	5-10	172	7	1/25/52	Hogansville, Ga.	Morris Brown	College Park, Ga.	16
37	Johnson, Kenny	S	5-10	176	2	1/7/58	Moss Point, Miss.	Mississippi State	Moss Point, Miss.	16
20	Jones, Earl	CB	6-0	178	2	7/19/57	Tuscaloosa, Ala.	Norfolk State	Norfolk, Va.	16
14	Jones, June	QB	6-4	200	4	2/19/53	Portland, Ore.	Portland State	Cumming, Ga.	0*
78	Kenn, Mike	T	6-6	257	6	2/9/56	Evanston, Ill.	Michigan	Buford, Ga.	16
54	Kuykendall, Fulton	LB	6-5	225	7	6/10/53	Coronado, Calif.	UCLA	Roswell, Ga.	10
51	Laughlin, Jim	LB	6-0	212	2	7/5/58	Lyndhurst, Ohio	Ohio State	Lyndhurst, Ohio	16
22	Lawrence, Rolland	CB	5-10	179	9	3/24/51	Franklin, Pa.	Tabor	Franklin, Pa.	16
39	Mayberry, James	RB	5-11	210	3	11/5/57	Amarillo, Tex.	Colorado	Decatur, Ga.	16
4	Mazzetti, Tim	K	6-1	175	4	2/1/56	Old Greenwich, Conn.	Pennsylvania	Lawrenceville, Ga.	16
52	McClain, Dewey	LB	6-1	236	6	4/25/54	Okmulgee, Okla.	East Central Oklahoma	Lawrenceville, Ga.	16
73	McKinney, Phil	DE	6-3	230	2	7/8/54	Berkeley, Calif.	West Virginia	Norcross, Ga.	16
87	Merrow, Jeff	DE	6-4	248	7	7/11/53	Akron, Ohio	West Virginia	Cumming, Ga.	7
75	Mikeska, Russ	TE	6-3	225	3	9/10/55	Temple, Tex.	Texas A&M	Temple, Tex.	15
80	Miller, Junior	TE	6-4	235	2	11/26/57	Midland, Tex.	Nebraska	Lincoln, Neb.	16
15	Moroski, Mike	QB	6-4	200	3	9/4/57	Novato, Calif.	Cal-Davis	Cumming, Ga.	3
81	Pearson, Dennis	WR	5-11	177	3	2/9/55	Seaside, Calif.	San Diego State	Seaside, Calif.	0*
59	Pennywell, Robert	LB	6-1	222	6	11/6/54	Shreveport, La.	Grambling	Alpharetta, Ga.	16
27	Pridemore, Tom	S	5-10	186	5	4/29/56	Ansted, W. Va.	West Virginia	Ansted, W. Va.	16
28	Reed, Frank	S	5-11	193	6	5/13/54	Seattle, Wash.	Washington	Decatur, Ga.	16
56	Richardson, Al	LB	6-2	206	2	9/23/57	Miami, Fla.	Georgia Tech	Decatur, Ga.	16
82	†Ryckman, Billy	WR	5-11	172	4	2/28/55	Lafayette, La.	Louisiana Tech	Decatur, Ga.	0*
70	Scott, Dave	G	6-4	265	6	12/26/53	Paterson, N.J.	Kansas	Decatur, Ga.	16
65	Smith, Don	DE	6-5	248	3	5/9/57	Oakland, Calif.	Miami	Norcross, Ga.	16
86	Smith, Mike	WR	5-10	194	6	4/28/58	Kingston, N.C.	Grambling	Decatur, Ga.	8
16	Smith, Reggie	WR	5-4	168	2	7/15/56	Bastrop, La.	North Carolina Central	Bastrop, La.	5
25	Strong, Ray	RB	5-9	184	5	7/15/56	Berkeley, Calif.	Nevada-Las Vegas	Charlotte, N.C.	16
68	Thielemann, R.C.	G	6-4	247	5	8/12/55	Houston, Tex.	Arkansas	Odessa, Fla.	16
57	Van Note, Jeff	C	6-2	247	13	2/7/46	South Orange, N.J.	Kentucky	Decatur, Ga.	16
58	Williams, Joel	LB	6-0	215	3	12/13/56	Miami, Fla.	Wisconsin-LaCrosse	Norcross, Ga.	16
79	Yeates, Jeff	DE	6-3	248	10	8/3/51	Buffalo, N.Y.	Boston College	Roswell, Ga.	16
63	Zele, Mike	DT	6-3	236	3	7/3/56	Euclid, Ohio	Kent State	Euclid, Ohio	11

*Bean, Easterling, Jones, Pearson, Ryckman missed '80 season due to injury; Fortner active for 16 games but did not play.

†Option playout, subject to developments.

Also played with Falcons in '80—LB Jonathan Brooks (4 games), CB Jerome King (2), DT Calvin Miller (2), LB Stan Sysma (2).

ATLANTA FALCONS 1981 FIRST-YEAR ROSTER

Name	Pos.	Ht.	Wt.	Birth-date	Birthplace	College	Residence	How Acq.
Allen, Dallas	WR	5-11	190	7/30/58	Dublin, Ga.	Morehouse	Atlanta, Ga.	FA
Baker, Herbert	QB	6-1	200	8/27/57	Pasadena, Tex.	Stephen Austin	Pasadena, Tex.	FA
Brockhaus, Jeff	P-K	6-3	200	4/15/59	St. Louis, Mo.	Missouri	Columbia, Mo.	FA
Butler, Bobby	CB	5-11	170	5/28/59	Boynton Beach, Fla.	Florida State	Tallahassee, Fla.	D1
Cathey, James	T	6-4	260	12/31/58	Maywood, Ill.	Tulane	Maywood, Ill.	FA
Chappelle, Keith	WR	6-0	178	3/29/60	Los Angeles, Calif.	Iowa	Iowa City, Iowa	D11
Cooksey, Robert	LB	6-1	225	4/6/56	Tyrone, Ga.	Georgia Tech	Atlanta, Ga.	FA
Cosper, Billy	TE	6-5	235	10/20/58	Dallas, Tex.	Stephen Austin	Dallas, Tex.	FA
Donald, George	RB	6-1	200	7/12/59	Joliet, Ill.	Elmhurst	Joliet, Ill.	D9
Fance, Calvin	RB	6-1	200	7/6/59	Houston, Tex.	Rice	Houston, Tex.	FA
Gaison, Blane	CB-S	5-9	185	5/13/58	Kaneohe, Hawaii	Hawaii	Kaneohe, Hawaii	FA
Hawkins, Michael	RB	5-9	192	7/22/58	Manson, N.C.	East Carolina	Greenville, N.C.	FA
Hodge, Floyd	WR	6-0	195	7/18/59	Compton, Calif.	Utah	Salt Lake City, Utah	FA
Janakievski, Vlade	K	5-7	165	4/10/57	Columbus, Ohio	Ohio State	Columbus, Ohio	FA
Luckhurst, Mick	K	6-0	180	3/31/58	Redbourn, Eng.	California	Berkeley, Calif.	FA
McCants, Mark	S	6-0	190	7/12/58	Quakertown, Pa.	Temple	Allentown, Pa.	D12
Mitchell, William	LB	6-0	213	8/2/59	Los Angeles, Calif.	Long Beach State	Los Angeles, Calif.	FA
Murphy, Robert	S	6-1	198	7/22/58	Bakersfield, Calif.	Ohio State	Santa Ynez, Calif.	D10
Musser, James	LB	6-1	218	3/20/57	Elon, N.C.	North Carolina State	Elon, N.C.	FA
Puha, Dennis	G	6-2	260	11/9/58	Honolulu, Hawaii	Nevada-Reno	Reno, Nev.	FA
Sanders, Eric	T	6-6	255	10/22/58	Reno, Nev.	Nevada-Reno	Reno, Nev.	D5
Scully, John	C	6-5	255	8/2/58	Long Island, N.Y.	Notre Dame	Huntington, N.Y.	D4
Singleton, John (1)	DE	6-5	260	12/22/56	Houston, Tex.	Texas-El Paso	El Paso, Tex.	FA
Stanback, Harry	DT	6-5	255	8/17/58	Rockingham, N.C.	North Carolina	Carrboro, N.C.	D6
Talley, Stan	P	6-5	220	9/5/58	Torrance, Calif.	Texas Christian	Ft. Worth, Tex.	FA
Todd, Daniel	S	5-11	195	5/11/58	Lancaster, S.C.	Northern Iowa	Cedar Falls, Iowa	D8
Toney, Cliff	CB-S	5-11	185	12/17/58	Huntsville, Ala.	Auburn	Auburn, Ala.	FA
Walters, Peter	G	6-2	265	3/17/59	Shepherdsville, Ky.	Western Kentucky	Shepherdsville, Ky.	FA
White, Lyman	LB	6-0	217	1/3/59	Franklin, La.	Louisiana State	Franklin, La.	D2
White, Terry	CB-S	5-10	180	3/26/59	Thomasville, Ga.	Pittsburgh	Thomasville, Ga.	FA
Whitely, Derick	WR	5-10	183	10/2/57	Bessemer, Ala.	Jacksonville State	Jacksonville, Ala.	FA
Wise, William	TE	6-4	232	10/27/58	Johnson City, Tenn.	Mississippi	Johnson City, Tenn.	FA
Woerner, Scott	CB-S	6-0	195	12/18/58	Baintown, Tex.	Georgia	Jonesboro, Ga.	D3
Wright, Michael	RB	5-10	200	10/4/58	Dallas, Tex.	Texas Christian	Ft. Worth, Tex.	FA
Zidd, James (1)	LB	6-1	228	3/14/57	Cleveland, Ohio	Kansas	Lawrence, Kan.	FA

Players who report to an NFL team for the first time are designated on rosters as rookies (R). If a player reported to an NFL training camp in a previous year but was not on the active squad for three or more regular season or postseason games, he is listed on the first-year roster and designated by a (1). Thereafter, a player who is on the active squad for three or more regular season games is credited with an additional year of playing experience.

COACHING STAFF

Head Coach, Leeman Bennett

Pro Career: Begins fifth season as pro head coach after guiding Falcons to their first NFC Western title in 1980. Served seven years as a pro assistant, coaching offensive backs with St. Louis Cardinals 1970-71 and Detroit Lions 1972 and receivers with Los Angeles Rams 1973-76. No pro playing experience. Career record: 35-30.

Background: College quarterback and defensive back at University of Kentucky 1958-60. College coach at University of Kentucky 1961-62, 1965, University of Pittsburgh 1966, University of Cincinnati 1967-68, and U. S. Naval Academy 1969.

Personal: Born June 20, 1938, in Paducah, Kentucky. Leeman and his wife, Pat, live in Atlanta and have two sons—Paul and Greg.

ASSISTANT COACHES

Jerry Glanville, defensive coordinator-defensive backfield; born October 14, 1941, Detroit, lives in Atlanta. Guard-linebacker Northern Michigan 1961-63. No pro playing experience. College coach: Northern Michigan 1966, Western Kentucky 1967, Georgia Tech 1968-73. Pro coach: Detroit Lions 1974-76, fifth year with Falcons.

Mike McDonnell, administrative assistant; born August 3, 1952, Peoria, Ill., lives in Atlanta. Linebacker Drake University 1972-74. No pro playing experience. Pro coach: Falcons since 1978.

John North, offensive backfield; born June 17, 1921, Gilliam, La., lives in Atlanta. End Vanderbilt 1942, 1946-47. Pro end Baltimore Colts 1948-50. College coach: Tennessee Tech 1954-55, Kentucky 1956-61, Louisiana State 1962-64. Pro coach: Detroit Lions 1965-72, New Orleans Saints 1973-75 (head coach), fifth year with Falcons.

Jimmy Raye, wide receivers; born July 3, 1945, Fayetteville, N.C., lives in Atlanta. Quarterback Michigan State 1965-67. Pro defensive back Philadelphia Eagles 1969. College coach: Michigan State 1971-75, Wyoming 1976. Pro coach: San Francisco 49ers 1977, Detroit Lions 1978-79, second year with Falcons.

Doug Shively, linebackers; born March 18, 1938, Lexington, Ky., lives in Atlanta. End Kentucky 1955-58. No pro playing experience. College coach: Virginia Tech 1961-66, Kentucky 1967-69, Clemson 1970-72, North Carolina 1973. Pro coach: New Orleans Saints 1974-76, fifth year with Falcons.

Jim Stanley, defensive line; born June 22, 1934, Dunham, Ky., lives in Atlanta. Guard Texas A&M 1955-57. No pro playing experience. College coach: Southern Methodist 1961, Texas-El Paso 1962, Oklahoma State 1963-68, 1972-78 (head coach 1973-78), Navy 1969-70. Pro coach: Winnipeg Bombers (CFL) 1971, New York Giants 1979, second year with Falcons.

Bill Walsh, offensive line; born September 8, 1927, Philipsburg, N.J., lives in Atlanta. Center Notre Dame 1946-49. Pro center Pittsburgh Steelers 1950-55. College coach: Notre Dame 1956-58, Kansas State 1959. Pro coach: Kansas City Chiefs 1960-74, Falcons since 1975.

Dick Wood, quarterbacks; born February 29, 1936, Lanett, Ala., lives in Atlanta. Quarterback Auburn 1956-59. Pro quarterback Baltimore Colts 1960-61, San Diego Chargers 1962, Denver Broncos 1962, New York Jets 1963-64, Oakland Raiders 1965, Miami Dolphins 1966. College coach: Georgia 1967-68, Mississippi 1971-73. Pro coach: Oakland Raiders 1969-70, Cleveland Browns 1974, New Orleans Saints 1976-77, fourth year with Falcons.

NOTES

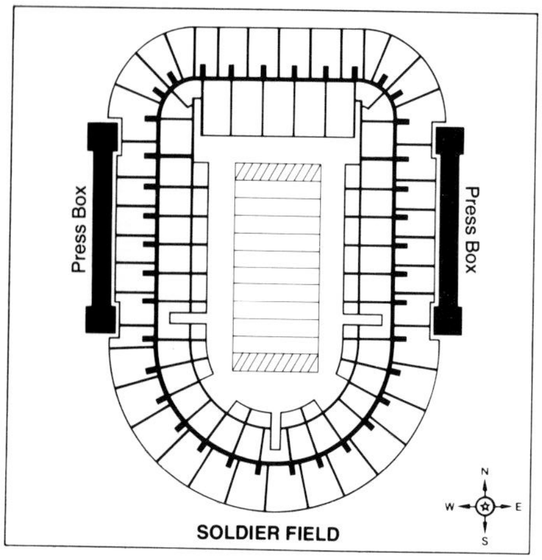

Chicago Bears

National Football Conference
Central Division

Team Colors: Orange, Navy Blue and White

Administrative and Ticket Offices:
55 E. Jackson Blvd., Chicago, Illinois 60604
Telephone: (312) 663-5100
Halas Hall (Coaching Staff, Personnel, Public Relations):
250 North Washington, Lake Forest, Illinois 60045
Telephone: (312) 295-6600

Club Officials

Chairman of the Board, President: George S. Halas
Executive Vice President-General Manager, Chief Operating Officer: Jim Finks
Vice President: Ed McCaskey
Assistant to General Manager: Bill McGrane
Director, College Scouting: Jim Parmer
Director, Pro Scouting: Bill Tobin
Stadium Operations-Admissions Director: George Arneson
Business Manager: Rudy Custer
Treasurer: Jerry Vainisi
Public Relations Director: Ted Haracz
Assistant Public Relations Director: Patrick McCaskey
Film Director: Mitch Friedman
Trainer: Fred Caito
Physical Coordinator: Clyde Emrich
Equipment Manager: Ray Earley

Stadium: Soldier Field • **Capacity:** 64,519
425 McFetridge Place
Chicago, Illinois 60605

Playing Surface: AstroTurf

Training Camp: Halas Hall
Lake Forest, Illinois 60045

1981 SCHEDULE

Preseason

Aug. 8	**New York Giants**	6:00
Aug. 15	at Kansas City	7:35
Aug. 22	**Cincinnati**	6:00
Aug. 29	at St. Louis	6:00

Regular Season

Sept. 6	**Green Bay**	1:00
Sept. 13	at San Francisco	1:00
Sept. 20	**Tampa Bay**	1:00
Sept. 28	**Los Angeles** (Monday)	8:00
Oct. 4	at Minnesota	12:00
Oct. 11	**Washington**	1:00
Oct. 19	at Detroit (Monday)	9:00
Oct. 25	**San Diego**	3:00
Nov. 1	at Tampa Bay	1:00
Nov. 8	at Kansas City	1:00
Nov. 15	at Green Bay	12:00
Nov. 22	**Detroit**	12:00
Nov. 26	at Dallas (Thanksgiving)	3:00
Dec. 6	**Minnesota**	12:00
Dec. 13	at Oakland	1:00
Dec. 20	**Denver**	12:00

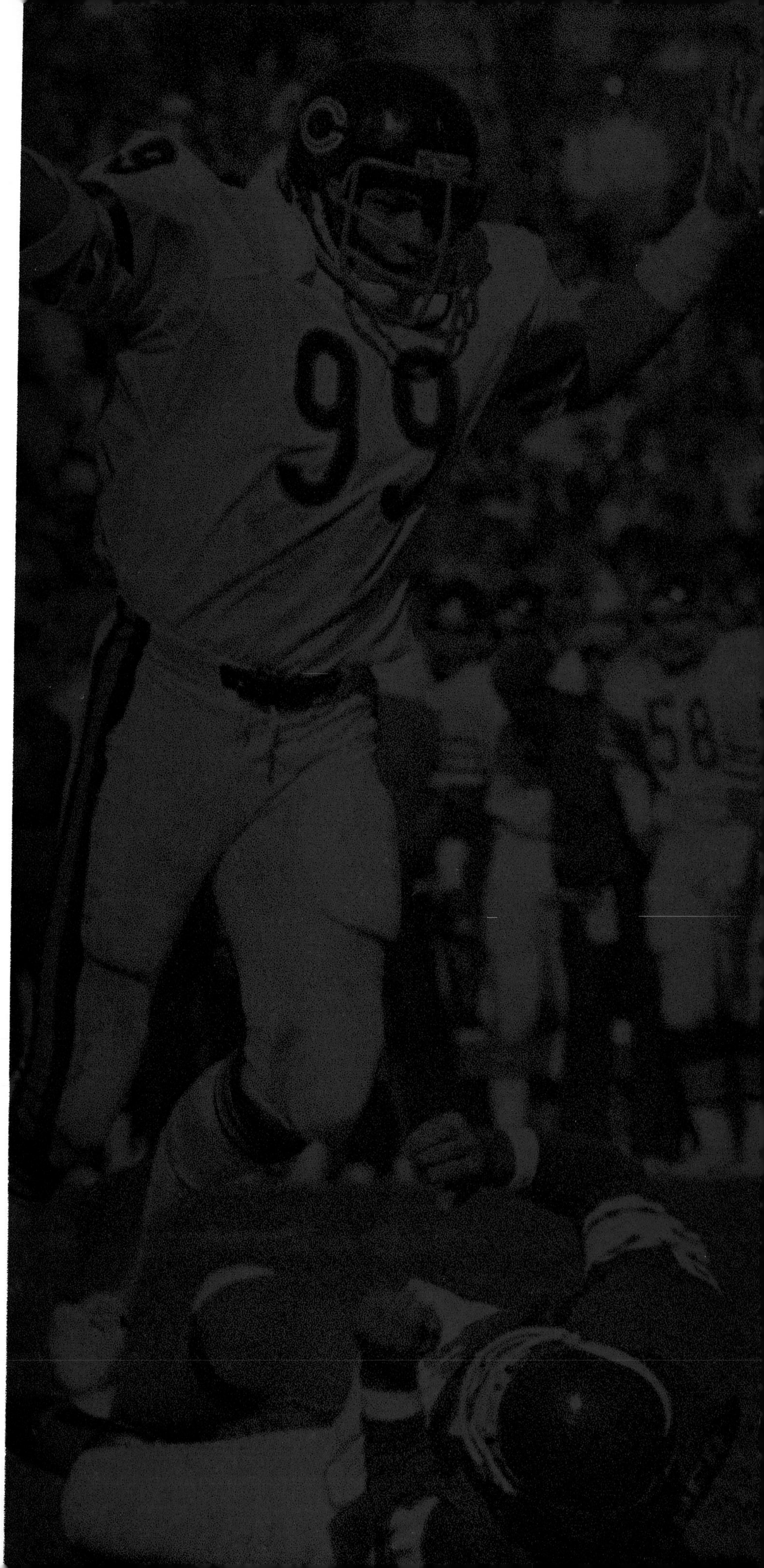

1980 TEAM STATISTICS

	Chicago	Opp.
Total First Downs	286	285
Rushing	139	111
Passing	121	149
Penalty	26	25
Third Down Efficiency	105/248	98/236
Third Down Percentage	42.3	41.5
Total Net Yards	4835	4907
Total Offensive Plays	1016	1003
Avg. Gain per Play	4.8	4.9
Avg. Gain per Game	302.2	306.7
Net Yards Rushing	2440	2015
Total Rushing Plays	579	506
Avg. Gain per Rush	4.2	4.0
Avg. Gain Rushing per Game	152.5	125.9
Net Yards Passing	2395	2892
Lost Attempting to Pass	33/274	46/379
Gross Yards Passing	2669	3271
Attempts/Completions	404/209	451/238
Percent Completed	51.7	52.8
Had Intercepted	25	17
Avg. Net Passing per Game	149.7	180.8
Punts/Avg.	79/40.6	82/39.0
Punt Returns/Avg.	41/6.8	46/9.0
Kickoff Returns/Avg.	56/20.6	58/21.6
Interceptions/Avg. Ret.	17/9.5	25/6.4
Penalties/Yards	100/842	129/1109
Fumbles/Ball Lost	23/14	32/14
Total Points	304	264
Avg. Points per Game	19.0	16.5
Touchdowns	38	32
Rushing	22	10
Passing	13	20
Returns and Recoveries	3	2
Field Goals	13/18	14/27
Conversions	35/37	30/31
Safeties	1	0

1980 TEAM RECORD

Preseason (1-3)

Chicago		Opponents
21	New York Jets	9
3	Cincinnati	21
31	Cleveland	33
13	St. Louis	21
68		84

Regular Season (7-9)

Chicago		Opponents	Att.
6	Green Bay (OT)	12	54,381
22	*New Orleans	3	62,523
14	*Minnesota	34	59,983
3	Pittsburgh	38	53,987
23	*Tampa Bay	0	61,350
7	Minnesota	13	46,751
24	*Detroit	7	58,508
14	Philadelphia	17	68,752
21	Cleveland	27	83,224
35	*Washington	21	57,159
6	*Houston	10	59,390
17	Atlanta	28	49,164
23	Detroit (OT)	17	75,397
61	*Green Bay	7	57,176
14	*Cincinnati (OT)	17	48,808
14	Tampa Bay	13	55,298
304		264	951,851

*Home Game (OT) Overtime

Score by Periods

							Total
Chicago	51	77	77	93	6	—	304
Opponents	57	79	51	68	9	—	264

Attendance

Home 464,897   Away 486,954   Total 951,851
Single game home record, 62,523 (9-14-80)
Single season home record, 951,626 (1980)

1980 INDIVIDUAL STATISTICS

Scoring

	TD	TD R	TD P	TD Rt	PAT	FG	TP
Thomas					35/37	13/18	74
Evans	8	8	0	0			48
Payton	7	6	1	0			42
Harper	5	5	0	0			30
Earl	3	3	0	0			18
Scott	3	0	3	0			18
Baschnagel	2	0	2	0			12
Fisher	2	0	2	0			12
Phipps	2	2	0	0			12
Watts	2	2	0	0			12
Page	1	0	0	1	(Safety)		8
McClendon	1	1	0	0			6
Walterscheid	1	0	0	1			6
Williams	1	1	0	0			6
Chicago	38	22	13	3	35/37	13/18	304
Opponents	32	10	20	2	30/31	14/27	264

Rushing

	Att	Yds	Avg	LG	TD
Payton	317	1460	4.6	69t	6
Harper	113	404	3.6	13	5
Evans	60	306	5.1	58	8
McClendon	10	88	8.8	48	1
Williams	26	57	2.2	14	0
Skibinski	13	54	4.2	8	0
Suhey	22	45	2.0	10	0
Phipps	15	38	2.5	9	2
Parsons	2	4	2.0		0
Watts	1	-16	-16.0	-16	0
Chicago	579	2440	4.2	69t	22
Opponents	506	2015	4.0	56t	10

Field Goal Success

Distance	1-19	20-29	30-39	40-49	50 Over
Made-Att.	1-1	5-5	4-8	3-4	0-0

Passing

	Att	Comp	Pct	Yds	TD	Int	LG	Tkld	Rate
Evans	278	148	53.2	2039	11	16	54t	26/205	66.1
Phipps	122	61	50.0	630	2	9	36t	7/69	39.8
Parsons	1	0	0.0	0	0	0		0/0	—
Payton	3	0	0.0	0	0	0		0/0	—
Chicago	404	209	51.7	2669	13	25	54t	33/274	57.6
Opponents	451	238	52.8	3271	20	17	76t	46/379	

Receiving

	No	Yds	Avg	LG	TD
Payton	46	367	8.0	54t	1
Scott	36	696	19.3	64t	3
Baschnagel	28	396	14.1	37	2
Watts	22	444	20.2	89t	4
Williams	22	132	6.0	18	0
Earl	18	223	12.4	28	2
Fisher	12	203	16.9	56t	3
Suhey	7	60	8.6	21	0
Harper	7	31	4.4	16	0
Skibinski	5	18	3.6	8	0
Haines	4	83	20.8	35	0
Cobb	2	16	8.0	9	0
Chicago	209	2669	12.8	89t	13
Opponents	238	3271	13.7	76t	20

Interceptions

	No	Yds	Avg	LG	TD
Walterscheid	4	84	21.0	36t	1
Campbell	3	36	12.0	15	0
Wilson	2	4	2.0	4	0
Muckensturm	2	2	1.0	2	0
Plank	1	20	20.0	20	0
Fencik	1	8	8.0	8	0
Hicks	1	8	8.0	8	0
Ellis	1	0	0.0	0	0
Page	1	0	0.0	0	0
Schmidt	1	0	0.0	0	0
Chicago	17	162	9.5	36t	1
Opponents	25	161	6.4	41t	1

Punting

	No	Yds	Avg	LG	In 20
Parsons	79	3207	40.6	61	16
Chicago	79	3207	40.6	61	16
Opponents	82	3197	39.0	65	20

Punt Returns

	No	FC	Yds	Avg	LG	TD
Walterscheid	33	11	239	7.2	25	0
Lusby	4	1	14	3.5		0
Watts	2	0	20	10.0	11	0
Suhey	1	0	4	4.0	4	0
Plank	1	0	0	0.0	0	0
Chicago	41	12	277	6.8	25	0
Opponents	46	7	415	9.0	56	0

Kickoff Returns

	No	Yds	Avg	LG	TD
Williams	27	666	24.7	95t	1
Suhey	19	406	21.4	31	0
Fisher	3	32	10.7	15	0
Walterscheid	1	12	12.0	12	0
Watts	1	12	12.0	12	0
Earl	1	11	11.0	11	0
McClendon	1	11	11.0	11	0
Herron	1	5	5.0	5	0
Haines	1	0	0.0	0	0
Ulmer	1	-2	-2.0	-2	0
Chicago	56	1153	20.6	95t	1
Opponents	58	1251	21.6	54	0

CHICAGO RECORD HOLDERS

Individual Records—Single Season

Category	Name	Performance
Rushing (Yds.)	Walter Payton, 1977	1852
Passing (Pct.)	Rudy Bukich, 1964	61.9
Passing (Yds.)	Bill Wade, 1962	3172
Passing (TDs)	Sid Luckman, 1943	28
Receiving (No.)	Johnny Morris, 1964	93
Receiving (Yds.)	Johnny Morris, 1964	1200
Interceptions	Roosevelt Taylor, 1963	9
Punting (Avg.)	Bobby Joe Green, 1963	46.5
Punt Ret. (Avg.)	Harry Clark, 1943	15.8
Kickoff Ret. (Avg.)	Gale Sayers, 1967	37.7
Field Goals	Mac Percival, 1968	25
Touchdowns (Tot.)	Gale Sayers, 1965	22
Points	Gale Sayers, 1965	132

Team Records—Single Game

Category	Opponent, Date	Performance
Offense		
First Downs	vs. GB, 12/7/80	33
Total Points	vs. SF, 12/12/65	61
	vs. SF, 12/12/65	61
Touchdowns	vs. GB, 12/7/80	9
Total Net Yards	vs. NYG, 11/14/43	682
Net Yards Rushing	vs. Brooklyn, 10/20/35	408
Net Yards Passing	vs. NYG, 11/14/43	488
Rushing Attempts	vs. Brooklyn, 10/20/35	72
Passing Attempts	vs. NYG, 10/23/49	59
Interceptions by	vs. GB, 9/22/40	7
	vs. Det, 11/22/42	7
	vs. Chi Cards, 12/5/54	7
	vs. StL, 9/19/67	7
Defense		
Net Yards Allowed	vs. Pitt, 10/2/39	54
Net Rushing Yards Allowed	vs. Chi Cards, 12/6/42	-17
Net Passing Yards Allowed	vs. GB, 11/4/73	-12

FIRST PLAYERS SELECTED

Year	Player, College, Position
1974	Waymond Bryant, Tennessee State, LB
1975	Walter Payton, Jackson State, RB
1976	Dennis Lick, Wisconsin, T
1977	Ted Albrecht, California, T
1978	Brad Shearer, Texas, DT (3)
1979	Dan Hampton, Arkansas, DT
1980	Otis Wilson, Louisville, LB
1981	Keith Van Horne, Southern California, T

BEARS COACHING HISTORY

Chicago Staleys 1921
(463-297-41)

1920-29	George Halas	85-30-18
1930-32	Ralph Jones	24-10-7
1933-42	George Halas*	89-25-4
1942-45	Hunk Anderson-Luke Johnsos**	24-13-2
1946-55	George Halas	77-42-2
1956-57	John (Paddy) Driscoll	14-10-1
1958-67	George Halas	75-53-6
1968-71	Jim Dooley	20-36-0
1972-74	Abe Gibron	11-30-1
1975-77	Jack Pardee	20-23-0
1978-80	Neill Armstrong	24-25-0

*Retired November 1 to re-enter Navy
**Co-coaches

CHICAGO BEARS 1981 VETERAN ROSTER

No.	Name	Pos.	Ht.	Wt.	NFL Exp.	Birth-date	Birthplace	College	Residence	Games in '80
64	Albrecht, Ted	T-G	6-4	250	5	10/8/54	Harvey, Ill.	California	Deerfield, Ill.	16
7	†Avellini, Bob	QB	6-2	210	7	8/28/53	Queens, N.Y.	Maryland	Northbrook, Ill.	0*
84	Baschnagel, Brian	WR-KR	6-0	184	6	1/8/54	Kingston, N.Y.	Ohio State	Shawnee Hills, Ohio	16
49	Becker, Dave	S	6-2	190	2	1/15/57	Atlantic, Iowa	Iowa	Atlantic, Iowa	11
59	Campbell, Gary	LB	6-1	220	5	3/4/52	Colorado	Colorado	Schaumburg, Ill.	16
20	Childs, Jim	WR	6-2	195	3	8/9/56	Honolulu, Hawaii	Cal Poly-SLO	West Covina, Calif.	0*
87	Cobb, Mike	TE	6-5	243	5	12/10/55	El Dorado, Ariz.	Michigan State	Riverwoods, Ill.	4
81	Earl, Robin	TE	6-5	240	5	3/18/55	Boise, Idaho	Washington	Hoffman Estates, Ill.	16
48	Ellis, Allan	CB	6-0	177	8	8/19/51	Los Angeles, Calif.	UCLA	Riverwoods, Ill.	16
8	Evans, Vince	QB	6-2	212	5	6/14/55	Greensboro, N.C.	Southern California	Chicago, Ill.	16
45	†Fencik, Gary	S	6-1	197	6	6/11/54	Chicago, Ill.	Yale	Chicago, Ill.	15
86	Fisher, Bob	TE	6-3	240	4	3/17/58	Los Angeles, Calif.	Southern Methodist	Vernon Hills, Ill.	13
36	†Gaines, Wentford	CB	6-0	185	4	2/4/57	Chicago, Ill.	Cincinnati	Chicago, Ill.	8
83	Haines, Kris	WR-KR	5-11	180	3	7/23/57	Akron, Ohio	Notre Dame	Chicago, Ill.	8
99	Hampton, Dan	DT-DE	6-5	255	3	9/19/57	Oklahoma City, Okla.	Arkansas	Lake Bluff, Ill.	12
35	Harper, Roland	RB	5-11	210	6	12/31/56	Seguin, Tex.	Louisiana Tech	Gurnee, Ill.	16
90	Harris, Al	DE	6-5	240	3	2/28/53	Bangor, Maine	Arizona State	Phoenix, Ariz.	16
73	Hartenstine, Mike	DE	6-3	243	7	7/27/53	Allentown, Pa.	Penn State	Lake Bluff, Ill.	16
51	Herron, Bruce	LB	6-2	220	4	4/14/54	Victoria, Tex.	New Mexico	Chicago, Ill.	16
54	Hicks, Tom	LB	6-4	235	6	12/18/52	Oak Park, Ill.	Illinois	Elmhurst, Ill.	11
47	Hoke, Jonathan	CB	5-11	175	2	1/24/57	Hamilton, Ohio	Ball State	Kettering, Ohio	14
65	†Jackson, Noah	G	6-2	265	7	4/14/51	Jacksonville, Fla.	Tampa	Lake Forest, Ill.	15
74	Jiggetts, Dan	T	6-5	270	6	3/10/54	Brooklyn, N.Y.	Harvard	Chicago, Ill.	16
57	Kunz, Lee	LB	6-2	225	3	4/21/57	Lakewood, Calif.	Nebraska	Golden, Colo.	16
88	Latta, Greg	TE	6-3	225	6	10/13/52	Newark, N.J.	Morgan State	Roselle, Ill.	0*
70	Lick, Dennis	T	6-3	265	6	4/26/54	Chicago, Ill.	Wisconsin	Northbrook, Ill.	16
29	Lusby, Vaughn	KR-CB	5-10	181	2	8/23/56	Ft. Polk, La.	Arkansas	Lawton, Okla.	2
37	McClendon, Willie	KR-RB	6-1	205	3	9/13/57	Brunswick, Ga.	Georgia	Highland Park, Ill.	16
71	Moore, Rocco	G	6-5	276	2	3/31/55	Charlotte, Mich.	Western Michigan	Potterville, Mich.	7
58	Muckensturm, Jerry	LB	6-4	205	6	10/13/53	Belleville, Ill.	Arkansas State	Jonesboro, Ark.	16
52	†Neal, Dan	C	6-4	255	9	8/30/49	Corbin, Ky.	Kentucky	Deerfield, Ill.	15
68	Osborne, Jim	DT	6-3	245	10	9/7/49	Sylvania, Ga.	Southern	Olympia Fields, Ill.	16
82	Page, Alan	DT	6-4	225	15	8/7/45	Canton, Ohio	Notre Dame	Minneapolis, Minn.	16
86	Parsons, Bob	P	6-5	225	10	6/29/50	Bethlehem, Pa.	Penn State	Wind Gap, Pa.	16
34	†Payton, Walter	RB	5-10	202	7	7/25/54	Columbia, Miss.	Jackson State	Arlington Heights, Ill.	16
15	†Phipps, Mike	QB	6-3	209	12	11/19/47	Shelbyville, Ind.	Purdue	Boca Raton, Ill.	12
46	Plank, Doug	S-KR	5-11	202	7	3/4/53	Greensburg, Pa.	Ohio State	Buffalo Grove, Ill.	16
76	Rydalch, Ron	DT	6-4	250	7	1/1/52	Tooele, Utah	Utah	Grantsville, Utah	7
44	†Schmidt, Terry	CB	6-0	177	8	5/28/52	Columbus, Ind.	Ball State	Lake Forest, Ill.	16
72	Shearer, Brad	DT	6-3	247	4	8/10/55	Houston, Tex.	Texas	Austin, Tex.	7
30	Simpson, Nate	RB	5-11	190	4	11/30/54	Nashville, Tenn.	Tennessee State	Nashville, Tenn.	0*
69	Skibinski, John	RB	6-0	222	3	4/27/55	Chicago, Ill.	Purdue	Vernon Hills, Ill.	13
62	Sorey, Revie	G	6-2	260	7	9/10/53	Brooklyn, N.Y.	Illinois	Chicago, Ill.	16
26	Suhey, Matt	RB-KR	5-11	212	2	7/7/58	Bellefonte, Pa.	Penn State	Chicago, Ill.	16
53	Tabor, Paul	C-G	6-4	241	2	11/30/56	Little Rock, Ariz.	Oklahoma	Houston, Tex.	16
16	Thomas, Bob	K	5-10	175	7	7/8/52	Rochester, N.Y.	Notre Dame	Lisle, Ill.	16
23	Walterscheid, Lenny	S-KR	6-0	190	5	9/13/54	Gainesville, Tex.	Southern Utah State	Chicago, Ill.	16
80	Watts, Rickey	WR-KR	6-1	203	3	5/16/57	Longview, Tex.	Tulsa	Vernon Hills, Ill.	15
22	Williams, Dave	RB-KR	6-2	217	5	3/10/54	Minden, La.	Colorado	San Mateo, Calif.	15
55	Wilson, Otis	LB	6-2	222	2	9/15/57	New York, N.Y.	Louisville	Libertyville, Ill.	16

* Avellini active for 16 games but did not play; Childs last active with St. Louis in '79; Latta missed '80 season due to injury; Simpson last active with Green Bay in '79.

† Option playout; subject to developments.

Also played with Bears in '80 — WR James Scott (15 games), S. Mike Ulmer (3).

COACHING STAFF

Head Coach, Neill Armstrong

Pro Career: Starts fourth season as NFL head coach after spending eight seasons as defensive coordinator for the Minnesota Vikings. In 1979, guided Bears to a 10-6 record and a playoff appearance. Assistant coach with Houston Oilers 1962-63, and was head coach of the Edmonton Eskimos (CFL) for six years prior to joining the Vikings in 1970. Played for the Philadelphia Eagles 1947-51 and Winnipeg Blue Bombers (CFL) 1951, 1953-54 as an end and defensive back. Career record: 24-25.

Background: Was an outstanding end and play caller on Oklahoma State teams (then Oklahoma A&M) 1943-46. Received All-America honors at the conclusion of senior year. Assistant coach at Oklahoma State 1955-61.

Personal: Born March 9, 1926, Tishomingo, Okla. Neill and wife, Jane, live in Chicago and have three children—Neill Jr., David, and Gail.

ASSISTANT COACHES

Dale Haupt, defensive line; born April 12, 1929, Manitowic, Wis., lives in Chicago. Guard Wyoming 1951-53. Pro guard Green Bay Packers 1954. College coach: Tennessee 1960-63, Iowa State 1964-65, Richmond 1966-71, North Carolina State 1972-76, Duke 1977. Pro coach: Fourth year with Bears.

Hank Kuhlmann, running backs-special teams; born October 6, 1937, St. Louis, Mo., lives in Chicago. Running back Missouri 1955-59. No pro playing experience. College coach: Missouri 1963-71, Notre Dame 1975-77. Pro coach: Green Bay Packers 1972-74, fourth year with Bears.

Jim LaRue, defensive backfield; born August 11, 1925, Clinton, Okla., lives in Chicago. Halfback Carson-Newman 1943, Duke 1944-45, Maryland 1947-49. No pro playing experience. College coach: Maryland 1950, Kansas State 1951-54, Houston 1955-56, SMU 1957-58, Arizona 1959-66 (head coach), Utah 1967-73, Wake Forest 1974-75. Pro coach: Buffalo Bills 1976-77, fourth year with Bears.

Ted Marchibroda, offensive coordinator; born March 15, 1931, Franklin, Pa., lives in Chicago. Quarterback St. Bonaventure 1950-51, Detroit 1953. Pro quarterback Pittsburgh Steelers 1953, 1955-56, Chicago Cardinals 1957. Pro coach: Washington Redskins 1961-65, 1971-73, Los Angeles Rams 1970, Baltimore Colts (head coach) 1975-79, first year with Bears.

Ted Plumb, receivers; born August 20, 1939, Reno, Nev., lives in Chicago. End Baylor 1959-61. No pro playing experience. College coach: Cerritos Junior College 1966-67, Texas Christian 1968-70, Tulsa 1971, Kansas 1972-73. Pro coach: New York Giants 1974-76, Atlanta Falcons 1977-79, second year with Bears.

Buddy Ryan, defensive coordinator; born February 16, 1934, Frederick, Okla., lives in Chicago. Guard Oklahoma State 1952-55. No pro playing experience. College coach: Buffalo 1961-65, Vanderbilt 1966, University of Pacific 1967. Pro coach: New York Jets 1968-75, Minnesota Vikings 1976-77, fourth year with Bears.

Dick Stanfel, offensive line; born July 20, 1927, San Francisco, Calif., lives in Chicago. Guard San Francisco 1948-51. Pro guard Detroit Lions 1952-55, Washington Redskins 1956-58. College coach: Notre Dame 1959-62, California 1963. Pro coach: Philadelphia Eagles 1964-70, San Francisco 49ers 1971-75, New Orleans Saints 1976-80 (head coach, 4 games in '80), first year with Bears.

CHICAGO BEARS 1981 FIRST-YEAR ROSTER

Name	Pos.	Ht.	Wt.	Birth-date	Birthplace	College	Residence	How Acq.
Bell, Todd	CB-KR	6-1	207	11/28/58	Middletown, Ohio	Ohio State	Middletown, Ohio	D4
Buckner, Rennie (1)	T	6-3	291	10/25/57	Chicago, Ill.	Boise State	Chicago, Ill.	FA
Clifford, Tim	QB	6-1	207	11/28/58	Ft. Thomas, Ky.	Indiana	Cincinnati, Ohio	D10
Cox, Martin (1)	WR	6-0	180	8/12/56	Mullin, S.C.	Vanderbilt	Plantation, Fla.	FA
Ditta, Frank	G	6-2	264	4/9/58	Houston, Tex.	Baylor	Houston, Tex.	D9
Ehlebracht, Tim	WR	6-1	174	2/10/58	Homewood, Ill.	North Central	Homewood, Ill.	FA
Fisher, Jeff	CB-KR	5-11	188	2/25/58	Culver City, Calif.	Southern California	Woodland Hills, Calif.	D7
Geske, John	TE	6-2	238	7/25/59	Chicago, Ill.	St. Joseph's	Wheeling, Ill.	FA
Henderson, Reuben	CB	6-1	200	10/3/58	Santa Monica, Calif.	San Diego State	San Diego, Calif.	D6
Hilgenberg, Jay	C	6-3	230	3/21/59	Iowa City, Iowa	Iowa	Iowa City, Iowa	FA
Johnson, Lonnie	RB	6-1	206	6/7/59	Frankfurt, Germany	Indiana	Bloomington, Ind.	D11
Margerum, Ken	WR	5-11	170	10/5/58	Fountain Valley, Calif.	Stanford	Palo Alto, Calif.	D3
McGhee, Scott	WR	5-9	165	3/15/59	Chicago, Ill.	Eastern Illinois	Charleston, Ill.	FA
Mullaney, Ryan (1)	LB-DE	6-4	243	7/29/56	Denver, Colo.	Nevada-Las Vegas	Denver, Colo.	FA
Noonan, Joe (1)	WR	6-2	190	12/11/58	Bloomington, Minn.	Nebraska-Omaha	Omaha, Neb.	FA
Pinckney, Mike	WR	5-10	182	11/22/58	Sumter, S.C.	Northern Illinois	Washington, D.C.	FA
Reid, Brad (1)	WR	5-11	175	12/23/57	Cedar Rapids, Iowa	Iowa	Marion, Iowa	FA
Rosenthal, Ken (1)	P	5-9	178	6/15/58	Philadelphia, Pa.	Southern Methodist	St. Louis, Mo.	FA
Sheets, Todd	WR	6-0	183	7/22/57	South Bend, Ind.	Northwestern	Evanston, Ill.	FA
Shupryt, Bob	LB	6-1	206	9/29/58	Chicago, Ill.	New Mexico	County Club Hills, Ill.	D12
Singletary, Mike	LB	5-11	230	10/9/58	Houston, Tex.	Baylor	Waco, Tex.	D2
Van Horne, Keith	T	6-7	265	11/6/57	Mt. Lebanon, Pa.	Southern California	Clarendon Hills, Ill.	D1
Zettek, Scott	DT	6-5	240	4/13/58	Chicago, Ill.	Notre Dame	Elk Grove Village, Ill.	D8

Players who report to an NFL team for the first time are designated on rosters as rookies (R). If a player reported to an NFL training camp in a previous year but was not on the active squad for three or more regular season or postseason games, he is listed on the first-year roster and designated by a (1). Thereafter, a player who is on the active squad for three or more regular season games is credited with an additional year of playing experience.

NOTES

Dallas Cowboys

National Football Conference
Eastern Division

Team Colors: Royal Blue, Metallic Blue, and White

6116 North Central Expressway
Dallas, Texas 75206
Telephone: (214) 369-8000

Club Officials

Chairman of the Board: Clint W. Murchison, Jr.
President-General Manager: Texas E. Schramm
Vice President-Personnel Development: Gil Brandt
Vice President-Treasurer: Don Wilson
Vice President-Administration: Joe Bailey
Administrative Assistant: Dan Werner
Director of Public Relations: Doug Todd
Assistant Public Relations Director: Greg Aiello
Ticket Manager: Kay Lang
Trainers: Don Cochren, Ken Locker
Equipment Manager: William T. (Buck) Buchanan
Cheerleaders Director: Suzanne Mitchell
Director of Promotions: Fred Hoster

Stadium: Texas Stadium • **Capacity:** 65,101
Irving, Texas 75062

Playing Surface: Texas Turf
Training Camp: California Lutheran College
Thousand Oaks, California 91360

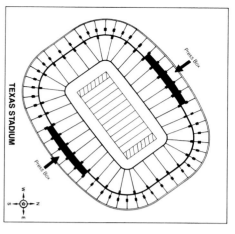

TEXAS STADIUM

1981 SCHEDULE

Preseason

Aug. 8	**Green Bay**	8:00
Aug. 15	at Los Angeles	5:30
Aug. 22	**Pittsburgh**	8:00
Aug. 29	**Houston**	8:00

Regular Season

Sept. 6	at Washington	1:00
Sept. 13	**St. Louis**	3:00
Sept. 21	at New England (Monday)	9:00
Sept. 27	**New York Giants**	3:00
Oct. 4	at St. Louis	12:00
Oct. 11	at San Francisco	1:00
Oct. 18	**Los Angeles**	8:00
Oct. 25	**Miami**	3:00
Nov. 1	at Philadelphia	4:00
Nov. 9	**Buffalo** (Monday)	8:00
Nov. 15	at Detroit	4:00
Nov. 22	**Washington**	3:00
Nov. 26	**Chicago** (Thanksgiving)	3:00
Dec. 6	at Baltimore	2:00
Dec. 13	**Philadelphia**	3:00
Dec. 19	at New York Giants (Saturday)	12:30

1980 TEAM STATISTICS

	Dallas	Opp.
Total First Downs	337	286
Rushing	143	98
Passing	171	160
Penalty	23	28
Third Down Efficiency	120/243	89/222
Third Down Percentage	49.4	40.1
Total Net Yards	5482	5279
Total Offensive Plays	1075	996
Avg. Gain per Play	5.1	5.3
Avg. Gain per Game	342.6	329.9
Net Yards Rushing	2378	2069
Avg. Gain per Rush	4.0	4.4
Avg. Gain Rushing per Game	148.6	129.3
Total Rushing Plays	595	469
Net Yards Passing	3104	3210
Lost Attempting to Pass	31/252	43/358
Gross Yards Passing	3356	3568
Attempts/Completions	449/265	484/231
Percent Completed	59.0	47.7
Had Intercepted	25	27
Avg. Net Passing per Game	194.0	200.6
Punts/Avg.	71/40.9	76/43.5
Punt Returns/Avg.	55/10.1	32/6.7
Kickoff Returns/Avg.	58/21.7	73/21.5
Interceptions/Avg. Ret.	27/19.4	25/7.2
Penalties/Yards	109/908	106/989
Fumbles/Ball Lost	26/14	33/20
Total Points	454	311
Avg. Points per Game	28.5	19.4
Touchdowns	60	38
Rushing	26	15
Passing	30	21
Returns and Recoveries	4	2
Field Goals	11/17	15/28
Conversions	59/60	38/38
Safeties	1	0

1980 TEAM RECORD

Preseason (3-1)

Dallas		Opponents
17	Green Bay	14
19	Los Angeles	16
20	Houston	13
10	Pittsburgh	31
66		74

Regular Season (12-4)

Dallas		Opponents	Att.
17	Washington	3	55,045
41	Denver	20	74,919
28	*Tampa Bay	17	62,750
28	Green Bay	7	54,776
24	*New York Giants	3	59,126
59	*San Francisco	14	63,399
10	Philadelphia	17	70,696
42	*San Diego	31	60,639
27	St. Louis	24	50,701
35	New York Giants	38	68,343
31	*St. Louis	21	52,567
14	*Washington	10	58,809
51	*Seattle	7	57,540
19	Oakland	13	53,194
14	Los Angeles	38	65,154
35	*Philadelphia	27	62,548
454		311	970,206

*Home Game

Score by Periods

Dallas	96	153	86	119	—	454
Opponents	59	130	44	78	—	311

Attendance

Home 477,378   Away 492,828   Total 970,206
Single game home record, 80,259 (11-24-66)
Single season home record, 508,965 (1979)

1980 INDIVIDUAL STATISTICS

Rushing

	Att	Yds	Avg	LG	TD
Dorsett	278	1185	4.3	56	11
Newhouse	118	451	3.8	29t	6
Springs	89	326	3.7	20t	6
J. Jones	41	135	3.3	9	1
D. White	27	114	4.2	48	2
Newsome	25	79	3.2	23	0
D. Pearson	2	30	15.0	32	0
Hill	4	27	6.8	15	0
DuPree	4	19	4.8	11	0
P. Pearson	3	6	2.0	2	0
Carano	4	6	1.5	5	0
Dallas	595	2378	4.0	56	26
Opponents	469	2069	4.4	61	15

Field Goal Success

Distance	1-19	20-29	30-39	40-49	50 Over
Made-Att.	1-1	3-4	6-6	0-3	1-3

Passing

	Att	Comp	Pct	Yds	TD	Int	LG	Tkld	Rate
D. White	436	260	59.6	3287	28	25	58t	30/352	80.8
Carano	12	5	41.7	69	2	0	30	1/0	100.4
Dorsett	1	0	0.0	0	0	0		0/0	—
Dallas	449	265	59.0	3356	30	25	58t	31/252	81.4
Opponents	484	231	47.7	3568	21	27	69t	43/358	—

Receiving

	No	Yds	Avg	LG	TD
Hill	60	1055	17.6	58t	8
D. Pearson	43	568	13.2	30	6
Dorsett	34	263	7.7	27	0
DuPree	29	312	10.8	39	7
Saldi	25	311	12.4	43	1
P. Pearson	20	213	10.7	20	2
Johnson	19	263	13.8	29t	4
Springs	15	212	14.1	58t	0
Newhouse	8	75	9.4	18	0
J. Jones	5	39	7.8	16	0
Newsome	4	43	10.8	16	0
Cosbie	2	11	5.5	6	0
D. White	1	-9	-9.0	-9	0
Dallas	265	3356	12.7	58t	30
Opponents	231	3568	15.4	69t	21

Interceptions

	No	Yds	Avg	LG	TD
Thurman	5	114	22.8	78t	1
Waters	5	78	15.6	29	0
Wilson	4	82	20.5	35	0
Mitchell	3	56	18.7	56	0
Breunig	3	34	11.3	15	0
Dickerson	2	46	23.0	34	0
Hegman	2	2	1.0	2	0
Cole	1	43	43.0	43t	1
Dutton	1	38	38.0	38t	1
Barnes	1	30	30.0	30	0
Dallas	27	523	19.4	78t	3
Opponents	25	179	7.2	36	1

Punting

	No	Yds	Avg	In 20	LG	TD
D. White	71	2903	40.9	17	58	0
Dallas	71	2903	40.9	17	58	0
Opponents	76	3303	43.5	12	58	0

Punt Returns

	No	FC	Yds	Avg	LG	TD
J. Jones	54	4	548	10.1	52	0
Solomon	1	0	8	8.0	8	0
Dallas	55	4	556	10.1	52	0
Opponents	32	10	215	6.7	53	0

Kickoff Returns

	No	Yds	Avg	LG	TD
J. Jones	32	720	22.5	41	0
Newsome	12	293	24.4	36	0
Wilson	7	139	19.9	34	0
Hurt	4	71	17.8	24	0
Saldi	1	23	23.0	23	0
Cosbie	1	13	13.0	13	0
Waters	1	0	0.0	0	0
Dallas	58	1259	21.7	41	0
Opponents	73	1568	21.5	53	0

Scoring

	TD R	TD P	TD Rt	PAT	FG	TP
Septien				59/60	11/17	92
Dorsett	11					66
Hill		8				48
DuPree		7				42
Springs	6	1				42
Newhouse	6					36
D. Pearson		6				36
Johnson		4				24
Newsome			2			12
P. Pearson		2				12
Cole			1			6
Cosbie		1				6
Dutton			1			6
Hegman			1			6
Saldi		1				6
Thurman			1			6
D. White	1					6
Team						2 (Safety)
Dallas	26	30	4	59/60	11/17	454
Opponents	15	21	2	38/38	15/28	311

DALLAS RECORD HOLDERS

Individual Records—Single Season

Category	Name	Performance
Rushing (Yds.)	Tony Dorsett, 1978	1325
Passing (Pct.)	Roger Staubach, 1973	62.6
Passing (Yds.)	Roger Staubach, 1979	3586
Passing (TDs)	Danny White, 1980	28
Receiving (No.)	Frank Clarke, 1964	65
Receiving (Yds.)	Bob Hayes, 1966	1232
Interceptions	Mel Renfro, 1969	10
Punting (Avg.)	Ron Widby, 1969	43.3
Punt Ret. (Avg.)	Bob Hayes, 1968	20.8
Kickoff Ret. (Avg.)	Mel Renfro, 1965	30.0
Field Goals	Toni Fritsch, 1975	22
Touchdowns (Tot.)	Dan Reeves, 1966	16
Points	Dan Villanueva, 1966	107

Team Records—Single Game

Category	Opponent, Date	Performance

Offense

Category	Opponent, Date	Performance
First Downs	vs. Phil, 10/9/66	32
	vs. NYG, 9/10/78	32
	vs. GB, 11/12/78	32
Total Points	vs. Det, 9/15/68	59
	vs. SF, 10/12/80	59
Touchdowns	vs. SF, 10/12/80	8
	vs. Det, 9/15/68	8
	vs. Phil, 10/9/66	8
Total Net Yards	vs. SF, 10/12/80	652
Net Yards Rushing	vs. GB, 11/12/78	313
Net Yards Passing	vs. Phil, 10/9/66	440
Rushing Attempts	vs. SF, 10/12/80	59
Passing Attempts	vs. Phil, 10/26/75	50
Interceptions by	vs. Phil, 9/30/60	7
	vs. Phil, 9/26/71	7

Defense

Category	Opponent, Date	Performance
Net Yards Allowed	vs. GB, 10/24/65	63
Net Rushing Yards Allowed	vs. Pitt, 10/30/66	7
Net Passing Yards Allowed	vs. GB, 10/24/65	-1
	vs. NYJ, 12/21/75	-1

FIRST PLAYERS SELECTED

Year	Player, College, Position
1966	John Niland, Iowa, G
1967	Phil Clark, Northwestern, DB (3)
1968	Dennis Homan, Alabama, WR
1969	Calvin Hill, Yale, RB
1970	Duane Thomas, West Texas State, RB
1971	Tody Smith, So. California, DE
1972	Bill Thomas, Boston College, RB
1973	Billy Joe DuPree, Michigan St., TE
1974	Ed Jones, Tennessee State, DE
1975	Randy White, Maryland, LB
1976	Aaron Kyle, Wyoming, DB
1977	Tony Dorsett, Pittsburgh, RB
1978	Larry Bethea, Michigan State, DE
1979	Robert Shaw, Tennessee, C
1980	Bill Roe, Colorado, LB (3)
1981	Howard Richards, Missouri, T

COWBOYS COACHING HISTORY (201-120-6)

1960-80	Tom Landry	201-120-6

DALLAS COWBOYS 1981 VETERAN ROSTER

No.	Name	Pos.	Ht.	Wt.	NFL Exp.	Birth-date	Birthplace	College	Residence	Games in '80
31	Barnes, Benny	CB	6-1	195	10	3/3/51	Lufkin, Tex.	Stanford	Dallas, Tex.	11
76	Bethea, Larry	DT	6-5	254	4	7/21/56	Florence, S.C.	Michigan State	Richardson, Tex.	11
53	Breunig, Bob	LB	6-2	225	7	7/4/53	Inglewood, Calif.	Arizona State	Dallas, Tex.	16
59	Brown, Guy	LB	6-4	228	5	6/1/55	Houston	Houston	Richardson, Tex.	16
18	Carano, Glenn	QB	6-3	202	5	11/18/55	San Pedro, Calif.	Nevada-Las Vegas	Dallas, Tex.	15
47	Clinkscale, Dextor	S	5-11	189	2	4/13/58	Greenville, S.C.	South Carolina State	Greenville, S.C.	16
61	Cooper, Jim	T	6-5	260	5	9/28/55	Philadelphia, Pa.	Temple	Philadelphia, Pa.	15
84	Cosbie, Doug	TE	6-6	230	3	3/27/56	Mountain View, Calif.	Santa Clara	Dallas, Tex.	16
51	Dickerson, Anthony	LB	6-2	214	2	6/9/57	Texas City, Tex.	Southern Methodist	Dallas, Tex.	16
67	Donovan, Pat	T	6-4	250	7	7/1/53	Helena, Mont.	Stanford	Wylie, Tex.	15
33	Dorsett, Tony	RB	5-11	190	5	4/7/54	Rochester, Pa.	Pittsburgh	Dallas, Tex.	15
89	DuPree, Billy Joe	TE	6-4	229	9	3/7/50	West Monroe, La.	Michigan State	Dallas, Tex.	16
78	Dutton, John	DT	6-7	265	8	2/6/51	Evansville, Ind.	Nebraska	Malcolm, Neb.	16
62	Fitzgerald, John	C	6-5	260	11	4/16/48	Southbridge, Mass.	Boston College	Richardson, Tex.	14
71	Frederick, Andy	T	6-6	255	5	7/25/54	Oak Park, Ill.	New Mexico	Plano, Tex.	16
58	Hegman, Mike	LB	6-1	225	6	1/17/53	Memphis, Tenn.	Tennessee State	Plano, Tex.	16
80	Hill, Tony	WR	6-2	198	5	6/23/56	San Diego, Calif.	Stanford	Dallas, Tex.	16
14	Hogeboom, Gary	QB	6-4	201	2	8/21/58	Grand Rapids, Mich.	Central Michigan	Dallas, Tex.	2
42	Hughes, Randy	S	6-4	207	7	4/3/53	Oklahoma City, Okla.	Oklahoma	Dallas, Tex.	5
57	Huther, Bruce	LB	6-1	220	5	7/23/54	Haledon, N.J.	New Hampshire	Dallas, Tex.	16
86	Johnson, Butch	WR	6-1	192	6	5/28/54	Los Angeles, Calif.	Cal-Riverside	Plano, Tex.	16
72	Jones, Ed	DE	6-9	270	7	2/23/51	Jackson, Tenn.	Tennessee State	Dallas, Tex.	16
23	Jones, James	RB	5-10	201	2	12/6/58	Vicksburg, Miss.	Mississippi State	Vicksburg, Miss.	16
50	†Lewis, D.D.	LB	6-1	215	13	10/16/45	Knoxville, Tenn.	Mississippi State	Richardson, Tex.	16
22	Manning, Wade	CB	5-11	190	2	7/25/55	Meadville, Pa.	Ohio State	Dallas, Tex.	2
79	Martin, Harvey	DE	6-5	250	9	11/16/50	Dallas, Tex.	East Texas State	Carrollton, Tex.	0*
34	Mitchell, Aaron	CB	6-1	196	3	12/15/56	Los Angeles, Calif.	Nevada-Las Vegas	Dallas, Tex.	15
44	Newhouse, Robert	FB	5-10	215	10	1/9/50	Longview, Tex.	Houston	Dallas, Tex.	16
30	Newsome, Timmy	FB	6-1	227	2	5/17/58	Ahoskie, N.C.	Winston-Salem State	Dallas, Tex.	16
88	Pearson, Drew	WR	6-0	183	9	1/12/51	South River, N.J.	Tulsa	Dallas, Tex.	16
26	†Pearson, Preston	RB	6-1	196	15	1/17/45	Freeport, Ill.	Illinois	Dallas, Tex.	11
65	Petersen, Kurt	G	6-4	251	2	6/17/57	St. Louis, Mo.	Missouri	Carrollton, Tex.	16
64	Rafferty, Tom	G	6-3	250	6	8/2/54	Syracuse, N.Y.	Penn State	Dallas, Tex.	16
56	Roe, Bill	LB	6-3	230	2	2/6/58	South Bend, Ind.	Colorado	Dallas, Tex.	2
87	Saldi, Jay	TE	6-3	227	6	10/8/54	White Plains, N.Y.	South Carolina	Dallas, Tex.	15
68	Scott, Herbert	G	6-2	252	7	1/18/53	Virginia Beach, Va.	Virginia Union	Plano, Tex.	16
1	Septien, Rafael	K	5-9	171	5	12/12/53	Mexico City, Mex.	Southwest Louisiana	Dallas, Tex.	16
52	Shaw, Robert	C	6-4	245	3	10/15/56	Tuscaloosa, Ala.	Tennessee	Plano, Tex.	16
20	Springs, Ron	FB	6-0	210	3	11/4/56	Williamsburg, Va.	Ohio State	Dallas, Tex.	16
77	Thornton, Bruce	DE	6-5	265	3	2/14/58	Detroit, Mich.	Illinois	Dallas, Tex.	13
32	Thurman, Dennis	S	5-11	170	4	4/13/56	Los Angeles, Calif.	Southern California	Dallas, Tex.	16
41	Waters, Charlie	S	6-2	200	11	9/10/48	Miami, Fla.	Clemson	Dallas, Tex.	16
66	Wells, Norm	G	6-5	261	2	9/8/57	Detroit, Mich.	Northwestern	Richardson, Tex.	16
11	White, Danny	QB-P	6-2	192	6	2/9/52	Mesa, Ariz.	Arizona State	Wylie, Tex.	3
54	White, Randy	DT	6-4	250	7	1/15/53	Wilmington, Del.	Maryland	Landenburg, Pa.	16
45	Wilson, Steve	CB	5-10	192	3	8/24/57	Durham, N.C.	Howard	Richardson, Tex.	16

*Manning missed '80 season due to injury.

†Option playout; subject to developments.

Retired—Larry Cole, 13-year defensive end, 16 games in '80.

Also played with Cowboys in '80—CB Eric Hurt (4 games), CB Roland Solomon (10).

COACHING STAFF

Head Coach, Tom Landry

Pro Career: Last year's 12-4 regular season record boosted the Cowboys into the playoffs for the 14th time in the past 15 years and gave Landry 15 winning seasons in succession. Cowboys became the fourth team in NFL to win a second Super Bowl. They defeated Denver 27-10 in Super Bowl XII on January 15, 1978 at Louisiana Superdome. Dallas has played in four other Super Bowls (V, VI, X, and XIII), winning Game VI 24-3 over Miami. Cowboys' only head coach in their 21-year history, compiling a 201-120-6 record. Pro defensive back with New York Yanks (AAFC) 1949, New York Giants 1950-55. Player-coach with Giants 1954-55, named all-pro in 1954. Defensive assistant coach with Giants 1956-59 before moving to Dallas as head coach in 1960.

Background: Halfback, University of Texas 1947-48, and played in Longhorns' victories over Alabama in 1948 Sugar Bowl and Georgia in 1949 Orange Bowl.

Personal: Born September 11, 1924 in Mission, Tex. World War II bomber pilot. Tom and his wife, Alicia, live in Dallas and have three children—Tom Jr., Kitty, and Lisa.

ASSISTANT COACHES

Ermal Allen, special assistant-research and development; born December 25, 1920, Sneedsville, Tenn., lives in Dallas. Quarterback Kentucky 1939-41. Pro back Cleveland Browns (AAFC) 1947. College coach: Kentucky 1948-61. Pro coach: Cowboys since 1962.

Mike Ditka, special teams-tight ends; born October 18, 1939, Carnegie, Pa., lives in Dallas. End Pittsburgh 1958-60. Pro tight end Chicago Bears 1961-66, Philadelphia Eagles 1967-68, Dallas Cowboys 1969-72. Pro coach: Cowboys since 1973.

Al Lavan, running backs; born September 13, 1946, Pierce, Fla., lives in Dallas. Defensive back Colorado State 1965-67. Pro defensive back Philadelphia Eagles 1968, Atlanta Falcons 1969-70. College coach: Colorado State 1972, Louisville 1973, Iowa State 1974, Georgia Tech 1977-78, Stanford 1979. Pro coach: Atlanta Falcons 1975-76, second year with Cowboys.

John Mackovic, quarterbacks; born October 1, 1943, Barberton, Ohio, lives in Dallas. Quarterback Wake Forest 1961-64. No pro playing experience. College coach: Army 1968, 1971-72, San Jose State 1969-70, Arizona 1973-76, Purdue 1977, Wake Forest 1978-80 (head coach). Pro coach: First year with Cowboys.

Jim Myers, assistant head coach-offensive line; born November 12, 1921, Madison, W. Va., lives in Dallas. Guard Tennessee 1941-42, 1946, Duke 1943. No pro playing experience. College coach: Wofford 1947, Vanderbilt 1948, UCLA 1949-56, Iowa State 1957 (head coach), Texas A&M 1958-61 (head coach). Pro coach: Cowboys since 1962.

Gene Stallings, defensive backs; born March 2, 1935, Paris, Tex., lives in Dallas. End Texas A&M 1954-57. No pro playing experience. College coach: Texas A&M 1957, 1965-71 (head coach), Alabama 1958-64. Pro coach: Cowboys since 1972.

Ernie Stautner, defensive coordinator-defensive line; born April 2, 1925, Kham, Bavaria, lives in Dallas. Guard Boston College 1946-49. Pro defensive tackle Pittsburgh Steelers 1950-63. Pro coach: Pittsburgh Steelers 1963-64, Washington Redskins 1965, Cowboys since 1966.

Jerry Tubbs, linebackers; born January 23, 1935, Breckenridge, Tex., lives in Dallas. Center-linebacker Oklahoma 1954-56. Pro linebacker Chicago Cardinals 1957, San Francisco 49ers 1958-59, Dallas Cowboys 1960-67. Pro coach: Cowboys since 1965.

Bob Ward, conditioning; born July 4, 1933, Huntington Park, Calif., lives in Dallas. Fullback-quarterback Whitworth College 1952-54. Doctorate in physical education, Indiana University. No pro playing experience. College coach: Fullerton CC (track) 1965-75. Pro coach: Cowboys since 1975.

DALLAS COWBOYS 1981 FIRST-YEAR ROSTER

Name	Pos.	Ht.	Wt.	Birth-date	Birthplace	College	Residence	How Acq.
Donley, Doug	WR	6-0	180	2/6/59	Cambridge, Ohio	Ohio State	Cambridge, Ohio	D2
Fellows, Ron	CB-S	6-0	173	11/7/58	South Bend, Ind.	Missouri	South Bend, Ind.	D7
Graham, Pat	DT	6-4	272	4/21/59	Palo Alto, Calif.	California	San Jose, Calif.	D10
Grimmett, Richard (1)	T	6-7	270	6/23/55	Dixmoor, Ill.	Illinois	Dallas, Tex.	FA
Kirk, Richard (1)	LB	6-2	233	10/2/56	Columbus, Ohio	Denison	Lawrenceville, N.J.	FA
Lundy, Nate	WR	6-0	162	10/15/58	Great Lakes, Ill.	Indiana	North Chicago, Ill.	D12
McLaughlin, Tom (1)	P	6-0	195	2/13/56	Dubuque, Iowa	Iowa	Dubuque, Iowa	FA
Morrison, Tim	T-G	6-4	259	2/8/58	Boaz, Ala.	Georgia	Suwanee, Ga.	D11
Nelson, Derrie	LB	6-2	216	12/10/58	York, Neb.	Nebraska	Fairmont, Neb.	D4a
Pelluer, Scott	LB	6-2	214	4/28/59	Yakima, Wash.	Washington State	Bellevue, Wash.	D4
Pennella, Richard (1)	P	6-2	210	10/1/55	Port Chester, N.Y.	Louisville	Port Chester, N.Y.	FA
Piurowski, Paul	LB	6-3	232	3/16/59	Danville, Ill.	Florida State	Sarasota, Fla.	D8
Richards, Howard	T-G	6-5	262	8/7/59	St. Louis, Mo.	Missouri	St. Louis, Mo.	D1
Skillings, Vince	CB-S	5-11	183	5/3/59	Latrobe, Pa.	Ohio State	Derry, Pa.	D6
Smerek, Don (1)	DE	6-7	250	12/20/57	Waterford, Mich.	Nevada-Reno	Dallas, Tex.	FA
Spradlin, Danny	LB	6-1	228	3/3/59	Detroit, Mich.	Tennessee	Maryville, Tenn.	D5
Titensor, Glen	T	6-4	256	2/21/58	Bellflower, Calif.	Brigham Young	Garden Grove, Calif.	D3
White, Allen (1)	P	6-2	196	5/9/59	Windsor, N.C.	North Carolina State	Windsor, N.C.	FA
Wilson, Mike	WR	6-3	210	12/19/58	Los Angeles, Calif.	Washington State	Carson, Calif.	D9

Players who report to an NFL team for the first time are designated on rosters as rookies (R). If a player reported to an NFL training camp in a previous year but was not on the active squad for three or more regular season or postseason games, he is listed on the first-year roster and designated by a (1). Thereafter, a player who is on the active squad for three or more regular season games is credited with an additional year of playing experience.

NOTES

Detroit Lions

**National Football Conference
Central Division**

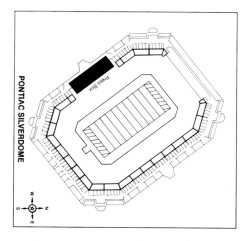

PONTIAC SILVERDOME

Team Colors: Honolulu Blue and Silver
Pontiac Silverdome
1200 Featherstone Road—Box 4200
Pontiac, Michigan 48057
Telephone: (313) 335-4131

Club Officials

President-Owner: William Clay Ford
Executive Vice-President-General Manager:
  Russell Thomas
Director of Football Operations-Head Coach:
  Monte Clark
Director of Player Personnel: Tim Rooney
Controller: Charles Schmidt
Consultant: Lyall Smith
College Scouts: Jerry Neri (Western Area),
  Joe Bushofsky (Eastern Area), Dirk Dierking
  (Central Area)
Director of Public Relations: Don Kremer
Publicity Assistant: Brian Muir
Ticket Manager: Fred Otto
Trainer: Kent Falb
Strength and Conditioning: Gary Wade
Equipment Manager: Dan Jaroshewich
Stadium: Pontiac Silverdome • **Capacity:** 80,638
  1200 Featherstone Road
  Pontiac, Michigan 48057
Playing Surface: AstroTurf
Training Camp: Oakland University
  Rochester, Michigan 48063

1981 SCHEDULE

Preseason

Aug. 8	at Buffalo	....	6:00
Aug. 15	**Cincinnati**	....	7:00
Aug. 22	**Miami**	....	7:00
Aug. 29	at New Orleans	....	7:00

Regular Season

Sept. 6	**San Francisco**	....	1:00
Sept. 13	at San Diego	....	1:00
Sept. 20	at Minnesota	....	12:00
Sept. 27	**Oakland**	....	1:00
Oct. 4	at Tampa Bay	....	4:00
Oct. 11	at Denver	....	2:00
Oct. 19	**Chicago** (Monday)	....	9:00
Oct. 25	**Green Bay**	....	1:00
Nov. 1	at Los Angeles	....	1:00
Nov. 8	at Washington	....	1:00
Nov. 15	**Dallas**	....	4:00
Nov. 22	at Chicago	....	12:00
Nov. 26	**Kansas City** (Thanksgiving)	....	12:30
Dec. 6	at Green Bay	....	12:00
Dec. 12	**Minnesota** (Saturday)	....	4:00
Dec. 20	**Tampa Bay**	....	1:00

1980 TEAM STATISTICS

	Detroit	Opp.
Total First Downs	308	265
Rushing	143	100
Passing	143	143
Penalty	22	22
Third Down Efficiency	106/237	84/223
Third Down Percentage	44.7	37.7
Total Net Yards	5540	4533
Total Offensive Plays	1040	955
Avg. Gain per Play	5.3	4.7
Avg. Gain per Game	346.3	283.3
Net Yards Rushing	2599	1599
Total Rushing Plays	572	449
Avg. Gain per Rush	4.5	3.6
Avg. Gain Rushing per Game	162.4	99.9
Net Yards Passing	2941	2934
Lost Attempting to Pass	45/346	44/300
Gross Yards Passing	3287	3234
Attempts/Completions	423/248	462/256
Percent Completed	58.6	55.4
Had Intercepted	12	23
Avg. Net Passing per Game	183.8	183.4
Punts/Avg.	73/41.6	93/41.6
Punt Returns/Avg.	56/8.3	38/7.9
Kickoff Returns/Avg.	57/20.5	64/20.1
Interceptions/Avg. Ret.	23/7.3	12/14.4
Penalties/Yards	104/844	98/815
Fumbles/Ball Lost	40/19	20/11
Total Points	334	272
Avg. Points per Game	20.9	17.0
Touchdowns	36	32
Rushing	21	9
Passing	13	14
Returns and Recoveries	2	9
Field Goals	27/42	16/21
Conversions	35/36	30/31
Safeties	1	1

1980 TEAM RECORD

Preseason (3-1)

Detroit		Opponents
7	Miami	17
24	Buffalo	17
40	New Orleans	17
15	Cincinnati	10
86		61

Regular Season (9-7)

Detroit		Opponents
41	Los Angeles	20
29	Green Bay	7
20	*St. Louis	7
27	*Minnesota	7
28	Atlanta	43
24	*New Orleans	13
7	Chicago	24
17	Kansas City	20
17	*San Francisco	13
0	Minnesota	34
9	*Baltimore	10
24	Tampa Bay	10
17	*Chicago (OT)	23
23	St. Louis	24
27	*Tampa Bay	14
24	*Green Bay	3
334		272

*Home Game   (OT) Overtime

Score by Periods

	1	2	3	4	OT		Total
Detroit	40	93	59	142	0	—	334
Opponents	61	98	36	71	6	—	272

Attendance

Home 621,353   Away 451,748   Total 1,073,101
Single game home record, 80,291 (9-28-80)
Single season home record, 621,353 (1980)

1980 INDIVIDUAL STATISTICS

Rushing

	Att	Yds	Avg	LG	TD
Sims	313	1303	4.2	52	13
Bussey	145	720	5.0	40	3
Danielson	48	232	4.8	33	2
Kane	31	125	4.0	22	1
Scott	5	86	17.2	48t	1
L. Thompson	6	61	10.2	30	0
King	18	57	3.2	8	1
R. Williams	2	17	8.5	11t	1
Robinson	3	2	0.7	4	0
J. Thompson	1	-4	-4.0	-4	0
Detroit	572	2599	4.5	52	21
Opponents	449	1599	3.6	21	9

Field Goal Success

Distance	1-19	20-29	30-39	40-49	50 Over
Made-Att.	0-1	9-9	10-13	7-15	1-4

Passing

	Att	Comp	Pct	Yds	TD	Int	Tkid	Rate
Danielson	417	244	58.5	3223	13	11	44/338	82.6
Komlo	4	2	50.0	26	0	0	0/0	—
Skladany	2	2	100.0	38	0	0	0/0	—
Detroit	423	248	58.6	3287	13	12	45/346	
Opponents	462	256	55.4	3234	14	23	44/300	

Receiving

	No	Yds	Avg	LG	TD
Scott	53	834	15.7	43t	4
Sims	51	621	12.2	87t	3
Hill	39	424	10.9	29	3
Bussey	39	364	9.3	30	0
L. Thompson	19	511	26.9	79t	3
King	19	184	9.7	29	0
J. Thompson	11	137	12.5	29	1
R. Williams	10	146	14.6	22t	1
Kane	5	26	5.2	9	0
Friede	1	21	21.0	21	0
Callicutt	1	19	19.0	19	0
Detroit	248	3287	13.3	87t	13
Opponents	256	3234	12.6	67t	14

Interceptions

	No	Yds	Avg	LG	TD
Allen	6	38	6.3	23	0
Hunter	6	20	3.3	13	0
Oldham	3	39	13.0	29t	1
White	2	22	11.0	15	0
Smith	1	23	23.0	23	0
W. Williams	1	19	19.0	19	0
Fantetti	1	10	10.0	10	0
Baker	1	0	0.0	0	0
Bradley	1	0	0.0	0	0
Weaver	1	-3	-3.0	-3	0
Detroit	23	168	7.3	29t	1
Opponents	12	173	14.4	67t	1

Punting

	No	Yds	Avg	LG	In 20
Skladany	72	3036	42.2	67	16
Detroit	73	3036	41.6	67	16
Opponents	93	3865	41.6	56	16

Punt Returns

	No	FC	Yds	Avg	LG	TD
R. Williams	27	4	259	9.6	53	0
Arnold	28	6	204	7.3	19	0
Callicutt	1	0	0	0.0	0	0
Detroit	56	10	463	8.3	53	0
Opponents	38	8	300	7.9	57t	1

Kickoff Returns

	No	Yds	Avg	LG	TD
Kane	23	495	21.5	62	0
Callicutt	16	301	18.8	31	0
R. Williams	9	228	25.3	91t	1
Arnold	9	145	16.1	33	0
Detroit	57	1169	20.5	91t	1
Opponents	64	1289	20.1	101t	3

Scoring

	TD	TD R	TD P	TD Rt	PAT	FG	TP
Murray					35/36	27/42	116
Sims	16	13	3				96
Scott	5	1	4				30
Bussey	3	3					18
L. Thompson	3		3				18
R. Williams	3	1	1	1			18
Danielson	2	2					12
King	2	2					12
Hill	1		1				6
Oldham	1			1			6
Cole							2 (Safety)
Detroit	36	21	13	2	35/36	27/42	334
Opponents	32	9	14	9	30/31	16/21	272

DETROIT RECORD HOLDERS

Individual Records—Single Season

Category	Name	Performance
Rushing (Yds.)	Billy Sims, 1980	1303
Passing (Pct.)	Gary Danielson, 1980	58.5
Passing (Yds.)	Gary Danielson, 1980	3223
Passing (TDs)	Bobby Layne, 1951	26
Receiving (No.)	Pat Studstill, 1966	67
Receiving (Yds.)	Pat Studstill, 1966	1266
Interceptions	Don Doll, 1950	12
	Jack Christiansen, 1953	12
Punting (Avg.)	Yale Lary, 1963	48.9
Punt Ret. (Avg.)	Jack Christiansen, 1952	21.5
Kickoff Ret. (Avg.)	Tom Watkins, 1965	34.4
Field Goals	Ed Murray, 1980	27
Touchdowns (Tot.)	Billy Sims, 1980	16
Points	Doak Walker, 1950	128

Team Records—Single Game

Category	Opponent, Date	Performance
Offense		
First Downs	vs. Wash, 9/30/51	30
Total Points	vs. GB, 11/22/51	52
	vs. GB, 10/26/52	52
Touchdowns	vs. NY Yanks, 11/23/50	7
	vs. GB, 11/22/51	7
	vs. GB, 10/26/52	7
Total Net Yards	vs. NY Yanks, 11/23/50	582
Net Yards Rushing	vs. Pitt, 11/4/34	426
Net Yards Passing	vs. Pitt, 9/27/53	375
Rushing Attempts	vs. Pitt, 11/9/52	59
Passing Attempts	vs. NYG, 12/11/55	49
Interceptions by	vs. Chi, 9/22/68	8
Defense		
Net Yards Allowed	vs. SF, 10/6/63	61
Net Rushing Yards Allowed	vs. Pitt, 11/9/52	-3
Net Passing Yards Allowed	vs. TB, 9/9/78	-31

FIRST PLAYERS SELECTED

Year	Player, College, Position
1974	Ed O'Neil, Penn State, LB
1975	Lynn Boden, South Dakota State, G
1976	James Hunter, Grambling, DB
1977	Walt Williams, New Mexico State, DB
1978	Luther Bradley, Notre Dame, DB
1979	Keith Dorney, Penn State, T
1980	Billy Sims, Oklahoma, RB
1981	Mark Nichols, San Jose State, WR

LIONS COACHING HISTORY

Portsmouth Spartans 1930-33
(323-303-31)

1939	Gus Henderson	6-5-0
1940	George (Potsy) Clark	5-5-1
1941-42	Bill Edwards*	4-9-1
1942	John Karcis	0-8-0
1943-47	Charles (Gus) Dorais	20-31-2
1948-50	Alvin (Bo) McMillin	12-24-0
1951-56	Raymond (Buddy) Parker	47-23-2
1957-64	George Wilson	55-45-6
1965-66	Harry Gilmer	10-16-2
1967-72	Joe Schmidt	43-35-7
1973	Don McCafferty	6-7-1
1974-76	Rick Forzano**	15-17-0
1976-77	Tommy Hudspeth	11-13-0
1978-80	Monte Clark	18-30-0

*Resigned after three games in 1942
**Resigned after four games in 1976

DETROIT LIONS 1981 VETERAN ROSTER

No.	Name	Pos.	Ht.	Wt.	NFL Exp.	Birth-date	Birthplace	College	Residence	Games in '80
40	Allen, Jimmy	S	6-2	194	8	3/6/52	Clearwater, Fla.	UCLA	Los Angeles, Calif.	15
47	Arnold, John	KR-WR	5-10	170	3	10/5/55	Shizaka, Japan	Wyoming	Rochester, Mich.	10
60	Baker, Al	DE	6-6	250	4	12/9/56	Jacksonville, Fla.	Colorado State	Southfield, Mich.	15
76	Baldischwiler, Karl	T	6-5	265	4	1/19/56	Okmulgee, Okla.	Oklahoma	Oklahoma City, Oklahoma	16
73	Bolinger, Russ	G	6-5	255	5	9/10/54	Wichita, Kan.	Long Beach State	Irvine, Calif.	16
27	Bradley, Luther	CB	6-2	195	4	5/7/55	Florence, S.C.	Notre Dame	Detroit, Mich.	8
24	Bussey, Dexter	RB	6-2	210	8	3/11/52	Dallas, Tex.	Texas Arlington	Bloomfield Township, Mich.	16
31	Callicutt, Ken	RB	6-0	190	4	8/20/55	Chester, S.C.	Clemson	Clarkston, Mich.	8
53	Cobb, Garry	LB	6-2	220	3	3/16/57	Stamford, Conn.	Southern California	Rochester, Mich.	13
50	Cole, Eddie	LB	6-2	235	3	12/16/56	Clarksdale, Miss.	Mississippi	Clarksdale, Miss.	13
16	Danielson, Gary	QB	6-2	195	6	9/10/51	Detroit, Mich.	Purdue	Rochester, Mich.	16
72	Dieterich, Chris	T	6-3	269	2	7/27/58	Freeport, N.Y.	North Carolina State	Raleigh, N.C.	16
70	Dorney, Keith	T	6-5	265	3	12/3/57	Allentown, Pa.	Penn State	Irvine, Calif.	9
61	Elias, Homer	G	6-3	255	4	5/1/55	Ft. Benning, Ga.	Tennessee State	Rochester, Mich.	14
57	Fantetti, Ken	LB	6-2	230	3	4/7/57	Toledo, Ore.	Wyoming	Waterford, Mich.	16
65	Fowler, Amos	C	6-3	250	4	2/11/56	Pensacola, Fla.	Southern Mississippi	Rochester, Mich.	16
79	Gay, William	DE	6-3	250	4	5/28/55	San Francisco, Calif.	Southern California	Rochester, Mich.	13
66	Ginn, Tommie	G	6-3	255	2	1/25/58	Scotia, Calif.	Arkansas	Fayetteville, Ark.	14
51	Harrell, James	LB	6-2	215	3	2/19/57	Tampa, Fla.	Florida	Rochester, Mich.	5
81	Hill, David	TE	6-2	230	6	1/1/54	San Antonio, Tex.	Texas A&I	Rochester, Mich.	14
17	Hipple, Eric	QB	6-1	196	2	9/16/57	Lubbock, Tex.	Utah State	Logan, Utah	15
28	Hunter, James	S	6-2	195	6	3/8/54	Silsbee, Tex.	Grambling	Southfield, Mich.	16
32	†Kane, Rick	RB	6-0	200	5	3/5/53	Concord, Calif.	San Jose State	Pontiac, Mich.	16
25	King, Horace	RB	6-0	210	7	7/30/56	Athens, Ga.	Georgia	Rochester, Mich.	16
19	Komlo, Jeff	QB	5-10	200	4	11/12/54	Cleverly, Md.	Delaware	Rochester, Mich.	16
68	†Lawless, Burton	G	6-4	256	6	12/28/48	Houston, Tex.	Florida	Rochester, Mich.	4
48	Lewis, Eddie	CB	6-0	175	8	5/27/56	LaMesa, Tex.	Kansas	North Hollywood, Calif.	9
58	†Luce, Derrell	LB	6-3	227	7	9/29/52	Lake Jackson, Tex.	Baylor	Waco, Tex.	13*
64	Mendenhall, John	DT	6-1	255	10	12/15/53	Mobile, Ala.	Grambling	Rochester, Mich.	14
3	Murray, Ed	K	5-9	164	2	8/29/56	Halifax, Nova Scotia	Tulane	Madison Hts., Mich.	16
80	Norris, Ulysses	TE	6-4	230	3	1/15/57	Monticello, Ga.	Georgia	Lake Orion, Mich.	16
23	†Oldham, Ray	S	5-11	192	9	2/23/51	Chattanooga, Tenn.	Middle Tennesee	Signal Mountain, Tenn.	16
62	†Parker, Willie	C	6-3	245	10	12/28/48	Houston, Tex.	North Texas State	Baytown, Tex.	4
75	Pureifory, Dave	DE	6-1	255	10	7/12/49	Merced, Calif.	Eastern Michigan	Ypsilanti, Mich.	9
36	Robinson, Bo	RB	6-2	225	3	5/27/56	LaMesa, Tex.	West Texas State	LaMesa, Tex.	14
87	Scott, Fred	WR	6-2	175	8	8/5/52	Grady, Ark.	Amherst	North Hollywood, Calif.	16
68	Simmons, Davie	LB	6-4	218	3	9/18/55	Wayne, N.C.	North Carolina	Southfield, Mich.	1
20	Sims, Billy	RB	6-0	212	2	9/18/55	St. Louis, Mo.	Oklahoma	Waco, Tex.	16
15	Skladany, Tom	P	6-0	195	5	6/29/55	Castle Shannon, Pa.	Ohio State	Madison Hts., Mich.	16
14	Smith, Wayne	S	6-0	170	2	5/9/57	Chicago, Ill.	Ohio State	Chicago, Ill.	15
84	†Thompson, Jesse	WR	6-1	185	3	3/12/56	Merced, Calif.	California	Merced, Calif.	11
39	Thompson, Leonard	WR	5-11	190	7	7/28/52	Tucson, Ariz.	Oklahoma State	Pontiac, Mich.	16
71	Tuinei, Tom	DT	6-4	251	2	2/21/58	Oceanside, Calif.	Hawaii	Nanakulu, Hawaii	16
55	Turnure, Tom	G	6-3	243	5	7/9/57	Seattle, Wash.	Washington	Pontiac, Mich.	3
67	†Walters, Rod	G	6-2	258	5	2/27/54	Richmond, Calif.	Iowa	Utica, Mich.	9*
59	Weaver, Charlie	LB	6-2	225	11	7/12/49	Lansing, Mich.	Southern California	Cockeysville, Md.	16
52	White, Stan	LB	6-1	223	10	10/24/49	Kent, Ohio	Ohio State	Cockeysville, Md.	16
74	Whited, Mike	T	6-4	249	2	3/30/58	Chico, Calif.	Pacific	Auburn Hts., Mich.	16
30	Williams, Ray	KR-WR	5-9	173	2	9/22/58	Welch, W.Va.	Washington State	Pacoima, Calif.	6
21	Williams, Walt	CB	6-1	185	5	7/10/54	Bedford Hills, N.Y.	New Mexico State	Las Cruces, N.M.	16

* Luce played 4 games with Minnesota, 9 with Detroit; Walters played 6 with Kansas City, 1 with Miami, 2 with Detroit.

† Option playout; subject to developments.

Also played with Lions in '80—DT Curley Culp (3 games), WR Mike Friede (4), T Vernon Holland (2), DT Alva Liles (1), DT Mike McCoy (4), S Prentice McCray (7), LB John Mohring (1), C Wally Pesuit (1).

COACHING STAFF

Head Coach, Monte Clark

Pro Career: Starts his fourth season as Lions head coach. Directed Lions to 9-7 mark in 1980. Was head coach of San Francisco 49ers in 1976, guiding them to 8-6 record. Was an assistant under Don Shula in Miami 1970-75 as offensive line coach. Drafted fourth by 49ers in 1959. Played defensive tackle until 1962 when he was traded to Dallas and switched to offensive tackle. Clark was traded to Cleveland and played for the Browns from 1963-69. Career record: 26-36.

Background: Three-year letterman who played offense and defense at Southern California 1956-58, co-captain of the 1958 squad.

Personal: Born January 24, 1937 in Fillmore, Calif. Monte and his wife, Charlotte, live in Bloomfield Township, Mich. and have three children—Bryan, Randy, and Eric.

ASSISTANT COACHES

Maxie Baughan, defensive coordinator-linebackers; born August 3, 1938, Forkland, Ala., lives in Pontiac, Mich. Linebacker Georgia Tech 1957-59. Pro linebacker Philadelphia Eagles 1960-65, Los Angeles Rams 1966-70, Washington Redskins 1971, 1974. College coach: Georgia Tech 1972-73. Pro coach: Baltimore Colts 1975-79, second year with Lions.

John Brunner, offensive backfield; born September 6, 1937, Perkesie, Pa., lives in Pontiac, Mich. Running back East Stroudsburg State 1957-59. No pro playing experience. College coach: Villanova 1967-69, Princeton 1974-75, Temple 1970-73, 1976-79. Pro coach: Second year with Lions.

Don Doll, special assignments; born August 29, 1926, Los Angeles, Calif., lives in Detroit. Defensive back Southern California 1944, 1946-48. Pro defensive back Detroit Lions 1949-52, Washington Redskins 1953, Los Angeles Rams 1954. College coach: Washington 1955, Contra Costa JC 1956, Southern California 1957-58, Notre Dame 1959-62. Pro coach: Detroit Lions 1963-64, Los Angeles Rams 1965, Washington Redskins 1966-70, Green Bay Packers 1971-73, Baltimore Colts 1974, Miami Dolphins 1975-76, rejoined Lions in 1978.

Fred Hoaglin, offensive line; born January 28, 1944, Alliance, Ohio, lives in Detroit. Center Pittsburgh 1965-67. Pro center Cleveland Browns 1966-72, Baltimore Colts 1973, Houston Oilers 1974-75, Seattle Seahawks 1976. Pro coach: Fourth year with Lions.

Joe Madden, special teams; born March 5, 1935, Washington, D.C., lives in Pontiac, Mich. Back Maryland 1954-56. No pro playing experience. College coach: Mississippi State 1962, Morehead State 1963, Wake Forest 1964-67, Iowa State 1968-71, Kansas State 1972, Pittsburgh 1973-76, Tennessee 1977-79. Pro coach: Second year with Lions.

Floyd Peters, defensive line; born May 21, 1936, Council Bluffs, Iowa, lives in Pontiac, Mich. Defensive tackle San Francisco State 1954-57. Pro defensive tackle Baltimore Colts 1958, Cleveland Browns 1959-62, Detroit Lions 1963, Philadelphia Eagles 1964-69, Washington Redskins 1970. Pro coach: Washington Redskins 1970, New York Giants 1974-75, San Francisco 49ers 1976-77, fourth year with Lions.

Mel Phillips, defensive backfield; born January 6, 1942, Shelby, N.C., lives in Pontiac, Mich. Defensive back North Carolina A&T 1963-65. Pro defensive back San Francisco 49ers 1966-76. Pro coach: Second year with Lions.

Bob Schnelker, offensive coordinator-quarterbacks; born October 17, 1928, Galion, Ohio, lives in Detroit. End Bowling Green 1946-50. Pro end Cleveland Browns 1953, New York Giants 1954-60, Minnesota Vikings 1961. Pro coach: Los Angeles Rams 1963-64, Green Bay Packers 1965-71, San Diego Chargers 1972-73, Miami Dolphins 1974, Kansas City Chiefs 1975-77, fourth year with Lions.

Larry Seiple, receivers; born February 14, 1945, Allentown, Pa., lives in Pontiac, Mich. Punter-tight end Kentucky 1964-66. Pro punter Miami Dolphins 1967-77. College coach: Miami 1979. Pro coach: Second year with Lions.

DETROIT LIONS 1981 FIRST-YEAR ROSTER

Name	Pos.	Ht.	Wt.	Birth-date	Birthplace	College	Residence	How Acq.
Alpuche, Charles	DE	6-4	235	5/11/59	Abington, Pa.	Delaware Valley	Jenkintown, Pa.	FA
Barnes, Robert	C-G	6-4	255	4/20/58	Corpus Christi, Tex.	Southern Methodist	Corpus Christi, Tex.	FA
Cannavino, Andy	LB	6-1	225	4/20/58	Cleveland, Ohio	Michigan	Cleveland, Ohio	D10
Columbia, Paul	TE	6-5	230	12/3/57	Mt. Sterling, Ky.	Villanova	Winchester, Ky.	FA
Gipson, Ron	FB	5-11	235	2/2/58	Everett, Wash.	Washington	Lynwood, Wash.	FA
Greco, Don	G	6-3	260	4/1/59	St. Louis, Mo.	Western Illinois	St. Louis, Mo.	D3
Green, Curtis	DT	6-3	256	6/3/57	Quincy, Fla.	Alabama State	Quincy, Fla.	D2
Hall, Alvin	CB	5-11	190	8/12/58	Dayton, Ohio	Miami, Ohio	Dayton, Ohio	FA
Hardy, Don	G	6-2	250	5/10/57	Wilkes-Barre, Pa.	Westchester State	Wilkes-Barre, Pa.	FA
Hartman, Dennis	RB	6-0	228	2/14/59	Buffalo, N.Y.	Syracuse	West Seneca, N.Y.	FA
Jackson, Willie	CB	5-10	194	10/9/57	Ocean Spring, Miss.	Mississippi State	Ocean Spring, Miss.	D11
Jernigan, Hugh	S	5-11	175	8/28/59	Little Rock, Ark.	Arkansas	Little Rock, Ark.	D9
Jett, DeWayne (1)	WR	6-2	194	2/24/58	Minneapolis, Minn.	Hawaii	Northridge, Calif.	D9 ('80)
Johnson, Sam	S	6-1	195	5/18/59	Ft. Bragg, N.C.	Maryland	Gambrills, Md.	D6
Katnik, Norman	C	6-1	241	11/10/57	Orange, Calif.	Arizona	Tucson, Ariz.	FA
Kirkland, Freddie	WR	5-9	160	9/4/57	Detroit, Mich.	Ferris State	Detroit, Mich.	FA
Lee, Larry	G	6-2	274	9/10/59	Dayton, Ohio	UCLA	Beverly Hills, Calif.	D5
Mathews, Melvin	WR	6-0	170	1/6/59	Detroit, Mich.	Saginaw Valley	Detroit, Mich.	FA
Martin, David	CB	5-10	185	3/15/59	Philadelphia, Pa.	Villanova	Philadelphia, Pa.	D9
Nichols, Mark	WR	6-2	210	10/29/59	Bakersfield, Calif.	San Jose State	Dallas, Tex.	D1
Niziolek, Bob	TE	6-4	220	6/30/58	Chicago, Ill.	Colorado	Boulder, Colo.	D8
Olivieri, Gino	RB	6-0	205	5/18/59	Batavia, N.Y.	Delaware	Batavia, N.Y.	FA
Pope, Russell	RB	5-11	184	10/10/57	Rockford, Ill.	Purdue	Rockford, Ill.	FA
Porter, Tracy	WR	6-1	196	6/1/59	Baton Rouge, La.	Louisiana State	Baton Rouge, La.	D4
Reeves, Bruce	RB	5-9	180	11/23/58	Columbia, S.C.	Michigan State	Irmo, S.C.	FA
Schramm, Andy	RB	6-2	216	6/22/59	Abington, Pa.	Michigan State	Findlay, Ohio	FA
Searcey, Bill	G-T	6-2	265	3/3/58	Savannah, Ga.	Alabama	Savannah, Ga.	FA
Smith, Ken	S	5-10	181	10/9/58	New Brunswick, N.J.	Rutgers	Somerset, N.J.	FA
Spengler, John	K	5-9	167	12/5/59	Toledo, Ohio	Bowling Green	Bowling Green, Ohio	FA
Spivey, Lee	G-T	6-2	270	12/7/57	Houston, Tex.	Southern Methodist	Houston, Tex.	D7
Stachowicz, Bob	QB	6-2	200	1/18/58	Cleveland, Ohio	Michigan State	Broadview Hts., Ohio	FA
Stiver, Chuck	DE	6-2	253	6/6/58	Port Huron, Mich.	Central Michigan	Port Huron, Mich.	D4
Thompson, Vince	RB	5-11	230	2/21/57	Trenton, N.J.	Villanova	Levittown, Pa.	FA
Walker, Bruce	DE	6-3	230	9/8/57	Indianapolis, Ind.	Tennessee State	Detroit, Mich.	FA
Wood, Charles	LB	6-1	207	4/20/58	Ashland, Ala.	Auburn	Auburn, Ala.	FA

Players who report to an NFL team for the first time are designated on rosters as rookies (R). If a player reported to an NFL training camp in a previous year but was not on the active squad for three or more regular season or postseason games, he is listed on the first-year roster and designated by a (1). Thereafter, a player who is on the active squad for three or more regular season games is credited with an additional year of playing experience.

NOTES

GREEN BAY PACKERS 1981 VETERAN ROSTER

No.	Name	Pos.	Ht.	Wt.	NFL Exp.	Birth-date	Birthplace	College	Residence	Games in '80
60	Allerman, Kurt	LB	6-2	222	5	8/30/55	Glenridge, N.J.	Penn State	Ballwin, Mo.	13
59	Anderson, John	LB	6-3	221	4	2/14/56	Waukesha, Wis.	Michigan	New Berlin, Wis.	9
44	Anderson, Vickey Ray	RB	6-0	205	2	5/3/56	Pampa, Tex.	Oklahoma	Oklahoma City, Okla.	7
42	Atkins, Steve	RB	6-0	216	2	6/22/56	Spotsylvania, Va.	Maryland	Upper Marlboro, Md.	9
62	Aydelette, Buddy	T	6-4	250	2	8/19/56	Mobile, Ala.	Alabama	Green Bay, Wis.	9
77	Butler, Mike	DE	6-5	265	5	4/4/54	Washington, D.C.	Kansas	Madison, Wis.	16
65	Cabral, Brian	LB	6-1	224	3	6/23/56	Ft. Benning, Ga.	Colorado	Boulder, Colo.	7
88	Cassidy, Ron	WR	6-0	185	3	7/23/57	Ventura, Calif.	Utah State	Green Bay, Wis.	15
82	Coffman, Paul	TE	6-3	218	4	3/29/56	St. Louis, Mo.	Kansas State	Manhattan, Kan.	16
52	Cornelius, Charles	CB	5-9	178	5	7/27/52	Boynton Beach, Fla.	Bethune-Cookman	Miami, Fla.	16*
12	Cumby, George	LB	6-0	215	2	7/5/56	Gorman, Tex.	Oklahoma	Green Bay, Wis.	9
53	Dickey, Lynn	QB	6-4	220	11	10/19/49	Osawatomie, Kan.	Kansas State	Lenexa, Kan.	16
31	Douglass, Mike	LB	6-0	224	4	3/15/55	St. Louis, Mo.	San Diego State	San Diego, Calif.	16
57	Ellis, Gerry	FB	5-11	216	2	11/12/57	Columbia, Mo.	Missouri	Columbia, Mo.	15
24	Gofourth, Derrel	G	6-3	260	5	3/20/55	Lake Charles, La.	Oklahoma State	Stillwater, Okla.	16
51	Gray, Johnnie	S	5-11	185	7	12/18/53	Parsons, Kan.	Cal State-Fullerton	Green Bay, Wis.	16
69	Gueno, Jim	LB	6-2	220	6	1/15/54	Crowley, La.	Tulane	Lafayette, La.	15
51	Harris, Leotis	G	6-1	267	4	6/28/55	Little Rock, Ark.	Arkansas	Little Rock, Ark.	16
24	Hood, Estus	CB	6-1	180	5	11/14/55	Hattiesburg, Miss.	Illinois State	Kankakee, Ill.	16
90	Huckleby, Harlan	RB	6-1	199	2	12/30/57	Detroit, Mich.	Michigan	Detroit, Mich.	16
99	Ivery, Eddie Lee	RB	6-1	210	3	7/30/57	McDuffie, Ga.	Georgia Tech	Decatur, Ga.	16
40	Johnson, Charles	DT	6-1	262	3	6/29/57	Baltimore, Md.	Maryland	Baltimore, Md.	16
25	Johnson, Ezra	DE	6-4	240	5	10/5/55	Detroit, Mich.	Morris Brown	College Park, Ga.	14
38	Jolly, Mike	S	6-3	185	2	3/19/58	Sandersville, Ga.	Alabama	Tuscaloosa, Ala.	15
69	Jones, Terry	DT	6-2	259	2	11/8/56	Orange, N.J.	Michigan	Winston-Salem, N.C.	16
72	Kitson, Syd	G	6-4	252	5	9/27/58	Bethesda, Md.	Wake Forest	Green Bay, Wis.	16
22	Koch, Greg	T	6-4	265	2	6/14/55	Shreveport, La.	Arkansas	Melvindale, Mich.	16
80	Koncar, Mark	T	6-5	268	5	5/5/53	Murray, Utah	Colorado	Sandy, Utah	9
46	Larson, Bill	TE	6-4	225	5	10/7/53	Greenfield, Iowa	Colorado State	Adair, Iowa	1
54	Lathrop, Kit	DT	6-5	253	5	5/10/56	San Jose, Calif.	Arizona State	Colorado Springs, Colo.	9
29	Lee, Mark	CB	5-11	180	3	3/20/58	Hanford, Calif.	Washington	Seattle, Wash.	16
78	Lofton, James	WR	6-3	187	2	7/5/56	Los Angeles, Calif.	Stanford	Los Angeles, Calif.	16
34	Luke, Steve	S	6-2	205	7	9/4/53	Massillon, Ohio	Ohio State	Columbus, Ohio	16
18	McCarren, Larry	C	6-3	238	9	11/9/51	Chicago, Ill.	Illinois	Green Bay, Wis.	16
84	McCoy, Mike	CB	6-4	255	6	8/16/53	Memphis, Ariz.	Colorado	Diablo, Calif.	13
56	Merrill, Casey	DE	6-4	255	3	7/16/57	Oakland, Calif.	Cal-Davis	Lafayette, Colo.	16
87	Middleton, Terdell	RB	6-0	195	5	4/8/55	Memphis, Tenn.	Memphis State	Memphis, Tenn.	16
70	Miller, Mark	QB	6-2	191	4	8/13/56	Canton, Ohio	Bowling Green	Grand Rapids, Ohio	0*
10	Nixon, Fred	WR	5-11	185	2	9/22/58	Camila, Ga.	Oklahoma	Green Bay, Wis.	15
76	O'Neil, Ed	LB	6-3	235	8	9/8/52	Warren, Pa.	Penn State	Rochester, Mich.	6
67	Perkins, Horace	CB	5-11	180	2	3/15/54	El Campo, Tex.	Colorado	Lafayette, Colo.	0*
89	Rudzinski, Paul	LB	6-2	225	4	7/28/56	Detroit, Mich.	Michigan State	Farmington, Mich.	6
83	Stenerud, Jan	K	6-1	190	15	11/26/43	Fetsund, Norway	Montana State	Overland Park, Kan.	12
26	Stokes, Tim	T	6-5	252	8	3/16/50	Elmhurst, Ill.	Oregon	Eugene, Ore.	15
20	Swanke, Karl	T-C	6-3	251	2	12/29/57	Dallas, Tex.	Boston College	Newington, Conn.	15
17	Thompson, Aundra	WR	6-0	186	5	1/2/53	Jackson, Miss.	East Texas State	Green Bay, Wis.	16
50	Thompson, John	TE	6-3	228	3	1/18/57	Troy, N.Y.	Utah State	Green Bay, Wis.	7
	Torkelson, Eric	RB	6-2	210	8	3/3/52	Dallas, Tex.	Connecticut	Oakland, Calif.	0*
	Turner, Wylie	CB	6-2	182	2	4/19/57	Los Angeles, Calif.	Angelo State	Dallas, Tex.	15
	Vaughan, Ruben	DT	6-2	263	2	8/5/56	Baumholder, Germany	Colorado	Foster City, Calif.	0*
	Whitehurst, David	QB	6-2	204	5	4/27/55	Decatur, Ga.	Furman	Decatur, Ga.	16
	Wingo, Rich	LB	6-1	230	3	7/16/56	Elkhart, Ind.	Alabama	Green Bay, Wis.	0*

*Cornelius played 16 games with San Francisco in '80; Miller active for 1 game but did not play; Torkelson, Wingo missed '80 season due to injuries; Perkins last active with Kansas City in '79; Vaughan last active with San Francisco in '79.

Retired—Mike Hunt, 4-year linebacker, 3 games in '80; Barty Smith, 7-year running back, 1 game.

Also played with Packers in '80—LB Dave Beekley (15 games), P Dave Beverly (16), C Ken Brown (6), G Mel Jackson (6), K Tom Birney (7), DT Mike Lewis (10), K Chester Marcol (5), QB Steve Pisarkewicz (1), QB Bill Troup (2), C Mike Wellman (4).

COACHING STAFF

Head Coach, Bart Starr

Pro Career: Starts seventh season as Green Bay head coach following a six-year record of 31-57-2. Packers quarterback from 1956-71, leading Green Bay to five world titles, 1961-62, 1965-67. Named NFL most valuable player in 1966 and MVP of Super Bowl I and II. Holds the NFL record for most consecutive passes without an interception, 294. Packers assistant coach in charge of quarterbacks in 1972 following his retirement as a player.

Background: A high school All-America who became a four-year letter winner at Alabama. Quarterbacked Alabama to victory over Syracuse in 1953 Orange Bowl. Was the second leading punter in the nation in 1953. Played in Blue-Gray game in 1955.

Personal: Born January 9, 1934 in Montgomery, Ala. Partner in two automobile dealerships in Birmingham, Ala. Bart and his wife, Cherry, live in DePere, Wis., and have two sons—Bart and Bret.

ASSISTANT COACHES

Zeke Bratkowski, offensive backfield-quarterbacks; born October 20, 1931, Danville, Ill., lives in DePere, Wis. Quarterback Georgia 1951-53. Pro quarterback Chicago Bears 1954, 1957-60, Los Angeles Rams 1961-63, Green Bay Packers 1963-68, 1971. Pro coach: Green Bay Packers 1969-70, Chicago Bears 1972-74, rejoined Packers in 1975.

Lew Carpenter, receivers; born January 12, 1932, Hayti, Mo., lives in Green Bay. Running back-defensive back Arkansas 1950-52. Pro running back-defensive back-end Detroit Lions 1953-55, Cleveland Browns 1957-58, Green Bay Packers 1959-63. Pro coach: Minnesota Vikings 1964-66, Atlanta Falcons 1967-68, Washington Redskins 1969-70, St. Louis Cardinals 1971-72, Houston Oilers 1973-74, Packers since 1975.

Ross Fichtner, defensive backs; born October 26, 1938, McKeesport, Pa., lives in Green Bay. Quarterback Purdue 1957-59. Pro defensive back Cleveland Browns 1960-67, New Orleans Saints 1968. Pro coach: Florida Blazers (WFL) 1974, Chicago Bears 1975-77, second year with Packers.

Pete Kettela, special assistant; born May 28, 1938, Buffalo, N.Y., lives in Green Bay. Running back Cal-Riverside 1958-60. No pro playing experience. College coach: Cal-Riverside 1965-69 (head coach), Cal-Santa Barbara 1970, Pacific 1971, Stanford 1972-76, San Jose State 1977. Pro coach: First year with Packers.

John Marshall, linebackers; born October 2, 1945, Arroyo Grande, Calif., lives in Green Bay. Oregon 1960. No pro playing experience. College coach: Oregon 1970-76, Southern California 1977-79. Pro coach: Joined Packers in 1980.

Ernie McMillan, offensive line; born February 21, 1938, Chicago Heights, Ill., lives in Green Bay. Tackle Illinois 1958-60. Pro tackle St. Louis Cardinals 1961-74, Green Bay Packers 1975-77. Pro coach: Fourth year with Packers.

John Meyer, defensive coordinator; born February 20, 1942, Chicago, lives in Green Bay. Linebacker Notre Dame 1963-64. Pro linebacker St. Louis Cardinals 1965-66, Houston Oilers 1967-68. Pro coach: Houston Oilers 1968, New England Patriots 1969-72, Detroit Lions 1973-74, Packers since 1975.

Dick Rehbein, special teams; born November 22, 1955, Green Bay, Wis., lives in Green Bay. Center Ripon 1973-76. No pro playing experience. Pro coach: Fourth year with Packers.

Richard (Doc) Urich, defensive line; born September 10, 1928, Toledo, Ohio, lives in Green Bay. End Miami, Ohio 1948-50. No pro playing experience. College coach: Miami, Ohio 1951-54, Northwestern 1955-63, Notre Dame 1964-65, Buffalo 1966-68, Northern Illinois 1969-70. Pro coach: Buffalo Bills 1971, Denver Broncos 1972-77, Washington Redskins 1978-80, first year with Packers.

GREEN BAY PACKERS 1981 FIRST-YEAR ROSTER

Name	Pos.	Ht.	Wt.	Birth-date	Birthplace	College	Residence	How Acq.
Braggs, Byron	DT	6-4	290	10/10/59	Los Angeles, Calif.	Alabama	Montgomery, Ala.	D5
Campbell, Rich	QB	6-4	224	12/22/58	Coral Gables, Fla.	California	Berkeley, Calif.	D1
Chambers, Steve (1)	T	6-6	265	1/24/56	S. Luis Obispo, Calif.	Arizona State	Scottsdale, Ariz.	FA
Chrest, Craig	WR	6-1	180	12/20/55	St. Paul, Minn.	Wisconsin-LaCrosse	LaCrosse, Wis.	FA
Coombs, Larry (1)	C-G	6-3	260	8/9/57	Arcata, Calif.	Idaho	Olympia, Wash.	FA
Garcia, Frank (1)	P	6-1	190	6/5/57	Tucson, Ariz.	Arizona	Tucson, Ariz.	FA
Hall, Nickie	QB	6-4	205	8/1/59	Lake Charles, La.	Tulane	Kenner, La.	D10
Huffman, Tim	T	6-5	277	8/31/59	Canton, Ohio	Notre Dame	South Bend, Ind.	D9
Johnston, William (1)	P	6-1	175	8/8/57	Opelika, Ala.	Auburn	Auburn, Ala.	FA
Kehr, Richard	G	6-3	265	6/18/59	Phoenixville, Pa.	Carthage	Steamwood, Ill.	FA
Lewis, Cliff	LB	6-1	226	11/9/59	Brewton, Ala.	Southern Mississippi	Ft. Walton Beach, Fla.	D12
Lewis, Gary	TE	6-5	234	12/30/58	Mt. Pleasant, Tex.	Texas-Arlington	Arlington, Tex.	D2
Mancuso, Mike (1)	QB	6-3	207	12/26/57	Omaha, Neb.	Nebraska-Omaha	Omaha, Neb.	FA
Mohr, Richard	DE	6-3	250	7/2/59	San Francisco, Calif.	Cal-Davis	Davis, Calif.	FA
Murphy, Mark (1)	S	6-2	199	4/22/58	Canton, Ohio	West Liberty State	N. Canton, Ohio	FA
Perkins, Calvin (1)	WR	6-2	192	6/22/57	Los Angeles, Calif.	Tennessee State	Gardena, Calif.	FA
Petway, David	S	6-1	207	10/17/55	Chicago, Ill.	Northern Illinois	Chicago, Ill.	FA
Prather, Guy (1)	LB	6-2	230	3/28/58	Olney, Md.	Grambling	Gaithersburg, Md.	FA
Reaves, Willard	RB	5-11	198	8/17/59	Flagstaff, Ariz.	Northern Arizona	Flagstaff, Ariz.	FA
Savich, Rade (1)	K	5-8	175	12/11/55	Yugoslavia	Central Michigan	St. Clair Shores, Mich.	FA
Scott, Randy	LB	6-1	220	1/31/59	Atlanta, Ga.	Alabama	Decatur, Ga.	FA
Shackelford, Robert	G	6-3	255	5/17/59	Ft. Benning, Ga.	St. Norbert	Ft. Benning, Ga.	FA
Smith, Tim (1)	CB-S	6-1	194	8/17/57	Corona, Calif.	Oregon State	Santa Ana, Calif.	FA
Stachowicz, Ray	P	5-11	185	2/14/59	Cleveland, Ohio	Michigan State	E. Lansing, Mich.	D3
Sweet, Don	K	6-0	189	7/13/48	Vancouver, B.C.	Washington State	Kirland, Que.	FA
Thomas, Troy (1)	DE	6-6	260	10/11/56	Shreveport, La.	Grambling	Vivian, La.	FA
Thompson, Pete	WR	6-0	185	5/8/57	Milwaukee, Wis.	Carroll	East Troy, Mich.	FA
Turner, Richard	DT	6-2	260	2/14/59	Hugo, Okla.	Oklahoma	Norman, Okla.	D4
Valora, Forrest	LB	6-0	236	3/28/59	Wilkes-Barre, Pa.	Oklahoma	Norman, Okla.	D11
Vernon, Skip (1)	K	5-10	175	10/12/56	Inglewood, Calif.	New Mexico State	Albuquerque, N.M.	FA
Werts, Larry	LB	6-2	231	2/28/58	Newberry, S.C.	Jackson State	Newberry, S.C.	D8
Whitaker, Bill	CB-S	6-0	182	11/18/59	Kansas City, Mo.	Missouri	Kansas City, Mo.	D7

Players who report to an NFL team for the first time are designated on rosters as rookies (R). If a player reported to an NFL training camp in a previous year but was not on the active squad for three or more regular season or postseason games, he is listed on the first-year roster and designated by a (1). Thereafter, a player who is on the active squad for three or more regular season games is credited with an additional year of playing experience.

NOTES

Los Angeles Rams

National Football Conference
Western Division

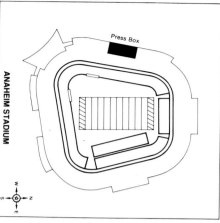

ANAHEIM STADIUM

Press Box

Team Colors: Royal Blue, Gold, and White

Business Address:
2327 West Lincoln Ave.
Anaheim, California 92801

Ticket Office:
Anaheim Stadium
1900 State College Blvd.
Anaheim, California 92806
Telephone: (714) 535-7267 or (213) 585-5400

Club Officials
President: Georgia Frontiere
Vice President and General Manager:
    Don Klosterman
Secretary-Treasurer: John Shaw
Director of Operations: Dick Beam
Assistant General Manager: Jack Faulkner
Director of Player Personnel: John Math
Director of Public Relations: Jerry Wilcox
Assistant Director of Public Relations: Geno Effler
Trainers: Gary Tuthill, George Menefee
Equipment Manager: Don Hewitt

Stadium: Anaheim Stadium
        Capacity: 69,005
        Anaheim, California 92806

Playing Surface: Grass
Training Camp: California State University
        Fullerton, California 92634

1981 SCHEDULE

Preseason

Aug. 10	**New England**		8:00
Aug. 15	**Dallas**		5:30
Aug. 21	at San Diego		6:00
Aug. 27	**Minnesota**		8:00

Regular Season

Sept. 6	**Houston**		1:00
Sept. 13	at New Orleans		12:00
Sept. 20	**Green Bay**		1:00
Sept. 28	at Chicago (Monday)		8:00
Oct. 4	**Cleveland**		8:00
Oct. 11	at Atlanta		1:00
Oct. 18	at Dallas		8:00
Oct. 25	at San Francisco		1:00
Nov. 1	**Detroit**		1:00
Nov. 8	**New Orleans**		1:00
Nov. 15	at Cincinnati		1:00
Nov. 22	**San Francisco**		1:00
Nov. 29	at Pittsburgh		1:00
Dec. 6	at New York Giants		1:00
Dec. 14	**Atlanta** (Monday)		6:00
Dec. 20	**Washington**		1:00

1980 TEAM STATISTICS

	Los Angeles	Opp.
Total First Downs	316	281
Rushing	144	112
Passing	157	141
Penalty	15	28
Third Down Efficiency	113/256	70/230
Third Down Percentage	44.1	30.4
Total Net Yards	6006	4546
Total Offensive Plays	1095	1011
Avg. Gain per Play	5.5	4.5
Avg. Gain per Game	375.4	284.1
Net Yards Rushing	2799	1945
Total Rushing Plays	615	445
Avg. Gain per Rush	4.6	4.4
Avg. Gain Rushing per Game	174.9	121.6
Net Yards Passing	3207	2601
Lost Attempting to Pass	29/234	56/496
Gross Yards Passing	3441	3097
Attempts/Completions	451/261	510/245
Percent Completed	57.9	48.0
Had Intercepted	23	25
Avg. Net Passing per Game	200.4	162.6
Punts/Avg.	77/39.0	90/42.1
Punt Returns/Avg.	47/6.7	42/8.4
Kickoff Returns/Avg.	53/18.5	78/19.9
Interceptions/Avg. Ret.	25/21.8	23/13.3
Penalties/Yards	118/973	
Fumbles/Ball Lost	29/13	30/17
Total Points	424	289
Avg. Points per Game	26.5	18.1
Touchdowns	54	38
Rushing	17	13
Passing	31	23
Returns and Recoveries	6	2
Field Goals	16/30	9/20
Conversions	52/54	34/38
Safeties	0	0

1980 INDIVIDUAL STATISTICS

Rushing

	Att	Yds	Avg	LG	TD
Bryant	183	807	4.4	20	3
Peacock	164	777	4.7	36	7
J. Thomas	65	427	6.6	61	2
Guman	100	410	4.1	17	3
Tyler	30	157	5.2	17	0
E. Hill	39	120	3.1	19	0
Ferragamo	15	34	2.3	15	1
Dennard	2	20	10.0	21	0
Hicks	7	19	19.0	19	1
Mitchell	7	16	2.3	5	0
Haden	3	12	4.0	6	0
D. Hill	1	4	4.0	4	0
Cromwell	2	−1	−1.0	−1	0
Lee	1	−1	−1.0	−1	0
Waddy	1	−2	−2.0	−2	0
Miller					
Los Angeles	615	2799	4.6	61	17
Opponents	445	1945	4.4	65	13

Field Goal Success

Distance	Made-Att.
1-19	1-1
20-29	11-12
30-39	2-5
40-49	2-9
50 Over	0-3

Passing

	Att	Comp	Pct	Yds	TD	Int	Tk/Yds	Rate
Ferragamo	404	240	59.4	3199	30	19	23/191	89.7
Haden	41	19	46.3	185	0	4	4/30	19.9
Cromwell	1	0	0.0	0	0	0	0/0	—
Guman	1	1	100.0	31	1	0	1/5	—
Rutledge	4	1	25.0	26	0	0	1/8	—
LA	451	261	57.9	3441	31	23	29/234	83.9
Opponents	510	245	48.0	3097	23	25	56/496	—

Receiving

	No	Yds	Avg	LG	TD
Bryant	53	386	7.3	25	3
Waddy	38	670	17.6	44t	5
Dennard	36	596	16.6	44	6
Peacock	25	213	8.5	59t	2
Hicks	23	318	13.8	32t	2
Miller	19	416	21.9	74t	8
D. Hill	14	131	9.4	41	1
Guman	10	168	16.8	37	1
Moore	5	75	15.0	33	1
Arnold	5	30	6.0	11	1
J. Thomas	4	29	7.3	11	1
E. Hill	3	22	7.3	12	0
Nelson	3	21	10.5	13	0
Mitchell					
Tyler	2	8	4.0	5	0
Los Angeles	261	3441	13.2	74t	31
Opponents	245	3097	12.6	60	23

Interceptions

	No	Yds	Avg	LG	TD
Cromwell	8	140	17.5	34	1
Perry	5	115	23.0	83t	1
J. Johnson	3	102	34.0	99t	1
P. Thomas	3	14	4.7	14	0
Irvin	2	80	40.0	80	0
Delaney	2	42	21.0	27	0
Ji. Youngblood	1	33	33.0	33t	1
Reynolds	1	20	20.0	20	0
Los Angeles	25	546	21.8	99t	4
Opponents	23	307	13.3	47t	1

Punting

	No	Yds	Avg	LG	In 20
Corral	76	3002	39.5	65	14
Los Angeles	77	3002	39.0	65	14
Opponents	90	3789	42.1	63	28

Punt Returns

	No	FC	Yds	Avg	LG	TD
Irvin	42	7	296	7.0	26	0
Waddy	2		10	5.0	10	0
Guman	2	1	6	3.0	3	0
J. Johnson	1	4	3	3.0	3	0
Cromwell	0	2	0	0.0	0	0
Los Angeles	47	14	315	6.7	26	0
Opponents	42	5	353	8.4	32	0

Kickoff Returns

	No	Yds	Avg	LG	TD
D. Hill	43	880	20.5	98t	1
Sully	4	36	9.0	20	0
Guman	2	25	12.5	13	0
J. Thomas	2	21	10.5	15	0
P. Thomas	1	12	12.0	12	0
Irvin	1	5	5.0	5	0
Los Angeles	53	979	18.5	98t	1
Opponents	78	1553	19.9	88	0

Scoring

	TD R	TD P	TD Rt	PAT	FG	TP
Corral				51/52	16/30	99
Peacock	7	2				54
Miller		8				48
Bryant	3	3				36
Dennard		6				36
Waddy		5				30
Guman	3	1				24
Hicks	1	2				18
D. Hill		1	2			18
J. Thomas	2	1				18
Cromwell			1	1*		7
Arnold		1				6
Ferragamo	1					6
J. Johnson			1			6
Moore		1				6
Perry			1			6
Ji. Yngblood			1			6
Los Angeles	17	31	6	52/54	16/30	424
Opponents	13	23	2	34/38	9/20	289

* scored PAT on run

LOS ANGELES RECORD HOLDERS

Individual Records—Single Season

Category	Name	Performance
Rushing (Yds.)	L. McCutcheon, 1977	1238
Passing (Pct.)	Vince Ferragamo, 1980	59.4
Passing (Yds.)	Vince Ferragamo, 1980	3199
Passing (TDs)	Vince Ferragamo, 1980	30
Receiving (No.)	Tom Fears, 1950	84
Receiving (Yds.)	Elroy Hirsch, 1951	1495
Interceptions	Dick Lane, 1952	14
Punting (Avg.)	Dan Villanueva, 1962	45.5
Punt Ret. (Avg.)	Woodley Lewis, 1952	18.5
Kickoff Ret. (Avg.)	Vitamin T. Smith, 1950	33.7
Field Goals	David Ray, 1973	30
Touchdowns (Tot.)	Elroy Hirsch, 1951	17
Points	David Ray, 1973	130

Team Records—Single Game

Category	Opponent, Date	Performance
Offense		
First Downs	vs. Sea, 11/4/79	38
Total Points	vs. Balt, 10/22/50	70
Touchdowns	vs. Balt, 10/22/50	10
Total Net Yards	vs. NY Yanks, 9/28/51	735
Net Yards Rushing	vs. NY Yanks, 11/18/51	371
Net Yards Passing	vs. NY Yanks, 9/28/51	554
Rushing Attempts	vs. Minn, 9/19/76	65
Passing Attempts	vs. Phil, 10/8/50	55
Interceptions by	vs. SF, 10/18/64	7
	vs. Chi Bears, 10/9/49	7
Defense		
Net Yards Allowed	vs. Sea, 11/4/79	−7
Net Rushing Yards Allowed	vs. Chi, 10/26/52	1
Net Passing Yards Allowed	vs. Sea, 11/4/79	−30

FIRST PLAYERS SELECTED

Year	Player, College, Position
1979	George Andrews, Nebraska, LB
1980	Johnnie Johnson, Texas, DB
1981	Mel Owens, Michigan, LB

RAMS COACHING HISTORY
Cleveland 1937-45 (305-245-20)

		W-L-T
1937-38	Hugo Bezdek*	1-13-1
1938	Art Lewis	4-4-0
1939-42	Earl (Dutch) Clark	16-26-2
1944	Aldo (Buff) Donelli	4-6-0
1945-46	Adam Walsh	15-5-1
1947	Bob Snyder	6-6-0
1948-49	Clark Shaughnessy**	14-7-3
1950-52	Joe Stydahar**	18-9-0
1952-54	Hamp Pool	23-11-2
1955-59	Sid Gillman	28-32-1
1960-62	Bob Waterfield***	9-24-1
1962-65	Harland Svare	14-31-3
1966-70	George Allen	49-19-4
1971-72	Tommy Prothro	14-12-2
1973-77	Chuck Knox	57-20-1
1978-80	Ray Malavasi	35-19-0

*Resigned after three games in 1938
**Resigned after one game in 1952
***Resigned after eight games in 1952

1980 TEAM RECORD

Preseason (2-2)

Los Angeles	Opponent	
35	New England	41
19	Dallas	10
13	Denver	21
17	San Diego	7
84		

Regular Season (11-5)

Los Angeles	Opponent	Att.
20	*Detroit	64,892
9	Tampa Bay	66,576
51	*Green Bay	63,850
28	New York Giants	73,414
48	*San Francisco	62,188
21	St. Louis	50,230
31	San Francisco	55,360
10	Atlanta	57,401
45	*New Orleans	59,909
14	*Miami	62,198
17	New England	60,609
27	New Orleans	53,448
38	*New York Jets	59,743
7	Buffalo (OT)	77,133
38	*Dallas	65,154
20	Atlanta (OT)	62,469
424	Opponents 289	994,574

*Home Game (OT) Overtime

Score by Periods

	1	2	3	4	OT	Total
Los Angeles	95	172	92	62	3	424
Opponents	30	89	54	113	3	289

Attendance

Home 500,403   Away 494,171   Total 994,574
Single game home record, 102,368 (11-10-57; L.A. Coliseum), 65,154 (12-15-80; Anaheim Stadium)
Single season home record, 519,175 (1973; L.A. Coliseum), 500,403 (1980; Anaheim Stadium)

LOS ANGELES RAMS 1981 VETERAN ROSTER

No.	Name	Pos.	Ht.	Wt.	NFL Exp.	Birth-date	Birthplace	College	Residence	Games in '80
52	Andrews, George	LB	6-3	223	3	11/28/55	Omaha, Neb.	Nebraska	Anaheim, Calif.	13
84	Arnold, Walt	TE	6-3	225	2	8/31/58	Galveston, Tex.	New Mexico	Los Alamos, N.M.	16
62	Bain, Bill	G	6-4	277	6	8/9/52	Pico Rivera, Calif.	Southern California	Westminster, Calif.	16
90	Brooks, Larry	DT	6-3	253	10	6/10/50	Philadelphia, Pa.	Va. State-Petersburg	Fountain Valley, Calif.	16
32	Bryant, Cullen	FB	6-1	236	9	5/20/51	Fort Sill, Okla.	Colorado	Broomfield, Colo.	16
†	Childs, Henry	TE	6-2	220	6	4/16/51	Thomasville, Ga.	Kansas State	Lenexa, Kan.	13
3	Corral, Frank	K-P	6-2	228	4	6/16/55	Chihuahua, Mex.	UCLA	Riverside, Calif.	16
21	Cromwell, Nolan	S	6-1	198	5	1/30/55	Smith Center, Kan.	Kansas	Lawrence, Kan.	16
41	Delaney, Jeff	S	6-0	195	2	10/25/56	Pittsburgh, Pa.	Pittsburgh	Upper St. Clair, Pa.	16
88	Dennard, Preston	WR	6-1	183	4	12/7/56	Mobile, Ala.	New Mexico	Fountain Valley, Calif.	16
71	Doss, Reggie	DE	6-4	267	4	11/28/55		Hampton Institute	Huntington Beach, Calif.	16
89	Dryer, Fred	DE	6-6	231	13	7/6/46	Hawthorne, Calif.	San Diego State	Long Beach, Calif.	16
55	Ekern, Carl	LB	6-3	223	6	5/27/54	Richland, Wash.	San Jose State	Fountain Valley, Calif.	16
79	Fanning, Mike	DT	6-6	252	7	2/2/53	Mt. Clemens, Mich.	Notre Dame	Tulsa, Okla.	15
77	France, Doug	T	6-5	270	7	4/26/53	Dayton, Ohio	Ohio State	Fountain Valley, Calif.	16
44	Guman, Mike	RB	6-2	210	2	4/21/58	Allentown, Pa.	Penn State	Bethlehem, Pa.	16
11	Haden, Pat	QB	5-11	185	6	1/23/53	Westbury, N.Y.	Southern California	San Marino, Calif.	7
9	Hare, Eddie	P	6-4	209	2	5/30/57	Ulysses, Kan.	Tulsa	Tulsa, Okla.	0*
60	Harrah, Dennis	G	6-5	255	7	3/9/53	Charleston, W. Va.	Miami	Long Beach, Calif.	16
51	Harris, Joe	LB	6-1	224	2	12/6/52	Fayetteville, N.C.	Georgia Tech	Fayetteville, N.C.	15
81	Hicks, Victor	TE	6-3	250	2	1/19/57	Lubbock, Tex.	Oklahoma	Anaheim, Calif.	16
87	Hill, Drew	WR-KR	5-9	170	3	10/5/56	Newnan, Ga.	Georgia Tech	College Park, Ga.	16
24	Hill, Eddie	RB-KR	6-2	210	3	3/7/57	Nashville, Tenn.	Memphis State	Huntington Beach, Calif.	15
72	Hill, Kent	G	6-5	260	6	5/13/57	Americus, Ga.	Georgia Tech	Americus, Ga.	16
63	Horton, Irv	G-C	6-4	248	2	1/1/51	San Bernardino, Calif.	Colorado	Redlands, Calif.	3
47	Irvin, LeRoy	CB-PR	5-11	180	2	9/15/57	Fort Dix, N.J.	Kansas	Augusta, Ga.	16
20	Johnson, Johnnie	S	6-1	185	2	10/8/56	La Grange, Tex.	Texas	Austin, Tex.	16
76	Jones, Cody	DT	6-5	244	7	5/3/51	San Francisco, Calif.	San Jose State	Huntington Beach, Calif.	16
19	Lee, Bob	QB	6-2	190	13	8/7/46	Columbus, Ohio	Pacific	San Francisco, Calif.	16
54	McGlasson, Ed	C	6-4	260	2	7/11/56	Annapolis, Md.	Youngstown State	Potomac, Md.	1
82	Miller, Willie	WR	5-9	172	6	4/26/48	Birmingham, Ala.	Colorado State	Fort Collins, Colo.	16
86	Moore, Jeff	WR	6-1	200	2	9/26/57	Memphis, Tenn.	Tennessee	Anaheim, Calif.	14
95	Murphy, Phil	DT	6-5	280	2	3/2/57	New London, Conn.	South Carolina State	Middletown, Conn.	1
83	Nelson, Terry	TE	6-2	240	8	5/20/51	Arkadelphia, Ark.	Arkansas-Pine Bluff	Arkadelphia, Ark.	16
75	Pankey, Irv	T	6-4	269	2	2/15/58	Aberdeen, Md.	Penn State	Aberdeen, Md.	16
34	Peacock, Elvis	RB	6-1	208	3	11/7/56	Miami, Fla.	Oklahoma	Huntington Beach, Calif.	4
49	Perry, Rod	CB	5-9	182	7	9/11/53	Fresno, Calif.	Colorado	Fresno, Calif.	16
8	Rutledge, Jeff	QB	6-2	202	3	1/22/57	Birmingham, Ala.	Alabama	Huntington Beach, Calif.	13
61	Saul, Rich	C	6-3	245	12	2/5/48	Butler, Pa.	Michigan State	Newport Beach, Calif.	16
78	Slater, Jackie	T	6-4	271	6	5/27/54	Jackson, Miss.	Jackson State	Meridian, Miss.	16
56	Smith, Doug	C-G	6-3	255	4	11/25/56	Columbus, Ohio	Bowling Green	Laguna Hills, Calif.	16
23	Smith, Lucious	CB	5-10	190	2	1/17/57		Cal State-Fullerton	Fullerton, Calif.	8
37	Sully, Ivory	S	6-0	193	4	6/20/57	Salisbury, Md.	Delaware	Brea, Calif.	16
33	Thomas, Jewerl	RB	5-10	223	2	9/10/57	Hanford, Calif.	San Jose State	Hanford, Calif.	16
27	Thomas, Pat	CB	5-9	182	6	9/1/54	Plano, Tex.	Texas A&M	Plano, Tex.	14
26	Tyler, Wendell	RB	5-10	195	5	5/20/55	Shreveport, La.	UCLA	West Covina, Calif.	4
80	Waddy, Billy	WR	5-11	188	5	2/19/54	Warton, Tex.	Colorado	Huntington Beach, Calif.	16
57	Westbrooks, Greg	LB	6-3	220	7	2/24/53	Chicago, Ill.	Colorado	Kansas City, Mo.	6
85	Youngblood, Jack	DE	6-4	244	11	1/26/50	Jacksonville, Fla.	Florida	Orange, Calif.	15
53	Youngblood, Jim	LB	6-3	231	9	2/23/50	Union, S.C.	Tennessee Tech	Fountain Valley, Calif.	15

*Hare last active with New England in '79.

†Option playout; subject to developments.

t-Rams traded for Childs (New Orleans through Washington).

Also played with Rams in '80—LB Bob Brudzinski (9 games), QB Vince Ferragamo (16), RB Lydell Mitchell (2), LB Jack Reynolds (16), G Conrad Rucker (2).

LOS ANGELES RAMS 1981 FIRST-YEAR ROSTER

Name	Pos.	Ht.	Wt.	Birth-date	Birthplace	College	Residence	How Acq.
Alexander, Robert	RB	6-0	185	4/21/58	Charleston, W. Va.	West Virginia	S. Charleston, W. Va.	D10
Anderson, John	DE	6-6	254	9/16/54	Attand, Fla.	Bethune-Cookman	Sanford, Fla.	FA
Anderson, Marcus	WR	6-0	178	6/12/59	Port Arthur, Tex.	Tulane	Lake Charles, La.	FA
Battle, Ron	TE	6-3	220	3/27/59	Shreveport, La.	North Texas State	Shreveport, La.	D7
Brant, Mike	WR	5-10	190	1/3/59	Tuscaloosa, Ala.	UCLA	Pacoima, Calif.	FA
Carson, Howard (1)	LB	6-2	233	2/11/57	Hico, Tex.	Howard Payne	Grapevine, Tex.	FA
Clark, Mike	DE	6-4	240	3/30/59	Dothan, Ala.	Florida	Graceville, Fla.	D7a
Cobb, Bob	DE	6-4	248	10/12/57	Cincinnati, Ohio	Arizona	Cincinnati, Ohio	D3a
Colbert, Stacy	WR-KR	5-7	165	4/23/59	Athens, Ga.	Utah State	Athens, Ga.	FA
Collins, Jim	LB	6-2	230	6/11/58	Orange, N.J.	Syracuse	Morristown, N.J.	D2
Collins, Kirk (1)	CB	5-11	185	7/18/58	San Antonio, Tex.	Baylor	San Antonio, Tex.	D7a ('80)
Daniels, William	DE-DT	6-3	250	2/13/58	Chicago, Ill.	Alabama State	Chicago, Ill.	D6
Dozier, Ricky (1)	T	6-7	287	3/22/57	San Francisco, Calif.	San Jose State	San Francisco, Calif.	FA
Farmer, George (1)	WR	5-10	175	12/5/58	Los Angeles, Calif.	Southern	Los Angeles, Calif.	D9 ('80)
Gruber, Bob (1)	T	6-5	250	6/7/58	Del Rio, Tex.	Pittsburgh	Anaheim, Calif.	D10 ('80)
Kemp, Jeff	QB	6-0	200	7/11/59	Santa Ana, Calif.	Dartmouth	Bethesda, Md.	FA
Kendra, Dan (1)	QB	6-2	200	9/24/56	Wilkes-Barre, Pa.	West Virginia	Allentown, Pa.	FA
Lilja, George	C	6-4	250	3/3/58	Evergreen Park, Ill.	Michigan	Palos Park, Ill.	D4
McLain, Jerry	LB	6-3	234	10/30/58	Monroe, Wash.	Washington	Snohomish, Wash.	FA
Meisner, Greg	DT	6-3	250	4/23/59	New Kensington, Pa.	Pittsburgh	New Kensington, Pa.	D3
Minyard, Rick	S	6-1	193	5/5/59	Santa Rosa, Calif.	Cal State-Northridge	Chatsworth, Calif.	FA
Owens, Mel	LB	6-2	230	12/7/58	Detroit, Mich.	Michigan	DeKalb, Ill.	D1
Parma, Rick	WR	5-11	180	12/4/57	Anaheim, Calif.	San Jose State	Buena Park, Calif.	FA
Penaranda, Jairo	FB	5-11	208	6/15/58	Barranquilla, Colom.	UCLA	Burbank, Calif.	D12
Petrosian, Ralph	K	5-7	163	6/28/59	Los Angeles, Calif.	Long Beach State	Montebello, Calif.	FA
Pettigrew, Tom (1)	T	6-4	262	12/26/56	Roanoke, Va.	Eastern Illinois	Fullerton, Calif.	D8 ('80)
Plunkett, Art	T	6-7	260	3/8/59	Chicago, Ill.	Nevada-Las Vegas	Salt Lake City, Utah	D8
Rakhshani, Vic	TE	6-3	230	7/7/58	Long Beach, Calif.	Southern California	Huntington Beach, Calif.	FA
Roberts, Elbert	CB	6-2	195	11/30/59	New York, N.Y.	Savannah State	Savannah, Ga.	FA
Seawell, Ron	LB	6-1	207	1/20/59	Portland, Ore.	Portland State	Milwaukie, Ore.	D9
Taylor, Robert	WR	6-0	187	2/17/59	San Diego, Calif.	San Diego State	Chula Vista, Calif.	FA
Whiteside, Mike	WR	5-11	175	10/29/58	Los Angeles, Calif.	Fresno State	Los Angeles, Calif.	FA
Wilson, Greg (1)	RB	6-0	185	4/16/57	Orlando, Fla.	East Tennessee	Orlando, Fla.	FA
Yancy, Billy	CB	5-10	170	6/16/58	Limestone, Mass.	Fresno State	Los Angeles, Calif.	FA

Players who report to an NFL team for the first time are designated on rosters as rookies (R). If a player reported to an NFL training camp in a previous year but was not on the active squad for three or more regular season or postseason games, he is listed on the first-year roster and designated by a (1). Thereafter, a player who is on the active squad for three or more regular season games is credited with an additional year of playing experience.

NOTES

COACHING STAFF

Head Coach, Ray Malavasi

Pro Career: Starts fourth season as NFL head coach after directing Rams to an 11-5 mark in 1980. Guided Rams to NFL record seventh straight division title and first Super Bowl appearance in 1979. Was Rams defensive coordinator from 1973-77 before elevation to top job. Started pro coaching career as Denver Broncos defensive line coach in 1963 and was named Broncos interim head coach in 1966. He was Canada's Hamilton Tiger-Cats defensive line coach in 1967-68 before taking same job with Buffalo Bills in 1969-70. He joined Oakland's staff in 1971. Although he was drafted by the Philadelphia Eagles in 1953, he decided to forego a pro playing career to become a player-coach at Fort Belvoir, Va. Career record: 39-27.

Background: Played collegiately at Army and Mississippi State where he was a lineman from 1950-52. Later became an assistant coach at Minnesota (1956-57), Memphis State (1958-60), and Wake Forest (1961).

Personal: Born November 8, 1930, Passaic, N.J. Graduated from Clifton (N.J.) High in 1948. Ray and his wife Mary live in Huntington Beach, Calif. and have two daughters—Maureen and Sheila—and three sons—Dennis, Bill, and Bryce.

ASSISTANT COACHES

Bud Carson, defensive coordinator; born August 28, 1931, Brackenridge, Pa., lives in Los Angeles. Defensive back North Carolina 1948-52. No pro playing experience. College coach: North Carolina 1957-64, South Carolina 1965, Georgia Tech 1966-71 (head coach). Pro coach: Pittsburgh Steelers 1972-77, fourth year with Rams.

Clyde Evans, conditioning specialist; born April 10, 1943, Watsonville, Calif., lives in Long Beach, Calif. Defensive back Cabrillo J.C. 1961-62. No pro playing experience. College coach: San Diego State 1972-73. Pro coach: San Diego Chargers 1974-77, fourth year with Rams.

Hewritt Dixon, offensive backfield; born January 8, 1940, Alachua, Fla., lives in Anaheim. Running back Florida A&M 1960-62. Pro running back Denver 1963-65, Oakland 1966-70. Pro coach: Joined Rams in 1980.

Paul Lanham, quarterbacks; born July 31, 1930, Ripley, W. Va., lives in Los Angeles. Linebacker Glenville State 1951-53. No pro playing experience. College coach: Delaware 1960, Dayton 1961, Colorado State 1962-69, Arkansas 1970-71. Pro coach: St. Louis Cardinals 1972, Washington Redskins 1973-77, fourth year with Rams.

Frank Lauterbur, defensive line; born August 8, 1925, Cincinnati, lives in Los Angeles. Guard Oberlin 1943, Camp Pendleton Marines 1945, Mount Union 1946-48. No pro playing experience. College coach: Kent State 1953-54, Army 1957-61, Pittsburgh 1962, Toledo 1963-70 (head coach), Iowa 1971-73 (head coach). Pro coach: Baltimore Colts 1955-56, 1974-77, fourth year with Rams.

Herb Paterra, linebackers; born November 8, 1940, Grassport, Pa., lives in Diamond Bar, Calif. Offensive guard-linebacker Michigan State 1960-62. Pro linebacker Buffalo Bills 1963-64, Hamilton Tiger Cats (CFL) 1965-68. College coach: Michigan State 1969-71, Wyoming 1972-74. Pro coach: Charlotte Hornets (WFL) 1975, Hamilton Tiger Cats (CFL) 1978-79, joined Rams in 1980.

Dan Radakovich, offensive line; born November 27, 1935, Duquesne, Pa., lives in Huntington Beach, Calif. Center-linebacker Penn State 1954-56. College coach: Penn State 1960-69, Cincinnati 1970, Colorado 1972-73. Pro coach: Pittsburgh Steelers 1971, 1974, San Francisco 49ers 1978, third year with Rams.

Lionel Taylor, offensive coordinator; born August 15, 1936, Kansas City, Mo., lives in Los Angeles. End New Mexico Highlands 1955-58. Pro receiver Chicago Bears 1959, Denver Broncos 1960-66, Houston Oilers 1967-68. Pro coach: Pittsburgh Steelers 1970-76, fifth year with Rams.

Jim Vechiarella, special teams; born February 20, 1937, Youngstown, Ohio, lives in Anaheim. Linebacker Youngstown State 1955-57. No pro playing experience. College coach: Youngstown State 1964-74, Southern Illinois 1976-77, Tulane 1978-80. Pro coach: Charlotte Hornets (WFL) 1975, first year with Rams.

MINNESOTA VIKINGS 1981 VETERAN ROSTER

No.	Name	Pos.	Ht.	Wt.	NFL Exp.	Birth-date	Birthplace	College	Residence	Games in '80
59	Blair, Matt	LB	6-5	229	8	9/20/51	Honolulu, Hawaii	Iowa State	Prior Lake, Minn.	14
62	Boyd, Brent	G	6-3	260	2	3/23/57	La Habra, Calif.	UCLA	Los Angeles, Calif.	16
23	Brown, Ted	RB	5-10	198	3	2/2/57	High Point, N.C.	North Carolina State	Burnsville, Minn.	16
82	Bruer, Bob	TE	6-5	235	5	5/2/53	Madison, Wis.	Mankato State	Edina, Minn.	14*
24	Brune, Larry	S	6-2	202	2	5/4/53	San Diego, Calif.	Rice	Houston, Tex.	14*
20	†Bryant, Bobby	CB	6-1	170	13	1/24/44	Macon, Ga.	South Carolina	Bloomington, Minn.	14
26	Cobb, Marvin	S	6-0	188	7	8/6/53	Detroit, Mich.	Southern California	Los Angeles, Calif.	8*
8	Coleman, Greg	P	6-0	178	5	9/9/54	Jacksonville, Fla.	Florida A&M	Jacksonville, Fla.	16
7	Danmeier, Rick	K	6-0	183	4	4/8/52	White Bear Lake, Minn.	Sioux Falls	Burnsville, Minn.	16
12	Dils, Steve	QB	6-1	190	3	12/8/55	Vancouver, Wash.	Stanford	Sunnyvale, Calif.	13
61	Hamilton, Wes	G	6-3	255	5	4/24/53	Texas City, Tex.	Tulsa	Burnsville, Minn.	13
45	Hannon, Tom	S	5-11	193	5	3/5/55	Massillon, Ohio	Michigan State	Massillon, Ohio	16
75	Holloway, Randy	DE	6-5	245	4	8/26/55	Sharon, Pa.	Pittsburgh	Burnsville, Minn.	10
51	Hough, Jim	C	6-2	267	4	8/4/56	Lynwood, Calif.	Utah State	Eden Prairie, Minn.	16
56	Huffman, Dave	C	6-6	255	3	4/4/57	Canton, Ohio	Notre Dame	Dallas, Tex.	16
52	Johnson, Dennis	LB	6-3	230	2	6/19/58	Flint, Mich.	Southern California	Los Angeles, Calif.	12
53	Johnson, Henry	LB	6-2	235	2	3/20/58	Wrens, Ga.	Georgia Tech	College Park, Ga.	16
25	Knoff, Kurt	S	6-2	188	5	4/6/54	East Grand Forks, Minn.	Stanford	Stafford, Tex.	16
9	Kramer, Tommy	QB	6-1	199	5	3/7/55	San Antonio, Tex.	Rice	Lakeville, Minn.	15
58	Langer, Jim	C	6-2	253	12	5/16/48	Little Falls, Minn.	South Dakota State	Lakeville, Minn.	16
80	LeCount, Terry	WR	5-10	172	4	7/9/56	Jacksonville, Fla.	Florida	Royalton, Minn.	16
79	Martin, Doug	DE	6-3	258	2	5/22/57	Fairfield, Calif.	Washington	Fairfield, Calif.	16
54	†McNeill, Fred	LB	6-2	229	8	5/6/52	Durham, Calif.	UCLA	Los Angeles, Calif.	11
87	Miller, Kevin	WR	5-10	180	4	3/21/55	Weirton, W.Va.	Louisville	Bloomington, Minn.	16
77	Mullaney, Mark	DE	6-6	242	8	4/30/53	Denver, Colo.	Colorado State	Denver, Colo.	4
49	Nord, Keith	S	6-0	197	3	3/13/57	Minneapolis, Minn.	St. Cloud State	Minnetonka, Minn.	16
40	Paschal, Doug	RB	6-2	219	2	3/5/58	Greenville, N.C.	North Carolina	Greenville, N.C.	16
36	Payton, Eddie	KR	5-6	179	5	8/3/51	Columbia, Miss.	Jackson State	Jackson, Miss.	16
28	Rashad, Ahmad	WR	6-2	200	9	11/19/49	Portland, Ore.	Oregon	Lakeville, Minn.	16
78	Riley, Steve	T	6-6	253	8	11/23/52	Chula Vista, Calif.	Southern California	Tustin, Calif.	16
76	Roller, Dave	DT	6-2	270	8	10/28/49	Dayton, Tenn.	Kentucky	Dayton, Tenn.	16
89	Sanders, Ken	DE	6-5	246	10	8/22/50	Valley Mills, Tex.	Howard Payne	Valley Mills, Tex.	15
81	Senser, Joe	TE	6-4	238	2	8/18/56	Philadelphia, Pa.	West Chester State, Pa.	Bloomington, Minn.	16
50	Siemon, Jeff	LB	6-3	237	10	6/2/50	Rochester, Minn.	Stanford	Edina, Minn.	16
55	Studwell, Scott	LB	6-2	224	5	8/27/54	Evansville, Ind.	Illinois	Lakeville, Minn.	16
69	Sutherland, Doug	DT	6-3	250	12	4/1/48	Superior, Wis.	Superior State, Wis.	Burnsville, Minn.	16
67	Swilley, Dennis	G	6-3	241	5	6/28/55	Bossier City, La.	Texas A&M	Burnsville, Minn.	16
37	Teal, Willie	CB	5-10	195	2	12/20/57	Texarkana, Tex.	Louisiana State	Baton Rouge, La.	16
27	Turner, John	CB	6-0	199	4	9/22/56	Miami, Fla.	Miami	Bloomington, Minn.	16
71	Vella, John	T	6-4	260	10	4/21/50	Cleveland, Ohio	Southern California	Castro Valley, Calif.	1
72	White, James	DT	6-3	263	6	10/26/53	Hot Springs, Ark.	Oklahoma State	Hot Springs, Ark.	16
85	White, Sammy	WR	5-11	189	6	3/16/54	Winnsboro, La.	Grambling	Monroe, La.	16
73	Yary, Ron	T	6-6	255	14	8/16/46	Chicago, Ill.	Southern California	Cerritos, Calif.	14
34	Young, Rickey	RB	6-2	195	7	12/12/53	Mobile, Ala.	Jackson State	San Diego, Calif.	16

*Bruer played 2 games with 49ers, 12 with Vikings; Cobb played 6 games with Pittsburgh, 2 with Vikings.

†Option playout; subject to developments.

Retired—Jimmy Edwards, 2-year running back-kick returner, 15 games; Charles Goodrum, 8-year tackle, 15 games in 1980; Wally Hilgenberg, 17-year linebacker, 7 games; Paul Krause, 17-year safety, 16 games; Robert Miller, 7-year running back, 16 games in 1980.

Also played with Vikings in '80—T Nick Bebout (1 game), LB Derrel Luce (4), G Mel Mitchell (6), TE Stu Voigt (3).

MINNESOTA VIKINGS 1981 FIRST-YEAR ROSTER

Name	Pos.	Ht.	Wt.	Birth-date	Birthplace	College	Residence	How Acq.
Berg, Mitch	S	6-2	205	9/7/59	Minneapolis, Minn.	St. John's	Collegeville, Minn.	FA
Bergeland, Nate (1)	DT	6-3	225	10/21/58	Livingston, Mont.	St. Olaf	Minneapolis, Minn.	FA
Coccimiglio, Ron	CB-S	6-0	194	5/24/58	Martinez, Calif.	California	Concord, Calif.	FA
Farra, Bob	QB	6-2	195	11/12/56	Seattle, Wash.	Claremont	Placentia, Calif.	FA
Fisher, Marcus	CB-S	6-0	185	3/8/57	Detroit, Mich.	Montana	Detroit, Mich.	FA
Gutzke, Dave	CB-S	6-3	205	8/3/58	Minneapolis, Minn.	Princeton	Waverly, Minn.	FA
Harris, Ken (1)	RB	6-2	240	8/18/58	Fairburn, Ga.	Alabama	Fairburn, Ga.	D3
Irwin, Tim	T	6-6	275	12/13/56	Knoxville, Tenn.	Tennessee	Knoxville, Tenn.	FA
Lewis, Leo (1)	WR	5-8	170	9/17/56	Columbia, Mo.	Missouri	Columbia, Mo.	D2
McDole, Mardye	WR	5-11	195	5/1/59	Pensacola, Fla.	Mississippi State	Starkville, Miss.	D2
Murphy, James	WR	5-10	177	10/10/59	Deland, Fla.	Utah State	Logan, Utah	D10
Murtha, Greg (1)	T	6-6	268	4/23/57	Minneapolis, Minn.	Minnesota	Minneapolis, Minn.	FA
Ray, Wendell	DE	6-4	233	10/19/56	St. Louis, Mo.	Missouri	St. Louis, Mo.	D5
Redwine, Jarvis	RB	5-10	198	5/16/57	Los Angeles, Calif.	Nebraska	Lincoln, Neb.	D2
Sendlein, Robin	LB	6-3	224	12/1/58	Las Vegas, Nev.	Texas	Austin, Tex.	D2
Shaver, Don	RB	5-11	222	5/6/59	Long Island, N.Y.	Kutztown State	Sea Cliff, N.Y.	D7
Smith, Freddie	RB	5-11	210	3/17/57	Athens, Ala.	Auburn	Athens, Ala.	FA
Stephanos, William	T	6-4	262	3/24/57	Lynn, Mass.	Boston College	Lynn, Mass.	D11
Swain, John	LB	6-1	195	9/4/59	Miami, Fla.	Miami	Opa-Locka, Fla.	D4
Wagner, Vince	K	5-11	175	7/16/59	Bozeman, Mont.	Northwestern, Minn.	Roseville, Minn.	FA
Williams, Brian	TE	6-4	226	10/14/57	Des Allemanda, La.	Southern	Baton Rouge, La.	D12
Wilson, Wade	QB	6-3	212	2/1/59	Greenville, Tex.	East Texas State	Commerce, Tex.	D8

Players who report to an NFL team for the first time are designated on rosters as rookies (R). If a player reported to an NFL training camp in a previous year but was not on the active squad for three or more regular season or postseason games, he is listed on the first-year roster and designated by a (1). Thereafter, a player who is on the active squad for three or more regular season games is credited with an additional year of playing experience.

COACHING STAFF

Head Coach, Bud Grant

Pro Career: Has guided Minnesota to 11 NFC Central titles in last 13 years (1968-71, 1973-78, 1980) and postseason play 11 of 14 seasons as head coach, including NFL champions in 1969 and NFC champions in 1973, 1974, and 1976. Head coach at Winnipeg of the Canadian Football League for 10 years before joining the Vikings in 1967. Grant's Winnipeg teams won six Western Conference championships and four Grey Cup championships. Played for the Philadelphia Eagles 1951-52 and ranked as the number 2 receiver in NFL in 1952. Played 1953-56 with Winnipeg before being named head coach in 1957. NFL record: 140-77-5.

Background: Attended University of Minnesota and was two-time All-Big Ten end. Won four letters in football, two in basketball (forward), and three in baseball (pitcher-outfielder). Played football and basketball at Great Lakes in 1945, first year out of high school. Played 1950-51 with Minneapolis Lakers of the National Basketball Association. Canadian coach of the year in 1965; named Minnesota athlete of the half-century in 1951.

Personal: Born Harry P. Grant on May 20, 1927, Superior, Wis. Bud and his wife, Pat, live in Bloomington, Minn., and have six children—Kathleen, Laurie, Peter, Michael, Bruce, and Dan.

ASSISTANT COACHES

Jerry Burns, offense; born January 24, 1927, Detroit, lives in Eden Prairie, Minn. Quarterback Michigan 1947-50. No pro playing experience. College coach: Hawaii 1951, Whittier 1952, Iowa 1954-65 (head coach 1961-65). Pro coach: Green Bay Packers 1966-67, Vikings since 1968.

Jim Carr, defensive backs; born March 25, 1933, Kayford, W. Va., lives in Bloomington, Minn. Running back-defensive back Morris Harvey 1952-54. Pro defensive back-linebacker Chicago Cardinals 1955-57, Montreal Alouettes 1958, Philadelphia Eagles 1959-63, Washington Redskins 1964-65. Pro coach: Minnesota Vikings 1966-68, Chicago Bears 1969, 1973-74, Philadelphia Eagles 1970-72, Detroit Lions 1975-76, Buffalo Bills 1977, San Francisco 49ers 1978, rejoined Vikings in 1979.

Tom Cecchini, defensive line; born September 12, 1944, Detroit, Mich., lives in Bloomington, Minn. Linebacker-center Michigan 1963-65. No pro playing experience. College coach: Michigan 1968-69, Xavier 1970-73 (head coach 1972-73), Iowa 1974-75, 1978-79, Tulane 1976-77. Pro coach: Second year with Vikings.

Bob Hollway, defense; born January 29, 1926, Ann Arbor, Mich., lives in Edina, Minn. End Michigan 1947-49. No pro playing experience. College coach: Maine 1951-52, Eastern Michigan 1953, Michigan 1954-66. Pro coach: Minnesota Vikings 1967-70, St. Louis Cardinals 1971-72 (head coach), Detroit Lions 1973-74, San Francisco 49ers 1975, Seattle Seahawks 1976-77, rejoined Vikings in 1978.

Bus Mertes, offensive backs; born October 6, 1923, Chicago, lives in Edina, Minn. Running back Iowa 1939-41. Pro running back Chicago Cardinals 1945, Los Angeles Dons (AAFC) 1946. Baltimore Colts (AAFC) 1947-48, New York Giants 1949-50. College coach: Bradley 1951-52, Kansas State 1953-59, Drake 1960-64. Pro coach: Denver Broncos 1965-66, Vikings since 1967.

John Michels, offensive line; born February 15, 1931, Philadelphia, lives in Bloomington, Minn. Guard Tennessee 1949-52. Pro guard Philadelphia Eagles 1953, 1956, Winnipeg Bombers (CFL) 1957. College coach: Texas A&M 1958. Pro coach: Winnipeg Bombers (CFL) 1956-66, Vikings since 1967.

Floyd Reese, linebackers; born August 8, 1948, Springfield, Mo., lives in Bloomington, Minn. Defensive tackle UCLA 1967-69. No pro playing experience. College coach: UCLA 1970-73, Georgia Tech 1974. Pro coach: Detroit Lions 1975-77, San Francisco 49ers 1978, third year with Vikings.

Les Steckel, receivers; born July 1, 1946, in Whitehall, Pa., lives in Bloomington, Minn. Running back Kansas 1964-67. No pro playing experience. College coach: Colorado 1972-76, Navy 1977. Pro coach: San Francisco 49ers 1978, third year with Vikings.

NOTES

New Orleans Saints

National Football Conference
Western Division

Team Colors: Old Gold, Black, and White
1500 Poydras Street
New Orleans, Louisiana 70112
Telephone: (504) 587-3034

Club Officials
President: John W. Mecom, Jr.
Assistant to the President: Fred Williams
Director of Operations: Harry Hulmes
Director of Player Negotiations: Pat Peppler
Director of Pro Personnel: Ernie Hefferle
Director of Player Personnel: Bob Whitman
Director of Public Relations: Greg Suit
Assistant Director of Public Relations:
  Rusty Kasmiersky
Ticket Manager: Don Johnson
Controller: Bobby Landry
Marketing Director: Barra Bircher
Administrative Assistant: Jack Cherry
Trainer: Dean Kleinschmidt
Equipment Manager: Dan Simmons

Stadium: Louisiana Superdome • **Capacity:** 71,330
  1500 Poydras Street
  New Orleans, Louisiana 70112
Playing Surface: AstroTurf
Training Camp: Dodgertown
  Vero Beach, Florida 32960

1981 SCHEDULE

Preseason
Aug. 8	**Baltimore**	7:00
Aug. 15	**Houston**	7:00
Aug. 23	vs. Philadelphia (Syracuse)	1:00
Aug. 29	**Detroit**	7:00

Regular Season
Sept. 6	at Atlanta	1:00
Sept. 13	**Los Angeles**	12:00
Sept. 20	at New York Giants	4:00
Sept. 27	at San Francisco	1:00
Oct. 4	**Pittsburgh**	1:00
Oct. 11	**Philadelphia**	12:00
Oct. 18	at Cleveland	1:00
Oct. 25	**Cincinnati**	1:00
Nov. 1	**Atlanta**	12:00
Nov. 8	at Los Angeles	1:00
Nov. 15	at Minnesota	12:00
Nov. 22	at Houston	12:00
Nov. 29	**Tampa Bay**	1:00
Dec. 6	at St. Louis	12:00
Dec. 13	**Green Bay**	12:00
Dec. 20	**San Francisco**	1:00

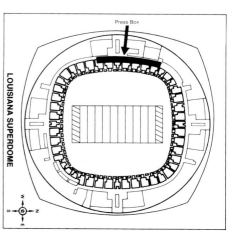

LOUISIANA SUPERDOME

Press Box

1980 TEAM STATISTICS

	New Orleans	Opp.
Total First Downs	285	360
Rushing	80	178
Passing	183	155
Penalty	22	27
Third Down Efficiency	65/203	95/225
Third Down Percentage	32.0	42.2
Total Net Yards	5010	6218
Total Offensive Plays	960	1102
Avg. Gain per Play	5.2	5.6
Avg. Gain per Game	313.1	388.6
Net Yards Rushing	1362	3106
Total Rushing Plays	348	630
Avg. Gain per Rush	3.9	4.9
Avg. Gain Rushing per Game	85.1	194.1
Net Yards Passing	3648	3112
Lost Attempting to Pass	46/362	27/229
Gross Yards Passing	4010	3341
Attempts/Completions	566/334	445/255
Percent Completed	59.0	57.3
Had Intercepted	22	12
Avg. Net Passing per Game	228.0	194.5
Punts/Avg.	89/39.3	64/38.5
Punt Returns/Avg.	22/8.0	48/10.2
Kickoff Returns/Avg.	88/22.4	58/20.0
Interceptions/Avg. Ret.	12/16.3	22/9.9
Penalties/Yards	98/837	79/690
Fumbles/Ball Lost	28/13	27/12
Total Points	291	487
Avg. Points per Game	18.2	30.4
Touchdowns	37	60
Rushing	9	28
Passing	26	31
Returns and Recoveries	2	1
Field Goals	12/22	23/31
Conversions	33/37	56/60
Safeties	0	1

1980 TEAM RECORD

Preseason (1-3)

New Orleans		Opponents
17	St. Louis	13
17	Houston	20
26	*Detroit	40
0	Miami	20
51		93

Regular Season (1-15)

New Orleans		Opponents	Att.
23	*San Francisco	26	58,621
22	Chicago	22	62,523
26	*Buffalo	35	51,154
16	Miami	21	40,946
7	*St. Louis	40	45,388
13	Detroit	24	78,147
14	*Atlanta	41	62,651
14	Washington	22	51,375
31	Los Angeles	45	59,909
21	*Philadelphia	34	44,340
21	Atlanta	31	53,871
7	*Los Angeles	27	53,448
20	*Minnesota	23	30,936
35	San Francisco (OT)	38	37,949
27	*New England	20	38,077
291		487	807,612

*Home Game   (OT) Overtime

Score by Periods

	1	2	3	4	OT	
New Orleans	55	90	71	75	0	291
Opponents	67	151	108	158	3	487

Attendance

Home 384,815   Away 422,797   Total 807,612
Single game home record, 84,728 (11-3-68; Tulane Stadium), 70,940 (11-4-79; Louisiana Superdome)
Single season home record, 550,578 (1971)

1980 INDIVIDUAL STATISTICS

Rushing

	Att	Yds	Avg	LG	TD
Rogers	80	366	4.6	24	1
Galbreath	81	308	3.8	26	3
Wilson	63	188	3.0	15	1
Muncie	40	168	4.2	24	2
Manning	23	166	7.2	24	0
Holmes	38	119	3.1	20	2
Strachan	20	41	2.1	10	0
Chandler	1	9	9.0	9	0
Mauti	1	2	2.0	2	0
Banks	1	-5	-5.0	-5	0
New Orleans	348	1362	3.9	26	9
Opponents	630	3106	4.9	69t	28

Field Goal Success

Distance	1-19	20-29	30-39	40-49	50 Over
Made-Att.	0-0	2-3	7-10	3-8	0-1

Passing

	Att	Comp	Pct	Yds	TD	Int	Tkld	Rate
Manning	509	309	60.7	3716	23	20	41/311	81.8
Scott	33	16	48.5	200	2	1	4/41	75.6
Benjamin	17	7	41.2	28	0	0	0/0	24.3
Chandler	1	1	100.0	43	0	0	1/10	—
Erxleben	1	0	0.0	0	0	0	0/0	—
Galbreath	2	0	0.0	0	0	0	0/0	—
Holmes	3	1	33.3	23	1	0	0/0	79.8
N. Orleans	566	334	59.0	4010	26	22	46/362	—
Opponents	445	255	57.3	3341	31	12	27/229	—

Receiving

	No	Yds	Avg	LG	TD
Chandler	65	975	15.0	50	6
Galbreath	57	470	8.2	21	2
Harris	37	692	18.7	44t	6
Childs	34	463	13.6	30	6
Wilson	31	241	7.8	42	1
Holmes	29	226	7.8	16	1
Rogers	27	267	9.9	43	2
Williams	26	351	13.5	56	2
Hardy	13	197	15.2	44	0
Muncie	7	25	3.6	8	0
Strachan	5	60	12.0	23	0
T. Owens	1	26	26.0	26	0
Mauti	1	10	10.0	10	0
Banks	1	7	7.0	7	0
New Orleans	334	4010	12.0	56	26
Opponents	255	3341	13.1	71t	31

Interceptions

	No	Yds	Avg	LG	TD
Myers	5	96	19.2	48	0
Brown	2	31	15.5	29	0
Marshall	2	17	8.5	17	0
Grooms	1	37	37.0	37	0
Mathis	1	15	15.0	15	0
Kovach	1	0	0.0	0	0
New Orleans	12	196	16.3	48	0
Opponents	22	217	9.9	34	0

Punting

	No	Yds	Avg	LG	In 20
Erxleben	89	3499	39.3	57	23
New Orleans	89	3499	39.3	57	23
Opponents	64	2466	38.5	57	20

Punt Returns

	No	FC	Yds	Avg	LG	TD
Mauti	11	5	111	10.1	18	0
Chandler	8	6	36	4.5	11	0
Waymer	3	0	29	9.7	14	0
Myers	0	1	—	—	—	0
New Orleans	22	12	176	8.0	18	0
Opponents	48	20	490	10.2	57t	1

Kickoff Returns

	No	Yds	Avg	LG	TD
Mauti	31	798	25.7	52	0
Rogers	41	930	22.7	88	0
Wilson	9	159	17.7	27	0
Galbreath	6	86	14.3	20	0
Holloway	1	0	0.0	0	0
New Orleans	88	1973	22.4	88	0
Opponents	58	1159	20.0	62	0

Scoring

	TD R	TD P	TD Rt	PAT	FG	TP
Ricardo				31/34	10/17	61
Chandler		6				36
Childs		6				36
Harris		6				36
Galbreath	3	2				30
Holmes	2	1				18
Rogers	1	2				18
Muncie	2					12
Williams		2				12
Wilson	1	1				12
Erxleben				2/2	2/5	8
Price			1			6
Reese			1			6
New Orleans	9	26	2	33/37	12/22	291
Opponents	28	31	1	56/60	23/31	487

NEW ORLEANS RECORD HOLDERS

Individual Records—Single Season

Category	Name	Performance
Rushing (Yds.)	Chuck Muncie, 1979	1198
Passing (Pct.)	Archie Manning, 1978	61.8
Passing (Yds.)	Archie Manning, 1980	3716
Passing (TDs.)	Archie Manning, 1980	23
Receiving (No.)	Tony Galbreath, 1978	74
Receiving (Yds.)	Wes Chandler, 1979	1069
Interceptions	Dave Whitsell, 1967	10
Punting (Avg.)	Tom McNeill, 1967	42.9
Punt Ret. (Avg.)	Gil Chapman, 1975	12.2
Kickoff Ret. (Avg.)	John Gilliam, 1967	30.1
Field Goals	Tom Dempsey, 1969	22
Touchdowns (Tot.)	Chuck Muncie, 1979	11
Points	Tom Dempsey, 1969	99

Team Records—Single Game

Category	Opponent, Date	Performance
Offense		
First Downs	vs. GB, 9/9/79	29
Total Points	vs. Sea, 11/21/76	51
	vs. StL, 11/2/69	51
Touchdowns	Six times; most recent, vs. Det, 10/21/79	4
Total Net Yards	vs. SF, 12/7/80	519
Net Yards Rushing	vs. KC, 9/26/76	299
Net Yards Passing	vs. SF, 12/7/80	376
Rushing Attempts	vs. Atl, 10/20/74	55
Passing Attempts	vs. SF, 10/15/78	55
Interceptions by	vs. GB, 9/10/78	53
Defense		
Net Yards Allowed	vs. Atl, 10/10/76	158
Yards Rushing Allowed	vs. Wash, 10/28/73	24
Net Passing		
Yards Passing Allowed	vs. Chi, 12/1/68	46

FIRST PLAYERS SELECTED

Year	Player, College, Position
1971	Archie Manning, Mississippi, QB
1972	Royce Smith, Georgia, G
1973	Derland Moore, Oklahoma, DE (2)
1974	Rick Middleton, Ohio State, LB
1975	Larry Burton, Purdue, WR
1976	Chuck Muncie, California, RB
1977	Joe Campbell, Maryland, DE
1978	Wes Chandler, Florida, WR
1979	Russell Erxleben, Texas, P-K
1980	Stan Brock, Colorado, T
1981	George Rogers, South Carolina, RB

SAINTS COACHING HISTORY
(55-142-5)

1967-70	Tom Fears*	13-34-2
1970-72	J.D. Roberts	7-25-3
1973-75	John North**	11-23-0
1975	Ernie Hefferle	1-7-0
1976-77	Hank Stram	7-21-0
1978-80	Dick Nolan***	15-29-0
1980	Dick Stanfel	1-3-0

*Released after seven games in 1970
**Released after six games in 1975
***Released after 12 games in 1980

NEW ORLEANS SAINTS 1981 VETERAN ROSTER

No.	Name	Pos.	Ht.	Wt.	NFL Exp.	Birth-date	Birthplace	College	Residence	Games in '80
80	t-Adams, Sam	G	6-3	260	10	9/20/48	Jasper, Tex.	Prairie View	Houston, Tex.	15
	Banks, Gordon	WR	5-9	175	2	3/12/58	Los Angeles, Calif.	Stanford	Los Angeles, Calif.	7
63	Bennett, Barry	DT	6-4	257	4	12/10/56	Long Prairie, Minn.	Concordia	Buffalo, Minn.	15
50	Bordelon, Ken	LB	6-4	226	5	8/26/54	New Orleans, La.	Louisiana State	Kenner, La.	7
67	Brock, Stan	T	6-6	275	2	6/8/58	Portland, Ore.	Colorado	Beaverton, Ore.	16
89	Chandler, Wes	WR	5-11	186	4	8/22/56	New Smyrna Beach, Fla.	Florida	New Orleans, La.	16
43	Collins, Larry	RB	5-11	189	3	8/8/55	San Antonio, Tex.	Texas A&I	Houston, Tex.	8
14	Erxleben, Russell	P	6-4	219	2	1/13/57	Seguin, Tex.	Texas	Austin, Tex.	16
59	Evans, Chuck	LB	6-3	235	2	12/19/56	West Covina, Calif.	Stanford	San Bernardino, Calif.	10
58	Federspiel, Joe	LB	6-2	230	10	5/6/50	Louisville, Ky.	Kentucky	Lexington, Ky.	15
72	Fultz, Mike	DT	6-5	278	5	1/28/54	Lincoln, Neb.	Nebraska	Metairie, La.	12
34	Galbreath, Tony	RB	6-1	230	6	1/29/54	Fulton, Mo.	Missouri	Fulton, Missouri	16
	Green, Sammy	LB	6-2	230	5	10/12/54	Bradenton, Fla.	Florida	Bothell, Wash.	2*
78	Grooms, Elois	DE	6-4	250	7	5/20/53	Tompkinsville, Ky.	Tennessee Tech	Kenner, La.	16
	Hardeman, Don	LB	6-2	235	7	7/9/56	Killeen, Tex.	Texas A&I	Tampa, Fla.	0*
87	Hardy, Larry	TE	6-3	230	4	8/13/53	Mendenhall, Miss.	Jackson State	Kenner, La.	16
82	Harris, Ike	WR	6-3	210	7	11/27/52	West Memphis, Ark.	Iowa State	Des Moines, Iowa	16
62	Hill, John	C	6-2	246	10	4/16/50	East Orange, N.J.	Lehigh	Destrahan, La.	16
51	Holloway, Stan	LB	6-2	218	2	9/28/57	Chattanooga, Tenn.	California	Oakland, Calif.	16
45	Holmes, Jack	FB	6-0	210	4	6/20/53	Rolling Fork, Miss.	Texas Southern	Houston, Tex.	16
52	Kovach, Jim	LB	6-2	225	3	5/1/56	San Antonio, Tex.	Kentucky	Kenner, La.	15
64	Lafary, Dave	T	6-7	280	5	1/13/55	Parma Heights, Ohio	Purdue	Kenner, La.	11
8	Manning, Archie	QB	6-3	200	11	5/19/49	Drew, Miss.	Mississippi	New Orleans, La.	15
23	Marshall, James	CB	6-0	182	2	9/8/53	Magnolia, Miss.	Jackson State	Jackson, Miss.	16
56	Mathis, Reggie	LB	6-2	220	6	3/18/56	Chattanooga, Tenn.	Oklahoma	Kenner, La.	16
84	Mauti, Rich	WR	6-0	190	6	5/25/54	Hollis, N.Y.	Penn State	Kenner, La.	16
26	Merkens, Guido	CB-S	6-1	200	4	8/14/55	San Antonio, Tex.	Sam Houston State	Houston, Tex.	4*
74	Moore, Derland	DT	6-4	253	9	10/7/51	Poplar Bluff, Mo.	Oklahoma	Kenner, La.	16
37	Myers, Tommy	S	6-0	180	10	10/24/50	Cohoes, N.Y.	Syracuse	Eugene, Ore.	16
49	Owens, Artie	WR	5-11	182	6	1/14/53	Montgomery, Ala.	West Virginia	Stroudsburg, Pa.	3
83	Owens, Tinker	WR	5-11	170	6	10/3/54	Miami, Okla.	Oklahoma	Kenner, La.	7
96	Parker, Steve	DE	6-6	265	2	12/8/56	Spokane, Wash.	Idaho	Kenner, La.	16
76	Pietrzak, Jim	C	6-5	260	7	2/21/53	Hamtramck, Mich.	Eastern Michigan	Coeur d'Alene, Idaho	4
22	Ray, Ricky	CB	5-11	170	3	2/2/56	Waynesboro, Va.	Norfolk State	New Baltimore, Mich.	7
1	Ricardo, Benny	K	5-10	180	5	5/30/57	Asuncion, Paraguay	San Diego State	Arlington, Va.	16
41	Rogers, Jimmy	RB	5-10	190	2	6/29/55	Earle, Ark.	Oklahoma	Dearborn Heights, Mich.	13
48	Schwartz, Don	S	6-1	191	4	2/24/56	Billings, Mont.	Washington State	Norman, Okla.	14
12	Scott, Bobby	QB	6-1	197	10	4/2/49	Chattanooga, Tenn.	Tennessee	Seattle, Wash.	16
47	Spivey, Mike	CB	6-0	198	5	3/10/54	Houston, Tex.	Colorado	Concord, Tenn.	5
68	Sturt, Fred	G	6-4	255	4	1/6/51	Toledo, Ohio	Bowling Green	Denver, Colo.	2
71	Taylor, James	T	6-4	265	4	8/12/56	Peoria, Ill.	Missouri	Waterville, Ohio	16
44	Waymer, Dave	CB	6-1	195	2	12/7/54	Brooklyn, N.Y.	Notre Dame	Columbia, Mo.	13
88	Williams, Brooks	TE	6-4	226	4	8/12/56	Baltimore, Md.	North Carolina	Charlotte, N.C.	16
30	Wilson, Wayne	FB	6-3	208	3	9/4/57	Montgomery County, Md.	Shepherd	Columbia, Md.	12
79	Zanders, Emanuel	G	6-1	248	8	7/31/51	Demopolis, Ala.	Jackson State	Kenner, La.	15

*Dorsey last active with Kansas City in '78; Green played 2 games with Houston in '80; Hardeman last active with Baltimore in '79; Merkens played 3 games with Houston, 1 with New Orleans.

t-Saints traded for Adams (New England).

Traded—Quarterback Guy Benjamin to San Francisco, tight end Henry Childs to Los Angeles through Washington.

Retired—Dave Washington, 11-year linebacker, 16 games in '80.

Also played with Saints in '80 —S Ray Brown (15 games), QB Ed Burns (2 games), DE Joe Campbell (5), CB Clarence Chapman (12), TE Henry Childs (13), C Larry Coombs (1), WR Tom Donovan (5), DE Tommy Hart (15), RB Chuck Muncie (4), DT Elex Price (14), DE Don Reese (12), RB Mike Strachan (3), G Robert Woods (10).

COACHING STAFF

Head Coach, O.A. (Bum) Phillips

Pro Career: Starts seventh season in the NFL and first with the Saints after signing with New Orleans as head coach on January 22, 1981. He had a career 59-38 record with the Oilers and twice played the AFC bridesmaid role with championship game losses to the Steelers in 1978 and 1979. Has been a constant playoff threat and finished with an 11-5 regular season record last fall with Houston. Joined the Oilers on January 25, 1975 as head coach and general manager after serving as assistant coach with the San Diego Chargers 1967-71 and as defensive coordinator with Oilers in 1974 prior to being named head coach.

Background: Guard at Lamar Junior College 1941, 1946-47, Stephen F. Austin 1948-49. College assistant coach at Texas A&M 1957, Houston 1963-66, Southern Methodist 1971-72, and Oklahoma State 1973. Head coach at University of Texas at El Paso 1962.

Personal: Born September 29, 1923 in Orange, Tex. Bum and his wife, Helen, live in Destrahan, La., and have six children—Wade, Susan, Cicely, Dee Jean, Andrea and Kim Ann.

ASSISTANT COACHES

King Hill, offensive coordinator; born November 8, 1936, Freeport, Tex., lives in Ormonv, La. Quarterback Rice, 1954-58. Pro quarterback St. Louis Cardinals, 1958-60, 1969, Philadelphia Eagles 1961-67, Minnesota Vikings 1968. Pro coach: Oilers 1972-80, first year with Saints.

John Levra, offensive backfield; born October 2, 1937, Arkma, Kan., lives in Destrahan, La. Guard-linebacker Pittsburgh (Kan.) State 1963-65. No pro playing experience. College coach: Stephen F. Austin 1971-74, Kansas 1975-78, North Texas State 1979. Pro coach: British Columbia Lions (CFL) 1979, first year with Saints.

Lamar McHan, receivers; born December 16, 1932, Lake Village Ark., lives in Metairie, La. Offensive back Arkansas 1951-53. Pro quarterback Chicago Cardinals 1954-58, Green Bay Packers 1959-60, Baltimore Colts 1961-62, San Francisco 49ers 1963. College coach: Northern Arizona 1969-70, Texas-Arlington 1971-73. Pro coach: New Orleans Saints 1974-75, rejoined Saints in 1978.

Wade Phillips, defensive coordinator; born June 21, 1947, Orange, Tex., lives in Destrahan, La. Linebacker Houston 1966-69. No pro playing experience. College coach: Oklahoma State 1973-75. Pro coach: Houston Oilers 1976-80, first year with Saints.

Harold Richardson, special teams; born September 27, 1944, Houston, lives in Destrahan, La. Tight end Southern Methodist University 1964-67. No pro playing experience. College coach: SMU 1971-72, Oklahoma State 1973-76, Texas Christian 1977-78, North Texas State 1979-80. Pro coach: First year with Saints.

Joe Spencer, offensive line; born August 15, 1923, Cleveland County, Okla., lives in Destrahan, La. Tackle Oklahoma State 1942-47. Pro tackle Brooklyn Dodgers (AAFC) 1948, Cleveland Browns 1949 Green Bay Packers 1950-52. College coach: Austin (Tex.) College 1952-60, Kansas University 1972-73. Pro coach: Houston Oilers 1961-65, Edmonton Eskimos (CFL) 1966-67, New York Jets 1968-70, St. Louis Cardinals 1971, Chicago Fire (WFL) 1974, Kansas City Chiefs 1975-80, first year with Saints.

Lance Van Zandt, defensive backfield; born January 19, 1939, Amarillo, Tex., lives in Destrahan, La. Attended Lamar University. College coach: New Mexico Highlands 1966-67, West Texas State 1968-69, Texas A&M 1970-71, Rice 1972, Oklahoma State 1973-74, Nebraska 1976-80. Pro coach: First year with Saints.

John Paul Young, linebackers; born December 31, 1939, Dallas, Tex., lives in River Ridge, La. Linebacker Texas-El Paso 1959-61. No pro playing experience. College coach: Texas-El Paso 1962-63, Southern Methodist 1967-68, Oklahoma State 1969, Texas A&M 1970-77. Pro coach: Houston Oilers 1978-80, first year with Saints.

Willie Zapalac, defensive line; born December 11, 1922, Sealy, Tex., lives in Ormonv, La. Fullback Texas A&M 1941-42, 1946. No pro playing experience. College coach: Texas A&M 1953-60, Texas Tech 1961-62, Oklahoma State 1963, Texas 1964-75. Pro coach: St. Louis Cardinals 1976-77, Buffalo Bills 1978-80, first year with Saints.

NEW ORLEANS SAINTS 1981 FIRST-YEAR ROSTER

Name	Pos.	Ht.	Wt.	Birth-date	Birthplace	College	Residence	How Acq.
Boyarsky, Jerry	DT	6-3	290	5/15/59	Scranton, Pa.	Pittsburgh	Olyphant, Pa.	D5a
Boyd, Lester (1)	LB	6-2	220	9/12/57	Franklin, Ky.	Kentucky	Franklin, Ky.	D6 ('80)
Brenner, Hoby	TE	6-4	240	6/2/59	Linwood, Calif.	Southern California	Fullerton, Calif.	D3a
Bunch, James	C-G	6-1	255	3/10/56	Richmond, Va.	Alabama	Tuscaloosa, Ala.	FA
Christian, Marvin (1)	RB	5-11	207	1/18/58	Quincy, Fla.	Tulane	Titusville, Fla.	FA
Copeny, Jerry (1)	RB	5-10	186	1/4/56	Chattanooga, Tenn.	Utah State	Chattanooga, Tenn.	FA
Echols, Donnie (1)	TE	6-4	235	12/16/57	Dallas, Tex.	Oklahoma State	Stillwater, Okla.	D8a
Evans, Kevin	CB-S	6-1	205	4/5/58	Little Rock, Ark.	Arkansas	N. Little Rock, Ark.	D10
Gajan, Hokie	RB	5-11	214	9/6/59	Baton Rouge, La.	Louisiana State	Baton Rouge, La.	D2
Gary, Russell	CB-S	5-11	195	7/31/59	Minneapolis, Minn.	Nebraska	Lincoln, Neb.	D8
Gladys, Eugene	LB	6-0	216	11/13/57	Monessen, Pa.	Penn State	State College, Pa.	FA
Gordon, Joe (1)	DE	6-3	270	8/18/56	New Orleans, La.	Grambling	Avondale, La.	FA
Grabenhorst, Ted (1)	T	6-6	265	1/21/57	Flint, Mich.	Michigan State	Mt. Morris, Mich.	FA
Hudson, Grant (1)	G	6-5	280	4/20/58	Levittown, Va.	Virginia	Charlottesville, Va.	FA
Hudson, Nat	G	6-3	265	10/11/57	Rome, Ga.	Georgia	Athens, Ga.	D6
Jackson, Ricky	LB	6-2	217	3/20/58	Pahokee, Fla.	Pittsburgh	Pahokee, Fla.	D2a
Jamison, Larry (1)	LB	6-3	220	4/29/56	Jackson, Miss.	Jackson State	Jackson, Miss.	FA
Jones, Quinn (1)	RB	6-2	220	9/4/56	Warner, Okla.	Tulsa	Tulsa, Okla.	FA
Kearns, Tom (1)	G	6-4	265	5/6/58	Lexington, Ky.	Kentucky	Lexington, Ky.	FA
Long, Ben (1)	LB	6-2	230	8/13/58	Cedar Rapids, Iowa	South Dakota	Cedar Rapids, Iowa	FA
McCollins, Dennis (1)	DT	6-5	252	3/8/57	New York, N.Y.	Southern	Richmond, Calif.	FA
McConnaughey, Tom	WR	6-2	185	8/1/57	Amarillo, Tex.	Central Arkansas	Federal Way, Wash.	D11
Mickens, Lester	WR	5-11	173	9/9/58	Charleston, S.C.	Kansas	Lawrence, Kan.	D5
Oubre, Louis	T	6-4	262	5/15/58	New Orleans, La.	Oklahoma	Norman, Okla.	FA
Pensick, Dan (1)	DE	6-5	255	4/16/58	Columbus, Neb.	Nebraska	Columbus, Neb.	D6a
Poe, Johnnie	CB-S	6-1	182	8/29/59	St. Louis, Mo.	Missouri	Columbia, Mo.	FA
Ratliff, Ernest (1)	LB	6-3	230	3/9/54	New Orleans, La.	Tulane	New Orleans, La.	FA
Redd, Glen	LB	6-2	229	6/17/58	Ogden, Utah	Brigham Young	Orem, Utah	D6b
Rippentrop, Bob (1)	DE	6-6	245	8/19/56	San Mateo, Calif.	Fresno State	Fresno, Calif.	FA
Rogers, George	RB	6-2	220	12/8/58	Duluth, Ga.	South Carolina	Duluth, Ga.	D1
Simpson, Phillip (1)	TE	6-4	230	3/11/58	Nacogdoches, Tex.	Texas A&M	Nacogdoches, Tex.	FA
Tyler, Toussaint	RB	6-1	212	3/19/59	Los Angeles, Calif.	Washington	Seattle, Wash.	D9
Vaughn, Michael (1)	WR	5-11	180	11/12/57	Tuskegee, Ala.	Southern	Baton Rouge, La.	FA
Warren, Frank	DE	6-4	275	9/14/59	Birmingham, Ala.	Auburn	Birmingham, Ala.	D3
Washington, Burks (1)	LB	6-2	220	10/9/56	Port Arthur, Tex.	North Texas State	Port Arthur, Tex.	FA
Wilks, Jim	DT	6-4	252	3/12/58	Los Angeles, Calif.	San Diego State	San Diego, Calif.	D12
Williams, Kevin	WR	5-8	164	1/7/58	Los Angeles, Calif.	Southern California	Mar Vista, Calif.	D7
Williams, Mike (1)	S	5-11	186	12/21/55	Abilene, Tex.	Texas A&M	Abilene, Tex.	FA
Williams, Rickie (1)	RB	6-1	228	2/13/58	Houston, Tex.	McMurry	Houston, Tex.	FA
Wilson, Dave*	QB	6-3	213	4/27/59	Anaheim, Calif.	Illinois	Anaheim, Calif.	D1
Young, Ernest (1)	CB-S	5-9	182	2/13/54	Vicksburg, Miss.	Alcorn State	Vicksburg, Miss.	FA

*Selected in 1981 Supplemental Draft

Players who report to an NFL team for the first time are designated on rosters as rookies (R). If a player reported to an NFL training camp in a previous year but was not on the active squad for three or more regular season or postseason games, he is listed on the first-year roster and designated by a (1). Thereafter, a player who is on the active squad for three or more regular season games is credited with an additional year of playing experience.

NOTES

134

New York Giants

National Football Conference
Eastern Division

Team Colors: Blue, Red, and White

Giants Stadium
East Rutherford, New Jersey 07073
Telephone: (201) 935-8111

Club Officials

President: Wellington T. Mara
Vice President-Treasurer: Timothy J. Mara
Vice President-Secretary: Raymond J. Walsh
General Manager: George Young
Assistant General Manager: Terry Bledsoe
Director of Player Personnel: Tom Boisture
Director of Pro Personnel: Jim Trimble
Director of Media Services: Ed Croke
Director of Promotions: Tom Power
Director of Special Projects: Victor Del Guercio
Box Office Treasurer: Jim Gleason
Trainer Emeritus: John Dziegiel
Head Trainer: Ronnie Barnes
Trainers: John Johnson, Dave Barringer
Equipment Manager: Ed Wagner, Jr.

Stadium: Giants Stadium **Capacity:** 76,891
East Rutherford, N.J. 07073
Playing Surface: AstroTurf
Training Camp: Pace University
Pleasantville, New York 10570

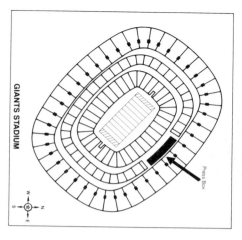

GIANTS STADIUM

Press Box

1981 SCHEDULE

Preseason

Aug. 8	at Chicago	6:00
Aug. 15	**Baltimore**	8:00
Aug. 22	**New York Jets**	8:00
Aug. 29	at Pittsburgh	6:00

Regular Season

Sept. 6	**Philadelphia**	1:00
Sept. 13	at Washington	1:00
Sept. 20	**New Orleans**	1:00
Sept. 27	at Dallas	3:00
Oct. 4	**Green Bay**	1:00
Oct. 11	**St. Louis**	4:00
Oct. 18	at Seattle	1:00
Oct. 25	at Atlanta	1:00
Nov. 1	**New York Jets**	1:00
Nov. 8	vs. Green Bay (Milwaukee)	12:00
Nov. 15	**Washington**	4:00
Nov. 22	at Philadelphia	1:00
Nov. 29	at San Francisco	1:00
Dec. 6	**Los Angeles**	1:00
Dec. 13	at St. Louis	12:00
Dec. 19	**Dallas** (Saturday)	12:30

1980 TEAM STATISTICS

	New York Giants	Opp.
Total First Downs	261	336
Rushing	100	156
Passing	136	160
Penalty	25	20
Third Down Efficiency	91/260	106/234
Third Down Percentage	35.0	45.3
Total Net Yards	4339	5752
Total Offensive Plays	1044	1060
Avg. Gain per Play	4.2	5.4
Avg. Gain per Game	271.2	359.5
Net Yards Rushing	1730	2507
Total Rushing Plays	483	584
Avg. Gain per Rush	3.6	4.3
Avg. Gain Rushing per Game	108.1	156.7
Net Yards Passing	2609	3245
Lost Attempting to Pass	47/322	28/224
Gross Yards Passing	2931	3469
Attempts/Completions	514/245	448/255
Percent Completed	47.7	56.9
Avg. Net Passing per Game	163.1	202.8
Punts/Avg.	94/44.8	70/40.3
Punt Returns/Avg.	37/8.2	58/8.7
Kickoff Returns/Avg.	71/18.6	52/20.1
Interceptions/Avg. Ret.	18/6.3	25/15.0
Penalties/Yards	98/962	108/862
Fumbles/Ball Lost	33/18	48/23
Total Points	249	425
Avg. Points per Game	15.6	26.6
Touchdowns	29	55
Rushing	10	31
Passing	19	22
Returns and Recoveries	0	2
Field Goals	16/24	27/29
Conversions	27/29	51/55
Safeties	0	1

1980 TEAM RECORD

Preseason (1-3)

New York Giants		Opponents
0	Pittsburgh	13
9	Denver	6
20	Baltimore	37
7	New York Jets	32
36		88

Regular Season (4-12)

New York Giants		Opponents	Att.
41	St. Louis	35	49,122
21	*Washington	23	73,343
3	Philadelphia	35	70,767
7	*Los Angeles	28	73,414
3	Dallas	24	59,126
16	*Philadelphia	31	71,051
7	San Diego	44	50,397
9	*Denver	14	67,598
13	Tampa Bay	30	68,256
38	*Dallas	35	68,343
27	*Green Bay	21	72,368
21	San Francisco	12	38,574
7	*St. Louis	23	65,852
27	Seattle	21	51,617
13	Washington	16	44,443
17	*Oakland	33	61,287
249		425	985,558

*Home Game

Score by Periods

New York Giants	37	94	37	81	— 249
Opponents	68	153	104	100	— 425

Attendance

Home 553,256   Away 432,302   Total 985,558

Single game home record, 76,490 (11-4-79)
Single season home record, 557,530 (1979)

1980 INDIVIDUAL STATISTICS

Rushing

	Att	Yds	Avg	LG	TD
Taylor	147	580	3.9	35	4
Heater	111	360	3.2	11	3
Perry	59	272	4.6	17	1
Simms	36	190	5.3	20	1
Matthews	64	180	2.8	18	0
Hicks	19	50	2.6	9	0
Hogan	22	46	2.1	9	1
Garrett	9	31	3.4	10	0
Brunner	10	18	1.8	12	0
Laidlaw	5	10	2.0	3	0
Pittman	1	-7	-7.0	-7	0
New York Giants	483	1730	3.6	35	10
Opponents	584	2507	4.3	56	31

Field Goal Success

Distance	1-19	20-29	30-39	40-49	50 Over
Made-Att.	0-0	5-6	4-6	5-6	2-6

Passing

	Att	Comp	Pct	Yds	TD	Int	LG	Tkld	Rate
Simms	402	193	48.0	2321	15	19	50t	36/233	58.9
Brunner	112	52	46.4	610	4	0	42	10/76	53.0
Jennings	0	0	0.0	0	0	0	—	1/13	—
N.Y. Giants	514	245	47.7	2931	19	25	50t	47/322	57.5
Opponents	448	255	56.9	3469	22	18	66t	28/224	—

Receiving

	No	Yds	Avg	LG	TD
Gray	52	777	14.9	50t	10
Taylor	33	253	7.7	42	0
Mullady	28	391	14.0	42	2
Pittman	25	308	12.3	22	0
Friede	21	350	16.7	48	0
Shirk	21	211	10.0	21	1
Matthews	19	86	4.5	12	0
Perkins	14	193	13.8	58t	3
Heater	10	139	13.9	43	0
Perry	8	84	10.5	25	0
Garrett	5	69	13.8	32t	1
Hogan	5	46	9.2	12	0
Laidlaw	2	16	8.0	8	0
Hicks	1	4	4.0	4	0
Martin	1	4	4.0	4t	1
New York Giants	245	2931	12.0	58t	19
Opponents	255	3469	13.6	66t	22

Interceptions

	No	Yds	Avg	LG	TD
Dennis	5	68	13.6	28	0
Reece	3	24	8.0	10	0
Van Pelt	2	3	1.0	3	0
Woolford	1	7	7.0	7	0
Marion	1	6	6.0	6	0
Haynes	1	5	5.0	5	0
Jackson	1	0	0.0	0	0
Hebert	1	0	0.0	0	0
Henry	1	0	0.0	0	0
New York Giants	18	113	6.3	28	0
Opponents	25	376	15.0	56	1

Punting

	No	Yds	Avg	LG	In 20	TD
Jennings	94	4211	44.8	66	16	0
New York Giants	94	4211	44.8	66	16	0
Opponents	70	2819	40.3	55	9	0

Punt Returns

	No	FC	Yds	Avg	LG	TD
Garrett	35	11	287	8.2	66	0
Reece	2	1	15	7.5	15	0
Henry						
New York Giants	37	13	302	8.2	66	0
Opponents	58	4	506	8.7	34	0

Kickoff Returns

	No	Yds	Avg	LG	TD
Reece	24	471	19.6	35	0
Garrett	28	527	18.8	41	0
Heater	5	103	20.6	29	0
N. Johnson	5	89	17.8	23	0
Pittman	2	41	20.5	18	0
Haynes	2	40	20.0	22	0
McLaughlin	2	27	13.5	15	0
Laidlaw	1	18	18.0	18	0
Lapka	1	3	3.0	3	0
Wyatt					
New York Giants	71	1319	18.6	41	0
Opponents	52	1047	20.1	40	1

Scoring

	TD R	TD P	TD Rt	PAT	FG	TP
Danelo				27/28	16/24	75
Gray		10				60
Taylor	4					24
Heater	3					18
Perkins		3				18
Mullady		2				12
Perry	1	1				12
Garrett		1				6
Hogan	1					6
Martin		1				6
Shirk		1				6
Simms	1					6
N.Y. Giants	10	19	0	27/29	16/24	249
Opponents	31	22	2	51/55	14/24	425

NEW YORK GIANTS RECORD HOLDERS

Individual Records—Single Season

Category	Name	Performance
Rushing (Yds.)	Ron Johnson, 1972	1182
Passing (Pct.)	Norm Snead, 1972	60.3
Passing (Yds.)	Y.A. Tittle, 1962	3224
Passing (TDs.)	Y.A. Tittle, 1963	36
Receiving (No.)	Del Shofner, 1961	68
Receiving (Yds.)	Homer Jones, 1967	1209
Interceptions	Otto Schnellbacher, 1951	11
	Jim Patton, 1958	11
Punting (Avg.)	Kay Eakin, 1941	47.4
Punt Ret. (Avg.)	Emlen Tunnell, 1951	14.4
Kickoff Ret. (Avg.)	Jack Salschneider,1949	31.6
Field Goals	Pete Gogolak, 1970	25
Touchdowns (Tot.)	Gene Roberts, 1949	17
Points	Pete Gogolak, 1970	107

Team Records—Single Game

Category	Opponent, Date	Performance
Offense		
First Downs	vs. StL, 12/7/69	33
Total Points	vs. Phil, 11/26/72	62
Touchdowns	vs. Phil, 10/15/33	8
	vs. Balt, 11/19/50	8
	vs. Phil, 11/26/72	8
Total Net Yards	vs. NY Yanks, 12/3/50	625
Net Yards Rushing	vs. Balt, 11/19/50	423
Net Yards Passing	vs. Wash, 10/28/62	505
Rushing Attempts	vs. Phil, 10/3/47	61
Passing Attempts	vs. Pitt, 12/5/48	53
Interceptions by	vs. GB, 11/21/48	8
	vs. NY Yanks, 12/16/51	8
Defense		
Net Yards Allowed	vs. Brk Dod, 10/17/43	48
Net Rushing Yards Allowed	vs. Brk Dod, 10/17/43	-24
Net Passing Yards Allowed	vs. Wash, 12/11/60	-6

FIRST PLAYERS SELECTED

Year	Player, College, Position
1970	Jim Files, Oklahoma, LB
1971	Rocky Thompson, W. Texas State, WR
1972	Eldridge Small, Texas A&I, DB
1973	Brad Van Pelt, Michigan St., LB (2)
1974	John Hicks, Ohio State, G
1975	Al Simpson, Colorado State, T (2)
1976	Troy Archer, Colorado, DE
1977	Gary Jeter, Southern California, DT
1978	Gordon King, Stanford, T
1979	Phil Simms, Morehead State, QB
1980	Mark Haynes, Colorado, DB
1981	Lawrence Taylor, North Carolina, LB

GIANTS COACHING HISTORY (382-325-31)

1925	Bob Folwell	8-4-0
1926	Joe Alexander	8-4-1
1927-28	Earl Potteiger	15-8-3
1929-30	LeRoy Andrews	26-5-1
1931-53	Steve Owen	154-108-17
1954-60	Jim Lee Howell	54-29-4
1961-68	Al Sherman	57-54-4
1969-73	Alex Webster	29-40-1
1974-76	Bill Arnsparger*	7-28-0
1976-78	John McVay	14-23-0
1979-80	Ray Perkins	10-22-0

*Released after seven games in 1976

NEW YORK GIANTS 1981 VETERAN ROSTER

No.	Name	Pos.	Ht.	Wt.	NFL Exp.	Birth-date	Birthplace	College	Residence	Games in '80
62	Apuna, Ben	LB	6-1	222	2	6/26/57	Honolulu, Hawaii	Arizona State	Mesa, Ariz.	10
60	Benson, Brad	T	6-3	258	4	11/25/55	Altoona, Pa.	Penn State	Altoona, Pa.	15
23	Blount, Tony	S	6-1	195	2	11/5/58	Atlanta, Ga.	Virginia	Passaic, N.J.	3
12	Brunner, Scott	QB	6-5	200	2	3/24/57	Sellersville, Pa.	Delaware	Livingston, N.J.	16
53	Carson, Harry	LB	6-2	235	6	11/26/53	Florence, S.C.	South Carolina State	Florence, S.C.	8
56	†Clack, Jim	C	6-3	250	11	10/26/47	Rocky Mount, N.C.	Wake Forest	Rocky Mount, N.C.	16
18	Danelo, Joe	K	5-9	166	7	9/2/53	Spokane, Wash.	Washington State	San Pedro, Calif.	16
46	Dennis, Mike	CB	5-10	190	2	6/6/58	Los Angeles, Calif.	Wyoming	Pasadena, Calif.	13
95	Donovan, Tom	WR	6-0	179	2	1/13/57	Flushing, N.Y.	Penn State	State College, Pa.	8*
48	Dove, Jerome	CB	6-2	193	5	10/3/53	Newport News, Va.	Colorado State	San Diego, Calif.	16*
63	Falcon, Terry	G	6-3	260	4	8/30/55	Culbertson, Mont.	Montana	Dumont, N.J.	13
22	Felton, Eric	S-CB	6-0	200	4	10/8/55	Austin, Tex.	Texas Tech	Dallas, Tex.	16
88	Friede, Mike	WR	6-3	205	2	9/22/57	Mineral Wells, Tex.	Indiana	Wayne, N.J.	8*
25	Garrett, Alvin	WR	5-7	178	2	10/1/56	Greenwood, Miss.	Angelo State	Greenwood, Miss.	16
83	Gray, Earnest	WR	6-3	195	3	3/2/57	Memphis, Tenn.	Memphis State	Memphis, Tenn.	16
37	Harris, Don	S	6-2	190	4	2/8/54	Elizabeth, N.J.	Rutgers	Reston, Va.	11
36	Haynes, Mark	CB	5-11	185	2	11/6/58	Kansas City, Kan.	Colorado	Boulder, Colo.	15
27	Heater, Larry	RB	5-11	205	2	1/9/58	Kansas City, Kan.	Arizona	Las Vegas, Nev.	14
26	Hebert, Bud	S	6-0	190	2	10/12/56	Beaumont, Tex.	Oklahoma	Beaumont, Tex.	16
47	Henry, Steve	S	6-2	190	3	3/5/57	St. Petersburg, Fla.	Emporia State	St. Petersburg, Fla.	5
79	Hughes, Ernie	G	6-3	250	3	1/24/55	Dallas, Tex.	Notre Dame	Sunnyvale, Calif.	3*
24	Jackson, Terry	CB	5-10	185	4	12/9/55	Sherman, Tex.	San Diego State	Edgewater, N.J.	8
13	Jennings, Dave	P	6-4	205	8	1/4/55	New York, N.Y.	St. Lawrence	Upper Saddle River, N.J.	16
33	Jeter, Gary	DE	6-4	260	5	6/11/51	Weirton, W. Va.	Southern California	Los Angeles, Calif.	14
70	Lapka, Myron	DT	6-4	255	2	5/10/56	Canonsburg, Pa.	Southern California	Seacaucus, N.J.	0*
71	Kotar, Doug	RB	5-11	205	8	1/24/55	New York, N.Y.	Kentucky	Weir, Mass.	16
54	Linnin, Chris	DT	6-4	250	2	5/4/57	Pasadena, Calif.	Southern California	Seattle, Wash.	0*
51	Lloyd, Dan	LB	6-3	232	5	11/9/53	Heber City, Utah	Washington	Rutherford, N.J.	10
72	Marion, Frank	LB	6-2	225	9	9/1/51	Dallas, Tex.	Florida A&M	Miami, Fla.	0*
55	Martin, George	DE	6-3	222	3	2/3/56	Madison, Wis.	Oregon	Vacaville, Calif.	11
84	Matthews, Bo	RB	6-3	228	5	3/16/51	Jersey City, N.J.	Colorado	Huntsville, Ala.	12
89	McGriff, Curtis	DT	6-4	245	2	2/16/53	Canonsburg, Pa.	Alabama	Huntsville, Ala.	16
44	McLaughlin, Joe	LB	6-3	228	7	11/16/51	Greenville, S.C.	Massachusetts	Gordon, Ala.	8
75	Mullady, Tom	TE	6-5	270	3	4/21/53	Mount Brook, Fla.	Southwestern at Memphis	Vacaville, Calif.	16
41	Olander, Cliff	QB	6-1	222	5	8/14/57	Franklin, Tex.	New Mexico State	Huntsville, Ala.	16
76	Patterson, Don	CB	6-3	205	8	4/21/53	Gloster, Miss.	Georgia Tech	Atlanta, Ga.	10
52	Perkins, Johnny	WR	6-1	205	2	11/15/51	Memphis, Tenn.	Abilene Christian	Granbury, Tex.	11
81	Perry, Leon	FB	6-2	224	5	5/17/58	Franklin, Tex.	Mississippi	Jackson, Miss.	10
15	Pittman, Danny	WR	6-2	205	2	7/1/57	Gloster, Miss.	Wyoming	Pasadena, Calif.	6
21	Reece, Beasley	S	5-11	195	6	1/30/57	Waco, Tex.	North Texas State	Washington Township, N.J.	16
86	Rivers, Nate	RB	6-2	215	3	4/22/55	Columbus, Ohio	South Carolina State	Orangeburg, S.C.	2
30	Saalfield, Kelly	C	6-1	246	5	10/31/57	Hartford, Conn.	Nebraska	Grand Island, Neb.	7
82	Shirk, Gary	TE	6-3	220	6	8/14/57	Gray, Ga.	Morehead State	Marysville, Ohio	16
28	Simmons, Roy	G	6-3	264	2	4/3/58	Savannah, Ga.	Georgia Tech	Atlanta, Ga.	3
59	Simms, Phil	QB	6-3	216	3	11/3/55	Springfield, Mass.	Morehead State	Lyndhurst, N.J.	13
34	Sinnott, John	T	6-4	275	2	11/8/56	Wexford, Ireland	Brown	Dedham, Mass.	0*
87	Skorupan, John	LB	6-3	225	9	5/17/51	Beaver, Pa.	Penn State	Beaver, Pa.	12
57	Small, George	DT	6-4	275	2	4/18/58	Shreveport, La.	North Carolina A&T	Englewood, N.J.	7
11	Tabor, Phil	DT	6-3	250	3	1/18/58	Houston, Tex.	Oklahoma	Norman, Okla.	12
69	Taylor, Billy	RB	6-0	215	4	1/18/56	San Antonio, Tex.	Texas Tech	Marysville, Ohio	16
65	Tobin, Steve	C	6-4	258	2	11/30/56	Columbus, Ohio	Houston	Carlstadt, N.J.	16
78	Turner, J.T.	G	6-3	250	2	7/6/56	Breckenridge, Minn.	Duke	Ringwood, N.J.	4
80	Turner, Kevin	LB	6-3	225	5	3/29/57	Fremont, Calif.	Pacific	Fargo, N.D.	12
38	Van Pelt, Brad	LB	6-5	235	9	4/17/53	Owosso, Mich.	Michigan State	Stockton, Calif.	16
52	Weston, Jeff	G	6-3	250	2	2/5/58	Philadelphia, Pa.	Notre Dame	Owosso, Mich.	3
68	Whittington, Mike	G	6-2	225	5	4/5/51	Louisville, Ky.	Notre Dame	Rochester, N.Y.	16
66	Wyatt, Kervin	LB	6-3	250	2	4/10/56	Jersey City, N.J.	Maryland	Miami, Fla.	15
10			6-3	235	9	4/5/51	Owosso, Mich.			6
73			6-2	220	2	8/9/58	Miami, Fla.	Miami, Fla.		16
58			6-1	235	2	10/17/57	Washington D.C.	Hillcrest Heights, Md.		4

*Donovan played 5 games with New Orleans; Dove played 16 games with San Diego in '80; Friede played 1 game with Detroit, 7 with Giants; Hughes played 3 games with San Francisco; Kotar, Lloyd missed '80 season due to injury/illness. Olander was active for 16 games but did not play; Sinnott was active for 10 games but did not play.

†Option playout; subject to developments.

Retired—Vernon Holland, 10-year tackle, 12 games in '80.

Also played with Giants in '80 —RB Art Best (1 game), LB Phil Cancik (5), RB Jim Culbreath (10), RB Eddie Hicks (3), RB Mike Hogan (6), RB Scott Laidlaw (7), DE Dale Markham (1), DT Mike McCoy (2), CB Doug Nettles (2), C Ralph Perretta (6), LB Whip Walton (3), S Garry Woolford (12).

COACHING STAFF

Head Coach, Ray Perkins

Pro Career: Starts third season as an NFL head coach. Came to Giants from San Diego Chargers, where he was offensive coordinator in 1978. Prior to that, he had been receivers and tight ends coach with New England Patriots from 1974-77. A seventh round draft choice of the Baltimore Colts, he spent five seasons (1967-71) with the Colts and played in two Super Bowls. In those five seasons, he caught 93 passes for 1,538 yards and 11 touchdowns. Career record: 10-22.

Background: Outstanding split end at Alabama from 1964-66, winning All-America honors in his junior season. Also was named most valuable player in the Southeastern Conference in 1966. Coached one year at Mississippi State in 1972 before entering pro coaching ranks.

Personal: Born November 6, 1941, Mount Olive, Miss. He and his wife Carolyn live in East Rutherford, N.J. and have two children — Tony and Mike.

ASSISTANT COACHES

Ernie Adams, offensive assistant; born March 31, 1953, Waltham, Mass. No college or pro playing experience. College coach: Northwestern 1973-75. Pro coach: New England Patriots 1976-78, third year with Giants.

Bill Austin, offensive line; born October 18, 1928, San Pedro, Calif., lives in East Rutherford, N.J. Tackle Oregon State 1947-49. Pro guard New York Giants 1949-50, 1953-57. College coach: Wichita 1958. Pro coach: Green Bay Packers 1959-64. Los Angeles Rams 1965, Pittsburgh Steelers (head coach) 1966-68, Washington Redskins 1969-70 (head coach) 1973-77, Chicago Bears 1971, St. Louis Cardinals 1972, second year with Giants.

Bill Belichick, special teams-linebackers; born April 16, 1952, Nashville, Tenn., lives in East Rutherford, N.J. Center-tight end Wesleyan 1972-74. No pro playing experience. Pro coach: Baltimore Colts 1975, Detroit Lions 1976-77, Denver Broncos 1978, third year with Giants.

Romeo Crennell, special assignments; born June 18, 1947, Lynchburg, Va., lives in East Rutherford, N.J., Defensive lineman Western Kentucky 1966-69. No pro playing experience. College coach: Western Kentucky 1970-74, Texas Tech 1975-77, Mississippi 1978-79, Georgia Tech 1980. Pro coach: First year with Giants.

Fred Glick, defensive backs; born February 25, 1937, Aurora, Colo., lives in East Rutherford, N.J. Quarterback-defensive back Colorado State 1955-57. Pro defensive back Chicago Cardinals 1959-60, St. Louis Cardinals 1960, Houston Oilers 1961-66. College coach: New Mexico State 1968, Arizona 1969-72, Arizona State 1973-77. Pro coach: Norfolk Neptunes (Continental League) 1967, St. Louis Cardinals 1978-79, New York Giants 1980, first year with Giants.

Pat Hodgson, receivers; born January 30, 1944, Columbus, Ga., lives in East Rutherford, N.J. Tight end Georgia 1963-65. Pro tight end Washington Redskins 1966. Minnesota Vikings 1967. College coach: Georgia 1968-70, 1972-77, Florida State 1971, Texas Tech 1978. Pro coach: San Diego Chargers 1978, third year with Giants.

Lamar Leachman, defensive line; born August 7, 1934, Cartersville, Ga., lives in East Rutherford, N.J. Center-linebacker Tennessee 1952-55. No pro playing experience. College coach: Richmond 1966-67, Georgia Tech 1968-71, Memphis State 1972, South Carolina 1973. Pro coach: New York Stars (WFL) 1974, Toronto Argonauts (CFL) 1975-77, Montreal Alouettes (CFL) 1978-79, second year with Giants.

Bob Lord, offensive backfield; born February 3, 1930, Brunswick, Maine, lives in East Rutherford, N.J. Running back-safety Colorado State 1954-56. No pro playing experience. College coach: Springfield 1958, Wesleyan 1959, North Park College 1960-63 (head coach), Macalester 1964-65 (head coach), Wake Forest 1966-68, Appalachian State 1969-71, Massachusetts 1972-73. Pro coach: Chicago Bears 1974, Green Bay Packers 1975-78, third year with Giants.

Bill Parcells, defensive coordinator-linebackers; born August 22, 1941, Englewood, N.J., lives in East Rutherford, N.J. Linebacker Wichita State 1961-63. No pro playing experience. College coach: Hastings, Neb. 1964, Wichita State 1965, Army 1966-69, Florida State 1970-72, Vanderbilt 1973-74, Texas Tech 1975-77, Air Force 1978 (head coach). Pro coach: New England Patriots 1980, first year with Giants.

NEW YORK GIANTS 1981 FIRST-YEAR ROSTER

Name	Pos.	Ht.	Wt.	Birth-date	Birthplace	College	Residence	How Acq.
Ard, Billy	G	6-3	250	3/12/59	East Orange, N.J.	Wake Forest	Watchung, N.J.	D8b
Ashley, Ralph (1)	LB	6-0	235	6/23/58	McComb, Miss.	Mississippi College	McComb, Miss.	FA
Barker, Mike	T	6-4	272	12/3/59	Bogalusa, La.	Grambling	Grambling, La.	D10
Bethea, Ken	WR	5-11	175	10/11/57	Jersey City, N.J.	St. Peters	Jersey City, N.J.	FA
Bowers, Sam (1)	TE	6-4	230	12/22/57	White Plains, N.Y.	Fordham	Hempstead, N.Y.	FA
Bright, Leon	RB	5-9	192	5/19/55	Merritt Island, Fla.	Florida State	Merritt Island, Fla.	FA
Brownlee, Cedric	FB	5-10	210	3/7/58	Fayetteville, Tenn.	Jacksonville State	Huntsville, Ala.	FA
Burt, Jim	DT	6-1	255	6/7/59	Buffalo, N.Y.	Miami	Orchard Park, N.Y.	FA
Carey, Dwight (1)	DE	6-3	247	9/16/54	Dallas, Tex.	Texas-Arlington	Arlington, Tex.	D4
Chatman, Clifford	RB	6-2	225	3/13/59	Clinton, Okla.	Central State	Oklahoma City, Okla.	D4
Cook, Chuck	S	6-1	193	11/29/58	Andulsia, Ala.	Southern Mississippi	Hattiesburg, Miss.	FA
Cornelius, Pat	C	6-3	250	3/17/58	Green Bay, Wis.	Utah State	Quincy, Mass.	FA
Edwards, N.L.	CB-S	5-9	175	4/13/59	Wichita Falls, Tex.	SE Oklahoma State	Wichita Falls, Tex.	FA
Flowers, Larry (1)	CB	6-1	190	4/19/58	Temple, Tex.	Texas A&I	Temple, Tex.	FA
Frageorgia, David	WR	5-11	185	12/19/57	Providence, R.I.	Rhode Island	Narragansett, R.I.	FA
Gordon, Bruce (1)	LB	6-1	225	11/27/57	Ridley Park, Pa.	Temple	Ridley Park, Pa.	FA
Hoover, Melvin	WR	5-11	171	9/21/59	Charlotte, N.C.	Southern Methodist	Charlotte, N.C.	D6
Hunt, Byron	LB	6-4	230	12/17/58	Longview, Tex.	Arizona State	Dallas, Tex.	D9
Ireland, Bob	CB-S	5-11	193	12/15/58	Brockport, N.Y.	Holy Cross	Brockport, N.Y.	D7
Jackson, Louis	RB	5-11	195	1/27/58	Fresno, Calif.	Cal Poly-SLO	Fresno, Calif.	FA
Johnson, Ray	RB	5-10	196	1/20/58	Charlottesville, Va.	Ferrum Jr. College	Charlottesville, Va.	FA
Jones, Craig (1)	K	5-11	170	7/22/58	Alexandria, Va.	VMI	Lexington, Va.	FA
Kimball, Bruce (1)	G	6-2	260	8/19/56	Beverly, Mass.	Massachusetts	Newbury, Mass.	FA
Kirchner, Bruce (1)	DT	6-2	255	8/7/56	Baltimore, Md.	Colorado	Longmont, Colo.	FA
Kurdyla, Kevin	T	6-3	260	6/14/59	East Orange, N.J.	Rutgers	Newark, N.J.	FA
Lazor, Jack (1)	LB	6-2	230	5/17/57	Warren, Ohio	Kent State	Kent, Ohio	D12
Maher, Mike	TE	6-5	230	8/5/59	Macomb, Ill.	Western Illinois	Macomb, Ill.	D3
Mistler, John	WR	6-2	186	10/28/58	Far Rockaway, N.Y.	Arizona State	Tucson, Ariz.	D3
Morucci, Mike (1)	RB	6-1	220	10/9/58	Bloomsburg, Pa.	Bloomsburg	Bloomsburg, Pa.	FA
Neill, Bill	DT	6-4	255	3/15/59	Norristown, Pa.	Pittsburgh	Bloomfield, N.J.	D5
O'Neal, Bill	RB	6-1	215	8/21/58	Sylacauga, Ala.	Tuskegee	Sylacauga, Ala.	D6a
Powers, John	G	6-3	265	4/6/58	Chicago, Ill.	Michigan	Oak Park, Ill.	D8
Reed, Mark	QB	6-3	195	2/21/59	Moorhead, Minn.	Moorhead	Moorhead, Minn.	D8a
Richardson, Dace	RB	5-11	205	6/21/59	Springfield, Ill.	Western Illinois	Springfield, Ill.	FA
Scott, George	RB	6-1	210	1/6/58	Far Rockaway, N.Y.	Maryland	Inwood, N.Y.	FA
Shantz, Joe	T-G	6-3	270	1/16/58	Springfield, Mo.	Arkansas	Buffalo, Mo.	FA
Slawson, Mike	WR	6-2	184	6/11/59	Sherman, Tex.	Citadel	Ladson, S.C.	FA
Snow, Mike (1)	S	6-1	195	9/20/57	Sunnyside, Wash.	Washington State	Forks, Wash.	FA
Stewart, Larry (1)	DT	6-4	274	8/17/57	Portsmouth, Va.	Maryland	Chesapeake, Va.	FA
Taylor, Lawrence	LB	6-3	237	2/4/59	Williamsburg, Va.	North Carolina	Williamsburg, Va.	D1
Young, Dave	TE	6-6	242	2/9/59	Akron, Ohio	Purdue	West Lafayette, Ind.	D2

Players who report to an NFL team for the first time are designated on rosters as rookies (R). If a player reported to an NFL training camp in a previous year but was not on the active squad for three or more regular season or postseason games, he is listed on the first-year roster and designated by a (1). Thereafter, a player who is on the active squad for three or more regular season games is credited with an additional year of playing experience.

NOTES

138

Philadelphia Eagles

National Football Conference
Eastern Division

Team Colors: Kelly Green, Silver, and White
Philadelphia Veterans Stadium
Broad Street and Pattison Avenue
Philadelphia, Pennsylvania 19148
Telephone: (215) 463-2500

Club Officials
President: Leonard H. Tose
General Manager: Jim Murray
Legal Counsel: Susan Fletcher
Business Manager: Jim Borden
Director of Public Relations: Jim Gallagher
Public Relations Assistant: Chick McElrone
Ticket Manager: Hugh Ortman
Director of Player Personnel: Carl Peterson
Player Personnel Consultant: Herman Ball
Assistant Director of Player Personnel: Jackie Graves
Sales and Marketing: Sam Procopio
Talent Scouts: Bill Baker, Jim Katcavage, Phil Neri
Trainer: Otto Davis
Equipment Manager: Rusty Sweeney

Stadium: Philadelphia Veterans Stadium •
Capacity: 71,524
Broad Street and Pattison Avenue
Philadelphia, Pennsylvania 19148
Playing Surface: AstroTurf
Training Camp: West Chester State College
West Chester, Pennsylvania 19380

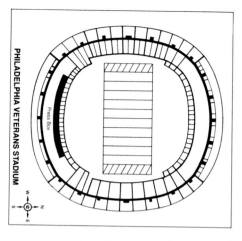

PHILADELPHIA VETERANS STADIUM

1981 SCHEDULE

Preseason
Aug. 6   at Houston   7:00
Aug. 15   **Pittsburgh**   6:00
Aug. 23   vs. New Orleans (Syracuse)   1:00
Aug. 29   vs. New York Jets (Giants Stadium)   8:00

Regular Season
Sept. 6   at New York Giants   1:00
Sept. 13   **New England**   4:00
Sept. 17   at Buffalo (Thursday)   8:30
Sept. 27   **Washington**   1:00
Oct. 5   **Atlanta** (Monday)   9:00
Oct. 11   at New Orleans   12:00
Oct. 18   at Minnesota   12:00
Oct. 25   **Tampa Bay**   1:00
Nov. 1   **Dallas**   4:00
Nov. 8   at St. Louis   12:00
Nov. 15   **Baltimore**   1:00
Nov. 15   **New York Giants**   1:00
Nov. 22   at Miami (Monday)   9:00
Nov. 30   at Washington   1:00
Dec. 6   at Dallas   3:00
Dec. 13   **St. Louis**   1:00
Dec. 20

1980 TEAM STATISTICS

	Philadelphia	Opp.
Total First Downs	326	270
Rushing	118	87
Passing	186	157
Penalty	22	26
Third Down Efficiency	89/217	84/245
Third Down Percentage	41.0	34.3
Total Net Yards	5519	4443
Total Offensive Plays	1036	1032
Avg. Gain per Play	5.3	4.3
Avg. Gain per Game	344.9	277.7
Net Yards Rushing	1995	1618
Total Rushing Plays	527	445
Avg. Gain per Rush	3.8	3.6
Avg. Gain Rushing per Game	124.7	101.1
Net Yards Passing	3524	2825
Lost Attempting to Pass	32/247	44/355
Gross Yards Passing	3771	3180
Attempts/Completions	477/275	543/265
Percent Completed	57.7	48.8
Had Intercepted	12	25
Avg. Net Passing per Game	220.3	176.6
Punts/Avg.	76/38.8	89/41.3
Punt Returns/Avg.	63/8.9	35/6.4
Kickoff Returns/Avg. Ret.	53/18.0	70/18.7
Interceptions/Avg. Ret.	25/6.8	12/18.3
Penalties/Yards	96/809	87/789
Fumbles/Ball Lost	29/16	27/10
Total Points	384	222
Avg. Points per Game	24.0	13.9
Touchdowns	48	26
Rushing	19	8
Passing	28	16
Returns and Recoveries	1	2
Field Goals	16/31	14/26
Conversions	48/48	24/26
Safeties	0	0

1980 TEAM RECORD

Preseason (3-1)

Philadelphia		Opponents
24	Buffalo	9
28	New York Jets	13
23	New England	17
23	Oakland	63
98		

Regular Season (12-4)

Philadelphia		Opponents	Att.
27	*Denver	6	70,307
42	Minnesota	7	46,460
35	*New York Giants	3	70,767
14	St. Louis	24	49,079
24	*Washington	14	69,044
31	New York Giants	16	71,051
17	*Dallas	10	70,696
27	Chicago	14	68,752
27	Seattle	20	61,047
34	New Orleans	21	44,340
24	Washington	0	51,897
10	*Oakland	7	68,585
21	San Diego	22	51,760
17	*Atlanta	20	70,205
17	*St. Louis	3	68,969
27	Dallas	35	62,548
384		222	995,507

*Home Game

Score by periods

Philadelphia	56	102	96	130	—	384
Opponents	63	60	55	44	—	222

Attendance

Home 557,325   Away 438,182   Total 995,507
Single game home record, 71,434 (12-8-79)
Single season home record, 557,325 (1980)

1980 INDIVIDUAL STATISTICS

Rushing

	Att	Yds	Avg	LG	TD
Montgomery	193	778	4.0	72t	8
Giammona	97	361	3.7	44	4
Harris	104	341	3.3	22	3
Harrington	32	166	5.2	19t	1
Campfield	44	120	2.7	9	1
Jaworski	27	95	3.5	19	1
Hogan	12	44	3.7	12	0
Smith	5	33	6.6	16	0
LeMaster	2	21	10.5	15	0
Fitzkee	1	15	15.0	15	0
Sciarra	3	11	3.7	11	0
Dixon	2	8	4.0	5	0
Culbreath	1	3	3.0	3	0
Krepfe	1	2			0
Pisarcik	3	-3	-1.0		0
Philadelphia	527	1995	3.8	72t	19
Opponents	445	1618	3.6	37t	8

Scoring

	TD R	TD P	TD Rt	PAT	FG	TP
Franklin				48/48	16/31	96
Montgomery	8	2				60
Carmichael		9				54
Giammona	4	1				30
Harris	3	1				24
Krepfe		4				24
Campfield	1	2				18
Smith		3				18
Spagnola		3				18
Fitzkee		2				12
Harrington	1					6
Hogan	1					6
Jaworski	1					6
Parker		1				6
Robinson			1			6
Philadelphia	19	28	1	48/48	16/31	384
Opponents	8	16	2	24/26	14/26	222

Field Goal Success

Distance	1-19	20-29	30-39	40-49	50 Over
Made-Att.	4-4	2-5	7-11	2-8	1-3

Passing

	Att	Comp	Pct	Yds	TD	Int	LG	Tkld	Rate
Jaworski	451	257	57.0	3529	27	12	56t	27/213	90.9
Pisarcik	22	15	68.2	187	0	0	26	5/34	94.3
Giammona	3	3	100.0	55	1	0	55	0/0	—
Montgomery	1	0	0.0	0	0	0		0/0	—
Philadelphia	477	275	57.7	3771	28	12	56t	32/247	90.9
Opponents	543	265	48.8	3180	16	25	86t	44/355	92.4

Receiving

	No	Yds	Avg	LG	TD
Montgomery	50	407	8.1	31	2
Carmichael	48	815	17.0	56t	9
Smith	47	825	17.6	46	3
Krepfe	30	450	15.0	27	4
Campfield	26	275	10.6	50	2
Spagnola	18	193	10.7	20	3
Giammona	17	178	10.5	30	1
Harris	15	207	13.8	51t	1
Parker	9	148	16.4	30t	1
Fitzkee	6	169	28.2	49	2
Henry	4	68	17.0	22	0
Harrington	3	24	8.0	17	0
Gilbert	1	7	7.0	7	0
Dixon	1	5	5.0	5	0
Philadelphia	275	3771	13.7	56t	28
Opponents	265	3180	12.0	86t	16

Interceptions

	No	Yds	Avg	LG	TD
Wilson	6	79	13.2	41	0
Young	4	27	6.8	26	0
Edwards	3	12	4.0	9	0
Johnson	3	9	3.0	9	0
Robinson	2	13	6.5	13	0
Blackmore	1	16	16.0	16	0
Logan	1	16	16.0	16	0
Bergey	1	7	7.0	7	0
LeMaster	1	7	7.0	7	0
Hairston	1	0	0.0	0	0
Wilkes	1	0	0.0	0	0
Philadelphia	25	170	6.8	41	0
Opponents	12	220	18.3	70t	1

Punting

	No	Yds	Avg	LG	In 20
Runager	75	2947	39.3	58	16
Philadelphia	76	2947	38.8	58	16
Opponents	89	3673	41.3	63	11

Punt Returns

	No	FC	Yds	Avg	LG	TD
Sciarra	36	1	330	9.2	32	0
Henry	26	1	222	8.5	30	0
Giammona	1	0	8	8.0	8	0
Philadelphia	63	2	560	8.9	32	0
Opponents	35	9	224	6.4	21	0

Kickoff Returns

	No	Yds	Avg	LG	TD
Campfield	26	540	20.8	33	0
Henry	7	154	22.0	39	0
Giammona	7	82	11.7	16	0
Harrington	6	104	17.3	30	0
Dixon	2	30	15.0	15	0
Montgomery	1	23	23.0	23	0
Blue	1	6	6.0	6	0
Baker	1	0	0.0	0	0
Clarke	1	0	0.0	0	0
Spagnola	1	0	0.0	0	0
Philadelphia	53	955	18.0	39	0
Opponents	70	1307	18.7	41	0

PHILADELPHIA RECORD HOLDERS

Individual Records—Single Season

Category	Name	Performance
Rushing (Yds.)	W. Montgomery, 1979	1512
Passing (Pct.)	Roman Gabriel, 1973	58.7
Passing (Yds.)	Sonny Jurgensen, 1961	3723
Passing (TDs)	Sonny Jurgensen, 1961	32
Receiving (No.)	Harold Carmichael, 1973	67
Receiving (Yds.)	Ben Hawkins, 1967	1265
Interceptions	Bill Bradley, 1971	11
Punting (Avg.)	Joe Muha, 1948	47.2
Punt Ret. (Avg.)	Steve Van Buren, 1944	15.3
Kickoff Ret. (Avg.)	Al Nelson, 1972	29.1
Field Goals	Tom Dempsey, 1973	24
Touchdowns (Tot.)	Steve Van Buren, 1945	18
Points	Bobby Walston, 1954	114

Team Records—Single Game

Category	Opponent, Date	Performance
Offense		
First Downs	vs. Wash, 12/2/51	32
Total Points	vs. Cin, 11/6/34	64
Touchdowns	vs. Cin, 11/6/34	10
Total Net Yards	vs. Cle, 11/7/65	582
Net Yards Rushing	vs. Wash, 11/21/48	376
Net Yards Passing	vs. NYG, 11/8/53	460
Rushing Attempts	vs. LA, 11/6/49	64
Passing Attempts	vs. Balt, 10/15/50	64
Interceptions by	vs. Wash, 12/1/40	9
Defense		
Net Yards Allowed	vs. Brk Dod, 12/3/44	29
Net Rushing Yards Allowed	vs. Brk Dod, 10/2/43	-33
Net Passing Yards Allowed	vs. Cin, 11/6/34	0
	vs. Chi Cards, 11/8/36	0
	vs. NY Bulldogs, 9/22/49	0
	vs. Cle, 12/3/50	0

FIRST PLAYERS SELECTED

Year	Player, College, Position
1977	Skip Sharp, Kansas, DB (5)
1978	Reggie Wilkes, Georgia Tech, LB (3)
1979	Jerry Robinson, UCLA, LB
1980	Roynell Young, Alcorn State, DB
1981	Leonard Mitchell, Houston, DE

EAGLES COACHING HISTORY (259-334-22)

Year		
1933-35	Lud Wray	9-21-1
1936-40	Bert Bell	10-44-2
1941-50	Earle (Greasy) Neale*	66-44-5
1951	Alvin (Bo) McMillin**	2-0-0
1951	Wayne Millner	2-8-0
1952-55	Jim Trimble	25-20-3
1956-57	Hugh Devore	7-16-1
1958-60	Lawrence (Buck) Shaw	20-16-1
1961-63	Nick Skorich	15-24-3
1964-68	Joe Kuharich	28-41-1
1969-71	Jerry Williams***	7-22-2
1971-72	Ed Khayat	8-15-2
1973-75	Mike McCormack	16-25-1
1976-80	Dick Vermeil	44-38-0

*Co-coach in Philadelphia-Pittsburgh merger in 1943
**Retired after two games in 1951
***Released after three games in 1971

PHILADELPHIA EAGLES 1981 VETERAN ROSTER

No.	Name	Pos.	Ht.	Wt.	NFL Exp.	Birthdate	Birthplace	College	Residence	Games in '80
63	Baker, Ron	G	6-4	250	4	11/19/54	Emerson, Ind.	Oklahoma State	Gary, Ind.	16
66	Bergey, Bill	LB	6-3	245	13	2/9/45	South Dayton, N.Y.	Arkansas State	Chadds Ford, Pa.	16
27	Blackmore, Richard	CB	5-10	174	3	8/14/56	Vicksburg, Miss.	Mississippi State	Vicksburg, Miss.	16
80	Blue, Luther	WR	5-11	180	5	10/21/55	Valdosta, Ga.	Iowa State	Bloomfield, Mich.	16
97	Brown, Thomas	DE	6-4	240	4	8/5/57	Galveston, Tex.	North Carolina	Galveston, Tex.	3
95	Bunting, John	LB	6-1	220	10	7/15/50	Portland, Maine	North Carolina	West Berlin, N.J.	16
67	Burnham, Lem	DE	6-4	240	4	3/30/47	Winter Haven, Fla.	U.S. International	Deptford, N.J.	0*
37	Campfield, Billy	RB	6-0	205	4	8/20/56	West Point, Ga.	Kansas	San Antonio, Tex.	15
17	Carmichael, Harold	WR	6-8	225	11	9/22/49	Jacksonville, Fla.	Southern	Cherry Hill, N.J.	16
59	Chesley, Al	LB	6-3	240	3	8/23/57	Washington, D.C.	Pittsburgh	Philadelphia, Pa.	16
71	Clarke, Ken	MG	6-2	255	4	8/28/56	Savannah, Ga.	Syracuse	Philadelphia, Pa.	16
46	Edwards, Herman	CB	6-0	190	5	4/27/54	Ft. Monmouth, N.J.	San Diego State	Philadelphia, Pa.	16
81	Fitzkee, Scott	WR	6-0	187	3	8/4/57	York, Pa.	Penn State	Westville, N.J.	7
1	Franklin, Tony	K	5-8	182	3	11/18/56	Big Spring, Tex.	Texas A&M	West Chester, Pa.	16
33	Giammona, Louie	RB-KR	5-9	180	5	3/3/53	St. Helena, Calif.	Utah State	Calistoga, Calif.	16
78	Hairston, Carl	DE	6-3	260	6	12/15/52	Martinsville, Va.	Maryland State	Virginia Beach, Va.	16
35	Harrington, Perry	FB	5-11	210	2	3/13/58	Bentonia, Miss.	Jackson State	Jackson, Miss.	4
20	Harris, Leroy	FB	5-9	230	4	7/3/54	Savannah, Ga.	Arkansas State	West Berlin, N.J.	15
68	Harrison, Dennis	DE	6-8	275	4	7/31/56	Cleveland, Ohio	Vanderbilt	Blackwood, N.J.	15
24	Henderson, Zac	S	6-1	190	2	10/14/55	Jena, La.	Oklahoma	Norman, Okla.	12
89	Henry, Wally	WR-PR	5-8	180	5	10/30/54	San Diego, Calif.	UCLA	Philadelphia, Pa.	7
16	Hertel, Rob	QB	6-2	198	3	2/21/55	Montebello, Calif.	Southern California	Newport Beach, Calif.	0*
30	Hicks, Eddie	RB	6-2	210	3	7/26/55	Henderson, N.C.	East Carolina	Henderson, N.C.	3*
87	Hogan, Mike	FB	6-2	215	6	11/1/54	Floyd County, Ga.	Tennessee at Chattanooga	Philadelphia, Pa.	13
†	Humphrey, Claude	DE	6-5	258	14	6/29/44	Memphis, Tenn.	Tennessee State	Oakland, Tenn.	8
7	Jaworski, Ron	QB	6-2	196	8	3/23/51	Lackawanna, N.Y.	Youngstown State	West Berlin, N.J.	16
65	Johnson, Charlie	MG	6-3	262	5	1/17/52	West Columbia, Tex.	Colorado	West Berlin, N.J.	16
73	Kenney, Steve	G	6-4	262	2	12/26/55	Wilmington, N.C.	Clemson	Deptford, N.J.	16
84	Krepfle, Keith	TE	6-3	230	7	2/4/52	Dubuque, Iowa	Iowa State	Cherry Hill, N.J.	13
55	LeMaster, Frank	LB	6-2	238	8	3/18/54	Lexington, Ky.	Kentucky	West Chester, Pa.	16
41	Logan, Randy	S	6-1	195	9	5/1/51	Detroit, Mich.	Michigan	Detroit, Mich.	16
31	Montgomery, Wilbert	RB	5-10	195	5	9/16/54	Greenville, Miss.	Abilene Christian	Philadelphia, Pa.	16
50	Morriss, Guy	C	6-4	255	9	5/13/51	Colorado City, Tex.	Texas Christian	Sicklerville, N.J.	16
83	Parker, Rodney	WR	6-1	190	2	7/18/53	Mobile, Ala.	Tennessee State	Philadelphia, Pa.	12
69	Peoples, Woody	G	6-2	260	13	8/16/43	Birmingham, Ala.	Grambling	Birmingham, Ala.	16
62	Perot, Petey	G	6-2	261	3	8/16/54	Natchitoches, La.	Northwest Louisiana	Natchitoches, La.	16
52	Phillips, Ray	LB	6-4	230	5	4/18/57	Fordyce, Ark.	Nebraska	Westville, N.J.	16
9	Pisarcik, Joe	QB	6-4	220	5	3/18/54	Wilkes Barre, Pa.	New Mexico State	Bradenton, Fla.	9
56	Powell, Steve	RB	5-11	186	3	1/2/56	Kirkwood, Mo.	Northeast Missouri State	Kirkwood, Mo.	0*
4	Robinson, Jerry	LB	6-2	218	3	12/18/56	San Francisco, Calif.	UCLA	West Chester, Pa.	16
21	Runager, Max	P	6-1	189	3	3/24/56	Greenwood, S.C.	South Carolina	West Chester, Pa.	16
76	Sciarra, John	S-PR	5-11	185	4	3/2/54	Los Angeles, Calif.	UCLA	La Canada-Flintridge, Calif.	16
61	Sisemore, Jerry	T	6-4	265	9	7/16/51	Olton, Tex.	Texas	Sicklerville, N.J.	16
85	Slater, Mark	C	6-2	257	4	2/1/55	Crosby, N.D.	Minnesota	Turnersville, N.J.	9
88	Smith, Charles	WR	6-1	185	9	7/26/50	Monroe, La.	Grambling	Monroe, La.	16
39	Spagnola, John	TE	6-4	240	3	8/1/57	Stroudsburg, Pa.	Yale	Philadelphia, Pa.	1
42	Torrey, Bob	FB	6-3	232	2	1/30/57	Olean, N.Y.	Penn State	Olean, N.Y.	16
75	Wagner, Steve	S	6-2	208	6	4/18/54	Milwaukee, Wis.	Wisconsin	Madison, Wis.	4
51	Walters, Stan	T	6-6	275	10	5/27/48	Rutherford, N.J.	Syracuse	West Chester, Pa.	16
22	Wilkes, Reggie	LB	6-4	230	4	5/27/56	Pine Bluff, Ark.	Georgia Tech	Philadelphia, Pa.	16
43	Wilson, Brenard	S	6-0	175	3	8/15/55	Daytona Beach, Fla.	Vanderbilt	Nashville, Tenn.	16
—	Young, Roynell	CB	6-1	181	2	12/1/57	New Orleans, La.	Alcorn State	New Orleans, La.	16

*Burnham missed '80 season due to injuries; Hertel was active for 11 games but did not play; Hicks played 3 games with N.Y. Giants in '80; Powell last active with Buffalo in '79.

†Option playout; subject to developments.

Also played with Eagles in '80 — RB Jim Culbreath (2 games), RB Zach Dixon (5), TE Ken Dunek (2), TE Lewis Gilbert (3).

PHILADELPHIA EAGLES 1981 FIRST-YEAR ROSTER

Name	Pos.	Ht.	Wt.	Birth-date	Birthplace	College	Residence	How Acq.
Asmus, Jim	P	6-2	195	12/2/58	Meppal, Holland	Hawaii	La Puente, Calif.	FA
Blair, Ken	WR	6-2	195	5/9/58	Oklahoma City, Okla.	Missouri	Oklahoma City, Okla.	FA
Brown, Gregory	DE	6-5	235	1/5/57	Washington, D.C.	Kansas State	Washington, D.C.	FA
Bubniak, Tony	C	6-4	250	6/6/58	Sayre, Pa.	Colgate	Sayre, Pa.	FA
Carhee, Artis	CB	5-9	190	11/12/58	Many, La.	Nevada-Las Vegas	Los Angeles, Calif.	FA
Casarino, Dario	P	6-7	245	9/30/57	St. Helena, Calif.	Washington	Reno, Nev.	FA
Caufield, Charles	S	6-0	198	9/8/58	Waco, Tex.	Tulsa	Stroud, Okla.	D9
Commiskey, Charles	C	6-5	280	3/2/58	Killeen, Tex.	Mississippi	Pascagoula, Miss.	D9
Curcio, Mike (1)	LB	6-1	237	1/24/57	Hudson, N.Y.	Temple	Mays Landing, N.J.	D8 (80)
Davis, Gail	DT	6-4	270	6/1/59	Washington, D.C.	Virginia Union	Marbury, Md.	D11
Day, Ron (1)	RB	6-0	191	9/21/57	Philadelphia, Pa.	Kutztown State	Philadelphia, Pa.	FA
Dottory, Michael	LB	6-2	230	8/2/55	Vicksburg, Miss.	Jackson State	Vicksburg, Miss.	FA
Duncan, Alan	K	5-11	182	11/13/58	Carthage, Tex.	Tennessee	Clinton, Tenn.	D7a
Dunek, Ken (1)	TE	6-6	235	6/20/57	Chicago, Ill.	Memphis State	Marengo, Ill.	FA
Ellis, Ray	CB	6-1	192	4/27/59	Canton, Ohio	Ohio State	Canton, Ohio	D12
Ensminger, Steve (1)	QB	6-3	211	9/15/58	Baton Rouge, La.	Louisiana State	Baton Rouge, La.	FA
Farris, Phil (1)	WR	6-2	195	10/18/58	Charlotte, N.C.	North Carolina	Burlington, N.C.	FA
Field, Doak	LB	6-2	226	10/8/58	Burnet, Tex.	Baylor	Lampasas, Tex.	D7
Gates, Todd	DT	6-5	265	6/17/59	Columbus, Ohio	Bowling Green	Columbus, Ohio	FA
Gower, Bill	FB	6-3	225	7/20/59	Pueblo, Colo.	Southern Colorado	Pueblo, Colo.	FA
Hooks, Alvin	WR	5-11	170	5/7/57	Los Angeles, Calif.	Cal State-Northridge	Los Angeles, Calif.	FA
James, Artis	DE	6-3	250	9/5/58	Waco, Tex.	Texas A&M	Bryan, Tex.	FA
Jones, Greg	DT	6-4	248	3/27/59	New Castle, Pa.	Penn State	New Castle, Pa.	FA
Junkman, Steve (1)	G	6-4	250	7/18/57	Ames, Iowa	North Carolina	Durham, N.C.	FA
LaFleur, Greg	TE	6-4	237	9/16/58	Lafayette, La.	Louisiana State	Ville Platte, La.	D3
Leong, Lyle	WR	5-10	170	1/18/58	Los Angeles, Calif.	Abilene Christian	Abilene, Tex.	FA
Lucky, Mark	C	6-0	250	5/22/58	Houston, Tex.	Oklahoma	Rosenberg, Tex.	FA
Luscinski, Jim (1)	T	6-4	273	12/16/58	Arlington, Mass.	Norwich	Hanover, Mass.	FA
Lush, Mike	S	6-2	261	4/18/58	Allentown, Pa.	East Stroudsburg	Allentown, Pa.	FA
Marren, Bill	G	6-3	258	2/23/58	Englewood, N.J.	Tennessee	Saddle Brook, N.J.	D2
Miraldi, Dean	G	6-5	254	4/8/58	Culver City, Calif.	Utah	Rosemead, Calif.	D1
Mitchell, Leonard	DE	6-7	272	10/12/58	Houston, Tex.	Houston	Houston, Tex.	D1
Moor, Buddy	DT	6-5	252	12/1/58	Greenville, Miss.	Eastern Kentucky	Valdosta, Ga.	D4
Murray, Calvin	RB	5-11	188	10/18/58	Middle Township, N.J.	Ohio State	Woodbine, N.J.	D4
Newsome, Edwin	WR	5-11	170	2/2/57	Houston, Tex.	Texas Tech	Houston, Tex.	FA
Obbema, Rick	LB	6-2	225	7/29/58	Los Angeles, Calif.	Hawaii	Buena Park, Calif.	FA
Oliver, Hubert	FB	5-10	212	11/12/57	Elyria, Ohio	Arizona	Elyria, Ohio	D10
Pitcock, Charles	G	6-4	270	2/20/58	Homestead, Fla.	Tulane	Richey, Fla.	FA
Pollard, Henry (1)	RB	6-3	226	8/2/57	Greenville, Miss.	Arizona State	St. Louis, Mo.	FA
Ralph, Stanley (1)	DT	6-2	245	3/14/57	Waterbury, Conn.	Illinois	Hempstead, N.Y.	FA
Schlecht, Mark	P	6-3	187	6/17/59	West Point, Neb.	Nebraska-Omaha	West Point, Neb.	FA
Schmitz, Doug	C	6-3	250	12/7/57	Paterson, N.J.	Widener	Easton, Pa.	FA
Sell, John	G	6-4	268	3/2/59	Gettysburg, Pa.	Shippensburg State	Littlestown, Pa.	FA
Sheets, Ken (1)	LB	6-3	225	5/9/57	Germany	North Carolina	Woodbridge, Va.	FA
Steinfeld, Al	T	6-4	256	10/28/58	Brooklyn, N.Y.	C.W. Post	Brooklyn, N.Y.	FA
Stonebrook, Tim	T	6-7	265	9/3/58	Akron, Ohio	Iowa State	Ames, Iowa	FA
Sydnor, Ray (1)	TE	6-8	225	4/9/58	Baltimore, Md.	Wisconsin	Westville, N.J.	FA
Tisdale, Brent	DE	6-4	248	4/10/58	Cleveland, Ohio	Indiana	Cleveland Hts., Ohio	FA
Ward, Terrell (1)	CB	5-9	190	11/17/57	San Francisco, Calif.	San Diego State	Westville, N.J.	D7 (80)
Ware, Reggie	CB-S	6-1	200	6/21/58	Birmingham, Ala.	Arizona	Tucson, Ariz.	FA
White, James	CB-S	6-0	185	5/21/58	Winnsboro, La.	Grambling	Monroe, La.	FA
Wise, Tom	WR	6-0	185	1/18/59	Washington, Pa.	Penn State	State College, Pa.	FA

Players who report to an NFL team for the first time are designated on rosters as rookies (R). If a player reported to an NFL training camp in a previous year but was not on the active squad for three or more regular season or postseason games, he is listed on the first-year roster and designated by a (1). Thereafter, a player who is on the active squad for three or more regular season games is credited with an additional year of playing experience.

COACHING STAFF

Head Coach, Dick Vermeil

Pro Career: Begins sixth season as Eagles' head coach. In 1980, guided Eagles to third straight playoff appearance climaxed by a 20-7 NFC championship victory over Dallas followed by 27-10 loss to Oakland in SB XV. Pro assistant with Los Angeles Rams for four years, serving under George Allen in 1969, Tommy Prothro in 1971-72, and Chuck Knox in 1973. No pro playing experience. Joined Eagles February 8, 1976. Career record: 44-38.

Background: Quarterback at Napa JC 1954-55 and San Jose State 1956-57. College assistant coach at College of San Mateo 1963, Stanford 1965-68, and UCLA 1970. Head coach Napa College 1964 and UCLA 1974-75. Led Bruins to the Pac-8 championship in 1975 and a 23-10 Rose Bowl victory over top-ranked Ohio State. UCLA record: 15-5-3.

Personal: Born October 30, 1936 in Calistoga, Calif. Dick and his wife Carolyn live in Bryn Mawr, Pa. and have three children—Richard, David, and Nancy.

ASSISTANT COACHES

John Becker, offensive backfield; born February 16, 1943, Alexandria, Va. lives in Philadelphia. Cal State-Northridge 1965. No pro playing experience. College coach: UCLA 1970-71, New Mexico CC 1972-73, Los Angeles Valley College (head coach) 1974-76, Oregon 1977-79. Pro coach: Eagles since 1980.

Chuck Bednarik, honorary coach; born May 1, 1925, Bethlehem, Pa. lives in Philadelphia. Center-linebacker Pennsylvania 1946-48. Center-linebacker Philadelphia Eagles 1949-62. Pro coach: Third year with Eagles.

Fred Bruney, defensive backfield; born December 30, 1931, Martins Ferry, Ohio, lives in Medford, N.J. Back Ohio State 1949-52. Pro defensive back San Francisco 49ers 1953-56, Pittsburgh Steelers 1957, Washington Redskins 1958, Boston Patriots 1960-62. College coach: Ohio State 1959. Pro coach: Boston Patriots 1963, Philadelphia Eagles 1964-68, Atlanta Falcons 1969-76, rejoined Eagles in 1977.

Marion Campbell, defensive coordinator; born May 25, 1929, Chester, S.C., lives in Medford, N.J. Tackle Georgia 1948-51. Pro defensive tackle San Francisco 49ers 1954-55, Philadelphia Eagles 1956-61. Pro coach: Boston Patriots 1962-63, Minnesota Vikings 1964-66, Los Angeles Rams 1967-68, Atlanta Falcons 1969-76 (head coach 1975-76), fifth year with Eagles.

Dick Coury, receivers; born June 23, 1929, Athens, Ohio, lives in Mount Laurel, N.J. Notre Dame 1948-51. No pro playing experience. College coach: Southern California 1961-63. Cal State-Fullerton 1969-71. Pro coach: Pittsburgh Steelers 1968, Denver Broncos 1972-73, Portland Storm (WFL) 1974 (head coach), San Diego Chargers 1975, Eagles since 1976.

Chuck Clausen, defensive line; born June 23, 1940, Anamosa, Iowa, lives in Mount Laurel, N.J. Defensive lineman New Mexico 1961-63. No pro playing experience. College coach: William & Mary 1969-70, Ohio State 1971-75. Eagles since 1976.

George Hill, linebackers; born April 28, 1933, Bay Village, Ohio, lives in Mt. Laurel, N.J. Tackle-fullback Denison 1954-57. No pro playing experience. College coach: Findlay 1959, Denison 1960-64, Cornell 1965, Duke 1966-70, Ohio State 1971-78. Pro coach: Eagles since 1979.

Ed Hughes, offensive assistant; born October 23, 1927, Buffalo, N.Y. lives in Philadelphia. Halfback Tulsa 1952-53. Pro defensive back Los Angeles Rams 1954-55, New York Giants 1956-58. Pro coach: Dallas Texans 1960-62, Denver Broncos 1963, Washington Redskins 1964-67, San Francisco 49ers 1968-70, Houston 1971 (head coach), St. Louis 1972, Houston 1973-76, Detroit 1977, New Orleans 1978-80, joined Eagles in 1981.

Ken Iman, offensive line-special teams; born February 8, 1939, St. Louis, Mo. lives in Mount Laurel, N.J. Center-linebacker Southeast Missouri State 1956-59. Pro center Green Bay Packers 1960-63, Los Angeles Rams 1964-74. Pro coach: Eagles since 1976.

Lynn Stiles, administrative assistant, special teams, tight ends; born April 12, 1941, Kermit, Tex., lives in Philadelphia. Offensive lineman and linebacker Utah 1959-62. No pro playing experience. College coach: Utah 1963-65, Iowa 1966-70, UCLA 1971-76, San Jose State 1976-78 (head coach). Pro coach: Third year with Eagles.

Jerry Wampfler, offensive line, running game; born August 6, 1932, New Philadelphia, Ohio, lives in Philadelphia. Tackle Miami, Ohio 1951-54. No pro playing experience. College coach: Presbyterian 1955, Miami, Ohio 1963-65, Notre Dame 1966-69, Colorado State 1970-72 (head coach). Pro coach: Philadelphia Eagles 1973-75, Buffalo Bills 1976-77, New York Giants 1978, rejoined Eagles in 1979.

NOTES

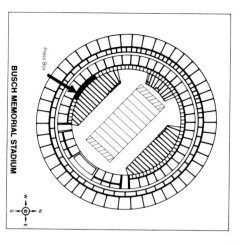

BUSCH MEMORIAL STADIUM

Press Box

St. Louis Cardinals

National Football Conference
Eastern Division

Team Colors: Cardinal Red, White, and
Black

200 Stadium Plaza
St. Louis, Missouri 63102
Telephone: (314) 421-0777

Club Officials

President: William V. Bidwill
Vice President-Operations: Joe Sullivan
Vice President-Administration: Bing Devine
Director of Pro Personnel: Larry Wilson
Treasurer: Charley Schlegel
Director of Player Personnel: George Boone
Media Coordinator: Marty Igel
Director of Community Relations: Adele Harris
Ticket Manager: Steve Walsh
Trainer: John Omohundro
Assistant Trainer: Jim Shearer
Equipment Manager: Bill Simmons

Stadium: Busch Memorial Stadium •
200 Stadium Plaza
St. Louis, Missouri 63102
Capacity: 51,392
Playing Surface: AstroTurf
Training Camp: The Lindenwood Colleges
St. Charles, Missouri 63301

1981 SCHEDULE

Preseason

Aug. 8	at San Diego		6:00
Aug. 14	at Seattle		7:30
Aug. 22	at Kansas City		7:35
Aug. 29	**Chicago**		6:00

Regular Season

Sept. 6	**Miami**		12:00
Sept. 13	at Dallas		3:00
Sept. 20	**Washington**		12:00
Sept. 27	at Tampa Bay		4:00
Oct. 4	**Dallas**		12:00
Oct. 11	at New York Giants		4:00
Oct. 18	at Atlanta		1:00
Oct. 25	**Minnesota**		12:00
Nov. 1	at Washington		4:00
Nov. 8	**Philadelphia**		12:00
Nov. 15	**Buffalo**		12:00
Nov. 22	at Baltimore		2:00
Nov. 29	at New England		1:00
Dec. 6	**New Orleans**		12:00
Dec. 13	**New York Giants**		12:00
Dec. 20	at Philadelphia		1:00

1980 TEAM STATISTICS

	St. Louis	Opp.
Total First Downs	281	311
Rushing	123	115
Passing	137	176
Penalty	21	20
Third Down Efficiency	96/240	101/252
Third Down Percentage	40.0	40.1
Total Offensive Plays	4859	5384
Total Net Yards	1039	1116
Avg. Gain per Play	4.7	4.8
Avg. Gain per Game	303.7	336.5
Net Yards Rushing	2183	2059
Total Rushing Plays	519	547
Avg. Gain per Rush	4.2	3.8
Avg. Gain Rushing per Game	136.4	128.7
Net Yards Passing	2676	3325
Lost Attempting to Pass	50/387	38/291
Gross Yards Passing	3063	3616
Attempts/Completions	470/239	531/287
Percent Completed	50.9	54.0
Had Intercepted	24	20
Avg. Net Passing per Game	167.3	207.8
Punts/Avg.	100/41.1	89/40.1
Punt Returns/Avg.	50/8.0	62/10.4
Kickoff Returns/Avg.	65/20.0	57/20.0
Interceptions/Avg. Ret.	20/16.4	24/10.3
Penalties/Yards	103/922	101/919
Fumbles/Ball Lost	24/13	27/14
Total Points	299	350
Avg. Points per Game	18.7	21.9
Touchdowns	37	43
Rushing	19	17
Passing	16	23
Returns and Recoveries	2	3
Field Goals	14/23	17/33
Conversions	35/37	41/42
Safeties	0	0

1980 TEAM RECORD

Preseason (2-2)

St. Louis		Opponents
13	New Orleans	17
21	Tampa Bay	14
10	Kansas City	20
21	Chicago	13
65		64

Regular Season (5-11)

St. Louis		Att.
35	*New York Giants	49,122
21	San Francisco (OT)	49,999
7	Detroit	79,587
24	*Philadelphia	49,079
40	New Orleans	45,388
13	*Los Angeles	50,230
21	Washington	51,060
0	Baltimore	33,506
17	*Dallas	50,701
24	*Atlanta (OT)	48,662
27	Dallas	52,567
21	*Kansas City	42,871
13	New York Giants	65,852
23	*Detroit	46,966
24	Philadelphia	68,969
3	*Washington	35,942
299		820,501

*Home Game   (OT) Overtime

Score by Periods

St. Louis	90	61	74	74	0	— 299
Opponents	27	115	75	124	9	— 350

Attendance

Home 373,573   Away 446,928   Total 820,501
Single game home record, 50,855 (9-2-79)
Single season home record, 376,771 (1979)

1980 INDIVIDUAL STATISTICS

Rushing

	Att	Yds	Avg	LG	TD
Anderson	301	1352	4.5	52	9
Morris	117	456	3.9	24	6
T. Brown	40	186	4.7	19	1
Harrell	42	170	4.0	26	3
Hart	9	11	1.2	12	0
Phillips	2	6	3.0	4	0
Love	1	3	3.0	3	0
Loyd	6	2	0.3	3	0
Gray	1	-3	-3.0	-3	0
St. Louis	519	2183	4.2	52	19
Opponents	547	2059	3.8	36	17

Field Goal Success

Distance	1-19	20-29	30-39	40-49	50 Over
Made-Att.	0-0	5-8	4-5	5-10	0-0

Passing

	Att	Comp	Pct	Yds	TD	Int	Tkd	Rate
Hart	425	228	53.6	2946	16	20	39/292	68.7
Loyd	28	5	17.9	49	0	1	7/48	24.6
Lisch	17	6	35.3	68	0	3	3/36	8.6
Wehrli	0	0	0.0	0	0	0	1/11	—
St. Louis	470	239	50.9	3063	16	24	50/387	61.8
Opponents	531	287	54.0	3616	23	20	38/291	—

Receiving

	No	Yds	Avg	LG	TD
Tilley	68	966	14.2	60t	6
Gray	40	709	17.7	69t	3
Anderson	36	308	8.6	35	0
Marsh	22	269	12.2	29	4
T. Brown	21	290	13.8	63	1
Stief	16	165	10.3	23	0
Morris	15	110	7.3	24	1
Harrell	9	52	5.8	14	0
Bell	8	123	15.4	34	0
Combs	2	52	26.0	38t	1
J. Lee	2	19	9.5	12	0
St. Louis	239	3063	12.8	69t	16
Opponents	287	3616	12.6	58t	23

Interceptions

	No	Yds	Avg	LG	TD
Stone	5	63	12.6	20	0
Greene	4	41	10.3	26	0
Allen	3	104	34.7	70t	1
E. Williams	2	31	15.5	20	0
Collier	2	22	11.0	22	0
Wehrli	1	25	25.0	25	0
Kearney	1	22	22.0	22	0
Green	1	10	10.0	10	0
R. Brown	1	9	9.0	9	0
St. Louis	20	327	16.4	70t	1
Opponents	24	246	10.3	78t	1

Punting

	No	Yds	Avg	LG	In 20
Swider	99	4111	41.5	66	12
St. Louis	100	4111	41.1	66	12
Opponents	89	3570	40.1	59	15

Punt Returns

	No	FC	Yds	Avg	LG	TD
Green	16	6	168	10.5	57t	1
Bell	21	3	195	9.3	54	0
Harrell	11	4	31	2.8	15	0
Nelson	1	0	5	5.0	5	0
Allen	1	0	0	0	0	0
Stone	0	1	0	—	0	0
St. Louis	50	14	399	8.0	57t	1
Opponents	62	12	645	10.4	75t	1

Kickoff Returns

	No	Yds	Avg	LG	TD
Green	32	745	23.3	37	0
Harrell	19	348	18.3	33	0
Love	3	46	15.3	27	0
Stone	3	34	11.3	13	0
Phillips	3	28	14.0	14	0
T. Brown	2	26	13.0	16	0
Clark	2	14	7.0	11	0
Nelson	1	29	29.0	29	0
Collins	1	0	0	0	0
Baker	0	27	—	27	0
St. Louis	65	1297	20.0	40	0
Opponents	57	1142	20.0	35	0

Scoring

	TD	TD R	TD P	TD Rt	PAT	FG	TP
Anderson	9	9	0	0			54
O'Donoghue	0	0	0	0	18/18	11/15	51
Morris	7	6	1	0			42
Tilley	6	0	6	0			36
Little					17/19	3/8	26
Marsh	4	0	4	0			24
Gray	3	0	3	0			18
Harrell	3	3	0	0			18
T. Brown	2	1	1	0			12
Allen	1	0	0	1			6
Combs	1	0	0	1			6
Green	1	0	1	0			6
St. Louis	37	19	16	2	35/37	14/23	299
Opponents	43	17	23	3	41/42	17/33	350

ST. LOUIS RECORD HOLDERS

Individual Records—Single Season

Category	Name	Performance
Rushing (Yds.)	Ottis Anderson, 1979	1605
Passing (Pct.)	Jim Hart, 1976	56.2
Passing (Yds.)	Charley Johnson, 1963	3280
Passing (TDs)	Charley Johnson, 1963	28
Receiving (No.)	Bobby Joe Conrad, 1963	73
Receiving (Yds.)	Jackie Smith, 1967	1205
Interceptions	Bob Nussbaumer, 1949	12
Punting (Avg.)	Jerry Norton, 1960	45.6
Punt Ret. (Avg.)	Red Cochran, 1949	20.9
Kickoff Ret. (Avg.)	Ollie Matson, 1952	35.5
Field Goals	Jim Bakken, 1967	27
Touchdowns (Tot.)	John David Crow, 1962	17
Points	Jim Bakken, 1967	117

Team Records—Single Game

Category	Opponent, Date	Performance
Offense		
First Downs	vs. NY Bulldogs, 11/13/49	32
Total Points	vs. NY Bulldogs, 11/13/49	65
Touchdowns	vs. Roch Jeff, 10/7/23	9
Total Net Yards	vs. NY Bulldogs, 11/13/49	589
Net Yards Rushing	vs. Phil, 12/16/62	330
Net Yards Passing	vs. NO, 10/5/80	430
Rushing Attempts	vs. GB, 12/5/48	70
Passing Attempts	vs. LA, 11/30/58	51
Interceptions by	vs. NY Bulldogs, 11/13/49	7
Defense		
Net Yards Allowed	vs. Pitt, 11/27/66	80
Net Yards Allowed	vs. NO, 10/5/80	80
Net Rushing Yards Allowed	vs. Det, 10/13/46	-24
Net Passing Yards Allowed	vs. Pitt, 10/17/65	-16

FIRST PLAYERS SELECTED

Year	Player, College, Position
1975	Tim Gray, Texas A&M, DB
1976	Mike Dawson, Arizona, DT
1977	Steve Pisarkiewicz, Missouri, QB
1978	Steve Little, Arkansas, K
1979	Ottis Anderson, Miami, RB
1980	Curtis Greer, Michigan, DE
1981	E. J. Junior, Alabama, LB

CARDINALS COACHING HISTORY

Chicago 1920-59 (305-406-33)

(Since 1949)

Year	Coach	Record
1949	Phil Handler-Buddy Parker*	6-5-1
1950-51	Earl (Curly) Lambeau	8-16-0
1952	Joe Kuharich	4-8-0
1953-54	Joe Stydahar	3-20-1
1955-57	Ray Richards	14-21-1
1958-61	Frank (Pop) Ivy	17-31-2
1962-65	Wally Lemm	27-26-3
1966-70	Charley Winner	35-30-5
1971-72	Bob Hollway	8-18-2
1973-77	Don Coryell	42-29-1
1978-79	Bud Wilkinson**	9-20-0
1979	Larry Wilson	2-1-0
1980	Jim Hanifan	5-11-0

*Co-coaches
**Released after 13 games in 1979

ST. LOUIS CARDINALS 1981 VETERAN ROSTER

No.	Name	Pos.	Ht.	Wt.	NFL Exp.	Birth-date	Birthplace	College	Residence	Games in '80
67	Acker, Bill	DT	6-2	255	2	11/7/56	Freer, Tex.	Texas	Freer, Tex.	16
27	†Allen, Carl	CB	6-0	186	5	12/21/55	Hattiesburg, Miss.	Southern Mississippi	St. Louis, Mo.	16
32	Anderson, Ottis	RB	6-2	215	3	1/19/57	West Palm Beach, Fla.	Miami	West Palm Beach, Fla.	16
52	Baker, Charles	LB	6-2	217	3	9/26/57	Mt. Pleasant, Tex.	Mt. Pleasant, Tex.	Odessa, Tex.	16
81	Bell, Mark	WR	5-9	175	3	6/14/57	Lynwood, Calif.	Colorado State	Ft. Collins, Colo.	11
71	Bostic, Joe	G	6-3	265	3	4/20/57	Greensboro, N.C.	Clemson	Greensboro, N.C.	16
51	†Brahaney, Tom	C	6-2	246	9	10/23/51	Midland, Tex.	Oklahoma	Midland, Tex.	16
55	Brooks, Jonathan	LB	6-2	215	3	6/22/57	Saluda, S.C.	Clemson	Saluda, S.C.	1
69	Brown, Rush	DT	6-2	257	2	6/27/54	Laurinburg, N.C.	Ball State	Muncie, Ind.	16
33	Brown, Theotis	RB	6-2	225	3	4/20/57	Chicago, Ill.	UCLA	Long Beach, Calif.	16
64	Clark, Randy	G-C	6-2	254	3	7/27/57	Chicago, Ill.	Northern Illinois	St. Peters, Mo.	8
61	Coder, Ron	G	6-4	250	5	5/24/54	Savannah, Ga.	Penn State	Redmond, Wash.	11
44	Collier, Tim	CB	6-0	174	6	5/31/54	Dallas, Tex.	East Texas State	St. Louis, Mo.	12
66	Collins, George	G-T	6-2	260	4	12/9/55	Macon, Ga.	Georgia	Athens, Ga.	16
80	Combs, Chris	TE	6-4	239	2	3/17/58	San Diego, Calif.	New Mexico	St. Louis, Mo.	16
60	Cotton, Barney	G	6-5	265	3	9/30/56	Omaha, Neb.	Nebraska	Omaha, Neb.	16
54	Criswell, Kirby	LB	6-5	238	2	8/31/57	Grinnell, Iowa	Kansas	Kellogg, Iowa	4
73	Dawson, Mike	DT	6-4	275	6	10/16/53	Tucson, Ariz.	Arizona	St. Louis, Mo.	4
72	†Deirdorf, Dan	T	6-3	288	11	6/29/49	Canton, Ohio	Michigan	St. Louis, Mo.	2
59	Favron, Calvin	LB	6-1	225	3	7/3/57	White Castle, La.	Southeast Louisiana State	Baton Rouge, La.	16
70	Goodspeed, Mark	T	6-5	270	2	12/1/56	Kansas City, Kan.	Nebraska	Omaha, Neb.	3
85	*Gray, Mel	WR	5-9	173	11	9/28/48	Fresno, Calif.	Missouri	St. Louis, Mo.	16
25	Green, Roy	S	5-11	190	3	6/30/57	Magnolia, Ark.	Henderson State	St. Louis, Mo.	15
37	Greene, Ken	S	6-3	203	4	5/8/56	Lewiston, Idaho	Washington State	Vancouver, Wash.	12
75	Greer, Curtis	DE	6-4	252	2	11/10/57	Detroit, Mich.	Michigan	Ann Arbor, Mich.	11
39	Harrell, Willard	RB	5-8	182	7	9/16/52	Stockton, Calif.	Pacific	Stockton, Calif.	16
17	†Hart, Jim	QB	6-1	210	16	4/29/44	Evanston, Ill.	Southern Illinois	St. Louis, Mo.	15
56	Kearney, Tim	LB	6-2	224	10	11/5/50	Kingsford, Mich.	Northern Michigan	St. Louis, Mo.	13
46	Lee, Jeff	WR	6-2	195	2	5/23/55	Racine, Wis.	Nebraska	Omaha, Neb.	4
16	Lisch, Rusty	QB	6-3	213	2	12/21/56	Belleville, Ill.	Notre Dame	Belleville, Ill.	2
40	Love, Randy	RB	6-1	205	3	9/30/56	Houston	Houston	Garland, Tex.	16
14	Loyd, Mike	QB	6-3	216	2	5/6/56	Joplin, Mo.	Missouri Southern	Joplin, Mo.	5
87	Marsh, Doug	TE	6-3	236	2	3/13/58	Akron, Ohio	Michigan	Ann Arbor, Mich.	16
76	Mays, Stafford	DE	6-2	242	2	6/18/58	Lawrence, Kan.	Washington	Tacoma, Wash.	16
50	McIntyre, Jeff	LB	6-3	232	4	9/20/55	Beaumont, Tex.	Arizona State	Tempe, Ariz.	10
24	Morris, Wayne	RB	6-0	208	6	5/3/54	Dallas, Tex.	Southern Methodist	Dallas, Tex.	16
53	†Neils, Steve	LB	6-2	218	8	5/2/51	St. Peter, Minn.	Minnesota	St. Louis, Mo.	14
38	Nelson, Lee	CB	5-10	185	6	1/30/54	Kissimee, Fla.	Florida State	Tallahassee, Fla.	16
11	†O'Donoghue, Neil	K	6-6	210	5	6/18/53	Dublin, Ireland	Auburn	Indian Rocks Beach, Fla.	10
36	†Phillips, Rod	RB	6-0	221	7	12/23/52	Meridian, Miss.	Jackson State	Jackson, Miss.	16
82	Pollard, Bob	DE	6-3	252	11	12/30/48	Beaumont, Tex.	Weber State	Metairie, La.	16
58	Seabron, Thomas	LB	6-3	215	2	5/24/57	Baltimore, Md.	Michigan	Southfield, Mich.	8*
84	Stief, Dave	WR	6-3	195	4	1/29/56	Portland, Ore.	Portland State	Gresham, Ore.	16
68	Stieve, Terry	G	6-2	265	6	3/10/54	Barboo, Wis.	Wisconsin	West Palm Beach, Fla.	0*
23	Stone, Ken	S	6-1	180	9	9/14/50	Cincinnati, Ohio	Vanderbilt	Pittsburgh	14
10	†Swider, Larry	P	6-2	195	3	2/1/55	Limestone, Maine	Pittsburgh	St. Louis, Mo.	16
83	Tilley, Pat	WR	5-10	175	6	2/15/53	Marshall, Tex.	Louisiana Tech	Shreveport, La.	14
22	Wehrli, Roger	CB	6-0	193	13	11/26/47	New Point, Mo.	Missouri	St. Louis, Mo.	16
55	Williams, Eric	LB	6-2	225	5	6/17/55	Sacramento, Calif.	Southern California	St. Louis, Mo.	12
62	Wortman, Keith	T	6-2	275	10	7/20/50	Billings, Mont.	Nebraska	St. Louis, Mo.	2
78	†Yankowski, Ron	DE	6-5	260	11	10/23/54	Arlington, Mass.	Kansas State	St. Louis, Mo.	14

*Seabron played 6 games with 49ers, 2 with St. Louis; Stieve missed entire 1980 regular season due to knee injury.

†Option playout; subject to developments.

Traded—Running back Terry Metcalf to Washington.

Retired—Mark Arneson, 10-year linebacker, 16 games in 1980.

Also played with Cardinals in '80—C Tom Banks (6 games), LB John Barefield (6 games), G Eric Cunningham (active for 2 games), K Steve Little (6 games), T Brad Oates (10 games), TE Gary Parris (1 game), CB Gerard Williams (4 games).

ST. LOUIS CARDINALS 1981 FIRST-YEAR ROSTER

Name	Pos.	Ht.	Wt.	Birth-date	Birthplace	College	Residence	How Acq.
Adams, Joe	G	6-5	240	11/2/57	Omaha, Neb.	Nebraska	Bellevue, Neb.	D12
Ahrens, Dave	LB	6-3	228	12/5/58	Cedar Falls, Iowa	Wisconsin	Oregon, Wis.	D6
Allman, John	CB-S	6-1	190	5/7/59	St. Louis, Mo.	Indiana State	St. Louis, Mo.	FA
Brazill, Tom	CB	6-1	205	5/12/59	Chicago, Ill.	Wisconsin-LaCrosse	Fond Du Lac, Wis.	FA
Donnalley, Kevin	S	5-11	177	1/17/58	Warren, Ohio	North Dakota State	Warren, Ohio	D7
Featherson, Vince	WR	5-10	165	12/9/57	St. Louis, Mo.	Missouri Southern	St. Louis, Mo.	FA
Fisher, Mike	WR	5-11	172	4/22/58	Gatesville, Tex.	Baylor	Gatesville, Tex.	D8
Gillen, John	LB	6-3	227	11/5/58	Arlington Heights, Ill.	Illinois	Arlington Heights, Ill.	D5
Griffin, Jeff	CB-S	6-0	185	7/19/58	Carson, Calif.	Utah	Carson, Calif.	D3
Joiner, Jim	WR	6-2	195	6/25/59	Detroit, Mich.	Miami	Detroit, Mich.	D10a
Junior, E.J.	LB	6-3	237	12/8/59	Sallsburg, N.C.	Alabama	Nashville, Tenn.	D1
Lomax, Neil	QB	6-3	215	2/17/59	Portland, Ore.	Portland State	Lake Oswego, Ore.	D2
Lukas, Don	WR	5-11	180	12/17/56	Detroit, Mich.	Michigan Tech	St. Clair, Minn.	FA
Mallard, James	WR	6-2	185	11/29/57	Tampa, Fla.	Alabama	Tampa, Fla.	D10
McCall, Ben	RB	6-0	202	7/31/59	Chicago, Ill.	Purdue	Chicago, Ill.	FA
Mitchell, Stump	RB	5-9	188	3/15/59	St. Mary's, Ga.	Citadel	St. Mary's, Ga.	D9
Rhodes, Steve	WR	6-0	191	12/26/57	Dallas, Tex.	Oklahoma	Dallas, Tex.	D4
Sherrod, Mike	TE	6-6	236	1/17/58	Robbins, Ill.	Illinois	Robbins, Ill.	D11
Williams, Ricky	RB	5-9	200	11/12/58	Springfield, Mo.	Central Missouri St.	Springfield, Mo.	FA

Players who report to an NFL team for the first time are designated on rosters as rookies (R). If a player reported to an NFL training camp in a previous year but was not on the active squad for three or more regular season or postseason games, he is listed on the first-year roster and designated by a (1). Thereafter, a player who is on the active squad for three or more regular season games is credited with an additional year of playing experience.

NOTES

Emmitt Thomas, receivers; born June 4, 1943, Angleton, Tex., lives in St. Louis. Quarterback-wide receiver Bishop College 1963-65. Pro defensive back Kansas City Chiefs 1966-78. College coach: Central Missouri State 1979-80. Pro coach: Joined Cardinals in 1981.

COACHING STAFF

Head Coach, Jim Hanifan

Pro Career: Named head coach on January 30, 1980 and posted 5-11 mark last season. No stranger to city of St. Louis, where he began his pro coaching career in 1973 as offensive line coach. Served Cardinals in that capacity until 1979 when he left to become assistant head coach of San Diego Chargers. During his first tenure at St. Louis, his offensive lines allowed fewest quarterback sacks in NFL for three straight years (1974-76), including an NFL record low of eight in 1975. Played end for the Toronto Argonauts in 1955.

Background: Played end for California 1952-54 and led the nation in receiving as a senior. Began coaching career at Charter Oak High School in Covina, Calif., in 1962. Was a college assistant for 14 years: Yuba JC 1959-61, Glendale JC 1964-65, Utah 1966-69, California 1970-71, San Diego State 1972.

Personal: Born September 21, 1933 in Compton, Calif. He and his wife, Mariana, live in St. Louis and have two children—Kathleen and James.

ASSISTANT COACHES

Bill Atkins, defensive backfield; born November 19, 1934, Millport, Ala., lives in St. Louis. Defensive back Auburn 1955-57. Pro defensive back Buffalo Bills 1960-62, New York Jets 1963, Denver Broncos 1964. College coach: Troy State 1966-71 (head coach). Pro coach: Buffalo Bills 1972-75, San Francisco 49ers 1976, Detroit Lions 1978-79, second year with Cardinals.

Chuck Banker, special teams; born March 12, 1941, Prescott Ariz., lives in St. Louis. Linebacker-tight end Pasadena City College 1959-60. No pro playing experience. College coach: Glendale JC 1962-65, Utah 1966-67, 1974-75, Westminster 1968-70, Boise State 1976-79. Pro coach: Second year with Cardinals.

Tom Bettis, defensive coordinator; born March 17, 1933, Chicago, lives in St. Louis. Guard Purdue 1951-54. Pro linebacker Green Bay Packers 1955-61, Pittsburgh Steelers 1962, Chicago Bears 1963. Pro coach: Kansas City Chiefs 1966-77 (head coach for final seven games of 1977), fourth year with Cardinals.

Rudy Feldman, defensive line; born May 18, 1932, San Francisco, lives in St. Louis. Guard UCLA 1950-53. No pro playing experience. College coach: Iowa State 1957, Oklahoma 1963-67, New Mexico 1968-73. Pro coach: San Diego Chargers 1974-77, fourth year with Cardinals.

Harry Gilmer, quarterbacks; born April 14, 1926, Birmingham, Ala., lives in St. Louis. Quarterback Alabama 1944-47. Pro back Washington Redskins 1948-52, 1954, Detroit Lions 1955-56. Pro coach: Pittsburgh Steelers 1957-60, Minnesota Vikings 1961-64, Detroit Lions 1965-66 (head coach), St. Louis Cardinals 1967-69, Atlanta Falcons 1970-74, rejoined Cardinals in 1975.

Dick Jamieson, offensive backfield; born November 13, 1937, Streator, Ill., lives in St. Louis. Quarterback Bradley 1955-58. Pro quarterback Baltimore Colts 1959, New York Titans 1960, Houston Oilers 1965. College coach: Utah 1967, 1972-76 (head coach 1974-76), Idaho State 1968-70, Stanford 1977-79. Pro coach: Saskatchewan Roughriders (CFL) 1971, Green Bay Packers 1980, first year with Cardinals.

Tom Lovat, offensive line; born December 28, 1938, Bingham, Utah, lives in St. Louis. Guard-linebacker Utah 1958-60. No pro playing experience. College coach: Utah 1967, 1972-76 (head coach 1974-76), Idaho State 1968-70, Stanford 1977-79. Pro coach: Bradley 1962-64, Missouri 1965. College coach: Bradley 1962-64. Pro coach: Second year with Cardinals.

Leon McLaughlin, special assistant; born May 30, 1925, San Diego, Calif., lives in St. Louis. Center-linebacker UCLA 1946-49. Pro center Los Angeles Rams 1951-55. College coach: Washington State 1956, Stanford 1959-65, San Fernando Valley State 1969-70 (head coach). Pro coach: Pittsburgh Steelers 1966-68, Los Angeles Rams 1971-72, Detroit Lions 1973-74, Green Bay Packers 1975-76, New England Patriots 1977, fourth year with Cardinals.

1980 TE

Total First I
Rushing
Passing
Penalty
Third Do
Third Do
Total Net Y
Total Offi
Avg. Gai
Avg. Gai
Net Yards
Total Ru
Avg. Gai
Avg. Gai
Net Yards
Lost Atte
Gross Ya
Attempts
Percent
Had Inte
Avg. Net
Punts/Avg.
Punt Retur
Kickoff Ret
Interceptio
Penalties/
Fumbles/B
Total Point:
Avg. Poi
Touchdo
Rushing
Passing
Returns
Field Go
Convers
Safeties

1980 TE

Preseas

San Franc

33	Oa	
17	Sa	
7	Se	
31	Ka	
88		

Regular

San Franc

26	Ne	
24	*St.	
37	Ne	
17	*Atl	
26	Lo	
14	Da	
17	Lo	
23	*Ta	
13	De	
16	Gr	
13	Mi	
12	*Ne	
21	*Ne	
38	Ne	
10	Atl	
13	*Bu	
320		

*Home Game

Score by

San Franci
Opponents

Attenda

Home 373,
Single gam
Single seas

SAN FRANCISCO 49ERS 1981 VETERAN ROSTER

No.	Name	Pos.	Ht.	Wt.	NFL Exp.	Birth-date	Birthplace	College	Residence	Games in '80
68	Ayers, John	G	6-5	255	5	4/14/53	Carrizo Springs, Tex.	West Texas State	Canyon, Tex.	16
77	†Barrett, Jean	T	6-6	250	9	5/24/51	Fort Worth, Tex.	Tulsa	Tulsa, Okla.	15
	†-Benjamin, Guy	QB	6-4	208	4	6/27/55	Hollywood, Calif.	Stanford	Sepulveda, Calif.	2
76	Bierdermann, Leo	T	6-7	275	2	10/19/55	Omaha, Neb.	California	Clayton, Calif.	0*
72	Board, Dwaine	DE	6-5	245	3	11/29/56	Union Hall, Va.	North Carolina A&T	Mt. View, Calif.	15
57	Bungarda, Kestutis	T	6-6	270	2	1/25/57	Roseville, Calif.	Missouri	Vista, Calif.	15
33	Bunz, Dan	LB	6-4	225	4	10/7/55	Pearland, Tex.	Cal State-Long Beach	Loomis, Calif.	16
87	Churchman, Ricky	S	6-1	193	2	3/14/58	Kingston, N.C.	Texas	Austin, Tex.	16
49	Clark, Dwight	WR	6-3	205	3	1/8/57	Lexington, Tex.	Clemson	Charlotte, N.C.	16
51	Cooper, Earl	FB	6-2	227	2	9/17/57	New York, N.Y.	Rice	Houston, Tex.	16
17	Cross, Randy	G	6-3	255	6	4/25/54	Oakland, Calif.	UCLA	Redwood City, Calif.	16
62	DeBerg, Steve	QB	6-2	205	5	1/19/54	Oakland, Calif.	San Jose State	Cupertino, Calif.	11
35	DeBernardi, Fred	DE	6-3	254	8	3/2/49	Santa Monica, Calif.	Texas-El Paso	Las Vegas, Nev.	6
71	Downing, Walt	C-G	6-3	254	3	6/11/56	Coatesville, Pa.	Michigan	Mt. View, Calif.	14
48	Elliott, Lenvil	RB	6-0	210	9	9/2/51	Richmond, Mo.	Northeast Missouri State	Fairfield, Ohio	14
82	Fahnhorst, Keith	T	6-6	263	8	2/6/52	St. Cloud, Minn.	Minnesota	St. Paul, Minn.	16
59	Francis, Phil	FB	6-0	205	3	1/10/57	Kewanee, Ill.	Stanford	Foster City, Calif.	5
44	Gilbert, Lewis	TE	6-4	225	3	5/24/56	Naples, Fla.	Florida	Norcross, Ga.	6
52	Harper, Willie	LB	6-1	215	8	7/30/50	Toledo, Ohio	Nebraska	Los Angeles, Calif.	16
3	Haslip, Wilbert	LB	6-1	215	2	12/8/56	El Centro, Calif.	Hawaii	Santa Ana, Calif.	3*
16	Hicks, Dwight	S	6-1	189	3	7/5/57	Mt. Holly, N.J.	Michigan	Sunnyvale, Calif.	16
89	Hilton, Scott	LB	6-1	215	2	6/11/56	Harrisburg, Pa.	No College	Hatboro, Pa.	6
42	Hofer, Paul	RB	6-0	195	6	5/13/52	Memphis, Tenn.	Mississippi	Foster City, Calif.	6
65	Huff, Gary	QB	6-1	200	8	4/27/51	Natchez, Miss.	Florida State	Tampa, Fla.	0*
54	Johnson, Charles	CB	5-10	180	3	5/5/56	Sacramento, Calif.	Grambling	Mansfield, La.	13
56	Leopold, Bobby	LB	6-1	215	2	10/18/57	Mansfield, La.	Notre Dame	Foster City, Calif.	16
80	Martin, Saladin	CB	6-1	180	2	1/17/56	San Diego, Calif.	San Diego State	San Diego, Calif.	3*
78	Miller, Jim	P	5-11	183	2	7/5/57	Ripley, Miss.	Mississippi	Ripley, Miss.	16
26	Montana, Joe	QB	6-2	200	3	6/11/56	Monongahela, Pa.	Notre Dame	Manhattan Beach, Calif.	15
88	Mucker, Larry	WR	5-11	188	5	12/15/54	Fresno, Calif.	Arizona State	Fresno, Calif.	0*
79	Owens, James	WR	5-11	192	4	7/5/55	Sacramento, Calif.	UCLA	Redwood City, Calif.	14
50	Patton, Ricky	RB	5-11	192	5	4/5/56	Hazelhurst, Miss.	Jackson State	Lithonia, Ga.	13
58	Pillers, Lawrence	DE	6-3	260	6	11/4/52	Hazelhurst, Miss.	Alcorn State	Port Gibson, Miss.	16
90	Puki, Craig	LB	6-1	231	2	1/18/57	Birmingham, Ala.	Tennessee	Tempe, Ariz.	16
74	Quillan, Fred	C	6-5	260	4	1/27/56	Portland, Ore.	Oregon	Beaverton, Ore.	16
14	Ramson, Eason	TE	6-2	234	3	4/30/56	Sacramento, Calif.	Washington State	Foster City, Calif.	16
60	Reese, Archie	DT	6-3	262	4	2/4/56	Mayesville, S.C.	Clemson	Clemson, S.C.	16
29	Rhodes, Ray	CB	5-11	185	8	10/20/50	Mexia, Tex.	Tulsa	Tampa, Fla.	16
23	Solomon, Freddie	WR	5-11	188	7	1/11/53	Sumter, N.C.	Tampa	Cayce, S.C.	14
47	Stuckey, Jim	DE	6-4	251	2	6/21/58	Jackson, Miss.	Clemson	Cayce, S.C.	16
86	Tautolo, Terry	LB	6-2	235	6	8/30/54	Corona, Calif.	UCLA	Long Beach, Calif.	8
	Turner, Keena	LB	6-2	219	2	10/22/58	Chicago, Ill.	Purdue	Chicago, Ill.	16
	Visger, George	DT	6-4	250	2	9/26/58	Stockton, Calif.	Colorado	Stockton, Calif.	3
	Washington, Harry	WR	6-0	180	3	7/30/56	Tacoma, Wash.	Colorado State	Tacoma, Wash.	0*
	Webb, Jimmy	DE	6-5	245	7	4/13/52	Jackson, Miss.	Mississippi State	Starkville, Miss.	16
	Wersching, Ray	K	5-11	210	9	8/21/50	Mondsee, Austria	California	Leucadia, Calif.	16
	Wilkinson, Jerry	DE	6-9	260	3	2/27/56	San Francisco, Calif.	Oregon State	Corvallis, Ore.	6
	Williams, Gerard	CB	6-1	184	5	5/25/52	Oklahoma City, Okla.	Langston	St. Louis, Mo.	4
	Williams, Herb	CB	6-0	198	2	8/30/58	Baton Rouge, La.	Southern	Baton Rouge, La.	9
	Woods, Don	RB	6-2	204	8	2/17/51	Denton, Tex.	New Mexico	San Diego, Calif.	10
	Young, Charle	TE	6-4	234	9	2/5/51	Fresno, Calif.	Southern California	Belmont, Calif.	16

*Bierderman last active with Cleveland in '78; DeBernardi last active with Kansas City in '74; Haslip last active with Kansas City in '79; Huff active for 16 games but did not play; Martin played 3 games with N.Y. Jets in '80; Mucker last active with Tampa Bay in '80; Washington last active with Chicago '80.

†Option playout; subject to developments.

†-49ers traded for Benjamin (New Orleans).

Traded—Defensive tackle Ted Vincent to Tampa Bay.

Retired—Bob Ferrell, 6-year running back, 12 games in 1980.

Also played with 49ers in '80—RB Jerry Aldridge (1 game), WR Terry Anderson (4), TE Bob Bruer (1), DT Mike Calhoun (4), CB Charles Cornelius (16), LB Thomas Henderson (1), G Ernie Hughes (3), DT Jim Krahl (2), DE Mel Land (3) CB Melvin Morgan (6), S Scott Perry (11), WR Jimmy Robinson (5), LB Thomas Seabron (6), T Ron Singleton (15), DT Ken Times (3).

1981
Prese...
Aug. 5
Aug. 15
Aug. 22
Aug. 29
Regu...
Sept. 6
Sept. 1
Sept. 2
Sept. 2
Oct. 4
Oct. 11
Oct. 18
Oct. 25
Nov. 1
Nov. 8
Nov. 15
Nov. 22
Nov. 29
Nov. 29
Dec. 6
Dec. 13
Dec. 20

San...
Natio... Westd...
Team...
711 Ne... Redw... Teleph...
Club O...
Preside...
Head C...
Directo...
Public I...
Busines...
Ticket I...
Co-Train...
Stadiu...
Equipm...
Playin...
Trainin...

Press Box

SAN FRANCISCO 49ERS 1981 FIRST-YEAR ROSTER

Name	Pos.	Ht.	Wt.	Birth-date	Birthplace	College	Residence	How Acq.
Adams, Joe	QB	6-3	185	5/4/58	Gulfport, Miss.	Tennessee State	Gulfport, Miss.	D12
Akers, Art	LB	6-2	223	5/14/59	Birmingham, Ala.	UCLA	Los Angeles, Calif.	FA
Barker, Larry	LB	5-11	215	8/3/58	Medford, Ore.	Idaho	Coeur D'Alene, Idaho	FA
Belluomini, Paul	C	6-0	225	3/31/57	Oakland, Calif.	Cal-Davis	Davis, Calif.	FA
Bouza, Matt	WR	6-2	205	4/8/58	San Jose, Calif.	California	Lafayette, Calif.	FA
Choma, John (1)	G-C	6-6	261	2/9/55	Cleveland, Ohio	Virginia	San Diego, Calif.	FA
Cole, Kevin (1)	RB	6-0	190	1/27/56	Benton Harbor, Mich.	San Jose State	Los Angeles, Calif.	D11
DeBose, Ron	TE	6-5	229	10/13/58	Los Angeles, Calif.	UCLA	Carson, Calif.	FA
Drake, Don	DT	6-2	234	9/20/59	Omaha, Neb.	Cal-Poly Pomona	Covina, Calif.	FA
Easley, Walt	FB	6-2	238	9/8/57	Charleston, W. Va.	West Virginia	Morgantown, W. Va.	FA
Gaines, Spider (1)	WR	6-3	190	4/14/57	Pittsburg, Calif.	Washington	Seattle, Wash.	FA
Gervais, Rick	CB-S	5-11	190	11/4/59	Bend, Ore.	Stanford	Bend, Ore.	FA
Graffis, Kevin	T	6-6	265	11/1/55	Wenatchee, Wash.	Washington State	Bridgeport, Wash.	FA
Harty, John	DT	6-4	253	12/17/58	Sioux City, Iowa	Iowa	Sioux City, Iowa	D2
Herring, Eric	WR	6-1	180	9/19/58	Houston, Tex.	Houston	Houston, Tex.	FA
Jensen, Bill	T	6-4	260	2/17/58	Madison, Wis.	Arizona	Mesa, Ariz.	D5
Jones, Arrington	FB	6-0	230	12/16/59	Richmond, Va.	Winston-Salem	Richmond, Va.	FA
Jones, Ray	RB	5-9	180	5/3/58	Pascagoula, Miss.	Pittsburgh	Pascagoula, Miss.	FA
Judie, Ed	LB	6-2	231	7/6/59	Tempe, Ariz.	Northern Arizona	Flagstaff, Ariz.	D6
Kugler, Pete	DT	6-4	255	8/9/59	Cherry Hill, N.J.	Penn State	Cherry Hill, N.J.	FA
Looney, Jim	LB	6-0	225	8/18/57	Bostrope, La.	Purdue	Los Angeles, Calif.	FA
Lott, Ronnie	CB-S	6-0	199	5/8/59	Albuquerque, N.M.	Southern California	Rialto, Calif.	D1
Marshall, Dupre	DT	6-3	250	12/2/58	San Francisco, Calif.	California	San Francisco, Calif.	FA
McCall, Ron (1)	WR	6-2	197	8/16/58	Bessemer, Ala.	Arkansas-Pine Bluff	Bessemer, Ala.	FA
Mitchell, Alan	WR	6-1	185	6/8/59	Detroit, Mich.	Michigan	Detroit, Mich.	FA
Morris, Rod	DT	6-3	242	6/8/52	Sharon, Pa.	Youngstown State	Youngstown, Ohio	FA
Nettling, Bill	TE	6-3	230	1/21/59	Akron, Ohio	Arizona	Cuyahoga Falls, Ohio	FA
Ogilvie, Major	RB	5-11	202	12/12/58	Birmingham, Ala.	Alabama	Birmingham, Ala.	D12
Parham, Gus (1)	DT	6-6	260	9/19/55	Detroit, Mich.	San Jose State	Inglewood, Calif.	FA
Ring, Bill (1)	RB	5-10	215	12/13/56	Des Moines, Iowa	Brigham Young	Acampo, Calif.	FA
Stauch, Scott	RB	5-11	204	1/3/59	Seattle, Wash.	UCLA	Los Angeles, Calif.	FA
Stone, Charles (1)	G	6-2	255	2/4/58	Bucyrus, Ohio	North Carolina State	Cary, N.C.	D5
Thomas, Lynn	CB	5-11	181	7/9/59	Pascagoula, Miss.	Pittsburgh	Pascagoula, Miss.	D5
White, Garry	RB	5-11	201	11/5/58	Rockdale, Tex.	Minnesota	Rockdale, Tex.	D8
Whitley, Eddy (1)	TE	6-3	230	2/12/58	Port Arthur, Tex.	Kansas State	Shawnee, Kan.	FA
Williams, Henry	WR	5-11	176	5/16/58	Blythe, Calif.	Cal. State-Long Bch.	Long Beach, Calif.	FA
Williamson, Carlton	CB	6-0	204	6/12/58	Atlanta, Ga.	Pittsburgh	Atlanta, Ga.	D3
Wolfson, David	RB	6-0	205	4/17/59	Pittsburgh, Pa.	Pittsburgh	Carnegie, Pa.	FA
Wright, Eric	CB	6-1	180	4/18/59	St. Louis, Mo.	Missouri	East St. Louis, Ill.	D2a

Players who report to an NFL team for the first time are designated on rosters as rookies (R). If a player reported to an NFL training camp in a previous year but was not on the active squad for three or more regular season or postseason games, he is listed on the first-year roster and designated by a (1). Thereafter, a player who is on the active squad for three or more regular season games is credited with an additional year of <u>playing experience</u>.

COACHING STAFF

Head Coach, Bill Walsh

Pro Career: Begins third season as an NFL head coach. Started pro coaching career in 1966 as offensive backfield coach for the Oakland Raiders. He then spent eight seasons (1967-75) in Cincinnati, where he was responsible for coaching the Bengals quarterbacks and receivers. His tenure in Cincinnati was followed by a season with the San Diego Chargers as offensive coordinator. While at Cincinnati he tutored Ken Anderson, who became the first NFL quarterback to lead the league in passing two straight years. At San Diego, he helped develop the talents of quarterback Dan Fouts. No pro playing experience. Career Record: 8-24.

Background: End at San Jose State in 1953-54. Started college coaching career at California, where he served under Marv Levy from 1960-62. In 1963 he joined John Ralston's Stanford staff and worked with the defensive backfield for three seasons. Returned to Stanford as head coach in 1977 and directed Cardinals to a two-year record of 17-7, including wins in the Sun and Bluebonnet Bowls. Received his master's degree in history from San Jose State in 1959.

Personal: Born November 30, 1931, in Los Angeles. He and his wife, Geri, live in Menlo Park and have three children—Steve, Craig, and Elizabeth.

ASSISTANT COACHES

Norb Hecker, linebackers; born May 26, 1927, Berea, Ohio, lives in San Francisco. End Baldwin-Wallace 1947-50. Pro end-defensive back Los Angeles Rams 1951-53, Toronto Argonauts (CFL) 1954, Washington Redskins 1955-57. College coach: Stanford 1972-78. Pro coach: Hamilton Tiger-Cats (CFL) 1958, Green Bay Packers 1959-65, Atlanta Falcons 1966-68 (head coach), New York Giants 1969-71, third year with 49ers.

Milt Jackson, special teams-receivers; born October 16, 1943, Groesbeck, Tex., lives in Foster City, Calif. Defensive back Tulsa 1966-67. Pro Quarterback Southern 1954-57. No pro playing experience. College coach: Kansas 1970, UCLA 1971-78. Pro coach: Third year with 49ers.

Billie Matthews, running backs; born March 15, 1930, Houston, Tex., lives in Redwood City. College coach: Westminster 1965 (head coach), Iowa 1966, Oregon 1967-71, Stanford 1972-74, 1977-79, Cornell 1975-76 (head coach). Pro coach: Second year with 49ers.

Bobb McKittrick, offensive line; born December 29, 1935, Baker, Ore., lives in San Mateo. Guard Oregon State 1955-57. No pro playing experience. College coach: Oregon State 1961-64, UCLA 1965-70. Pro coach: Los Angeles Rams 1971-72, San Diego Chargers 1974-78, third year with 49ers.

Bill McPherson, defensive line; born October 24, 1931, Santa Clara, Calif., lives in San Jose. Tackle Santa Clara 1950-52. No pro playing experience. College coach: Santa Clara 1963-74, UCLA 1975-77. Pro coach: Philadelphia Eagles 1978, third year with 49ers.

George Seifert, defensive backs; born January 22, 1940, San Francisco, Calif., lives in Sunnyvale, Calif. Linebacker Utah 1960-62. No pro playing experience. College coach: Westminster 1965 (head coach), Iowa 1966, Oregon 1967-71, Stanford 1972-74, 1977-79, Cornell 1975-76 (head coach). Pro coach: Second year with 49ers.

Chuck Studley, defensive coordinator; born January 17, 1929, Maywood, Ill., lives in Sunnyvale. Guard Illinois 1949-51. No pro playing experience. College coach: Massachusetts 1960, Cincinnati 1961-66. Pro Coach: Cincinnati Bengals 1969-78, third year with 49ers.

Al Vermeil, strength-conditioning; born February 4, 1945, Calistoga, Calif., lives in Fremont. Linebacker Utah State 1966-68. No pro playing experience. Pro coach: Third year with 49ers.

Sam Wyche, quarterbacks; born January 5, 1945, Atlanta, Ga., lives in Sunnyvale. Quarterback Furman 1962-65. Pro quarterback Cincinnati Bengals 1968-70, Washington Redskins 1971-73, Detroit Lions 1974-75, St. Louis Cardinals 1976, Buffalo Bills 1976. College coach: South Carolina 1967. Pro coach: Third year with 49ers.

NOTES

Tampa Bay Buccaneers

National Football Conference
Central Division

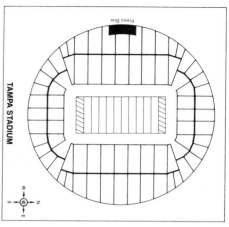

TAMPA STADIUM

Team Colors: Florida Orange, White with
Red Trim

One Buccaneer Place
Tampa, Florida 33607
Telephone: (813) 870-2700

Club Officials

Owner: Hugh F. Culverhouse
President: Hugh F. Culverhouse
Vice President: Joy Culverhouse
Vice President-Head Coach: John H. McKay
Secretary/Treasurer: Ward Holland
Director of Administration: Herbert M. Gold
Assistant to the President: Phil Krueger
Director of Player Personnel: Ken Herock
Director of Public Relations and Promotions: Bob Best
Assistant Director of Public Relations: Rick Odioso
Assistant Director of Promotions: Jim Rowe
Director of Ticket Operations: John Sheffield
Assistant Director of Ticket Operations: Terry Wooten
Ticket Staff: Earl Russell, Kitten Winchester
Pro Personnel Scout: Bill Muir
College Personnel: Jack Bushofsky, Craig Fertig,
Bill Groman,
Controller: Len Hessenauer
Trainer: Tom Oxley
Assistant Trainer: Scott Anderson
Equipment Manager: Pat Marcuccilo
Assistant Equipment Manager: Frank Pupello
Stadium: Tampa Stadium • **Capacity:** 72,128
Tampa, Florida 33607
Playing Surface: Grass
Training Camp: One Buccaneer Place
Tampa, Florida 33607

1981 SCHEDULE

Preseason

Aug. 8	**Cincinnati**	7:00
Aug. 15	**New England**	7:00
Aug. 22	**Houston**	7:00
Aug. 28	at Atlanta	8:30

Regular Season

Sept. 5	**Minnesota** (Saturday)	8:00
Sept. 13	at Kansas City	12:00
Sept. 20	at Chicago	1:00
Sept. 27	**St. Louis**	4:00
Oct. 4	**Detroit**	4:00
Oct. 11	at Green Bay	1:00
Oct. 18	at Oakland	1:00
Oct. 25	at Philadelphia	1:00
Nov. 1	**Chicago**	1:00
Nov. 8	at Minnesota	12:00
Nov. 15	**Denver**	1:00
Nov. 22	**Green Bay**	1:00
Nov. 29	at New Orleans	1:00
Dec. 6	**Atlanta**	4:00
Dec. 13	**San Diego**	1:00
Dec. 20	at Detroit	1:00

1980 TEAM STATISTICS

	Tampa Bay	Opp.
Total First Downs	281	313
Rushing	102	126
Passing	154	168
Penalty	25	19
Third Down Efficiency	99/241	110/250
Third Down Percentage	41.1	44.0
Total Net Yards	5059	5405
Total Offensive Plays	1031	1088
Avg. Gain per Play	4.9	5.0
Avg. Gain per Game	316.2	337.8
Net Yards Rushing	1839	2101
Total Rushing Plays	477	548
Avg. Gain per Rush	3.9	3.8
Avg. Gain Rushing per Game	114.9	131.3
Net Yards Passing	3220	3304
Lost Attempting to Pass	24/194	24/173
Gross Yards Passing	3414	3477
Attempts/Completions	530/256	516/328
Percent Completed	48.3	63.6
Had Intercepted	17	15
Avg. Net Passing per Game	201.3	206.5
Punts/Avg.	89/41.8	89/42.0
Punt Returns/Avg.	57/5.5	54/9.8
Kickoff Returns/Avg.	67/19.3	62/22.9
Interceptions/Avg. Ret.	15/11.9	17/10.9
Penalties/Yards	90/840	117/1077
Fumbles/Ball Lost	28/21	32/13
Total Points	271	341
Avg. Points per Game	16.9	21.3
Touchdowns	32	40
Rushing	9	20
Passing	20	17
Returns and Recoveries	3	3
Field Goals	16/23	20/33
Conversions	31/32	39/40
Safeties	0	1

1980 TEAM RECORD

Preseason (3-1)

Tampa Bay		Opponents
21	Houston	7
14	St. Louis	21
20	Cincinnati (OT)	14
11	Washington	6
66		48

Regular Season (5-10-1)

Tampa Bay		Opponents	Att.
17	Cincinnati	12	38,280
10	*Los Angeles	9	66,576
17	Dallas	28	62,750
27	*Cleveland	34	65,540
0	Chicago	23	61,350
14	*Green Bay (OT)	14	64,854
14	Houston	20	48,167
24	San Francisco	23	51,925
30	*New York Giants	13	68,256
21	*Pittsburgh	24	71,636
30	Minnesota	38	46,032
10	*Detroit	24	64,976
20	Green Bay	17	54,225
10	*Minnesota	21	65,649
14	Detroit	27	76,893
13	*Chicago	14	55,298
271			962,407

*Home Game (OT) Overtime

Score by Periods

Tampa Bay	73	88	34	76	0	—	271
Opponents	58	108	76	99	0	—	341

Attendance

Home 522,785   Away 439,622   Total 962,407

Single game home record, 71,636 (11-9-80)
Single season home record, 545,980 (1979)

1980 INDIVIDUAL STATISTICS

Rushing

	Att	Yds	Avg	LG	TD
Bell	174	599	3.4	40	2
Eckwood	149	504	3.4	35t	2
Williams	58	370	6.4	27	4
Berns	39	131	3.4	17	0
J. Davis	39	130	3.3	8	1
House	1	32	32.0	32	0
Hagins	3	24	8.0	32	0
T. Davis	5	24	4.8	26	0
G. Davis	7	21	3.0	8	0
Fusina	1	14	14.0	14	0
Jones	1	-10	-10.0	-10	0
Tampa Bay	477	1839	3.9	40	9
Opponents	548	2101	3.8	56	20

Field Goal Success

Distance	1-19	20-29	30-39	40-49	50 Over
Made-Att.	1-1	7-8	7-9	1-5	0-0

Passing

	Att	Comp	Pct	Yds	TD	Int	LG	Tkld	Rate
Williams	521	254	48.8	3396	20	16	40	23/194	69.7
Eckwood	4	2	50.0	18	0	0	—	0/0	—
Fusina	4	2	50.0	0	0	1	—	1/0	—
Hannah	1	0	0.0	0	0	0	—	0/0	—
Tampa Bay	530	256	48.3	3414	20	17		24/194	68.5
Opponents	516	328	63.6	3477	17	15		24/173	—

Receiving

	No	Yds	Avg	LG	TD
Jones	48	669	13.9	41t	5
Eckwood	47	475	10.1	40	1
Bell	38	292	7.7	22	1
Giles	33	602	18.2	51	5
House	24	531	22.1	61	2
Hagins	23	364	15.8	48	1
T. Davis	12	115	9.6	18	1
Obradovich	11	152	13.8	24	0
G. Davis	9	79	8.8	15	0
Shumann	4	75	18.8	25	1
J. Davis	4	17	4.3	9	0
Mucker	2	37	18.5	19	0
Berns	1	6	6.0	6	0
Tampa Bay	256	3414	13.3	61	20
Opponents	328	3477	10.6	50	17

Interceptions

	No	Yds	Avg	LG	TD
Washington	4	30	7.5	16	0
Wood	3	76	25.3	55t	1
Cotney	3	28	9.3	21	0
Colzie	1	39	39.0	39	0
Brantley	1	6	6.0	6	0
C. Brown	1	0	0.0	0	0
D. Lewis	1	0	0.0	0	0
Thomas	1	0	0.0	0	0
Tampa Bay	15	179	11.9	55t	1
Opponents	17	185	10.9	44	0

Punting

	No	Yds	Avg	LG	In 20
Blanchard	88	3722	42.3	62	18
Tampa Bay	89	3722	41.8	62	18
Opponents	89	3739	42.0	61	16

Punt Returns

	No	FC	Yds	Avg	LG	TD
Reece	57	1	313	5.5	19	0
T. Davis		1	0	0.0	0	0
Tampa Bay	57	2	313	5.5	19	0
Opponents	54	4	529	9.8	53t	1

Kickoff Returns

	No	Yds	Avg	LG	TD
G. Davis	44	951	21.6	54	0
Reece	7	128	18.3	23	0
Obradovich	5	46	9.2	15	0
Hagins	4	82	20.5	23	0
T. Davis	4	58	14.5	16	0
Berns	1	19	19.0	19	0
Samuels	1	10	10.0	10	0
Jordan	1	0	0.0	0	0
Tampa Bay	67	1294	19.3	54	0
Opponents	62	1417	22.9	91t	1

Scoring

	TD	TD R	TD P	TD Rt	PAT	FG	TP
Yepremian	0	0	0	0	31/32	16/23	79
House	5	0	5	0			30
Jones	5	0	5	0			30
Giles	4	0	4	0			24
Williams	4	4	0	0			24
Bell	3	2	1	0			18
Eckwood	3	2	1	0			18
Hagins	2	0	2	0			12
C. Brown	1	0	1	0			6
J. Davis	1	1	0	0			6
T. Davis	1	0	0	1			6
Logan	1	0	0	1			6
Shumann	1	0	1	0			6
Wood	1	0	0	1			6
Tampa Bay	32	9	20	3	31/32	16/23	271
Opponents	40	20	17	3	39/40	20/33	341

TAMPA BAY RECORD HOLDERS

Individual Records—Single Season

Category	Name	Performance
Rushing (Yds.)	Ricky Bell, 1979	1263
Passing (Pct.)	Steve Spurrier, 1976	50.2
Passing (Yds.)	Doug Williams, 1980	3396
Passing (TDs)	Doug Williams, 1980	20
Receiving (No.)	Gordon Jones, 1980	48
Receiving (Yds.)	Isaac Hagins, 1979	692
Interceptions	Cedric Brown, 1978	6
Punting (Avg.)	Tom Blanchard, 1980	42.3
Punt Ret. (Avg.)	Danny Reece, 1978	8.9
Kickoff Ret. (Avg.)	Isaac Hagins, 1977	23.5
Field Goals	Garo Yepremian, 1980	16
Touchdowns (Tot.)	Ricky Bell, 1979	9
Points	Garo Yepremian, 1980	79

Team Records—Single Game

Category	Opponent, Date	Performance
Offense		
First Downs	vs. Minn, 11/16/80	27
Total Points	vs. Chi, 10/22/78	33
Touchdowns	vs. Chi, 10/22/78	5
Total Net Yards	vs. Minn, 11/16/80	573
Net Yards Rushing	vs. KC, 12/16/79	244
Net Yards Passing	vs. NYG, 11/2/80	486
Rushing Attempts	vs. KC, 12/16/79	62
Passing Attempts	vs. Cle, 9/28/80	56
Interceptions by	vs. Minn, 11/16/80	56
	vs. NO, 12/11/77	6
Defense		
Net Yards Allowed	vs. KC, 12/16/79	80
Net Rushing Yards Allowed	vs. Det, 11/11/79	38
Net Passing Yards Allowed	vs. Cin, 9/7/80	16

FIRST PLAYERS SELECTED

Year	Player, College, Position
1976	Lee Roy Selmon, Oklahoma, DT
1977	Ricky Bell, Southern California, RB
1978	Doug Williams, Grambling, QB
1979	Greg Roberts, Oklahoma, G (2)
1980	Ray Snell, Wisconsin, G
1981	Hugh Green, Pittsburgh, LB

BUCCANEERS COACHING HISTORY (23-54-1)

1976-80	John McKay	23-54-1

TAMPA BAY BUCCANEERS 1981 VETERAN ROSTER

No.	Name	Pos.	Ht.	Wt.	NFL Exp.	Birth-date	Birthplace	College	Residence	Games in '80
69	Austin, Darrell	G-T	6-4	255	7	11/5/51	Union, S.C.	South Carolina	Tampa, Fla.	8
42	Bell, Ricky	RB	6-2	215	5	4/8/55	Houston, Tex.	Southern California	Los Angeles, Calif.	14
36	Berns, Rick	RB	6-2	205	3	2/5/56	Okinawa, Japan	Nebraska	Tampa, Fla.	16
16	Blanchard, Tom	P	6-0	185	11	5/28/49	Grants Pass, Ore.	Oregon	Grants Pass, Ore.	16
53	†Bonness, Rik	LB	6-3	220	5	3/20/54	Borger, Tex.	Nebraska	Tampa, Fla.	0*
52	Brantley, Scot	LB	6-1	230	2	2/24/58	Chester, S.C.	Florida	Ocala, Fla.	16
55	Brown, Aaron	LB	6-2	235	4	1/13/56	Warren, Ohio	Ohio State	Tampa, Fla.	0*
34	Brown, Cedric	S	6-2	205	5	5/6/54	Columbus, Ohio	Kent State	Tampa, Fla.	13
87	Carter, Gerald	WR	6-1	185	2	6/19/57	Bryan, Tex.	Texas A&M	Bryan, Tex.	3*
	Cesare, Bill	S	5-11	190	3	6/2/55	New York, N.Y.	Miami	Miami, Fla.	2*
20	†Colzie, Neal	S	6-2	195	7	2/28/53	Fitzgerald, Ga.	Ohio State	Tampa, Fla.	16
33	Cotney, Mark	S	6-0	205	7	6/26/52	Altus, Okla.	Cameron State	Tampa, Fla.	16
71	Crowder, Randy	NT	6-3	250	6	7/30/52	Farrell, Pa.	Penn State	Tampa, Fla.	2
28	Davis, Gary	RB	5-10	210	6	9/7/54	Los Angeles, Calif.	Cal Poly-SLO	Miami, Fla.	15
38	Davis, Johnny	RB	6-1	235	4	7/17/56	Montgomery, Ala.	Alabama	Tampa, Fla.	14
27	†Davis, Tony	RB	5-11	210	6	1/21/53	Tecumseh, Neb.	Nebraska	Tampa, Fla.	15
43	Eckwood, Jerry	RB	6-0	200	3	12/26/54	Brinkley, Ark.	Arkansas	Tampa, Fla.	15
14	Fusina, Chuck	QB	6-1	195	3	5/31/57	Pittsburgh, Pa.	Penn State	McKees Rocks, Pa.	2
88	Giles, Jimmie	TE	6-3	245	5	11/8/54	Greenville, Miss.	Alcorn State	Tampa, Fla.	16
81	Hagins, Isaac	WR	5-9	180	5	3/2/54	Shreveport, La.	Southern	Tampa, Fla.	16
73	Hannah, Charley	T	6-6	260	5	7/26/55	Albertville, Ala.	Alabama	Tampa, Fla.	16
59	Hawkins, Andy	LB	6-2	220	2	3/31/58	Bay City, Tex.	Texas A&I	Bay City, Tex.	14
89	House, Kevin	WR	6-1	175	2	12/20/57	St. Louis, Mo.	Southern Illinois	Tampa, Fla.	16
56	Johnson, Cecil	LB	6-2	230	5	8/19/55	Miami, Fla.	Pittsburgh	Tampa, Fla.	16
84	Jones, Gordon	WR	6-0	190	3	7/25/57	Buffalo, N.Y.	Pittsburgh	Tampa, Fla.	16
25	†Jordan, Curtis	CB-S	6-2	205	6	1/25/54	Lubbock, Tex.	Texas Tech	Tampa, Fla.	16
77	Kollar, Bill	DE-NT	6-4	250	8	11/12/52	Warren, Ohio	Montana State	Tampa, Fla.	16
62	Leonard, Jim	C	6-3	250	2	10/19/57	Santa Cruz, Calif.	Santa Clara	Santa Cruz, Calif.	6
57	Lewis, David	LB	6-4	245	5	10/15/54	Houston, Tex.	Southern California	Tampa, Fla.	15
79	Lewis, Reggie	DE	6-3	255	3	5/6/56	Port Arthur, Tex.	North Texas State	Tampa, Fla.	10
76	†Logan, David	NT	6-2	250	3	10/25/56	Pittsburgh, Pa.	Pittsburgh	Pittsburgh, Pa.	16
51	Natziger, Dana	LB	6-1	220	4	10/26/53	Woodstock, Ill.	Cal Poly-SLO	Pismo Beach, Calif.	0*
86	†Obradovich, Jim	TE	6-2	230	7	4/2/53	Los Angeles, Calif.	Southern California	Hermosa Beach, Calif.	16
78	Radford, Bruce	DE	6-5	260	2	9/5/55	Pineville, La.	Grambling	Pineville, La.	12
75	Reavis, Dave	T	6-5	260	7	6/19/50	Nashville, Tenn.	Arkansas	Tampa, Fla.	16
61	Roberts, Greg	G	6-3	260	3	11/19/56	Nacogdoches, Tex.	Oklahoma	Tampa, Fla.	16
80	†Samuels, Tony	TE	6-4	235	5	12/30/54	New Orleans, La.	Bethune-Cookman	Tampa, Fla.	10*
74	†Sanders, Gene	G-T	6-3	260	3	11/10/56	Eufaula, Okla.	Texas A&M	Tampa, Fla.	11
58	Selmon, Dewey	LB	6-1	240	6	11/19/53	Eufaula, Okla.	Oklahoma	Norman, Okla.	15
63	Selmon, Lee Roy	DE	6-3	250	6	10/20/54	Eufaula, Okla.	Oklahoma	Tampa, Fla.	16
82	Shumann, Mike	WR	6-0	175	6	10/13/55	Louisville, Ky.	Florida State	Redwood City, Calif.	6
72	Snell, Ray	G	6-3	255	2	2/24/58	Baltimore, Md.	Wisconsin	Tampa, Fla.	13
65	Stalls, Dave	DE	6-4	250	5	9/19/55	Madison, Wis.	Northern Colorado	Long Beach, Calif.	15
85	Stewart, Joe	WR	5-11	180	3	11/18/55	Evanston, Ill.	Missouri	Evanston, Ill.	0*
41	Thomas, Norris	CB	5-11	185	5	5/1/54	Inverness, Miss.	Southern Mississippi	Pascagoula, Miss.	15
40	†Vincent, Ted	NT	6-4	265	4	8/10/56	O'Fallon, Mo.	Wichita State	O'Fallon, Mo.	12
12	Washington, Mike	CB	6-2	200	6	7/1/53	Montgomery, Ala.	Alabama	Montgomery, Ala.	16
50	Williams, Doug	QB	6-4	215	4	8/9/55	Zachary, La.	Grambling	Tampa, Fla.	16
54	Wilson, Steve	C	6-3	265	6	5/19/54	Fort Sill, Okla.	Georgia	Tampa, Fla.	15
68	Wood, Richard	LB	6-2	230	7	5/31/53	Elizabeth, N.J.	Southern California	Tampa, Fla.	16
1	Yano, George	G-C	6-2	255	3	8/12/57	Spokane, Wash.	Washington State	Tampa, Fla.	16
	Yepremian, Garo	K	5-8	175	14	6/2/44	Larnaca, Cyprus	No College	Miami, Fla.	16

*Bonness and Natziger missed '80 season due to injuries; Carter played 3 games with N.Y. Jets in '80; Cesare played 2 games with Miami in '80; Samuels played 4 games with Kansas City, 6 with Tampa Bay; Stewart last active with Oakland in '79.

†Option playout; subject to developments.

‡Buccaneers traded for Vincent (San Francisco).

Also played with Buccaneers in '80—DE Mike Calhoun (3 games), WR Larry Mucker (7), CB Danny Reece (16), TE Conrad Rucker (2).

COACHING STAFF

Head Coach, John McKay

Pro Career: Starts sixth season as Buccaneers head coach. In 1979, guided Tampa Bay to NFC Central title and first playoff berth. Under his direction, Tampa Bay became the second expansion team to qualify for the playoffs in one of its first four seasons and the first expansion team to win 10 games in one of its first four seasons. Drafted by the New York Yankees (AAFC) in 1950 but turned down pro playing career. Career record: 23-54-1.

Background: Defensive back Purdue 1946, transferred to Oregon and played both ways 1947-49. Holds Oregon records for most touchdowns rushing in a game and highest career average per carry. Assistant coach at Oregon 1950-58 and Southern California 1959. Head coach at Southern California 1960-75. Directed Southern California teams to four national championships and nine Bowl appearances (Rose 8, Liberty 1). Southern California coaching record: 127-40-8.

Personal: Born July 5, 1923, Everettsville, West Virginia. John and his wife, Corky, live in Tampa and have four children—Michele, John Jr., Richard, and Terri.

ASSISTANT COACHES

Tom Bass, defensive coordinator; born August 2, 1936, Riverside, Calif., lives in Tampa. Linebacker San Jose State 1955-57. No pro playing experience. College coach: San Jose State 1958-59, San Diego State 1960-62. Pro coach: Ohio State 1968-78. Pro coach: Third year with Buccaneers.

George Chaump, running backs; born April 20, 1936, Scranton, Pa., lives in Tampa. Center Bloomsburg State 1956-58. No pro playing experience. College coach: Ohio State 1968-78. Pro coach: Third year with Buccaneers.

Boyd Dowler, receivers; born October 18, 1937, Rock Springs, Wyo., lives in Tampa. Quarterback Colorado 1955-58. Pro wide receiver Green Bay Packers 1959-69. Washington Redskins 1971. Pro coach: Los Angeles Rams 1970, Washington Redskins 1971-72, Philadelphia Eagles 1973-75, Cincinnati Bengals 1976-79, second year with Buccaneers.

Wayne Fontes, defensive secondary; born February 17, 1940, New Bedford, Mass., lives in Tampa. Defensive back Michigan State 1959-62. Pro defensive back New York Titans (AFL) 1963-64. College coach: Dayton 1968, Iowa 1969-71, Southern California 1972-75. Pro coach: Buccaneers since 1976.

Abe Gibron, chief assistant-defensive line; born September 22, 1925, Michigan City, Ind., lives in Tampa. Guard Purdue 1945-47. Pro guard Buffalo Bills (AAFC) 1949, Cleveland Browns 1950-55, Philadelphia Eagles 1956-57, Chicago Bears 1958-59. Pro coach: Washington Redskins 1960-64, Chicago Bears 1965-74 (head coach 1972-74), Chicago Wind (WFL) 1975 (head coach), Buccaneers since 1976.

Bill Johnson, offensive line; born July 14, 1926, Tyler, Tex., lives in Tampa. Center Texas A&M 1944-46. Pro center San Francisco 49ers 1948-55. Pro coach: San Francisco 49ers 1956-67, Cincinnati Bengals 1968-78 (head coach 1976-78), third year with Buccaneers.

Bill Nelsen, quarterbacks; born January 29, 1941, Los Angeles, lives in Tampa. Quarterback Southern California 1960-62. Pro quarterback Pittsburgh Steelers 1963-67, Cleveland Browns 1968-72. Pro coach: New England Patriots 1973-74, Atlanta Falcons 1975-76, fifth year with Buccaneers.

Howard Tippett, linebackers-special teams; born September 23, 1938, Tallassee, Ala., lives in Tampa. Quarterback-safety East Tennessee State 1955-57. No pro playing experience. College coach: Tulane 1963-65, West Virginia 1966, 1971, Houston 1967-70, Mississippi State 1972-73, 1979, Washington State 1976, Oregon 1977-78, UCLA 1980. Pro coach: Jacksonville Sharks (WFL) 1974-75, joined Buccaneers in 1981.

TAMPA BAY BUCCANEERS 1981 FIRST-YEAR ROSTER

Name	Pos.	Ht.	Wt.	Birth-date	Birthplace	College	Residence	How Acq.
Christiansen, Gregg	T	6-4	260	9/19/58	Encino, Calif.	UCLA	Canoga Park, Calif.	FA
Clark, David	DT	6-3	250	7/2/58	Rotan, Tex.	Nebraska	Junction City, Ore.	FA
Flowers, Jackie (1)	WR	6-0	190	3/4/58	Jacksonville, Fla.	Florida State	Jacksonville, Fla.	FA
Ford, Mike	QB	6-3	220	1/30/59	Clarksville, Tex.	Southern Methodist	Mesquite, Tex.	D9
Gettel, Steve	G	6-1	260	5/20/59	Daytona Beach, Fla.	South Carolina	Ormond Beach, Fla.	FA
Green, Hugh	LB	6-2	225	7/27/59	Natchez, Miss.	Pittsburgh	Natchez, Miss.	D1
Hamilton, Wayne (1)	DT	6-5	245	2/18/58	Okahumpka, Fla.	Alabama	Okahumpka, Fla.	FA
Henry, Forrest	CB-S	6-0	200	7/20/59	Philadelphia, Pa.	Utah	Salt Lake City, Utah	FA
Hersey, Richard	RB	6-1	200	3/24/59	Elgin, Ill.	Arizona	Tucson, Ariz.	FA
Holt, John	CB-S	5-11	180	5/14/59	Lawton, Okla.	West Texas State	Canyon, Tex.	D4
Johnson, Denver	T	6-6	250	10/17/58	Seminole, Okla.	Tulsa	Seminole, Okla.	D8
McCune, Ken	DE-DT	6-6	250	2/12/59	Freeport, Tex.	Texas	Austin, Tex.	D10
Menhardt, Herb	K	5-11	175	3/8/58	Philadelphia, Pa.	Penn State	Flourtown, Pa.	FA
Quinn, Jeff	QB	6-2	205	2/16/58	Ord, Neb.	Nebraska	Lincoln, Neb.	FA
Roveto, John (1)	K	5-11	175	2/20/58	Ft. Lauderdale, Fla.	Southwest Louisiana	Atlanta, Ga.	D11
Smith, Johnny Ray	CB-S	5-9	175	9/7/57	Crockett, Tex.	Lamar	Cleveland, Tex.	FA
Taylor, Bo (1)	WR	5-9	180	11/21/57	Dallas, Tex.	Baylor	Dallas, Tex.	FA
Thomas, Robert	RB	6-0	225	6/2/59	Cameta, Miss.	Texas Southern	Rolling Fork, Miss.	FA
White, Brad	DT-DE	6-2	250	10/18/58	Rexburg, Idaho	Tennessee	Knoxville, Tenn.	D12
Wilder, James	RB	6-2	220	5/12/58	Sikeston, Mo.	Missouri	Columbia, Mo.	D2

Players who report to an NFL team for the first time are designated on rosters as rookies (R). If a player reported to an NFL training camp in a previous year but was not on the active squad for three or more regular season or postseason games, he is listed on the first-year roster and designated by a (1). Thereafter, a player who is on the active squad for three or more regular season games is credited with an additional year of playing experience.

NOTES

154

Washington Redskins

**National Football Conference
Eastern Division**

Team Colors: Burgundy and Gold

Redskin Park,
P.O. Box 17247
Dulles International Airport,
Washington, D.C. 20041
Telephone: (703) 471-9100

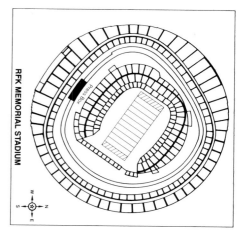

RFK MEMORIAL STADIUM

Club Officials

Chairman of the Board-Chief Operating Executive:
Jack Kent Cooke
President: Edward Bennett Williams
Senior Vice President: Gerard T. Gabrys
Board of Directors: Jack Kent Cooke, John Kent
Cooke, Lawrence Lucchino, W. Jarvis Moody,
Robert A. Schulman, William A. Shea,
Edward Bennett Williams
General Manager: Bobby Beathard
Assistant General Manager: Bobby Mitchell
Assistant General Manager: Joel Margolis
Assistant General Manager: Dick Myers
Director of Player Personnel: Mike Allman
Director of Pro Scouting: Kirk Mee
Director of College Scouting: Dick Daniels
Scouts: Charley Taylor, Charles Casserly
Public Relations Director: Joe F. Blair
Assistant Public Relations Director: Charles M. Taylor
Ticket Manager: George X. Christophel
Head Trainer: Lamar (Bubba) Tyer
Assistant Trainers: Joe Kuczo, Keoki Kamau
Director of Photography: Nate Fine
Equipment Manager: Jay Brunetti

Stadium: Robert F. Kennedy Stadium •
Capacity: 55,045
East Capitol Street
Washington, D.C. 20003
Playing Surface: Grass (PAT)
Training Camp: Dickinson College
Carlisle, Pennsylvania 17013

1981 SCHEDULE

Preseason

Aug. 7	**Kansas City**	7:30
Aug. 14	**Minnesota**	7:30
Aug. 22	at Baltimore	8:00
Aug. 30	at New England	12:30

Regular Season

Sept. 6	**Dallas**	1:00
Sept. 13	**New York Giants**	1:00
Sept. 20	at St. Louis	12:00
Sept. 27	at Philadelphia	1:00
Oct. 4	**San Francisco**	1:00
Oct. 11	at Chicago	1:00
Oct. 18	at Miami	4:00
Oct. 25	**New England**	1:00
Nov. 1	**St. Louis**	4:00
Nov. 8	**Detroit**	4:00
Nov. 15	at New York Giants	4:00
Nov. 22	at Dallas	3:00
Nov. 29	at Buffalo	1:00
Dec. 6	**Philadelphia**	1:00
Dec. 13	**Baltimore**	1:00
Dec. 20	at Los Angeles	1:00

1980 TEAM STATISTICS

	Washington	Opp.
Total First Downs	279	298
Rushing	109	144
Passing	148	127
Penalty	22	27
Third Down Efficiency	89/232	81/216
Third Down Percentage	38.4	37.5
Total Net Yards	4854	4695
Total Offensive Plays	1039	1020
Avg. Gain per Play	4.7	4.6
Avg. Gain per Game	303.4	293.4
Net Yards Rushing	2016	2524
Total Rushing Plays	517	585
Avg. Gain per Rush	3.9	4.3
Avg. Gain Rushing per Game	126.0	157.8
Net Yards Passing	2838	2171
Lost Attempting to Pass	36/333	43/333
Gross Yards Passing	3171	2504
Attempts/Completions	486/284	392/187
Percent Completed	58.4	47.7
Had Intercepted	18	33
Avg. Net Passing per Game	177.4	135.7
Punts/Avg.	85/39.2	84/40.7
Punt Returns/Avg.	48/10.1	52/6.8
Kickoff Returns/Avg.	57/21.1	60/18.4
Interceptions/Avg. Ret.	33/9.7	18/12.2
Penalties/Yards	114/1008	90/766
Fumbles/Ball Lost	35/18	25/12
Total Points	261	293
Avg. Points per Game	16.3	18.3
Touchdowns	30	36
Rushing	12	16
Passing	17	17
Returns and Recoveries	1	3
Field Goals	18/33	13/17
Conversions	27/30	36/36
Safeties	0	1

1980 TEAM RECORD

Preseason (3-1)

Washington			Opponents
3	Baltimore		3
12	Cleveland		3
34	Oakland		17
6	Tampa Bay		11
65			34

Regular Season (6-10)

Washington			Opponents	Att.
3	*Dallas		17	55,045
23	New York Giants		21	73,343
21	Oakland		24	45,163
0	*Seattle		14	53,263
14	Philadelphia		24	69,044
17	Denver		20	74,657
23	*St. Louis		0	51,060
14	*Minnesota		14	51,375
22	New Orleans		39	52,060
21	Chicago		35	57,159
0	*Philadelphia		24	51,897
10	Dallas		14	58,809
6	Atlanta		10	55,665
40	*San Diego		17	48,556
16	*New York Giants		13	44,443
31	St. Louis		7	35,942
261			293	877,481

*Home Game

Score by Periods

Washington	43	80	61	77	261
Opponents	80	101	34	78	293

Attendance

Home 407,699   Away 469,782   Total 877,481

Single game home record, 55,045 (9-8-80)
Single season home record, 427,651 (1979)

1980 INDIVIDUAL STATISTICS

Rushing

	Att	Yds	Avg	LG	TD
Jackson	176	708	4.0	55t	3
Harmon	128	484	3.8	23	0
Hammond	45	265	5.9	36	1
Claitt	57	215	3.8	16	3
Theismann	29	175	6.0	37	3
Hardeman	40	132	3.3	13	1
Forte	30	51	1.7	6	0
Kruczek	9	5	0.6	5	1
Walker	1	-8	-8.0	-8	0
Harrison	2	-11	-5.5	-3	0
Washington	517	2016	3.9	55t	12
Opponents	585	2524	4.3	50t	16

Field Goal Success

Distance	1-19	20-29	30-39	40-49	50 Over
Made-Att.	0-0	3-4	5-6	7-12	3-11

Passing

	Att	Comp	Pct	Yds	TD	Int	LG	Tkld	Rate
Theismann	454	262	57.7	2962	17	16	55t	31/282	75.1
Kruczek	31	22	71.0	209	0	2	36	5/51	62.3
Hardeman	1	0	0	0	0	0			
Washington	486	284	58.4	3171	17	18	55t	36/333	74.2
Opponents	392	187	47.7	2504	17	33	50t	43/333	—

Receiving

	No	Yds	Avg	LG	TD
Monk	58	797	13.7	54t	3
Harmon	54	534	9.9	45	0
Warren	31	323	10.4	35	0
Jackson	27	279	10.3	27	1
Hammond	24	203	8.5	38	1
Thompson	22	313	14.2	54t	5
Hardeman	16	178	11.1	46	0
Forte	15	174	11.6	28	1
McDaniel	14	154	11.0	18	0
Walker	10	88	8.3	15t	1
Harrison	8	66	8.3	12	0
Claitt	3	34	11.3	26	0
DuBois	1	16	16.0	16	0
Coleman	1	12	12.0	12	0
Washington	284	3171	11.2	54t	17
Opponents	187	2504	13.4	54t	17

Interceptions

	No	Yds	Avg	LG	TD
Parrish	7	13	1.9	9	0
Lavender	6	96	16.0	51t	1
Murphy	6	58	9.7	28	0
Peters	4	59	14.8	37	0
Milot	4	-8	-2.0	2	0
Coleman	3	92	30.7	41	0
White	2	1		8	0
Smith	1	8	8.0	8	0
Washington	33	319	9.7	51t	1
Opponents	18	219	12.2	52	0

Punting

	No	Yds	Avg	In 20	LG	TD
Connell	85	3331	39.2	11	64	0
Washington	85	3331	39.2	11	64	0
Opponents	84	3422	40.7	15	52	0

Punt Returns

	No	FC	Yds	Avg	LG	TD
Nelms	48	5	487	10.1	64	0
Washington	48	5	487	10.1	64	0
Opponents	52	14	351	6.8	52	0

Kickoff Returns

	No	Yds	Avg	LG	TD
Nelms	38	810	21.3	51	0
Jackson	8	204	25.5	35	0
Forte	4	114	28.5	53	0
McKinney	2	48	24.0	31	0
Claitt	2	18	9.0	11	0
Monk	1	10	10.0	10	0
Anderson	1	0	0.0	0	0
Thompson	1	0	0.0	0	0
Washington	57	1204	21.1	53	0
Opponents	60	1102	18.4	70t	1

Scoring

	TD R	TD P	TD Rt	PAT	FG	TP
Moseley				27/30	18/33	81
Harmon	8	4	4			48
Thompson	5	0	5			30
Jackson	4	3	1			24
Monk	3	0	3			18
Theismann	3	0	0			18
Claitt	2	1	1			12
Forte	2	1	1			12
Hammond	1	1	0			6
Lavender	1	0	1			6
Walker	1	0	1			6
Washington	30	12	17	27/30	18/33	261
Opponents	36	16	17	36/36	13/17	293

WASHINGTON RECORD HOLDERS

Individual Records—Single Season

Category	Name	Performance
Rushing (Yds.)	Larry Brown, 1972	1216
Passing (Pct.)	Sammy Baugh, 1945	70.3
Passing (Yds.)	Sonny Jurgensen, 1967	3747
Passing (TDs)	Sonny Jurgensen, 1967	31
Receiving (No.)	Bobby Mitchell, 1962	72
	Charley Taylor, 1966	72
Receiving (Yds.)	Bobby Mitchell, 1963	1436
Interceptions	Don Sandifer, 1948	13
Punting (Avg.)	Sammy Baugh, 1940	51.3
Punt Ret. (Avg.)	Dick Todd, 1941	17.0
Kickoff Ret. (Avg.)	Dick James, 1961	29.4
Field Goals	Curt Knight, 1971	29
Touchdowns (Tot.)	Charley Taylor, 1966	15
	Curt Knight, 1971	114
Points	Mark Moseley, 1979	114

Team Records—Single Game

Category	Opponent, Date	Performance
Offense		
First Downs	vs. Det, 11/18/48	29
	vs. NYJ, 12/5/76	29
Total Points	vs. NYG, 11/27/66	72
Touchdowns	vs. NYG, 11/27/66	10
Total Net Yards	vs. NY Yanks, 10/31/48	625
Net Yards Rushing	vs. NY Yanks, 11/25/51	352
Net Yards Passing	vs. NY Yanks, 10/31/48	501
Rushing Attempts	vs. LA, 11/25/51	64
Passing Attempts	vs. Chi, 10/25/64	57
Interceptions by	vs. NYG, 12/8/63	7
	vs. Phil, 12/21/75	7
Defense		
Net Yards Allowed	vs. NYG, 9/27/42	51
	vs. NYG, 12/11/60	51
Net Rushing Yards Allowed	vs. LA, 10/11/42	-29
Net Passing Yards Allowed	vs. StL, 12/21/80	-12

FIRST PLAYERS SELECTED

Year	Player, College, Position
1973	Charles Cantrell, Lamar, G (5)
1974	Jon Keyworth, Colorado, TE (6)
1975	Mike Thomas, Nevada-Las Vegas, RB (6)
1976	Mike Hughes, Baylor, G (5)
1977	Duncan McColl, Stanford, DE (4)
1978	Tony Green, Florida, RB (6)
1979	Don Warren, San Diego St., TE (4)
1980	Art Monk, Syracuse, WR
1981	Mark May, Pittsburgh, T

REDSKINS COACHING HISTORY

Boston 1932-36
(306-300-26)

1949	John (Billick) Whelchel**	2-4-1
1949-51	Herman Ball***	5-15-0
1951	Dick Todd	5-4-0
1952-53	Earl (Curly) Lambeau	10-13-1
1954-58	Joe Kuharich	26-32-2
1959-60	Mike Nixon	4-18-2
1961-65	Bill McPeak	21-46-3
1966-68	Otto Graham	17-22-3
1969	Vince Lombardi	7-5-2
1970	Bill Austin	6-8-0
1971-77	George Allen	69-35-1
1978-80	Jack Pardee	24-24-0

*Retired to enter Navy
**Released after seven games in 1949
***Released after three games in 1951

WASHINGTON REDSKINS 1981 VETERAN ROSTER

No.	Name	Pos.	Ht.	Wt.	NFL Exp.	Birth-date	Birthplace	College	Residence	Games in '80
79	†Bacon, Coy	DE	6-4	265	14	8/30/43	Cadiz, Ky.	Jackson State	Herndon, Va.	16
53	Bostic, Jeff	C	6-2	246	2	9/18/58	Greensboro, N.C.	Clemson	Greensboro, N.C.	16
69	Brooks, Perry	DT	6-3	260	4	12/4/54	Bogalousa, La.	Southern	Baton Rouge, La.	12
65	Butz, Dave	DT	6-7	285	9	6/23/50	Lafayette, Ala.	Purdue	Belleville, Ill.	16
35	Claitt, Rickey	RB	5-10	206	2	4/12/57	Sylvester, Ga.	Bethune-Cookman	Avon Park, Fla.	15
51	Coleman, Monte	LB	6-2	230	3	11/4/57	Pine Bluff, Ark.	Central Arkansas	Reston, Va.	16
10	Connell, Mike	P	6-1	200	2	3/15/56	Sharon, Pa.	Cincinnati	Reston, Va.	16
63	Dean, Fred	G	6-3	253	5	2/24/56	Gainesville, Fla.	Texas Southern	Houston, Tex.	12
86	Dimler, Rich	DT	6-6	260	2	7/18/56	Bayonne, N.J.	Southern California	Glendale, Calif.	0*
30	DuBois, Phil	TE	6-2	220	2	11/16/56	Rochester, Minn.	San Diego State	Whittier, Calif.	2
59	†Dusek, Brad	LB	6-2	223	8	12/13/50	Longview, Tex.	Texas A&M	Haymarket, Va.	16
34	†Forte, Ike	RB	6-0	211	6	3/8/54	Texarkana, Tex.	Arkansas	Texarkana, Tex.	12
22	†Hammond, Bobby	RB	5-10	170	6	2/20/52	Orangeburg, S.C.	Morgan State	Fairfax, Va.	15
38	Hardeman, Buddy	RB	6-0	202	5	10/21/54	Corpus Christi, Tex.	Iowa State	Vienna, Va.	15
71	Harmon, Clarence	RB	5-11	209	5	11/30/55	Kosciusko, Miss.	Mississippi State	Kosciusko, Miss.	15
89	Harrison, Kenny	WR	6-0	170	5	12/12/53	Beaumont, Tex.	Southern Methodist	Dallas, Tex.	9
75	Hermeling, Terry	T	6-5	255	12	4/25/46	Santa Monica, Calif.	Nevada-Reno	Reston, Va.	14
82	Hickman, Dallas	DE-LB	6-6	242	6	12/16/52	Martinez, Calif.	California-Berkeley	Leesburg, Va.	16
40	Jackson, Wilbur	RB	6-1	219	7	11/19/51	Ozark, Ala.	Alabama	Ozark, Ala.	16
54	Kuziel, Bob	C	6-5	255	7	7/24/50	New Haven, Conn.	Pittsburgh	Fairfax, Va.	15
20	Lavender, Joe	CB	6-4	185	9	2/10/49	Rayville, La.	San Diego State	Hillcrest Heights, Md.	16
80	Lorch, Karl	DE	6-3	258	6	6/14/50	Honolulu, Hawaii	Southern California	Honolulu, Hawaii	16
84	McDaniel, John	WR	6-0	197	8	9/23/51	Birmingham, Ala.	Lincoln	Birmingham, Ala.	16
11	McKinney, Zion	WR	6-0	200	2	2/10/58	Pickens, S.C.	South Carolina	Reston, Va.	10
26	†McQuilken, Kim	QB	6-3	203	8	2/26/51	Allentown, Pa.	Lehigh	Dunwoody, Ga.	0*
57	t-Metcalf, Terry	RB	5-10	185	7	9/24/51	Seattle, Wash.	Long Beach State	St. Louis, Mo.	0*
81	Milot, Rich	LB	6-3	209	3	1/30/57	Coraopolis, Pa.	Penn State	Herndon, Va.	16
3	Monk, Art	WR	6-4	230	2	12/5/57	White Plains, N.Y.	Syracuse	Arlington, Va.	16
29	Moseley, Mark	K	6-0	205	10	3/12/48	Laneville, Tex.	Stephen F. Austin	Haymarket, Va.	16
21	Murphy, Mark	S	6-4	210	5	7/13/55	Fulton, N.Y.	Colgate	Sterling, Va.	16
62	Nelms, Mike	S	6-1	185	2	4/8/55	Ft. Worth, Tex.	Baylor	Reston, Va.	16
52	†Nugent, Dan	G	6-4	227	5	8/22/53	Mt. Clemons, Mich.	Auburn	Fairfax, Va.	3*
24	Olkewicz, Neal	LB	6-0	250	3	1/30/57	Phoenixville, Pa.	Maryland	Herndon, Va.	16
56	Parrish, Lemar	CB	5-10	170	12	12/13/47	Riviera Beach, Fla.	Lincoln	Reston, Va.	15
23	†Peiffer, Dan	C	6-3	251	4	2/5/48	Sigourney, Iowa	Southeast Misri State	Oak Ridge, Mo.	8
44	Peters, Tony	S	6-1	177	7	8/4/53	Oklahoma City, Okla.	Oklahoma	Chantilly, Va.	16
56	Raba, Bob	TE	6-1	225	5	4/23/55	Bethesda, Md.	Maryland	Bethesda, Md.	3*
64	Riggins, John	RB	6-2	230	11	8/4/49	Seneca, Kan.	Kansas	Lawrence, Kan.	0*
76	Saul, Ron	G	6-3	254	12	1/4/48	Butler, Pa.	Michigan State	Chantilly, Va.	16
74	Scanlan, Jerry	T	6-5	270	2	1/4/57	Honolulu, Hawaii	Hawaii	Kaneohe, Hawaii	3
7	Starke, George	T	6-5	250	9	7/18/48	New Brunswick, N.J.	Columbia	Washington, D.C.	16
83	Theismann, Joe	QB	6-0	195	8	9/9/49	New York, N.Y.	Notre Dame	Vienna, Va.	16
47	Thompson, Ricky	WR	6-0	177	6	5/15/54	El Paso, Tex.	Baylor	Waco, Tex.	13
88	Waddy, Ray	CB	5-11	175	3	8/21/56	Freeport, Tex.	Texas A&I	Reston, Va.	7
85	Walker, Rick	TE	6-4	235	5	5/26/55	Santa Ana, Calif.	UCLA	Santa Ana, Calif.	15
25	Warren, Don	TE	6-4	236	3	5/5/56	Bellingham, Wash.	San Diego State	Long Beach, Calif.	16
45	t-Washington, Joe	RB	5-10	179	6	9/24/53	Crockett, Tex.	Oklahoma	Baltimore, Md.	13
99	White, Jeris	CB	5-10	188	8	9/3/52	Ft. Worth, Tex.	Hawaii	Sarasota, Fla.	16
—	t-Young, Wilbur	DE	6-6	290	11	4/20/49	New York, N.Y.	William Penn	Kansas City, Mo.	14

* Dimler active for 3 games with Green Bay; McQuilken active for 4 games but did not play; Metcalf last active with St. Louis in '77.; Raba played 3 games with Baltimore; Riggins last active with Washington in '79.

† Option playout; subject to developments.

t-Redskins traded for Metcalf (St. Louis), Washington (Baltimore), Young (San Diego).

Traded—Guard Jeff Williams to San Diego.

Retired—Ken Houston, 14-year safety, 13 games; Paul Smith, 13-year defensive end, 16 games in '80; Pete Wysocki, 6-year linebacker, 16 games.

Also played with Redskins in '80—G Gary Anderson (5 games), DE Joe Jones (7), QB Mike Kruczek (7), TE Grady Richardson (1), DT Diron Talbert (16).

COACHING STAFF

Head Coach,
Joe Gibbs

Pro Career: Named head coach on January 13, 1981 after spending eight years as an NFL assistant coach and nine years on the college level. Came to Redskins from the San Diego Chargers where he was offensive coordinator in 1979 and 1980. Prior to that, he was offensive coordinator for the Tampa Bay Buccaneers in 1978 and offensive backfield coach for the St. Louis Cardinals from 1973-77. While he was with San Diego, the Chargers won the AFC West title and led the NFL in passing two straight years. No pro playing experience.

Background: Played tight end, linebacker and guard under Don Coryell at San Diego State in 1961 and 1962 after spending two years at Cerritos (Calif.) J.C. (1959-60). Started his college coaching career at San Diego State (1964-66) followed by stints at Florida State (1967-68), Southern California (1969-72) and Arkansas (1971-72).

Personal: Born November 25, 1940, in Mocksville, N.C. Graduated from Santa Fe Springs High, California. Two-time national racquetball champion and ranked second in the over-35 category in 1978. He and his wife Pat live in Washington, D.C. and have two sons—J.D. and Coy.

ASSISTANT COACHES

Don Breaux, offensive backs; born August 3, 1940, Jennings, La.; lives in Washington, D.C. Quarterback McNeese State 1959-61. Pro quarterback Denver Broncos 1963, San Diego Chargers 1964-67. College coach: Florida State 1966-67, Arkansas 1968-71, 1977-80, Florida 1973-74, Texas 1975-76. Pro coach: First year with Redskins.

Joe Bugel, offensive coordinator; born March 10, 1940, Pittsburgh, Pa.; lives in Washington, D.C. Guard Western Kentucky 1960-62. No pro playing experience. College coach: Western Kentucky 1964-68, Navy 1969-72, Iowa State 1973, Ohio State 1974. Pro coach: Detroit Lions 1975-76, Houston Oilers 1977-80, joined Redskins 1981.

Dan Henning, assistant head coach; born June 21, 1942, Bronx, N.Y., lives in Washington, D.C. Quarterback William & Mary 1960-63. Pro quarterback San Diego Chargers 1964-67. College coach: Florida State 1968-70, 1974, Virginia Tech 1971, 1973. Pro coach: Houston Oilers 1972, New York Jets 1976-78, Miami Dolphins 1979-80, joined Redskins in 1981.

Bill Hickman, administrative assistant; born June 21, 1923, Baltimore, Md. lives in Washington, D.C. Halfback Virginia 1946-48. No pro playing experience. College coach: Virginia 1949, Duke 1950, N.C. State 1951, Vanderbilt 1953, North Carolina 1966-72. Pro coach: Washington Redskins 1973-77, Los Angeles Rams 1978-80, rejoined Redskins in 1981.

Larry Peccatiello, linebackers; born December 21, 1935, Newark, N.J., lives in Washington, D.C. Receiver William & Mary 1955-58. No pro playing experience. College coach: William & Mary 1961-68, Navy 1969-70, Rice 1971. Pro coach: Houston Oilers 1972-75, Seattle Seahawks 1976-80, joined Redskins in 1981.

Richie Petitbon, defensive coordinator; born April 18, 1938, New Orleans, lives in Washington, D.C. Back Tulane 1955-58. Pro defensive back Chicago Bears 1959-67, Los Angeles Rams 1969-70, Washington Redskins 1971-73. Pro coach: Houston Oilers 1974-77, fourth year with Redskins.

Wayne Sevier, special teams; born July 3, 1941, San Diego, lives in Washington, D.C. Quarterback Chaffey College 1960. San Diego State 1961-62. No pro playing experience. College coach: St. Louis Cardinals 1974-75, Atlanta Falcons 1976, San Diego Chargers 1979-80, joined Redskins in 1981.

Warren Simmons, tight ends; born February 25, 1942, Poughkeepsie, N.Y., lives in Washington, D.C. Center San Diego State 1963-65. No pro playing experience. College coach: Cal-State Fullerton 1972-75, Cerritos J.C. 1976-80. Pro coach: First year with Redskins.

LaVern Torgeson, defensive line; born February 28, 1929, LaCrosse, Wash., lives in Washington, D.C. Center-linebacker Washington State 1948-50. Pro linebacker Detroit Lions 1951-54. Washington Redskins 1955-58. Pro coach: Washington Redskins 1959-61, 1971-77, Pittsburgh Steelers 1962-68, Los Angeles Rams 1969-70, 1978-80, rejoined Redskins in 1981.

WASHINGTON REDSKINS 1981 FIRST-YEAR ROSTER

Name	Pos.	Ht.	Wt.	Birth-date	Birthplace	College	Residence	How Acq.
Allen, Chuck	DT	6-3	260	5/27/59	Anderson, S.C.	South Carolina	Columbia, S.C.	FA
Bell, Farley (1)	LB	6-4	248	11/22/56	Toledo, Ohio	Cincinnati	Reston, Va.	D6 ('80)
Brown, Charlie	WR	5-10	179	10/29/57	Charleston, S.C.	South Carolina State	John's Island, S.C.	D8
Didier, Clint	TE	6-5	244	7/14/59	Connell, Wash.	Portland State	Connell, Wash.	D12
Elshire, Neil	DE	6-5	256	3/8/58	Salem, Ore.	Oregon	Salem, Ore.	FA
Flick, Tom	QB	6-2	185	8/30/58	Patuxent River, Md.	Washington	Bellevue, Wash.	D4
Grant, Darryl	G	6-1	266	11/22/59	San Antonio, Tex.	Rice	San Antonio, Tex.	D9
Grimm, Russ	C	6-3	258	5/2/59	Scottsdale, Pa.	Pittsburgh	Scottsdale, Pa.	D3
Hill, Jerry	WR	6-1	177	2/17/59	Memphis, Tenn.	North Alabama	Killen, Ala.	D11
Hunter, Chuck (1)	RB	6-1	213	5/17/57	Wilksboro, N.C.	Ohio State	Columbus, Ohio	FA
Jacoby, Joe	T	6-7	282	7/6/59	Louisville, Ky.	Louisville	Louisville, Ky.	FA
Jones, Melvin (1)	G	6-2	276	9/27/55	Houston, Tex.	Houston	Houston, Tex.	D7 ('80)
Kaufman, Mel	LB	6-2	214	2/24/58	Los Angeles, Calif.	Cal Poly-SLO	San Luis Obispo, Calif.	FA
Kennedy, Allan	T	6-7	268	1/8/58	Vancouver, B.C.	Washington State	San Diego, Calif.	D10a
Kessell, Phil	QB	6-2	205	4/28/58	Ann Arbor, Mich.	Northern Michigan	Madison, Wis.	D10
Kubin, Larry	LB	6-2	230	2/26/59	Union, N.J.	Penn State	Union, N.J.	D6
McDaniel, LeCharles	S	5-9	169	10/15/58	Ft. Bragg, N.C.	Cal Poly-SLO	San Luis Obispo, Calif.	FA
Manley, Dexter	DE	6-3	240	7/2/59	Houston, Tex.	Oklahoma State	Houston, Tex.	D5
May, Mark	T	6-6	267	11/2/59	Oneonta, N.Y.	Pittsburgh	Pittsburgh, Pa.	D1
Megna, Jay (1)	CB-S	5-10	186	11/23/58	Westchester, N.Y.	East Tennessee St.	Ft. Lauderdale, Fla.	FA
Mendenhall, Mat (1)	DE	6-6	254	5/14/57	Salt Lake City, Utah	Brigham Young	Alpine, Utah	D2 ('80)
Mitchell, Ronald	TE	6-3	220	10/25/59	Los Angeles, Calif.	Northern Arizona	West Covina, Calif.	FA
Ogrin, Pat (1)	DE	6-5	265	2/10/58	Ft. Worth, Tex.	Wyoming	Reston, Va.	FA
Sayre, Gary	G	6-5	262	9/26/57	Upland, Calif.	Cameron State	Irving, Tex.	D5a
Seay, Virgil (1)	WR	5-7	177	1/1/58	Moultrie, Ga.	Troy State	Moultrie, Ga.	FA
Speelman, Brian	K	5-11	177	3/18/57	Columbus, Ohio	Capital University	San Jose, Calif.	FA
Spencer, Herb	LB	6-2	218	9/23/59	Charleston, S.C.	Newberry	Hanahan, S.C.	FA
Stewart, James (1)	CB	6-0	189	6/28/57	Memphis, Tenn.	Memphis State	Memphis, Tenn.	FA
Streater, Steve	CB	5-11	170	12/22/58	Sylva, N.C.	North Carolina	Carrboro, N.C.	FA
Taylor, Ken	S	6-1	187	4/10/58	Lakeland, Fla.	Georgia Tech	Atlanta, Ga.	FA
Vitiello, Sandro (1)	K	6-1	200	2/21/58	Broccostella, Italy	Massachusetts	East Meadow, N.Y.	FA
Walker, Lewis (1)	RB	6-0	190	12/12/58	Los Angeles, Calif.	Utah	Reston, Va.	D10 ('80)
Wells, Angelo (1)	DE	6-3	250	1/19/54	Annapolis, Md.	Morgan State	Baltimore, Md.	FA
Wonsley, Otis (1)	RB	5-10	214	8/13/57	Pascagoula, Miss.	Alcorn State	Moss Point, Miss.	FA

Players who report to an NFL team for the first time are designated on rosters as rookies (R). If a player reported to an NFL training camp in a previous year but was not on the active squad for three or more regular season or postseason games, he is listed on the first-year roster and designated by a (1). Thereafter, a player who is on the active squad for three or more regular season games is credited with an additional year of playing experience.

NOTES

1981 NFL Roster of Officials

Art McNally, Supervisor of Officials
Jack Reader, Assistant Supervisor of Officials
Nick Skorich, Assistant Supervisor of Officials
Stu Kirkpatrick, Officiating Assistant

*No.	Name	Position	College
23	Baetz, Paul	Back Judge	Heidelberg
14	Barth, Gene	Referee	St. Louis
16	Beeks, Bob	Line Judge	Lincoln
22	Bergman, Jerry	Head Linesman	Duquesne
5	Botchan, Ron	Umpire	Occidental
8	Boylston, Bob	Umpire	Alabama
8	Cashion, Red	Referee	Texas A&M
16	Cathcart, Royal	Side Judge	UC Santa Barbara
17	Clymer, Roy	Back Judge	New Mexico State
7	Conway, Al	Umpire	Army
15	Creed, Dick	Side Judge	Louisville
14	Demmas, Art	Umpire	Vanderbilt
18	DeSouza, Ron	Side Judge	Morgan State
15	Dodez, Ray	Head Linesman	Wooster
3	Dolack, Dick	Field Judge	Ferris State
19	Dooley, Tom	Referee	VMI
22	Douglas, Merrill	Side Judge	Utah
5	Douglas, Ray	Back Judge	Baltimore
12	Dreith, Ben	Referee	Colorado State
24	Everett, John	Line Judge	Illinois
15	Ferguson, Dick	Field Judge	West Virginia
9	Fette, Jack	Line Judge	No College
17	Fiftick, Ed	Umpire	Marquette
14	Frantz, Ernie	Head Linesman	No College
15	Frederick, Bob	Referee	Colorado
24	Gandy, Duwayne	Side Judge	Colorado
25	Gereb, Neil	Line Judge	California
10	Gierke, Terry	Head Linesman	Portland State
15	Glass, Bama	Line Judge	Colorado
20	Glover, Frank	Head Linesman	Morris Brown
4	Gosier, Wilson	Field Judge	Fort Valley State
7	Graf, Fritz	Field Judge	Western Reserve
24	Grier, Johnny	Field Judge	D.C. Teachers
9	Hagerty, Ligouri	Head Linesman	Syracuse
4	Haggerty, Pat	Referee	Colorado State
6	Hakes, Don	Field Judge	Bradley
12	Hamer, Dale	Referee	California State, Pa.
12	Hamilton, Dave	Head Linesman	Utah
18	Hantak, Dick	Umpire	Southeast Missouri
8	Harder, Pat	Back Judge	Wisconsin
22	Hawk, Dave	Umpire	Southern Methodist
18	Heberling, Chuck	Head Linesman	Washington and Jefferson
19	Hensley, Tom	Referee	Tennessee
25	Jacob, Vince	Side Judge	No College
16	Johnson, Jack	Head Linesman	Pacific Lutheran
3	Jones, Nathan	Side Judge	Lewis & Clark
6	Jorgensen, Dick	Referee	Wisconsin
14	Jury, Al	Back Judge	California
12	Kearney, Jim	Back Judge	Pennsylvania
4	Keck, John	Umpire	Cornell College
7	Kelleher, Tom	Back Judge	Holy Cross
8	Klemmer, Grover	Side Judge	California
11	Knight, Pat	Head Linesman	Southern Methodist
21	Kragseth, Norm	Head Linesman	Northwestern

*No.	Name	Position	College
6	Leimbach, John	Line Judge	Missouri
18	Lewis, Bob	Field Judge	No College
9	Look, Dean	Side Judge	Michigan State
16	Mace, Gil	Side Judge	Westminster
16	Mallette, Pat	Line Judge	Occidental
9	Marion, Ed	Head Linesman	Nebraska
19	Markbreit, Jerry	Referee	Illinois
20	Marshall, Vern	Line Judge	Pennsylvania
10	McCarter, Gordon	Referee	Western Reserve
8	McElwee, Bob	Referee	Navy
10	McKenzie, Dick	Line Judge	Ashland
3	McLaughlin, Bob	Field Judge	Xavier
20	Merrifield, Ed	Head Linesman	Missouri
3	Miles, Leo	Umpire	Virginia State
15	Morcroft, Ralph	Head Linesman	Ohio State
9	Moss, Dave	Umpire	Dartmouth
14	Murphy, Ron	Side Judge	Villanova
17	Musser, Charley	Field Judge	Penn State
3	Myers, Tom	Line Judge	Wabash
21	O'Brien, Bill	Side Judge	Indiana State, Pa.
16	Orem, Dale	Line Judge	Louisville
10	Orr, Don	Field Judge	Vanderbilt
20	Osborne, Jim	Line Judge	North Carolina State
3	Palazzi, Lou	Umpire	Penn State
21	Parry, Dave	Umpire	Purdue
21	Peters, Walt	Side Judge	San Diego State
7	Poole, Jim	Back Judge	Iowa State
24	Quinby, Bill	Side Judge	West Chester State
16	Reynolds, Bill	Line Judge	Denison
7	Rice, Bob	Side Judge	Auburn
19	Rosser, Jimmy	Back Judge	Southern Illinois
15	Sanders, J.W.	Back Judge	Winona State
17	Seeman, Jerry	Referee	Southern California
25	Semon, Sid	Head Linesman	San Jose State
7	Silva, Fred	Referee	Duke
20	Sinkovitz, Frank	Umpire	Vanderbilt
22	Smith, Boyce	Line Judge	Prairie View
5	Spencer, Willie	Side Judge	Redlands
6	Stanley, Bill	Field Judge	No College
20	Swanson, Bill	Back Judge	Lake Forest
11	Terzian, Armen	Field Judge	San Francisco
18	Toler, Burl	Head Linesman	Texas
4	Tompkins, Ben	Back Judge	Occidental
3	Tunney, Jim	Referee	Mississippi State
14	Vaughan, Jack	Field Judge	Southern Methodist
5	Veteri, Tony	Head Linesman	Ohio Wesleyan
8	Ward, Ed	Side Judge	Occidental
8	Wedge, Don	Back Judge	Houston
11	Wells, Gordon	Umpire	Cal State Northridge
9	Williams, Banks	Back Judge	Lake Forest
23	Williams, Dale	Head Linesman	West Virginia
12	Wortman, Bob	Field Judge	Findlay
11	Wyant, Fred	Referee	West Virginia

*Officials are numbered by position. There will be duplicate numbers in the listing.

Numerical Roster

No.

Referees
3 Jim Tunney
4 Pat Haggerty
5 Dick Jorgensen
7 Fred Silva
8 Gene Barth
9 Red Cashion
10 Gordon McCarter
11 Fred Wyant
12 Ben Dreith
15 Bob Frederick
17 Jerry Seeman
18 Bob McElwee
19 Tom Dooley
19 Jerry Markbreit
20 Tom Hensley

Head Linesmen
5 Tony Veteri
9 Ed Marion
9 Ligouri Hagerty
10 Terry Gierke
11 Pat Knight
12 Dave Hamilton
14 Ernie Frantz
15 Ray Dodez
15 Ralph Morcroft
16 Jack Johnson
18 Chuck Heberling
18 Burl Toler
20 Frank Glover
20 Ed Merrifield
21 Norm Kragseth
22 Jerry Bergman
23 Dale Williams
25 Sid Semon

Umpires
3 Lou Palazzi
3 Leo Miles
4 John Keck
5 Ron Botchan
7 Al Conway
8 Bob Boylston
9 Dave Moss
11 Gordon Wells
14 Art Demmas
17 Ed Fiftick
18 Dick Hantak
20 Frank Sinkovitz
21 Dave Parry
22 Dave Hawk

Line Judges
3 Tom Myers
6 John Leimbach
9 Jack Fette
10 Dick McKenzie
15 Bama Glass
16 Bob Beeks
16 Pat Mallette
16 Dale Orem
16 Bill Reynolds
20 Vern Marshall
20 Jim Osborne
22 Boyce Smith
24 John Everett
25 Neil Gereb

Back Judges
4 Ben Tompkins
5 Ray Douglas
7 Tom Kelleher
7 Jim Poole
8 Pat Harder
8 Don Wedge
9 Banks Williams
12 Jim Kearney
14 Al Jury
15 J.W. Sanders
17 Roy Clymer
19 Jimmy Rosser
20 Bill Swanson
23 Paul Baetz

Side Judges
3 Nathan Jones
5 Willie Spencer
7 Bob Rice
8 Ed Ward
8 Grover Klemmer
9 Dean Look
14 Ron Murphy
15 Dick Creed
16 Royal Cathcart
16 Gil Mace
18 Ron DeSouza
21 Walt Peters
22 Merrill Douglas
24 Duwayne Gandy
24 Bill Quinby
25 Vince Jacob

Field Judges
3 Dick Dolack
3 Bob McLaughlin
4 Wilson Gosier
6 Don Hakes
7 Fritz Graf
10 Don Orr
11 Armen Terzian
12 Bob Wortman
14 Jack Vaughan
17 Charley Musser
18 Bob Lewis
24 Johnny Grier
25 Dick Ferguson

1981 Officials at a Glance

Referees

Gene Barth, No. **14**, St. Louis University, president, oil company, 11th year.

Red Cashion, No. **8**, Texas A&M, chairman of the board, insurance company, 10th year.

Tom Dooley, No. **19**, VMI, General Contractor, 4th year.

Ben Dreith, No. **12**, Colorado State University, teacher-counselor, 22nd year.

Bob Frederic, No. **15**, Colorado, president, printing and lithographing company, 14th year.

Pat Haggerty, No. **4**, Colorado State College, teacher and coach, 17th year.

Chuck Heberling, No. **18**, Washington & Jefferson, executive administrator state high school athletic program, 17th year.

Dick Jorgensen, No. **6**, Wisconsin, president, commercial bank, 14th year.

Jerry Markbreit, No. **9**, University of Illinois, sales manager, 6th year.

Gordon McCarter, No. **20**, Western Reserve, industrial sales, 15th year.

Bob McElwee, No. **10**, U.S. Naval Academy, construction engineer, 6th year.

Jerry Seeman, No. **17**, Winona State, central office school administrator, 7th year.

Fred Silva, No. **7**, San Jose State, director of chain sales, 15th year.

Jim Tunney, No. **3**, Occidental, president of motivation company and professional speaker, 22nd year.

Fred Wyant, No. **11**, West Virginia, regional insurance sales director, former NFL player, 16th year.

Umpires

Ron Botchan, No. **22**, Occidental, college professor, former AFL player, 2nd year.

Bob Boylston, No. **5**, U. of Alabama, manufacturers representative, 4th year.

Al Conway, No. **7**, Army, polyester product manager, 13th year.

Art Demmas, No. **14**, Vanderbilt, investments and financial planning, insurance company, 14th year.

Ed Fiffick, No. **17**, Marquette University, podiatric physician, 3rd year.

Dave Hamilton, No. **12**, Utah University, hospital administrator, 7th year.

Pat Harder, No. **8**, Wisconsin, executive vice-president, automobile leasing company, former NFL player, 16th year.

Tommy Hensley, No. **19**, Tennessee, transportation sales representative, 15th year.

John Keck, No. **4**, Cornell College, petroleum and automobile parts distributor, 10th year.

Ralph Morcroft, No. **15**, Ohio State, baseball operations director, 21st year.

Dave Moss, No. **9**, Dartmouth, insurance, 2nd year.

Tom Myers, No. **10**, San Jose State, owner, auto leasing company, 3rd year.

Lou Palazzi, No. **3**, Penn State, landscape architect, former NFL player, 30th year.

Frank Sinkovitz, No. **20**, Duke, president, marketing company, former NFL player, 24th year.

Gordon Wells, No. **11**, Occidental, college professor physical education, 10th year.

Head Linesmen

Jerry Bergman, No. **17**, Duquesne, transportation manager, 16th year.

Ray Dodez, No. **15**, Wooster, telephone company executive, 14th year.

Ernie Frantz, No. **14**, vice president and manager, land title company, 1st year.

Terry Gierke, No. **10**, Portland State, real estate broker, 1st year.

Frank Glover, No. **20**, Morris Brown, assistant area superintendent, 10th year.

Ligouri Hagerty, No. **9**, Syracuse, manager sporting goods company, 6th year.

Dale Hamer, No. **12**, California St., Pa., senior planning specialist, 4th year.

Dave Hawk, No. **22**, SMU, vice president, manufacturing company, 10th year.

Jack Johnson, No. **16**, Pacific Lutheran, college coordinator, student programs, 6th year.

Norm Kragseth, No. **21**, Northwestern, physical education department chairman, 8th year.

Ed Marion, No. **6**, Pennsylvania, vice president, pension marketing, insurance company, 22nd year.

Leo Miles, No. **3**, Virginia State, university athletic director, former NFL player, 13th year.

Sid Semon, No. **25**, U. of Southern California, chairman of physical education department, 4th year.

Burl Toler, No. **18**, San Francisco, director of adult and community education, 17th year.

Tony Veteri, No. **7**, sales manager, consumer product, 21st year.

Dale Williams, No. **23**, Cal State Northridge, coordinator of athletic officials, 2nd year.

Line Judges

Bob Beeks, No. **16**, Lincoln, police community relations officer, 14th year.

John Everett, No. **14**, Illinois, assistant principal, 3rd year.

Jack Fette, No. **9**, district sales manager, sporting goods company, 17th year.

Neil Gereb, No. **25**, California, supervisor of division of aircraft company, 1st year.

Bama Glass, No. **15**, Colorado, owner consumer products, 3rd year.

Wilson Gosier, No. **4**, Fort Valley State, assistant director, professional practices commission, 2nd year.

John Leimbach, No. **6**, Missouri, school teacher, 1st year.

Vern Marshall, No. **19**, Linfield College, counseling coordinator, 6th year.

Dick McKenzie, No. **8**, Ashland, independent insurance agent, 4th year.

Bob McLaughlin, No. **3**, Xavier University, vice president sales, 4th year.

Dale Orem, No. **17**, Louisville, owner sporting goods company, 2nd year.

Jim Osborne, No. **20**, Villanova, sales marketing executive, 4th year.

Walt Peters, No. **24**, Indiana State, insurance broker, 14th year.

Bill Reynolds, No. **11**, West Chester State, junior high teacher and coach, 7th year.

Boyce Smith, No. **22**, Vanderbilt, president and general manager, steel company, 1st year.

Back Judges

Paul Baetz, No. **23**, Heidelberg, financial consultant, 4th year.

Roy Clymer, No. **17**, New Mexico State, area manager, gas company, 2nd year.

Ray Douglas, No. **5**, University of Baltimore, traffic manager, 14th year.

Dick Hantak, No. **18**, Southeast Missouri, state traffic officer, 4th year.

Al Jury, No. **14**, San Bernardino Valley, guidance counselor, 4th year.

Jim Kearney, No. **12**, Pennsylvania, account manager, 4th year.

Tom Kelleher, No. **7**, Holy Cross, president, marketing company, 22nd year.

Pat Knight, No. **11**, Southern Methodist, general manager, lumber company, former NFL player, 9th year.

Jim Poole, No. **16**, San Diego State, college physical education professor, 7th year.

Jimmy Rosser, No. **10**, Auburn, personnel director, 5th year.

J.W. Sanders, No. **15**, Southern Illinois, physical education professor, 2nd year.

Bill Swanson, No. **20**, Lake Forest, manufacturers representative, 18th year.

Ben Tompkins, No. **4**, Texas, attorney, 11th year.

Don Wedge, No. **8**, Ohio Wesleyan, national sales manager, 10th year.

Banks Williams, No. **9**, Houston, vice president-general sales manager, concrete company, 4th year.

Side Judges

Royal Cathcart, No. **16**, UC-Santa Barbara, commercial real estate broker, former NFL player, 11th year.

Richard Creed, No. **15**, Louisville, real estate management, 4th year.

Ron DeSouza, No. **18**, Morgan State, vice president-student affairs, 2nd year.

Merrill Douglas, No. **22**, Utah, deputy sheriff, former NFL player, 1st year.

Duwayne Gandy, No. **24**, Tulsa, regional manager, book company, 1st year.

Vince Jacob, No. **25**, wireman special apparatus, 7th year.

Nathan Jones, No. **3**, Lewis and Clark College, high school principal, 5th year.

Grover Klemmer, No. **8**, California, department chairman and athletic director, 19th year.

Dean Look, No. **9**, Michigan State, vice president, insurance company, former AFL player, 10th year.

Gil Mace, No. **5**, Westminster, national accounts manager, 8th year.

Ron Murphy, No. **14**, Austin State, manufacturers representative, 2nd year.

Dave Parry, No. **21**, Wabash, high school athletic director, 7th year.

William Quinby, No. **7**, Iowa State, industrial relations director, 4th year.

Bob Rice, No. **19**, Denison, teacher and coach, 13th year.

Willie Spencer, No. **6**, Prairie View, central office administrator, 4th year.

Ed Ward, No. **4**, Southern Methodist, executive director, motor freight association, 4th year.

Field Judges

Dick Dolack, No. **3**, Ferris State, pharmacist, 16th year.

Dick Ferguson, No. **15**, West Virginia, commissioner of officials, 8th year.

Fritz Graf, No. **7**, Western Reserve, area manager, medical and hospital equipment company, 22nd year.

Johnny Grier, No. **24**, D.C. Teachers, telephone company, 1st year.

Don Hakes, No. **6**, Bradley, high school dean of students, 5th year.

Bob Lewis, No. **18**, operations, air force base, 6th year.

Pat Mallette, No. **16**, Nebraska, real estate broker, 13th year.

Ed Merrifield, No. **20**, Missouri, sales manager, 7th year.

Charley Musser, No. **19**, North Carolina State, vice president, refining company, 17th year.

Bill O'Brien, No. **9**, Indiana, university department chairman-professor, 15th year.

Don Orr, No. **10**, Vanderbilt, executive vice president, machine company, 11th year.

Bill Stanley, No. **5**, Redlands, college athletic director, 8th year.

Armen Terzian, No. **11**, Southern California, director of physical education, 21st year.

Jack Vaughan, No. **14**, Mississippi State, real estate broker, 6th year.

Bob Wortman, No. **12**, Findlay, insurance agent, 16th year.

Official Signals

1
TOUCHDOWN, FIELD GOAL, or SUCCESSFUL TRY
Both arms extended above head.

2
SAFETY
Palms together above head.

3
FIRST DOWN
Arm pointed toward defensive team's goal.

4
DEAD BALL or NEUTRAL ZONE ESTABLISHED
One arm above head with an open hand.
With fist closed: **Fourth Down.**

5
BALL ILLEGALLY TOUCHED, KICKED, OR BATTED
Fingertips tap both shoulders.

6
TIME OUT
Hands crisscrossed above head.
Same signal followed by placing one hand on top of cap: **Referee's Time Out.**
Same signal followed by arm swung at side: **Touchback.**

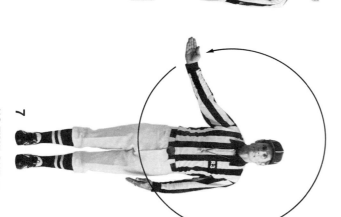

7
NO TIME OUT or TIME IN WITH WHISTLE
Full arm circled to simulate moving clock.

8
DELAY OF GAME or EXCESS TIME OUT
Folded arms.

9

FALSE START, ILLEGAL SHIFT, ILLEGAL PROCEDURE, ILLEGAL FORMATION, ILLEGAL MOTION, or KICKOFF OR SAFETY KICK OUT OF BOUNDS

Forearms rotated over and over in front of body.

10

PERSONAL FOUL

One wrist striking the other above head. Same signal followed by swinging leg: **Running into or Roughing Kicker.**

Same signal followed by raised arm swinging forward: **Roughing into Passer.** Same signal followed by hand striking back of calf: **Clipping.**

11

HOLDING

Grasping one wrist, the fist clenched, in front of chest.

12

ILLEGAL USE OF HANDS, ARMS, OR BODY

Grasping one wrist, the hand open and facing forward, in front of chest.

13

PENALTY REFUSED, INCOMPLETE PASS, PLAY OVER, or MISSED GOAL

Hands shifted in horizontal plane.

14

PASS JUGGLED INBOUNDS AND CAUGHT OUT OF BOUNDS

Hands up and down in front of chest (following incomplete pass signal).

15

ILLEGAL FORWARD PASS

One hand waved behind back followed by loss of down signal (number 23).

16

INTENTIONAL GROUNDING OF PASS

Parallel arms waved in a diagonal plane across body.

162

17

INTERFERENCE WITH FOWARD PASS or FAIR CATCH
Hands open and extended forward from shoulders with hands vertical.

18

INVALID FAIR CATCH SIGNAL
One hand waved above head.

19

INELIGIBLE RECEIVER or INELIGIBLE MEMBER OF KICKING TEAM DOWNFIELD
Right hand touching top of cap.

20

ILLEGAL CONDUCT
One open hand extended forward.

21

OFFSIDE or ENCROACHING
Hands on hips.

22

ILLEGAL MOTION AT SNAP
Horizontal arc with one hand.

23

LOSS OF DOWN
Both hands held behind head.

24

CRAWLING, INTERLOCKING INTERFERENCE, PUSHING, OR HELPING RUNNER
Pushing movement of hands to front with arms downward.

27

**ILLEGAL CUT or
BLOCKING BELOW
THE WAIST**
Hand striking front of thigh.

30

TRIPPING
Repeated action of right foot
in back of left heel.

26

**UNSPORTSMANLIKE
CONTACT (Non-contact fouls)**
Arms outstretched, palms down.
(Same signal means continuous
action fouls are disregarded.)

29

PLAYER DISQUALIFIED
Ejection signal.

25

**TOUCHING A FORWARD
PASS or SCRIMMAGE KICK**
Diagonal motion of
one hand across another.

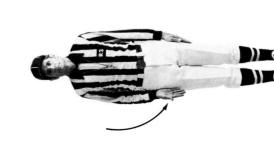

28

ILLEGAL CRACKBACK
Strike of an open right hand
against the right mid thigh.

NFL Digest of Rules

This Digest of Rules of the National Football League has been prepared to aid players, fans, and members of the press, radio, and television media in their understanding of the game.

It is not meant to be a substitute for the official rule book. In any case of conflict between these explanations and the official rules, the rules always have precedence.

In order to make it easier to coordinate the information in this digest with the topics discussed generally follow the order of the rule book.

Officials' Jurisdictions, Positions, and Duties

Referee—General oversight and control of game. Gives signals for all fouls and is final authority for rule interpretations. Takes a position in backfield 10 to 12 yards behind line of scrimmage, favors right side (if quarterback is right-handed passer). Determines legality of snap, observes deep back(s) for legal motion. On running play, observes quarterback during and after handoff, remains with him until action has cleared away, then proceeds downfield, checking on runner and contact behind him. When runner is downed, Referee determines forward progress from wing official and if necessary, adjusts final position of ball.

On pass plays, drops back as quarterback begins to fade back, picks up legality of blocks by near linemen. Changes to complete concentration on quarterback as defenders approach. Primarily responsible to rule on possible roughing action on passer and if ball becomes loose, rules whether ball is free on a fumble or dead on an incomplete pass.

During kicking situations, Referee has primary responsibility to rule on kicker's actions and whether or not any subsequent contact by a defender is legal.

Umpire—Primary responsibility to rule on players' equipment, as well as their conduct and actions on scrimmage line. Lines up approximately four to five yards downfield, varying position from in front of weakside tackle to strongside guard. Looks for possible false start by offensive linemen. Observes legality of contact by both offensive linemen while blocking and by defensive players while they attempt to ward off blockers. Is prepared to call rule infractions if they occur on offense or defense. Moves forward to line of scrimmage when pass play develops in order to insure that interior linemen do not move illegally downfield. If offensive linemen indicate screen pass is to be attempted, Umpire shifts his attention toward screen side, picks up potential receiver in order to insure that he will legally be permitted to run his pattern and continues to rule on action of blockers. Umpire is to assist in ruling on incomplete or trapped passes when ball is thrown overhead or short.

Head Linesman—Primarily responsible for ruling on offside, encroachment, and actions pertaining to scrimmage line prior to or at snap. Keys on closest setback on his side of the field. On pass plays, Linesman is responsible to clear this receiver approximately seven yards downfield as he moves to a point five yards beyond the line. Linesman's secondary responsibility is to rule on any illegal action taken by defenders on any delay receiver moving downfield. Has full responsibility for ruling on sideline plays on his side, e.g.; pass receiver or runner in or out of bounds. Together with Referee, Linesman is responsible for keeping track of number of downs and is in charge of mechanics of his chain crew in connection with its duties.

Linesman must be prepared to assist in determining forward progress by a runner on play directed toward middle or into his side zone. He, in turn, is to signal Referee or Umpire what forward point ball has reached. Linesman is responsible to rule on legality of action involving wide receiver on his side as well as that of other receivers who approach his side zone. He is to call pass interference when the infraction occurs and is to rule on legality of blockers and defenders on plays involving ball carriers, whether it is entirely a running play, a combination pass and run, or a play involving a kick.

Line Judge—Straddles line of scrimmage on side of field opposite Linesman. Keeps time of game as a backup for clock operator. Along with Linesman is responsible for offside, encroachment, and actions pertaining to scrimmage line prior to or at snap. Line Judge Keys on closest set back on his side of field. Line Judge is to observe his receiver until he moves at least seven yards downfield, Judge then moves toward backfield side, being especially alert to rule on any back in motion and on flight of ball when pass is made (he must rule whether forward or backward). Line Judge has primary responsibility to rule whether or not passer is behind or beyond line of scrimmage when pass is made. He also assists in observing actions by

blockers and defenders who are on his side of field. After pass is thrown, Line Judge directs attention toward activities that occur in back of Umpire. During punting situations, Line Judge remains at line of scrimmage to be sure that only the end men move downfield until kick has been made. He also rules whether or not the end men move downfield to cover the kick.

Back Judge—Operates on same side of field as Line Judge 17 yards deep. Keys on wide receiver on his side. Concentrates on path of end or back, observing legality of his potential block(s) or of actions taken against him. Has primary responsibility to make decisions involving sideline on his side of field, e.g.; pass receiver or runner in or out of bounds. Concentrates on path of end or back(s) for legal motion. On running play, observes quarterback during and after handoff, remains with him until action has cleared away, then proceeds to rule from deep position on holding or illegal use of hands by end or back or on defensive infractions committed by player guarding him. Has primary responsibility to make decisions involving sideline on his side of field, e.g.; pass receiver or runner in or out of bounds.

Side Judge—Operates on same side of field as Linesman 17 yards deep. Keys on wide receiver on his side. Concentrates on path of end or back, observing legality of his potential block(s) or of actions taken against him. Is prepared to rule from deep position on holding or illegal use of hands by end or back or on defensive infractions committed by player guarding him. Is prepared to rule from deep position on holding or illegal use of hands by end or back or on defensive infractions committed by player guarding him. Side Judge makes decisions involving catching, recovery, or illegal touching a loose ball beyond line of scrimmage; rules on plays involving pass receiver, including legality of catch or pass interference; assists in covering actions of runner, including blocks by teammates and that of defenders; and calls clipping on punt returns.

Field Judge—Takes a position 25 yards downfield. In general, favors the tight end's side of field. Keys on tight end, concentrates on his path and observes legality of tight end's potential block(s) or of actions taken against him. Is prepared to rule from deep position on holding or illegal use of hands by end or back or on defensive infractions committed by player guarding him.

Field Judge times interval between plays on 30-second clock plus intermission between plays for each half; makes decisions involving catching, recovery, or illegal touching of a loose ball beyond line of scrimmage; is responsible to rule on plays involving end line, calls pass interference, fair catch infractions, and clipping on kick returns; and, together with Back Judge, rules whether or not field goal attempts are successful.

Definitions

1. **Chucking:** Warding off an opponent who is in front of a defender by contacting him with a quick extension of arm or arms, followed by the return of arm(s) to a flexed position, thereby breaking the original contact.

2. **Clipping:** Throwing the body across the back of an opponent's leg or hitting him from the back while moving up from behind unless the opponent is a runner or the action is in close line play.

3. **Close Line Play:** The area between the positions normally occupied by the offensive tackles, extending three yards on each side of the line of scrimmage.

4. **Crackback:** Eligible receivers who take or move to a position more than two yards outside the tackle may not block an opponent below the waist if they then move back inside to block.

5. **Dead Ball:** Ball not in play.

6. **Double Foul:** A foul by each team during the same down.

7. **Down:** The period of action that starts when the ball is put in play and ends when it is dead.

8. **Encroachment:** When a player is in the neutral zone at the time of the snap or makes contact with an opponent before the ball is snapped.

9. **Fair Catch:** An unhindered catch of a kick by a member of the receiving team who must raise one arm full length above his head while the kick is in flight.

10. **Foul:** Any violation of a playing rule.

11. **Free Kick:** A kickoff, kick after a safety, or kick after a fair catch. It may be a placekick, dropkick, or punt, except a punt may not be used on a kickoff.

12. **Fumble:** The loss of possession of the ball.

13. **Impetus:** The action of a player that gives momentum to the ball.

14. **Live Ball:** A ball legally free kicked or snapped. It continues in play until the down ends.

10 Yards
1. Offensive pass interference.
2. Ineligible player downfield during passing down.
3. Holding, illegal use of hands by offense.
4. Tripping by a member of either team.

15 Yards
1. Clipping.
2. Fair catch interference.
3. Illegal batting or punching loose ball.
4. Deliberately kicking a loose ball.
5. Illegal crackback block by offense.
6. Piling on (automatic first down).
7. Roughing the kicker (automatic first down).
8. Roughing the passer (automatic first down).
9. Twisting, turning, or pulling an opponent by the face mask.
10. Unnecessary roughness.
11. Unsportsmanlike conduct.
12. Delay of game at start of either half.
13. Illegal blocking below the waist.

Five Yards and Loss of Down
1. Forward pass thrown from beyond line of scrimmage.

10 Yards and Loss of Down
1. Intentional grounding of forward pass (safety if passer is in own end zone).

15 Yards and Loss of Coin Toss Option
1. Team's late arrival on the field prior to scheduled kickoff.

15 Yards (and disqualification if flagrant)
1. Striking opponent with fist.
2. Kicking or kneeing opponent.
3. Striking opponent on head or neck with forearm, elbow, or hands.
4. Roughing kicker.
5. Roughing passer.
6. Malicious unnecessary roughness.
7. Unsportsmanlike conduct.
8. Palpably unfair act. (Distance penalty determined by the Referee after consultation with other officials.)

Suspension From Game
1. Illegal equipment. (Player may return after one down when legally equipped.)

Touchdown
1. When Referee determines a palpably unfair act deprived a team of a touchdown. (Example: Player comes off bench and tackles runner apparently en route to touchdown.)

Field
1. Sidelines and end lines are out of bounds. The goal line is actually in the end zone. A player with the ball in his possession scores when the ball is on, above, or over the goal line.
2. The field is rimmed by a white border, six feet wide, along the sidelines. All of this is out of bounds.
3. The hashmarks (inbound lines) are 70 feet, 9 inches from each sideline.
4. Goal posts must be single-standard type, offset from the end line and painted bright gold. The goal posts must be 18 feet, 6 inches wide and the top face of the crossbar must be 10 feet above the ground. Vertical posts extend at least 30 feet above the crossbar. A ribbon 4 inches by 42 inches long is to be attached to the top of each post. The actual goal is the plane extending indefinitely above the crossbar and between the outer edges of the posts.
5. The field is 360 feet long and 160 feet wide. The end zones are 30 feet deep. The line used in try-for-point plays is two yards out from the goal line.
6. Chain crew members and ball boys must be uniformly identifiable.
7. All clubs must use standardized sideline markers. Pylons must be used for goal line and end line markings.
8. End zone markings and club identification at 50 yard line must be approved by the Commissioner to avoid any confusion as to delineation of goal lines, sidelines, and end lines.

Ball
1. The home club must have 24 balls available for testing by the Referee one hour before game time. In case of bad weather, a playable ball is to be substituted on request of the offensive team captain.

---

15. **Loose Ball:** A live ball not in possession of any player.
16. **Muff:** The touching of a loose ball by a player in an unsuccessful attempt to obtain possession.
17. **Neutral Zone:** The space the length of a ball between the two scrimmage lines. The offensive team and defensive team must remain behind their end of the ball.
   Exception: The offensive player who snaps the ball.
18. **Offside:** A player is offside when any part of his body is beyond his scrimmage or free kick line when the ball is snapped.
19. **Own Goal:** The goal a team is guarding.
20. **Possession:** When a player holds the ball long enough to give him control when his second foot has clearly touched the ground inbounds. It is in flight.
21. **Punt:** A kick made when a player drops the ball and kicks it while it is in flight.
22. **Safety:** The situation in which the ball is dead on or behind a team's own goal if the impetus comes from a player on that team. Two points are scored for the opposing team.
23. **Shift:** The movement of two or more offensive players at the same time before the snap.
24. **Striking:** The act of swinging, clubbing, or propelling the arm or forearm in contacting an opponent.
25. **Sudden Death:** The continuation of a tied game into sudden death overtime in which the team scoring first (by safety, field goal, or touchdown) wins.
26. **Touchback:** When a ball is dead on or behind a team's own goal line, provided the impetus came from an opponent and provided it is not a touchdown or a missed field goal.
27. **Touchdown:** When any part of the ball, legally in possession of a player inbounds, is on, above, or over the opponent's goal line, provided it is not a touchback.
28. **Unsportsmanlike Conduct:** Any act contrary to the generally understood principles of sportsmanship.

Summary of Penalties
Automatic First Down
1. Awarded to offensive team on all defensive fouls with these exceptions:
   (a) Offside.
   (b) Encroachment.
   (c) Delay of game.
   (d) Illegal substitution.
   (e) Excessive time out(s).

Loss of Down (No yardage)
1. Second forward pass behind the line.
2. Forward pass strikes ground, goal post, or crossbar.
3. Forward pass goes out of bounds.
4. Forward pass is first touched by eligible receiver who has gone out of bounds and returned.
5. Forward pass accidentally touches ineligible receiver on or behind line.
6. Forward pass thrown from behind line of scrimmage after ball once crossed the line.

Five Yards
1. Crawling.
2. Defensive holding or illegal use of hands (automatic first down).
3. Delay of game.
4. Encroachment.
5. False start.
6. Illegal formation.
7. Illegal shift.
8. Illegal motion.
9. Illegal substitution.
10. Illegal substitution.
11. Kickoff out of bounds between goal lines and not touched.
12. Invalid fair catch signal.
13. More than 11 players on the field at snap for either team.
14. Less than seven men on offensive line at snap.
15. Offside.
16. Failure to pause one second after shift or huddle.
17. Running into kicker (automatic first down).
18. More than one man in motion at snap.
19. Grasping face mask of opponent (if by defense, automatic first down).
20. Player out of bounds at snap.
21. Ineligible member(s) of kicking team going beyond line of scrimmage before ball is kicked.
22. Illegal return.
23. Failure to report change of eligibility.
24. Helping the runner.

Coin Toss

1. The toss of coin will take place within three minutes of kickoff in center of field. The toss will be called by the visiting captain. The winner may choose one of two privileges and the loser gets the other:
   (a) Receive or kick
   (b) Goal his team will defend
2. Immediately prior to the start of the second half, the captains of both teams must inform the officials of their respective choices. The loser of the original coin toss gets first choice.

Timing

1. The stadium clock is official. In case it stops or is operating incorrectly, the Line Judge takes over the official timing on the field.
2. Each period is 15 minutes. The intermission between the periods is two minutes. Halftime is 15 minutes, unless otherwise specified.
3. On charged team timeouts, the Field Judge starts watch and blows whistle after 1 minute 30 seconds. However, Referee may allow two minutes for injured player and three minutes for equipment repair.
4. Each team is allowed three time outs each half.
5. Offensive team has 30 seconds to put the ball in play. The time is displayed on two 30-second clocks, which are visible to the players, officials, and fans. Field Judge is to call a delay of game penalty (five yards) when the time limit is exceeded. In case 30-second clocks are not operating, Field Judge takes over the official timing on the field.
6. Clock will start running when ball is snapped following all changes of team possession.

Sudden Death

1. The sudden death system of determining the winner shall prevail when score is tied at the end of the regulation playing time of all NFL games. The team scoring first during overtime play shall be the winner and the game automatically ends upon any score (by safety, field goal, or touchdown) or when a score is awarded by Referee for a palpably unfair act.
2. At the end of regulation time the Referee will immediately toss coin at center of field in accordance with rules pertaining to the usual pregame toss. The captain of the visiting team will call the toss.
3. Following a three-minute intermission after the end of the regulation game, play will be continued in 15-minute periods or until there is a score. There is a two-minute intermission between subsequent periods. The teams change goals at the start of each period. Each team has three time outs and general provisions for play in the last two-minutes of a half shall prevail. Disqualified players are not allowed to return.

Exception: In preseason and regular season games there shall be a maximum of 15 minutes of sudden death with two time outs instead of three. General provisions for play in the last two minutes of a half will be in force.

Timing in Final Two Minutes of Each Half

1. On kickoff, clock does not start until the ball has been legally touched by player of either team in the field of play. (In all other cases, clock starts with kickoff.)
2. A team cannot "buy" an excess timeout for a penalty. However, a fourth timeout is allowed without penalty for an injured player, who must be removed immediately. A fifth timeout or more is allowed for an injury and a five-yard penalty is assessed if the clock was running. Additionally, if the clock was running and the score is tied or the team in possession is losing, the ball cannot be put in play for at least 10 seconds on the fourth or more timeout. The half or game can end while those 10 seconds are run off on the clock.

Players-Substitutions

1. Each team is permitted 11 men on the field at the snap.
2. Unlimited substitution is permitted. However, players may enter the field only when the ball is dead. Players who have been substituted for are not permitted to linger on the field. Such lingering will be interpreted as unsportsmanlike conduct.
3. Players leaving the game must be out of bounds on their own side, clearing the field between the end lines, before a snap or freekick. If player crosses end line leaving field, it is delay of game (five-yard penalty).

Try-for-Point

1. After a touchdown, the scoring team is allowed a try-for-point during one scrimmage down. The ball may be spotted anywhere between the in-bounds lines, two or more yards from the goal line. The successful conversion counts one point, whether by run, kick, or pass.
2. The defensive team never can score on a try-for-point. As soon as defense gets possession, or kick is blocked, ball is dead.
3. Any distance penalty for fouls committed by the defense that prevent the try from being attempted can be enforced on the succeeding kickoff. Any foul committed on a successful try will result in a distance penalty being assessed on the ensuing kickoff.

Kickoff

1. The kickoff shall be from the kicking team's 35 yard line at the start of each half and after a field goal and try-for-point. A kickoff is one type of free kick.
2. Either a one-, two-, or three-inch tee may be used (no tee permitted for field goal or try-for-point plays). The ball is put in play by a placekick or dropkick.
3. If kickoff clears the opponent's goal posts it is not a field goal.
4. A kickoff is illegal unless it travels 10 yards OR is touched by the receiving team. Once the ball is touched by the receiving team it is a free ball. Receivers may recover and advance. Kicking team may recover but NOT advance UNLESS receiver had possession and lost the ball.
5. When a kickoff goes out of bounds between the goal lines without being touched by the receiving team, it must be kicked again. There is a five-yard penalty for a short kick or an out-of-bounds kick.
6. When a kickoff goes out of bounds between the goal lines and is touched last by receiving team, it is receiver's ball at out-of-bounds spot.

Free Kick

1. In addition to a kickoff, the other free kicks are a kick after a safety and a kick after a fair catch. In both cases, a dropkick, placekick, or punt may be used (a punt may not be used on a kickoff.)
2. On free kick after a fair catch, captain of receiving team has the option to put ball in play by punt, dropkick, or placekick without a tee, or by snap. If the placekick or dropkick goes between the uprights a field goal is scored.
3. On a free kick after a safety, the team scored upon puts ball in play by a punt, dropkick, or placekick without tee. No score can be made on a free kick following a safety, even if a series of penalties place team in position. (A field goal can be scored only on a play from scrimmage or a free kick after a fair catch.)

Field Goal

1. All field goals attempted and missed from scrimmage line beyond the 20 yard line will result in the defensive team taking possession of the ball at the scrimmage line. On any field goal attempted and missed from scrimmage line inside the 20 yard line, ball will revert to defensive team at the 20 yard line.

Safety

1. The important factor in a safety is impetus. Two points are scored for the opposing team when the ball is dead on or behind a team's own goal line if the impetus came from a player on that team.

Examples of Safety:

(a) Blocked punt goes out of kicking team's end zone. Impetus provided by punting team. The block only changes direction of ball, not impetus.
(b) Ball carrier retreats from field of play into his own end zone and is downed. Ball carrier provides impetus.
(c) Offensive team commits a foul and spot of enforcement is behind its own goal line.
(d) Player on receiving team muffs punt and, trying to get ball, forces or illegally kicks it into end zone where he or a teammate recovers. He has given new impetus to the ball.

Examples of Non-safety:

(a) Player intercepts a pass inside his own 5 yard line and his momentum carries him into his own end zone. Ball is put in play at spot of interception.
(b) Player intercepts a pass in his own end zone and is downed. Impetus came from passing team, not from defense. (Touchback)
(c) Player passes from behind his own goal line. Opponent bats down ball in end zone. (Incomplete pass)

Measuring

1. The forward point of the ball is used when measuring.

Position of Players at Snap

1. Offensive team must have at least seven players on line.
2. Offensive players, not on line, must be at least one yard back at snap. (**Exception:** player who takes snap.)
3. No interior lineman may move after taking or simulating a three-point stance.
4. No player of either team may invade neutral zone before snap.

5. No player of offensive team may charge or move, after assuming set position, in such manner as to lead defense to believe snap has started.

6. If a player changes his eligibility, the Referee must alert the defensive captain after player has reported to him.

7. All players of offensive team must be stationary at snap, except one back who may be in motion parallel to scrimmage line or backward (not forward).

8. After a shift or huddle all players on offensive team must come to an absolute stop for at least one second with no movement of hands, feet, head, or swaying of body.

9. A double shift is legal after it has been shown three times in the game outside an opponent's 20 yard line.

10. Linemen may lock legs only with the snapper.

11. Quarterbacks can be called for a false start penalty (five yards) if their actions are judged to be an obvious attempt to draw an opponent offside.

Use of Hands, Arms, and Body

1. No player on offense may assist a runner except by blocking for him. There shall be no interlocking interference.

2. A runner may ward off opponents with his hands and arms but no other player on offense may use hands or arms to obstruct an opponent by grasping with hands, pushing, or encircling any part of his body during a block.

3. Pass blocking is the obstruction of an opponent by use of that part of the body above the knees. During a legal block, hands (open or closed) must be inside the blocker's elbows and can be thrust forward to contact an opponent as long as the contact is inside the frame. Hands cannot be thrust forward above the frame to contact an opponent on the neck, face, or head. (**Note:** The frame is defined as that part of the opponent's body below the neck that is presented to the blocker.) Blocker cannot use his hands or arms to push from behind, hang onto, or encircle an opponent in a manner that restricts his movements as the play develops. By use of up and down action of arm(s), the blocker is permitted to ward off the opponent's attempt to grasp his jersey or arm(s) and prevent legal contact to the head.

4. A defensive player may not tackle or hold an opponent other than a runner. Otherwise, he may use his hands, arms, or body only:
(a) To defend or protect himself against an obstructing opponent.

Exception: An eligible receiver is considered to be an obstructing opponent ONLY to a point five yards beyond the line of scrimmage unless the player who receives the snap clearly demonstrates no further intention to pass the ball. Within this five-yard zone, a defensive player may make contact with an eligible receiver that may be maintained as long as it is continuous and unbroken. The defensive player cannot use his hands or arms to push from behind, hang onto, or encircle an eligible receiver in a manner that restricts movement as the play develops. Beyond this five-yard limitation, a defender may use his hands or arms ONLY to defend or protect himself against impending contact caused by a receiver. In such reaction, the defender may not contact a receiver who attempts to take a path to evade him.

(b) To push or pull opponent out of the way on line of scrimmage.
(c) In actual attempt to get at or tackle runner.
(d) To push or pull opponent out of the way in a legal attempt to recover a loose ball.
(e) During a legal block on an opponent who is not an eligible pass receiver.
(f) When legally blocking an eligible pass receiver above the waist.

Exception: Eligible receivers lined up within two yards of the tackle, whether on or immediately behind the line, may be blocked below the waist at or behind the line of scrimmage. NO eligible receiver may be blocked below the waist after he goes beyond the line.

5. A defensive player must not contact an opponent above the shoulders with the palm of his hand except to ward him off on the line. This exception is permitted only if it is not a repeated act against the same opponent during any one contact. In all other cases the palms may be used on head, neck, or face only to ward off or push an opponent in legal attempt to get at the ball.

6. Any offensive player who pretends to possess the ball or to whom a teammate pretends to give the ball may be tackled provided he is crossing his scrimmage line between the ends of a normal tight offensive line.

7. An offensive player who lines up more than two yards outside his own tackle or a player who, at the snap, is in a backfield position and subsequently takes a position more than two yards outside a tackle may not clip an opponent anywhere nor may he contact an opponent below the waist if the blocker is moving toward the ball and if contact is made within an area five yards on either side of the line.

8. A player of either team may block at any time provided it is not pass interference, fair catch interference, or unnecessary roughness.

9. A player may not bat or punch:
(a) A loose ball (in field of play) toward his opponent's goal line or in any direction in either end zone.
(b) A ball in player possession or attempt to get possession.
(c) A pass in flight forward toward opponent's goal line.

Exception: A forward or backward pass may be batted in any direction at any time by the defense.

10. No player may deliberately kick any ball except as a punt, dropkick or placekick.

Forward Pass

1. A forward pass may be touched or caught by any eligible receiver. All members of the defensive team are eligible. Eligible receivers on the offensive team are players on either end of line (other than center, guard, or tackle) or players at least one yard behind the line at the snap. A T-formation quarterback is not eligible to receive a forward pass during a play from scrimmage.

Exception: T-formation quarterback becomes eligible if pass is previously touched by an eligible receiver.

2. An offensive team may make only one forward pass during each play from scrimmage (Loss of down).

3. The passer must be behind his line of scrimmage (Loss of down and five yards, enforced from the spot of pass).

4. Any eligible offensive player may catch a forward pass. If a pass is touched by one offensive player and touched or caught by a second eligible offensive player, pass completion is legal. Further, all offensive players become eligible once a pass is touched by an eligible receiver or any defensive player.

5. The rules concerning a forward pass and ineligible receivers:
(a) If ball is touched accidentally by an ineligible receiver on or behind his line: loss of down.
(b) If touched or caught intentionally by an ineligible receiver on or behind his line: loss of 10 yards.
(c) If touched or caught (intentionally or accidentally) by ineligible receiver beyond the line: loss of 10 yards or loss of down.
(d) If ineligible receiver is illegally downfield: 10 yards.

6. If a forward pass is caught simultaneously by eligible players on opposing teams, possession goes to passing team.

7. Any forward pass becomes incomplete and ball is dead if:
(a) Pass hits the ground or goes out of bounds.
(b) Hits the goal post or the cross bar of either team.
(c) Is caught by offensive player after touching ineligible receiver.
(d) An illegal pass is caught by the passer.

8. A forward pass is complete when a receiver touches the ground with both feet inbounds while in possession of the ball. If a receiver is carried out of bounds by an opponent while in possession in the air, pass is complete at the out-of-bounds spot.

9. If an eligible receiver goes out of bounds accidentally or is forced out by a defender and returns to catch a pass, the play is regarded as a pass caught out of bounds. (Loss of down, no yardage.)

10. On a fourth down pass—when the offensive team is inside the opposition's 20 yard line—an incomplete pass results in a loss of down at the line of scrimmage.

11. If a personal foul is committed by the defense prior to the completion of a pass, the penalty is 15 yards from the spot where ball becomes dead.

12. If a personal foul is committed by the offense prior to the completion of a pass, the penalty is 15 yards from the previous line of scrimmage.

Intentional Grounding of Forward Pass

1. Intentional grounding of a forward pass is a foul: loss of down and 10 yards from previous spot if passer is in the field of play or safety if passer is in his own end zone when ball is released.

2. It is considered intentional grounding of a forward pass when the ball strikes the ground after the passer throws, tosses, or lobs the ball to prevent a loss of yards by his team.

Protection of Passer

1. By interpretation, a pass begins when the passer—with possession of

ball—starts to bring his hand forward. If ball strikes ground after this action has begun, play is ruled an incomplete pass. If passer loses control of ball prior to his bringing his hand forward, play is ruled a fumble.

2. No defensive player may run into a passer of a legal forward pass after the ball has left his hand (15 yards). The Referee must determine whether opponent had a reasonable chance to stop his momentum during an attempt to block the pass or tackle the passer while he still had the ball.

3. Officials are to blow the play dead as soon as the quarterback is clearly in the grasp of any tackler.

Pass Interference

1. There shall be no interference with a forward pass thrown from behind the line. The restriction for the passing team starts with the snap. The restriction on the defensive team starts when the ball leaves the passer's hand. Both restrictions end when the ball is touched by anyone.

2. The penalty for defensive pass interference is an automatic first down at the spot of the foul. If interference is in the end zone, it is first down for the defense's 1 yard line. If previous spot was inside the defense's 1 yard line, penalty is half the distance to the goal line. The penalty for offensive pass interference is 10 yards from the previous spot.

4. It is interference when any player's movement beyond the passing team's line hinders the progress of an eligible opponent in his attempt to reach a pass.

Exception: Such incidental movement or contact when two or more eligible players make a simultaneous and bona fide attempt to catch or bat the ball is permitted. "Simultaneous and bona fide" means the contact of an eligible receiver and a defensive player when each is playing the ball and contact is unavoidable and incidental to the act of trying to catch or bat the ball.

5. It must be remembered that defensive players have as much right to the path of the ball as eligible receivers. Any bodily contact, however severe, is not interference if a player is making a bona fide and simultaneous attempt to catch or bat the ball.

Backward Pass

1. Any pass not a forward pass is regarded as a backward pass or lateral. A pass parallel to the line is a backward pass. A runner may pass backward at any time. Any player on either team may catch the pass or recover the ball after it touches the ground.

2. A backward pass that strikes the ground can be recovered and advanced by offensive team.

3. A backward pass that strikes the ground can be recovered but cannot be advanced by the defensive team.

4. A backward pass caught in the air can be advanced by the defensive team.

Fumble

1. The distinction between a fumble and a muff should be kept in mind in considering rules about fumbles. A fumble is the loss of possession of the ball. A muff is the touching of a loose ball by a player in an unsuccessful attempt to obtain possession.

2. A fumble may be advanced by any player on either team regardless of whether recovered before or after ball hits the ground.

3. If an offensive player fumbles anywhere on the field during a fourth down play, or if a player fumbles on any down after the two-minute warning in a half, only the fumbling player is permitted to recover and/or advance the ball. If recovered by any other offensive player, the ball is dead at the spot of the fumble unless it is recovered behind the spot of the fumble. In that case, ball is dead at spot of recovery. Any defensive player may recover and/or advance any fumble.

Kicks From Scrimmage

1. Any punt or missed field goal that touches a goal post is dead.

2. During a kick from scrimmage, only the end men, as eligible receivers on the line of scrimmage at the time of the snap, are permitted to go beyond the line before the ball is kicked.
Exception: An eligible receiver who, at the snap, is aligned or in motion behind the line and more than one yard outside the end man on his side of the line, clearly making him the outside receiver, REPLACES that end man as the player eligible to go downfield after the snap. All other members of the kicking team must remain at the line of scrimmage until the ball has been kicked.

3. Any punt that is blocked and does not cross the line of scrimmage can be recovered and advanced by either team. However, if offensive team recoveries it must make the yardage necessary for its first down to retain possession if punt was on fourth down.

4. The kicking team may never advance its own kick even though legal recovery is made beyond the line of scrimmage. Possession only.

5. A member of the receiving team may not run or rough a kicker who recovers a loose ball. Ball is loose when kicker muffs snap or snap hits ground.
(a) Incidental to and after he had touched ball in flight.
(b) Caused by kicker's own motions.
(c) Occurs during a quick kick, or a kick made after a run, or after kicker recovers a loose ball. Ball is loose when kicker muffs snap or snap hits ground.
The penalty for running into the kicker is 5 yards; for roughing the kicker: 15 yards and disqualification if flagrant.

6. If a member of the kicking team attempting to down the ball on or inside opponent's 5 yard line carries the ball into the end zone, it is a touchback.

7. Fouls during a punt are enforced from the previous spot (line of scrimmage).
Exception: Illegal touching, illegal fair catch signal, invalid fair catch signal, and fouls by the receiving team during loose ball after ball is kicked.

8. While the ball is in the air or rolling on the ground following a punt or field goal attempt and receiving team commits a foul before gaining possession, receiving team will retain possession and will be penalized for its foul.

9. It will be illegal for a defensive player to jump on, stand on any player, or be picked up by a teammate or to use a hand or hands on a teammate to gain additional height in an attempt to block a kick (Penalty 15 yards, unsportsmanlike conduct).

10. A punted ball remains a kicked ball until it is declared dead or in possession of either team.

11. Any member of the punting team may down the ball anywhere in the field of play. However, it is illegal touching (Official's timeout and receiver's ball at spot of illegal touching). This foul does not offset any foul by receivers during the down.

12. Defensive team may advance all kicks from scrimmage (including unsuccessful field goal) whether or not ball crosses defensive team's goal line. Rules pertaining to kicks from scrimmage apply until defensive team gains possession.

Fair Catch

1. The member of the receiving team must raise one arm full length above his head while kick is in flight. (Failure to give proper sign: receivers' ball five yards behind spot of signal.)

2. No opponent may interfere with the fair catcher, the ball, or his path to the ball. Penalty: 15 yards from spot of foul and fair catch is awarded.

3. A player who signals for a fair catch is not required to catch the ball. However, if a player signals for a fair catch, he may not block or initiate contact with any player on the kicking team until the ball touches a player. Penalty: snap 15 yards behind spot of foul.

4. If ball hits ground or is touched by member of kicking team in flight, fair catch signal is off and all rules for a kicked ball apply.

5. Any undue advance by a fair catch receiver is delay of game. No specific distance is specified for "undue advance" as ball is dead at spot of catch. If player comes to a reasonable stop, no penalty. For violation, five yards.

6. If time expires while ball is in play and a fair catch is awarded, receiving team may choose to extend the period with one free-kick down. However, placekicker may not use tee.

Spot of Enforcement of Foul

1. There are four basic spots at which a penalty for a foul is enforced:
(a) Spot of foul: The spot where the foul is committed.
(b) Previous spot: The spot where the ball was put in play.
(c) Spot of snap, pass, fumble, return kick, or free kick: The spot where the act connected with the foul occurred.
(d) Succeeding spot: The spot where the ball next would be put in play if no distance penalty were to be enforced.

Foul on Last Play of Half or Game

1. On a foul by defense on last play of half or game, the down is replayed if penalty is accepted.

2. On a foul by the offense on last play of half or game, the down is not replayed and the play in which the foul is committed is nullified.
Exception: Fair catch interference, foul following change of possession, illegal touching. No score by offense counts.

3. On double foul on last play of half or game, down is replayed.

Guide for Statisticians

The chief statistician is selected by the individual club, subject to the Commissioner's approval. It is recommended that he have a minimum of two assistants plus a play-by-play typist. He shall have the responsibility to make decisions involving judgment, i.e., yardage on all plays, etc., and shall communicate such decisions to the press box via a loud speaker system. He is to provide the news media with a halftime summary score sheet and at the conclusion of the game with a final summary score sheet. These pre-printed forms are to be provided by the home club, which is responsible for the duplicating of all copy and the distribution in the press box.

In addition, the chief statistician shall prepare an official score blank provided by the league and, within an hour after the game, phone the league statisticians with the necessary information. This official score blank should then be mailed with two copies of the play-by-play to the statisticians. The chief statistician shall audit the statistics from the play-by-play and notify the league statisticians of any areas of disagreement between the play-by-play and the official score blank; such notification shall occur within 24 hours after completion of the game.

Games Played

A player is credited with a game played when he participates in at least one play, even if the only play in which he is involved is nullified by penalty, or even if no playing time is consumed.

Credit a player with a game started when he participates in Team A's first offensive play, or Team B's first offensive play. For purposes of this rule, the following plays are *not* regarded as offensive plays:

1. A kickoff
2. An extra point attempt
3. A punt or a field goal attempt from behind the line of scrimmage
4. A free kick following a safety

A play nullified by penalty shall be regarded as a play for purposes of this rule.

Example I: A player on Team A returns the opening kickoff to Team B's 2 yard line. On first down, Team A uses a double-tight end offense; the second tight end is used in place of a wide receiver, who is the usual starter. On first-and-goal, Team A is penalized for holding. On first-and-goal from the 12, the wide receiver replaces the second tight end in the lineup. *Scoring:* Credit the tight end with a game started; no game started for the wide receiver.

Determining the Yard Line

If any point of the football rests on or above any yard stripe, future action is to be computed from that yard line. However, if all of the football has been advanced beyond any yard stripe, future action is computed from the first yard line in advance of the football.

This principle is to be followed on all spotting situations, regardless of down, with the following exceptions:

1. In certain situations (any down but first) where there is less than a yard to gain for a first down, it may be necessary to spot the ball back one yard to conform with the principle that there must always be, for statistical purposes, at least one yard remaining to be gained for a first down.

2. When, on first down, the ball rests just outside a defensive team's 10 yard line, it will be necessary to designate the scrimmage line as the 11 inasmuch as it would be possible for the offensive team to advance for a first down without scoring a touchdown.

3. See field goal section for determining yard line of attempts.

First Downs

Statistics are to be compiled on all first downs made via rushing, passing, and penalties.

First downs are compiled only from plays originating from the line of scrimmage and a first down shall be credited to each scoring play resulting from rushes or forward passes, regardless of the distance covered.

If a fumble occurs on a scrimmage play and the resultant *fumble return* or *loose ball* yardage provides the yardage necessary for a first down or a touchdown, the first down shall be credited to the category initiating the action. (For a passing category to be initiated, a pass must be thrown.) A first down is never scored if the team loses possession of the ball on the play, even if the required distance is achieved.

On broken plays where there is a fumble and subsequent recovery, and advance results in a first down or a touchdown, it shall be considered a first down rushing. Similarly, if following a blocked punt or field goal attempt, a player on the kicking team recovers and runs for a first down or a touchdown, credit a *first down rushing*, even though any yardage

---

Exception: If foul occurs after a touchdown and before the whistle for a try-for-point, succeeding spot is spot of next kickoff.

2. All fouls committed by offensive team behind the line of scrimmage and in the field of play shall be penalized from the previous spot.

3. When spot of enforcement for fouls involving defensive holding or illegal use of hands by the defense is behind the line of scrimmage, any penalty to be assessed on that play shall be measured from the line.

Double Foul

1. If there is a double foul during a down in which there is a change of possession, the team last gaining possession may keep the ball unless its foul was committed prior to the change of possession.

2. If double foul occurs after a change of possession, the defensive team retains the ball at the spot possession was gained.

3. If one of the fouls of a double foul involves disqualification, that player must be removed, but no penalty yardage is to be assessed.

4. If the kickers foul during a punt before possession changes and the receivers foul after possession changes, penalties will be offset and the down is replayed.

Penalty Enforced on Following Kickoff

1. When a team scores by touchdown, field goal, extra point or safety and either team commits a personal foul, unsportsmanlike conduct or obvious unfair act during the down, the penalty will be assessed on the following kickoff.

gained is treated as miscellaneous yardage.

Example I. Passer attempting to pass fumbles, and advances to first down. This is a *first down rushing*, but yardage is *fumble yardage*. (See Fumble Section, paragraph 8, and Passing Plays, paragraph 12.)

Ordinarily, there can be only one first down on a play. However, if a team advances by scrimmage action enough yardage for a first down, and then a penalty that would ordinarily produce a first down (i.e., any *automatic first down* penalty or *15-yard penalty*) is assessed against the defense from the spot at which the scrimmage play concludes, two first downs (one by the scrimmage category initiating the action and one by penalty) shall be credited.

On the last play of the second or fourth quarter, or of an overtime period, if, in the scorer's judgment, the offensive team advances the ball to a first down, credit should be given whether or not the officials so signify.

Third Down Efficiency

A third down attempt is credited whenever the offensive team is credited with either a rushing attempt, a pass, or a "tackled attempting to pass" on its third down play. A third down conversion is credited whenever the offensive team is credited with either a first down rushing or a first down passing on its third down play.

EXCEPTION: Do not credit a third down attempt when the offensive team commits a foul (and the penalty is accepted by the defense), the spot of enforcement is in advance of the line of scrimmage, and the down remains the same.

Example I: Third-and-2 at midfield. Running back gains three yards but defense is offside. Offense elects to take the penalty; first-and-10 at the 45. *Scoring:* No entry is made in the third down efficiency category, since the first down was awarded by penalty.

Example II: Third-and-2 at midfield. Running back gains three yards, and defensive team is charged with facemask foul (not flagrant), moving the ball to the 42. *Scoring:* Two first downs are awarded (one rushing, one by penalty); credit a third down attempt and conversion, since the offense had made a first down without regard to the penalty.

Example III: Third-and-10 at midfield, offensive team ahead with 30 seconds remaining in the game. Quarterback falls to the ground after taking the snap, making no effort to gain yardage. *Scoring:* One third down attempt.

Example IV: Third-and-20 at offensive team's 1 yard line. Quarterback punts from behind the line of scrimmage. *Scoring:* No third down attempt.

Example V: Third-and-10 at midfield. Running back gains six yards, but a teammate is guilty of a personal foul, three yards in advance of the line of scrimmage. *Scoring:* Running back gets one rush for three yards, and his team is charged with a 15-yard penalty. No third down attempt is scored, since the spot of enforcement of the foul is ahead of the line of scrimmage. The next play is third-and-22 at the offensive team's 38.

Example VI: Third-and-10 at midfield. Quarterback scrambles one yard beyond the line, then throws a forward pass caught by a teammate. *Scoring:* Quarterback gets one rush for one yard, his team gets a five-yard penalty, and a third down attempt is scored, since the down changes. Next play is fourth-and-14 at the offensive team's 46.

Time of Possession

Time of possession is computed from the first play initiated by a team from the line of scrimmage until it scores, loses possession, or until the half or the game ends. When a change of possession (punt, fumble, interception, blocked kick) occurs during a play, consider the original team in possession until the play ends.

EXCEPTION: On a kickoff or on a free kick following a safety, all time consumed is credited to the team that first gains possession of the kick. (If neither team gains possession and the kick goes out of bounds, all time consumed is credited to the receiving team.)

Example I: Kickoff with 8:00 to play in the first quarter bounces off receiving team player and is recovered by kicking team with 7:50 to play. *Scoring:* Ten seconds of possession time is credited to kicking team, since it was the team that first *gained possession* of the kickoff.

Example II: Second-and-goal at the 1 yard line. Quarterback fumbles snap, defensive player recovers and runs the length of the field for a touchdown. Play consumes 25 seconds. *Scoring:* Original offensive team (the team that lost the fumble) is credited with 25 seconds of possession time.

Measuring a Scoring Drive

Scoring drive yardage is measured from the initial line of scrimmage to the goal line, in the event of a touchdown, or from the initial line of scrimmage to the last line of scrimmage for field goals, not the spot from which the kick is attempted. Penalty plays (where the down remains the same but the ball changes position) are not included in the total number of plays in a scoring drive. No scoring drive should exceed the total number of plays from the initial line to the goal line or to the last line of scrimmage for field goals.

Penalty Plays

Plays in which penalties are involved are scored as follows:

1. If the play is nullified in its entirety, and the penalty is to be assessed from the line of scrimmage, the penalty reflects the entire yardage. An example of this is a play nullified by offside, delay of game, offensive fouls behind the line of scrimmage, etc.

2. If a penalty occurs within the framework of a play and there is both yardage gained as well as penalty yardage assessed, the play is scored as follows in order to account for change in ball position:

Credit the offensive player(s) with yardage gained to the point of the infraction, and charge the offending team with the yardage specified by the infraction. This principle shall also apply in the case of a penalty occurring during a punting play (while the ball is in the air), if the penalty is assessed from the point of infraction, no return will be credited to receiving team. Offending (punting) team will be credited with downed punt and charged with penalty yardage specified.

Example I: Running back rushes for 25 yards, but a teammate is called for clipping 20 yards in advance of the line of scrimmage. *Scoring:* Running back gets one rushing attempt for 20 yards (to point of infraction). His team is penalized 15 yards. This accounts for forward movement of the ball of net 5 yards.

Example II: Quarterback completes pass for 17 yards to tight end and clipping occurs 15 yards in advance of line of scrimmage. *Scoring:* Quarterback gets one pass attempt, one pass completion for 15 yards. Tight end one pass reception for 15 yards. Team is charged with 15 yard penalty from point of infraction.

Example III: Running back gains 7 yards rushing, but offensive clipping occurs 5 yards in advance of line of scrimmage. Credit runner with 5 yards rushing (to point of infraction), team with 15 yards penalty from point of infraction even though play results in a 10-yard net loss from scrimmage.

Example IV: With ball at midfield, quarterback is tackled attempting to pass at his own 40, where the defensive team commits a facemask foul (not flagrant). Ball is moved back to midfield, according to rule, and offensive team is awarded a first down. *Scoring:* Tackled attempting to pass for a ten-yard loss. Then, defensive team is charged with one penalty for ten yards. Credit the offensive team with a first down by penalty.

If the overall movement of the ball on a first down play is to a point beyond that needed for a first down, score a first down on the play. (Such action on a second, third or fourth down play would be reflected by officials' awarding a first down.)

Caution: Do not be confused by the fact that the down does not change in above circumstances unless the net yardage of play and penalty exceeds that needed for a first down.

3. When a foul occurs behind the spot of possession on an interception, punt return, kickoff return, or miscellaneous yardage play, the player is given one return for no yards. Penalty yardage shall commence from the spot of enforcement.

Example: Player receives a punt on his own 40 and returns to his 48. His teammate is called for clipping at his 35. The 15-yard penalty is enforced from there, and the ball is moved to the 20. *Scoring:* Credit the returner with one return for no yards; his team is penalized 15 yards.

EXCEPTION: When the foul is in advance of the line of scrimmage, the normal spot of enforcement would be beyond the line of scrimmage, and credit yards gained to the spot of the foul. Charge the team with one penalty for *no yards.* Also, if on the last play of a half, the defensive team scores on a play during which the offensive team commits a foul, the play stands and the score counts, because the penalty is declined.

4. The receiving team commits an infraction while a punt is in the air and the yardage is enforced from the point of the infraction. *Scoring:* If ball is handled, one punt return for no yards or a fair catch, as the case may be. If the infraction occurs in front of the returner, the punt should be measured to the point at which the punt ends.

5. A pass interference call is wholly a penalty play and first downs are credited accordingly.

6. When an offensive foul occurs on the last play of a half and the offensive team gains yardage on the play, the play is *nullified* in its entirety. Charge the team with one penalty for *no yards.*

18, then pitches back to a teammate on the 22, where the teammate is downed. *Scoring:* Second player gets one rush, minus 2 yards.

Example II: First-and-10 on opponent's 20 yard line. Player runs to the 15, then pitches back to a teammate on the 18; teammate runs to the 8. *Scoring:* First player gets one rush, 2 yards; second player gets 10 yards rushing (*no* rushing attempt); credit a first down rushing.

Example III: First-and-10 on opponent's 20 yard line. Player runs to the 15, pitches back to a teammate on the 18, where he is downed. *Scoring:* First player gets one rush, 2 yards.

Example IV: First-and-10 on opponent's 20 yard line. Quarterback hands ball to runner, who is about to be tackled at 25 when he laterals or hands ball to a teammate on the 26, where the teammate is downed. *Scoring:* Last player handling ball gets one rush, minus 6 yards.

Example VI: First-and-10 on opponent's 20 yard line. Player runs to the 5, then laterals to a teammate on the 5, where the teammate is downed. *Scoring:* First player gets one rush, 15 yards; credit first down rushing.

Example IV: First-and-10 on opponent's 20 yard line. Player runs to the 3, then laterals to a teammate on the 5; teammate runs for a touchdown. *Scoring:* First player gets one rush, 15 yards; second player gets 5 yards and touchdown rushing (*no* rushing attempt); credit a first down rushing.

For fumbles on rushing plays see Fumbles section.

Passing

The passing category includes both the forward pass and the forward pass reception. (In this section, the word "pass" shall indicate "forward pass" unless otherwise noted.)

Passing yardage is computed from the line of scrimmage and includes the length of the pass plus the running yardage gained or lost by the receiver after the completion.

If a forward pass is completed behind the line of scrimmage and the receiver is downed, credit the passer with an attempt and completion and the minus yardage.

A forward pass ruled complete due to interference is not considered an attempt or a completion. It is a penalty play (yardage and first down).

Charge a player with a pass attempt when he:

1. Throws a completed pass;
2. Throws an intercepted pass;
3. Throws an incomplete pass, including when:

   A. The pass strikes the ground or goes out of bounds;

   B. The pass accidentally touches an ineligible offensive player on or behind the line of scrimmage;

   C. The pass is the second forward pass from behind the line of scrimmage and it is caught by an offensive player; when this occurs, no completion or yardage is credited for the original (completed) pass;

   D. The pass is caught by an ineligible offensive player on or behind the line of scrimmage;

   E. The pass is thrown from behind the line of scrimmage, after having been carried or passed backward from a spot beyond the line;

   F. The pass is touched by an eligible offensive player returning from out of bounds.

Do *not* charge a pass attempt when the acceptance of a penalty nullifies the play in its entirety (e.g., roughing the passer on an incomplete pass), if the penalty is for a continuing action foul.

At times, a penalty will be enforced *in addition* to the loss of down, which is the result of an incompletion. In these cases, charge a pass attempt as well as any penalty yardage that is enforced. *Examples:* Intentional grounding, ineligible receiver touches a pass beyond the line of scrimmage, etc.

When a player throws a forward pass from beyond the line of scrimmage, and the penalty is accepted, do *not* charge the passer with a pass attempt. Credit him with yards gained (in the category initiating the action) to the point of the pass; penalty yardage will commence from that spot.

Example I: Second-and-10 at own 30 yard line. Quarterback, back to pass, runs beyond line and throws forward pass at 34. *Scoring:* One rush for 4 yards; one penalty for 5 yards.

Example II: Second-and-10 at own 30 yard line. Pass is completed to 50, where the receiver, attempting to lateral, throws a forward pass. *Scoring:* One completion for 20 yards; one penalty for 5 yards. Credit a first down passing.

When the defense declines a penalty for a forward pass thrown in advance of the line of scrimmage, the scoring shall reflect the actual ball movement during the play.

Example III: Second-and-10 at own 30 yard line. Pass is completed to 50, where the receiver, attempting to lateral, throws a forward pass that is

---

Example I: Second-and-4 at offensive team's 20 yard line. On last play of half, player runs for 6 yards, but a teammate is offside. *Scoring:* The play is nullified (no rushing attempt). Charge one penalty for *no yards*.

Example II: Second-and-4 at offensive team's 20 yard line. On last play of half, player runs for 30 yards, but a teammate is called for clipping within his own 45 yard line. *Scoring:* Since this penalty occurred downfield within the framework of the play, player receives one rush for 25 yards (to point of foul) and his team gets a first down rushing. Charge the team with one penalty for *no yards*.

Example III: Second-and-4 at offensive team's 20 yard line. On last play of a half, a pass is incomplete. Offensive team is called for holding behind the line of scrimmage. *Scoring:* Since the offensive team did not gain yardage, charge the passer with one attempt. Do *not* charge a penalty.

Example IV: Second-and-4 at offensive team's 20 yard line. On last play of a half, quarterback is sacked for a loss of 12 yards; a teammate is called for holding behind the line of scrimmage. *Scoring:* Since the offensive team did not gain yardage, score one "tackled attempting to pass" for 12 yards. Do *not* charge a penalty.

Example V: Second-and-4 at offensive team's 20 yard line. On last play of a half, quarterback's pass is intercepted at the 50. The ball is returned to the 30, but a teammate of the interceptor is called for clipping at the 40. Meanwhile, the original offensive team was guilty of illegal motion at the snap. *Scoring:* The offensive team did not gain yardage, so the play stands; score an interception, and credit the interceptor with 10 return yards (to the spot of the foul). Charge *his* team with one penalty for *no yards*.

Example VI: Second-and-4 at offensive team's 20 yard line. On last play of a half, offensive team is guilty of illegal motion at the snap. Running back gains two yards and fumbles; defensive player recovers at the 22 and returns to the 10. *Scoring:* Since offensive team's runner gained yardage on the play, this play is nullified in its entirety. Charge the offensive team with one penalty for *no yards*.

Example VII: Second-and-4 at offensive team's 20 yard line. On last play of a half, offensive team is guilty of illegal motion at the snap. Running back fumbles at 22, but ball bounces back to the 18, where anyone recovers and is tackled. *Scoring:* Running back gets one rush for minus two yards. Do *not* charge a penalty.

7. Penalty yardage may be assessed on an extra point attempt.

Example I: Defensive team is offside as an extra point attempt is good. The penalty is assessed on the subsequent kickoff. *Scoring:* One penalty for 5 yards.

Example II: Offensive team is offside as an extra point attempt is good. Ball is moved back from the 2 to the 7 yard line for the next attempt. *Scoring:* One penalty for 5 yards.

Example III: Defensive team is offside as an extra point attempt is missed. The offensive team elects:

(a) to rekick, with the ball remaining at the 2 yard line. *Scoring:* Defensive team is charged with one penalty, no yards.

(b) to rekick, with the ball moved to the 1 yard line. *Scoring:* Defensive team is charged with one penalty for 1 yard.

Rushing

All plays from scrimmage are rushing plays unless:

1. There is a kick from behind the line of scrimmage; or
2. There is a pass from behind the line of scrimmage; or
3. A player makes an apparent attempt to pass at any time before he or a teammate is tackled, steps out of bounds or fumbles behind or at the line of scrimmage.

There is no separate category for "yards lost" rushing and the yards gained for both individual and team is determined by deducting the minus figures from the plus figures to arrive at *net yards gained.* For example, a player gains 5 yards on one attempt and minus 2 on another. His totals would be 2 rushing attempt's and a net gain of 3 yards.

A run from a fake punt or field goal formation is considered a rushing attempt.

On a rushing play, the last player to handle a pitchout, backward pass, handoff, or reverse is charged with a rushing attempt, and is responsible for any yardage gained or lost from scrimmage, *provided* that he receives a pitchout, backward pass, handoff, or reverse beyond the line of scrimmage. If a player receives a pitchout, backward pass, handoff, or reverse beyond the line of scrimmage, credit the player responsible with yardage gained to the point of the second player's possession.

Example I: First-and-10 on opponent's 20 yard line. Player runs to the

intercepted at opponent's 49 and returned for a touchdown. *Scoring:* One completion (reception) for 20 yards. Player receiving the original pass also gets one pass (intercepted). (Defense declines the penalty in order to score the touchdown.)

The same rules apply when a forward pass not from scrimmage is thrown (e.g., on a punt return): No pass attempt is charged, unless the ball is intercepted. Penalty yardage is assessed from the spot of the foul.

In passing statistics there is a category called "tackled and yards lost attempting to pass." It shall be determined by the following rules:

1. When the quarterback or a teammate, makes an apparent attempt to pass at any time before he or a teammate is tackled, steps out of bounds, or fumbles behind or at the line of scrimmage, the play is scored as "tackled" and any yards lost attempting to pass. (Should he advance the ball across the line of scrimmage, it is a rushing play.)

2. When the quarterback is tackled or, after *gaining possession of the snap*, he fumbles or falls down, while retreating to his normal passing position, it shall be scored as "tackled" and yards lost attempting to pass, even though he may not have assumed a passing position.

Example I: Second-and-1 at own 20 yard line. Quarterback, back to pass, fumbles the ball while standing in the pocket, without any defensive contact. He recovers at the 13. *Scoring:* One "tackled" and 7 yards lost, a fumble, and an own recovery.

Example II: Second-and-1 at own 20 yard line. Quarterback takes snap, then while retreating to pass, fumbles. Ball rolls to 10, and then is batted back to the 5, where a player recovers and is downed. *Scoring:* Charge one "tackled" and 10 yards lost (to point of first batting). The other 5 yards are the result of a loose ball. (See Fumbles, 6. E. (b).)

Example III: Third-and-25 at own 40 yard line. Quarterback fumbles snap on what appears to be a definite passing down. He recovers at the 35. *Scoring:* An aborted play; quarterback gets one rush for no yards, a fumble, an own recovery, and minus 5 (fumble yardage) yards.

3. When a quarterback rolls out, or a player other than the quarterback handles the ball on an option play, or takes the snap in a "shotgun" formation, and makes an *apparent attempt* to pass before being tackled or stepping out of bounds behind or at the line of scrimmage, it shall be scored as "tackled" and any yards lost attempting to pass. If the player makes no *apparent attempt* to pass, the play shall be considered a rushing play.

4. The individual passer shall not be charged with an attempted forward pass, or yardage lost, when the play is scored as "tackled...attempting to pass." However, the yardage lost on such plays *MUST* be deducted from his team's gross passing yardage to reflect *net yards gained passing*. For fumbles on passing plays see Fumbles section.

Lateral Passes

Lateral passes subsequent to the originating play are considered as part of the play from which they originate. The receiver of a lateral is given credit for the yardage he gains from the point of the lateral *BUT* he is not given an attempt, return or reception on the play. (See Exceptions listed under Punt Returns and under Kickoff Returns.) For example, a forward pass is completed and the receiver advances the ball an additional 20 yards, then laterals to a teammate who advances the ball 40 yards, then laterals to a teammate who advances the ball an additional 20 yards. This is considered a 60-yard pass play. The first receiver is credited with the reception and 40 yards gained; his teammate, although not credited with a reception, would appear in the pass receiving section with 20 yards gained, annotated with an asterisk ("Lateral). If a touchdown is scored as a result of such a play, the player who scores shall be credited with a touchdown via receiving. In any case the original play determines in what category the touchdown was made.

When the receiver of a backward pass, or lateral, is beyond the line of scrimmage, it is *his* position that determines the yardage gained by each of the individuals involved. The player who throws the pass is credited with yards gained only to the point at which the pass is caught or (if muffed) is recovered, provided this point is behind the spot of the pass.

Example: Second-and-20 on own 20 yard line. Player catches a forward pass at his own 40, then throws a backward pass to a teammate on the 38. The teammate then:

(a) is downed at the 38. *Scoring:* First player gets one reception for 18 yards.

(b) runs to the 45. *Scoring:* First player gets one reception for 18 yards; second player gets 7 yards in pass receiving category, but is not credited with a reception. Credit a first down passing.

(c) muffs the ball and an opponent recovers on the 33. *Scoring:* First player gets one reception for 13 yards and a fumble. Opponent gets a fumble recovery.

Interceptions

Interception yardage is computed from the point where the impetus of the act of interception ends and the intercepting player begins forward or backward movement on his own. This *includes* the end zone area of the intercepting player, except that a player making an interception in his own end zone shall not be credited with any return yardage if the ball becomes dead behind his own goal line.

Example I: Player intercepts the ball five yards deep in his end zone, and returns to his 7 yard line. *Scoring:* 12 yard return.

Example II: Player intercepts the ball five yards deep in his end zone, starts to run, but stops one yard short of the goal line, where he downs the ball or is tackled for a touchback. *Scoring:* One interception for no yards; the ball never left the end zone.

Punts

All punts from behind or on the line of scrimmage shall be measured from the line of scrimmage to the point at which the impetus of the punt ends, or the ball goes out of bounds, or is downed. If a punt goes into the end zone, measure its length to the goal line, unless the ball is fielded and returned out of the end zone by the receiving team (in such a case, measure the punt to the spot of possession in the end zone by the receiver). All punts from beyond the line of scrimmage, and all punts following an exchange of possession ("return kicks") shall be measured from the spot of the kick to the point at which the impetus of the punt ends, or the ball goes out of bounds or is downed.

EXCEPTION: If a punt is touched (but not possessed) by the receiving team and is recovered by the kicking team in the end zone, measure the punt to the point at which the ball is spotted on the field of play (either the spot of the touch or the 1 yard line).

The impetus of a punt continues until the receiving team is in possession or the kickers legally recover, unless:

(a) the ball is batted or kicked by the kicking team (measure the punt to the spot of the bat or kick); or

(b) the receiving team has touched the ball, causing the ball to change direction and bounce toward the kickers' goal line; measure the punt to the spot of the touch.

Example I: A punt from the 50 touches a receiver on the 10, and is recovered by the kickers in the end zone. *Scoring:* A 40-yard punt; kickers' ball, first-and 10 at the 10.

Example II: A punt from the 50 goes into the end zone (three yards deep), where a receiving team player fields it and returns to the 7. *Scoring:* A 53-yard punt and a 10-yard return.

Example III: A punt from the 50 is muffed by a receiver on the 10. The ball bounces upfield where it is recovered by anyone at the 18. *Scoring:* A 40-yard punt (to the spot of the first touch by receivers).

Example IV: A punt from the 50 is rolling slowly on the 10 when a kicking team player running downfield accidentally knocks the ball into the end zone for a touchback. *Scoring:* A 40-yard punt.

A blocked punt is scored *only* when the punted ball fails to go beyond the line of scrimmage. A "partially blocked" punt that travels beyond the line of scrimmage is *not* a blocked punt. A blocked punt is charged to the team, but not to the individual punter.

Do not charge a player with a punt unless he actually punts the ball. Note that if the center snap is *satisfactory* and the punter does not fumble, but is tackled before he punts or while attempting to run, the play is a rushing play. If the play develops as action off a fake punt play, score the play as a rush, pass, or tackled attempting to pass consistent with the basic scoring rules on scrimmage plays.

Credit a player with an inside-20 when his punt is not returned to the receivers' 20 yard line or beyond. A touchback is *not* an inside-20. When there is a penalty during the return, the point at which the return ends statistically is the determining spot for crediting an inside-20.

If, following a punt or punt return, the ball is positioned between the receivers' 19 and 20 yard lines, *no inside 20 is scored* if the ball is statistically determined to be on the 20 yard line.

Example V: A punt from the 50 is caught on the 15 and returned to the 30. Receivers commit a clipping foul at the 30, and the ball is moved back to the 15. *Scoring:* A 35-yard punt, 15-yard return, and 15-yard penalty. Do not credit an inside-20, since the return took the ball to the 30. First-and-10 at the 15.

Beginning in 1976, a Punting Game category was devised to help illustrate team punting effectiveness. To compile the net punting average of each punter, divide the total number of punts (including blocked punts not charged against him individually) into his gross punting yardage minus touchbacks (delete 20 yards per touchback) and minus return yardage. *Example:* Player punts 59 times for 2,536 gross yards, a 43.0 average. Two additional punts are blocked, for which he is not charged. Of his 59 punts, 11 result in touchbacks and 29 are returned for 179 yards. To compute his Punting Game effectiveness, divide 61 punts into net yardage of 2,137 (2,536 minus 220 for touchbacks minus 179 return yardage). His team's Punting Game effectiveness when he is punting is 35.3.

Blocked Kicks

When a punt or a field goal attempt is blocked and recovered by the offensive team behind the line of scrimmage any running advance is treated as miscellaneous yardage. In the rare case when the offensive player attempts a forward pass after a blocked kick include it as a passing attempt and any completion as passing yardage. However, if the player is tackled behind the line of scrimmage *do not* treat this as yards lost attempting to pass. In the latter case merely note the player recovered a blocked kick. NOTE: Regardless of any subsequent action the original blocked punt or field goal must be recorded.

Punt Returns

A punt return is credited to the first player on the receiving team who gains possession of the punt.

EXCEPTION: If, prior to the receiving team gaining possession of the punt, the ball is muffed or touched by a receiver *who is trying to gain possession*, then the punt return is credited to the player who first muffed or touched the ball. (Note that this exception does *not* apply if the ball touches a player who was *not trying to gain possession*.)

If the punt is legally recovered by the kicking team before any receiving team player gains possession, then charge a punt return to the first player on the receiving team who touched (or was touched by) the ball, whether or not he was trying to gain possession.

Example I: Punt from the 50. Receiver tries to catch the ball on the 20, but it bounces off (or through) his hands and is recovered by a teammate on the 12. *Scoring:* a 38-yard punt (the impetus of the punt continued to the 12 yard line). The punt return is credited to the player who muffed the ball at the 20; he also gets a fumble, and the recovering player is credited with an own recovery.

Example II: Punt from the 50. Ball is touched by a receiver on the 20 (whether or not he was trying to gain possession), and kicking team player recovers at the 15. *Scoring:* a 35-yard punt (the impetus of the punt continued to the 15 yard line). The punt return is credited to the player who touched (or was touched by) the ball at the 20; he also gets a fumble, since the prior touching was *not by a* player who was trying to gain possession.

Do not charge a punt return to a player who:

(1) signals for, and safely makes, a fair catch; or

(2) is interfered with before having the opportunity to catch the punt (with or without a fair catch signal).

In both of the above circumstances, credit a fair catch. Do *not* credit a fair catch if the player muffs the ball following a fair catch signal, regardless of who recovers the ball. Credit the player with a punt return and fumble; the appropriate player is credited with a fumble recovery.

Example III: Punt from the 50. Ball bounces at the 25, and after taking an unusual bounce, strikes the leg of a receiver who is trying to avoid the ball. The ball rolls to the 20, where it is recovered by another receiving team player. *Scoring:* a 30-yard punt (the impetus of the punt continued to the 20 yard line). The punt return is credited to the player who recovered (and first possessed) the ball, since the prior touching was *not by a* player who was trying to gain possession.

Example IV: Receiver does not signal for a fair catch and runs toward the punted ball in an attempt to catch it. Player from kicking team is in the receiver's way on the receiver's 30 yard line; the receiver cannot reach the ball. The ball rolls to the 20 where it is downed. *Scoring:* Fair catch is awarded to the receiver because of opponent's interference. Punt is measured to the 30 yard line, and kickers are penalized 15 yards.

The distance of a punt return shall be measured from the point at which the impetus of the punt ends and the receiver is able to initiate forward progress.

Example V: A player takes a punt on his own 30, runs back 10 yards to his own 20, then forward to the 35. The punt return is measured as five yards.

Example VI: A player takes a punt on his own 30 but retreats 3 yards to the 27 because the impetus of the punt requires him to move backward. He then advances back to the 30. The punt is recorded to the 27, and the punt return is measured as 3 yards.

Example VII: A player catches the ball on his own 30, runs back 20 yards and is tackled on his own 10. The punt return is recorded as minus 20 yards, and the punt is recorded ONLY to the 30 yard line.

Return by a defensive player of a blocked punt is not considered a punt return. The player and the yardage gained shall be noted on the back of the official score blank under "remarks."

On the score blank the total punts for the team should equal the total punt returns, plus the fair catches, plus the punts out of bounds, plus the punt touchbacks, plus punts downed, and punts blocked. Official scorers should always reconcile these figures on score blank.

For fumbles on punt returns see Fumbles section.

Kickoff Returns

A kickoff return is credited to the first player on the receiving team who gains possession of the kickoff, except:

(1) if the player who fields the kickoff makes no effort to advance an apparent onside kick, and if the first touching of the ball is within 15 yards of the spot of the kick, *no kickoff return is credited.*

(2) when the receiver of a kickoff *makes no advance* of the ball, but instead laterals or hands off to a teammate. If there is no fumble during the exchange (meaning if the ball does *not* touch the ground), the second player is given credit for any return and the yardage is computed from the point at which he gains possession.

(3) when the receiver of the kickoff gains less than 10 yards before he laterals or hands off to a teammate, and that teammate gains more yardage than the original handler of the kickoff. In such a case, the second player receives credit for a kickoff return and yardage; the first player gets no return but does get return yards (not more than nine).

(4) if, prior to the receiving team gaining possession of the kickoff, the ball is muffed or touched by a receiver *who is trying to gain possession*, and the first player who gains possession makes no effort to advance the ball, then the kickoff return and a fumble are credited to the player who first muffed or touched the ball.

(5) if the receiver downs the ball in the end zone for a touchback.
Note that a kickoff return is credited on any kickoff that is first touched by the receivers more than 15 yards from the spot of the kick, except if the receiver downs the ball in the end zone for a touchback. When no player on the receiving team gains possession of a kickoff, do not credit a kickoff return unless the ball goes out of bounds or is recovered by the kicking team *after* touching (or having been touched by) a receiving team player, *and* the first such touching is more than 15 yards from the spot of the kick. In such a case, credit a kickoff return and a fumble to the player on the receiving team who touched (or was touched by) the ball.

The distance of a kickoff return shall be measured from the point at which the impetus of the kickoff ends and the receiver *gains possession and is able to initiate forward progress.* This includes the *end zone area.*

For example, a player takes the kickoff on the 10, runs back to the 5 and then advances to the 20. He is credited with a 10-yard return. Another example: A player takes the kickoff on the 10, but retreats to the 7 because the impetus of the kickoff requires him to do so. He then advances to the 20. He is credited with a 13-yard return. A third example: A player takes the ball on the 10, but runs back to the 5, where he is tackled. He is credited with one kickoff return for MINUS 5 yards.

Example I: A player receives the kickoff on the 20, makes no attempt to advance but laterals to a teammate on the 15, who then advances to the 17. The first player is not credited with a kickoff return, but his teammate is credited with one return for 2 yards.

Example II: A player receives the kickoff on the 20, makes no attempt to advance, but laterals to a teammate on the 15. The teammate then retreats and is tackled on the 12. The first player is not credited with a return, but the teammate is credited with one return for MINUS 3 yards.

Example III: A player receives the kickoff on the 20 and then runs laterally across the field and hands off to a teammate on the 18. The teammate returns to the 25 and is credited with one return for 7 yards.

Example IV: A player receives the kickoff on the 20, *then advances to the* 22 before lateralling to a teammate on the 15. The teammate advances to the 30. The first player is credited with no return for 2 yards and the second player one return for 8 yards.

Example V: A player receives the kickoff on the 20, *then advances to the* 22 before lateraling to a teammate on the 15. The teammate is tackled on the 17. The first player is credited with one kickoff return for *minus 3* yards and the second player one return for 8 yards.

Example VI: A player receives a kickoff on the 20, then advances to the 22 before handing off to a teammate, who then retreats and is tackled on the 19. The first player is credited with one kickoff return for no yards and the second player with no kickoff return with MINUS 1 yard.

Example VII: A player receives a kickoff on the 20, then advances to the 22 before handing off to a teammate. The teammate then runs to the 30. In this instance, the first player is credited with one kickoff return with no return for yardage.

If the lateral is a bad pass or the handoff is fumbled, then the first player is credited with one return for no yardage and the remainder of the play is treated as a fumble. For this and other fumbles on kickoff returns, see Fumbles section.

The general provisions for scoring a fair catch, which appear in the Punt Returns section, also apply to kickoff returns.

Free Kicks

Free kicks shall be scored as kickoffs in all instances, regardless of whether they are punted or made from placement. The receiver gets credit for a kickoff return in all cases.

EXCEPTION: When a free kick is called for (following a fair catch of a punt) to attempt a field goal, the kicker shall be charged with a field goal attempt. Any yardage on a runback by an opposing player shall be credited as miscellaneous yardage, as with any other field goal attempt.

Fumbles

Definitions of Fumbles and Recoveries

1. A fumble is an act that results in an individual's loss of possession of the ball or his failure to handle a ball which has been properly centered or handed to him. EXCEPTIONS: No fumble shall be charged (a) on an attempted point-after-touchdown, or (b) on a momentary bobble of the ball at the point of reception if in the scorer's judgment the bobble had no effect on the continuing action, provided that the ball has not touched the ground or another player. A fumble is also charged in certain instances in which a player *muffs* a ball punted to him. See Punt Returns section.

2. If a fumbled ball (a) goes out of bounds and remains in possession of the team fumbling, or (b) goes over the end line for a touchback or safety, score the play as a fumble and also note it as "fumble out of bounds" under the fumbles section.

3. "Own recovery" designates a fumble recovered by any member of the team committing the fumble. "Opponents' recovery" designates a fumble recovered by any member of the team *not* committing the fumble. Note that there must be a "recovery" for every fumble charged except for fumbles that go out of bounds.

4. When a fumbled ball is touched by several players, only the player who lost possession originally shall be charged with a fumble and only the player who ultimately gains possession shall be credited with a recovery. There can be more than one fumble and more than one recovery on a single play only if possession is clearly established following the original fumble.

5. When a bobbled ball is recovered out of the air by a teammate or an opponent, it shall be scored as a fumble and a recovery. EXCEPTION: If a receiver juggles a pass without establishing possession and a teammate or an opponent gains possession in the air, it shall be scored as a completed pass or interception as the case may be.

Principles of Scoring Yardage on Fumble Plays

6. Any yardage gained or lost on a rushing play in which a fumble occurs—except on Aborted Plays described in Number 7—shall be recorded as follows:

A. When a player recovers his own fumble, credit him with the net yardage gained or lost on the play in the category initiating the action. (Charge him with a fumble and credit him with "own recovery.")

B. When a teammate recovers:
(a) Behind (or on) the line of scrimmage, charge the player who fumbled with all yardage lost, if any, to the point of recovery or the new line of scrimmage, whichever is less. (Charge him with a fumble and credit him with "own recovery.")
(b) Beyond the line of scrimmage, credit the player who fumbled with yardage gained to the point of recovery, whichever is less.

C. When an opponent recovers:
(a) Behind (or on) the line of scrimmage, charge the player who fumbled with yardage lost, if any, to the point of recovery.
(b) Beyond the line of scrimmage, credit the player who fumbled with yardage gained to the point of his advance or the point of recovery, whichever is less.

D. A teammate or opponent who recovers shall be credited with fumble yardage for any gain or loss from the point of recovery. If a teammate recovers behind the line of scrimmage and advances a teammate may make behind the line of scrimmage. The theory is that the player who fumbled shall benefit from any advance a teammate makes behind the line of scrimmage. (Note that no minus yardage can be charged unless the teammate opponent causes the minus yardage by running or throwing the ball after gaining possession of it.)

E. (a) When a fumbled ball rolls free and is recovered beyond the point of the fumble (by either a teammate or an opponent), any yardage between the spot of the fumble and the spot of recovery is loose ball yardage.
(b) When a fumbled ball is legally batted or kicked by either team, charge the player who fumbled with yardage lost to the spot of the first such bat or kick; the rest of the yardage is loose ball yardage. If an opponent eventually gains possession, his fumble yardage shall be credited from the spot at which he gains possession. If a teammate gains possession, his fumble yardage shall commence at the spot of the fumble or the spot of possession (whichever is nearer the opponents' goal line).

Scoring of Fumble Plays
ABORTED PLAYS

7. An *aborted play* is a play from scrimmage which falls into one of the following categories:

A. the ball is *clearly* centered improperly;
B. the intended ball-handler fumbles the snap from center;
C. a player hands off or laterals improperly, behind the line of scrimmage;
D. a backward pass behind the line of scrimmage is muffed.

In each of these cases, charge a rush for no yards. In A. and B., the rush is charged to the player who receives, or intended to receive, the snap from center. In C. and D., the rush is charged to the player who hands off or laterals improperly, or who throws a backward pass which is muffed.

EXCEPTION: If the player charged with the rush recovers the loose ball and advances beyond the line of scrimmage, credit any advance as rushing yardage.

When the ball is clearly centered improperly, charge the center with a fumble and any yards lost as fumble yardage. On any other aborted play, the player charged with the rush is also charged with a fumble and any yards lost as fumble yardage.

If an opponent recovers beyond the line of scrimmage, charge fumble yardage to the offensive player to the point of recovery only.

If a teammate recovers behind the line of scrimmage and advances beyond the line, credit that player with fumble yardage equal to the distance between the old and new lines of scrimmage.

If a player from either team (other than the player charged with the rush) makes the initial recovery beyond the line of scrimmage, the ball movement to the point of recovery shall be treated as loose ball yardage. If the player charged with the rush makes such a recovery, credit him with rushing yardage equal to the point of recovery only.

Example I: Second-and-10 at own 20 yard line. Quarterback fumbles the snap, and a teammate recovers at the 15, where he is downed. *Scoring:* Quarterback gets one rush for no yards, a fumble, and minus 5 yards as fumble yardage. Teammate gets an own recovery.

Example II: Same play as above, except that the teammate advances to:

A. the 18 yard line. *Scoring:* Quarterback gets one rush for no yards, a fumble and minus 2 yards as fumble yardage. Teammate gets an own recovery.

B. the 30 yard line. *Scoring:* Quarterback gets one rush for no yards and a fumble. Teammate gets an own recovery, 10 yards (fumble yardage) and team is credited with a first down *rushing.*

Example III: Second-and-10 at own 20 yard line. Quarterback fumbles the snap, then recovers and advances to the 24. *Scoring:* Quarterback gets one rush for 4 yards, a fumble, and an own recovery.

Example IV: Fourth-and-10 at own 20 yard line. Punter intends to receive snap, but it is clearly centered improperly. *Scoring:* Center gets one rush for no yards, a fumble, and an own recovery. Punter recovers at the 5, where he is downed. *Scoring:* Center

tacklers, is tackled at the 40 — a net loss of 10 yards on the play. *Scoring:* Running back is charged with one rushing attempt for minus 6 yards and a fumble. Teammate is charged with minus 4 fumble yards because he caused the additional loss.

10. When an opponent recovers:

Example I: With ball on opponent's 30, running back rushes to 28, where he is tackled and fumbles. Opponent recovers the ball on the 25. *Scoring:* Running back is credited with one rush for 2 yards and is charged with a fumble.

Example II: With ball on opponent's 30, running back rushes to 28, where he is tackled and fumbles. Opponent recovers the ball on the 32. *Scoring:* Running back is charged with one rush for minus 2 yards and also with a fumble.

Example III: With ball on opponent's 30, running back rushes to 28, where he is tackled and fumbles. Opponent recovers the ball at the 25 and returns it to the 32 before being tackled. *Scoring:* Running back is credited with one rush for 2 yards and is charged with a fumble; opponent is credited with 7 yards of fumble yardage.

Example IV: With ball on opponent's 30, running back is tackled at the 32 and fumbles. Opponent recovers the ball at the 28. *Scoring:* Running back is charged with one rush for no yards and also with a fumble.

Example V: With ball on opponent's 30, running back rushes to the 25, where he is tackled and fumbles. An opponent picks up the ball at the 25 and runs it back and fumbles at the 30, where the ball is recovered. *Scoring:* Regardless of which team recovers the second fumble, credit the original ball carrier with one rush for 5 yards and also with a fumble; credit the opponent who recovered the first fumble with plus 5 yards of fumble yardage and also charge him with a fumble.

PASSING PLAYS

11. When a passer fumbles while attempting to pass, charge him with "tackled" and a fumble and with all yardage lost to the point of recovery as yards lost attempting to pass.

EXCEPTION 1: If a teammate or an opponent legally bats, or kicks, or deflects a ball the yardage lost is to the point of the first touch. (See Rule 6 par. b)

EXCEPTION 2: If the point of recovery is in advance of the original line of scrimmage or if the player recovering the fumble advances the ball beyond the line of scrimmage, charge the passer with "tackled" for no yards and also with a fumble, and credit the player who advanced the ball with fumble yardage equal to the distance between the old and the new lines of scrimmage.

Example I: With ball on opponent's 30, quarterback goes back to pass and is hit by defense at 38, fumbles and ball bounces backward to 41, where he, a teammate, or an opponent recovers. *Scoring:* Charge quarterback with "tackled," 11 yards lost attempting to pass, and a fumble.

Example II: In the same circumstances as Example I, the ball is recovered at the 35, 3 yards in advance of the spot where the fumble occurred. *Scoring:* Charge quarterback with "tackled," 5 yards lost attempting to pass, and a fumble.

Example III: In the same circumstances as Example I, the quarterback or a teammate recovers and advances the ball to the opponent's 28. *Scoring:* Charge quarterback with "tackled," no yards lost attempting to pass, and a fumble; credit player recovering with 2 yards of fumble yardage.

Example IV: In the same circumstances as Example I, the ball bounces backward to the 41 where it is deflected by an opponent and eventually recovered by the quarterback himself on the 50 yard line. *Scoring:* Charge the quarterback with a "sack" and 11 yards lost attempting to pass plus a fumble and an own recovery. The additional 9 yards lost are the result of a loose ball.

Example V: In the same circumstances as Example I, the ball bounces backward to the 41, where an opponent picks it up and runs to midfield before being tackled. *Scoring:* Charge quarterback with "tackled," 11 yards lost attempting to pass and a fumble; credit opponent recovering with 9 yards of fumble yardage.

RECEPTIONS, INTERCEPTIONS, AND RETURNS

12. When a player fumbles after catching or intercepting a pass or on a punt return or kickoff return, he shall be credited with a gain or loss to (a) his original point of advance or (b) the point of fumble recovery, whichever is less. *EXCEPTION:* If the player recovers his own fumble, all yardage gained or lost shall be credited in the category initiating the action.

Example I: A receiver, after catching a pass, is 40 yards in advance of the line of scrimmage when he fumbles. He, a teammate, or an opponent

---

gets a fumble and minus 15 as fumble yardage. Punter gets one rush for no yards and an own recovery.

B. Punter recovers at the 5 and runs to the 22. *Scoring:* Center gets a fumble. Punter gets an own recovery, and a rush for 2 yards.

C. Blocking back recovers at the 5, where he is downed or the ball is declared dead. *Scoring:* Center gets a fumble and minus 15 as fumble yardage. Punter gets a rush for no yards. Blocking back gets an own recovery.

D. Blocking back recovers at the 5, runs to the 35. *Scoring:* Center gets a fumble. Punter gets one rush for no yards. Blocking back gets an own recovery, 15 yards (fumble yardage), and team is credited with a first down *rushing.*

Example V: Second-and-10 at own 20 yard line. Quarterback takes snap, turns to hand off to running back, and the exchange is mishandled. The ball bounces free and is recovered by anyone at the 12. *Scoring:* Quarterback gets one rush for no yards, a fumble, and minus 8 as fumble yardage. Credit the recovery to the appropriate player.

Example VI: Second-and-10 at own 20 yard line. Quarterback receives snap and tosses a backward pass (pitchout or lateral). The pass is satisfactory, but the ball bounces off the running back's hands and is recovered by an opponent at the 11. *Scoring:* Quarterback gets one rush for no yards and a fumble for minus 9 (fumble yardage). Credit the player recovering the ball with an opponents' recovery.

Example VII: Second-and-10 at own 20 yard line. Same play as Example VI, except that when the running back muffs the ball, it bounces forward, and an offensive tackle recovers on the 25 and runs to the 35. *Scoring:* Quarterback gets one rush for no yards and a fumble. Tackle gets an own recovery and 10 yards (fumble yardage). Credit a first down *rushing.*

Example VIII: Second-and-10 at own 20 yard line. Quarterback hands off to running back; running back's handoff to wide receiver is mishandled. The ball is recovered at the 12. *Scoring:* running back gets one rush for no yards and a fumble for minus 8 (fumble yardage).

RUSHING PLAYS

8. When a player recovers his own fumble:

Example I: With ball on opponent's 30, running back rushes to 20, where he is tackled and fumbles. He recovers on the 25 and advances to the 21. *Scoring:* Running back is credited with one rush for 9 yards and is charged with a fumble.

Example II: With ball on opponent's 30, running back rushes to the 29, where he is tackled and fumbles. He falls on his own fumble at the 31. *Scoring:* Running back is credited with one rush for minus 1 yard and is charged with a fumble.

9. When a teammate recovers:

Example I: With ball on opponent's 30, running back rushes to the 20, where he is tackled and fumbles. A teammate recovers the ball on the 25. *Scoring:* Running back is credited with one rush for 5 yards and is charged with a fumble.

Example II: With ball on opponent's 30, running back rushes to the 20, where he is tackled and fumbles. A teammate recovers the ball on the 15. *Scoring:* Running back is credited with one rush for 10 yards and is charged with a fumble. Teammate is credited with no yardage.

Example III: With ball on opponent's 30, running back rushes to the 28, where he is tackled and fumbles. A teammate recovers at the 31 — a net loss of 1 yard. *Scoring:* Running back is credited with one rush for minus 1 yard. Teammate is charged with a fumble.

Example IV: With ball on opponent's 30, running back is tackled 2 yards behind line of scrimmage and fumbles. A teammate recovers the ball at the 34 — a net loss of 4 yards. *Scoring:* Running back is charged with one rushing attempt for minus 4 yards and a fumble.

Example V: With ball on opponent's 30, running back is tackled 4 yards behind line of scrimmage and fumbles. A teammate recovers the ball at the 34 and advances it to the 29 — a net gain of 1 yard on the play. *Scoring:* Running back is charged with one rushing attempt for no gain and with a fumble. Teammate is credited with plus 1 yard of fumble yardage.

Example VI: With ball on opponent's 30, running back is tackled four yards behind line of scrimmage and fumbles. A teammate recovers the ball at the 34 and advances it to the 32 — a net loss of 2 yards on the play. *Scoring:* Running back is charged with one rushing attempt for minus 2 yards and also with a fumble.

Example VII: In the same circumstances as Example VI, the teammate recovers the ball at the 36 and, while retreating in an attempt to elude

recovers the ball 37 yards in advance of the line of scrimmage. *Scoring:* Play is listed as a 37-yard pass.

Example II: In the same situation as Example I, the receiver recovers his own fumble and advances to a point 45 yards in advance of the line of scrimmage before being tackled. *Scoring:* Play is listed as a 45-yard pass.

Example III: In the same situation as Example I, a teammate recovers and advances the ball to a point 45 yards in advance of the line of scrimmage before being tackled. *Scoring:* Play is listed as a 40-yard pass; teammate who recovered is credited with 5 yards of fumble yardage.

Example IV: Kick return man receives a punt on his own 10, and returns to his 35, where he fumbles. The ball bounces forward to the 40, where he recovers his own fumble. *Scoring:* Kick returner is credited with a punt return of 30 yards.

Example V: In the same situation as Example IV, the ball is recovered at the 40 by a teammate or an opponent. *Scoring:* Kick returner is credited with a punt return of 25 yards; the remaining yardage is treated as being the result of a loose ball.

Example VI: In the same situation as Example IV, the ball bounces back to the 30, where the kick returner, a teammate, or an opponent recovers. *Scoring:* Kick returner is credited with a punt return of 20 yards.

Example VII: Kick return man receives a punt on his own 20, retreats trying to elude a tackler and is tackled at the 17, where he fumbles. The ball bounces back to the 15, where it is recovered. *Scoring:* Kick returner is charged with a punt return of minus 5 yards, regardless of who recovers.

Note: No rushing attempt, or pass attempt, or completion, shall be credited on an extra point attempt.

Touchdowns

There are three types of touchdowns—rushing, passing, and returns. The only touchdowns considered touchdowns passing are those that result from a completed forward pass from a teammate. On the score blank all touchdowns should be noted in their respective categories according to the manner made (rushing, passing, punt returns, fumbles recovered, etc.)

Extra Points

Players attempting conversions shall not be charged with an extra point missed when a bad pass from center, or a muff by the ball holder, prevents an opportunity to kick. However, attempts at conversion that are blocked shall be scored as extra points missed. (*EXCEPTION:* If, in the judgment of the official scorer, an error in the center snap or placement of the ball by the holder is the direct cause of a blocked attempt, the kicker shall not be charged with an attempt. The same exception may be applied to field goal attempts.) No fumble should be charged on an attempted conversion.

Field Goals

Field goals shall be measured from the spot of the kick. Spot of an attempt is dictated by the same principle as used in determining the line of scrimmage.

Example: If any point of the football when kicked rests on or above any yard stripe, credit distance from that yard stripe. If all of the ball rests between yard stripes, credit distance from the yard line nearest the intended goal.

Kicker is not charged with a field goal attempt if he does not actually kick. If player holding the ball juggles it long enough to prevent kicker from making an attempt, charge ball holder with a rush and yardage lost as fumble yardage, plus a fumble and his own fumble recovered. (Also see the exception paragraph in Extra Points section regarding blocked field goals).

SPECIAL NOTE—If the center snap is *satisfactory* and the holder *does not fumble* the snap or mishandle the placement of the ball, but is instead smothered at the spot or tackled after he attempts to run, charge the holder with a rush and any yards lost as rushing yardage.

If the play develops as action off a fake field goal attempt, charge the holder with a rush, or pass or "tackled" consistent with the basic scoring rules on scrimmage plays.

All yardage gained by a player in returning an unsuccessful field goal attempt should be noted on the back of the score blank under "remarks." For blocked field goal attempts, see Blocked Kicks section.

Safeties

Credit a player with a safety when:

A. He downs an opponent behind the opponent's goal line;

B. He causes an opponent to step out of bounds behind the opponent's goal line;

C. He blocks a kick or deflects a backward pass and the ball goes out of the end zone behind the opponent's goal line.

Example I: Fourth-and-10 at own 4 yard line. Defensive tackle blocks a punt. The ball is recovered in the end zone by the punter, and cornerback downs the punter there. *Scoring:* Credit the cornerback with a safety.

Example II: Fourth-and-10 at own 4 yard line. Offensive team decides to allow a safety rather than to kick on fourth down. Punter lingers near end line, consuming time until defensive tackle chases him out of bounds. *Scoring:* Credit defensive tackle with a safety.

Unless a safety falls into one of the categories listed above, no credit shall be given to any individual.

Qualifications for Individual Leaders

Rushing: Most net yards gained (minimum 100 carries to qualify for highest average gain).

Passing: Minimum average of 12 passes attempted per each team's games to qualify. Standings are based on percent of completions, percent of touchdown passes per attempt, percent of pass attempts intercepted, and average gain per attempted pass. Passers are rated against a standard in each of the four categories and the passer with most rating points is the leader.

Pass Receptions: Most receptions (minimum 32 to qualify for highest average gain).

Pass Interceptions: Most interceptions.

Scoring: Most total points scored.

Punting: Longest average distance per punt (minimum average of 2½ punts per each of team's games, 40 for season). Blocked punts are not charged to individual punter.

Punt Returns: Average per return (minimum average of one return per each of team's games).

Kickoff Returns: Average per return (minimum average of one return per each of team's games).

1981 Schedule and Note Calendar

All times P.M. local daylight.
Nationally televised games in parentheses. CBS and NBC television doubleheader games in the regular season to be announced.

Preseason/First Week

Date	Game		TV	Time
Saturday, August 1	Cleveland	vs. Atlanta — at Canton, Ohio	(ABC)	3:30
Wednesday, August 5	San Francisco	at Seattle		7:30
Thursday, August 6	Philadelphia	at Houston		7:00
Friday, August 7	Kansas City	at Washington		7:30
	New York Jets	at Denver		7:30
Saturday, August 8	Atlanta	at Oakland		6:00
	Baltimore	at New Orleans		7:00
	Cincinnati	at Tampa Bay		7:00
	Detroit	at Buffalo		6:00
	Green Bay	at Dallas		8:00
	Miami	at Minnesota		8:00
	New York Giants	at Chicago		6:00
	Pittsburgh	at Cleveland		7:30
	St. Louis	at San Diego		6:00
Monday, August 10	New England	at Los Angeles		8:00

Preseason/Second Week

Date	Game		TV	Time
Friday, August 14	Minnesota	at Washington		7:30
	St. Louis	at Seattle		7:30
Saturday, August 15	Baltimore	at New York Giants		8:00
	Chicago	at Kansas City		7:35
	Cincinnati	at Detroit		7:00
	Cleveland	at Buffalo		6:00
	Dallas	at Los Angeles	(CBS)	5:30
	Denver	at Miami		8:00
	Houston	at New Orleans		7:00
	New England	at Tampa Bay		7:00
	New York Jets	at Atlanta		7:00
	Oakland	vs. Green Bay — at Milwaukee		7:00
	Pittsburgh	at Philadelphia		6:00
	San Diego	at San Francisco		6:00

Preseason/Third Week

Date	Game		TV	Time
Friday, August 21	Los Angeles	at San Diego	(ABC)	6:00
Saturday, August 22	Atlanta	at Minnesota		8:00
	Buffalo	at Cleveland		7:30
	Cincinnati	at Chicago		6:00
	Green Bay	at Denver		7:30
	Houston	at Tampa Bay		7:00
	Miami	at Detroit		7:00
	New York Jets	at New York Giants		8:00
	Oakland	at New England		2:00
	Pittsburgh	at Dallas	(NBC)	8:00
	St. Louis	at Kansas City		7:35
	Seattle	at San Francisco		6:00
	Washington	at Baltimore		8:00
Sunday, August 23	New Orleans	vs. Philadelphia — at Syracuse	(NBC)	1:00

Preseason/Fourth Week

First Week

Thursday, August 27

Minnesota ___	at Los Angeles ___	8:00

Friday, August 28

Baltimore ___	at Seattle ___	7:30
Buffalo ___	at San Diego ___	6:00
Kansas City ___	at Miami ___	8:00
Tampa Bay ___	at Atlanta ___	8:30

Saturday, August 29

Chicago ___	at St. Louis ___	6:00
Cleveland ___	at Green Bay ___	7:00
Denver ___	at Cincinnati ___	7:00
Detroit ___	at New Orleans ___	7:00
Houston ___	at Dallas ___	(CBS) 8:00
New York Giants ___	at Pittsburgh ___	6:00
Philadelphia ___	vs. New York Jets ___ at Giants Stadium	8:00
San Francisco ___	at Oakland ___	6:00

Sunday, August 30

Washington ___	at New England ___	(ABC) 12:30

Second Week

Saturday, September 5
Sunday, September 6
(NBC-TV doubleheader)

Minnesota ___	at Tampa Bay ___	8:00
Baltimore ___	at New England ___	1:00
Dallas ___	at Washington ___	1:00
Green Bay ___	at Chicago ___	1:00
Houston ___	at Los Angeles ___	1:00
Kansas City ___	at Pittsburgh ___	12:00
Miami ___	at St. Louis ___	4:00
New Orleans ___	at Atlanta ___	1:00
New York Jets ___	at Buffalo ___	4:00
Oakland ___	at Denver ___	2:00
Philadelphia ___	at New York Giants ___	1:00
San Francisco ___	at Detroit ___	1:00
Seattle ___	at Cincinnati ___	1:00

Monday, September 7

San Diego ___	at Cleveland ___	(ABC) 9:00

Third Week

Thursday, September 10
(NBC-TV doubleheader)

Pittsburgh ___	at Miami ___	(ABC) 8:30

Sunday, September 13

Atlanta ___	at Green Bay ___	12:00
Buffalo ___	at Baltimore ___	2:00
Chicago ___	at San Francisco ___	1:00
Cincinnati ___	at New York Jets ___	4:00
Denver ___	at Seattle ___	4:00
Detroit ___	at San Diego ___	1:00
Houston ___	at Cleveland ___	1:00
Los Angeles ___	at New Orleans ___	12:00
New England ___	at Philadelphia ___	4:00
New York Giants ___	at Washington ___	1:00
St. Louis ___	at Dallas ___	3:00
Tampa Bay ___	at Kansas City ___	12:00

Monday, September 14

Oakland ___	at Minnesota ___	(ABC) 8:00

Thursday, September 17

Philadelphia ___	at Buffalo ___	(ABC) 8:30

Sunday, September 20
(CBS-TV doubleheader)

Baltimore ___	at Denver ___	2:00
Cleveland ___	at Cincinnati ___	1:00
Detroit ___	at Minnesota ___	12:00
Green Bay ___	at Los Angeles ___	1:00
Miami ___	at Houston ___	12:00
New Orleans ___	at New York Giants ___	4:00
New York Jets ___	at Pittsburgh ___	1:00
San Diego ___	at Kansas City ___	1:00
San Francisco ___	at Atlanta ___	1:00
Seattle ___	at Oakland ___	1:00
Tampa Bay ___	at Chicago ___	1:00
Washington ___	at St. Louis ___	12:00

Monday, September 21

Dallas ___	at New England ___	(ABC) 9:00

Fourth Week

**Sunday, September 27
(CBS-TV doubleheader)**

Atlanta — at Cleveland —		1:00
Buffalo — at Cincinnati —		1:00
Houston — at New York Jets —		1:00
Kansas City — at Seattle —		1:00
Miami — at Baltimore —		2:00
Minnesota — vs. Green Bay — at Milwaukee		1:00
New England — at Pittsburgh —		1:00
New Orleans — at San Francisco —		1:00
New York Giants — at Dallas —		3:00
Oakland — at Detroit —		1:00
St. Louis — at Tampa Bay —		4:00
San Diego — at Denver —		2:00
Washington — at Philadelphia —		1:00

Monday, September 28

Los Angeles — at Chicago —	(ABC) 8:00

Fifth Week

**Sunday, October 4
(NBC-TV doubleheader)**

Baltimore — at Buffalo —		1:00
Chicago — at Minnesota —		12:00
Cincinnati — at Houston —		1:00
Cleveland — at Los Angeles —		1:00
Dallas — at St. Louis —		12:00
Denver — at Oakland —		1:00
Detroit — at Tampa Bay —		4:00
Green Bay — at New York Giants —		1:00
Kansas City — at New England —		1:00
New York Jets — at Miami —		4:00
Pittsburgh — at New Orleans —		1:00
San Francisco — at Washington —		1:00
Seattle — at San Diego —		1:00

Monday, October 5

Atlanta — at Philadelphia —	(ABC) 9:00

Sixth Week

**Sunday, October 11
(CBS-TV doubleheader)**

Cincinnati — at Baltimore —		2:00
Cleveland — at Pittsburgh —		1:00
Dallas — at San Francisco —		1:00
Detroit — at Denver —		2:00
Los Angeles — at Atlanta —		1:00
Minnesota — at San Diego —		1:00
New England — at New York Jets —		1:00
Oakland — at Kansas City —		1:00
Philadelphia — at New Orleans —		12:00
St. Louis — at New York Giants —		4:00
Seattle — at Houston —		1:00
Tampa Bay — at Green Bay —		1:00
Washington — at Chicago —		1:00

Monday, October 12

Miami — at Buffalo —	(ABC) 9:00

Seventh Week

**Sunday, October 18
(CBS-TV doubleheader)**

Buffalo — at New York Jets —		1:00
Denver — at Kansas City —		3:00
Houston — at New England —		1:00
Los Angeles — at Dallas —		(ABC) 8:00
New Orleans — at Cleveland —		1:00
New York Giants — at Seattle —		1:00
Philadelphia — at Minnesota —		12:00
Pittsburgh — at Cincinnati —		1:00
St. Louis — at Atlanta —		1:00
San Diego — at Baltimore —		2:00
San Francisco — vs. Green Bay — at Milwaukee		12:00
Tampa Bay — at Oakland —		4:00
Washington — at Miami —		4:00

Monday, October 19

Chicago — at Detroit —	(ABC) 9:00

Eighth Week

Sunday, October 25
(NBC-TV doubleheader)

Baltimore ___	at Cleveland ___	1:00
Cincinnati ___	at New Orleans ___	1:00
Denver ___	at Buffalo ___	1:00
Green Bay ___	at Detroit ___	1:00
Kansas City ___	at Oakland ___	1:00
Los Angeles ___	at San Francisco ___	3:00
Miami ___	at Dallas ___	12:00
Minnesota ___	at St. Louis ___	12:00
New England ___	at Washington ___	1:00
New York Giants ___	at Chicago ___	1:00
San Diego ___	at Atlanta ___	3:00
Seattle ___	at New York Jets ___	1:00
Tampa Bay ___	at Philadelphia ___	1:00

Monday, October 26

Houston ___	at Pittsburgh ___	(ABC) 9:00

Ninth Week

Sunday, November 1
(CBS-TV doubleheader)

Atlanta ___	at New Orleans ___	12:00
Baltimore ___	at Miami ___	1:00
Chicago ___	at Tampa Bay ___	1:00
Cleveland ___	at Buffalo ___	1:00
Dallas ___	at Philadelphia ___	4:00
Detroit ___	at Los Angeles ___	1:00
Houston ___	at Cincinnati ___	1:00
Kansas City ___	at San Diego ___	1:00
New England ___	at Oakland ___	1:00
New York Jets ___	at New York Giants ___	1:00
St. Louis ___	at Washington ___	4:00
San Francisco ___	at Pittsburgh ___	1:00
Seattle ___	at Green Bay ___	1:00

Monday, November 2

Minnesota ___	at Denver ___	(ABC) 7:00

Tenth Week

Sunday, November 8
(NBC-TV doubleheader)

Atlanta ___	at San Francisco ___	1:00
Chicago ___	at Kansas City ___	1:00
Cincinnati ___	at San Diego ___	1:00
Cleveland ___	at Denver ___	2:00
Detroit ___	at Washington ___	1:00
Miami ___	at New England ___	1:00
New Orleans ___	at Los Angeles ___	1:00
New York Giants ___	vs. Green Bay ___ at Milwaukee	12:00
Oakland ___	at Houston ___	4:00
Philadelphia ___	at St. Louis ___	12:00
Pittsburgh ___	at Seattle ___	1:00
Tampa Bay ___	at Minnesota ___	12:00

Monday, November 9

Buffalo ___	at Dallas ___	(ABC) 8:00

Eleventh Week

Sunday, November 15
(CBS-TV doubleheader)

Baltimore ___	at Philadelphia ___	1:00
Buffalo ___	at St. Louis ___	12:00
Chicago ___	at Green Bay ___	12:00
Cleveland ___	at San Francisco ___	1:00
Dallas ___	at Detroit ___	4:00
Denver ___	at Tampa Bay ___	1:00
Houston ___	at Kansas City ___	12:00
Los Angeles ___	at Cincinnati ___	1:00
New Orleans ___	at Minnesota ___	12:00
New York Jets ___	at New England ___	1:00
Oakland ___	at Miami ___	1:00
Pittsburgh ___	at Atlanta ___	1:00
Washington ___	at New York Giants ___	4:00

Monday, November 16

San Diego ___	at Seattle ___	(ABC) 6:00

Twelfth Week

Sunday, November 22
(NBC-TV doubleheader)

Denver	at Cincinnati	1:00
Detroit	at Chicago	12:00
Green Bay	at Tampa Bay	1:00
Miami	at New York Jets	4:00
New England	at Buffalo	1:00
New Orleans	at Houston	12:00
New York Giants	at Philadelphia	1:00
Pittsburgh	at Cleveland	1:00
St. Louis	at Baltimore	2:00
San Diego	at Oakland	1:00
San Francisco	at Los Angeles	1:00
Seattle	at Kansas City	1:00
Washington	at Dallas	3:00

Monday, November 23

Minnesota	at Atlanta	(ABC) 9:00

Thirteenth Week

Thursday, November 26
(Thanksgiving Day)

Chicago	at Dallas	(CBS) 3:00
Kansas City	at Detroit	(NBC) 12:30

Sunday, November 29
(CBS-TV doubleheader)

Atlanta	at Houston	3:00
Baltimore	at New York Jets	1:00
Cincinnati	at Cleveland	1:00
Denver	at San Diego	1:00
Green Bay	at Minnesota	12:00
Los Angeles	at Pittsburgh	1:00
New York Giants	at San Francisco	1:00
Oakland	at Seattle	1:00
St. Louis	at New England	1:00
Tampa Bay	at New Orleans	1:00
Washington	at Buffalo	1:00

Monday, November 30

Philadelphia	at Miami	(ABC) 9:00

Fourteenth Week

Thursday, December 3

Cleveland	at Houston	(ABC) 8:00

Sunday, December 6
(NBC-TV doubleheader)

Atlanta	at Tampa Bay	4:00
Buffalo	at San Diego	1:00
Dallas	at Baltimore	2:00
Detroit	at Green Bay	12:00
Kansas City	at Denver	2:00
Los Angeles	at New York Giants	1:00
Minnesota	at Chicago	12:00
New England	at Miami	1:00
New Orleans	at St. Louis	12:00
New York Jets	at Seattle	1:00
Philadelphia	at Washington	1:00
San Francisco	at Cincinnati	1:00

Monday, December 7

Pittsburgh	at Oakland	(ABC) 6:00

Fifteenth Week

Saturday, December 12

Minnesota	at Detroit	(CBS) 4:00
New York Jets	at Cleveland	(NBC) 12:30

Sunday, December 13
(CBS-TV doubleheader)

Baltimore	at Washington	1:00
Buffalo	at New England	1:00
Chicago	at Oakland	1:00
Cincinnati	at Pittsburgh	1:00
Green Bay	at New Orleans	12:00
Houston	at San Francisco	1:00
Miami	at Kansas City	1:00
New York Giants	at St. Louis	12:00
Philadelphia	at Dallas	3:00
San Diego	at Tampa Bay	1:00
Seattle	at Denver	2:00

Monday, December 14

Atlanta	at Los Angeles	(ABC) 6:00

Sixteenth Week

First Round Playoff Games

Site Priorities

Two wild card teams (fourth- and fifth-best records) from each conference will enter the first round of the playoffs. The wild cards from the same conference will play each other. Home clubs will be the clubs with the best won-lost-tied percentage in the regular season. If tied in record, the tie will be broken by the tie-breaking procedure already in effect.

Saturday, December 19

Buffalo ___	at Miami ___	(NBC)	4:00
Dallas ___	at New York Giants ___	(CBS)	12:30

Sunday, December 20 (NBC-TV doubleheader)

Cincinnati ___	at Atlanta ___	1:00
Cleveland ___	at Seattle ___	1:00
Denver ___	at Chicago ___	12:00
Green Bay ___	at New York Jets ___	1:00
Kansas City ___	at Minnesota ___	12:00
New England ___	at Baltimore ___	2:00
Pittsburgh ___	at Houston ___	3:00
St. Louis ___	at Philadelphia ___	1:00
San Francisco ___	at New Orleans ___	1:00
Tampa Bay ___	at Detroit ___	1:00
Washington ___	at Los Angeles ___	1:00

Monday, December 21

Oakland ___	at San Diego ___	(ABC) 6:00

Sunday, December 27

American Football Conference ___ at ___ (NBC)

National Football Conference ___ at ___ (CBS)

Divisional Playoff Games

Site Priorities

In each conference, the two division winners with the highest won-lost-tied percentage during the regular season will be the home teams. The division winner with the best percentage will be host to the wild card winner from the first round playoff, and the division winner with the second best percentage will be host to the third division winner, unless the wild card team is from the same division as the winner with the highest percentage. In that case, the division winner with the best percentage will be host to the third division winner and the second best division winner will be host to the wild card.

Saturday, January 2, 1982

American Football Conference ___ at ___ (NBC)

National Football Conference ___ at ___ (NBC)

Sunday, January 3, 1982

American Football Conference ___ at ___ (CBS)

National Football Conference ___ at ___ (NBC)

Conference Championship Games, Super Bowl XVI, and AFC-NFC Pro Bowl

Site Priorities for Championship Games

The home teams will be the surviving divisional playoff winners with the best won-lost-tied percentage during the regular season. The wild card team will never be the home team, in either the divisional playoffs or the championship games. Any ties in won-lost-tied percentage will be broken by the tie-breaking procedures already in effect.

Sunday, January 10, 1982

American Football Conference Championship Game ___ at ___ (CBS)

National Football Conference Championship Game ___ at ___ (NBC)

Sunday, January 24, 1982

Super Bowl XVI at Silverdome, Pontiac, Michigan ___ at ___ (CBS)

Sunday, January 31, 1982

AFC-NFC Pro Bowl at Honolulu, Hawaii ___ vs. ___ (CBS)

AFC ___ vs. NFC ___ (ABC)

NOTES

NOTES